Publications of the Milman Parry Collection
of Oral Literature No. 7

# SINGERS AND TALES
# IN THE TWENTY-FIRST CENTURY

# SINGERS AND TALES IN THE TWENTY-FIRST CENTURY

edited by
David F. Elmer and Peter McMurray

Published by
THE MILMAN PARRY COLLECTION OF ORAL LITERATURE
Harvard University

Distributed by
HARVARD UNIVERSITY PRESS
Cambridge, Massachusetts & London, England
2024

*Singers and Tales in the Twenty-First Century*

Published by The Milman Parry Collection of Oral Literature, Harvard University
Distributed by Harvard University Press, Cambridge, Massachusetts & London, England




Production Team of the Center for Hellenic Studies

Production Manager for Publications: Jill Curry Robbins
Web Producer: Noel Spencer
Cover Design: Joni Godlove
Production: Kristin Murphy Romano

ISBN: 978-0-674-278547

*The editors and contributors dedicate this book to the memory of John Miles Foley.*

ἔνθεν δὲ προτέρω πλέομεν ἀκαχήμενοι ἦτορ

# Table of Contents

# Introduction

## Parry, Lord, and the Polyphonic Archive

DAVID F. ELMER AND PETER MCMURRAY

THIS VOLUME IS AN EXPLORATION of the legacies of the pioneering scholars of oral literature, Milman Parry (1902–1935) and Albert Lord (1912–1991). The essays included here have their origin in a conference convened at Harvard in 2010 to commemorate the fiftieth anniversary of the publication of Lord's landmark book, *The Singer of Tales*, and the seventy-fifth anniversary of the death of Milman Parry. The conference was deliberately framed in as broad a way as possible, in order to capture a wide range of topics. Its breadth is reflected in the essays here assembled, which, despite their divergent approaches, are all inspired by the work of Parry and Lord. Much time has now passed since the authors met in Cambridge, Massachusetts, to exchange ideas. The intervening years have brought the usual mix of joys and sorrows including, most poignantly, the loss of John Miles Foley (1947–2012), to whom this volume is dedicated. Nevertheless, even with the passage of time, or perhaps in virtue of it, it has seemed desirable to publish these essays, both for their individual contributions and for the testimony they collectively provide to the wide-ranging and continuing impact of the scholarship of Parry and Lord. In addition, we hope that the volume offers a kind of comparative conspectus, showing some of the breadth and richness of the ongoing study of orality, verbal arts, and sung poetry across a range of cultural and historical contexts.[1] In hopes of achieving these intertwined aims—considering the legacy of Parry and Lord, while also exploring what the study of oral poetry in the twenty-first century might mean—we begin this introduction with a review

1 Oral poetry and the idea of orality more generally continue to give rise to important research across a range of disciplines. Some recent work of note includes Bohlman and Petković 2011, Minchin 2012, Ochoa Gautier 2014, Saussy 2016, Macintosh et al. 2018, Ready 2019, Vayntrub 2019, and Lang et al. 2019. The emergence of voice studies, with its emphasis on voice, vocality, and embodiment from a number of disciplinary perspectives, also offers important points of intellectual confluence; see Fisher 2016, Yasar 2018, Eidsheim and Meizel 2019.

of the physical archive that anchors the legacies of Parry and Lord, and from which their work in large part derives its continuing authority: the Milman Parry Collection of Oral Literature, housed in Room C of Harvard University's Widener Library.[2] We then situate the contributions in this volume within that archival and intellectual history.

## Archival Beginnings

Contrary to appearances, archives can be very unstable things—and the Parry Collection is no exception. The core of the Parry Collection comes from the research trips of Milman Parry and his student/assistant Albert Lord, especially their work from 1934–1935, conducted with the collaboration of Nikola Vujnović.[3] Parry undertook two field expeditions, a short one to survey the terrain in the summer of 1933, and a longer one from June 1934 through August 1935. Parry died shortly after returning from his second trip and Vujnović died a little after World War II, while Lord continued to conduct research in southeastern Europe through the 1960s. The Collection was augmented by the materials of the James A. Notopoulos Collection of Modern Greek Ballads and Songs, recorded in 1952–1953, and the Whitman-Rinvolucri Collection (1962–1971), comprising recordings and films documenting Greek shadow puppet plays. The shelves and cabinets of Room C contain also a kind of para-archive, items not formally accessioned by the Collection. This para-archive includes tapes and other materials given to Lord over the years by students and colleagues, a large number of which were presented to Lord by Dwight Reynolds, whose essay appears in this volume, at the 1988 annual meeting of the American Folklore Society. By the time of Lord's death, however, the Parry Collection seemed to be a mostly static object, poised to be digitized to allow increased circulation of materials online and through new publications (e.g. on Albanian-language materials in the Collection), but not otherwise likely to change substantially.[4]

2 For a concise overview of the history and contents of the Collection, see Elmer 2013. The editors of this volume have both served on the Collection's curatorial staff.

3 According to information related to Michael Nardone (to whom we are grateful for sharing his field notes) by Dragan Vujnović on July 29, 2019, Nikola Vujnović was born in 1908. Dragan Vujnović believes that Nikola was killed by Tito's Partisans in 1945, but in a letter to Parry's widow, dated November 27, 1949, Lord claims to have had recent news from Nikola, who was at that time living in Stolac, though suffering from an illness that Lord believed to be tuberculosis. (The letter is among the papers described below.)

4 A comprehensive introduction to the Albanian materials in the Collection is now available in Scaldaferri 2021.

Yet in the past two decades, the Parry Collection has seen some crucial additions and reassessments that have reshaped what the Collection is and how it may be used for future scholarship. Key aspects of those reassessments have been tied directly to digitization, suggesting an archival corollary to McLuhan's dictum that "the medium is the message": there are ways in which the ontology of the archive is defined by the mechanisms of access to it. Many of the most dramatic shifts in the Collection's archival contours, however, have come through "old media," including aluminum discs and correspondence written on paper. Three examples of significant additions to the Collection that have simultaneously expanded and destabilized the archive include: test recordings Milman Parry made between his two expeditions; correspondence and personal papers documenting aspects of Parry's personal and professional life in the 1920s and 1930s; and family and local histories from the former Yugoslavia relating to the work of Parry, Lord, and Vujnović, in many cases made possible by ongoing efforts to digitize the Parry Collection. We briefly discuss each of these additions under headings corresponding to the media that made them possible.

## Aluminum

Visiting the Parry Collection in 2014, media theorist Wolfgang Ernst emphasized the value of physical media that occupy the interstices of the catalogued collection, such as uncatalogued tapes that might have been left in tape recorders.[5] The remark proved prescient: in 2016, we came across a record sleeve tucked away in the bottom corner of the set of shelves housing Parry's field recordings. In place of the serial numbers by which the catalogued recordings are organized was the simple, if cryptic, label "These discs have Milman Parry's voice on them." The four aluminum discs in the sleeve turned out to contain a variety of test recordings, presumably made around the spring of 1934 between Parry's two research trips to Yugoslavia as he explored the possibilities of recording on his newly-commissioned recording device. (Physically, in terms of the current housing of the discs, and temporally, in terms of the date of recording, these discs occupy an interstitial position in relation to Parry's fieldwork.) The recordings show Parry testing different recording set-ups: standing closer or farther from the microphone, trying out different cutting heads on the recording apparatus, and so on. He explores a variety of different ways of vocalizing, including reciting

5 Ernst has written widely on archival media, including those in the Milman Parry Collection: see, for example, his books *Digital Memory and the Archive* (2013, especially 59–65) and *Sonic Time Machines* (2016, especially 71–82). Peter McMurray elaborates further on interactions with Ernst at the Parry Collection in McMurray 2015.

poetry in Ancient Greek and Bosnian/Croatian/Serbian, reading written prose (a French text on Sophocles, an article from a student newspaper, and a letter from a former professor at Berkeley, who advises him not to be seduced by the "siren song of a Yugoslavian bard"; one detects a note of mirth in Parry's voice as he recites this phrase), and even a recording of someone playing *gusle*, albeit rather badly. The most striking recordings, however, are those featuring Parry's own singing, including excerpts of a Bach mass and several excerpts from music composed by recent Harvard graduate Elliott Carter for the Harvard Classical Club's 1933 production of Sophocles's *Philoctetes*, which Parry had directed.

Numerically speaking, adding four discs to the thousands already in the Parry Collection does not change much. Yet these materials offer important insight into Parry's thinking and recording practice that would otherwise be largely left to speculation. For instance, in the aluminum disc recordings made in Yugoslavia, Parry actively monitors how loudly singers speak and how people arrange themselves around the microphone. It is clear from these earliest test records that Parry was keenly interested in maintaining adequate sound quality and particularly in ensuring the intelligibility of speech and song, something he found difficult to do on the wax cylinder recordings he made in the summer of 1933 (Lord 1954:7). At the same time, these records suggest that Parry was himself quite engaged with the question of vocal performance; whether or not he was singing Bach and Carter from memory, he clearly knew the music for both well, if not necessarily to a professional standard. In the 1980s, anthropologists began grappling with the so-called "crisis of representation," questioning the role of the anthropologist/fieldworker in the forms of knowledge that were produced during such encounters. In recent decades, scholars have posed related questions about the Parry Collection (e.g. García 2001, Tate 2010, Ranković 2012). These recordings offer an important moment of methodological reflexivity in understanding how Parry conceived of his work and especially the act of audio recording: they simultaneously give concrete archival traces of Parry's direct involvement in the practice of recording verbal arts (understood broadly) and deepen our understanding of Parry's methodological concerns, made audible through the act of making preliminary recordings.

## Paper

The musical skill that Parry demonstrated in his test recordings was partially contextualized by documents donated to the Collection in 2018 by two of Parry's grandchildren, Laura and Andrew Feld. For over a decade prior to this donation, we, as curators, had sought to establish a broader context for the Collection's catalogued materials by conducting interviews with individuals who had been personally involved in the fieldwork of Parry and Lord. These included Marian Parry, daughter of Milman, who traveled as a ten-year-old child with him and their family to Yugoslavia in 1934; Miloš Velimirović, Lord's Serbian assistant during his field research in the early 1950s; and Mary Louise Lord, who also traveled with her husband Albert in those years. The reminiscences of Marian Parry were particularly remarkable, narrated as they were from the viewpoint of an exceptionally observant child, and recounted with the visual richness one would expect from a celebrated watercolorist.[6] The documents donated in 2018 by Marian's children are in many ways even more remarkable. In addition to correspondence, personal photos and other documents, and biographical notes collected by Sterling Dow as well as an interview conducted by Pamela Newhouse with Milman Parry's wife, also named Marian, these documents include the diary kept by 10-year-old Marian during the year she spent with her family in Yugoslavia.[7] In those pages she describes a generally happy life in Dubrovnik, alternating between periods of anxious waiting while Parry was away collecting material and the long stretches of days after his return, when their house would be filled with the voices of singers as his assistants worked to transcribe his recordings. Among the details that the young Marian recorded from her youthful perspective is the fact that, clean shaven, Parry (who wears a moustache or goatee in nearly every available photograph) resembled Bela Lugosi's villainous character Roxor in *Chandu the Magician*, a 1932 film Marian saw in Dubrovnik.

With regard to Parry's own musicianship, the new materials reveal that Parry acquired his musical literacy from his mother, who worked as a piano teacher and taught her son piano. He put this musical ability to work by helping to compose the Senior Extravaganza, a theatrical production, at the University of California, Berkeley, in the spring of 1923. This experience doubtless served him well when he directed *Philoctetes* at Harvard ten years later (although one imagines that the two productions differed widely in character). The new documents also provide fascinating glimpses of the austere life led by the Parrys in France during Milman's doctoral studies. And they give an indication of where Parry saw his research leading at the time of his death: in a letter to his sister

6 Marian Parry shared some of her recollections at the conclusion of the conference in which this volume originates.

7 Both Sterling Dow, who retired from Harvard as the John E. Hudson Professor of Archaeology, and Pamela Newhouse (Mensch), who became a distinguished translator of classical texts, were contemplating writing a biography of Parry. Their ambitions have lately been fulfilled by Robert Kanigel, whose biography of Parry, *Hearing Homer's Song: The Brief Life and Big Idea of Milman Parry*, appeared in 2021.

written just two and a half weeks before his death, Parry states that he intends to spend the coming summer in Albania, presumably to follow up on the Albanian-language materials he had collected the year before (on which, see Neziri and Scaldaferri in this volume). One of the most precious aspects of the new papers, however, is the strikingly personal portrait they provide of Parry as he was seen by several of the people closest to him (his wife, his daughter, his sister). His wife recalled that Parry was fond of making up stories for his children featuring a villain named Clifford Moore (the name of the Dean of the Faculty of Arts and Sciences during Parry's years at Harvard). Concluding a letter to Sterling Dow, his sister Addison wrote: "Milman was of a warm and affectionate nature and he loved us all. His family took great joy and pride in him. And he was fun—he was such fun!"

## Digital media

At the suggestion of Asim Vrcić, a local historian in Sjenica, Serbia, Peter McMurray traveled in 2004 to visit Zaim Međedović, son of Avdo, as part of a research project on the legacies of Parry's and Lord's work in the former Yugoslavia.[8] A key aspect of that visit (and subsequent visits in 2005 and 2012), described in greater detail in McMurray's article in this volume, was bringing recordings from the archive back to the Međedović family. Since then, re-engagements between the "field" and the "archive" have become all the more common, especially in connection with ongoing efforts to digitize the Parry Collection holdings and to make them available online. Very often, exchanges between what John Miles Foley has called the "agoras" of digital archives and oral traditions have proceeded along the same lines: in his last book, Foley recounts his own experience with the digital afterlives of archives (2012:141), highlighting his electronic correspondence with a descendant of Halil Bajgorić who had contacted him regarding his electronic edition (Foley 2004) of an epic performed by Bajgorić and recorded by Parry in 1935.

In the past two decades, several families and other scholars in the former Yugoslavia have likewise contacted the Parry Collection. At a minimum, such contacts offer a chance at fostering a digital form of repatriating the materials in the Collection. But more often than not, the sharing is a reciprocal process in which families recount additional details from family histories about local singing traditions that do not appear in the Parry Collection holdings, often offering new ways of understanding the holdings. For instance, Indira Fazlijević

8 That project served as the basis for McMurray's 2005 undergraduate senior thesis, "'The Singer after 70 Years: A Dialogic Restudy of Parry, Lord, and The Family Međedović" (archived in the Harvard University Archives).

Jusić, a relative of Jusuf Smajić's living in Texas, contacted the Collection after hearing from a friend who lived nearby, Enver Spahalić, himself a relative of Mujo Kukuruzović. Both Smajić and Kukuruzović had recorded songs for Parry and his team, and both families had been interested in the singing traditions in their families. The Smajić family shared some stories from Jusuf's life that added considerable texture to our understanding of what kinds of songs a singer might know (e.g. religious songs and other kinds of recitation), while also highlighting some of the political difficulties that swept through the region during World War II and its aftermath. The testimony of the Smajić family also helped to make sense of an archival document, a photograph showing Smajić "playing" a cane or walking stick as though it were a *tambura*: Smajić evidently used the cane as a performative aid or kinetic mnemonic device (McMurray 2019). Along similar lines, Aaron Tate has written about local memories of a particular day during Parry's research in Kijevo, in present-day Croatia (Tate 2010), while Michael Nardone has documented family lore about Nikola Vujnović, Parry's indispensable collaborator (see footnote 3, above).

From a technical point of view, examples such as these may appear to represent the expansion of archival metadata—the information *about* certain objects held in the Collection. But one of the striking aspects of Parry's work was the way he intertwined what we now would call "data" with "metadata," recording not only songs (data) but also interviews with singers about their lives and their poetic practices (ostensibly metadata), often with songs interspersed. In addition, his archival records (metadata) are typically extremely clear and precise. These mixings of genre blurred any clear boundaries between data and metadata, but so too did the collection of interviews themselves, which have in recent years become of particular interest to scholars as an archive in their own right (Vidan 2003, Elmer 2010, and Alexander in this volume). In short, these new archival additions offer an important reminder of the uniqueness of Parry's research approach and the rich and complex archive he and Lord left behind.

## Rumbling and Polyphony as Archival Legacies

What then do these changes mean? On the most fundamental (perhaps even banal) level, they indicate that archives are rarely, if ever, fixed entities. That lack of fixity and the slight shifts within the archive—something akin to what Wolfgang Ernst has called the "stirrings" or "rumbling" (*das Rumoren*) of the archives (Ernst 2015)—yield new insights even while calling into question the undergirding structure of archives that has made knowledge possible. In many cases, such as Parry's test recordings, these new materials simultaneously offer clarity and raise new questions: for instance, the newly-uncovered discs add crucial documentation of Parry's thinking and practice between the two trips, as he responded to challenges he faced in summer 1933; yet they also remind us of questions not yet posed, such as the relation between Parry's own musicianship and his fieldwork.

Ernst claims, provocatively, "The gaps are the archive" (2015:13), suggesting that the archive "is not so much what is left behind so much as it is the already extant screen for an indexed reality" (14). That is, for Ernst, the ways archives organize knowledge help clarify how human activity already follows a kind of archival logic. Postcolonial theorists and historians have also long reflected on archival gaps, highlighting the silence/silencing that archives can generate (Trouillot 1995) among other forms of absence (Falzetti 2015), all of which require particular ways of reading (or listening) that foreground the archive "as a site of knowledge production, an arbiter of truth, and a mechanism for shaping the narratives of history" (Burton 2005:2; see also Stoler 2008). For media archaeologists like Ernst as well as postcolonial historians, gaps and silences are defining features of archives.

In this case, recent developments within the Parry Collection suggest a similar argument, though one that has always been explicit in Parry's and Lord's writing: this particular collection of singers and tales is only one possible version of the broader archive of song repertoires and singers' lived experiences. It is an attempt at a snapshot of an expansive culture at a single historical moment (i.e. South Slavic epic singing ca. 1933–1935), a kind of synchronic slice; yet even that slice did not entail recording all singers singing every song they knew. By naming this subset of material both "oral" and "traditional," as Lord took pains to emphasize repeatedly toward the end of his career (e.g. Lord 1991), Parry and Lord effectively pointed to the gaps in their archive as *the* broader historical archive of this tradition. Silence, gaps, and archival "grains" remain, but in this case, the Parry Collection has always highlighted those as necessary conditions for conceptualizing an archive of oral poetry. As such, the Parry Collection has an unexpected timeliness for the archival turn across the humanities in recent years.

Finally, these stirrings or rumblings in the Parry Collection also highlight what we might call the *polyphony of the archive*. Parry's and Lord's analyses of oral poetry as a shared tradition explicitly required an encounter with many singers and many voices to establish patterns in transmission and formulaic language. This more literal polyphony is suggestive of the ways in which arguably all archives emerge from the multiplicity of utterances they contain. Again, the aforementioned gaps and silences in the archives remind us that every voice in the resulting archival polyphony is not given equal prominence. In an encouraging shift, many of those voices that had previously been less audible have attracted attention in recent scholarship such as Aida Vidan's groundbreaking book on women's poetic traditions in the region (2003) and research by Nicola Scaldaferri and Zymer Neziri on Albanian-language materials in the Parry Collection and beyond (see their contribution to this volume, as well as their essays in Scaldaferri 2021). Of course, explorations of oral tradition were never confined to southeastern Europe, or the West more generally, and one of the important challenges that remains even decades after the publication of *The Singer of Tales* is to continue exploring different cultural contexts in which the precise mechanisms of sung poetry and other tales offer new and distinctive ways of understanding the concept of orality.

## Singers and Tales

As mentioned at the outset, the principal aim of this volume is to (re)consider the legacies of Milman Parry and Albert Lord, including the idea of "orality," the life of the Milman Parry Collection of Oral Literature since Lord's death, and more broadly, the application of Parry's and Lord's thinking to other poetic traditions. The volume is inherently comparative not only because it brings together scholars working in a variety of disciplines but also because so many of the central ideas Parry and Lord proposed emerged from comparative study. The plurality of the title—singers and tales, rather than an individual "singer of tales"—signals, again, the sense of polyphony in oral traditions more generally but also the proliferation of methodologies and cultural contexts that have grown from Parry and Lord. Their notion of what has become known as the Oral-Formulaic Theory remains a necessary starting point—but only a starting point—for research on a whole range of verbal and musical arts, as the essays here make clear.

The conference in which the seeds of these essays germinated was framed in a deliberately broad fashion. As a result, although there are many shared topics, themes, and approaches, the essays gathered here are predictably heterogeneous, and could have been organized in a variety of different ways. We have chosen to organize them into six categories, each of which corresponds to a key intervention made by Parry and Lord or an important aspect of their work. In many, if not most, cases, an essay could easily have been included in more than one category. Our organizational scheme is intended primarily as a way of highlighting six particularly significant facets of the legacies of Parry and Lord. These are, in the order of their appearance in this volume:

1. **"Formula and theme."** At the heart of the approach to oral poetry pioneered by Parry and Lord is their model of composition in performance, which relies on the verbal formula—itself the realization in words of a unit of meaning (a "theme" or "motif")—as its most fundamental mechanism. Parry's famous definition of the formula as "a group of words which is regularly employed under the same metrical conditions to express a given essential idea" has been subject to a good deal of criticism and revision over the years, but the concept remains among the most useful for the analysis and interpretation of oral poetry.[9] The concept of the "theme" as developed and elaborated by Lord has similarly proven to be of fundamental importance.[10] The first section of this book assembles essays that engage in different ways with these fundamental concepts. Taking up Lord's term for texts composed using techniques of formula and theme—"patterned narrative"—Minna Skafte Jensen ("Menelaus in the *Odyssey*: Introducing the 'Doubled Pattern' ") explores a special form of patterning in the *Odyssey,* one that doubles a thematic sequence in order to produce effects of emphasis and contrast. Françoise Létoublon ("The Trojan Formulaic Theater") explores the system of formulas referring to the city of Troy, confirming Parry's notions of the "economy" and "extension" of such systems but showing also how an economical and extensive formulaic system can be shaped by poetic concerns and the broader mythical context. Dwight Reynolds ("Composition in Performance, Arab Style"), summarizing results of his fieldwork among the Bani Hilal Bedouins of Northern Egypt in the 1980s, examines formulaic systems shaped by a very different kind of constraint, namely end-rhyme. Rhyme does not function as a constraint either in Homeric poetry or in the South Slavic traditions documented by Parry and Lord, but it does turn out to be the most significant constraint for the singers of the Arabic oral epic *Sīrat Banī Hilāl*, with important consequences for their techniques of composition in performance.

2. **"Comparative approaches."** Parry's initial fieldwork was founded on the notion that comparison with a living tradition of oral poetry could

[9] Parry 1971:272. For a sampling of some key views in the ongoing debate about the idea of the formula in oral poetry, see Finnegan 1992, Nagy 1996, and Friedrich 2019. Despite these lively debates over the course of decades, even prominent critics of Parry's formulation such as Finnegan have tended to conclude that the "basic insights remain stimulating and fruitful" (1992:72).

[10] Lord's delineation of the "theme" and its function in the composition of oral poetry represents his most important contribution to the "Parry-Lord Theory"; see Lord 2019:71–104.

illuminate the poetry of the distant past; his project as a whole was conceived in a fundamentally comparative spirit, insofar as he aimed to articulate a model of an oral style that would permit entirely unrelated texts, in different languages, to be brought into relation with each other as examples of oral composition in performance. Over the course of his long career, Lord made good on the promise of Parry's comparative methodology, bringing his ideas and those of Parry to bear on *Beowulf* and other Anglo-Saxon texts, the *Chanson de Roland*, the Byzantine epic *Digenis Akritas*, the *Kalevala*, Latvian *dainas*, Turkic epics, and other texts and traditions. The essays in Section Two all employ an explicitly comparative approach to shed new light on texts derived from oral traditions. Margaret Beissinger's discussion of the theme of incest in Romanian epic songs customarily sung at weddings ("Spiritual Kinship, Incest, and Traditional Weddings: Honor, Shame, and Cultural Boundaries in Romanian Marriage Songs") makes illuminating connections with similar themes in South Slavic epics and Anglo-Scots ballads, with the result that a fuller, more generalized picture is established of the relation between taboo violations in performed narratives and the social practices in which those performances are embedded. Anna Bonifazi and David F. Elmer ("Visuality in Bosniac and Homeric Epic") revisit the classic comparison made by Parry and Lord between South Slavic and Homeric epic but shift the *tertium comparationis* from formula and theme to the mediation of visual experience—which turns out to play an equally important role in traditional techniques of composition in performance. Joseph Falaky Nagy ("Heroes and Their Snakes") likewise makes use of South Slavic epic to cast light on the folkloric and mythological background of a medieval Irish tale; the point of comparison is in this case the remarkable motif of snakes inhabiting the multiple hearts of the hero's antagonist. Nikolay P. Grintser ("Common Grief: Weeping Over Hector and Rāma") undertakes a comparative analysis of lamentation as represented in Homeric and Sanskrit epic, tracing both common typologies and significant differences. His discussion reveals, among other things, the existence of an Indo-European ritual paradigm that the sequencing of laments in the *Iliad* both reflects and departs from for special effect.

3. **"Multiformity."** One of Lord's more important and lasting contributions to the study of oral traditional narrative is his insistence that one must think in terms of "multiformity" as a fundamental condition of oral tradition and discard the notion of "variation" with its implied

concept of an "original" from which the "variant" departs.[11] Each of the four essays of Section Three explores a different kind of multiformity, each fundamental to the tradition to which it belongs. Casey Dué and Mary Ebbott ("The Homer Multitext and the System of Homeric Epic") argue that the multiformity of the Homeric tradition, understood as a feature of oral composition in performance, demands, in the editing of the written records of that tradition, a different kind of textual criticism, one that takes full account of the systematic character of traditional multiformity. They offer their Homer Multitext project as an example of this new "digital criticism." In a theoretically and ethnographically rich discussion of the ecology of genres in the Finnish-Karelian region, Lotte Tarkka ("The 'Field of Song' and the Four-Legged Horse: On the Dialogue of Genres in Kalevala-Meter Poetry") provides numerous examples of the ways in which a generic system can provide a kind of matrix within which multiformity, as the recurrence of traditional elements in novel forms or contexts, becomes a mechanism of creative innovation: by hybridizing traditional generic forms or "translating" traditional content from one genre into another, performers are able to express themselves in new ways within the constraints of a traditional communicative system. In turn, Mirsad Kunić ("The Many Deaths of Mustaj Beg of Lika") draws on the Milman Parry Collection and other published song texts to explore different accounts of the death of a key Bosnian hero, Mustaj Beg of Lika, and the unique narrative practices that emerge in the *Krajina* frontier region at the western edge of the Ottoman Empire. His approach illustrates how a multiform-based reading of oral epic can enable a more granular analysis of local poetics that also suggests some of the cultural complexities of Muslim and Christian coexistence along the frontier. Finally, in a posthumously published essay, John Miles Foley explores the realization of epic song as the product of an individual singer's negotiation of regional and supra-regional traditions, applying the concept of "distributed authorship" to the kinds of creativity evident in epics from Stolac, Herzegovina. John's presentation was one of the highlights of the conference in which this volume originated, and his influence can be felt in many of the essays in this book. We are pleased to be able to include his own contribution.

4. **"Orality and Textuality."** As a scholar who had argued for the oral character of the Homeric poems on the basis of the evidence provided

11 Lord 2019:106–107; 1995:23.

by written texts, Parry was acutely aware of the complexity of the relationship between orality and writing. In Yugoslavia he found that many singers had been influenced in various ways by written texts. If only so that he could identify and focus his attention on the singers who were least influenced by the culture of writing, Parry made a great effort to document the circulation of printed texts, collecting hundreds of volumes of published songs (now part of the collections of Widener Library). Even so, one of the landmark products of Parry's own fieldwork, Avdo Međedović's "Wedding of Smailagić Meho," represents a song that the singer had learned via a written text.[12] Lord, in his own writing, likewise wrestled with the relationship between orality and writing, particularly in connection with the notion of the "transitional text."[13] The three authors whose essays appear in Section Four each explore a particular intersection of orality with writing. The writing in question in Olga M. Davidson's essay ("The Written Text as a Metaphor for the Integrity of Oral Composition in Classical Persian Traditions and Beyond") is, in the first instance, a metaphorical one: an archetypal Ur-text that serves as the basis, in terms of the poet's own mythologization, for the oral traditions that are textualized in Ferdowsi's *Shāhnāma*. Gísli Sigurðsson ("The Oral Background of the Eddas and Sagas") argues for the necessity of taking into consideration underlying oral traditions for a proper understanding of Old Norse Eddic poetry and sagas; he demonstrates how much is to be gained by appreciating the operation of "traditional referentiality" even in the case of the prose sagas, whose referential networks have too often been understood strictly in terms of relationships between written texts. In a similar way, Aida Vidan ("Držić's Magician and Lucić's Captive Maiden") employs a "palimpsestuous" reading of two plays of the Croatian Renaissance to uncover elements taken over from folklore and oral tradition, elements that are critical for understanding those plays' political subtexts.

12 Međedović learned this song by listening to a friend read aloud from a published version of a song originally collected in 1884 from a singer named Ahmed Isakov Šemić (Lord 2019:83). The version Međedović dictated for Parry ran to over 12,000 verses.

13 A "transitional text" suggests a text that occupies an intermediate position between orality and writing: for example, a text composed with the aid of writing, but which nevertheless exhibits a style that indicates "oral" methods of composition. Lord denied the possibility of such a text in *The Singer of Tales* (Lord 2019:138–141), but later came to accept it as a reality (Lord 1986:479–480, 491–494; 1995).

5. **"Performance and Context."** While the contemporary study of oral poetry naturally focuses on performances in their traditional contexts, Parry was ahead of his time in recording and studying actual performances of oral epic. Earlier scholars had to rely on texts gathered by dictation or taken down by teams of scribes transcribing the texts of performed songs; even in his own day, available recording technologies generally allowed the capture only of relatively short segments of a performance. Parry's innovative use of dual recording heads allowed him, by alternating between one turntable and the other, to make recordings of virtually any length: for the first time it was possible to record a song or a narrative exactly as the performer wished to sing or tell it. Parry went to great lengths to make these recording sessions feel as "natural" as possible for the performer, but of course singing into a microphone hardly represented a traditional context. Nevertheless, in their writings both Parry and Lord spend a good deal of time thinking about the ways in which context shapes performance. Section Five gathers four essays that touch on the dynamics of performance, the relationship between performance and context, or the documentation of performances in context. Thomas A. DuBois ("Performances, Texts, and Contexts: Olaus Sirma, Johan Turi, and the Dilemma of Reifying a Context-Dependent Oral Tradition") discusses two other pioneers in the study of oral poetry as an event inextricably embedded in a social context, Olaus Sirma and Johan Turi, writing in the seventeenth and early twentieth centuries, respectively. Working against the grain of contemporary tendencies to "itemize" folksong, these writers sought ways to present Sámi *joik* as "an embedded, context-dependent ethnographic event." In "The Poetics of Immanence in the American Mountain *Märchen*," Carl Lindahl offers us a precious glimpse of "the private dimensions of public performance" as he explores the inner worlds and domestic environments of the tellers of tales in an eastern Kentucky family. We learn about the striking and terrifying image of "Rawhead and Bloodybones" conjured in the mind of one future tale-teller and about the particular configurations of domestic life that shape both the content of the family's tales and the rituals of their performance. A pair of essays by Gejin Chao ("Indigenized Applications of the Oral-Formulaic Theory in China") and Qubumo Bamo ("The Institute of Ethnic Literature's Institutionalized Approaches to Living Oral Traditions") together describe past and present efforts to document and study oral traditions in China, where the extraordinary wealth of living traditions, many of them threatened by disruptions of traditional ways of

life brought about by modernization, demands an ambitious program of context-sensitive documentation. As Chao and Bamo both show, the strategies that have been employed in the Chinese context have been heavily influenced by the pioneering approaches of Parry and Lord, even as these approaches have been adapted and "indigenized" in various ways.

6. **"Audible Archives."** A central, if sometimes tacit, part of Parry's and Lord's work was conceiving of oral traditions as sonic practices and, indeed, as a kind of audible archive distributed among many singers across the topographies of a given tradition. In turn, their research practices generated audible archives as well: as described above, Parry commissioned a special pair of phonographs to allow for the continuous, real-time documentation of a singer's tale as sound. Lord managed that archive and built on it with many more recordings of his own (on wire spools and eventually magnetic tape) but also collaborated with composer/musicologist/pianist Béla Bartók to produce a book of song texts (transcribed by Vujnović and translated/annotated by Lord) and musical transcriptions (by Bartók). That resulting publication, *Serbo-Croatian Folk Songs* (Bartók and Lord 1951), was, in fact, the first book emerging from the Parry Collection materials, preceding the series of published song texts, *Serbocroatian Heroic Songs* (starting in 1953), and Lord's *The Singer of Tales* (1960, new editions in 2000 and 2019).[14] But more important than the question of chronological precedent is simply the emphasis Parry and Lord—each in his own way—placed on the sonic aspects of epic tradition. Indeed, we might reframe their broader intervention into ancient Greek epic studies as a challenge to understand Homeric poetry *as sound*, rather than as text—an audible tradition composed in real-time performance and transmitted orally/aurally across generations, rather than (just) a textualized corpus. The essays in this final section begin from this premise of *listening* to the archives, both figurative (as repertoire) and literal (as recordings), of oral poetry. Karl Reichl ("The Singing of Tales: The Role of Music in the Performance of Oral Epics in Turkey and Central Asia") opens his essay by looking briefly at the history of engagement (or lack thereof) with the musi-

[14] The various volumes of *Serbocroatian Heroic Songs* were numbered not according to their order of publication but according to their content: even-numbered volumes contained the original texts and odd-numbered ones translations, with volume numbers assigned in advance depending on the region in which the material for a planned volume was collected. As a result, the bibliographic record displays apparent anomalies: Volume 2 was the first to appear, in 1953, followed by Volume 1 in 1954, and there are gaps in the numbering.

> cal aspects of epic, ultimately offering an extended analysis of music and singing in Turkish and Central Asian Turkic epic traditions, with special attention to Âşık Şeref Taşlıova, a renowned singer of tales from Turkey who performed at the 2010 conference and sadly passed away in 2014. Zymer U. Neziri and Nicola Scaldaferri ("From the Archive to the Field: New Research on Albanian Epic Songs") explore the dialectic between archival holdings and fieldwork in the context of Albanian epic, a tradition that played an important role in Parry's research and was then taken up more overtly in Albert Lord's 1937 research trip to Northern Albania. Their essay culminates with a focus on one particular epic singer, Isa Elezi-Lekëgjekaj, a Kosovar Albanian with an expansive knowledge of tradition and a highly embodied performance practice. Ronelle Alexander's essay ("Tracking the South Slavic Epic Register") looks at intersections of sound and archive beyond the notion of music by revisiting the large body of interviews Parry and his assistants recorded in the 1930s. She examines these interviews as a linguistic archive that further elucidates oral poetics through its particular language "registers," a term John Miles Foley and others have previously explored in the context of oral poetry. Finally, Peter McMurray ("There Are No Oral Media? Multisensory Perceptions of South Slavic Epic Poetry") suggests that attending to sound within oral poetry quickly leads to a broader constellation of multisensory experiences, in which listening, vision, and spatiality become interconnected, even more intensely so once oral poetry is recorded.

Taken altogether, these essays suggest, again, a rich polyphony of both oral traditions and research approaches to those traditions. The volume, we hope, will point to important continuities extending from Parry's and Lord's research to the present, as well as to areas and themes where further work is needed. For instance, the contributions from authors dealing with the geographies/periods that primarily interested Parry and Lord—ancient Greece, modern Yugoslavia and its successor states—show how lively those conversations remain today and how much work might continue to be done there. At the same time, that historical legacy suggests a latent Euro- or Western-centrism within the study of oral traditions that calls for a more expansive engagement with scholars (both past and present) working outside of Europe and North America. On a related note, we are pleased to be able to include essays in this volume from several contributors who themselves come from the regions they study and as such highlight a different set of questions—of cultural and economic power, of insider/outsider dynamics, of repatriation—that have perhaps not been interrogated as thoroughly in oral traditional studies as they could or should be.

According to Albert Lord, the first paper Milman Parry planned to publish after his fieldwork in Yugoslavia was supposed to focus on what Parry called "the singer's rests" in epic songs—that is, the possibility that after singing some part of a tale, a South Slavic singer "will pause at almost any point in the narrative to rest himself or to put off the singing to another occasion" (Lord 1936:106). In that same spirit, we hope that this book of essays can act as a collective utterance by this group of scholars and the artists and poets whose work animates our research, knowing that after the "rest," other poets and scholars will carry these discussions further in a whole range of ways.

## Editorial Note

Because the contributions in this book deal with so many different languages and styles of transliteration, many of which are not universally agreed upon, there remains some discrepancy between spellings/transliteration of names and key terms across different chapters. Unless otherwise specified, translations are by the author of each chapter.

## Bibliography

Bartók, B., and A. B. Lord. 1951. *Serbo-Croatian Folk Songs: Texts and Transcriptions of Seventy-Five Folk Songs from the Milman Parry Collection and a Morphology of Serbo-Croatian Folk Melodies*. With a foreword by G. Herzog. New York.

Bohlman, P. V., and N. Petković. 2011. *Balkan Epic: Song, History, Modernity*. Lanham, MD.

Burton, A. 2005. *Archive Stories: Fact, Fiction, and the Writing of History*. Durham, NC.

Eidsheim, N. S., and K. Meizel, eds. 2019. *The Oxford Handbook of Voice Studies*. New York.

Elmer, D. F. 2010. "*Kita* and *Kosmos*: The Poetics of Ornamentation in Bosniac and Homeric Epic." *The Journal of American Folklore* 123/489:276–303.

———. 2013. "The Milman Parry Collection of Oral Literature." *Oral Tradition* 28:341–354.

Ernst, W. 2013. *Digital Memory and the Archive*. Ed. J. Parikka. Minneapolis.

———. 2015. *Stirrings from the Archive: Order from Disorder*. Trans. A. Siegel. Lanham, MD. Orig. pub. 2002.

———. 2016. *Sonic Time Machines: Explicit Sound, Sirenic Voices, and Implicit Sonicity*. Amsterdam.

Falzetti, A. G. 2015. "Archival Absence: The Burden of History." *Settler Colonial Studies* 5:128–144.

Finnegan, R. 1992. *Oral Poetry: Its Nature, Significance, and Social Context*. 2nd ed. Bloomington. Orig. pub. 1977.

Fisher, D. 2016. *The Voice and Its Doubles: Media and Music in Northern Australia*. Durham, NC.

Foley, J. M. 2004. *The Wedding of Mustajbey's Song Bećirbey: As performed by Halil Bajgorić*. Helsinki.

———. 2012. *Oral Tradition and the Internet: Pathways of the Mind*. Urbana, IL.

Friedrich, R. 2019. *Postoral Homer: Orality and Literacy in the Homeric Epic*. Stuttgart.

García, J. F. 2001. "Milman Parry and A. L. Kroeber: Americanist Anthropology and the Oral Homer." *Oral Tradition* 16:58–84.

Kanigel, R. 2021. *Hearing Homer's Song: The Brief Life and Big Idea of Milman Parry*. New York.

Lang, A., M. Murat, and C. Pardo. 2019. *Archives sonores de la poésie*. Dijon.

Lord, A. B. 1936. "Homer and Huso I: The Singer's Rests in Greek and Southslavic Heroic Song." *Transactions and Proceedings of the American Philological Association* 67:106–113.

———, ed. 1954. *Serbocroatian Heroic Songs*. Vol. 1, *Novi Pazar: English Translations*. With musical transcriptions by B. Bartók and prefaces by J. H. Finley, Jr. and R. Jakobson. Cambridge, MA.

———. 1986. "Perspectives on Recent Work on the Oral Traditional Formula." *Oral Tradition* 1:467-503.

———. 1991. *Epic Singers and Oral Tradition*. Ithaca.

———. 1995. "The Transitional Text." In *The Singer Resumes the Tale,* ed. M. L. Lord, 212-237. Ithaca.

———. 2019. *The Singer of Tales*. 3rd ed. Ed. D. F. Elmer. Hellenic Studies 77. Publications of the Milman Parry Collection of Oral Literature 4. Washington, DC. Orig. pub. Cambridge, MA, 1960.

Macintosh, F., J. McConnell, S. Harrison, and C. Kenward, eds. 2018. *Epic Performances from the Middle Ages into the Twenty-First Century.* Oxford.

McMurray, P. 2015. "Archival Excess: Sensational Histories Beyond the Audiovisual." *Fontes Artis Musicae* 62:262–275.

———. 2019. "After the Archive: An Archaeology of Bosnian Voices." In *The Oxford Handbook of Musical Repatriation*, ed. F. Gunderson, R. C. Lancefield, and B. Woods, 607–626. New York.

Minchin, E., ed. 2012. *Orality, Literacy and Performance in the Ancient World.* Leiden.

Nagy, G. 1996. *Homeric Questions*. Austin.

Ochoa Gautier, A. M. 2014. *Aurality: Listening and Knowledge in Nineteenth-Century Colombia*. Durham, NC.

Parry, M. 1971. *The Making of Homeric Verse: The Collected Papers of Milman Parry.* Ed. A. Parry. Oxford.

Ranković, S. 2012. "Managing the 'Boss': Epistemic Violence, Resistance, and Negotiations in Milman Parry's and Nikola Vujnović's *Pričanja* with Salih Ugljanin." *Oral Tradition* 27:5–66.

Ready, J. L. 2019. *Orality, Textuality, and the Homeric Epics: An Interdisciplinary Study of Oral Texts, Dictated Texts, and Wild Texts*. Oxford.

Saussy, H. 2016. *The Ethnography of Rhythm: Orality and Its Technologies*. New York.

Scaldaferri, N., ed. 2021. *Wild Songs, Sweet Songs: The Albanian Epic in the Collections of Milman Parry and Albert Lord.* Milman Parry Collection of Oral Literature 5. Cambridge, MA.

Stoler, A. L. 2008. *Along the Archival Grain: Epistemic Anxieties and Colonial Common Sense.* Princeton.

Tate, A. 2010. "'There Were Two Foreigners and One of Ours': Parry and Lord in Kijevo, Croatia, 24 September 1934." *Folklore* 121: 311-320.

Trouillot, M.-R. 1995. *Silencing the Past: Power and the Production of History*. Boston.

Vayntrub, J. 2019. *Beyond Orality: Biblical Poetry on Its Own Terms.* London.

Vidan, A. 2003. *Embroidered with Gold, Strung with Pearls: The Traditional Ballads of Bosnian Women*. Milman Parry Collection of Oral Literature 1. Cambridge, MA.

Yasar, K. 2018. *How the Telephone, Phonograph and Radio Shaped Modern Japan, 1868–1945*. New York.

# PART I

# FORMULA AND THEME

# 1

# Menelaus in the *Odyssey*: Introducing the "Doubled Pattern"

Minna Skafte Jensen

## Introduction

In *The Singer of Tales*, Albert Lord introduced the term "patterned narrative" for texts composed by formulas and themes. In his introductory discussion of patterns, Lord identified patterning on the level of rhythm, word-boundaries, syntax, sound, and thought, and further on he also spoke of patterns of formulas, themes, groups of themes, and songs.[1] By drawing an analogy with "formulas" he defined "themes" as "the groups of ideas regularly used in telling a tale in the formulaic style of traditional song."[2] Thus, Lord's themes are less abstract and generalized than Vladimir Propp's thirty-one functions that constitute the Russian fairy tale[3] and, especially, they are not limited to a fixed number. Already in 1963 Patricia Arant, in her study of Russian *byliny,* felt the need to distinguish between "theme" = typical scene and "story pattern" = sequence of events, and she arranged the various formulaic units according to size, positing the scale, formula—theme—story pattern—song.[4] The patterns I am concerned with in the present paper are such story patterns as Arant describes.

A possible description of Homeric poetry is that it consists of a surface narrative built on underlying patterns, and in this sense the difference between theme (= typical scene) and story pattern is not only one of size but also of level: themes belong to the surface narrative and are often expressed with the same

1 Lord 2019:42-46 (patterning on many levels), 45-46 (patterning of formulas), 71-72 (of themes), 119 (of groups of themes), 128 (of songs).

2 Lord 2019:71.

3 Propp 1968:25–65.

4 Arant 1990:10, 65, 118.

words whenever they recur, whereas patterns may work without any such similarities in phrasing. The distinction between the two elements is fluid.

There are general patterns and more particularized ones, and there are patterns within patterns. The *Odyssey* as such is a return song and follows a pattern known from many parts of the world; a particularly close parallel is to be found in the Turkic *Epic of Alpāmïš*.[5] Among the songs collected by Parry and Lord in the former Yugoslavia, return songs constitute a subgenre, and John Miles Foley has analyzed them as a parallel to the *Odyssey*.[6] Recently, Anna Bonifazi has compared ancient non-Greek return stories to the *Odyssey*, especially some Egyptian prose tales.[7] On a global scale, the *Odyssey* is related to motif no. 974 in Aarne-Thompson-Uther's index of folklore motifs, the story of the absent lover or husband who returns to his beloved exactly when she is on the point of being wedded to another man. Considered as a more particularized pattern in the complex of stories about the Trojan War, the *Odyssey* is a *nostos*, a tale of what happened to the Greek heroes on their journeys home after the sack of Troy. When in Books 3 and 4 of the *Odyssey* Nestor and Menelaus tell what happened to them and most of the other heroes on their voyages back, these tales are *nostoi* within the *nostos*, and when the tales Menelaus offers are actually accounts of what the monstrous sage Proteus told him, these *nostoi* are part of Menelaus' *nostos* which is again part of Odysseus' *nostos*.

The Finnish folklorist Lauri Honko introduced the term "pool of tradition" for the sum of formulas and story patterns common to all singers in a given epic tradition.[8] According to how well-trained and competent singers are, their individual pools of tradition or "epic idiolect" may compare to the common pool or only parts of it.

Most patterns were probably age-old contributions to the rhapsodes' common pool of tradition. In an epic tradition, formulas and themes are analogs to the lexicon of natural languages and the patterns to the syntax, and just as in a natural language new words and phrases are introduced with relative ease while syntax tends to remain stable, new formulas are probably coined more frequently than patterns. An epic singer may activate known patterns endlessly, introducing new actors and building up new narratives, and sometimes this may change a pattern so much that a new pattern is born. Only if such a new pattern is accepted by other singers will it enter the shared pool. In general, there is no more sense in investigating the age of a pattern than in discussing the origin of languages.

5 For a modern edition, see Reichl 2001.

6 Foley 1990, especially 12–13.

7 Bonifazi 2009:481–484.

8 Honko 1998:70–73, with a reference to Ruth Finnegan.

For the various songs epic singers have in their repertories, they have "mental texts" that may be expanded, abbreviated, or varied in other ways to meet the expectations of a given audience, and any performance is a multiform of this mental text.[9] Whenever a singer of epic wishes to add volume to his mental text, he may multiply his patterns.[10] The method is well known in the two surviving Homeric epics. For instance, in the *Iliad*, the poet is able to base an overwhelming variety of battle scenes on a few patterns.[11] Similarly, in the *Odyssey*, the *nostos* is a generously multiplied story pattern. In Honko's terminology, the poets activate patterns from their pool of tradition and flesh them out as it suits the context.

This way of composition raises a fundamental problem for the interpreter: when is the use of a formula or pattern general or particular? Over the decades, scholars have given different answers. In 1974, Michael Nagler stated: "All is traditional on the generative level, all original on the level of performance."[12] I accept this as the basic answer: the poet/singer is responsible for choosing what formulas and patterns to activate and how to do it. Still, also on the level of performance, they may be more or less particularized.

An unusually clear position is taken by Maureen Alden in the case of what she calls "para-narratives": "All the narratives which do not advance the main plot ... are nevertheless related to it or to an episode within it, and shed light on its interpretation," she states, and she proceeds to show how every passage which might be considered just a digression is important for understanding the *Iliad* and the *Odyssey*.[13] She is an acute and careful reader; even so, her standpoint gives me an uneasy feeling compared to the very common experience of fieldworkers that epic singers often let more or less relevant episodes enter their performance merely, or at least mainly, in order to expand it. The respect for quantity, for grand performances, is widespread and, I think, shared by the Homeric poets, and I find it difficult to believe that they never succumbed to the temptation of adding to their text by, for example, repeating a pattern with suitable variation. Besides, we have the problem of the listeners. How did they react to para-narratives? Alden has an impressive demonstration of how Achilles' meetings with Aeneas and Hector in *Iliad* Book 20 follow the same patterns as Diomedes' meetings with Glaucus and Hector in Books 6 and 11 respectively.[14] What was the poet's message? Did he expect his audience on listening to Book

9 Honko 1998:92–99.

10 Singers of epic tend to be male, and as far as our sources go, Greek rhapsodes were men.

11 Fenik 1968.

12 Nagler 1974:26.

13 Alden 2000:10. See also Alden 2010 and 2017. Grethlein 2017 offers similar interpretations.

14 Alden 2000:173–178.

20 to think back to Diomedes and Glaucus and realize that these heroes foreshadowed what was now happening to Achilles? Such questions are, of course, beyond clear answering. Nevertheless, they are implied when we, as readers, discuss general or particular activation of patterns, and our understanding is in each case dependent on special interpretation.

Sometimes the parallelism of patterns is explicitly referred to in the surface narrative. In the *Odyssey*, that is most conspicuously the case of Agamemnon's *nostos*. Agamemnon, Clytemnestra, Aegisthus, and Orestes are in various contexts compared to Odysseus, Penelope, the suitors, and Telemachus, often recommended as a moralistic-rhetorical paradigm for Telemachus. Georg Danek has pointed to the fact that the narrator often gives Agamemnon's story a special twist in order to make it fit as a model for Odyssean events.[15] However, most multiplied patterns are just there, without any explicit comment on their function.

In some cases, the *Odyssey* displays two multiforms of a pattern that are particularly close, as in the case of the just-mentioned use of Agamemnon's homecoming as a foil to that of Odysseus. In other respects, Menelaus' *nostos* is the one most similar to Odysseus'. Particularly in the story of Proteus, Menelaus' *nostos* activates a pattern that recurs in Books 10–12 as part of Odysseus' *nostos*: the hero has troubles in finding his way home—a goddess (Eidothea, Circe) explains to him that he has to ask a sage what to do (Proteus, the dead soul of Teiresias)—the sage is only accessible by means of great efforts (Proteus has to be caught and kept from escaping into other shapes, Teiresias must be raised from Hades) but the goddess explains how to proceed—the advice the sage offers is to give a sacrifice. Whether this double has particularized significance remains unclear.

In the wealth of multiforms of the pattern "arrival of a guest," the two activations in which a young host manages to receive an unexpected guest—Telemachus in Book 1 and Nausicaa in Book 6—make a particularly interesting doubling of the pattern, since they are not only young but also perform their duties under unusual circumstances. Telemachus must bid his guest welcome while the suitors have occupied his home, and Nausicaa is not even at home and approached by a starkly naked guest. Both succeed blamelessly, but the reader who compares the two youngsters might well be especially impressed by Nausicaa's resourcefulness. Recently, Joel Christensen has argued for interpreting Telemachus in Book 1 as a foil to Odysseus in Book 5.[16] Both are met by Athena in a situation in which they have lost confidence in solving their

15 Danek 1998:40, 42, 78.

16 Christensen 2020:47–70.

problems and are overwhelmed by "Learned Helplessness," and Telemachus' development towards agency prepares audiences for what happens later on with his father. I accept Christensen's interpretation of Telemachus as a foil to Odysseus and think the young man has a similar function in relation to Nausicaa. That he is remembered by the listeners of Books 5 and 6 seems probable simply because the first scenes of the poem are likely to remain present in their minds.

In all these cases, two activations of one and the same pattern are closer to each other than what is implied in a general multiplying of patterns. The doubled pattern is related to one of the "Laws of Folk Narrative" which Axel Olrik once established, "Two to a Scene": folk narrative "only reluctantly brings more than two characters on stage at the same time."[17] Such character doubles occur often in the *Odyssey.* Among the three enchantresses who pose a risk to Odysseus' homecoming, two are particularly close—Calypso and Circe—and it is exactly the similarity between them that brings out their deeply different natures.[18] Another interesting pair is constituted by Odysseus and his swineherd Eumaeus. In a sophisticated analysis of the relationship between them, Tim Wright demonstrates how the two characters mirror each other: "We do not just have a swineherd hosting a beggar; we have a swineherd who used to be a *basileus* (unknowingly) hosting a beggar who also used to be a *basileus* in the very household in which he is now being hosted."[19]

Just as two protagonists in a scene serve to bring out clearly their contrasting characters and standpoints, two activations of the same story pattern may call attention to the elements that distinguish the two. Their confrontation calls forth their individuality, a common enough feature in the *Iliad* and the *Odyssey*. On the basis of her narratological approach, Irene de Jong speaks of "the technique of juxtaposition."[20] Compared to the *Iliad*, however, the use of the doubled pattern as described here seems to belong to the *Odyssey* poet's individual pool of tradition, his idiolect.

In what follows, I shall argue that the visits Odysseus' son Telemachus pays to Nestor and Menelaus (*Odyssey* 3.1–4.623 and 15.1–181) constitute such a doubled pattern, and that this special example works in such a way that its first activation serves as a foil for the second one. I have argued elsewhere for the opinion that the *Iliad* and the *Odyssey* are oral poems in the full sense of the term—orally composed, performed, and transmitted—and this will here be taken for granted.[21] Accordingly, just before they hear Book 4, the audience has

17 Olrik 1992:43.

18 Jensen 1994.

19 Wright 2019, quote p. 12.

20 de Jong 2001:68.

21 Jensen 1980; cf. Jensen 2011.

listened to Book 3. What I am concerned with in this paper is the narrative[22] of the *Odyssey*, this particular multiform of the rhapsode's mental text.

## The Doubled Pattern of *Odyssey* 3–4

The very similarity of the two passages underlines the individuality of protagonists and behavior. Nestor and Menelaus are both impressive heroes, each in his own way, but the harmony in Pylos is in marked contrast to the tensions in Sparta, and the cheerful atmosphere in Nestor's palace underlines the melancholy that pervades Menelaus' surroundings. The fact that the two parallel passages occur in immediate sequel is included as an element of the interpretation: to the audience that was present at the original composition-in-performance of the *Odyssey*, an understanding of Menelaus on the background of Nestor must have offered itself naturally.

Single elements in the chain of events may themselves be analyzed as patterns and themes, more or less generalized. For instance, the themes of the bath, the greeting, and the feast have been analyzed by Foley,[23] and they lend themselves to analysis as potential parts of an often-recurring arrival pattern.

Menelaus and Helen are, of course, among the absolute protagonists of the Trojan War, with detailed stories in the pool of tradition shared by all Homeric rhapsodes, and Nestor is a figure with a history that goes back to Indo-European prehistory.[24] This means that the poet's narrative was conditioned and restricted by fixed elements of their stories. There was a "*Faktenkanon*" (in Wolfgang Kullmann's sense)[25] that could not be significantly changed, and it seems to have contained at least the following details: they all survived the war, but Nestor lost his son Antilochus there—Menelaus took his wife back—they returned safely to their homes, Nestor by direct voyage, Menelaus and Helen after many years of adventurous roaming.

Such stories constituted the very material with which the poet built his narrative and which, at the same time, restricted his creativity and compelled him to remain within a fixed framework. What he was free to decide, however, was how he would describe the characters and the events in which they were involved, what kind of interest he would make his audience take in them, and especially, whether he would make his listeners sympathize with them. The great Athenian tragedians handled the myths in a similar way.

22 For the distinction between story and narrative (*histoire*/*récit*), see Genette 1980:25–27.

23 Foley 1990:247–277.

24 Frame 1978 and 2009.

25 Kullmann 1960:12–13.

In comparison, Nestor's youngest son Pisistratus seems to have had little or no existence in myth—no stories are known of him, and in Hesiod's list of Nestor's offspring he is not included.[26] This impression may, of course, be misguided. Most of Greek epic and storytelling has been lost, and we cannot say with any certainty whether this young man also had a place in the *Faktenkanon*. But this does not seem to have been the case, and the suspicion is reinforced by the fact that he is relatively pale and uninteresting as a character. To an oral poet, the traditional stories are the very thread of which the fabric of his narrative is woven, and the richer the material is in the pool of tradition, the more detailed and nuanced the narrative becomes.

The course of events in the two narratives is closely similar: Telemachus arrives accompanied by a friend. In Book 3 the friend is the goddess Athena disguised as an elderly man, in Book 4, Pisistratus. The guests arrive just as the host is engaged in a great celebration: Nestor is making a sacrifice to Poseidon surrounded by his sons and subjects, and Menelaus is celebrating a wedding. The arrival of the newcomers is reported to the host, and he acts with the utmost correctness, caring for the wellbeing of his guests before asking them about their identity. In both cases, Telemachus is the inexperienced young man from a relatively humble court at the margins of the Greek world, who visits a rich and famous man, a protagonist from the War of Troy. During their stay, the host tells the guests of the adventures of the various Greek heroes on their voyages back from Troy after the sack of the city. The guests stay overnight and are sent off with caring solicitude.

In her commentary, Stephanie West points to the melancholic atmosphere of Menelaus' household as compared to that of Nestor's, and Irene de Jong states her impression that "underneath the glitter and glamour of the palace, much sorrow lies hidden."[27] I agree with both of them. But I think that this observation can be carried much further, and that when the two books are read as a doubled activation of the same pattern, the components of the sorrow and melancholy come out especially clearly.

A special sophistication in the narrative is the fact that the narrator does not comment upon the proceedings but lets them speak for themselves. Nestor is presented almost as in a painting, surrounded by sons and companions as he presides over the sacrifice to Poseidon. He is the epitome of an old and venerable king, head of a flourishing community and a large and respected family. Besides Antilochus, who was killed fighting courageously in the war, he has six sons and at least one daughter. The atmosphere is peaceful and uncomplicated:

26 Aloni 2006:73–75.

27 West 1988:158, 192–195, 200; de Jong 2001:91; cf. Danek 1998:96.

when the guests arrive, people flock around them, and the youngest son, Pisistratus, spontaneously invites them to approach the king. Nestor's behavior is respectful and considerate, and after suitable hospitality, when he begins to ask the guests about their names and errands, he does so in a simple and direct fashion. Besides that, his piety is underlined both in the sacrificial procedure in which he is engaged on their arrival and in his reaction toward the end of the day when he understands that one of his guests was the goddess Athena herself in disguise. That he is also well-to-do is clear from the impressive number of cattle being sacrificed the first morning, as well as from the detail that, when a heifer is sacrificed to the goddess the next day, a goldsmith is fetched to cover her horns with gold.

From beginning to end, Nestor's every act is completely natural and satisfactory. On the morning before Telemachus departs for Sparta accompanied by Pisistratus, the king is, again, depicted as on a canvas but this time in more detail. He is described seated in his father's official seat and surrounded by his many sons, whose names are listed. In this way, he stands out as the quintessence of human perfection, a man who has had a life in harmony with gods and men, the son of a hero and himself the father of a prosperous lineage.

The festivities at Menelaus' court are occasioned by a double wedding: Menelaus is celebrating that his daughter with Helen is being wedded to Achilles' son, and that his son with a slave woman is being wedded to a local bride. This is briefly stated at the beginning of the poem, and commentators have been bewildered by the fact that, as the evening develops, the double wedding seems to be forgotten while the narrative concentrates on Telemachus and Pisistratus and their conversation with Menelaus and Helen. Instead of asking, "Why is the wedding forgotten?" I prefer to ask, "Why is it there?" The answer, I submit, is that it underlines an important difference between Nestor and Menelaus.

At the arrival in Pylos, Pisistratus observed the newcomers and went to inform his father. At the arrival in Sparta, one of Menelaus' attendants, a certain Eteoneus, goes to inform the king and asks how the two young guests should be treated, and Menelaus gives him a small lecture on the rules of hospitality. What is a simple, natural process in Pylos is a question of rules and forms in Sparta. At the root of this difference is the fact that Nestor is the proud father of a large family. In Sparta there is no young son to point out the arrival. Menelaus has a daughter, as beautiful as Aphrodite herself, and her wedding to the son of the foremost fighter from Troy is the best possible match—high society if ever there was one! Except for her, his only child is an illegitimate son whose name is Megapenthes ("Whose sorrow is great"), a name which might have been an epithet of his father.[28] The narrator does not comment on this, but compared with Nestor, Menelaus lacks what is most important of all, sons—to continue his lineage—and in Sparta the wedding, however noble, makes this fact painfully evident.

## The Silent Telemachus

Readers have focused on the stories that Helen and Menelaus tell as evening entertainment, and they are, of course, among the strangest elements of the narrative, in themselves an obvious example of such character doubles that bring forth the different natures of the two speakers.[29] Besides, this element of the event constitutes a significant distinction between the two multiforms of the pattern of Telemachus' visits.

Here, however, I am more interested in the difference to be found between the dialogues that develop between host and guest. Whereas Telemachus approaches Nestor with a short, dignified speech, he does not utter a word to Menelaus until the end of the evening when he asks to be allowed to go to bed. In striking contrast to his young guest (but with reminiscences of Nestor as he is represented in the *Iliad*), Menelaus talks and talks. Why is Telemachus so silent and Menelaus so talkative?

In Pylos the guests were asked their names and errand in so many words, and when Nestor heard that Telemachus was Odysseus' son, he recognized in him an intellectual similarity to his father. In Sparta things are less simple. In his first address to his guests, Menelaus mentions that he will ask them questions when they have had their meal, but the conversation develops differently. Telemachus, who is overwhelmed by the richness and elegance of Menelaus' hall, whispers to Pisistratus that this must be how the gods live on Olympus. Menelaus hears this and, while he assures them that mortals should not compete with gods, he allows that he may be perhaps the richest man in the world. However, he states that he would be content with a third of his riches if it would bring back to life his dead companions (4.97–103). This is the only passage in which it is stated directly that Menelaus, for all his riches and his elegant court, is not a very happy man.

Finally, he speaks of Odysseus, whose life remains in question. When he mentions how hard the situation must be for his wife and son, Telemachus breaks into tears. In this passage, another pattern is activated with the following sequence: X mentions Y, who is present – Y cries and hides his head – Z notices and reacts. This sequence recurs in Book 8.521–534, when Odysseus asks the

28 Nagy 1979:146n2.

29 Alden 2017:158.

Phaeacian bard to perform the song of the Wooden Horse. In that passage, the incident leads Odysseus to reveal his identity, which had until then been unknown to the others.

In Sparta the pattern also triggers the identification of the guest but in a strangely muddled way. It is stated that Menelaus has not yet decided how to react when his gorgeous wife makes her grand appearance. She immediately steals the show and, looking at the guests, recognizes Telemachus as Odysseus' son. When she mentions this, her husband admits that he had thought so himself. The reader may well speculate: if Menelaus realizes all along who the young man is, why then does he not say so? Instead he provokes the guest to reveal himself by mentioning his father and how much he has worried about him and his family. The suspicion that Menelaus postpones his question on purpose is reinforced by the strange wording of his thoughts at Telemachus' crying: should he let the young man himself mention his father or, rather, ask him first and investigate everything (4.117–119)?

Telemachus remains silent, but Pisistratus speaks for them both, and Menelaus continues, stating in rather exaggerated terms how dear a friend Odysseus was to him, which makes everybody cry. Menelaus does not, however, answer Pisistratus' questions. Instead, Menelaus seems to have his mind focused upon something different. The conversation ends with Menelaus asserting that he and Telemachus will speak to each other the next morning. Again, the reader may ask: why not now?

Except for the whispered remark to his friend, Telemachus is silent throughout the evening. Pisistratus is the one to confirm that his friend is actually Odysseus' son and to state that he has come to ask for Menelaus' help in words or deed (4.163). Now, this was not actually the purpose of Telemachus' journey. He was to gather information about his father, not ask for help. In my understanding, this detail reveals that Pisistratus, on hearing that Menelaus does not know where Odysseus is, changes the errand accordingly,[30] and I take Telemachus' silence as an opposite reaction to the same remark. Pisistratus reacts to what is said: Menelaus has no information to give but may be helpful in other ways. Telemachus, instead, reacts to what is not said and suspects that there is something fishy about Menelaus' remark: perhaps he knows something that he does not want to tell. In this detail, then, we have the two friends, Pisistratus and Telemachus, compared according to Olrik's law.

Menelaus in his speech and Telemachus in his silence both show a similar kind of empathy: on seeing the young man, Menelaus guesses not

[30] In this I follow the scholiast on verse 163.

only his identity but also his errand, and Telemachus understands that Menelaus has understood but that the information he asks for will be unpleasant to him.[31]

The conversation goes back to the Trojan War, and host and hostess each tell of a famous incident in which Odysseus was the protagonist. Helen recalls his dangerous expedition when he entered Troy in disguise, and Menelaus tells of his stratagem, the Trojan Horse. Alden points out the similarity of the two speeches: "The deliberate correspondences and repeated motifs require them to be taken as a pair, revealing the characters of the two narrators, and something of their relationship,"[32] and I agree with her; otherwise, her discussion of the scene is concerned with other aspects of it. They are strange stories to tell as entertainment to this small, intimate audience, for Helen actually asserts that Odysseus revealed the Greek plan to her, and Menelaus, for his part, describes how Helen did her best to betray the Greek warriors—Menelaus himself and Odysseus among them—while they were hiding in the horse. In short, the stories tell how Odysseus and Helen respectively acted as traitors to the Greeks. Menelaus' story is insulting to Helen, as has often been pointed out, but it might be maintained that Helen's story is just as insulting to Odysseus' son: his father was clever enough to enter Troy in disguise but not clever enough to deceive Helen and not principled enough not to talk. The scholiast on verse 4.256 understands the plan Odysseus revealed to be the stratagem of the horse, which is an attractive interpretation that links the two parallel speeches together and explains how Helen could betray the warriors in the horse.[33] However, before the storytelling, Helen has doctored the wine, inserting a drug that protects the drinkers against any form of sadness—the adjective is *nēpenthes* "without sorrow." Gregory Nagy has underlined its effect: it makes storytellers and audience forget their personal involvement in what is told.[34]

After the storytelling, Telemachus—not the host—suggests that it is time to go to bed. Drugged or not, the entertainment seems not to have pleased him.

31 At a conference in Hamburg, in October 2010, Ruth Scodel drew attention to a series of examples of such empathy between Homeric actors.

32 Alden 2017:158.

33 West 1988:210 also follows the scholiast. Ann Bergren's sophisticated interpretation of the two speeches is thought-provoking, but I remain unconvinced by her reading of Helen's story, especially when she suggests that with the bathing scene Helen may be trying "to seduce her young guest with glimpses of a sexual scene with his father" (Bergren 2009:326). Compare 3.464–465 (Telemachus bathed by Nestor's daughter).

34 Nagy 1979:100.

## The Talkative Menelaus

The next morning, Menelaus wakes up, goes straight to where Telemachus and Pisistratus are sleeping, and asks Telemachus what his errand is. In the long ensuing bedside conversation, Pisistratus is not mentioned, and we must assume that he is asleep so that now, finally, Telemachus and Menelaus are alone and can speak freely. Telemachus puts his question exactly as he did to Nestor (3.92–101 = 4.322–331), in both cases underlining that he wants to be told the truth even if it is unpleasant, and Menelaus embarks upon the long tale of his many adventures during the eight years after the fall of Troy before he reached his home. The most exciting is the tale of how he succeeded in finding Proteus—the sea-monster who knows all but escapes into ever-shifting forms—and made him tell what he knew of the *nostoi* of Ajax, Agamemnon, and Odysseus. It is a long and colorful speech, 260 verses in all, of which merely ten contain the information sought by Telemachus (4.551–560). After that extremely brief passage, Menelaus proceeds immediately to what Proteus said about Menelaus himself, how he would never die but live in eternity in Elysium because he was the son-in-law of Zeus. So the information about Odysseus almost disappears in the wealth of tales told by Menelaus.

However, it reveals that Menelaus does actually know, and that when, on the young men's arrival, he stated that Odysseus' fate was unknown, he was lying. Here, then, the question is: why does Menelaus postpone his story until the two are alone, and why does he talk and talk of things about which Telemachus does not ask, while answering his question so briefly?

At the end of the speech, Menelaus invites Telemachus to stay in Sparta. Telemachus' reaction is remarkable: he praises Menelaus for being a great storyteller but declines his invitation, and he comments not a single word about the sensational information he, at long last, has had of his father (4.594–599). Menelaus accepts the young man's wish to return, and just as at the arrival of the guests, he gives a small lecture on the duties of a host.[35] Here this action is interrupted, only to resume at the beginning of Book 15.

Other readers have emphasized other aspects of the proceedings, but it seems to me that the story of Telemachus and Menelaus is that of a kind older man who keeps beating about the bush in order to avoid having to tell a young guest the unpleasant news that, when his lost father has not returned to his mother, the reason is that he is spending his time on a distant island with a lady.

When much later Telemachus tells his mother of his journey, his report of the visit to Menelaus reduces the hero's long speech to the few verses about Odysseus,

[35] The brevity of the crucial passage and the fact that Telemachus does not comment upon it are my main arguments for not seeing Menelaus' postponement as just a "series of retardations," as stated by de Jong 2001:89.

including a direct quote of the crucial words about Odysseus and Calypso but leaving out the detail of his father's crying (4.557–560 = 17.143–146). Unlike Menelaus, the young man shows no regard for the feelings of his addressee.

At the beginning of his long speech, Menelaus had expressed his wish that Odysseus would soon return, strong and powerful as he had known him in former days and take revenge on the suitors (4.341–346). How different was the description Proteus gave! The image of the returning father with which Menelaus opened his speech must have met the son's every wish, but the passive, crying Odysseus who perhaps makes the audience feel compassion would, to his son, appear simply pathetic.

However much Menelaus lets Proteus state that Odysseus stays with Calypso against his will, the son may have his doubts. The listeners have been told by Athena herself at the beginning of the poem that Odysseus does, as a matter of fact, wish to get away, which builds up the expectation that he is the goddess's sex prisoner. But in Book 4 Telemachus has only Menelaus' word for it and may well suspect that his host is trying to veil unpleasant facts. When, in Book 5, the tale of Calypso's relations to Odysseus is told, it actually turns out that the hero has not always been so eager to get away. The notion that the mention of Calypso must have been shocking to Telemachus is reinforced when we compare what Athena/Mentes said to him to begin with, that his father was probably detained on some faraway island by hostile men (1.197–199). The father Telemachus wishes for is the returning, powerful avenger. A dead father would also be acceptable. A father who is alive but does not return, whether against his will or not, is a catastrophe.

Book 15 begins early in the morning, before daybreak (and here another pattern makes itself felt, that a book of the *Odyssey* normally begins in the morning).[36] Commentators have disagreed about how to understand the link to Book 4. Formally, Telemachus has now spent many days in Sparta while the parallel storyline has brought his father from Calypso's island back to Ithaca: "While one storyline is in the foreground, the others usually remain stationary, i.e. time ticks on, but nothing important happens."[37] The narrator leaves Telemachus after his morning talk with Menelaus, and when he finally resumes this storyline at the beginning of Book 15, he concentrates on the essence of the development in Book 4, that Telemachus was told that his father was living with Calypso on her island, just as if nothing had happened in the meantime. To me,

[36] Jensen 2011:350–360.
[37] de Jong 2001:590.

Telemachus lying awake at the beginning of Book 15 has just had his shocking conversation with Menelaus.

While his friend Pisistratus is still asleep, Telemachus receives a visit from Athena, who urges him to return home to Ithaca as soon as possible. His mother, she argues, is at the point of remarrying, and that might lead to a total loss of livelihood on his part. Further, she informs him of the fact that the suitors plan to waylay him on his way back and gives him advice on how to evade the ambush.

Epiphanies have their patterns, too, and when gods interfere, they may be helpful, as Athena is at the beginning of the poem; adverse, as Hermes is to Calypso in Book 5; or even deceitful, as when Zeus sends Agamemnon a misleading dream at the beginning of *Iliad* 2. When gods are helpful, their advice often resembles what, in modern times, would be understood as a mental process: a person has a good idea or is developing a passion. To a modern mind, Hera making Achilles convene the assembly in Book 1 of the *Iliad* (1.55–56) would be understood as the hero's independent reaction to the fact that his comrades were dying without the supreme leader taking action; and, when later on Athena restrains him from drawing his sword and attacking Agamemnon (1.193–196), her arguments against the impulsive act are such as Achilles himself might have had on second thought.[38] Similarly, the first half of Athena's speech to Telemachus in *Odyssey* 15 may be interpreted as the kind of thoughts the young man would naturally have, lying in bed in the early morning and trying to cope with the unpleasant piece of information he just received. His father will never return, his mother will accept a new husband, and he must necessarily reach home before she has emptied the house of its valuables.

In what follows, Telemachus is all the time intent on precipitating his departure, whereas Menelaus tries to keep him back, even suggesting that the two of them could go on a sightseeing tour around the region, meeting people and receiving gifts. It seems that Menelaus is convinced that Odysseus will never return, and as the kind and caring man he is, he makes a constructive first effort to help his young guest set up a life of his own. When on Telemachus' departure an omen occurs, Menelaus cannot decide how it should be interpreted. Helen, however, who is Zeus' daughter, feels no restraint against assuring the guest that his father will actually return and do away with the suitors—as will eventually happen. However, with the knowledge accessible to them at the beginning of Book 15, it seems to me that the two men's reactions, Telemachus' eagerness to depart, as well as Menelaus' procrastination and hesitation, demonstrate that they have both lost the hope of Odysseus' return. Based on the information

[38] Snell 1975:35–36.

Menelaus had been given from Proteus, there is no reason for them to expect that Odysseus will ever come back to Ithaca.

## Conclusion

Analyzed as a doubled pattern, the visits to Nestor and Menelaus handle the hosts' storytelling in a way that underlines the difference between the messages of the two *nostos*-stories, which on the surface are so very similar and together tell a continued story of the homecomings. Whereas Nestor simply informs Telemachus of what he knows, Menelaus' story is full of twists and turns that serve to veil an unpleasant fact.

Furthermore, the doubled pattern reveals the sad fate of Menelaus. He may be immensely rich and have the most beautiful woman in the world as his wedded wife, but he is not at home in his palace and cannot speak freely as he pleases. His relations with Helen seem happy enough but require potent drugs when the past is mentioned.

Nestor's name is cognate with *nostos*. Douglas Frame, who underscores the derivative *-tor* and translates the name as "Homebringer" rather than "Homecomer," argues that the name was still so understood in "the Homeric era."[39] However, in the specific narrative of the *Odyssey*, I cannot find traces of the active sense. In my reading of *Odyssey* 3, Nestor is the homecomer, the hero of the Trojan cycle who really comes home, in all senses of the word. He survives the war and escapes the dangers of the sea on his homeward journey. In general, he steers his voyage through life so that, on reaching old age, he arrives safely and happily at his proper destination. Compared to that, Menelaus remains unsettled, despite returning to his Spartan kingdom and regaining his famous wife.

The comparison with Nestor makes clear the tragedy of Menelaus. In the Homeric world there are two kinds of afterlife available to mortals. One is the continuation of the family line, the other the fame bestowed by epic songs. Nestor will have both: he has always been a respected warrior and has generated a wealth of stories. In addition, he is the father to many sons. Menelaus has his daughter Hermione, but her offspring will continue Achilles' line, not his. While he has been adequate as a warrior, his main story will be that he was the husband from whom Helen ran away. He may look forward to eternal bliss in Elysium, but through no merit of his own. Even in the afterlife, Helen steals the show.

[39] Frame 2009:182n78.

## Bibliography

Alden, M. 2000. *Homer Beside Himself: Para-Narratives in the* Iliad. Oxford.

———. 2017. *Para-narratives in the Odyssey: Stories in the Frame*. Oxford.

Aloni, A. 2006. *Da Pilo a Sigeo: Poemi cantori e scrivani al tempo dei Tiranni*. Alessandria.

Arant, P. M. 1990. *Compositional Techniques of the Russian Oral Epic, the Bylina*. Harvard Dissertations in Folklore and Oral Tradition. New York. Reprint of PhD diss., Harvard University, 1963.

Bergren, A. 2009. "Helen's 'Good Drug': *Odyssey* iv 1–305." In Doherty 2009:314–335. Orig. pub. 1981 in *Contemporary Literary Hermeneutics and the Interpretation of Classical Texts*, ed. S. Kresic, 201–214.

Bonifazi, A. 2009. "Inquiring into *Nostos* and its Cognates." *American Journal of Philology* 130:481–510.

Christensen, J. 2020. *The Many-Minded Man: The* Odyssey, *Psychology, and the Therapy of Epic*. Ithaca.

Danek, G. 1998. *Epos und Zitat: Studien zu den Quellen der* Odyssee. Wiener Studien, Beiheft 22. Vienna.

Doherty, L. E., ed. 2009. *Oxford Readings in Classical Studies: Homer's* Odyssey. Oxford.

Eriksen, R., ed. 1994. *Contexts of Pre-Novel Narrative: The European Tradition*. Berlin.

Fenik, B. 1968. *Typical Battle Scenes in the* Iliad*: Studies in the Narrative Techniques of Homeric Battle Description*. Hermes Einzelschriften 21. Wiesbaden.

Foley, J. M. 1990. *Traditional Oral Epic: The* Odyssey, Beowulf, *and the Serbo-Croatian Return Song*. Berkeley.

Frame, D. 1978. *The Myth of Return in Early Greek Epic*. New Haven.

———. 2009. *Hippota Nestor*. Hellenic Studies 37. Washington, DC.

Genette, G. 1980. *Narrative Discourse: An Essay in Method*. Trans. J. E. Lewin. Ithaca.

Grethlein, J. 2017. *Die* Odyssee*: Homer und die Kunst des Erzählens*. Munich.

Heubeck, A., S. West, J. B. Hainsworth, eds. 1988. *A Commentary on Homer's* Odyssey. Vol. I, *Introduction and Books I-VIII*. Oxford.

Honko, L. 1998. *Textualising the Siri Epic*. Folklore Fellows Communications 264. Helsinki.

Jensen, M. S. 1980. *The Homeric Question and the Oral-Formulaic Theory*. Opuscula Graeco-Latina 20. Copenhagen.

———. 1994. "Homer's Portrayal of Women: A Discussion of Homeric Narrative from an Oralist Point of View." In Eriksen 1994:27–46.

———. 2011. *Writing Homer: A Study Based on Results from Modern Fieldwork*. Copenhagen.

Jong, I. J. F. de. 2001. *A Narratological Commentary on the* Odyssey. Cambridge.

Kullmann, W. 1960. *Die Quellen der* Ilias *(Troischer Sagenkreis)*. Hermes Einzelschriften 14. Wiesbaden.

Lord, A. B. 2019. *The Singer of Tales*. 3rd ed. Ed. D. F. Elmer. Hellenic Studies 77. Publications of the Milman Parry Collection of Oral Literature 4. Washington, DC. Orig. pub. Cambridge, MA, 1960.

Nagler, M. N. 1974. *Spontaneity and Tradition: A Study in the Oral Art of Homer*. Berkeley.

Nagy, G. 1979. *The Best of the Achaeans: Concepts of the Hero in Archaic Greek Poetry*. Baltimore. Repr. 1999.

Olrik, A. 1992. *Principles for Oral Narrative Research*. Trans. K. Wolf and J. Jensen. Bloomington. Orig. pub. as *Nogle Grundsaetninger for Sagnforskning*. Copenhagen, 1921.

Propp, V. 1968. *Morphology of the Folktale*. 2nd ed. Trans. L.A. Wagner, intro. A. Dundee. Austin. Orig. pub. 1928.

Reichl, K. 2001. *Das usbekische Heldenepos Alpomish: Einführung, Text, Übersetzung*. Wiesbaden.

Snell, B. 1975. *Die Entdeckung des Geistes: Studien zur Entstehung des europäischen Denkens bei den Griechen*. 4th ed. Göttingen. Orig. pub. 1946.

Uther, H. J., et al. 2004. *The Types of International Folktales: A Classification and Bibliography. Based on the System of Antti Aarne and Stith Thompson*. 3 vols. Folklore Fellows Communications 284–286. Helsinki.

West, S. 1988. "The Transmission of the Text. Prefatory Note. Introduction. Books 1–4." In Heubeck, West, and Haisworth 1988:33–248.

Wright, T. 2019. "Eumaeus as Odysseus' Double in the *Odyssey*." *Quaderni Urbinati di Cultura Classica* 121:11–32.

## 2

# The Trojan Formulaic Theater[1]

Françoise Létoublon

THIS PAPER STUDIES the epithets used in Homer for the city of Troy, called either Ἴλιος or Τροίη, in order to evaluate their role in the poems. We count thirteen epithets that can be considered "fixed epithets" in Parry's terminology, a number comparable to the figures for Homeric gods or heroes, which might lead us to consider the city a "character" in the epics. It is thus worthwhile to review the uses of the epithets with a view to their metrical value, place in the hexameter, and possible equivalence with another form.

Milman Parry emphasized the epithets for heroes, distinguishing fixed epithets and particularized ones and subdividing the first category into generic vs. distinctive epithets[2]; but he was not as confident in regard to epithets for objects and places. In his first dissertation, he actually considered some *generic* epithets for cities,[3] and

1 Many thanks to the organizers of the Parry-Lord Conference and the editors of the book, to Stephen Rojcewicz who carefully checked my English, and to the kind reviewer who read the first version of the text with a very positive *akribeia*. David Elmer deserves the epithet ταλασίφρων for his patience in several states of this paper.

2 In the *thèses* he submitted for the degree of Docteur-ès-Lettres at the University of Paris, Parry makes a series of binary distinctions between various possible kinds of epithet. He distinguishes in the first place between the *épithète fixe* or *ornementale* and the *épithète particularisée*; then, as subdivisions of the first category, he distinguishes the *épithète générique* from *the épithète spéciale*. (See, for example, Parry 1928a:25, 80-81.) "Distinctive" is the standard English translation, originating with Adam Parry, for Parry's label *spéciale*; we adopt it here, although the complementary relationship with the *épithète générique* might be better captured by rendering *spéciale* as "specific."

3 Parry 1971: "If we take a generic epithet of a hero, δαΐφρονος, which is said of 15 heroes, or μεγαλήτορος, which is said of 13 heroes, that each of these epithets, and each alone, presents one of the 21 different metrical values attested for generic epithets of heroes in the genitive case, may be regarded as certain proof that both epithets are integral parts of a traditional system. Or again, we have a certain proof of the traditional character of πολύτλας δῖος Ὀδυσσεύς in that this formula is, first, unique in metre among the 14 noun-epithet formulae used in the nominative case for this hero, and second, is of the same metrical value with a great many other noun-epithet formulae of heroes—we pointed out 40 of them (TE p. 10–13). But when we try to determine whether the epithets εὐρυάγυια and τειχιόεσσαν, to choose two examples, are traditional or original, whether

gave a list of them in a note,[4] but the combination of epithets with proper city-names did not particularly interest him, and he did not consider the possibility that a city might have a distinctive epithet.[5] After a historical examination of scholarship on the question, I will attempt, through a close examination of the formulaic epithets for cities, to show the system of epithets used for Troy and to determine whether it corresponds to the law of economy, as does the system of epithets used with the names of the epic heroes and gods demonstrated by Parry.[6] We shall try to see how the metrical distinction between the names Τροίη and Ἴλιος determines the choice of the epithets and their placement in the verse, being thus far in line with Parry's insights. But our study will show that the epithets used for Troy play a role in the construction of meaning for the epic plot, thus contradicting Parry's strong affirmation that the fixed epithets are "purely ornamental." The argument will lead us to concluding observations on the importance of the space between the Achaean ships and the city walls as the theater of war and a highly dramatized center of the epic.

## 1. A Survey of Scholarship

The formulaic phrases under examination here have not, to date, received sufficient attention in a Parryan perspective or otherwise. We must, however, mention Stephen Scully, who brilliantly pleads the *expressivity* of the epithets.[7] Scully actually takes the formulaic system of epithets for Troy into account, but he chooses to leave the Parryan distinctions aside and leans on Vivante, Amory Parry, and Finkelberg for developing the idea of the contextual

they are generic or distinctive, we no longer have this certainty. The different epithets of cities which are beyond doubt generic amount to only seven, in all the five cases" (102).

4 Parry 1971: "In the genitive: ἐυκτιμένης (2), ἐρατεινῆς (2), ἱεράων (1). In the dative: ἐυκτιμένηι (3), ἠγαθέηι (3), ἱερῆι (2), εὖ ναιομένωι (1). In the accusative: ἐυκτίμενον πτολίεθρον (4), ἐρατεινήν (7), ἐρατεινάς (1), ἐυκτιμένην (2), ζαθέην (4), ἱερόν, ἱερήν (3), ἠγαθέην (1), εὖ ναιομένον (2)" (102). As Parry notes, "The figures indicate the number of different cities described by each form."

5 An interesting historical view on the formula before Parry, in his work and afterwards, is found in Russo 1997.

6 On this system, see Nagy 1990:22–23, esp. 23: "A distinctive epithet is like a small theme song that conjures up a thought-association with the traditional essence of an epic figure, thing, or concept. To cite an example that has deservedly become commonplace: Odysseus is πολύτλας 'much-suffering' throughout the *Iliad* because he is already a figure in an epic tradition about adventures that he will have after Troy."

7 Scully 1990:4: "Epithets are generally considered to be the least expressive element in Homeric poetics. I argue for a contrary view. For epithets of place, one can claim that their use in speech, and occasionally in narrative, responds to the dramatic pressure of each particular episode. In addition to their metrical utility, they can be keys to interpretation. For example, the Iliadic epithet for Troy, *euteikheos* ('well-walled'), occurs only in speech, uttered only by those eager, but thwarted, in their desire to take the city." Compare with Whallon 1961:191 on epithets for heroes.

congruence of epithets (see particularly Scully 1990:74–80). We shall come back to his ideas later.

While William M. Sale's 1987 article, "The Formularity of the Place-Phrases in the *Iliad*," very deeply interested in epithets for cities, is very accurate and will be often quoted here, it may appear surprising that Sale does not check the system of formulaic epithets, though he still intends, in this paper, to *defend* Parry. The author seems to have ignored—not without good reason, in my opinion—a paper by C. M. Bowra published in 1960 (note the coincidence with the date of Lord's *The Singer of Tales*) in the *Journal for Hellenic Studies*, under the title "Homeric Epithets for Troy," which does not even mention Parry, nor German scholars such as Düntzer, whose importance in the analysis of fixed epithets Parry had recognized.[8] Bowra leans on archaeology and Mycenean studies for such assertions as the following:

> It is out of the question that Homer saw Troy in its heyday or even enough ruins of it to give him a clear notion of what it had been some five hundred years before his own lifetime. But this does not mean that he did not know the country round the hill where Troy had once stood. Indeed it is difficult to imagine how he could have composed the *Iliad* unless he had in his mind a far clearer picture of the Troad than that of Ithaca in the *Odyssey*, and the clarity of the picture, which helped him to some of his dramatic effects, must have been due in some degree to personal knowledge.[9]

However, without mentioning either Parry[10] or earlier German scholarship like that of Düntzer's and Witte's, Bowra somehow rediscovers the importance of the various kinds of generic epithets for Troy. His first section bears the heading "Conventional Epithets for Places," with the following list for Troy (without any questioning of the Greek form of the city name): ἐυκτιμένον πτολίεθρον, ἐρίβωλος, ἐριβῶλαξ, ἐρατεινή, εὐρεία, ἱρή (this last case will be discussed below, since it is more complex than it seems in Bowra's paper: I see it rather as a distinctive epithet). Bowra's second section consists of "Epithets Confined to Troy," and contains the following, which could correspond to

8 Düntzer is quoted at least six times in Parry's theses, as well as Witte.

9 Bowra 1960:22-23.

10 I first thought that Bowra did not read Parry or the German scholarship, but the anonymous reviewer of this paper remarked that he quoted Parry's theses written "some 40 years ago" in his posthumously published book entitled *Homer* (1972) and considered them fruitful. I recognize that Bowra endorsed Parry's findings in this book (particularly in Chapter 2, titled "Oral Composition"). However, he still believed that the epithets with place-names correspond to an essentially archaeological reality.

Parry's "distinctive" epithets: ἐΰδμητος, εὐτείχεος, εὔπυργος, ὀφρυόεσσα. Bowra connects this last with expressions such as ἐπ' ὀφρύσι Καλλικολώνης (*Iliad* 20.151), and notes that "ὀφρυόεσσα is explained by the Townleian scholiast as ἐπὶ ὀφρυώδους τόπου κειμένη. It was used in the seventh or sixth century by a Delphic oracle for Acrocorinth (Herodotos 5.92 β 3)."[11] Bowra also mentions as relevant here ἄστυ μέγα and εὔπωλος. About εὐτείχεος and εὔπυργος, he writes:

> The walls of Troy VI, which survived with some patching in Troy VIIA, show how well deserved the epithet is, and it helps to explain why the Achaeans took ten years to capture the city.[12]

In his 1972 book, Bowra summarizes his position about epithets for places, staying faithful—while devoting a chapter to "Oral Composition," with reference to Parry 1971—to his belief in the concordance between poetic terms and archaeological findings:

> In dealing with places it was obviously convenient to have certain epithets which would be right almost anywhere, such as "goodly," "well-built," "beloved," "holy." But sometimes a real knowledge is displayed and confers a special prominence. The ruins of Tiryns show that it deserves "walled"; Pylos, with its enclosed bay, is certainly "sandy"; excavation has proved that Mycenae amply justifies "rich in gold"; Lacedaemon, under the mass of Taygetus, is aptly "hollow"; Egyptian Thebes, outside Greek experience, is "hundred-gated"; Boeotian Thebes, "seven-gated," accords with legend; Dodona is "stormy"; Calydon is "rocky." ... Troy presents a more interesting case. It shares with other cities such epithets as "lovely," "well-built," and "holy," and these do not mean very much. Much more distinctive are "steep," "with good horses," "well-walled," "with good towers," "beetling," "windy," "with lofty gates," "wide-streeted," all of which have been justified by the excavation of the site and show that the tradition was well informed on the look of Troy from without and within.[13]

Coming back to his earlier paper, we will see once more that the question is much more complex.

[11] Bowra 1960:18.

[12] Bowra 1960:18.

[13] Bowra 1972:21, in the very chapter entitled "Oral Composition."

His third category, "Epithets Suitable to Troy but not Confined to It," seems rather confused, with αἰπή, αἰπύ, αἰπεινή, ὑψίπυλος, ἠνεμόεσσα, εὐρυάγυια, εὖ ναιόμενον.

The main problem is, of course, that Bowra does not see that these more or less recurrent epithets necessarily imply a formulaic analysis and theory rather than a confrontation with some *reality* or with archaeological remains. We also note that he does not mention the peculiarity of the existence of multiple names for the same city nor the role of metrical constraints, whereas both of these facts absolutely need to be taken into account in this kind of study.

It may seem easy to mock such a way of finding epithets more or less *suitable* for the remains discovered by Schliemann, Blegen, and their successors, but this is still the kind of evidence used by the archaeological team on the site today (Korfmann 2001), albeit in a much more sophisticated manner (I am thinking, for example, of the exhibition *Troia: Traum und Wirklichkeit* ["Troy: Dream and Reality"], shown in Stuttgart in 2001).[14] We see there a very general tendency to look at landscapes through the mirror of well-known texts and, conversely, to illustrate those texts with pictures taken from *reality*.[15]

It is thus necessary to study the whole set of epithets used with each of the names given to Troy as precisely as possible. In Parry's writing, we think that the distinction between generic and distinctive epithets was a point very finely observed, though maybe not enough stated.[16] In the following study, we will try to apply this distinction to the city, starting with generic epithets in the first part and then discuss what would be called, after Parry, the "distinctive" epithets as seen above (n. 2). The specificity of Troy as a place will be eventually posited as the heroic space of the narrative.

Following the path opened by William Whallon (1961, 1969), we may now dismiss one of Parry's main assertions, that the fixed epithet is "purely ornamental," and admit its importance in constructing the *meaning* of the

14 For more nuanced positions on this point, see Kullmann 2002 and Montanari 2005, among a huge number of references.

15 See. for instance, Luce 1999.

16 See Parry 1971:88–96 on epithets "reserved for a single hero," 145–153 on generic epithets, and 153–165 on particularized ones. Edwards 1986:193–197 appears particularly clear on these distinctions. Parry does not say much about this use apart from the "thrift of the diction" mentioned in his 1930 paper, which for Nagy "is not really a conditioning principle," "not a cause but an effect of traditional diction" (Nagy 1990:23). Nagy goes further: "As for epithets that still function in a distinctive phase, one sees them from the diachronic standpoint as capsules of traditional themes associated with the noun described. A distinctive epithet is like a small theme song that conjures up a thought-association with the traditional essence of an epic figure, thing, or concept" (Nagy 1990:23), which fits with our analysis.

whole epic corpus: some epithets are used "almost exclusively for Hector and never for Odysseus," for example, "man-slaying" (ἀνδροφόνος), or "for Hector and a number of other men, but never for Odysseus," for example, "horse-taming" (ἱππόδαμος), whereas "counter-god" (ἀντίθεος) is used most often for Odysseus and never for Hector (Whallon 1961:134). On the same page, Whallon writes:

> The three epithets cannot be thought jejune, for the epic matter illustrates the appropriateness of their use. Hector seems destined to slay many men until he is himself slain in revenge for the slaying of one particular man; Odysseus throughout his career also slays many men, but is not so redoubtable in hand-to-hand fighting as Hector, and would not so fittingly be called *man-slaying*. Hector is closely associated with horses in two passages, and as a prince of a land of horses must himself be skilled with horses; but Odysseus comes from a land unsuitable for horses, and would not fittingly be called *horse-taming*. Hector on the other hand is not shown equal to the gods in cunning or an enemy of more than human hostility, and would not fittingly be called a *counter-god*. Parry found it notable that *counter-god* but not *horse-taming* should be used for Odysseus, yet the epic matter seems clearly to show that epithets cannot successfully be interchanged merely because they are metrically equivalent.

One of the finest discussions of the ornamental value of fixed epithets came from Richard Sacks, who studied "traditional phrasing and the characterization of Hector" through the distribution of the same epithets ἀνδροφόνος and ἱππόδαμος, as well as φαίδιμος, in the *Iliad* (Sacks 1987:105–226): used with other heroes' names and with υἱός, φαίδιμος is generic, whereas the nominative κορυθαίολος is the distinctive epithet for Hector. However, φαίδιμος Ἕκτωρ occurs in "a certain marked ring. ... The most concentrated instances of it were in passages overtly emphasizing his defeats, delusions, and ultimate death" (Sacks 1987:142). Thus the epithet appears non-ornamental. For ἀνδροφόνος, it is used only in the genitive, "at moments of lamentation when he is not slaying, but slain," which assures us, it seems, of its ornamental nature. However,

> though the *Iliad* contains passage after passage depicting Hector's "man-slaying" exploits, only his deeds while dressed as Achilles are interspersed with the phrase Ἕκτορος ἀνδροφόνοιο. Elsewhere in the poem the phrase appeared either in lamentations over his death—real or imagined—or on the lips of his slayer—again, real or imagined. But it is totally excluded from other battle narratives in which he is

> involved. ... Such a distribution cannot be either ornamental or, to repeat Parry's words, "an unconscious habit."[17]

Hector is said to be "man-slaying" when he is about to die at the "man-slaying" hands of Achilles (χεῖρας / δεινὰς ἀνδροφόνους 24.479, see Sacks 1987:175).

A third author, John Miles Foley, contributes to this discussion of the ornamental value of the fixed epithet. The meaning of the epithets may have been particularly relevant for an episode of the cyclic poems which is lost.[18] The Homeric epithets appear then to have a *metonymic* value, alluding to episodes and adventures other than those in which they are met. This is what Foley later called the "traditional referentiality" of an "immanent art."[19] We will try to test Whallon's, Sacks's, and Foley's insights by applying them to the system of formulae and formulaic phrases referring to Troy in the *Iliad*.

## 2. Generic Epithets for Τροίη / Ἴλιος

I propose to analyze αἰπεινή, ὑψίπυλος, εὐρείη, ἐρίβωλος and the derived form ἐριβῶλαξ as generic epithets, insofar as they also occur with other city names.

### αἰπεινή 'lofty'

The data for αἰπεινή show the formula Ἴλιος αἰπεινή (always in this word order) declined at the beginning of the hexameter. We find it in the nominative in

> Ἴλιος αἰπεινή· νῦν τοι σῶς αἰπὺς ὄλεθρος (*Iliad* 13.773)

in the accusative in

> Ἴλιον αἰπεινὴν ἑλέειν κτάσθαι τε πολίτας (15.558; cf. 17.327)

and in the genitive in

> Ἰλίου αἰπεινῆς· μάλα γάρ ἑθεν εὐρύοπα Ζεὺς (9.419 = 686; cf. 15.215)

17 Sacks 1987:170.

18 Whallon 1961:139: "If the lays had survived, we might better realize why Hermes is *the slayer of Argus* (Ἀργειφόντης) or why Priam is described as a man *who has the good ash* (ἐυμμελίης)."

19 Foley 1991:xv: "As firsthand experience with the oral traditional epic of the South Slavs will show, any single performance merely instances an unexpressed, and inexpressible, whole, a larger story that will forever remain beyond the reach of acoustically recorded, oral-dictated, or even written textualization. In that instancing, however, each performance also summons its traditional referent according to the contract that governs the generation of meaning in this art form, so that the necessarily partial reflection of the larger story is actually never incomplete. Even in the case of the ancient Greek and Anglo-Saxon epics . . . the whole tradition is still manifestly prominent."

We do not encounter the dative, but it is clear that nothing formally rules out Ἰλίῳ αἰπεινῇ, and its absence may be thus due to accident, though such scholars as Sale actually rely on a correspondence between semantic need and the existence of formulas more than we do.[20]

This epithet, αἰπεινή, is also met in conjunction with other city names, either at the same place in the verse, as in

> Πήδασον αἰπεινήν. Φύλακον δ' ἕλε Λήϊτος ἥρως (*Iliad* 6.35)

or at a different place in the verse, as for other places like Calydon and Gonoessa:

> οἵ θ' Ὑπερησίην τε καὶ αἰπεινὴν Γονόεσσαν (2.573)
> ὃς πάσῃ Πλευρῶνι καὶ αἰπεινῇ Καλυδῶνι (13.217; cf. 14.116)

This epithet never appears with the name Τροίη, but no holder of the *realist* theory like Bowra would say that Ἴλιος was *lofty* and Τροίη was not.

## ὑψίπυλος 'with high gates'

With Τροίη, the compound adjective ὑψίπυλος seems generic, since the formulaic hemistich ἔνθά κεν ὑψίπυλον, which occurs twice in the repeated verse ἔνθά κεν ὑψίπυλον Τροίην ἕλον υἷες Ἀχαιῶν (*Iliad* 16.698 = 21.544), has a metrical shape very similar to the beginning of 6.416, where the epithet occurs with Θήβην but in reverse order (Θήβην ὑψίπυλον· κατὰ δ' ἔκτανεν Ἠετίωνα).

These few occurrences do not allow a strong conclusion but still suggest that ὑψίπυλος is generic with Τροίη, as αἰπεινή is with Ἴλιος.

## εὐρείη 'wide'

More numerous instances draw more confidence for the adjective meaning "wide," though the relevance of this meaning may appear troublesome. It occurs with Τροίη as well as with other place names, hence its generic status: in addition to the 4 Iliadic and 3 Odyssean instances in which the epithet is applied to Τροίη (in the phrase ἐνὶ Τροίῃ εὐρείῃ at the end of the verse or Τροίῃ ἐν εὐρείῃ at the beginning), there is a series of instances with the names Λυκίη, Κρήτη, and Σπάρτη and occasionally other ones like Κνωσός. With Τροίη we find examples such as:

[20] Sale 1987, 1996.

γῆμεν ἀνὴρ ὤριστος ἐνὶ Τροίῃ εὐρείῃ (*Iliad* 13.433; cf. 24.774, *Odyssey* 11.499, 12.189)
Τροίῃ ἐν εὐρείῃ, τῶν δ' οὔ τινά φημι λελεῖφθαι (*Iliad* 24.256 = 494; cf. *Odyssey* 1.62, 4.99, 5.307)

Line-final ἐνὶ Τροίῃ εὐρείῃ is built on the same fundamental schema as ἐν Λυκίῃ εὐρείῃ (*Iliad* 6.210), Λυκίης εὐρείης (*Iliad* 6.173), ἐν Κρήτῃ εὐρείῃ (*Odyssey* 13.256, etc.), and (with an even closer resemblance) ἐνὶ Σπάρτῃ εὐρείῃ (*Odyssey* 11.460) and ἐνὶ Κνωσῷ εὐρείῃ (*Odyssey* 18.591), all at line-end. With Λυκίῃ another schema is possible, exemplified by:

κρίνας ἐκ Λυκίης εὐρείης φῶτας ἀρίστους (*Iliad* 6.188; cf. 16.455, 16.673, 16.683)

We observe here a "grammar of the formula,"[21] with three main possibilities, corresponding to spondaic place-names like Κρήτη and Τροίη or those with short vowels like Λυκίῃ:

a. at verse beginning: ἐν εὐρείῃ – –

b. at verse end: ἐνὶ / ἐν – – εὐρείῃ·

c. Names with the shape ⏑ ⏑ –, like Λυκίῃ, can be situated at various positions in the verse, including in line-final formulas.

## ἐρίβωλος 'fertile'

The epithet ἐρίβωλος forms with Τροίη a formulaic hemistich. The accusative is usual with the verb ἱκέσθαι,[22] as in Τροίην ἐρίβωλον ἵκοντο (*Iliad* 18.67) and Τροίην ἐρίβωλον ἱκέσθην (*Iliad* 23.215). As a variant of this formula, we find the second hemistich with the prepositional complement in the verse ending κατὰ Τροίην ἐρίβωλον (*Iliad* 9.329), unless the reverse could be said, since statistics are not proof with so few examples.

As evidence for the generic status of this epithet, we find it applied to the names Φθίῃ (*Iliad* 9.363), Σχερίη (*Odyssey* 5.34), Παιονίη (*Iliad* 21.154), and the common noun ἄρουρα (*Iliad* 21.232).

21 The notion of "declension of the formula" is owed to the German scholar Kurt Witte (1913); see de Lamberterie 1997:18. As Edwards 1986:197–198 recognizes, Chantraine 1932 was the first application of Parry's ideas, "and for a long time the only one apart from Parry's own later work." We consider Nagler 1967 and 1974 an important step in taking a "generative" view of formulas. See Létoublon 1992a (on the phrase ἥβης μέτρον with various forms of ἱκέσθαι, in contrast with other phrases for the coming of old age, with such phrases as γῆρας ἱκάνει).

22 Létoublon 1985:144–146.

## ἐριβῶλαξ 'fertile'

Formally and semantically close to ἐρίβωλος appears the derived adjective ἐριβῶλαξ, with an interesting case of declension of the formula (we find accusative, genitive, and dative forms with different verbs). Alongside the first-hemistich formulas with the accusative

> ναίοιτε Τροίην ἐριβώλακα (*Iliad* 3.74; cf. 3.257)

we find interesting examples of the (locative) dative with preposition ἐν/ἐνὶ in a central position, for example:

> ἦσαν ἐνὶ Τροίῃ ἐριβώλακι τέκτονες ἄνδρες (*Iliad* 6.315)
> φθίσειν ἐν Τροίῃ ἐριβώλακι τηλόθι πάτρης (*Iliad* 16.461; cf. 24.86)

The generic status of this epithet is evident from the following examples of its use with other nouns:

> οὐδέ ποτ' ἐν Φθίῃ ἐριβώλακι βωτιανείρῃ (*Iliad* 1.155; cf. 9.479)
> τῆλ' ἀπὸ Λαρίσης ἐριβώλακος, οὐδὲ τοκεῦσι (*Iliad* 17.301; cf. 2.841)
> Βώρου, ὃς ἐκ Τάρνης ἐριβώλακος εἰληλούθει (*Iliad* 5.44)
> ὅι ῥ' ἐξ Ἀσκανίης ἐριβώλακος ἦλθον ἀμοιβοὶ (*Iliad* 13.793)
> τῶν ὅσσοι Λυκίην ἐριβώλακα ναιετάουσι (*Iliad* 16.172)
> ὅς ῥ' ἐκ Παιονίης ἐριβώλακος εἰληλούθει (*Iliad* 17.350)
> Ῥίγμον, ὃς ἐκ Θρῄκης ἐριβώλακος εἰληλούθει (*Iliad* 20.485; cf. 11.222)
> κεῖθ' ἁλὶ κεκλιμένη ἐριβώλακος ἠπείροιο (*Odyssey* 13.325)

We may note that, while the epithet occurs in the genitive case with many toponyms (Λαρίσης, Τάρνης, Ἀσκανίης, Παιονίης, Θρῄκης) and with the common noun ἠπείροιο, there are no occurrences with the genitive Τροίης.

## εὐρυάγυια 'with wide streets'

With the epithet εὐρυάγυια, the most frequent formulas in the *Iliad* employ forms of the verb αἱρέω "take, capture." So, for example:

> πανσυδίῃ νῦν γάρ κεν ἕλοι πόλιν εὐρυάγυιαν / Τρώων (*Iliad* 2.12–13; cf. 2.29–30, 2.66–67)
> οὐ γὰρ ἔτι Τροίην αἱρήσομεν εὐρυάγυιαν (*Iliad* 2.141 = 9.28)
> τῷ δεκάτῳ δὲ πόλιν αἱρήσομεν εὐρυάγυιαν (*Iliad* 2.329)[23]

[23] Note also *Iliad* 14.88–89: οὕτω δὴ μέμονας Τρώων πόλιν εὐρυάγυιαν / καλλείψειν.

In the *Odyssey*, other city names warrant the generic status of the epithet (including Πριάμου πόλις "Priam's city," which of course refers to Troy):

> ἵκετο δ' ἐς Μαραθῶνα καὶ εὐρυάγυιαν Ἀθήνην (*Odyssey* 7.80)
> ἠὲ διεπράθετο πτόλις ἀνδρῶν εὐρυάγυια (*Odyssey* 15.384)
> σῇ δ' ἥλω βουλῇ Πριάμου πόλις εὐρυάγυια (*Odyssey* 22.230)

The epithet also occurs once with Μυκήνη at the end of the verse:

> Ἄργος τε Σπάρτη τε καὶ εὐρυάγυια Μυκήνη (*Iliad* 4.52)

Even though this is its only attestation within the Homeric corpus, εὐρυάγυια Μυκήνη should very likely be counted as a formula.[24] If we take into account Whallon's remark that an epithet may have been relevant in the cyclic epics, it is easy to suppose that Mycenae's wealth was concerned.

It would be relatively easy to exclude the examples with Ἀθήνην (and Μαραθῶνα) as more recent, and to observe that most other examples imply Troy in an indirect way, but it may seem more plausible to characterize the epithet as generic; its use with Μυκήνη seems a strong argument in this direction. Any wealthy city in the archaic period could likely merit a description as "having wide streets."

## 3. εὐτείχεος 'With Strong Walls': Generic or Distinctive?

The case of εὐτείχεος shows an interesting paradigmatic complementarity between Ἴλιος and Τροίη. The epithet occurs with no other toponym, which poses a challenge for Bowra's reasoning: why do we not find it describing Tiryns or Mycenae, where the walls are still now very impressive, and must have been impressive in antiquity?[25] This case is peculiar because the distinctive epithets mentioned by Parry generally correspond to one and the same name rather than one and the same reality, whereas this epithet could be specific for the city referred to by both names, Ἴλιος and Τροίη. The walls of the city, however, figure prominently in the Troy story: witness the myth of the gods Poseidon and Apollo together building them for king Laomedon (*Iliad* 21.441–446)[26] and

24 See de Lamberterie 1997:19–20 for an analysis of formulas that occur only once, as at 1.554.

25 See Polychronopoulou 1999:275–294, "Les murailles des Cyclopes." King Proitos of Tiryns was thought to have called the Cyclopes from Lydia or Thrakia to build the walls. In other traditions, they were built by the Pelasgoi.

26 See Scully 1990:51. Scully's chapter 3, entitled "The Walled City" (41–53) deals with this question, noting first that only nine cities are said to be walled in the *Iliad*: Troy (Ilios), Thebes (in Egypt and in Boeotia), Lyrnessos, Tiryns, Kalydon, Phaia, and Gortyn. But none of these walls matter

Andromache's mention of a weak part of the wall, which may allude to the future fall of the city (*Iliad* 6.433–439).[27] Thus εὐτείχεος with reference to Τροίη or Ἴλιος represents a kind of "traditional referentiality," as John Foley would have said.[28]

The most frequent formula is a whole formulaic verse with the name Ἴλιος appearing four times in the *Iliad*:

> Ἴλιον ἐκπέρσαντ' εὐτείχεον ἀπονέεσθαι (*Iliad* 2.113, 2.288, 5.716, 9.20)

We also find two instances with Τροίην εὐτείχεον:

> αἴ κέ ποθι Ζεὺς / δῷσι πόλιν Τροίην εὐτείχεον ἐξαλαπάξαι (*Iliad* 1.129)
> ἱέμενος Τροίην εὐτείχεον ἐξαλαπάξαι (*Iliad* 8.241)

We may also note the alternative form εὐτειχής without either of the proper names, but with a clear reference to Troy through the word πόλιν in

> δουρὶ δ' ἐμῷ κτεάτισσα πόλιν εὐτείχεα πέρσας (*Iliad* 16.57)

Arguably related is an isolated use of εὔπυργος "with strong towers" in

> εἰς ὅ κεν ἢ ὑμεῖς Τροίην εὔπυργον ἕλητε (*Iliad* 7.71)

Τροίην εὔπυργον has a different metrical shape from the more usual Τροίην εὐτείχεον, necessitating a different placement in the verse, but both phrases exhibit a similar distribution around the caesura (penthemimeral or hepthemimeral). Therefore Τροίην εὔπυργον may reasonably be considered a formula, entering the complex system of the formulaic epithets for Troy.

Εὐτείχεος and εὔπυργος refer to the walls and the towers of the Trojan city; they emphasize the strong defense apparatus, which should succeed in protecting the city against enemies. Therefore the more εὐτείχεος and εὔπυργος the city, the more tragic the Achaean attack against it appears. The interpretation of these words as distinctive epithets for Troy with both of its proper names seems possible, but we deem it more interesting to conclude that an ambiguity exists. Though we do not know any other cases in which the same epithet is used with two different names for one and the same reality, it cannot be formally

---

as much for the epics as Troy's wall. Scully devotes one section of his book to *euteikheos*, another to *hiera teikhea*. The formal complementarity of Ἴλιον ... εὐτείχεον, Τροίην εὐτείχεον, and Τροίην εὔπυργον at different places in the verse, corresponding to Parry's law of economy, is not made clear enough in Scully's discussion, in my opinion.

27 Kirk 1990:217–218.

28 Foley 1991:38–60.

proven that the epithet is not generic. Anyhow, the reality of the walls and towers of Troy does not really matter here: rather, we are dealing with a kind of "traditional referentiality." We suggest that Troy's strong walls are not a specific characteristic of this city in themselves, since we know other cities that were endowed with very impressive walls and gates at that time; however, they take on great importance in the *Iliad*'s narrative because of the events that occur around them, and that could explain why these epithets seem quasi-specific for both of the names of the city.[29] Let us recall Scully's important remark quoted above: all of those examples occur in speeches by the Achaeans and carry a strong emotional weight.[30]

Before dealing with the possible cases of distinctive epithets, it must be noted that both Ἴλιος and Τροίη also occur without any epithet, as in

> Τροίῃ δὲ πεφήσεται αἰπὺς ὄλεθρος (*Iliad* 17.153)

Here, however, the adjective αἰπύς, modifying ὄλεθρος, could substitute for αἰπεινή (attested with Ἴλιος, not with Τροίη; see above) or αἰπύς, which also occurs once with Ἴλιος:

> ... εἰς ὅ κ' Ἀχαιοὶ
> Ἴλιον αἰπὺ ἕλοιεν Ἀθηναίης διὰ βουλὰς (*Iliad* 15.70–71)

Note also the lines

> νῦν ὤλετο πασῆς κατ' ἄκρης
> Ἴλιος αἰπεινή· νῦν τοι σῶς αἰπὺς ὄλεθρος (*Iliad* 13.772–773)

in which the formula Ἴλιος αἰπεινὴ at the beginning of the verse occurs in close proximity with the final formula αἰπὺς ὄλεθρος. We may consider this an indication of the relation between the elevation of the city and the abruptness of its destiny in the poet's mind. Thus the *abruptness* of the city becomes a

29 A similar argument might be made for ἐρίβωλος and ἐριβῶλαξ: the epithets do not indicate that the Troad was an especially fertile territory, although the frequent emphasis on horses (see below on εὔπωλος) might suggest this, as for Pylos and Sparta.

30 Scully 1990:4, quoted above; see also 74: "There are two formulaic phrases: 'to go home after having utterly destroyed well-walled Troy' (*Ilion ekpersant' euteikheon aponeesthai*), and 'if Zeus / grants us' (or 'desiring') 'to sack well-walled Troy' (*dōisi polin* [or *hiemenos*] *Troiēn euteikheon exalapaxai*). Thus it *always* appears in a context where desire (human or divine) plays against the seemingly impregnable defense of the city. Even more than highlighting a general sense of Troy's existence, the epithet with almost verbal energy of its own struggles against the sentence's actual verb, thwarting its telos. ... Counterpoint between verb and epithet not only is forceful but appears intentional as it sustains much of the dramatic tension within the line. When we recognize that all these examples occur only in the speeches by the Achaeans, it is hard to deny that the epithet carries emotional weight."

metaphor of its destiny, and the metaphor is achieved in the traditional formulaic style. In 17.153 (quoted above) the application of the epithet to ὄλεθρος alone, with the dramatic dative Τροίῃ standing alone at the beginning of the same verse, could thus emphasize the metaphorical value of the epithet, the high city becoming the victim of a high fall, as if there were a fitting proportion between its high walls and the fall. It is of course possible that we attach too much importance to the usual way an epithet occurs and to the contrast with the occurrence where it is missing: we just want to point out a possible stylistic and rhetorical device.[31]

Both Ἴλιος and Τροίη also occur without an epithet in a use we could call *neutral*, mostly with a preposition: compare, for instance, *Iliad* 8.131: κατὰ Ἴλιον; 21.295: κατὰ Ἰλιόφι; 24.67: ἐν Ἰλίῳ; 24.145: Ἴλιον εἴσω; 22.478: ἐν Τροίῃ; and particularly the following formulaic verse ending, which seems more expressive:

> ... οἳ Ἰλίῳ ἐγγεγάασιν (*Iliad* 6.493, 17.145)

Note that this is particularly the case for locative expressions: this could lead to support for Sale's observation that there are no formulas for the locative meaning "in Troy" and for departing from it, and for his hypothesis: the dramatization of the plot inside the city would correspond to the poet's period, when no more formulas were created anew.[32] We will come back to this issue.

## 4. Possible Distinctive Epithets and the Holy City

### ἠνεμόεσσα 'windy'

Few epithets may be said to be distinctive of Troy, as either Ἴλιος or Τροίη, in the strong Parryan sense. It seems possible, however, to consider ἠνεμόεσσα a quasi-specific epithet for Ἴλιος since, apart from one instance in which it modifies another city-name, Ἐνίσπη, the epithet occurs (in the *Iliad*) only with Ἴλιος, in a formula confined to the second hemistich. The single exception, from the Catalogue of Ships, is:

[31] Those formulas with αἰπ- in diverse forms appear interesting in a comparative way: as C. Watkins remarked, Ἰλίου αἰπεινῆς could have a parallel in a Luvian phrase meaning "when they came from steep Wilusa" (1986:58–62). It is tempting to dream about a very ancient poetic use of the qualification of the city as steep before the Homeric epics. Quoting this article, Sale (1987:35n8) remarks: "If this phrase was an ancestor of Homer's, it went through several changes as it descended; for Homer speaks of Ἰλίου αἰπεινῆς only in formulae for the city's destruction, never for motion from the city."

[32] Sale 1987:32–38.

> Ῥίπην τε Στρατίην τε καὶ ἠνεμόεσσαν Ἐνίσπην (*Iliad* 2.606)

All of the other Iliadic instances reverse the order of name and epithet, as in

> ἤτοι ἐγὼν εἶμι προτὶ Ἴλιον ἠνεμόεσσαν (*Iliad* 3.305; cf. 8.499, 12.115, 13.724, 18.174, 22.64, 23.297)

In the *Odyssey* the same epithet occurs in the same position with common nouns:

> ᾤκεον ἐν σπήεσσι δι᾽ ἄκριας ἠνεμόεσσας (*Odyssey* 9.400; cf. 16.365)
> Παρνησοῦ, τάχα δ᾽ ἵκανον πτύχας ἠνεμόεσσας (*Odyssey* 19.432)

As in the *Iliad*, the epithet occupies the last position in the verse, but the association with ἄκριας or πτύχας instead of Ἴλιος seems to indicate a disregard of the traditional formulaic system.

The formula προτὶ / ὑπὸ Ἴλιον ἠνεμόεσσαν, as Sale notes,[33] occurs mostly in the "motion-to" use, which for him proves the role of semantic values of the formula.

## εὔπωλος 'abounding in horses'

εὔπωλος occurs only with Ἴλιος, in a formula confined to the first hemistich. The hemistich, which occurs five times in the *Iliad* and the *Odyssey*, is exemplified by the line

> Ἴλιον εἰς εὔπωλον ἅμ᾽ Ἀργείοισιν ἑπέσθην (*Iliad* 5.551; cf. 16.576, *Odyssey* 2.18, 14.71, 11.169)[34]

Thus εὔπωλος could be a distinctive epithet for this city, known in mythology for the divine horses given by Zeus to Tros as compensation for the taking of his son Ganymede (*Iliad* 5.266). That is not to say that other places were not also known for their horses, such as Argos, for which the epics use other formulas, especially employing the epithet ἱππόβοτος (the word probably characterizes Argos as a large country rather than a city, as may be the case for Ἴλιος when it is said to be εὔπωλος).[35]

[33] Sale 1987:30.

[34] Note that in several of these examples, going "to Ilios abounding in horses" is associated with the idea of combat (cf. ἵνα Τρώεσσι μάχοιτο / μαχοίμην in *Iliad* 16.576, *Odyssey* 11.169, 14.71), in accordance with the Achaean point of view. On Homeric formulae with horses, see Whallon's "Equestrian Epithets" (1961:118-120), Fagan 2001, and Platte 2014 and 2017. Though old-fashioned, let us also mention the "lexique du cheval" of Delebecque 1951.

[35] Two formulaic schemes are found for Argos, the horse-nourishing place. The first occurs at the end of the verse with a genitive: ἀπ᾽ Ἄργεος ἱπποβότοιο (*Iliad* 2.287, 19.329); μυχῷ Ἄργεος ἱπποβότοιο (*Iliad* 6.152); ἑκὰς Ἄργεος ἱπποβότοιο (*Iliad* 9.246). The second occurs at the beginning

It is not surprising to find formulas that likewise associate the Trojan people with horses. Phrases with the epithet ἱππόδαμος "horse-taming" in the first part of the verse in the dative or the accusative exhibit variations showing how the formula may adapt to both meter and morpho-syntax:

> Τρωσὶν ἐφ' ἱπποδάμοις (*Iliad* 8.110, 8.516)
> Τρωσὶν ἐφ' ἱπποδάμοισιν (*Iliad* 4.355, 19.237, 318)
> Τρῶας ἐς ἱπποδάμους (*Iliad* 17.230)
> Τρῶας θ' ἱπποδάμους καὶ ἐϋκνήμιδας Ἀχαιούς (*Iliad* 3.343, 4.80)
> Τρώων ἱπποδάμων (*Iliad* 2.230, 4.355, 6.461, 11.568)
> Τρώων θ' ἱπποδάμων καὶ Ἀχαιῶν (χαλκοχιτώνων) (*Iliad* 3.127, 3.131, 4.352, 8.71)

In the whole-verse formulas Τρώων θ' ἱπποδάμων καὶ Ἀχαιῶν χαλκοχιτώνων and Τρῶας θ' ἱπποδάμους καὶ ἐϋκνήμιδας Ἀχαιούς, *clustered* in Books 3 and 4, and each denoting the same two groups, note that, although the first hemistich is identical, the second shows a change of both word-order and epithet.

The nominative proper is not attested, but the vocative occurs twice in a verse-initial formula that exhibits a significant shift in both meter and word-order:

> ὄρνυσθ' ἱππόδαμοι Τρῶες (*Iliad* 4.509, 12.440)

The other formulas quoted above may also, with slight variations, be encountered at other places in the verse, as in

> αὐτὰρ ἐγὼ Τρώεσσι μεθ' ἱπποδάμοις ἀγορεύσω (*Iliad* 7.361, 8.525)
> πῶς γὰρ νῦν Τρώεσσι μεμιγμένοι ἱπποδάμοισιν (*Iliad* 10.424; cf. 17.418, 20.180)

The epithet also occurs with the names of several individuals, including Hector and Antenor among the Trojans, and Tydeus, Diomedes, Nestor, Thrasymedes, and Atreus among the Achaeans (all fighters in the Trojan War or their ancestors) but with no other collective name. So it can be concluded that it is a distinctive epithet for the Trojans, as εὔπωλος is with Ἴλιος, showing once more the complementarity between Ἴλιος and Τροίη.

---

of the verse with an accusative: Ἄργος ἐς ἱππόβοτον (*Iliad* 3.75, 3.258, 15.30). Cf. also the formula Δαναῶν ταχυπώλων at the end of the verse (*Iliad* 4.232 etc.), and one occurrence of Μυρμιδόνες ταχύπωλοι at its beginning (*Iliad* 23.6): all of this material seems to obey Milman Parry's laws.

## ὀφρυοέσσα 'with overhanging brows'

The very intriguing epithet ὀφρυόεσσα, with the nominative Ἴλιος, is a *hapax*:

> τῷ δὲ μάλιστ' ἄρ' ἔην ἐναλίγκιον ὡς εἰ ἅπασα
> Ἴλιος ὀφρυόεσσα πυρὶ σμύχοιτο κατ' ἄκρης (*Iliad* 22.410–411)

The phrase Ἴλιος ὀφρυόεσσα at the beginning of the verse looks like a formula, and though we find no other instance of it, we would be less confident than most "hard Parryist" scholars about excluding its formulaic status:[36] in a tradition that can be traced back to Meillet,[37] we admit the possibility of formulas that occur only once in the Homeric corpus and could perhaps have had an important role in the Cyclic poems. Nevertheless, the opacity of the epithet, already problematic in antiquity for the scholiast quoted by Bowra (above, p. 44), leads us to conclude that this epithet may be very ancient and not at all an invention of "Homer," whatever its meaning is. The formal relation of ὀφρυόεσσα to ὀφρῦς seems clear, but does it mean "eyebrow" with an anthropomorphic meaning? Or is the meaning of "eyebrow" for the substantive itself derived from another meaning, which could be attributed to natural features as well as to eyebrows (as seems to be the case in English for *brow*)?[38] It happens elsewhere that semantically opaque expressions that can be illuminated by comparison with other languages and/or literatures appear in Homer, Hesiod, Pindar, etc., as very ancient formulas that were obviously not very well understood. Could ὀφρυόεσσα, then, be the sole attested instance of an old epithet distinctive of Ἴλιος? If we take into account the masculine form ὀφρυόεντα found in an oracle for Corinth preserved by Herodotos,[39] the epithet would be distinctive of this city situated on a steeper rock than Troy. It is impossible to go further with such evidence. But it might be important that this passage with a distinctive epithet deals in a very solemn tone with the tragic loss of the city, as was the case above with the "high disaster" (αἰπὺς ὄλεθρος) coming to the high city with its high walls. It might also be important to mention that *Ophryneion* is a toponym known in the Troad, at least through Strabo, who situates a grove sacred to Hector there (13.1.29):[40] our hypothesis would be that this name

36 See Sale 1987; 1996.

37 de Lamberterie 1997:19; see above.

38 LSJ s.v. ὀφρυόεις: "on the brow or edge of a steep rock, beetling."

39 Herodotos 5.92 (ὀφρυόεντα Κόρινθον). See also Strabo 8.6.23: χώραν δ' ἔσχεν οὐκ εὔγεων σφόδρα, ἀλλὰ σκολιάν τε καὶ τραχεῖαν, ἀφ' οὗ πάντες ὀφρυόεντα Κόρινθον εἰρήκασι καὶ παροιμιάζονται "Κόρινθος ὀφρυᾷ τε καὶ κοιλαίνεται." Note also Strabo's use of ὀφρύς in geographical descriptions at 12.6.5.19, 17.1.33.2, 17.3.14.7.

40 See Cook 1973:72–77, and particularly 74: "The Ophryneion site lies 1.5 km from the centre of Erenköy and just north of a precipitous ravine with banks of oolitic drift in which Calvert

derives from the same ὀφρῦς as the epithet ὀφρυόεσσα, based on a similar meaning of ὀφρυ-, let us say "brow" or "ravine," itself relatively frequent in geographical descriptions.

## ἱερή / ἱρή 'sacred'

Let us develop a little more the association of Troy with two adjectives that seem very close one to another but nevertheless display very different behavior, ἱερή and ἱρή.[41] The first adjective occurs with other city-names or place-names, like Thebe, city of Eetion, Andromache's father. Though the location of this city might suggest that it is close to Troy and included in the Troad, this is not the case for Euboea, Zeleia, and Pylos, all places that receive the epithet.[42] ἱερή therefore appears to be a generic epithet, which also occurs with certain common nouns. It occurs with Ἴλιος only once:

> Ἴλιον εἰς ἱερήν· τῇ δ' ἀντίος ὄρνυτ' Ἀπόλλων (*Iliad* 7.20)

Especially worthy of note is the line

> Περγάμῳ εἰν ἱερῇ, ὅθι οἱ νηός γε τέτυκτο (*Iliad* 5.446)

Although, as we will see shortly, Πέργαμος is the name of the Trojan acropolis, ἱερὴ is a generic epithet in reference to the city of the Trojans.

In strong contrast, its apparent allomorph ἱρή seems strictly limited to Troy under the name Ἴλιος; metrically, it is strictly limited to the verse-final position. The whole formulaic verse

> ἔσσεται ἦμαρ ὅτ' ἂν ποτ' ὀλώλῃ Ἴλιος ἱρή (*Iliad* 4.164, 6.448)

occurs twice in the *Iliad*. There are other instances of the phrase in the nominative case:

> Κτίσσε δὲ Δαρδανίην, ἐπεὶ οὔ πω Ἴλιος ἱρὴ (*Iliad* 20.216; cf. 4.46, 24.27)[43]

as well as in the genitive:

> ὥς κεν Τύδεος υἱὸν ἀπόσχῃ Ἰλίου ἱρῆς (*Iliad* 6.96 ~ 6.277; cf. 21.128)

discovered remains of various creatures of the pliocene."

41 See Scully 1990, Ch. 2 ("The Sacred City"); Scully does not contrast ἱερή and ἱρή.

42 See *Iliad* 1.366, 2.535, 4.103, 4.121, *Odyssey* 21.108.

43 This instance proves that for the poet, Ἴλιος is different from Δαρδανίη, the first establishment known in the region. See below.

The epithet is most frequent in the accusative case. We observed two recurring whole-line formulas, and in these instances its *formularity* is evident:

> τεύχεα συλήσας οἴσω προτὶ Ἴλιον ἱρήν (*Iliad* 7.82; cf. *Iliad* 7.413, 7.429, 13.657, 17.193)
> βῆ δὲ κατ᾽ Ἰδαίων ὀρέων εἰς Ἴλιον ἱρήν (*Iliad* 15.169; cf. *Iliad* 24.143, *Odyssey* 11.86, 17.293)

There are, as well, a number of instances of the verse-final formula Ἴλιον ἱρήν in other contexts (*Iliad* 5.648, 6.416, 18.270, 21.515, 24.383).

This clear evidence of a declined formula in the strongest Parryian sense (without any examples in the dative, which could support Sale's remarks on the absence of the locative value for "Troy-city") contrasts with the other name of the city, Τροίη, which does not occur at all with ἱρή, and is used with ἱερός only in the periphrases Τροίης ἱερὰ κρήδεμνα (*Iliad* 16.100) and Τροίης ἱερὸν πτολίεθρον (*Odyssey* 1.2). Might we detect in this difference of usage a difference in meaning? ἱρός is usually understood to mean "sacred," like ἱερός, but some have proposed that it means, instead, "mighty, powerful."[44] ἱρή seems distinctive with the name Ἴλιος whereas ἱερή is generic with both of the city's names.

City-names are often constructed as derivatives of the name of the city's founder.[45] The famous genealogy of Aeneas in *Iliad* Book 20 (214–231) gives the list of his ancestors but does not seem to provide a key to Ἴλιος ἱρή: the main figures in the royal lineage outlined there are successively Dardanos (219), Erichthonios (219), Tros (231), his sons Ilos, Assarakos, and Ganymedes (232), Ilos' son Laomedon (236) and grandson Priam (237), and Assarakos' son Kapys and grandson Anchises (239).[46] Ἴλιος appears to relate to Ilos, Τροίη to Tros. The specificity of Tros' three sons, Ilos, Assarakos, and Ganymedes, excludes the hypothesis of a mistake or change in the tradition of which Aeneas preserves the memory. Pseudo-Apollodorus' *Bibliotheca* (3.140), perhaps more accurately than the *Iliad*, mentions a first Ilos, eldest son of Dardanos, who died without heir so that his brother Erichthonios became king.

The tradition of the Palladion, which comes from the Epic Cycle but is not referred to in Homer, derives the origin of the statue either from Dardanos, the very first ancestor mentioned in *Iliad* 20 (who in most detailed traditions came

44 See Chantraine 2009:1309.

45 In this case, the city-names Ἴλιος and Τροίη both with suffix *-yo/ya*, as well as Δαρδανίη deriving from *Dardanos*.

46 On this genealogy, see Wathelet 1989:97–101 and 1988:1.399–407 on Dardanos; 606–611, on Ilos, where he argues that, although Apollodorus mentions another person called Ilos, this Ilos is a "doublet" of Tros' son. Wathelet says that the city-name preexists the founder, which seems morphologically difficult. See also 1988:2.1028–1031 on Tros.

from Greece through Samothrace, still another problem that we cannot deal with here), or from Ilos, but never from Tros or Erichthonios. The point cannot be developed in this frame,[47] but the statue of the Palladion played a crucial role for the city as a protective talisman until a night expedition by Diomedes and Odysseus succeeded in stealing it. Therefore, I propose a strong link between the magical power of the statue and Ilos, recalling that he had his tomb in the plain near Troy, an important landmark in the surroundings of the city for the chiefs and soldiers of both camps. This Ilos could be the son of Dardanos omitted in Aeneas' genealogy rather than the son of Tros, about whom he has explicit knowledge.

The formulaic theater—located in our minds rather than reality—could then be first the place where oral poetry is still now "fighting" against the defenders of that "astonishing degree of reality" (Bowra's phrasing) found in the Homeric poems. But a step further can be possible with the help of Jenny Strauss Clay's studies of "Homer's Trojan Theater,"[48] in which the space between the Achaean ships and the city walls is described as a theater where the episodes of fighting move the narrative along with higher and higher intensity until Hector's men set the ships on fire, which leads Achilles to accept Patroklos' demand and send him to war in his own armor. It could be assumed that the formulaic style stresses and emphasizes this theater of war: the Achaeans want to take the city which, protected by its high walls and doors, is relatively safe. Conversely, the Trojans want to defend their holy city at all costs. In this connection, I would like to study more closely expressions such as the following:

> νῦν γάρ κεν ἕλοι πόλιν εὐρυάγυιαν / Τρώων (*Iliad* 2.12–13; cf. 2.29–30, 2.66–67)
> εἴ κεν Ἀχαιοὶ / Τρῷας δηώσωσιν ἕλωσί τε Ἴλιον ἱρήν (*Iliad* 4.415–416)
> εἰ γᾶρ νῦν Τρώεσσι μένος πολυθαρσὲς ἐνείη / ... αἶψά κε Πάτροκλον ἐρυσαίμεθα Ἴλιον εἴσω (*Iliad* 17.156–159)[49]

Sale aptly remarks that typical formulas exist for expressing a move towards the city (compare the examples of προτὶ Ἴλιον ἠνεμόεσσαν and προτὶ/εἰς Ἴλιον ἱρήν, noted above),[50] whereas there are virtually no formulas corresponding to the locative meaning of "in the city," nor to the expression of the movement away from the city. Sale explains this by a hypothesis concerning the relative

47 See Faraone 1992, Létoublon 2009, 2014b.

48 Clay 2007 and 2011. See Létoublon 2018.

49 See Wakker 1994:388–389 for the relation of the wish with the conditional.

50 Sale 1987:37.

chronology of the text, the Troy-scenes that imply the locative being composed, in his opinion, more or less at the date of "Homer." This conclusion might be in harmony with that of the importance of the space between the Achaean ships and the city walls as the theater of war, which we are exploring.

## 5. The Names of Troy and Formulaic Economy

In its sole occurrence in the *Iliad*, the name Δαρδανίη is given to the first settlement in the Troad, founded by Dardanos higher on the heights of Mount Ida than the future site of Troy (*Iliad* 20.215–218).[51] Six formulaic uses of the name Πέργαμος show that this was the name of the acropolis of Troy, standing in the same relation to the city as the Kadmeia to Thebes, for example:

> νεμέσησε δ' Ἀπόλλων / Περγάμου ἐκκατιδών (*Iliad* 4.507–508; cf. 7.20–21)
> Αἰνείαν δ' ἀπάτερθεν ὁμίλου θῆκεν Ἀπόλλων / Περγάμῳ εἰν ἱερῇ (*Iliad* 5.445–446)
> ὣς εἰπὼν αὐτὸς μὲν ἐφέζετο Περγάμῳ ἄκρῃ (*Iliad* 5.460, with reference to Ares; cf. 6.512–513)
> Πέργαμον εἰσαναβᾶσα φίλον πατέρ' εἰσενόησεν (*Iliad* 24.700, with reference to Cassandra)

While *Pergamos* appears to be the proper name of Troy's acropolis, ἐν πόλει ἄκρῃ can be considered a "minimal formula" for this part of the city.[52] Pergamos was probably the solemn, official name contrasting with the quotidian use of ἐν πόλει ἄκρῃ.

The uses of the names of peoples are also very interesting: they seem to imply that Dardanians were a distinct population of inhabitants of the Troad, different from the Trojans but constantly fighting with them because of their close kinship.[53] Why no ethnonym deriving from the name of Ilos occurs in Homer, although Ἴλιος appears more sacred than Τροίη, remains a mystery.

To conclude with this point, Ἴλιος and Τροίη refer to one and the same city under the name of a different founder: the more sacred Ἴλιος very probably refers to the first Ilos, whom Aeneas did not mention in his genealogy, rather than to the second Ilos, whom he remembers because that Ilos is closer to his own lineage, whereas the founder died without posterity. The use of the formulaic epithets implies that the city of Troy is, along with the Achaean camp,

51 There is no entry for Dardania in the OCD, but the city is mentioned in the entry on Dardanus.

52 Sale 1987:33n25. Occurrences of ἐν πόλει ἄκρῃ: *Iliad* 6.88. 6.297, 6.317, 7.345. See also *Iliad* 20.52.

53 Space does not permit me to consider here the available research on the formulaic status of the names of Trojans and Dardanians, but see on this question Sale 1989.

the very center of the epics: its name occurs with some generic epithets that occur with other city names as well, but some epithets might have a distinctive status, just as heroes and gods have some distinctive epithets. This might mean, not that Troy is uniquely windy, rich in horses, or even holy, but rather that in the ongoing course of the epic plot, the whole interest of the characters, and by extension that of the audience, focuses on this very city. Meanwhile, the particular form ἱρή, associated solely with the name Ἴλιος, could be explained by particular features of Trojan myth, as extensively told in the Epic Cycle and alluded to in Homer's *Iliad* and *Odyssey*.[54]

Let us conclude with remarks on the formulaic system and its economy. The epithets for both Ἴλιος and Τροίη correspond to a very extensive and economic formulaic system, since no formulas expressing the same essential idea fit exactly the same metrical conditions. This system can be sketched as follows:[55]

Generic Epithets

> Τροίην ἐρίβωλον ἵκοντο [P 6–12] 1x
> Τροίην ἐρίβωλον ἱκέσθην [P 6–12] 1x
>
> ναίοιτε Τροίην ἐριβώλακα [P 1–8] 1x
> ναίοιμεν Τροίην ἐριβώλακα [P 1–8] 1x
>
> ἐνὶ Τροίῃ ἐριβώλακι [P 2b–8] 1x
> ἐν Τροίῃ ἐριβώλακι [P 3–8] 2x
>
> Τροίην αἱρήσομεν εὐρυάγυιαν [P 4–12] 2x
> πόλιν εὐρυάγυιαν [P 8a–12] 5x[56]

54 See Fantuzzi and Tsagalis 2015, Létoublon 2011. The myth of Troy may have begun with the Judgment of Paris in the *Cypria* and may have included the construction of the walls by Poseidon and Apollo, hired by Laomedon; it ended with the sack of the city and the murder of Trojan males while women were enslaved in the part of the Cycle we know under the name of *Iliou Persis*.

55 In the following list, I use the system outlined by Sicking 1993:69 (a modification of O'Neill 1942) to indicate the localization of phrases within the hexameter. Sicking's system assigns a number to each position in the hexameter as follows:

| 1 | 2a | 2b | 3 | 4a | 4b | 5 | 6a | 6b | 7 | 8a | 8b | 9 | 10a | 10b | 11 | 12 |
|---|---|---|---|---|---|---|---|---|---|---|---|---|---|---|---|---|
| − | ∪ | ∪ | − | ∪ | ∪ | − | ∪ | ∪ | − | ∪ | ∪ | − | ∪ | ∪ | − | x |

Thus "P 6–12," for example, indicates that the first syllable of the phrase falls in Sicking's Position 6 and the last syllable in Position 12 (which is the last syllable of the verse). The "masculine" (penthemimeral), "feminine," and hepthemimeral caesurae fall at the boundaries between positions 5 / 6a, 6a / 6b, and 7 / 8a, respectively.

56 In four of five instances, the city is further specified as Τρώων "of the Trojans"; in the fifth instance (*Odyssey* 4.246), it is clear from the context that the city is Troy.

Ἴλιος αἰπεινή [P 1–5] 1x
Ἴλιον αἰπεινὴν [P 1–5] 2x
Ἰλίου αἰπεινῆς [P 1–5] 3x[57]

ὑψίπυλον Τροίην [P 3–7] 2x

With the idea "broad" appears a subsystem in the dative:

ἐνὶ Τροίῃ εὐρείῃ [P 6b–12] 4x
Τροίῃ ἐν εὐρείῃ [P 1–5] 5x

Another interesting subsystem appears with εὐτείχεος, which occurs with both names in different metrical patterns:

Ἴλιον ἐκπέρσαντ' εὐτείχεον ἀπονέεσθαι [P 1–12] 4x
Τροίην εὐτείχεον [P 4–8b] 2x[58]

Possible distinctive epithets:

προτὶ Ἴλιον ἠνεμόεσσαν [P 6a–12] 5x
ὑπὸ Ἴλιον ἠνεμόεσσαν [P 6a–12] 1x

Ἴλιον εἰς εὔπωλον [P 1–6a] 2x

ἱππόδαμοι Τρῶες [P 3–7] 2x
Τρώων (θ') ἱπποδάμων [P 1–5] 9x
Τρωσὶν ἐφ' ἱπποδάμοισι(ν) [P 1–6] 4x[59]
Τρῶάς θ' ἱπποδάμους [P 1–5] 3x
Ἴλιος ὀφρυόεσσα [P 1–6a] 1x

ἱερή and ἱρή:

Ἴλιον ἱρήν [P 9–12] 13x
Ἰλίου ἱρῆς [P 9–12] 3x

Ἴλιον εἰς ἱερήν [P 1–5] 1x
Τροίης ἱερὰ κρήδεμνα [P 4–10a] 1x

57 Ἴλιον αἰπὺ [P 1–4a] (*Iliad* 15.71) might be a variant, linked to the notion of αἰπὺς ὄλεθρος "steep destruction"; see above.

58 This formula, whose constituents stand on either side of the penthemimeral caesura, is in an apparently complementary relationship with Τροίην εὔπυργον [P 6–10a, x 1], whose constituents are on either side of the hepthemimeral caesura.

59 There are an additional 6 instances of Τρωσίν / Τρώεσσι with ἱπποδάμοις / ἱπποδάμοισι(ν) in various positions in the verse.

Τροίης ἱερὸν πτολίεθρον [P 6a–10a] 1x in the *Odyssey*
Περγάμῳ εἰν ἱερῇ [P 1–5] 1x

Most of these epithets indicate that Ἴλιος and Τροίη, though located in the same geographical place, refer to different realities, maybe because they have different founders. Or possibly the poets used different metrical shapes, associated with different epithets, to single out different periods in the city's stratified history. We cannot explain why only Ἴλιος occurs in the nominative, but it might have to do with the fact that, in several cases, the formulas relative to this name are declined (Ἴλιος αἰπεινή and Ἴλιος ἱρή) whereas those with Τροίη are not, and with the fact that Ἴλιος and its paradigm often appear at the beginning of the verse, in an apparently emphatic position. Thus the formulaic system clearly functions according to Parry's characterization:

> The uses of noun-epithet formulae are varied and many, but their common utility lies in the fact that they fill exactly a certain portion of the verse where the noun, or its synonym, would not fit. The technique of the use of the fixed epithet as we find it in Homer reveals plainly an ancient and intense development. In those cases where the importance of a word, or a category of words, has brought about its use frequently, and in different combinations of words, we find that the noun-epithet formulae constitute systems characterized by a great complexity and by a strict economy.[60]

The numerous epithets that occur with both Ἴλιος and Τροίη (ἐρίβωλος, ἐριβῶλαξ, εὐρυάγυια, etc.) exhibit a variety of metrical shapes, providing considerable flexibility when joined with either name.

One last comment concerns Sale's analysis of place-name formulas. In his 1987 paper, he remarks on the strange absence of formulas with the locative meaning of the dative. I first believed I had discovered an error in this analysis with two cases: ἐν(ὶ) Τροίῃ ἐριβώλακι and ἐνὶ Τροίῃ εὐρείῃ / Τροίῃ ἐν εὐρείῃ. After looking more closely both at the whole list of the examples and his paper, it seems to me that the situation is more complicated.[61] Let us first quote his accurate phrasing:

> We have established, then, that there are few or no pre-Homeric formulae for "in Troy-city" and none for "from Troy." The formulaic tradition did not say these things. But what about the whole epic

60 Parry 1971:246. The anonymous reviewer is once more to be thanked for having drawn my attention to this paper; I did not remark its importance.

61 And the reviewer of my first version of the paper encouraged me to think so.

> tradition, formulaic and non-formulaic?—for it is evident from Homer that not every time an idea is expressed will it be expressed in a formula. Did no poet before Homer ever say "from Troy"? Such an extreme view is surely very unattractive. What we *can* argue is this: in the last few generations before the composition of the *Iliad*, the oral poets did not *frequently* say "in Troy" or "from Troy." If they had, formulae would have developed.[62]

Sale then takes a further step (1987:37):

> ... pre-Homeric poetry did not say "in Troy" frequently because it did not frequently place the action in Troy. It did not say "from Troy" because, being rarely inside the city, it rarely had occasion to leave it. This would mean that the bulk of the *Iliad*'s Trojan scenes—there are 33 in all—could safely be attributed to Homer's own invention. Note that this does *not* mean that the Trojan scenes will be significantly less formulaic than the rest. Hector's helmet is just as bright, and the Achaean chitons just as brazen, whether referred to inside the city or out of it. It certainly does not make Homer a pen-poet who inherited the rest of the *Iliad*. It *does* mean that the parts of Troy which are not visible from outside will lack formulae—and this is in fact the case.

Sale does not analyze the formulaic system of the names for Troy because he is interested in what he calls the *formularity* of place-names (more generally than Troy) in the *Iliad*, which means the statistical proportion of formulas vs. non-formulaic uses of words. He concludes that "in Troy" does not occur in formulas, but he introduces a note of caution with the qualifiers "often" and "frequently." It is true that the uses of ἐν(ὶ) Τροίῃ with both ἐριβώλακι and εὐρείῃ are formulaic and are used to express that some event happened "in Troy." Nevertheless, in my opinion, these uses do not imply that Sale's intuition is wrong: they do not belong to the real *Trojan scenes* he had in mind, for instance the scenes on the wall in Books 6 and 22, in Priam's palace, etc. Rather, they all refer to the period before the war, when the "best man who was in Troy married Hippodameia" (*Iliad* 13.433), when Priam's sons were born, or when Hector was still protecting his family (three examples in Book 24), and further in the Odyssean examples. They all belong to a timespan before the period narrated in the *Iliad*, and they derive from that a nostalgic tone. The poet never uses those phrases when he tells, for instance, of Helen inside the palace or on the walls, of Hector's quest for Andromache and their meeting, or of the sacrifice scene to Athena. Actually,

62 Sale 1987:37.

Sale does not notice some formulaic uses meaning "in Troy," but this does not compromise his conclusions.

Thus the various uses of fixed epithets with different names of the city of Troy show that the city can be counted as one of the heroic "characters" of the *Iliad*. We do not meet any other place with so many qualifications, which by itself contributes to the crystallization of the Myth of Troy, telling the city's "steep fall." We may quote Scully once more: "The *Iliad's* true center of gravity is Troy, the point where the threads of events crisscross and the metaphysical place on which the sacred fiction of the poem turns."[63] Moreover, Sale's analysis might show that the scenes inside Troy constitute the very bulk of Homer's work, distinct from the more traditional and formulaic theater of the war.

Is it possible that Parry's analysis of generic vs. distinctive epithets is still relevant, even as Scully's remarks about the role of Troy as the "well-walled city" in the speeches of the Achaeans who wish to sack and destroy it remain valid, as well as Sale's argument about a formulaic step in the evolution of epic language, contrasting with a greater freedom of the poet in the latest period? I do not see actual incompatibility between them, and my research in the linguistic field of motion verbs[64] taught me to accept different and even opposed theories according to the different issues that we have to confront.

[63] Scully 1990:118–119.
[64] Létoublon 1985.

# Bibliography

Antonaccio, C. 1995. *An Archaeology of Ancestors: Tomb Cult and Hero Cult in Early Greece*. Lanham, MD.

Bakker, E. J. 1997. "The Study of Homeric Discourse." In Morris and Powell 1997:284–304.

Bakker, E. J., and A. Kahane, eds. 1997. *Written Voices, Spoken Signs: Tradition, Performance and the Epic Text.* Cambridge, MA.

Bowra, C. M. 1960. "Homeric Epithets for Troy." *Journal of Hellenic Studies* 80:16–23.

———. 1972. *Homer*. London.

Bremer, J. M., I. J. F. de Jong, and J. Kaiff, eds. 1987. *Beyond Oral Poetry: Recent Trends in Homeric Interpretation*. Amsterdam.

Chantraine, P. 1932. "Remarques sur l'emploi des formules dans le premier chant de *l'Iliade*." *Revue des Études Grecques* 45:121–154.

———. 2009. *Dictionnaire étymologique de la langue grecque. Histoire des mots*. New editon. Ed. A. Blanc, C. de Lamberterie, and J.-L. Perpillou. Paris. Orig. pub. 1968.

Clay, J. S. 2007. "Homer's Trojan Theater." *Transactions of the American Philological Association* 137:233–252.

———. 2011. *Homer's Trojan Theater: Space, Vision, and Memory in the* Iliad. Cambridge.

Cook, J. M. 1973. *The Troad: An Archaeological and Topographical Study*. Oxford.

Delebecque, E. 1951. *Le Cheval dans l'Iliade*. Paris.

Dowden, K., and N. Livingstone, eds. 2011. *A Companion to Greek Mythology*. Malden, MA.

Edwards, M. W. 1986 "Homer and the Oral Tradition: The Formula. Part I." *Oral Tradition* 1:171–230.

———. 1988. "Homer and the Oral Tradition: The Formula. Part II." *Oral Tradition* 3:11–60.

———. 1997. "Homeric Style and Oral Poetics." In Morris and Powell 1997:261–283.

Fagan, P. L. 2001. *Horses in the Similes of the* Iliad*: A Case Study*. Toronto.

Fantuzzi, M., and C. Tsagalis, eds. 2015. *The Greek Epic Cycle and its Ancient Reception: A Companion*. Cambridge.

Faraone, C. 1992. *Talismans and Trojan Horses: Guardian Statues in Ancient Greek Myth and Ritual*. New York.

Fenik, B., ed. 1978. *Homer: Tradition and Invention*. Leiden.

Foley, J. M. 1991. *Immanent Art: From Structure to Meaning in Traditional Oral Epic*. Bloomington.

Giuliani, L. 2003. *Bild und Mythos: Geschichte der Bilderzählung in der griechischen Kunst.* Munich.
Hajnal, I. 2003. "U̯iluša—Tarhuiša. Sprachwissentschaftliche Nachbetrachtungen zum Beitrag von Susaenne Heinhold-Kramer." In Ulf 2003:169–173.
Heinhold-Kramer, S. 2003. "Zur Gleichsetzung der Namen Ilios-Wiluša und Troia-Tarhuiša." In Ulf 2003:146–168.
Kampakoglou, A., and A. Novokhatko, eds. 2018. *Gaze, Vision and Visuality in Ancient Greek Literature: Concepts, Contexts and Reception.* Berlin.
Kirk, G. S. 1990. *The Iliad: A Commentary.* Vol. 2, *Books 5–8.* Cambridge.
Korfmann, M. 2001. "Troia, Traum und Wirklichkeit: Eine Einleitung in das Thema." In *Troia: Traum und Wirklichkeit,* 4–23. Stuttgart.
Kullmann, W. 2002. *Realität, Imagination und Theorie. Kleine Schriften zu Epos und Tragödie in der Antike.* Ed. A. Rengakos. Stuttgart.
Lamberterie, C. de. 1997. "Milman Parry et Antoine Meillet." In Létoublon 1997:9–22.
Leaf, W. 1900–1902. *The Iliad.* 2nd ed. London.
Létoublon, F. 1983. "Défi et combat dans l'*Iliade*." *Revue des Études Grecques* 96:27–48.
———. 1985. *Il allait, pareil à la nuit. Les verbes de mouvement en grec: supplétisme et aspect verbal.* Études et commentaires 98. Paris.
———. 1992a. "De la syntaxe à la poétique générative, ou grammaire et mesure." In Létoublon 1992b:93–103.
———, ed. 1992b. *La langue et les textes en grec ancien. Actes du colloque Pierre Chantraine (Grenoble, 5–8 Septembre 1989).* Amsterdam.
———, ed. 1997. *Hommage à Milman Parry. Le style formulaire de l'épopée homérique et la théorie de l'oralité poétique.* Amsterdam.
———. 2009. "Athéna et son double." *Pallas* 81:179-190.
———. 2011. "Homer's Use of Myth." In Dowden and Livingstone 2011:27–45.
———. 2014a. "Athena and Pallas, Image, Copies, Fakes and Doubles." In Martinez 2014:143–161.
———. 2014b. "Le Palladion dans la Guerre de Troie: un talisman du Cycle épique, un tabou de l'*Iliade*." In Scafoglio 2014:59–84.
———. 2018. "War as Spectacle in the *Iliad*." In Kampakoglou and Novokhatko 2018:3–32.
Luce, J. V. 1999. *Celebrating Homer's Landscapes: Troy and Ithaca Revisited.* New Haven.
Martínez, J., ed. 2014. *Fakes and Forgers of Classical Literature: Ergo decipiatur!* Leiden.
Mellink, M. J., ed. 1986. *Troy and the Trojan War: A Symposium held at Bryn Mawr College (October 1984).* Bryn Mawr.

Montanari, F. 1998. "Antichi commenti a Omero. Alcune riflessioni." In *Omero. Gli aedi, i poemi, gli interpreti*, 1–17. Florence.

———. 2005. "Les poèmes homériques entre réalité et fiction." *Gaia* 9:9–24.

Morris, I., and B. Powell, eds. 1997. *A New Companion to Homer*. Leiden.

Nagler, M. 1967. "Towards a Generative View of the Formula." *Transactions of the American Philological Association* 98:269–311.

———. 1974. *Spontaneity and Tradition: A Study in the Oral Art of Homer*. Berkeley.

Nagy, G. 1990. *Greek Mythology and Poetics*. Ithaca.

O'Neill, E. 1942. *The Localization of Metrical Word-types in the Greek Hexameter: Homer, Hesiod, and the Alexandrians*. New Haven.

Parry, M. 1928a. *L'épithète traditionnelle dans Homère*. Paris.

———. 1928b. "The Homeric Gloss: A Study in Word-sense." *Transactions of the American Philological Association* 59:233—247.

———. 1930. "Studies in the Epic Technique of Oral Verse-Making. I. Homer and Homeric Style." *Harvard Studies in Classical Philology* 41:73–147. Repr. in Parry 1971:266–324.

———. 1971. *The Making of Homeric Verse: The Collected Papers of Milman Parry*. Ed. A. Parry. Oxford.

Platte, R. 2014. "Hades' Famous Foals and the Prehistory of Homeric Horse Formulas." *Oral Tradition* 29:149–162.

———. 2017. *Equine Poetics*. Hellenic Stuidies 74. Washington, DC.

Polychronopoulou, O. 1999. *Archéologues sur les pas d'Homère: la naissance de la protohistoire égéenne*. Paris.

Richardson, N. J. 1993. *The* Iliad*: A Commentary*. Vol. 6, *Books 21–24*. Ed. G. S. Kirk. Cambridge.

Russo, J. 1997. "The Formula." In Morris and Powell 1997:238–260.

Sacks, R. 1987. *The Traditional Phrase in Homer. Two Studies in Form, Meaning and Interpretation*. Leiden.

Sale, W. M. 1987. "The Formularity of the Place-Phrases of the *Iliad*." *Transactions of the American Philological Association* 117:21–50.

———. 1989. "The Trojans, Statistics, and Milman Parry." *Greek, Roman, and Byzantine Studies* 30:341–410.

———. 1996. "In Defense of Milman Parry: Renewing the Oral Theory." *Oral Tradition* 11:314–417.

Scafoglio, G., ed. 2014. *Studies on the Greek Epic Cycle*. Philologia Antiqua 7. Pisa.

Scully, S. 1990. *Homer and the Sacred City*. Ithaca.

Sicking, C. M. J. 1993. *Griechische Verslehre*. Handbuch der Altertumswissenschaft II–4. Munich.

Ulf, C., ed.2003. *Der neue Streit um Troja: Eine Bilanz*. Munich.

Vet, T. de. 1996. "The Joint Role of Orality and Literacy in the Composition, Transmission, and Performance of the Homeric Texts: A Comparative View." *Transactions of the American Philological Association* 126:43–76.

Wakker, G. C. 1994. *Conditions and Conditionals: An Investigation of Ancient Greek.* Amsterdam.

Watkins, C. 1986. "When They Came from Steep Wilusa: The Language of the Trojans." In Mellink 1986:45–62.

Wathelet, P. 1988. *Dictionnaire des Troyens de l'*Iliade. 2 vols. Liège.

———. 1989. *Les Troyens de l'*Iliade. *Mythe et Histoire*. Paris.

Whallon, W. 1961. "The Homeric Epithets." *Yale Classical Studies* 17:95-142.

———. 1969. *Formula, Character, and Context: Studies in Homeric, Old English and Old Testament Poetry.* Washington, DC.

Whitman, W. 1951. *Homer and the Heroic Tradition.* Cambridge, MA. Repr. New York, 1965.

Witte, K. 1913. "Homeros. B) Sprache." *Real-Enzyklopädie*, vol. 8, col. 2213–2247.

———. 1972. *Zur homerischen Sprache.* Darmstadt.

# 3

# Composition in Performance, Arab Style

Dwight F. Reynolds

For researchers who conduct ethnographic fieldwork on oral traditions, one of the most exciting aspects of *The Singer of Tales* is Albert Lord's accounts of *experimentation in the field*, the various ways in which he and Milman Parry interrogated living traditions by comparing performances, setting up encounters between poets, asking poets to repeat performances, asking them to sing about new themes and so forth, all with the aim of understanding the nitty-gritty details of how poets learned, composed, and performed their tales. Together, they developed fieldwork techniques that had a profound influence on all later researchers. Where others before them had been content to collect "texts," Parry and Lord opened up the question of *how* oral compositions come into being and *how* they are transmitted from one generation to the next.

These techniques so excited me as an undergraduate, and later graduate, student that when I went into the field to do my dissertation research on the Arabic oral epic poem *Sīrat Banī Hilāl* (The Epic of the Bani Hilal Bedouin Tribe) in Northern Egypt in the mid-1980s, I sought to replicate those experiments as much as possible.[1] I hoped even to carry their innovative methods a bit further by engaging in an "apprenticeship" with an epic singer and trying to learn to sing a portion of the epic, not in an attempt to become a singer but, rather, as a means of exploring and understanding the techniques of oral epic composition and performance. It seemed worthwhile, not only to test the concepts of "oral formula" and "composition in performance" in a different oral epic tradition but also to replicate the fieldwork methods Parry and Lord had developed in a different cultural context. In effect, I hoped to create a laboratory in which to test their ideas and hypotheses about the processes of transmission,

1 The research described here was made possible by the generous support of grants from the Center for Arabic Studies Abroad (CASA 1980–1981, 1982–1983); the Harvard Society of Fellows (1986–1990); a Fulbright-Hays international dissertation grant (1986–1987); and an American Council of Learned Societies (ACLS) Digital Humanities grant (2008–2009).

composition, and variation in performance by using the same techniques they had used. I offer this brief summary of the modest results of my own work as an homage to their remarkably innovative fieldwork and as a means of reminding ourselves that Parry and Lord were not only groundbreaking scholars in the conclusions they drew from their materials but also in *how* they collected them. It is quite possible that they might not have reached the conclusions they did if they had not conducted their research the way they did, for fieldwork methods to a great extent predetermine the intellectual outcomes they produce.

## 1. The Structure of Classical Arabic Poetry

The vast majority of written and oral Arabic poetry over the past 1,500 years has been composed within one basic form (*qarīḍ* in Arabic), in which each verse consists of two equal-length hemistichs separated by a medial caesura, and the rhyme established at the end of the first verse is found at the end of every verse thereafter for the duration of the poem, an arrangement commonly termed "mono-endrhyme":

-------------------- -------------------A
-------------------- -------------------A
-------------------- -------------------A
(etc.)

The interaction between written and oral in the Arabic literary tradition is too complex to treat in detail here; suffice it to say that in the pre-Islamic and early Islamic eras it was quite common to compose and recite poems orally and only later, selectively, set them down in writing. In other words, even the written corpus of classical Arabic poetry that has come down to us is deeply intertwined with the processes of oral composition and performance.[2]

Given that classical Arabic verses typically average between twenty-two and thirty-two syllables in length, depending on the meter, the medial caesura

[2] "Classical Arabic" refers here to a specific register of formal Arabic that is defined by its adherence to a set of grammatical norms, including a complex system of desinential case-endings. It contrasts with "colloquial Arabic," a term that refers to the various spoken forms of Arabic, which differ from "classical Arabic" in a number of ways, among which is the general lack of a case system. In this regard, colloquial Arabic dialects differ from classical Arabic in ways similar to how the Romance languages differ from Latin. The rules of classical Arabic prosody were codified already in the eighth century CE and were strictly adhered to with remarkable consistency until the twentieth century; whereas colloquial poetry, on the other hand, appears always to have been more flexible. Both "classical" and "colloquial" Arabic poetry can be composed, performed, and transmitted orally, so the linguistic register of an Arabic poem provides little evidence as to whether it was composed orally or as a written text.

is virtually a performative necessity because it creates a brief pause in which the reciter can take a breath. In classical Arabic poetry, it was considered a "defect" to repeat a rhyme word unless it was used with a different meaning, a rule that effectively limited most classical Arabic poems to a maximum of some 120 lines. Although the exact nature of meter in early classical Arabic poetry has remained a source of discussion, the centrality of end-rhyme to the Arabic poetic tradition is unchallenged.[3] Mandatory mono-endrhyme is a feature of the earliest Arabic poetry known to us (ca. fifth century CE) and may have existed in Himyaritic in Yemen for a number of centuries before that.[4] With the exception of some polyrhymed strophic song forms that emerged in the Middle Ages, obligatory mono-endrhyme remained a constant feature of nearly all classical Arabic poetic production until the introduction of "free verse" in the twentieth century.

For the first few centuries of the Islamic period, there is little evidence that oral *colloquial* or *folk* poetry differed in its basic structure from the classical poetry described above; in other words, even colloquial poetry appears to have been composed as mono-endrhymed poems with medial caesurae. Beginning in the later Middle Ages, however, a number of new poetic genres begin to appear in the written record that are composed in colloquial or semi-colloquial Arabic and are multi-rhymed in a wide variety of patterns.[5] These new forms appear to reflect the diversity of colloquial oral traditions, such as are currently found in modern times in oral folk poetry around the Arab world.

The *Sīrat Banī Hilāl* oral epic in Northern Egypt and the scattered written fragments of epic verse that have been recorded from the late fourteenth century to the present, however, all use the classical mono-endrhyme with medial caesura form, which therefore sets it apart from most other genres of Arabic oral folk poetry.[6] *Sīrat Banī Hilāl* epic poetry is thus colloquial in language but composed in the same form as classical Arabic poetry. It should be noted that narratives about the Bani Hilal tribe are also performed in many regions as folk tales, that is, in prose rather than verse and without musical accompaniment, but these

3 Whether pre-Islamic poetry was composed within a strict metrical system or whether the extant metrical patterns were conceived of at a later date and early compilers then "regularized" the versions that have come down to us, as well as the role of stress-access versus quantitative meters, all remain topics of vigorous debate. See Weil 1958 for a concise and reliable summary; also Heinrichs 1987.

4 See ʿAbdallah 1988.

5 See Larkin 2006.

6 The Southern Egyptian tradition of singing *Sīrat Banī Hilāl* in rhymed quatrains seems to be a unique regional variant—thus references to "Arabic oral epic singing" in the remainder of this essay do not necessarily hold true for the Southern Egyptian tradition. For an account of pre-twentieth-century written records, see Reynolds 1995:1–13; for a study of the Southern Egyptian quatrain tradition, see Slyomovics 1987.

are not of concern to us here.[7] The tradition examined in this essay is one in which the tales of the Bani Hilal have been unified into a single lengthy narrative which is performed almost entirely in sung rhymed verse with musical accompaniment, punctuated with occasional prose passages that are used primarily for scene-setting, rapid summarization of events, or comic interjections. The classical rule that a rhyme-word should not be repeated, however, is not used in oral epic singing, which allows singers to produce sequences of hundreds of verses with the same end-rhyme before switching to a different rhyme. In the twentieth century and today, the tradition of performing the epic in sung verse with musical accompaniment is found *only* in Egypt, though it may have been more widespread in earlier centuries.

The epic of the Bani Hilal is of prodigious length—a master singer in Egypt can take between 60 and 140 hours to sing his version—and consists of a complicated story involving a cluster of some eight to twelve key characters. The story is divided in performance into segments or episodes (Ar. *qiṣaṣ*, sing. *qiṣṣa*) of four to ten hours in duration, typically sung over one or two evenings. With its focus on a constellation of main characters, the overall narrative of the Bani Hilal epic more closely resembles, say, the *Iliad*, the *Nibelungenlied*, or the King Arthur cycle, rather than mirroring "single hero" epics such as the *Odyssey*, *Beowulf*, or *The Song of Roland*. Although it has been clear for some time from the fragmentary pre-modern written records and from ethnographic materials collected in the late nineteenth and early twentieth centuries that Arabic epic poetry is to a great extent oral-formulaic in nature, it has also been apparent that oral formulae function rather differently in Arabic than in either the South Slavic epic traditions or the classical Greek tradition. What follows is a description of some of the key differences.

## 2. Of Rhyme and Reason

Parry and Lord were far ahead of their time in stressing the importance of understanding the processes of transmission and in their exploration of how young men learned to sing epic poems. Unfortunately, I was not afforded the opportunity to observe young singers learning to sing, nor did I have the opportunity to record singers at various stages of their lives as they mastered and developed their craft. Already in the 1980s the sons of epic singers in northern Egypt were going to school and learning other trades rather than doing a traditional apprenticeship of ten or more years with older male relatives.

7 There are also proverbs and riddles that derive from the tale of the Bani Hilal.

The singing of the Bani Hilal epic in this region has been almost entirely a hereditary, professional craft restricted to specific social groups, a sharp contrast with the South Slavic traditions where young men learned the craft by attending performances, rather than being trained by family members. Although there had been a few examples in the not-too-distant past of men in northern Egypt who had learned the epic purely out of their love for it, these singers had all passed away before I undertook my research. The most famous singer of this type in northern Egypt was Sayyid Hawwas, who had become a local "superstar" by performing selected scenes from the epic on the western violin, accompanied by several other musicians, with highly amplified sound and at times with painfully strong "reverb," standing on a stage like an urban singer.[8] All of the singers I worked with were instead hereditary professional singers from a single distinct social group, one of several groups in Egypt that have at times been labeled "Gypsies," but who are not, however, directly related to the Roma of Europe. In this social group, there have been, until the last 30 years or so, two traditional occupations for males: epic singing or blacksmithing. There was no choice between the two—one was either the member of an epic-singing family or a blacksmithing family, and one inherited the occupation of one's father and grandfather. (Women engage in a variety of different informal trades such as selling vegetables in the marketplaces, weaving baskets or mats, etc., and in recent decades young men have sought a wide variety of jobs including in construction, carpentry, and even the local police force.) Because of this clear knowledge that boys from given families would grow up to be singers, the learning process began quite early, sometimes by the age of five or six.

Older poets all described a very similar process of apprenticeship that involved attending performances with male relatives from an early age, learning to play drone notes on the *rabāb* (the two-string spike fiddle that is the traditional musical instrument for epic singing), then simple melodies, next learning to sing shorter song genres such as praise songs to the prophet Muhammad and *mawwāls* (short lyric songs), and finally scenes and later full episodes from the epic itself. Most said that they started out performing the shorter genres during breaks in the epic performance while their father or uncle or grandfather smoked a cigarette and had a glass of tea before picking up the epic tale again. Later they would perform a scene or two during an evening's performance, and by their late teens they were capable of singing a full episode (i.e. a performance of four to ten hours). Some struck out on their own to perform as itinerant poets at a young age while others continued to play "second fiddle" to an older male relative for many years.

8 See Reynolds 1989.

After several months of attending and recording performances of oral epic singing in the northern Egyptian village in which I did my dissertation fieldwork, I decided to expand my research by attempting to learn to sing the epic from a master poet. Ethnomusicology as a discipline has long stressed the value of learning to perform the traditions one studies on the principle that there are many elements about musical structures, ideas, and techniques that only become apparent in actual performance and because it is necessary to understand a performer's conception of what he or she does and observe how the tradition is transmitted.[9] My very first lesson, however, was an abysmal failure—my teacher sang perhaps twenty to twenty-five verses and then asked me to sing them back to him. I, unfortunately, could scarcely remember the first few words of the first verse. On the other hand, having just heard the rather simple melody twenty or more times, I had no difficulty playing the tune back to him on the *rabāb*. He found this quite surprising and at a later point asked me pointedly why I was able to play the instrument so easily when, in his words, my tongue was "made of wood." When I first asked permission to record our lessons, he refused since he naturally only wanted good, full performances to be recorded, but I finally persuaded him. I would then spend hours after my lesson listening to the tape over and over again, and although I at first tried to memorize my lessons orally, I simply was not able to learn more than a few verses at a time in this manner. I eventually accepted the fact that I was hopelessly literate and resorted to writing down passages on scraps of paper that I could refer to during the day to jog my memory. Mine was therefore not a traditional apprenticeship—but it was never intended to be.

What taking "lessons" did allow me to do was to test the boundaries of acceptable variation. For example, I soon found out that my teacher did not necessarily expect me to sing passages back to him in my next lesson to the same melody he had used. If I chose a known melody that worked with the length of the line, he voiced no objections. As any scholar of oral tradition might have predicted, he also did not have a word-for-word or even line-for-line recollection of what he had taught me in previous lessons—if I got the story right (in other words, retold the events of the story as he had taught them to me), everything was fine. I am convinced that he was also unaware that at times I memorized passages as closely as I possibly could, producing a nearly word-for-word replication in which I memorized even the slight melodic variations from his performance. This type of "verbatim" imitation drew no comments from him.

But then I tried to change something that *did* matter to him. Battle scenes in the epic are very repetitive. The heroes always challenge each other to single

9 See Hood 1960.

combat; they always taunt and insult each other before beginning to fight; the bad guy always appears to get the upper hand at first; and the good guy always wins in the end. So one time I substituted passages from a battle-scene in one episode for a scene in another. My teacher immediately cocked his head and said to me, "That is not from this episode." I asked how he knew this, and the answer was deceptively simple—the rhyme was wrong. As we discussed the matter, he was astonished that I had never noticed that each episode had a set rhyme scheme. When I asked him what he meant, he immediately rattled off the rhyme scheme of the episode I was learning: it starts in one rhyme, and then, when such-and-such happens in the narrative, it changes to a different rhyme, and later when so-and-so sings his poem about X, that poem is in a different rhyme, and so forth. For several months I had been listening, recording, transcribing, and translating texts and I had failed to notice the single most important structural element in the minds of the poets—the rhyme scheme! Of course I had paid quite a bit of attention to rhyme, but I had failed to notice that the same poet from one performance to the next, and even different poets performing the same episode, followed a traditional, inherited rhyme scheme.

## 3. Oral Formulaic Systems

Milman Parry defined an "oral formula" as "a group of words which is regularly employed under the same metrical conditions to express a given essential idea."[10] This definition certainly holds true for traditions that feature strict metrical constraints, but what about poetic traditions in which meter is not the primary structuring device of epic verse?[11] In Arabic oral epic poetry in northern Egypt, end-rhyme is strictly observed, as is the overall length of each line (typically twenty-six to thirty syllables), but the metrical system is rather flexible. Classical Arabic poetry, as it has come down to us in written versions, possesses a complex system of quantitative meter based on alternating patterns of long and short syllables, but even in this seemingly rigid system, it is completely acceptable at most points within a verse to substitute two short syllables for one long syllable or vice versa; the classical metrical system was thus fixed but somewhat elastic in nature. This metrical elasticity is even more apparent in the sung tradition of oral epic poetry, where poets have additional musical resources that further allow the "stretching" of a single syllable via *melisma* (singing a single syllable over several notes) or the "squeezing" of several syllables into a single note. In this tradition, which has notably long verses and a relatively malleable

10 Parry 1930:80 (reprinted as Parry 1971:272).

11 A number of scholars have questioned the applicability of a strict definition of "oral formula" across cultures; see, for example, Finnegan 1977:58–73; Sowayan 1985:183–195; Caton 1990:86–99.

metrical structure, it is therefore not surprising to find the most easily identified oral formulae clustered at the end of lines where the singers face their greatest compositional challenge—the generation of end-rhyme. The poets of Northern Egypt refer to this as *al-mashī bi-l-ḥarf*, walking or going along with the "letter," perhaps better rendered as "sticking to the letter" in colloquial English.

One of the techniques that poets have developed for generating end-rhyme while singing their tales is the use of what might be termed "oral-formulaic systems" (clusters of related oral formulae) that consist of a stem-phrase plus a choice of different rhyme words that all express a similar idea. This is a mechanism that allows poets to express the same or very similar ideas with different rhymes, the way South Slavic oral formulae allow poets to express the same idea in different metrical contexts. They also use closely related stem-phrases of different lengths, so that one can use the formula to fill out anywhere from a few syllables at the end of a verse to an entire hemistich of twelve to fifteen syllables. The linchpin of the system, however, is always the rhyme word.

A common example of this system is an expression in the archaic diction of the epic for losing control of oneself from grief, anger, surprise, or some other intense emotion, which is very similar to the English phrase "to lose one's mind." This idea occurs almost exclusively in final (i.e. rhyme) position and the many variants of this idea form an "oral formulaic system" that can be used to express the same idea in all of the most common rhyme schemes. Below are examples of this simple formula attached to "stem phrases" of various lengths so that the same idea can be expressed in various different rhymes in phrases that range from six to eleven syllables:

1. His mind from him + rhyme word

A. *il-ʿaql-I*[12] *minnuh: tāh / rāḥ / ṭār / hām / iḥtār* [6–7 syllables]
His mind[13] from him: strayed / departed / flew /
wandered / grew confused

B. *il-ʿaql-I min dimāghuh: tāh / rāḥ / ṭār / hām / iḥtār* [8–9 syllables]
His mind from his skull: strayed / departed /
flew / wandered / grew confused

[12] The "-I" here represents an obligatory helping vowel which occurs to prevent the clustering of three consonants.

[13] Literally "the mind" since Arabic often does not use possessive endings for body parts (i.e. "the hand" for "my hand").

C. *il-'aql-I min juwwa dā rāsuh: tāh / rāḥ / ṭār / hām / iḥtār* [10–11 syllables]
His mind from inside his head: strayed / departed / flew / wandered / grew confused

The very simple cluster of formulae in set A, when used at the end of the verse, makes it possible to express the same basic idea with many different rhymes. Demonstrated above are *-āh*, *-āḥ*, *-ār*, and *-ām*, with an additional option of a two-syllable final word within the "r" rhyme (*iḥtār*), all of which are appended to a five-syllable stem phrase (*il / 'aq / l-I / min / nuh*). In set B, the same rhyme words are appended to a seven-syllable stem phrase, and in set C to a nine-syllable stem phrase. There are many other rhyme words that can occur in this position such that this particular formulaic system allows oral poets to express this same idea in almost any rhyme environment. But there are also closely related formulae that express very similar ideas with slightly more complex or different imagery. These occur somewhat less frequently than the phrases in the example above:

2. His mind departed from ...

*il-'aql-I rāḥ min: ḥimāh / il-maṭāriḥ*
His mind departed from: its sanctuary / these places

3. His mind ...

*'aqluh: fāriq il-mīzān / ghāyib / ikhtalaṭ bi-jinān*
His mind: tipped the scale / (is/was) absent / mixed with madness

Thus, if South Slavic oral formulae exist to assist the expression of ideas with "the same metrical contexts," we might make a slight alteration of the definition for these Arabic formulaic systems as existing to help poets express ideas in the same "rhyme contexts." The change is quite logical—in South Slavic oral epic, meter is the primary structural constraint upon the singer, whereas in Arabic the primary structural constraint is end-rhyme.

These systems of verse-final formulae were readily apparent to me even in the early part of my research. The work of Parry and Lord had already provided an effective model for identifying, marking, and calculating the percentages of such formulae, and these were therefore the first elements of compositional technique I was able to identify. Their research also suggested one of the first fieldwork "experiments" that I conducted. Every now and then, I took to asking a poet to re-sing a passage immediately under some pretext so I could study the amount of variation. I would, for example, say, "Oh no! That tape was bad," or offer some other excuse, and then ask if the poet could please re-sing the part of the story that he had just finished.

One time it suddenly occurred to me to ask Shaykh Taha Abu Zayd, my teacher, if he would repeat a section—but on a different rhyme. This occurred during a performance in a private home in front of about a dozen adult male listeners, and I made my request while Shaykh Taha was taking a break, sipping tea, and smoking a cigarette. He stopped, looked me squarely in the eye and asked, "What rhyme do you want?" He had sung this section on the rhyme /*-ār*/, a rather common rhyme, so I chose another common rhyme /*-ām*/.[14] He again looked me in the eye, which made me feel that I was being a rather impertinent, perhaps even disrespectful student, but he immediately picked up his *rabāb* and re-sang sixty-five verses of poetry without a pause, changing the rhyme in every verse but with almost no changes in the narrative.[15] I was amazed and enthusiastically asked if he could do it again on a *third* rhyme, but the audience members objected, saying, "Doktoor, what didn't you understand? We have already heard this part twice!" The poet looked at me and smiled, as if to underline that although he and I were aware of what he had just done, the audience members were totally oblivious to the virtuosity that had just been demonstrated (a thought that he confirmed in our conversation the following day) and were instead focused entirely on the story. The resulting two versions of the same scene provide ample testimony to Shaykh Taha's mastery both of the art of epic singing and of the versatility of the system of end-rhyme formulae. Six verses from these two parallel performances are compared below; each performance was a half-hour in length (i.e. the side of one cassette tape) and they were almost exactly the same number of verses in length, though Shaykh Taha started the second performance with a few introductory verses that were not part of the original version. Verbatim repetitions are underlined, nearly verbatim repetitions are marked with broken underlining, passages that have been changed are unmarked, and the rhyme phrase appears in English between slashes and thereafter the rhyme word appears in Arabic transliteration.

14 In Arabic, a rhyme is referred to only by its rhyming consonant, not by the vowels that precede or follow it, so I literally asked Sheikh Taha to sing on an "m-rhyme" (Ar. *Mīm*).

15 Looking back at this moment after even just a few days, I realized that my request might well have been perceived as disrespectful, primarily because it took place in front of others, and that it might have been more diplomatic to have made this request in private during a lesson. I was, however, simply carried away with the excitement of the moment. We may certainly wonder whether the various tasks Parry and Lord placed before their singers might also have been perceived as lacking in appropriate decorum.

In this scene, the hero Abu Zayd[16] (also known as Salama) is arriving in a city after a long journey across the desert and he poses as an epic poet (a common motif in this tradition); he introduces himself to the group of men he finds there and is asked to sing, but while he is singing, the city is attacked by enemy forces and the alarm is sounded. Abu Zayd then doffs his poet's garb, mounts a horse, rides with the men of the city into battle and slays their enemy. Thus, the "lowly poet" is revealed to be, in truth, a valiant hero and vice versa.[17] The audio recordings of these two performances can be accessed at the Sirat Bani Hilal Digital Archive (siratbanihilal.ucsb.edu)—the passages below are quoted from recording 118-B (starting at 15:56) and recording 119-A (starting at 3:10):

Text 1 / Line 5: **Rhyme**

Abu Zayd reached them: "My greetings to the Arabs,
My greetings to those on the right, yes, and are repeated /to those on the left/ **yasār**

*Ṭabb 'aleyhum Abū Zeyd: "Salāmī 'al-'arab / salāmī 'ala l-yumne aywa ti'ūd yasār"*

Text 2 / Line 11:

"My greetings to you, O Bedouin,
My greetings to those on the right and I repeat /my greetings/ **salām**

*"Salāmī 'aleykum ayyuhā l-bawādī / salāmī 'al-yumnā wi-a'īd is-salām*

Text 1 / Line 6:

Abū Zayd recounted to them what had befallen him;
They welcomed him /from right and left/ **yasār**

*Ḥakā lhum Abū Zeyd bi-mā qad jarā luh / dōl raḥḥabū min yamīn wi-yasār*

[16] Shaykh Taha Abu Zayd, like a number of other epic singers, incorporates the name of one of the heroes of the epic into his own personal name, in this case because it was the name of his father.

[17] I have analyzed the interplay of poets and heroes in the Bani Hilal epic in detail in Reynolds 1995.

Text 2 / Line 13:

Abu Zayd recounted to them what had happened to him,
And they welcomed him, O Nobles, not just with /words/ **kalām**

*Ḥakā lhum Abū Zeyd bi-mā qad ḥaṣal luh / wa-raḥḥabū yā agāwīd min ghayr-I kalām*

Text 1 / Line 8:

"What is your craft, O Uncle, and what is your profession?"
So Salāma [Abū Zayd] said, "I am a poet /of princes/" **umār**

*"Mā ṣan'itak yā 'amm wi-ēh mihnitak?" / fa-qāl Salāma, "Dā anā shā'ir al-umār"*

Text 2 / Line 14:

"What is your profession and what is your craft?"
He said to them, "I am a poet /I measure words/." **kalām**

*"Mā mihnitak wi-ēh ṣan'itak?" / fa-qāla, "Shā'ir anā bawzin il-kalām*

Text 1 / Line 9:

They said to him, "Poet, take out your rabāb,
Let us hear, man, praise of the Prophet, /the Chosen One/. **mukhtār**

*Gālū*[18] *luh, "Shā'ir, ḥill-I rabābak / sammi'nā yā rāgil madḥ in-nabī il-mukhtār*

Text 2 / Line 16:

They said to him, "Poet, O Uncle, take out your rabāb,
Let us hear praise of the Arab Prophet, /the High, the Leader/." **miqdām**

*Qālū luh, "Shā'ir yā 'amm-I, ḥill-I rabābak / sammi'nā fī madḥ in-nabī il-'arabī al-'ālī al-miqdām*

[18] Shaykh Taha alternates between the more classical pronunciation of the verb "to say" (pronounced with an initial "q") and the colloquial pronunciation (pronounced with a "g").

Text 1 / Line 11:

Abū Zayd was making poetry when suddenly the horses of the foreigners
Came out from the mountains, /men of King Ṣaymūl, strong of refuge-seeker/[19] **al-jār**

*Abū Zeyd biyish'ir illā wi-khēl il-'agam ṭālla min ig-gabal / rigāl malik Ṣaymūl 'azīz il-jār*

Text 2 / Line 19:

Abū Zayd was making poetry when suddenly the horses of the foreigners Came out from the mountains,
/each warrior like seven at the time of weighing/ **mīzān**

*Abū Zeyd biyish'ar illā wi-khēl il-'agam ṭāllū min ig-gabal / min kull-I fāris sab' waqt-I mīzān*

Text 1 / Line 14:

Put up your rabāb—Ah! Ah! Ah!—O poet of the Arabs
The horses of the foreigners have come to us,
they have seized /the regions/ **al-ashṭār**

*Tāwī rabābak āh āh āh yā shā'ir il-'arab / khēl il-'agam gātnā itmalakū l-ashṭār*

Text 2 / Lines 21 and 22:

"O poet of the Arabs, listen as we speak to you,
Stop your rabāb and cut short your words **kalām**

The horses of the foreigners have come to us, right and left,
The foreigners have come to us and have seized
/the fronts/ **aqdām**

*Yā shā'ir il-'urbān w-isma' nikallimak / baṭṭal rabābak wi-qill il-kalām*
*Khēl il-'agam gātnā yamīnan wi-maysara / gātnā il-'agam w-itmalikū l-aqdām*

[19] An epithet that indicates that he is so powerful that even the strong seek refuge with him in times of need.

Most of the verses in this performance were converted from one rhyme to another through a simple substitution of the final rhyme word or phrase utilizing precisely the type of "oral-formulaic system" demonstrated above. But, in a few cases, Shaykh Taha made no attempt to "convert" the image from his first performance by changing the rhyme word but, rather, shifted to an entirely different image that nevertheless described the same action. These passages, upon inspection, turn out to be some of the most common stock motifs of the epic, for example, the hero dressing, arming himself, and then riding into battle. Below are the four verses from the first performance and the two and a half verses in the second performance that describe these actions:

Text 1 / Lines 24–28:

Salāma [Abū Zayd] dressed, possessor of audacity,
    Tall of stature, sugar of the skirmish,
He put on brocade, and then silk, and then chainmail,
    Then he girded himself with an Indian [sword] that splits stones,
Plates of steel on the chest of Salāma,
    With them he deflects the arrows of the heathens,
Plates of steel, plates and arm-guards on his right arm,
    With them he deflects attack when taking revenge.

Text 2 / Lines 30–32:

When the Hilālī [Abū Zayd] had dressed with resolve,
    In his hand was a Yemeni [sword] with a well-sharpened
    blade-edge.
God is Great! Abū Zayd when he mounted!
    Like the sail of a ship on the seas as it wanders.
Or a tall dovecot tower filled with doves.[20]

It turns out that the poets possess what might be called "templates" for the most common stock scenes in different rhyme schemes. If one is singing in the rhyme *-ār*, the "dressing for battle" scene leads almost inevitably to the image of a sword that "splits stones" [*yiflaq al-aḥjār*], an image that is not found in other rhymes, perhaps for lack of other words that fit the image of "splitting." It is a "rhyme-specific" formula. The substituted image

20 Shaykh Taha here sang two rhyming hemistichs in a row, which he did not consider an "error" because the rhyme fell into place.

in the second performance ("a well-sharpened blade-edge"), in contrast, does generate a number of other possibilities, due to the richness of Arabic vocabulary for swords, blades, edges, etc. (nearly forty terms for swords and blades occur in the epic); it is part of an "oral-formulaic system."

In sum, the experiment of asking Shaykh Taha to re-sing a section of the epic on a different end-rhyme revealed several things about the role of oral formulae in this tradition: 1) oral formulae occur most frequently at the end of verses, that is, in "rhyme position"; 2) many of these formulae operate within formulaic systems that allow poets to substitute different end-rhymes with a fair amount of ease by changing only one or two words; 3) there are also certain formulae that occur in rhyme-specific environments, that is, they occur only with a specific rhyme; and 4) sequences of formulae constitute a form of "template" for expressing stock scenes in a particular rhyme. If all stock scenes were sung using the same images and phrases with changes only in the rhyme words, Arabic epic singing would be boring and repetitive in the extreme, so this final element, the different rhyme "templates" as I have termed them, plays an important role in creating a richer, more varied set of phrases, images, and details for embellishing common narrative scenes. I only came to realize the centrality of these rhyme templates, however, when I tried out another fieldwork "experiment," again inspired by the example of Parry and Lord.

## 4. Two Poets Compared

The example below presents a comparison of two different poets singing the same episode—the birth of the hero Abu Zayd. The epic is performed with short passages in spoken prose in between much longer passages of sung verse. The transition from prose to sung verse can only take place at the beginning of a character's speech or song; that is, the junction between speaking and singing is always at the opening of a quotation of direct speech. Once he has begun to sing, however, the poet can use sung verse for first-person speech, dialogue, reported narrative, external commentary, or description. He can switch from sung verse back to spoken prose whenever he wishes, and this is sometimes used to speed up a performance by summarizing events quickly or for the insertion of some comic material, both of which are more easily done in spoken prose. In the chart below, it is easy to see that these two poets use almost exactly the same rhymes for the same narrative material, and they also insert their brief prose passages in nearly the same places. It should be noted, however, that whenever a performance is interrupted, a poet must use a prose introduction to get back into the story, so not all prose passages are the result of the poet's aesthetic choices but may instead reflect external factors in the performance situation.

## Rhyme Scheme Comparison

| Shaykh Taha | Shaykh Biyeli | Story |
|---|---|---|
| prose | prose | 1) Introduction of characters; Rizq has married eight women but does not yet have a son to be his heir. |
| -āXiḥ | -āXiḥ[21] | 2) Rizq's complaint about his state; he marries Ghanim's daughter, but she bears a girl, then a crippled boy; he sends her back to her father; Rizq goes hunting with Sarhan; in the desert a dervish shaykh tells Rizq to go to Mecca and marry Khadra, daughter of the Sharif of Mecca, and she shall bear him a son. |
| prose | prose | 3) The Bani Hilal tribe arrives in Mecca and are welcomed by the ruler, Qirda; Rizq wishes to marry his daughter. |
| -ālhā | -ān[22]<br>prose | 4) the Hilali Qadi [judge] proposes marriage and describes the dowry; they marry; seven years pass and they still have no children. |
| " | -ālhā[23] | 5) Ghanim tells Rizq to divorce Khadra and marry another. |
| -āh | -āh | 6) Rizq goes to Khadra and confronts her; she greets him and calms him saying that all is in the hands of God; Rizq grows angry and strikes her; she leaves her tent and goes to Shamma, another barren woman of the tribe; they go to the desert and wish upon birds—Shamma for a son as beautiful as a white bird, Khadra for a son as strong as a black bird she sees; her servant wishes also for a son; at their return they are reconciled with their husbands. |

21 This is a two-syllable rhyme in which the two vowels and the final consonant are set, but the penultimate consonant is variable, marked here as X (for example, *wāḍiḥ*, *rāyiḥ*, *maṭāriḥ*).

22 Shaykh Biyeli interpolates a six-verse section on the rhyme *-ān* before breaking into a rapid prose summary of the subsequent events, perhaps because he started off on the wrong rhyme. He then switched to the "proper" rhyme a few moments later.

23 The disjunct /*-ālhā*/ section in these two performances is a comic passage in which the speaker describes what type of girls one should and should not marry. Shaykh Taha places it in the mouth of the Hilali Qadi who is addressing the ruler of Mecca on Rizq's behalf; Shaykh Biyeli places it in the mouth of Ghanim who is advising Rizq to divorce Khadra since she has borne him no children and to take another wife.

| | | |
|---|---|---|
| prose | prose | 7) Shamma bears Ḥasan, Khadra gives birth, but the boy is black; Rizq is ridiculed by the men of the tribe who say that Khadra has committed adultery with a black slave; Khadra's servant bears a son to Rizq's servant, Najah. |
| -āra | —[24] | 8) Najah goes to his master Rizq with the good news. |
| -āh | -ālī | 9) Rizq grows angry and confronts his wife; they argue. |
| -ālī | " | 10) She protests her innocence, but he casts her out. |
| -āh | prose | 11) They propose to divide the herds by throwing a spear; a dervish shaykh appears and takes the spear; he casts it and wins for Khadra all of Rizq's livestock and half of Ghanim's. |
| —[25] | " | 14) Rizq in his grief leaves the tribe to live alone among the wild beasts of the desert; Khadra seeks refuge with the other nobles of the tribe but is refused. |
| -āh | " | 15) Khadra is escorted into the desert by a shaykh. |
| " | -āh | 16) Khadra complains of her fate; they come to cross-roads, and she chooses the road to the Zahlan tribe, the enemies of the Bani Hilal; the shaykh cannot take her further and leaves; she is alone and lost in the wilderness with her newborn son. |

The above comparison covers thirty minutes of performance and Shaykh Taha's version includes 184 verses of rhymed poetry.[26] We can see that although the rhyme scheme is not absolutely fixed, these two poets do share a basic rhyme scheme in their minds. They shift from prose to poetry and back again at the same points in the narrative. At a few points, one poet uses prose when the other uses verse, but during the verse passages, there are only a few verses where the end-rhyme in the two performances are not in agreement.

In discussions with the poets about rhyme schemes, I came to realize that they possessed an additional concept that I had failed to grasp: *farsh al-qiṣṣa* or "the bedding of the story," by which they mean that the overall story is based

24 This short scene is not present in Shaykh Biyeli's performance.

25 This scene is not found in this performance by Shaykh Taha but is part of other performances sung by him.

26 The audio recordings of both performances are available online at: www.siratbanihilal.ucsb.edu: Shaykh Taha 101A and Shaykh Biyeli 003A. Shaykh Taha's performance is also presented there in Arabic transcription and English translation, as well as in the "Virtual Performance" section where one can hear the performance and read a synchronized line-by-line text.

on a sequence of common rhymes that are rather easy to improvise in, but that specific poems stand out against this background because they are composed in rhymes that are more unusual and more difficult to use. In essence, there is an "aria and recitativo" structure to the epic. The "arias" are in more difficult rhymes and the "recitativo" passages are in easy rhymes. It is also clear that the "recitativo" sections (which include all of the more banal stock scenes such as travels, descriptions of gardens, descriptions of beautiful maidens, battle-scenes, and so forth) also vary more from one performance to the next in their wording and length—exactly as we understand oral-formulaic composition in performance from the work of Parry and Lord. But there also exist contrasting passages, the "arias," which vary much less and are also much better known by the audience. These "arias" appear most frequently at dramatic or highly emotional points in the narrative. Audience members wait for these moments with almost palpable anticipation, and poets will occasionally take the opportunity to liven up the performance by singing the best-known verses several times over, encouraging listeners to sing along.[27] I several times heard audience members criticize the performance of one of these "arias" for having left out a favorite line or group of lines, a level of familiarity and consistency that is not possible with the "recitativo" sequences. It is not that these "arias" contain no oral formulae—they do; but because the rhymes in these passages are used much more rarely and for shorter periods of time, their oral-formulaic quality is much less evident.[28]

The "bedding" of "The Birth of Abu Zayd" consists of two rhymes /*-āh*/ and /*-ān*/, to which the poets return again and again. The opening "aria" is a *shakwā* or complaint against Fate and Destiny, sung by the father of the future hero who has sired a dozen daughters but has no son to carry on his name. This passage is composed in a double rhyme (i.e. where the two final syllables rhyme) in the pattern /*-āXiḥ*/ (where X stands for any consonant, for example, *wāḍiḥ*, *sāyiḥ*, *maṭāriḥ*); later, when the mother of the hero is accused of adultery and thrown out of the tribe because her son is black, she sings a poignant defense of her honor and requests God to protect her and her son in another double-rhymed "aria" on the pattern /*-alī*/, and so forth. Some of these "arias" are even further embellished by internal rhymes.

This overall rhyme structure also helps explain my inability to replicate one of the experiments that Lord recounts in *The Singer of Tales*. Try as I might, I could never get the poets I worked with to compose on new themes, and even more baffling to me was that they knew episodes from the epic that they could

27 For an analysis of one such passage, see Reynolds 1991:308–311.

28 Cf. Lord's analysis of "oft repeated blocks of lines (a stable, but not fixed, core of wording)" in Lord 1995, Chapter 2 (summarized by M. L. Lord on pp. 62–63).

recount in prose, but which they said they could not sing in poetry. The poets even repeatedly referred to these episodes in their introductions to evening performances. For example, they might say: "Now after Abu Zayd had stolen the famous Mare of Jabir al-'Uqayli and married his daughter 'Alya, he traveled back to the camps of the Bani Hilal tribe ..." and here the performance began. I was particularly eager to record a performance of this particular episode because Lady Anne Blunt and her husband Wilfred Scawen Blunt had recorded and translated a version in Egypt in the nineteenth century with which I hoped to compare a version recorded from oral tradition a century later.[29] But to my frustration, my teacher and all of the other poets in the village simply said: "I don't sing that episode." They could tell me the story, in full detail, in prose, but consistently said they could not sing it. The work of Parry and Lord, however, made me believe that they *should* be able to sing it, so I pressed my teacher until he finally said, "I have never heard it sung—I don't know its rhymes."

It is interesting to note that Parry encountered a somewhat similar situation where poets refused to sing rhymed poems when they had forgotten the rhyme, but this was because their method of oral-formulaic composition did not include techniques for creating rhyme. Unrhymed poetry was never sung exactly the same by two different singers, but rhymed poetry had to be memorized: "The poem in rhyme, however, must be learned by heart, and when forgotten it cannot be re-improvised on the instant, since the rhymes present too great an obstacle to such improvisation."[30] Epic poets in Egypt, however, *are* able to improvise in rhyme because their oral-formulaic methods of composition are specifically geared to that goal. Their objection was rather to trying to recreate an episode by creating *new* rhymes since they did not know the traditional rhyme scheme.

In the ensuing discussion with Shaykh Taha, it became clear that he felt strongly that one did not just go about creating new episodes—this went against his own sense of transmitting what he had been taught by his father and grandfather. This poet was a master improviser within a performance, as we have seen above, but "creating" an episode went against his concept of the epic itself. His statements that he was transmitting what he had been taught were not just a rhetorical stance; rather, they represented a very real understanding of the tradition, and this element makes the Arabic process of "composition in performance" rather different from that so wonderfully and richly documented by Parry and Lord among South Slavic singers.

29 Blunt and Blunt 1892, reprinted in Blunt 1914:129–217.

30 Parry 1971:442.

## Conclusion

The poets who sing the Arabic oral epic poem of *Sīrat Banī Hilāl* learn a basic narrative structure coupled with the technique of "composition in performance" that allows them, for example, to expand or contract passages in response to their audience's reactions by a method very similar to the techniques described by Parry and Lord. But there are also at least two additional levels of structure to *Sīrat Banī Hilāl* that do not seem to exist in the South Slavic tradition: first, there is a historically transmitted rhyme scheme for each episode that the singers preserve and pass on from generation to generation; and, second, there are individual passages (that I have here termed "arias") that are more tightly—and more distinctively—composed, that remain more stable over time, and that appear to be somewhat less formulaic than other passages. With this essay, I would therefore like to pose the question to scholars of other oral poetic traditions whether the texts and performances they study are entirely of the same texture—cut from the same type of cloth, so to speak—or whether there are passages that stick out from the overall flow of the poem, similar to these "arias," that is, passages that are more fixed, or are in some other manner distinctive and separate from the larger poem.

Parry and Lord were ground-breaking scholars not only in the conclusions that they drew from their research but also in the manner in which they conducted their research. Without their innovative and experimental research techniques, they might never have discovered the key ideas that have proved so fruitful and so productive in the study of so many different traditions, oral and written, the world over. Their ideas about "composition in performance" and "oral-formulaic composition" have been compelling contributions to the study of oral poetry; but it should not be forgotten that their fieldwork methods are equally deserving of notice and emulation.

## Bibliography

ʿAbdallah, Y. 1988. "Der Sonnengesang von Saba: ein Stück religiöser Literatur aus dem antiken Jemen." In *Die Königin von Saba: Kunst, Legende und Archäologie zwischen Morgenland und Abendland*, ed. W. Daum, 185–192. Stuttgart.

Blunt, A., and W. S. Blunt, eds. 1892. *The Celebrated Romance of the Stealing of the Mare*. London.

Blunt, W. S. 1914. *The Poetical Works of Wilfred Scawen Blunt: A Complete Edition* II. London.

Caton, S. C. 1990. *"Peaks of Yemen I Summon": Poetry as Cultural Practice in a North Yemeni Tribe*. Berkeley.

Finnegan, R. 1977. *Oral Poetry: Its Nature, Significance, and Social Context*. Cambridge.

Heinrichs, W. 1987. "Poetik, Rhetorik, Literaturkritik, Metrik und Rheimlehre." In *Grundriss der arabischen Philologie II: Literaturwissenschaft*, ed. H. Gätje, 177–207. Wiesbaden.

Hood, M. 1960. "The Challenge of 'Bi-musicality.'" *Ethnomusicology* 4:55–59.

Larkin, M. 2006. "Popular Poetry in the Post-classical Period, 1150–1850." In *Arabic Literature in the Post-Classical Period*, ed. R. Allen and D. S. Richards, 189–242. Cambridge.

Lord, A. B. 1995. *The Singer Resumes the Tale*. Ed. M. L. Lord. Ithaca.

Parry, M. 1930. "Studies in the Epic Technique of Oral Verse-Making. I. Homer and Homeric Style." *Harvard Studies in Classical Philology* 41:73–147. Repr. in Parry 1971:266–324.

———. 1971. *The Making of Homeric Verse: The Collected Papers of Milman Parry*. Ed. A. Parry. Oxford.

Reynolds, D. F. 1989. "Tradition Replacing Tradition in Egyptian Oral Epic-Singing: The Creation of a Commercial Image." *Pacific Review of Ethnomusicology* 5:1–14.

———. 1991. "The Interplay of Genres in Oral Epic Performance: Differently Marked Discourse in a Northern Egyptian Tradition." In *The Ballad and Oral Literature*, ed. J. Harris, 292–317. Cambridge, MA.

———. 1995. *Heroic Poets, Poetic Heroes: The Ethnography of Performance in an Arabic Oral Epic Tradition*. Ithaca.

Slyomovics, S. E. 1987. *The Merchant of Art: An Egyptian Hilali Oral Epic Poet in Performance*. Berkeley.

Sowayan, S. A. 1985. *Nabati Poetry: The Oral Poetry of Arabia*. Berkeley.

Weil, G. 1958. "ʿArūḍ." In *Encyclopedia of Islam*, new ed., vol. 1, fasc. 11, 667–677. Leiden.

# PART II

# COMPARATIVE APPROACHES

# 4

# Spiritual Kinship, Incest, and Traditional Weddings

## Honor, Shame, and Cultural Boundaries in Romanian Marriage Songs

MARGARET H. BEISSINGER

A YOUNG GROOM-TO-BE, along with a celebratory band of Romani (Gypsy) musicians and a throng of wedding guests, arrives after a lengthy journey at the faraway residence of his soon-to-be bride, eager to take her home, where she will become his wife and join his family. The bride's father, however, has other plans. He insists, before relinquishing his daughter, that the groom successfully accomplish a series of tasks in order to win her. The groom is reluctant to undertake the trials, upon which a substitute for him steps in and masterfully completes them. The guests, in a jubilant procession, then return with the bride to the home of the groom, where his family awaits them, and the festive, several-day-long wedding takes place.

The narrative pattern that relates the successful execution of the tasks of the bridegroom by a substitute is widespread throughout the Balkans. It is a quintessential example of what Albert Lord called *wedding songs*: "heroic tales of bride capture that end with an elaborate wedding."[1] In the Romanian tradition, the substitute hero is the couple's godfather; the song is often titled "Cântecul naşului" ("The Godfather's Song").[2] It was, until very recently, performed at virtually every traditional wedding in southern Romania.[3] It portrays a caring and supportive godfather representing, in a larger sense, the constructive social ties that bind and uphold traditional communities. It is also an ethnographic

1 Lord 1991:110.

2 It is also called "Letinul bogat" (The Rich Latin/Infidel).

3 After the Romanian Revolution of 1989, narrative song performances at weddings became infrequent.

"text" that endorses out-group marriage and expresses the tensions evoked when kin relations shift at weddings. Spiritual kin at Romanian weddings, however, do not appear only in positive, upbeat narratives. They are also present in songs about marriage that offer the reverse of the story just recounted: negative, destructive tales in which godparents violate established relationships and norms of conduct through sexual deviance. In one, in addition to flouting the customary practices of gift-giving during the wedding rituals, a godfather also violates the bride (his goddaughter). She is shamed, and he is put to death by the groom. In another, a godmother brazenly attempts to seduce her godson who repeatedly rejects her advances. The broken honor and disgrace of both are publicly exposed, and each commits suicide or is killed. In these tales, shame and revenge are close to the surface; honor, trust, status, and generosity are dramatically distorted and lead to violent, unsettling ends. But, as we will see, these songs also articulate culturally-constructed rules of marriage.

In this essay, I explore spiritual kinship in Romanian marriage songs—traditional narrative songs about weddings and marriage.[4] Godparents, because they are sponsors at baptisms and weddings, play vital roles in Romanian families and communities and are highly respected. Their representation in marriage songs reflects the significance of their roles in the *real* nuptial rituals and marriages of their godchildren. Substitute-bridegroom narratives performed at weddings depict godfathers as compassionate and honorable, offering reassurance and inspiration to couples as they get married. But why songs of incest between spiritual kin, especially at weddings? I argue that while incest between spiritual kin in marriage songs at weddings may seem inauspicious, it furnishes compelling counterexamples of the behavior that substitute-bridegroom narratives promote and thus important cautionary tales. More often than not, it is shame that characterizes the negative conduct in these stories. Moreover, incest in the marriage songs furnishes a symbolic vehicle for the expression of the cultural boundaries that traditional marriage assumes, among them: exogamy, endogamy, and the taboo on adultery. It metaphorically frames one of the most fundamental questions in traditional society and one that is in the forefront during weddings: who can and should marry whom?

Weddings are intermediary periods during which virtually all kin relations are shifting, new kin bonds are forming, and reversals of standard behavior are temporarily sanctioned. Like other traditional celebrations that mark life- or calendrical-cycle changes, weddings offer openings during which aberrant social behavior or discourse, such as anomalous marriage songs, may be

4 I use "marriage song" instead of "wedding song" since the latter can also refer to lyric and ritual songs performed at weddings.

expressed.[5] I suggest that the rituals and events that take place during weddings allow for the inverted relations—both constructive and subversive—depicted in marriage songs about spiritual kin, where identities, relationships, and perspectives are in flux and, in some cases, reversed. Furthermore, Romanian marriage songs about spiritual kin are sung during *real* weddings: stories are tied, through performance, to events. Narrated as wedding rituals are transpiring, the songs speak to concerns right as they are happening: the bride's eventful rite of passage, the crucial role of godparents, the banquet, gift-giving, and the challenges and tensions within marriage. In other words, the immediate context of the performance is simultaneously mirrored in the stories being sung. Thus, performance plays a critical role in generating the messages embedded in real time. Performance mediates between story and event and organically brings meaning to both the verbal and the ritual narratives.

In the pages ahead, I discuss kinship and incest as well as traditional Romanian weddings, and then explore seven Romanian oral narratives, including multiple song texts from various sources, some from my own fieldwork.[6] I also offer comparative commentary from Slavic Balkan epic and Anglo-Scots ballad.[7]

## Kinship and Incest

After a hiatus, the study of kinship has received renewed attention in the past two decades and has been approached more recently as a culturally-constructed, not only biological, process. With this reorientation have also come reassessments of incest. The universality of the incest taboo, famously affirmed by Claude Lévi-Strauss in 1949, as the exchange of exogamous women by and for men, has been re-examined.[8] More than sixty years later, anthropologists consider that while a taboo on sexual relations between primary kin (parent/child and siblings) is extremely widespread, it is not absolutely universal.[9] Maurice Godelier defines incest as "sexual relations prohibited between consanguineous kin or between affines considered to be too close or too similar."[10] The incest taboo on primary

5 Compare the transitional calendrical-cycle rituals *căluş* (Romania) or *kukeri* (Bulgaria), where "normal" behavior is temporarily subverted; see Kligman 1981, Creed 2011.

6 Sources include published texts as well as epic songs that I collected in Bucharest (1979) and in villages in southern Romania: Blejeşti (1980), Celei (1987), and Mârşa (2002). All of the translations into English are mine.

7 South Slavic sources include Kačić-Miošić 1946; Karadžić 1969, 1975; Vidan 2003 (some, though not all, of the translations into English are mine). The ballads are from Child 1965; see also Bronson 1969, Buchan 1972.

8 See Lévi-Strauss 1969.

9 Godelier 2011:78–79.

10 Godelier 2011:566.

kin compels individuals to seek partners and marry outside of their immediate families; thus, incest rules may be viewed as a corollary of exogamy.

Kinship groups in traditional Romanian society are based on descent (consanguinity), marriage (affinity), and sponsorship (spiritual kinship).[11] Traditional marriage, permitted after the third degree of relatedness (in some communities after the fourth), is exogamous with preferred local endogamy.[12] As Nicolae Constantinescu notes,

> The rules of exogamy and the prohibition of incest are strictly observed in traditional Romanian society ... Romanians practice a type of endogamous exogamy, in which the marital couple comes from two different families but belongs to the same community: neighborhood, village, or region.[13]

By contrast, "spiritual kinship" is a "fictitious kin tie created by the religious bonds that are established for instance in Christianity between the child ... and the persons who agreed to be his or her godfather and godmother."[14] It was first associated with baptism in the Catholic Church; *spiritual* parents were sponsors and played central roles in the lives of *reborn* babies. Baptismal sponsorship also ensured the security of godchildren should they be orphaned.[15] It generated close, albeit artificial, bonds between individuals and families, reinforced by the ritual character of baptism.[16] Orthodox and Catholic godparenthood developed along similar lines until the reforms of the Council of Trent (1545–1563), at which point the Western Church introduced modifications, while the Eastern Church continued to implement previous policies.[17]

Godparenthood (*năşie*) in Romania "institutionalizes between two families a ritual-spiritual relationship predicated primarily on social and economic obligations,"[18] offering security and stability to godchildren and their families. As their sponsors, godparents

> officiate at ... birth and marriage. Generally, the ritual sponsor at a marriage is also the ritual sponsor for the children born to the couple.

11 Pop 1979:136–140.
12 Pop 1976:16.
13 Constantinescu 2000:212.
14 Godelier 2011:570.
15 Stone 2010:246.
16 Alfani and Gourdon 2012:20.
17 Alfani 2009:231.
18 Kligman 1988:35.

> The relationship between godparents and godchildren is ... enduring and ... establishes ritual kin bonds between the two families.[19]

The significance of spiritual kin is invoked at weddings, where godparents specifically *join* the couple in marriage by placing the crowns on their heads and thus generate their union. Through the godparents, the marriage is recognized not only in a religious sense but also in a communal one. Assuming a public role, godparents occupy an important and influential social position; thus, spiritual kinship provides alliances between families and security in the community. Spiritual kin relations strengthen social ties both horizontally as well as vertically, across generations as well as from one to the next.

The practices of spiritual kin among Orthodox believers throughout Eastern Europe are embedded in both religious and secular culture. The role of folk customs in spiritual kinship is significant. Godparenthood in the Balkans preceded Christianity;[20] Barbara and Joel Halpern maintain that it was "pre-Christian in origin but [was] adapted into church practice."[21] In Russia, "folk tradition viewed baptism as one of the principal rites of passage and treated spiritual kinship as an important social network within kinship relationships."[22] Russian peasants of the eighteenth and nineteenth centuries "respected spiritual kinship and treated it as even more important than blood kinship."[23] For centuries the Church has recognized impediments to marriage between godparents, godchildren, and their relations up to the third degree of relatedness.[24] In Russia, "[s]piritual kinship ... excluded all sexual activity between spiritual kin. Popular tradition viewed those as the worst type of incest."[25] In the Balkans as well, godparents cannot be related by blood or marriage to their godchildren.[26] Thus marriage between sponsors and sponsored is "precluded on the grounds of ritual kinship."[27] The violation of spiritual kinship through sexual relations is socially unique because, unlike family-kin incest, it throws into disarray the larger communal, ritual bonds that spiritual kinship assumes (produced at baptism and wedding and perpetuated through marriage). It shatters trust and security on a public stage, affecting individuals, marriages, and families.

19 Kligman 1988:36.

20 Hammel 1968:5. Sponsorship in Balkan folk belief is more formalized and hierarchical than in the Orthodox canon (Hammel 1968:8); see also Filipović 1960:77.

21 Halpern and Kerewsky-Halpern 1986:122.

22 Muravyeva 2012:262.

23 Muravyeva 2012:262.

24 Alfani 2009:231. The earliest written record documenting a ban on marriage between spiritual kin dates from the year 530 (Lynch 1986:219).

25 Muravyeva 2012:262.

26 Vuković 2004:70.

27 Kligman 1988:36.

## Traditional Romanian Weddings

In order to appreciate the ethnographic content of marriage songs, I present a generic wedding description drawn mainly from the weddings I have attended during fieldwork in southern Romania.[28] Romani poet-musicians known as *lăutari* (sg. *lăutar*)—professional (hired), male, traditional singers—are indispensable to the wedding. They provide all of the music for the rituals and celebrations.[29] The social biases of patriarchy and patrilocality permeate traditional Balkan weddings and marriage. Emblems of exogamy are embedded in traditional society and are symbolically represented in wedding rituals, songs, and practices, as are fertility symbols and metaphors of separation, transition, and incorporation.[30]

In addition to the bride and groom, the most important participants in the wedding are the godparents from the groom's side (*naşi*, sg. *naş/naşă*), typically called "great," e.g. *naşul mare* "the great godfather." In his 1890 monograph on weddings, S. F. Marian states that "[t]he great godfather ... exercises absolute control during the entire wedding ... Everyone must do as he says ... The great godmother, in addition to assisting her husband," tends to the bride.[31] In fact, the godparents are so vital to the wedding that they are present throughout all of the events, while the couple's parents are present at only a select number of them and do not even attend the church ceremony.[32] Gendered female and male activities, each frequently with the godmother or godfather, respectively, occur throughout the wedding.

On the morning of the ceremony, the bride, at her home, is "prepared" by a small company of female kin, both family and spiritual, of which the godmother is the most important. As she places the crown on the bride's head, a *lăutar* sings "Cântecul miresei" (The Bride's Song), a poignant reminder that the bride will no longer be a maiden at her parents' home but will be joining the ranks of married women as a "stranger" in her husband's—a stirring example of the patrilocality of traditional marriage.[33]

In the meantime, the groom sets out with his godfather and the wedding guests in a procession to the bride's home. Sometimes, upon arriving, obstacles

28 In Bucharest and many towns and villages (1980–2013). See also Kligman 1988, Constantinescu 1999, Marian 2000, and Pop 1976.

29 A female vocalist also often joins the male bands. On *lăutari and weddings*, see Beissinger 1991, 2005, and 2016.

30 See Van Gennep 1960 for his well-known tripartite structure of rituals. There are many customs and genres in the wedding that I do not discuss.

31 Marian 2000:142.

32 See Kligman 1988:96–149 on godparents' roles in Romanian weddings.

33 See Beissinger 2020 for a fuller discussion of this poetry.

are imposed by the bride's father for the groom. Symbolic "tests" include questions posed to the groom, which he must answer cleverly.[34] Once the bride is secured, the groom and company return with her to his home. The celebratory wedding processions, complete with *lăutari*, are important as the status of the couple, their godparents, and families is on display. Following the church ceremony, the wedding party gathers in the evening at the home of the groom for a lengthy, festive banquet at which the *lăutari* perform. At traditional weddings, it was at this time that guests, including the godfather, would tip the *lăutari* with requests for narrative songs. Also called *cântece bătrânești* ("ancient songs" or epic songs), they were sung, until the late twentieth century, at every banquet. They are still sung on occasion today.[35] "The Godfather's Song" was a requisite part of the banquet repertoire.[36]

The guests eat, drink, dance, and celebrate for many hours, often all night long. At one point, gifts for the couple are individually announced and presented. This affords another show of status and wealth. Particularly important are the gifts given to the couple by the godparents. Later, after the meal, the godmother oversees the bride's ritual transition from unmarried maiden to married woman during the public removal of her crown, accompanied again by "The Bride's Song." The godmother then ceremoniously ties a "married woman's" kerchief on the bride's head, indicating her new role as wife. At traditional weddings, the couple would then retire to a room where they would consummate their marriage. At this juncture, another "test" had to be passed: the bride had to prove her virginity by displaying her blood on the bedsheets. In former times, this was extremely important, since it demonstrated the bride's honor, which reflected on the groom and both of their families.[37]

## Substitute Bridegrooms

"The Godfather's Song" is the only Romanian marriage song involving spiritual kin that does not include incest. It has been collected and transcribed numerous times since the mid-nineteenth century.[38] In Communist Romania

34 Pop 1976:22.

35 Epic is also performed at other life-cycle celebrations such as baptisms. On Romanian epic, see Beissinger 1991 and 2012.

36 Like elsewhere in the Balkans, the Romanian epic tradition was influenced by the centuries-long Ottoman period. Many of the narratives are heroic. Songs are rarely longer than 500 verses; the meter is generally trochaic, and verses are octosyllabic.

37 In some very conservative communities (especially among Roma), "showing the sheets" is still practiced.

38 Over 100 versions are found in publications and archives (Constantinescu 1999:93). Twenty texts form the materials for my observations: Amzulescu 1964(1):401–411; 1974:108–113; Bălășel 1967:130–136, 136–141; Gregorian 1967:562–564; Popescu 1970:70–75, 76–79, 80–83, 84–87;

and earlier, it was standard at traditional weddings for the musicians to sing this song. In 1987, a *lăutar* from a village in south-central Romania told me that "The Godfather's Song" was still sung "at every wedding!"[39] In today's world it is performed only rarely.

The substitute-bridegroom narrative is also well-known in the South Slavic tradition, where epic was likewise sung at weddings, the *Slava* (feast day of a family's patron saint), coffee-houses, and at home.[40] One of the best-known texts is "Ženidba Sibinjanina Janka" (The Wedding of Sibinjanin Janko),[41] in which Janko is assisted in passing the tests of the bridegroom by his sister's youngest son, Sekul, in disguise as a Bulgarian. Sekul represents bonds of kin loyalty in the groom's extended family as well as fertility as a young, unmarried man.[42]

This pan-Balkan narrative promotes strong networks of spiritual and family kin, stability, and continuity. It offers a symbolic tale that projects a mutually reinforcing society, especially at weddings, when social boundaries are shifting, and kin ties are in flux. This is true for the bride, but it also pertains to the groom, whose identity is also changing as his role reversal with the godfather (or nephew) reveals. In the Romanian text below, the godfather advocates an explicit swapping of identities with his godson in order to pass the tests of the bridegroom and warmly assures him that the wedding will take place:[43]

> "Taci, fine, nu te speria,
> Fii tu naş în locul meu,
> Şi eu fin în locul tău ...
> Că te-om scăpa de belea
> Şi pe fina om lua,
> Ca să faci casă cu ea."[44]

> "Be silent, Godson, don't be afraid,
> You be the godfather in my place,
> And I'll be the godson in yours ...

Rădulescu-Codin 1986(1):18–19, 19–21, 21–23; Teodorescu 1982:704–707, 707–709; Tocilescu 1980(1):95–97, 97–98, 98–100, 101; two epic songs collected during fieldwork in Bucharest (1979) and the village of Celei (1987).

39 Conversation with Marin Candoi, Celei, July 7, 1987.

40 Lord 1995:2.

41 Kačić-Miošić 1946:107–109.

42 Janko is Sekul's uncle on his mother's side (*ujak*); Sekul aids the groom in most South Slavic versions. In some Balkan cultures, the nephew-maternal uncle relationship is highly regarded, hence the significance of the nephew's role in the wedding (Constantinescu 2000:21–23).

43 Janko is similarly promised by his nephew: "Ne plaši se, Sibinjanin Janko! / Ja ću strilat na kopju jabuku." ("Don't be afraid, Sibinjanin Janko! I will shoot the apple on the spear," Kačić-Miošić 1946:108, ll. 59–60)

44 Amzulescu 1964(1):406–407, ll. 219–221, 224–226.

Because we'll rescue you from this predicament
And we'll get the goddaughter,
So you can marry [make a house with] her."

The metaphoric journey to and from the bride's home is richly symbolic, pointing to patrilocality and exogamy. The bride is the daughter of *Letinul bogat* "the Rich Latin/Infidel'" from Dobrogea (a region in eastern Romania on the Black Sea), home to the largest Turkish population in the country—a hyperbolic example of exogamous identity from the perspective of Orthodox ethnic Romanians. Not only do names and places speak to the bride's out-group identity, but the journey itself—occurring "from Saint Peter's Day" (June 29) "to Saint Dumitru's" (October 26)—represents metaphorically how suitable an out-group bride she is by how *far away* she lives.[45]

"The Godfather's Song" is a type of metanarration[46] or metanarrative performance, in which varying levels of narration and communication are embedded within each other, a marriage song performed during an actual wedding. In other words, two "narratives" are taking place, one inside the other. The sung narrative occurs within the event narrative. The story features a "perfect" godfather, who smooths out wrinkles in the wedding events, resolving the obstacles that arise when the wedding party arrives at the bride's home. He does symbolically in the narrative what he is expected to do in actuality—be there for the nuptial couple, aid them in any difficulties, and provide a bedrock of security. *Lăutari* typically present complimentary depictions of godfathers in this song. And so the magnanimous godfathers in the epic poetry and the flattered godfathers at the *real* weddings connect in performance, effecting the dynamics of the metanarrative pair—godfather in song and godfather in person. This also sometimes results in bigger tips for the *lăutar*. As Gail Kligman observes, traditional Romanian "society generates marriage through the godparents, shifting interpersonal relations to the communal level."[47] Indeed, this performance event provides a strong affirmation in public of the role of the godfather as a dedicated spiritual parent who aids and protects his spiritual *children*, the wedding couple.

Metanarration also functions in smaller, more rhetorical ways. Commenting on how words are adapted for metanarrative effect, Barbara Babcock notes that beginnings and endings of stories provide "one of the ways in which a narrator

45 Janko also searches for a bride far and wide, finally finding "Janja" from Temišvar (Timişoara) in the Banat (western Romania).

46 See Babcock 1977:62, Bauman 1986:98–101.

47 Kligman 1988:149.

sets up an interpretative frame" as "*explicit* metanarration"[48] and that a "shift in pronouns ... implicitly comments on the story or the storytelling by effecting a transfer from an internal point of view to an external one."[49] The wedding banquet in the text below is described as the banquet in the *real* wedding is simultaneously taking place. The internal perspective becomes external, the pronouns shift from third-person to first- and second-person forms, and the song and event merge:

O horă mare prindea,
Lăutarii tot cînta,
Aluneasca o juca.
Şi a fost o nuntă mare,
De la munte pîn' la mare!
Şi a fost nuntă domnească,
De veci să se pomenească,
Cu mari boieri şi cocoane,
Ca la astă nuntă mare.
La boieri ca dumneavoastră
Noi facem cîntarea noastră,
Tutora ca să fie
Cu bine şi cu bucurie![50]

They assembled a great circle dance,
The *lăutari* continued to sing and play,
They danced "the little hazelnut" [folkdance],
And it was a great wedding,
From the mountains to the sea!
And it was a royal wedding
That will be remembered forever,
With great boyars and great ladies,
Just like at this great wedding.
To boyars like you
We sing this song
So that all of you
Will enjoy it and be happy!

This recalls what Dwight Reynolds terms "overlapping performances" in Arabic oral epic, where "narrative strategies" enable the poet "effective means of

48 Babcock 1977:71.
49 Babcock 1977:73.
50 Amzulescu 1964:1.411, ll. 400–412.

moving back and forth through the boundaries of the story world."[51] *Lăutari* likewise cross boundaries of verbal and cultural "texts" and organically bring "story, performance, and event" to life.[52]

## Counterexamples: Incest and Spiritual Kin

Two narratives in the Romanian epic tradition involve incestuous designs by godparents on their godchildren. They distort the standard "story" of weddings and marriage and turn conventional behavior on its head, employing the trope of incest in dramatic and violent ways. The first narrative charts how a godfather shuns gift etiquette at a wedding banquet and forces himself sexually on his goddaughter, while the second exposes how dishonor destroys families linked by spiritual kin when a godmother recklessly determines to seduce her godson. Shame and the loss of honor result from incest between spiritual kin—both for the individuals and the community, representing a complete breakdown of society.

### Gift-giving and reciprocity

The shame that ensues when public gift-giving and reciprocity are inverted is fundamental to "Radu-vodă şi Drăgan" (Prince Radu and Drăgan).[53] Godparents' functions at weddings include, among other things, ritual gift-giving. As Kligman notes, wedding "[g]ifts are not simply expected; they are mandatory"; indeed, "[g]ift-giving is an expression of social interaction."[54] In this song, Radu-vodă, the godfather, fails to offer adequate gifts to the nuptial couple during the public gift-giving at the wedding banquet. In a metanarrational moment, the *lăutar* references the ritual gift-giving in the example below, corresponding to the actual banquet at which the wedding guests—including the godfather—are seated. The context of gift-giving that is evoked parallels the public display of gifts during the *real* wedding feast:

> Că, cînd Radu l-a cununat,
> Cînd a fost la masa mare,
> Toţi boierii i-a dat
> Care vii, care moşii,
> Care galbeni pe tipsii.

[51] Reynolds 1999:156, 164.

[52] See Bauman 1986.

[53] Two texts form the materials for my observations: Amzulescu 1964:3.74–76 and Tocilescu 1980:1.305–306.

[54] Kligman 1988:101.

Numai Radu nu i-a dat
Nici o vie, nici o moşie
Şi nici galbeni pă tipsie.[55]

So, when Radu was sponsor for [Drăgan],
When he was at the great banquet,
All of the boyars gave [things] to [Drăgan]:
Some [gave] vineyards, some estates,
Some gold coins on trays.
Only Radu didn't give him anything:
Not a single vineyard, nor a single estate,
And not even gold coins on a tray.

Social status and responsibility are transparently reflected in public gift-giving. Radu-vodă's disregard of the etiquette of this event is a breach of duty for a godparent. Moreover, his understanding of reciprocity is totally inverted: he gives little or nothing and then, in return, takes far more than his share—his goddaughter's virginity and honor and, importantly, Drăgan's esteem as well. Radu-vodă commits incest with the bride in the garden: a place that represents nature and disorder, away from the cultural and more ordered space of the wedding proper and outside of the rules of the household. Drăgan furiously accuses him:

"Pe fina ta ţi-ai luat,
În grădină te-ai băgat,
Făcuşi voia trupului,
Lăcomia ochilor!"[56]

"You took your goddaughter,
You shoved her into the garden,
You enjoyed the pleasures of the flesh,
You feasted your greedy eyes!"

As punishment, Drăgan threatens to behead not only Radu-vodă but sometimes Radu-vodă's son Vlăduţ as well, predicting that if he were to spare Vlăduţ, the boy would simply grow up to repeat the sins of his father. Drăgan's obliteration of both father and son speaks to the importance of honor within families over time, since a godfather in the Balkans "marries and christens, and his obligation

55 Tocilescu 1980:1.305, ll. 9–16.
56 Amzulescu 1964:3.75, ll. 49–52.

passes from one generation to the next."[57] In an attempt to salvage himself (and his son), Radu-vodă reminds Drăgan of their obvious spiritual kin relationship and recalls the important ritual moments they have shared, hoping that the memory of these purportedly inviolate ritual bonds will change his mind: "Că la mic te-am botezat, / La mare te-am cununat" ("Because when you were little I baptized you, / When you were big, I was sponsor for you [in marriage]").[58] Unmoved, Drăgan decapitates Radu-vodă (and his son) and sticks his head onto a stake, placing it on the main road to air Radu-vodă's shame in public.

In the comparable South Slavic "Ženidba Marka Kraljevića"[59] ("The Wedding of Marko Kraljević"), shame, also generated as the vulnerability of the bride on her metaphoric journey from her home (maidenhood) to that of her groom (wifehood), is interwoven with themes of exogamy and the importance of honor and trust. Like the substitute-bridegroom narrative, the journey to and from the out-group bride's faraway home provides the context for the story. But like "Radu-vodă," the ostensibly honorable godfather turns on his goddaughter in order to seduce her. Endogamy also enters the picture. On incest and literature, Susan Stewart remarks that "[o]ne must travel to find a mate. That is, one must not look too closely, and one must not look too far afield."[60] While the daughter of the Bulgarian king is a duly exogamous bride for Marko in this song, the traitorous Catholic (infidel) godfather (the Doge of Venice) and best man (*djever*) "should have been" more in-group, as the bride's mother earlier warned Marko: "[N]emoj vodit tudjina djevera" ("Don't bring a stranger as best man").[61] Marriage choices in traditional society entail a delicate balance of exogamous and endogamous matching.[62]

The bride's honor is vulnerable as she progresses in her journey from one secure cultural space to another. As Kligman points out, among the central themes of the traditional wedding are the bride's honor and shame and her virginity.[63] The bride's mother is deeply anxious about her daughter's perilous journey to the groom's house, telling Marko that "Bojimo se goleme sramote" ("We fear some deed of shame").[64] David Atkinson notes that incest in ballads occurs "in liminal settings like the 'greenwood' with its connotation of being

57 Vuković 2004:70.

58 Tocilescu 1980:306, ll. 54–55.

59 Karadžić 1969:208–214.

60 Stewart 1991:173.

61 Karadžić 1969:209, l. 62.

62 As Stewart notes, the prohibition on incest "is simultaneously endogamous (defining those within the marriage pool) and exogamous (defining those without it)" (1991:174).

63 Kligman 1981:145.

64 Karadžić 1969:209, l. 65.

somewhere outside the law,"[65] such as in the Anglo-Scots "Babylon" and "The King's Dochter Lady Jean," where brothers unwittingly hope to marry or rape their sisters.[66] Radu-vodă rapes Drăgan's bride in the garden, an "irrational" and "ungovernable" natural space.[67] The godfather also tries to seduce Marko's bride "outside the law," en route between her house and Marko's, but she cleverly exposes him, and Marko kills him. In another, shorter variant of this song, "Ženidba Imroara Nenada" ("The Wedding of Nenad Imroar"), the plucky bride singlehandedly slays her assailant (the groom's bloodbrother, also spiritual kin) during a similar journey.[68] In both South Slavic texts, the honor of both bride and groom is barely upheld. By contrast, in "Radu-vodă," the bride's honor and life are shattered; she is polluted and humiliated. And Drăgan, who cannot return to her, simply wanders endlessly without purpose.

What the godfathers (and bloodbrother) do in the incest narratives contrasts clearly with what the exemplary godfather does in "The Godfather's Song." But there is another subtext. Substituting the godfather for the groom (and "winning" the bride) symbolically also evokes incest, even if it does not actually entail the risk of it.[69] One could argue that although the threat of incest lurks below the surface in "The Godfather's Song," it is managed constructively and, in fact, complements the negative tales of incest by the godfather—a meaning, I believe, that is augmented by an ethnographic reading. Constantinescu remarks that in the past, on the night of the wedding, the godfather had the right to sleep with his goddaughter, the bride.[70] Hammel also notes that "sexual privilege" with the bride was sometimes extended to the groom's *kum* (godfather), notwithstanding that "the moral of these [stories] is always that such a relationship is a sinful one."[71] In other words, these tales sung at weddings may have served as uneasy forewarnings even of the hours or days to

65 Atkinson 2002:115.

66 In "Babylon" (Child 1965:14), a brother kills two of his sisters with his "pen-knife" in the woods when they refuse to marry him and then himself when their identities are disclosed. In "The King's Dochter Lady Jean" (Child 1965:52), a brother rapes his then-unidentified sister in the woods. When it is revealed who they are, he kills her with his knife and later dies himself.

67 Syndergaard 1993:136.

68 Karadžić 1975:498–500. *Pobratimstvo* 'bloodbrotherhood' (Serbian) entails the exchange of blood between unrelated boys and/or men, a tradition rooted in antiquity (Constantinescu 1999:91–92). It establishes a close spiritual bond that prohibits marriage between their families (Vuković 2004:71–72).

69 Thanks to David Elmer for sharing this reading.

70 Constantinescu 2000:223–224. Kligman also makes reference to godfathers sometimes sleeping with the bride/goddaughter (1981:337n26).

71 Hammel 1968:34. Vuković 2004 points out that "[t]here was, at one time, the custom that on the first night, the *dever* (best man) slept with the bride to guard her from the bridegroom" (48). It seems that on occasion at traditional weddings in the Balkans, the *dever* had the right to sleep with the bride before the wedding ceremony; the groom's brother is often said to "sleep

follow. Constantinescu implies that it was "a right of the godfather that had to be accepted."[72] The fact that this liberty was sometimes taken, however, does not mean that it did not cause a great deal of anger, anguish, and even violence.

## Cultural boundaries violated

The cultural boundaries that inform possible marriage partners and adultery, as well as honor and shame, are central to "Vartici."[73] A godmother repeatedly attempts to seduce her young godson and servant, Vartici, who rejects her amorous advances on the basis of their spiritual kin bond.[74] The incestuous nature of this relationship scars the principal actors and their families permanently, and the tale ends with the miserable deaths of both godmother and godson.

"Vartici" is a tale full of transpositions—performed, appropriately, when the interim moments and role reversals of *real* weddings take place. In a hypothetical union of the godmother (Ileana) and her godson (Vartici), most of the normal social boundaries in marriage are overturned, creating a caricature that accentuates the prohibitions that form impediments to wedlock. One could say that it is an inverted marriage song, with genders and outcomes reversed: Ileana wishes to "win" Vartici, not with the symbolic help of a substitute, but rather on her own, by seducing him. Ironically, while in normal weddings the godmother is devoted to the bride, in "Vartici" she is "devoted" to the "groom." But her "proposal" is turned down, so there is no wedding at the end but rather a funeral, since both "bride" and "groom" die. The transitional nature of wedding celebrations temporarily permits the sounding out of this violation of the marriage story, in which virtually every component of the customary wedding is turned on its head. A much older "bride" attempts to win a younger "groom," both of whom are already married and belong to different social classes. Moreover, they are godmother and godson. As Stewart maintains, the prohibition of incest in narrative has to do with the "articulation and maintenance of cultural boundaries in time and space";[75] the taboo on incest in narratives "extends spatially

with" the bride on her way to the wedding or to take minor sexual liberties with her after her marriage" (Hammel 1968:33–34).

72 Constantinescu 2000:224.

73 Five texts form the materials for my observations: Amzulescu 1964:3.82–85; 1974:457–465; Păsculescu 1910:195–196; Rădulescu-Codin 1986:36–37, 37–40.

74 "Vartici" is a version of the ancient tale, "Potiphar's wife" (K2111 in the *Motif-Index of Folk Literature*): "A woman makes vain overtures to a man and then accuses him of attempting to force her" (Thompson 1960:474). In the Biblical form (Genesis 39:1–20), the woman is the wife of Potiphar (a prominent figure in the community), while the young man she wishes to seduce is Joseph, their slave. See Balotă 1958 for a historical reading of "Vartici."

75 Stewart 1991:173.

to the boundaries of social groups and temporally through the organization of generations."[76] "Vartici" includes a recognition of the marriage limitations imposed by spiritual kinship, previous marriage commitments, class distinctions, and age, offering a tale of cultural, social, and generational groups that are either forbidden or at least strongly discouraged from mixing. "Vartici," like rules of incest, spells out "whom it is possible or forbidden to marry" and offers a commentary on the dynamics of trust in marriage,[77] as well as the consequences of adultery, all topics relevant at weddings, where finding suitable marriage partners is both explicitly and implicitly acknowledged.

In "real" relationships, class and spiritual kinship overlap, since godparents are frequently from a higher economic and social class than their godchildren.[78] Underscoring class divisions, "Doamna" (Lady) Ileana is portrayed at home at the outset of the narrative, presiding over an aristocratic all-female banquet, while Vartici, her godson, is serving the meal. Her husband, Ştefan-vodă (Prince Stephen), has gone hunting.[79] The initial scene is reminiscent of banquets in heroic epic. Yet it is a parody of them: it is attended only by women and headed by Ileana, producing an uncharacteristic, caricatured, female-dominated space, the inverse of typical all-male banquet assemblies. In heroic epic, after the meal-assembly, the men typically set off in pursuit of someone or something, while in "Vartici," Ileana suddenly cuts her banquet short, dismissing all of her lady guests so that she can "pursue" Vartici and seduce him alone. In the example below, the *lăutar* "calls attention to the narrative performance as performance" through a metanarrative "interpretive frame" as he "steps outside" of the banquet by parodying it:[80]

> În curte la dom' Dumitraşe, [verse repeated] ...
> Mîndră masă-mi este-ntins',
> Săvai masă dă batis'
> Cu dalbe făclii aprinse.
> Jur-prejuru mesiei
> Şade-m' <u>vere</u>, şade-m' <u>dragă</u>
> F-o cinzăj' dă priotese,
> Patruzăj' dă jupînese,
> Cei mai mari căimăcănese ...
> <u>Iar cu pahar cin' le da</u>?

[76] Stewart 1991:173.
[77] Godelier 2011:79.
[78] Hammel 1968:77–78, 80.
[79] Ştefan cel mare (Stephen the Great) (1433–1504), whose name is frequently (and fictionally) attached to heroic epic songs, ruled Moldova (northeastern Romania) 1457–1504.
[80] Babcock 1977:71.

Săvai finu-său Vartici. [verse repeated]
Iar în capu mesiei [verse repeated]
Șade-m' vere, șade-m' dragă,
Șade doamna Ileana,
Frumoasă ca icoana ...[81]

In the court of King Dumitrașe, [verse repeated] ...
A wonderful table is set,
Even a table [covered with a cloth] of printed silk
With lighted white torches [surrounding it].
All around the table
Are sitting, Cousin, are sitting, My dear,
Fifty or so priests' wives,
Forty boyar wives,
The greatest wives of the caimacans ...
But who is serving them glasses [of wine]?
Even [Ileana's] godson Vartici. [verse repeated]
And at the head of the table [verse repeated]
She sits, Cousin, she sits, My dear,
Lady Ileana sits,
As beautiful as an icon ...

Questions that propel the story forward that the *lăutar* poses to the public (as in the underlined verse) are also metanarrative devices for connecting with the listeners as are the vocative nouns addressed to them (also underlined).[82] The banquet in the narrative paradoxically relates to the "real" banquet at the wedding. Moreover, as an unconventional feast it immediately sets up the story as a series of unexpected, inverted events in which boundaries of all kinds are transgressed. Ileana frames her desire for Vartici with "Vino lîngă mine-aici"[83] ("Come here close to me"), accentuating the physical, which becomes the moral boundary that she is violating. She knows that this path may take her beyond another even more imposing boundary as she tells Vartici: "Chiar de azi să intru-n iad, / Dar să iubesc ce mi-e drag!" ("Even if I go this day to Hell, / Just let me love what is dear to me!").[84] The boundaries created between Ileana and Vartici by spiritual kinship are the principal obstacles to a sexual relationship from Vartici's perspective. Employing verses that are reminiscent

81 Amzulescu 1974:457, ll. 2, 4–11, 13–18.

82 These are common rhetorical devices in Romanian oral epic.

83 Amzulescu 1964:3.83, l. 47.

84 Rădulescu-Codin 1986:38, ll. 84–85. In several texts, Ileana promises Vartici that if he agrees to sleep with her, she will give richly to the Church and charity in order to atone for her sins.

of Radu-vodă's plea for mercy from Drăgan, Vartici makes clear what Ileana also knows: that she has been a godmother for two generations in his family and that these spiritual kin bonds preclude the intimacy that she desires:

> "Că mai mic, m-ai botezat,
> Mai mare m-ai cununat,
> La mijloc m-ai retezat,[85]
> Trei copii mi-ai botezat ...
> Nu ţ-o fi, naşă, păcat
> Şi frică dă blestemat?!"[86]
>
> "Because when I was young, you christened me,
> When I was older, you were sponsor for me [in marriage],
> In between you [ritually] cut my hair,
> You christened my three children ...
> Wouldn't you be sinning, Godmother,
> And aren't you afraid of being cursed?!"

The momentous rituals that a godparent performs in the life of his or her godchild and the ensuing boundaries that spiritual kinship entails are concisely summed up by Vartici's four consecutive references to Ileana's past godparenting roles.

Atkinson points out that in ballads, incest typically happens to "characters separated from the continuity of everyday life and its relations."[87] In "Vartici," the attempted seduction also occurs in a marked space. But with genders switched, it becomes a domestic, female space (immediately following a "female banquet"). For Vartici, it is an uncomfortable realm: a seductive, women's arena in which he could lose control. In one text, for her planned seduction, Ileana takes Vartici to an even more private spot: a secluded space she calls "sus în casă" ("upstairs in the house"), where she mixes sensual suggestions that they eat and drink together with climbing into bed.[88]

In a metaphor (in all of the "Vartici" texts) for social boundaries that threaten to be crossed, Vartici deceptively tells Ileana that he will go home to change clothes so that he can return to her in attire more fitting for what she has in mind. The clothing ironically epitomizes the distance between culture and nature in the ostensibly upper-class ("princely") Ileana. In order for Vartici

85 This refers to *moţul* (Romanian), a child's ritual first haircut, performed by the family's godparents; it is a widespread pre-Christian Balkan custom that is still practiced (Hammel 1968:8).

86 Amzulescu 1974:459, ll. 68–72, 77–78.

87 Atkinson 2002:115.

88 Rădulescu-Codin 1986:38, l. 40.

to "connect with" her, he will need to "come down to her level" and don "whoring" clothes:

> "Lapăd haine d-al' domneşti
> Să-mbrac ieu d-ale curveşti,
> Pintru tine mă gătesc,
> Prea frumos să te iubesc!"[89]

> "I'll take off these princely clothes
> And put on my whoring clothes
> In order to get myself ready for you,
> So I can make love with you just right!"

Although Vartici returns home, he immediately departs, heading for yet another, distant boundary, into the unknown—to the "Tatar land," "Armenian region," or "Ţaligrad"[90]—where he hopes to evade Ileana as well as his own family forever. Here he echoes the disconsolate Drăgan in "Radu-vodă" and the dejected brother in the Anglo-Scots ballad "Lizie Wan" (who, after mortally stabbing his sister, pregnant with his child, aimlessly sets out to sea).[91] All of these figures are shamed and eternally wandering. Incest destroys relationships and families with a certain finality. As Larry Syndergaard notes, incest ballads "offer no strategy for mitigation or recovery, or for continuance of life in any endurable form after the incest itself."[92] Once Vartici has departed, Ileana goes in search of him, usually finding him far away, living with a new wife. She drugs Vartici, and when he awakens to realize that he has been wed to her against his will, he promptly grabs a dagger and stabs himself "Să scape de naşă-sa" ("So he could escape his godmother").[93] Ileana follows suit. In incest ballads, as Atkinson observes, stabbing "is a potent symbol of sexual assault, combining penetration with destruction"; and the "phallic nature [of the knife] as a weapon of penetration is more or less inescapable in these texts."[94] In "Vartici," the knife as a weapon of suicide is clearly associated with incest—although initiated by a woman, not the usual male perpetrator. In the South Slavic "Wedding of Nenad

89 Amzulescu 1974:460, ll. 107–110.

90 Constantinople.

91 Child 1965:51.

92 Syndergaard 1993:133.

93 Păsculescu 1910:196, l. 106.

94 Atkinson 2002:115. A knife is employed for murder or suicide in most of the best-known Anglo-Scots incest ballads: "Babylon," "Lizie Wan," "The King's Dochter Lady Jean," and "The Bonny Hind," in which brother and sister unknowingly sleep together; when they realize their relationship, she fatally stabs herself, and he mourns (Child 1965:50).

Imroar," when the bloodbrother attempts to seduce the bride, she kills him with a knife: also a metaphor in reverse.

"Vartici" exposes the tensions between nature and culture, what Stewart calls the "cultural rule of the natural."[95] "Vartici" is not only about Ileana's persistent attempts to indulge in illicit desire, but also, I believe, Vartici's near inability to curb his own instincts and maintain the boundaries he objectively recognizes. In the example below, he tells his wife that when Ileana propositioned him, he almost "crossed the line" himself—evocatively called *prag* ("threshold"):

> "Am lăsat-o şi-am fugit!
> De mai stam niţel pe prag,
> Chiar mă dedea de păcat!"[96]
>
> "I left her and fled!
> If I had stood on the threshold even a little bit longer,
> She would have led me to sin!"

And once Ileana has declared her love, Vartici deserts his wife and children, unable to fit any longer into his own world—or hers, for that matter. He simply flees "Ca să scape de păcat"[97] ("In order to keep from sinning"). Ileana sometimes denounces Vartici, claiming that he desired an adulterous affair.[98] She reverses the guilt and portrays her own shame as Vartici's, for which Ştefan-vodă hangs, beheads, or mercilessly stabs him. Ileana then takes her own life.[99]

"Vartici" is also about the anxiety generated within marriage by the rules that forbid adultery. A criss-crossing of spouses and would-be spouses characterizes the complex of marriages in the narrative. Ileana and Ştefan-vodă, as well as Vartici and his wife, are (happily) married at the outset. Soon Ileana wishes to couple illicitly with Vartici, whose wife consequently loses her equilibrium. Meanwhile, Vartici departs and finds another wife, far away from Ileana (and his first wife, if she is not already dead), while Ileana unlawfully tries to marry Vartici and actually succeeds momentarily. By the end, all are deceased

95 Stewart 1991:174. As Stewart notes, "Exogamous relations therefore pose a contradictory set of cultural solutions. On the one hand, they define one's membership, and by completing one's need for otherness pose an imaginary wholeness ... But on the other hand ... they define one's subjection, the renunciation of 'spontaneous' desires, the 'castration' one experiences under the rule of all cultural law" (175).

96 Rădulescu-Codin 1986:38, ll. 110–112.

97 Amzulescu 1964:1.84, l. 79.

98 This aspect of the story is less prominent in "Vartici" than in other Potiphar narratives.

99 She is not the only woman to kill herself over Vartici's death; when his wife sees him dead in some texts, she kills herself.

except Ştefan-vodă and Vartici's (second) wife. The web of secrecy, deception, infidelity, and cowardice has been intentionally manufactured by the central actors and results in chaos. A strong normative message denouncing adultery surely emerges when this song is performed at weddings.

In today's Romania, contemporary song genres have, for the most part, replaced epic at traditional weddings. This includes *manele* (sg. *manea*), the extremely popular Balkan pop-song genre performed by *lăutari* at weddings since the 1990s.[100] *Manele* are often requested and dedicated to significant guests at the wedding banquet (such as the godfather). The songs are sung in the first person as the *lăutar* takes on the identity of the person to whom the song is dedicated. The lyrics typically include superlative characterizations that flatter him (generating, in turn, more baksheesh for the singer). *Manele* are songs that speak of love, sex, money, and power. Embedded in these topics are songs about infidelity. The parallels with the marriage songs about incest are intriguing. The male voices typically admit, in the *manea* lyrics of infidelity, to having fine wives and decent conditions at home. But they also confess—with a good bit of bravura—to indulging in extramarital affairs. They are somewhat like "male Ileanas," driven by sexual desire and power despite adequate marriages. While the lyrics consciously defy paradigmatic monogamy, *manele* are not cautionary tales, however, since male egos are glorified but never rebuked. Perhaps such *manele* are permissible violations of the norm, included along with other inverted behavior, during the frenzied celebrations at weddings. They may very well also be expressions of male power in a liberated, post-communist age of secular modernity, markets, and globalization.

## Family versus Spiritual Incest in Oral Narrative Song

Incest between primary kin in Romanian epic is rendered in four distinct narratives. Three of them concern siblings. Resembling an explanatory myth, "Soarele şi luna"[101] (The Sun and the Moon), recounts the Sun's unrequited love for his sister, the Moon. The cosmos itself opposes this union, hence the Sun's eternal "punishment"—to chase the Moon across the sky. "Iovan Iorgovan,"[102] a dragon-slayer wondertale in verse, recounts how Iovan searches for his sister, who has fled due to his incestuous advances. He finds her captured by a dragon that he kills. In some texts, the sister eventually curses Iovan, who becomes a stone, after which she often turns into a flower. And in "Nevasta vândută" (The Wife Who Was Sold), in order to obtain money to pay taxes to the Turks, a man

[100] On *manele*, see Beissinger 2005 and 2007; also Beissinger, Rădulescu, and Giurchescu 2016.

[101] Amzulescu 1964:1.283–293.

[102] Amzulescu 1964:1.311–319, 319–323.

sells his wife to a man who turns out to be her brother (the siblings having been separated at birth).[103] The brother returns his sister to her husband. South Slavic narratives of sibling incest—brothers pursuing unwilling sisters—include comparable outcomes.[104]

The Romanian "Ursitoare"[105] (Fate), analogous in some degree to "Vartici," involves a mother and son. It is an Oedipal story in which a son unwittingly kills his father and marries his mother. Appropriately called "Fate," not only does one of the three Fates predict at the son's birth that he will marry his mother but, "fatefully," just before son and mother consummate their marriage, they intuit that they resemble each other "too much" and are related.[106] They resolve to live together instead as mother and son. The best-known South Slavic mother-son parallel is the religious legend "Nahod Simeuna" (Simeun the Foundling).[107]

The Balkan narratives of family incest, which are generally neither tragic nor violent, are resolved by and large by nature, fate, and curses that invoke nature. And although "Fate," about "real" mother-son incest, corresponds to "Vartici," about "metaphoric" (god)mother-(god)son incest, they are quite different. In "Fate," where the events and outcomes are determined by destiny, the mother and son are easily reconciled to their situation. By contrast, in "Vartici," the role of agency is central. Intention and transgression underlie the tale as a godmother fights to the death to "have" her godson. Since the almost-incest in "Fate" is not purposely committed, and there is no penalty, one could argue that it is not really a cautionary tale. "Vartici," on the other hand, is. The prohibition on incest is explicitly disregarded, resulting in calamity and providing a dramatic warning that resonates in the context of wedding rituals.

## Conclusion

Weddings furnish quintessential public occasions for the singing of narratives about marriage. The expression of narrative within event, with the arsenal of metanarrative devices that *lăutari* wield as part of their trade, empowers the performative experience, enlivening both the song and the rituals and

[103] Amzulescu 1964:3.281–287, 287–291, 292–294.

[104] See "Dušan hoće sestru da uzme" (Dušan Wishes to Marry His Sister) (Karadžić 1969:81–83), "Udaja sestre Dušanove" (The Marriage of Dušan's Sister) (Karadžić 1969:84–85), "Senjanin Ivo i Njegova sestra" (Senjanin Ivo and his Sister) (Karadžić 1975:549–550); Vidan 2003:188–191, #18; see also Krstić 1984:275–277.

[105] Amzulescu 1983:441–442.

[106] There are some formulaic similarities between this and "The Wife Who Was Sold."

[107] Simeun and his mother unknowingly sleep together, for which Simeun is thrown into prison. The keys to the prison are deposited in the river, and he is told that he will be released when the keys are found. Ten years later, they are discovered and presented to Simeun, still in prison, reading the Bible (Karadžić 1969:43–47, 47–50); see also Krstić 1984:277.

intensifying the meanings of both. In the joyous substitute-bridegroom narratives, the expectations of marriage are confidently celebrated as grooms seek and, with help, ultimately win exogamous brides, while constructive social alliances are publicly reproduced through the deeds of spiritual kin. Quite the reverse, however, are the destructive and disturbing portrayals in alternative narratives of subversive behavior on the part of godparents articulated through the trope of incest, where honor and trust are broken and futures dashed. "Radu-vodă" and "Vartici" are devastating tales, providing explicit counterexamples to the optimistic substitute-bridegroom narratives at weddings. They offer incisive cautionary tales in which godparents fully recognize the prohibitions on incest, but selfishly disregard them and are punished. Incest in narrative songs also articulates cultural boundaries that spell out obligations within marriage, through which honor is sustained. In the midst of these perspectives on human behavior—both positive and negative—are important subtexts that offer insight on their most profound question: who can/should marry whom? The tales of spiritual kin articulate and endorse obligations relating to exogamy, endogamy, and other social boundaries, especially with regard to categories of culture, class, and generation.

Each of the spiritual-kin narratives of incest is unique. While in all of the other narratives incest is only a threat or suggestion of sexual relations, in "Radu-vodă," rape actually takes place. In this way, it is the most destructive and sobering narrative about incest, and perhaps the most tragic. Like the maidens in the Anglo-Scots ballads "Bonny Hind" and "The King's Dochter Lady Jean," it concerns the pitiful fate of a female victim. As for "Vartici," it is a tale, not about male gender as power as are all the other incest narratives but, rather, about female gender and power in terms of cultural, social, and generational advantage. As a marriage song that is thoroughly inverted, "Vartici" ends up, through counterexample, pronouncing powerful taboos on incest and adultery.

As a pair of tales, the two narratives jointly convey yet another important meaning. Godparents, ideally, provide unwavering support to their nuptial godchildren. While so many significant changes take place during weddings—parents sorrowfully let go of their daughters, brides timorously move to new families, parents-in-law brashly permit them as "strangers" into their homes, and sons appropriate new roles as able husbands—it is godparents who remain steadfast. They are, ideally, stable and persistent anchors of security in the midst of all the transitions for the couple and their families (as "The Godfather's Song" so ably demonstrates). Godparents join the bride and groom from outside the family and are not "natural" kin but rather "fictional," thus bringing to the relationship a deliberately adopted sense of moral obligation, ritually reinforced by baptisms, weddings, and the traditions of cooperative and honorable relationships. Thus tales that involve the breakdown of godparents' integrity and honor also represent the breakdown of the moral commitment of spiritual kinship, with implications for individuals, families, and the community. It is no wonder that this prospect makes for narratives that are both powerful and threatening.

Both the productive and destructive tales of spiritual kin provide profound narrative confirmations of society's convictions and truths but also its conflicts and contradictions. As Albert Lord so poignantly stated:

> Oral traditional epic is not merely entertainment ... but has a serious function in its society. It contains the ideals and values of the society, as well as a regard for the fundamental problems of both the community and the individual and for how they may be met and accepted if they cannot be solved.[108]

The Romanian (and other Balkan) epic songs of incest warn of the fallout from crossing forbidden boundaries. They advocate, through example and counterexample, behavior that reinforces the foundation of social groups—interpersonal and group relations based on alliances and trust—and the cultural boundaries that are so vital to social survival. The narratives uphold in dramatic, symbolic, and sometimes inverted terms the stability and continuity that are essential to traditional society—where marriage, family, and spiritual kin generate critical bonds that can falter and dissolve, bringing devastation and anguish, but where they also have the power to create, reinforce, and sustain social order and communal cohesion.

108 Lord 1995:106.

## Bibliography


Alfani, G. 2009. *Fathers and Godfathers: Spiritual Kinship in Early-Modern Italy*. Trans. C. Calvert. Surrey.

Alfani, G., and V. Gourdon, eds. 2012a. *Spiritual Kinship in Europe, 1550–1900*. London.

———. 2012b. "Spiritual Kinship and Godparenthood: An Introduction." In Alfani and Gourdon 2012a:1–44.

Amzulescu, A. I. 1964. *Balade populare romînești*. 3 vols. Bucharest.

———. 1974. *Cîntece bătrînești*. Bucharest.

———. 1983. *Balada familială: Tipologie și corpus de texte poetice*. Bucharest.

Atkinson, D. 2002. *The English Traditional Ballad: Theory, Method, and Practice*. Aldershot.

Babcock, B. A. 1977. "The Story in the Story: Metanarration in Folk Narrative." In *Verbal Art as Performance*, ed. R. Bauman, 61–79. Prospect Heights, IL.

Bălăşel, T. 1967. *Folclor din Oltenia şi Muntenia: Texte alese din colecţii inedite* II. Bucharest.

Balotă, A. 1958. "Funcţiunea socială a cîntecului bătrînesc: Balada lui Vartici." *Revista de folclor* 3:101–112.

Bauman, R. 1986. *Story, Performance, and Event: Contextual Studies of Oral Narrative*. Cambridge.

Beissinger, M. H. 1991. *The Art of the Lăutar: The Epic Tradition of Romania*. New York.

———. 2005. "Romani (Gypsy) Music-Making at Weddings in Post-Communist Romania: Political Transitions and Cultural Adaptations." *Folklorica* 10:39–51.

———. 2007. "'Muzica Orientală': Identity and Popular Culture in Post-Communist Romania." In *Balkan Popular Culture and the Ottoman Ecumene: Music, Image, and Regional Political Discourses*, ed. D. A. Buchanan, 95–141. Lanham, MD.

———. 2012. "Court Poetry, Village Verse: Romanian Oral Epic in the Medieval World." In *Medieval Oral Literature*, ed. K. Reichl, 386–408. New York.

———. 2016. "Romani Performance and the Music of Celebration: Traditional Weddings in Pre-and Post-1990 Southern Romania." In *Von Hora, Doina und Lautaren: Einblicke in die rumänische Musik und Musikwissenschaft*, ed. T. Kahl, 129–141. Berlin.

———. 2020. "Nature as metaphor in Romanian and Slavic ritual wedding poetry." *Philologica Jassyensia* 16:187–204.

Beissinger, M. H., S. Rădulescu, and A. Giurchescu, eds. 2016. *Manele in Romania: Cultural Expression and Social Meaning in Balkan Popular Music*. Lanham, MD.

Bronson, B. H. 1969. *The Ballad as Song*. Berkeley.

Buchan, D. 1972. *The Ballad and the Folk*. London.
Child, F. J. 1965. *The English and Scottish Popular Ballads* I. Boston. Orig. pub. 1882.
Constantinescu, N. 1999. *Romanian Folk-Culture: An Introduction*. Bucharest.
———. 2000. *Etnologia şi folclorul relaţiilor de rudenie*. Bucharest.
Creed, G. W. 2011. *Masquerade and Postsocialism: Ritual and Cultural Dispossession in Bulgaria*. Bloomington.
Filipović, M. S. 1960. "Forms and Functions of Ritual Kinship among South Slavs." *Vie Congrès international des Sciences anthropologiques et ethnologiques* II, 77–80. Paris.
Godelier, M. 2011. *The Metamorphoses of Kinship*. Trans. N. Scott. London. Orig. pub. as *Métamorphoses de la parenté*. Paris, 2004.
Gregorian, M. 1967. *Folclor din Oltenia şi Muntenia: Texte alese din colecţii inedite* I. Bucharest.
Halpern, J. M., and B. Kerewsky-Halpern. 1986. *A Serbian Village in Historical Perspective*. Prospect Heights, IL.
Hammel, E. A. 1968. *Alternative Social Structures and Ritual Relations in the Balkans*. Englewood Cliffs.
Kačić-Miošić, A. 1946. *Razgovor ugodni naroda slovenskoga*. Zagreb. Orig. pub. 1756.
Karadžić, V. S. 1969. *Srpske narodne pjesme: Knjiga druga*. Belgrade. Orig. pub. 1845.
———. 1975. *Srpske narodne pjesme: Knjiga prva*. *Sabrana dela Vuka Karadžića: Knjiga četvrta*. Belgrade. Orig. pub. 1841.
Kligman, G. 1981. *Căluş: Symbolic Transformation in Romanian Ritual*. Chicago.
———. 1988. *The Wedding of the Dead: Ritual, Poetics, and Popular Culture in Transylvania*. Berkeley.
Krstić, B. 1984. *Indeks motiva narodnih pesama Balkanskih Slovena*. Belgrade.
Lévi-Strauss, C. 1969. *The Elementary Structures of Kinship*. Trans. J. H. Bell and J. R. von Sturmer. Boston. Orig. pub. as *Les structures élémentaires de la parenté*, Paris, 1949.
Lord, A. B. 1991. *Epic Singers and Oral Tradition*. Ithaca.
———. 1995. *The Singer Resumes the Tale*. Ed. M. L. Lord. Ithaca.
Lynch, J. 1986. *Godparents and Kinship in Early Medieval Europe*. Princeton.
Marian, S. F. 2000. *Nunta la români: Studiu istorico-comparativ etnografic*. Bucharest. Orig. pub. 1890.
Muravyeva, M. 2012. "Godparenthood in the Russian Orthodox Tradition: Custom against the Law." In Alfani and Gourdon 2012:247–274.
Păsculescu, N. 1910. *Literatura populară românească*. Bucharest.
Pop, M. 1976. *Obiceiuri tradiţionale româneşti*. Bucharest.
———. 1979. "The Relationship Between the System of Kinship Relations and the System of Customs." In *Europe as a Cultural Area*, ed. J. Cuisenier, 135–146. The Hague.

Popescu, A. I. 1970. *Cîntece bătrîneşti din Oltenia* II. Craiova.
Rădulescu-Codin, C. 1986. *Literatură populară.* Vol. 1, *Cîntece şi descîntece ale poporului.* Bucharest. Orig. pub. 1913.
Reynolds, D. 1999. "Problematic Performances: Overlapping Genres and Levels of Participation in Arabic Oral Epic-Singing." In *Epic Traditions in the Contemporary World: The Poetics of Community*, ed. M. Beissinger, J. Tylus, and S. Wofford, 155–168. Berkeley.
Stewart, S. 1991. *Crimes of Writing: Problems in the Containment of Representation.* New York.
Stone, L. 2010. *Kinship and Gender: An Introduction.* 4th ed. Boulder. Orig. pub. 1997.
Syndergaard, L. 1993. "Incest Ballads in the English and Scottish Popular Ballads: Pattern and Meaning." *Southern Folklore* 50:127–141.
Teodorescu, G. D. 1982. *Poezii populare române.* Bucharest. Orig. pub. 1885.
Thompson, S. 1960. *Motif-Index of Folk Literature* IV. Bloomington.
Tocilescu, G. G. 1980. *Materialuri folclorice* I. Bucharest. Orig. pub. 1900.
Van Gennep, A. 1960. *The Rites of Passage.* Trans. M. B. Vizedom and G. L. Caffee. Chicago. Orig. pub. as *Rites de passage*, Paris, 1909.
Vidan, A. 2003. *Embroidered with Gold, Strung with Pearls: The Traditional Ballads of Bosnian Women.* Milman Parry Collection of Oral Literature 1. Cambridge, MA.
Vuković, M. T. 2004. *Narodni običaji, verovanja, i poslovice kod Srba.* Belgrade.

# 5

# Visuality in Bosniac and Homeric Epic

ANNA BONIFAZI AND DAVID F. ELMER

## 1. Introduction

HOMERIC POETRY is an intensely visual art, as numerous studies have shown.[1] This intense visuality is a feature that Homeric poetry shares with many other oral narrative traditions.[2] The affinity of oral narrative for optically rich modes of presentation can be explained by the usefulness of visual techniques in composition and performance. Various writers have stressed the importance of visual and spatial information as facilitators of memory and recall: from the point of view of the oral performer, the cultivation of a detailed mental vision, which can then be scanned and presented in speech—what Albert Lord called "the living eye of the singer's imagination"—is an essential support for the cognitively demanding process of realizing a traditional narrative in performance.[3] At the same time, visual cues

1 See, for example, Andersson 1976:15–52 on the visual emphasis on characters rather than on scenery; Richardson 1990:110–123 on changes of scene and bird's eye views; Bakker 1993 on the "presence" of the narrator through visualization; Minchin 2001:132–160 and Bakker 2001 on the visual impact of similes; Scodel 2002 on special signs to be recognized and the cognitive notion of flashbulb memory; de Jong and Nünlist 2004 on scenic standpoints; Turkeltaub 2005 on the relevance of the description of glowing eyes; Slatkin 2007 on tragic visualizations in the *Iliad*; Nagy 2009:97–105 on the association between Homeric poetry and non-verbal visual arts; Purves 2010:24–64 on the different ways in which the *Iliad* is "eusynoptic"; Strauss Clay 2011 on the "theater" of Troy; Tsagalis 2012 on the *Iliad*'s visual spaces.

2 See, among others, Fleischman 1990:265–266. A Gaelic storyteller interviewed in the 1970s, when asked about "viewing" the events, asserts: "You've got to see it as a picture in front of you or you can't remember it properly ... You're as if the picture were in front of you here and all you do is follow the thing as it is" (MacDonald 1978:15). Zeman 2016 offers a more recent discussion of visualization as a feature of oral epic poems.

3 Lord 2019:98. Rubin 1995 provides an excellent overview of relevant work in cognitive psychology and applies it to the particular problems faced by oral performers. For the application of such work to the Homeric poems in particular, see Minchin 2001 and 2008. Among earlier writers on

are equally indispensable to the audience in the face of their own, equally demanding cognitive task. By fostering involvement in the shared vision communicated by performance, such cues assist the audience in tracking the movement of the unfolding narrative. The cognitive importance of visual elements to the successful realization and comprehension of the performance helps to explain the prominence and structural significance of visually intense moments in many narrative traditions. Visual imagery often seems to function as a kind of "motor" of narrative movement, with important moments being heavily coded for visualization.[4]

It is this "architectonic" function of visual techniques that we would like to explore in this paper, with reference to both Homeric and Bosniac epic. The fruitful comparison between these two traditions established by Parry and Lord has tended to focus on the utility of traditional formulas as expressions of traditional themes, but the comparison can be extended in any number of directions, including the one suggested here. We will suggest some convergences and divergences between these traditions by examining a Bosniac epic song performed for Milman Parry by the Albanian singer Alija Fjuljanin in 1934, with an eye to its heuristic value as a guide to the understanding of the visual strategies employed by Homeric poetry.[5] The value of Fjuljanin's song as a comparandum for Homer consists in the fact that, as a much shorter composition—with a "mere" 1,000 lines—it permits us to observe the use of compositional devices on a much smaller and more easily comprehensible scale.

We will begin by reviewing examples of some techniques deployed by Fjuljanin and their Homeric analogues. These techniques relate to visuality at two theoretically distinct but practically interrelated levels. The first

Homer, one of the most influential proponents of the importance of visuality in the "psychological effort of recall" was Eric Havelock, who remarked, "[epic] units of meaning are highly visualized in order that vision may lead on to vision" (1963:188).

4 Bakker's analysis of narrative progression in Homeric poetry provides numerous illustrations of this motor function (Bakker 1997:54–122). Bakker describes a "syntax of movement" articulated in terms of visual framings, close-ups, and elaborations of detail, where narration and description cannot be disjoined.

5 We use the term "Bosniac" to refer to the traditional culture of those Muslim inhabitants of the republics of the former Yugoslavia who speak a South Slavic language. Following the usage of the majority of Parry's Muslim informants, we refer to their language as "Bosnian." In contemporary usage, "Bosniac" generally indicates a cultural identity, while "Bosnian" refers to a political one, i.e. to the identity of residents of Bosnia-Herzegovina. Fjuljanin, ethnically Albanian, was from the village of Leskova, some thirty kilometers southwest of Novi Pazar in today's Serbia. According to his own testimony in an interview recorded by Parry, although the residents of Leskova were mainly Albanian, they all spoke Bosnian (which Fjuljanin refers to as *jugoslavenski*, "Yugoslavian")—and sang epics only in Bosnian (Lord 1954:292).

concerns the visual dimension of the narrative content—the visual aspects of the events themselves and the act of seeing as experienced by characters and narrated by the performer. Visuality at this level can be termed "propositional visuality." The second level, which can be designated as the level of "pragmatic visuality," relates to the way the narrator presents this content, that is, the way his language encodes and cues the visual processing of the narrative. These two levels are distinct both conceptually and in terms of the particular devices they involve. Their practical independence, moreover, can be detected in the fact that the "mind's-eye" experiences of narrators and listeners—the domain in which the effects of pragmatic visuality are felt—often exceed in richness of detail the descriptive content of a narrative.[6] Nevertheless, propositional and pragmatic visuality often work together. That is, the visual relevance of what is told may be connected to the visual relevance of *how* it is told.

## 2. Relevant Features in a Bosniac Epic and Comparable Features in the Homeric Poems

Alija Fjuljanin's song "Halil Hrnjičić and Miloš the Highwayman" tells the story of the kidnapping of a certain Hajkuna, sister of the Muslim heroes Mujo and Halil, by a Christian villain and Halil's subsequent rescue of her.[7] What we have termed "propositional visuality" can be observed, at its most basic level, in any of the text's many descriptive passages. Bosniac epic is a visually rich medium; it shares with Homeric poetry a preference for the accumulation of ornamental details.[8] Fjuljanin, however, has a noticeable tendency to draw attention to the visual content of his narrative, for instance by using semantic redundancy to make the action of seeing as explicit as possible (l. 348):

6 See, for example, the comments of Lindahl 2009:212–13 on the way the Muncy family tales, in spite of an extremely sparing use of visual detail, produced vivid images in the minds of narrator and listener. For more on Jane Muncy and her family's tales, see Lindahl, this volume.

7 Fjuljanin's song is PN 662 in the Milman Parry Collection of Oral Literature. The song was recorded by Milman Parry on 19 aluminum phonograph discs (numbers 1087–1105) on November 21, 1934, in Novi Pazar. The text has been published in Lord 1953 and a complete translation in Lord 1954. The translations presented here are by D. F. Elmer. The original recordings and a transcription by Nikola Vujnović can be accessed through the website of the Milman Parry Collection of Oral Literature (http://mpc.chs.harvard.edu).

8 For a comparison of the "poetics of ornamentation" in Bosniac and Homeric epic, see Elmer 2010. On the "optic poetics" of the Homeric tradition, see Bakker 2005:63.

uh kad vide crnjo sa oćima

Oh! When that black one saw with his eyes ...[9]

The "black one" is Halil, who has been chasing after his sister's abductors and just now realizes—after careful inspection of the grass for signs of passing horses—that they have made good their escape.

The Homeric poems likewise employ redundant expressions to emphasize the impact of visual experience on the characters. These mostly formulaic expressions typically combine the instrumental ὀφθαλμοῖσι(ν) "by means of eyes" with a form of the verb ὁρᾶν "to see," as in the formula:

ἐπεὶ ἴδον ὀφθαλμοῖσι

(*Odyssey* 10.414 = 2.155; cf. 11.615, 23.92)

when they saw with their eyes[10]

When considering the significance of these devices, it is essential to keep in mind the correlation between the visual perception of the characters and the mental vision of the audience. Every time characters are said to have seen, noticed, or spotted something or someone, listeners are invited to make the same object appear to their minds (and to their mind's eyes). The narrative unfolds for the listener as a sequence of mental images that are largely coextensive with the characters' visual experiences. Moreover, the links between these images—which is to say, the sequential steps that advance the plot—are often constructed precisely in terms of the act of seeing: in battle scenes, for instance, the narrative moves from killing to killing by describing how one hero observes another's death and so is motivated to seek vengeance.[11] In this way, the characters' vision becomes the very force that drives the plot forward. We glimpse here already an initial indication of the interrelationship between propositional and pragmatic visuality. Insofar as it animates the listeners' mental experience of the story—advances the frames, so to speak, of their mental film-strips—the propositional visuality of the characters' experiences takes on a pragmatic dimension.

9 Compare the similar formulations at ll. 878 (*uh kad vide gospa sa oćima*), 935 (*a kad vide Miloš sa oćima*), 981 (*aj da vidiš ćuda sa očima*), and 986 (*uh kad Mujo vide sa očima*), all of which exhibit the same semantically redundant formulation "X saw with his/her eyes." Note that Vujnović alternates between the spellings *oćima*/*očima*.

10 Other comparable examples: *Iliad* 3.28, 13.99 (= 15.286, 20.344, 21.54), 17.466, 23.202; *Odyssey* 3.373, 4.47.

11 Slatkin 2007:19–20. Slatkin observes that the *Iliad*'s most decisive plot development—Achilles' decision to send Patroklos into battle in his place—is precipitated by precisely such an act of seeing.

A special case of the interplay between the visual experience of the characters and the mental experience of the listeners is presented by the motif of *disguise and recognition*, which is as prominent and important a device in the Bosniac tradition as it is in the Homeric. Regardless of whether the disguised character is recognized or not, the special narrative pleasure of this device derives from the contrast between strictly visual phenomena and the extradiegetic knowledge with which the listeners are able to enrich their mental vision. In "Halil and Miloš," Halil disguises himself as an unmarried girl and enters the palace of his enemies in the company of his helper, Ruža. The Christian *ban* (the potentate whom Miloš serves) is completely taken in by the deception:

> 'aman Ružo grom te pogodijo
> đe s ovaku curu nabavila
> nabavila sa sela devojku'
>
> PN 662, ll. 748–750

> '*Aman*, Ruža—may lightning strike you!—
> where did you find such a girl?
> Where did you find this maiden from the country?'

Scenes such as these produce delight because they invite listeners to share in a vision that they know to be false, and simultaneously establish the superiority of the audience's state of knowledge over that of the participants in the action. The *Odyssey*, of course, exploits this technique to the full, repeatedly presenting Odysseus to the gaze of unrecognizing spectators. Strategic usages of deictic or anaphoric markers heighten the effect by emphasizing the sameness of the referent "Odysseus" even as he is visualized or recalled as a different individual by internal and external spectators.[12]

Considered in isolation from the propositional level, pragmatic visuality encompasses all the techniques employed by the performer in order to help himself and the listeners visually construe and/or process the ongoing narration. As the narrative unfolds and the visual focus switches from object to object and place to place, the performer must mark these shifts in focus in order to facilitate cognitive tracking of the story in progress. The linguistic means for performing this function is provided in both Bosnian and Greek by lexemes known as "particles," which, though not in themselves necessarily visual, may

12 See, for example, the deictic use of ὅδε at *Odyssey* 16.57, where Telemachus—still unaware of his father's presence—asks Eumaeus about the beggar: πόθεν τοι ξεῖνος ὅδ' ἵκετο; "from where did this stranger come to you?" Deictic devices such as this facilitate the convergence of the audience's mental vision with the perceptual sphere of the characters.

nevertheless indicate varying degrees of discontinuity in the mental vision shared by performer and audience.[13] In Bosnian, for example, the particle *a* marks the moderately discontinuous shift between two characters who are visualized sequentially, as in the following example, where the particle triggers a shift from the leader of the raiding party (Mujo) to the hero directly behind him (Osman):

> e okrenu poljom zeljenijem
> a za njime Arnaut Osmane
>
> PN 662, ll. 14–15

> So, he set off over the green plain,
> and behind him was Osman the Albanian.[14]

Since both characters act within the same temporal and spatial setting, the shift from one to the other is relatively smooth—more like a pan of the camera than a cut. Homeric poetry employs similar means to accomplish the same task, as when the narrator of the *Odyssey* employs the particle αὐτάρ to accomplish the visual switch from Demodokos to Odysseus:

> ... μετὰ δέ σφιν ἐμέλπετο θεῖος ἀοιδός,
> Δημόδοκος, λαοῖσι τετιμένος. αὐτὰρ Ὀδυσσεὺς
> πολλὰ πρὸς ἠέλιον κεφαλὴν τρέπε παμφανόωντα,
> δῦναι ἐπειγόμενος· δὴ γὰρ μενέαινε νέεσθαι.
>
> *Odyssey* 13.27–30

> ... and among them sang the godlike singer
> Demodokos, honored by the people. But Odysseus
> often turned his head toward the radiant sun,
> anxious for it to set, for he was very eager to set out for home.

Here the camera shifts from Demodokos to Odysseus and then continues to follow his gaze toward the setting sun.

A similar technique for marking visual discontinuity is deployed whenever a general description is followed by single details or a sequence of

13 See Bonifazi 2016 for a general discussion of the pragmatic functions of particles in PN 662 and in the Homeric poems.

14 The particle *a*, here translated "and," is in fact a mild adversative particle. Canakis 2011, pointing out parallels between this particle and modern Greek *kai* "and," observes that *a* can sometimes have a "deictic function" when it "marks a change of person." This "deictic function" matches well the function we ascribe to *a* here and elsewhere, where it marks or implies a visual shift.

details.[15] In the next example, the image of a wounded hero is followed by a kind of zooming-in on the details of his frightful appearance; once again, each visual shift, each cut of the mental "montage," is marked by a particle or interjection:

> ej kakav se momak nagrdijo
> a na njega ruha ni beljaja
> sve mu brza zrnad raznijela
> ej krvava va sablja do balćaka
> a krvava ruka do ramena
>
> PN 662, ll. 158–162

> Hey, how the young man had been disfigured!
> And on him there was not a scrap of clothing,
> swift bullets had torn it all away.
> Hey, his sword was bloody to the hilt,
> and his arm was bloody to the shoulder.

Homeric poetry offers many comparable examples as, for instance, in the famous scene of Agamemnon's arming in Book 11 of the *Iliad*. In this case as well, a broad descriptive statement ("he himself donned the gleaming bronze," 11.16) gives way to a sequence of details about the individual pieces of Agamemnon's equipment:

> Ἀτρεΐδης δ' ἐβόησεν ἰδὲ ζώννυσθαι ἄνωγεν
> Ἀργείους· ἐν δ' αὐτὸς ἐδύσετο νώροπα χαλκόν.
> κνημῖδας μὲν πρῶτα περὶ κνήμῃσιν ἔθηκε
> καλὰς ἀργυρέοισιν ἐπισφυρίοις ἀραρυίας
> δεύτερον αὖ θώρηκα περὶ στήθεσσιν ἔδυνε
> . . . . . . . . . . . . . . . . . . . . . . . . . . . . . . . . .
> ἀμφὶ δ' ἄρ' ὤμοισιν βάλετο ξίφος· ...
> . . . . . . . . . . . . . . . . . . . . . . . . . . . . . . . . .
> κρατὶ δ' ἐπ' ἀμφίφαλον κυνέην θέτο τετραφάληρον
> ἵππουριν· δεινὸν δὲ λόφος καθύπερθεν ἔνευεν.
> εἵλετο δ' ἄλκιμα δοῦρε δύω κεκορυθμένα χαλκῷ
> ὀξέα·
>
> *Iliad* 11.15–19, 29, 41–43

15 Tannen (1989:134–166) analyzes the role of imagery and the functions of detailing in conversational narratives. Details, in particular, "fire the individual imagination" (136); their accumulation may mark the climax of a story "contributing to its main point" (141). Detailing may be seen as a way of evaluating (141); it is a powerful means of triggering memories and emotions (150). Examples from PN 662 reviewed below illustrate some of these points.

The son of Atreus cried out and bid the Argives
to arm themselves, and he himself donned the gleaming bronze.
First he put on his legs beautiful greaves,
fitted with silver ankle-pieces.
Then he put a corselet around his chest
. . . . . . . . . . . . . . . . . . . . . . . . . . . . . . . . .
And over his shoulders he hung his sword ...
. . . . . . . . . . . . . . . . . . . . . . . . . . . . . . . . .
And on his head he set a helmet with bosses on both sides, four
buckles,
and a horse-hair crest; and the crest swayed terrifyingly above it.
And he gripped two stout spears tipped with bronze
and sharp.

Each successive shift to a new detail in this description is linguistically marked by means of a particle (μέν, αὖ, ἄρα, δέ, δέ).

As mentioned earlier, propositional visuality and pragmatic visuality not infrequently converge. So, in the following example, the visual wonder of the character Mujo yields immediately to the visual surprise engineered by the performer, who uses a direct address to the audience to communicate a sense of amazement at the sudden arrival of a new character (Osman) on the scene:

taman Mujo u tom razgovoru
dok ugljeda ćudo sa oćima
kad evo ti Arnautovića

PN 662, ll. 148–150

Mujo had just spoken these words
when he caught sight of a wonder—
here you are, the Albanian's son.

The performer may also bridge the gap between the visual experience of characters and that of the audience by means of another strategy, which involves embedded visualizations—descriptions of the content of a character's vision. These embedded visualizations fuse the characters' attempts to perceive a remarkable event with those of the audience. In fact, this device invites the listeners not only to share but also to relive the perceptual and emotional experiences of the characters. The following excerpt, in which Mujo uses his spyglass to survey the landscape and look for signs of the danger that he fears threatens his city of Kladuša, provides an excellent example of this technique:

e sve gljeda kulje i avljije
a gljedaše ka ešći Kladuše
pa gljedaše sobom govoraše
Bože mijo na svemu ti fala
svuđe vedro jeste havajima
nigđe maglje nema ravninama
sem Kladušu tama ufatila
dalj je magla al' je pala tama
dal to puši kula serdareva

PN 662, ll. 139–147

Well, he [Mujo] looked over all the towers and courtyards,
and he looked toward ancient Kladuša,
and while he looked he said to himself,
"Dear God, thanks be to you in all things,
everywhere the skies are clear,
nowhere is there fog upon the plains—
a dark cloud has enveloped Kladuša alone.
Is it fog or a dark cloud that has come down,
or is it the *serdar's* tower smoking?"

The redundant repetition of the verb *gl(j)edati* "to look" in lines 139–141 lays considerable stress on Mujo's anxious attempts to obtain clear visual information about what is happening. His efforts to see become a kind of figure or *mise-en-abyme* for the audience's own drive to visualize events in anticipation of a major turning point in the action. What Mujo struggles to make out turns out to be exactly what he most fears: Kladuša is on fire; it has been sacked by the Christian warrior Miloš. A certain dilation of narrative time intensifies the audience's visual experience: the literal zooming in on the mysterious cloud (through Mujo's eyes) is emphasized by the retardation of the narrative pace.

In his lengthy study of Bosniac epic, the slavist Alois Schmaus draws attention to the way in which the Bosniac tradition develops such scenes of embedded visualization into a major compositional device that not only contributes to a more concrete and realistic "chronotope" but also provides an important means by which singers structure their narratives.[16] Of the spyglass motif in particular, Schmaus notes that it functions as an alternative way of introducing into the

[16] Schmaus 1979:79, 140–146. Mikhail Bakhtin's influence on Schmaus's thinking in these pages is evident. For more on Schmaus's contribution to the study of Bosniac epic, see Kunić, this volume.

narrative information about events happening at a distance.[17] In other words, it is a substitute for the various kinds of messenger-figures that appear throughout the Christian and Muslim epic traditions. This functional equivalence is in a sense made explicit in Fjuljanin's song, when Mujo's use of the spyglass leads directly to the appearance of Osman, who brings news of the attack on Mujo's home.

Schmaus makes a further observation with significance for our discussion: he compares the embedded visualizations of the Bosniac tradition to the *Teikhoskopia*, or "Viewing from the Walls," of *Iliad* Book 3.[18] In this famous scene, the Trojan king Priam, in the company of Helen, gazes down at the battlefield below and asks his daughter-in-law to identify the warriors he singles out. Priam's vision structures this scene: as he directs his gaze at several visually prominent figures in succession, he directs the listener's mental gaze as well. We will return shortly to the structural significance of Priam's vision. For now it is sufficient to stress that, once again, a visualization from afar focuses attention on the enemy threat at a crucial moment in the development of the action by zooming in on a succession of details.

## 3. Visual and Narrative Landmarks in "Halil and Miloš"

The spyglass episode allows us to take our argument a step further by evaluating the function of such devices within the overall narrative economy of the song. The visualization of the cloud over Kladuša occupies an important narrative position: it serves as the trigger for the complicating action. This corresponds to a broader storytelling strategy employed by Fjuljanin, who often uses propositional or pragmatic visuality to establish visual "landmarks" at narrative turning points.

An outstanding example of the use of visual techniques in connection with narrative landmarks and emotional peaks is provided by the character Osman's account of the abduction of Hajkuna. Fjuljanin employs an embedded flashback, a highly marked device, to record this crucial event, which must be fixed vividly in the listener's mind in order to establish the character of the story's antagonist. At the pivotal moment in the standoff between attackers and defenders, Fjuljanin's Osman pauses to provide a detailed description of the villain's mount.

[17] Schmaus 1979:79, 91.

[18] Schmaus calls song no. 26 in the Matica Hrvatska collection of Muslim epic (vols. 3–4 of *Hrvatske narodne pjesme*, first published in 1898 and 1899, respectively) "a humble variant of the Homeric *Teikhoskopia*" (143). Although Schmaus does not develop this point further, it should be noted that the connection between embedded visualization and messenger-figures is apparent in the *Iliad* as well: the *Teikhoskopia* concludes with the arrival of the Trojan herald Idaios, who brings news of developments on the battlefield.

This description almost literally launches the action forward, by transitioning directly into the preternatural leap with which the animal carries its rider into the courtyard:

> e to reče zasede alata
> kakav beše zakljali ga vuci
> ćetiri mu noge putaljaste
> a cijela glava baljatasta
> e zinuo ka da pobesnijo
> iz noždara maven plamen bije
> pripaljuje travu detelinu
> nagna konja preskoći avljiju
> uh kad dušman pade u avljiju
> doćeka' ga puškom od obraza
> što je fajda helj ga pogodijo
> ne hoće ga gvožđe ni olovo
> sve od njega zrnad odlećuju
> udaraju kulji u duvaru
> gotovo mi oči isteraše
> ja potego sablju ađemkinju
> na troje se sablja prelomila
> tako Ajka pa ga doćekala
> što je fajda helj ga doćekala
> ne hoće ga gvožđe ni olovo
> pruži ruku dofati Hajkunu
> pa je baci za se na alata
>
> PN 662, ll. 252–273

> Well, saying this he mounted his chestnut horse.
> What was [the horse] like, may wolves devour him?
> His four legs had white markings
> but his head was entirely black,
> and he bared his teeth as though he were mad.
> From his nostrils a blue flame darts;
> it sets the clover grass aflame.
> He spurred the horse, lept over the courtyard wall.
> Oh! When the enemy descended into the courtyard,
> I met him with my rifle at my shoulder.
> What use, even if I struck him?
> Neither iron nor lead has any purchase on him.

Every bullet flies off him,
strikes the wall of the tower.
They nearly struck out my own eyes.
I drew my Persian sword;
my sword broke into three pieces.
Ajka faced him in the same way.
What use, even if she faced him?
Neither iron nor lead has any purchase on him.
He stretched out his arm, he seized Hajkuna
and he set her behind him on the chestnut horse.

In a manner similar to the cinematographic "design for terror" discerned by Alain Renoir (1962) in *Beowulf*, the scene cuts from a vision of the villain on his terrifying horse to a sequence of shots of Osman and Hajkuna as they attempt to defend themselves. The singer's effort to invest this visually intense sequence with an emotional, as well as narrative, significance is likewise evident in the use of a rhetorical question coupled with an expressive curse ("What was the horse like, may wolves devour him?").

The initiation of the complicating action is by no means the only narrative high point that is singled out by means of visual devices. The *denouement* is similarly marked. The song's concluding scene hinges on an embedded visualization that is also a visual deception—which is to say, a kind of variation on the recognition motif. Halil "disguises" the disembodied head of Miloš as the whole, living person, and fools his brother into thinking that Miloš has returned to attack again. Note that redundant references to Mujo's vision bracket the scene:

e moj brate Kladuški serdare
aj da vidiš ćuda sa očima
e đe stiže Miloš ćesedžija
. . . . . . . . . . . . . . . . . . . . . .
uh kad Mujo vide sa očima
a kad vide na kapiju glavu
aman što ga nemir ufatijo
pa bežaše redom odajama
a smije se Mujović Haljile
baka baka pa dobra junaka
kako bi joj živoj udarijo
kad se boji posećene glave
a smije se Haljil po odajidots

e kad vide Mujo sa oći(ma)

PN 662, ll. 980–982, 986–995

"Hey, my brother, *serdar* of Kladuša,
ah, see a wonder with your eyes,
hey, how Miloš the Highwayman approaches.
. . . . . . . . . . . . . . . . . . . . . .
Oh! When Mujo saw with his eyes,
and when he saw the head at the gate,
*aman*! What distress took hold of him.
And he ran in flight through room after room.
But Mujo's Halil laughed:
"Just look, what a noble hero!
How would he have met him if he were still alive,
when he's afraid of his severed head!"
But Halil laughed in the chamber,
hey, when Mujo saw with his eyes.

A number of narrative turning points in Fjuljanin's song are, in fact, accomplished by means of recognition scenes, a fact that attests to the satisfaction and pleasure produced by these moments of recalibration, when the visual experience of a character or characters is synchronized with the point of view of the audience.[19]

## 4. Back to Homer

What new perspectives on Homer are opened up by this examination of Fjuljanin's performance? The techniques on display in "Halil and Miloš" help to focus attention on comparable features of Homeric discourse at both the propositional and pragmatic levels, and on an instructive difference as well.

At the propositional level, Fjuljanin's use of visually intense scenes to articulate his narrative suggests that we look for a similar "architectural" strategy in Homer. In fact, we can detect an indication of just such a strategy, played out in terms of propositional visuality, in a scene that has already been mentioned—the *Teikhoskopia*. This scene—which is itself a significant narrative landmark—establishes a motif that plays an essential role in the subsequent development

[19] Cf. the recognitions of Halil by Anđelija (ll. 447–458), Miloš (ll. 616–638), Ruža (ll. 657–670), and Ajkuna (ll. 815–828). Schmaus 1979:135, discussing Bosniac epic's pronounced affinity for disguise and recognition, notes the "special charm" of the disjunction between the experiences of the characters, on the one hand, and of the performer and audience on the other.

of the song. The motif centers on Priam's visual observation of the enemy. One might expect the narrative complications leading up to Hektor's fatal duel with Achilles to be focused on Hektor's experience of his antagonist; in actuality, however, the progress toward Hektor's death is articulated in terms of *Priam*'s experience of Achilles, as we see in the following two passages:

> ἑστήκει δ' ὃ γέρων Πρίαμος θείου ἐπὶ πύργου,
> ἐς δ' ἐνόησ' Ἀχιλῆα πελώριον· αὐτὰρ ὑπ' αὐτοῦ
> Τρῶες ἄφαρ κλονέοντο πεφυζότες ...
>
> *Iliad* 21.526–528

> And aged Priam stood upon the divinely-built tower,
> and noticed huge Achilles: before him
> the Trojans, put to flight, rushed wildly.

> τὸν δ' ὃ γέρων Πρίαμος πρῶτος ἴδεν ὀφθαλμοῖσι
> παμφαίνονθ' ὥς τ' ἀστέρ' ἐπεσσύμενον πεδίοιο,
> ὅς ῥά τ' ὀπώρης εἶσιν, ἀρίζηλοι δέ οἱ αὐγαὶ
> φαίνονται πολλοῖσι μετ' ἀστράσι νυκτὸς ἀμολγῷ
> . . . . . . . . . . . . . . . . . . . . . . . . . . . . . . . . . . . . . .
> ὣς τοῦ χαλκὸς ἔλαμπε περὶ στήθεσσι θέοντος.
>
> *Iliad* 22.25–28, 32

> Aged Priam first saw him [Achilles] with his eyes,
> shining as he sped over the plain like the star
> that rises in late summer, and its bright rays
> are conspicuous among the many stars in the dark of night
> . . . . . . . . . . . . . . . . . . . . . . . . . . . . . . . . . . . . . .
> Just so did the bronze about his chest flash as he ran.

In the first of these passages, the king singles out Achilles from the wall: Achilles occupies the visual center of attention, the Trojans, the periphery. More strikingly, in the second passage, from the beginning of Book 22, Priam's vision of Achilles is likened to the vision of the evening rising of Sirius, the Dog-Star.[20]

[20] On the narratological impact of the simile, see de Jong 2004:126; on its architectonic function in terms of signaling "long-range narrative design," see Moulton 1974:26. The suggestion of this long-range design can be discerned already in the words with which Priam concludes his involvement in the events of Book 3 (an involvement that began with the *Teikhoskopia*): "Never will I endure to see with my eyes my dear son engaged in combat with Menelaos, beloved of Ares" (3.306–307; note the redundancy of ἐν ὀφθαλμοῖσι ὁρᾶσθαι).

The reason for this emphasis on Priam's visual experience becomes clear when we situate these passages in the context of the overall trajectory of the Iliadic narrative. This resonant simile and, more generally, the emphasis on the fixture of Priam's gaze on Achilles look forward to the climactic visual experience of the poem, the reciprocal gaze of Priam and Achilles that caps the scene of Hektor's ransom in Book 24:

> ὡς δ' ὅτ' ἂν ἄνδρ' ἄτη πυκινὴ λάβῃ, ὅς τ' ἐνὶ πάτρῃ
> φῶτα κατακτείνας ἄλλων ἐξίκετο δῆμον
> ἀνδρὸς ἐς ἀφνειοῦ, θάμβος δ' ἔχει εἰσορόωντας,
> ὣς Ἀχιλεὺς θάμβησεν ἰδὼν Πρίαμον θεοειδέα.
> θάμβησαν δὲ καὶ ἄλλοι, ἐς ἀλλήλους δὲ ἴδοντο.
>
> *Iliad* 24.480–484

> As when overwhelming derangement takes hold of a man who,
> having killed another in his own land, comes to a foreign country,
> to the house of a rich man, and wonder grips those who behold him:
> so Achilles wondered as he gazed at godlike Priam;
> the others wondered, too, and they looked at each other.

This moment of intense propositional visualization concludes one of the poem's highest emotional peaks as well as the principal narrative arc.

A masterpiece of late-sixth-century Athenian art, the famous hydria (water jar) in Boston's Museum of Fine Arts depicting the dragging of Hektor's corpse (MFA 63.473), may attest to the impact this architectural device had on early audiences. By an artful combination of pictorial motifs, the painter has integrated into a single image several distinct moments in the plot of the *Iliad*: Achilles' initial disfiguring of the corpse (22.395ff.), the dragging of the body around the tomb of Patroklos (24.12–18), and the goddess Iris' mission to bring about the ransoming of Hektor's remains (24.159ff.).[21] These three narrative moments are synchronized, so to speak, by the visual engagement of the figures. Priam and Achilles, both painted with very prominent eyes, stare intently at each other while Iris, approaching from the right and balanced by the figure of Hekabe on the left, gazes along the same line of sight toward the ensemble. Hektor seems almost completely unnoticed; the scene's dramatic intensity derives from the ricocheting glances that originate with Priam at the far left of the image but that never touch his son. In the words of Emily Vermeule, "the painter forces the parents ... to stare into the eyes of the enemy who had just killed their son

21 For a sensitive description of the scene and the various motifs the painter has employed to capture these various moments in the plot, see Vermeule 1965:40–47.

and they do not even see the head of dead Hektor as it passes along the ground at their feet."[22] The pointed use of the figures' interlocking gazes to coordinate this synopsis of the *Iliad*'s last books recalls the way that Priam's sighting of Achilles articulates the Iliadic narrative.[23]

At the level of pragmatic visuality, Fjuljanin's techniques reinforce the idea that the performance of epic poetry ought to be understood as a process of mediating between past and present. In his investigations of the "immediacy" effect of the Homeric reenactment of the past, Egbert Bakker has demonstrated the many ways in which the Homeric performer may use the resources of language to bring it about that "the mountain comes to Mohammed"—that is, to bring the past into the present of performance.[24] Among the linguistic resources useful in this regard, Bakker includes the particle *ara* and the aorist tense, both of which are employed in the following example to render particularly vivid Penelope's retrieval of a weapon that plays a crucial role in the plot[25]:

> ἡ δ' <u>ἄρ'</u> ἐφ' ὑψηλῆς σανίδος <u>βῆ</u>· ἔνθα δὲ χηλοὶ
> ἕστασαν, ἐν δ' <u>ἄρα</u> τῇσι θυώδεα εἵματ' ἔκειτο.
> ἔνθεν ὀρεξαμένη ἀπὸ πασσάλου αἴνυτο τόξον
> αὐτῷ γωρυτῷ, ὅς οἱ περίκειτο φαεινός.
>
> *Odyssey* 21.51–54

> She went up to the raised platform: there stood
> the chests in which fragrant clothing was kept.
> Then, stretching out her hand, she lifted from its peg the bow
> along with the gleaming case that enclosed it.

Fjuljanin "presents" a similar moment—the retrieval and disabling of Miloš's rifle by Anđelija, another of Halil's helpers—with an even more explicit token of immediacy:

22 Vermeule 1965:44.

23 Vermeule notes (1965:44) that the painter, in adapting the conventions of departure scenes, has put Priam and Hekabe in the position normally occupied by the departing warrior's parents. This surprising arrangement may be an attempt to capture graphically the analogical relationship between Priam and Peleus, which plays an important role in the ransoming of Hektor's corpse. Immediately after they have exchanged their reciprocal looks of wonder, Priam begins his plea to Achilles: "Remember your father" (μνῆσαι πατρὸς σοῖο, 24.486). A similar emphasis on the reciprocal gaze of Priam and Achilles can be found in the depiction of the ransom of Hektor on an amphora attributed to the Rycroft Painter (Toledo 1972.54).

24 Bakker 2005:156.

25 On "Mohammed and the Mountain," see Bakker 2005:154–176. For Bakker's inclusion of ἄρα among the linguistic devices that foster immediacy, see Bakker 1993:16–25; 2005:97–100. For more on ἄρα, see Bonifazi, Drummen, and de Kreij 2016:II.4§§38–41, §§50–53; II.5§§51–62; III.2§96; IV.4§§171–172; II.3§§65–67; II.5§§51–62; IV.4§§169–170.

pa dofati brešku granajliju
evo brešku vinom natoćila

PN 662, ll. 857–858

Then she took his engraved rifle;
here [you are], she filled the rifle with wine

The deictic marker *evo* "here" is a compressed version of a "presentation formula," a device that enables Bosniac epic singers to summon events linguistically before their audience.[26] Elsewhere in the song, a similar effect is achieved by means of the deictic marker *sad(e)* "now."[27]

Even though Homeric narrative does not make use of spatial or temporal markers that are explicitly tied to the "here and now" of performance, we may observe the use of linguistic strategies that appear consciously designed to bridge the gap between past event and present telling. Some of these involve the use of lexical items other than those noted by Bakker to heighten the vividness and immediacy of the narrative. In the following passage, for example, the collocation καὶ δή singles out a visual and temporal zooming in on a new detail:[28]

ἦ τοι ὁ καλὸν ἄλεισον ἀναιρήσεσθαι ἔμελλε,
χρύσεον ἄμφωτον, καὶ δὴ μετὰ χερσὶν ἐνώμα
. . . . . . . . . . . . . . . . . . . . . . . . . . . . . . . . . . . . . . . .
τὸν δ' Ὀδυσεὺς κατὰ λαιμὸν ἐπισχόμενος βάλεν ἰῷ

*Odyssey* 22.9–10, 15

He [Antinoos] was just about to raise a beautiful cup,
golden, with two handles, and now he was holding it in his hands
. . . . . . . . . . . . . . . . . . . . . . . . . . . . . . . . . . . . . . . .
But Odysseus, aiming for the throat, shot him with an arrow

26 For presentation formulas, see Elmer 2009. An uncompressed version of the formula in PN 662 is quoted below.

27 In lines 774 and 780, for example, *sad(e)* brings Ruža's actions into proximity with the present time of the performance, even though the verb tense is past.

28 In tragedy, καὶ δή frequently marks the entry of an actor—obviously a visually remarkable event. See van Erp Taalman Kip 2009, which argues that καὶ δή marks an expected new entry, while the cognate collocation καὶ μήν is used for an unexpected new entry. Καὶ μήν is used already in Homer to mark unexpected new entries (cf. *Odyssey* 11.582 and 593, where Tantalus and Sisyphus appear to Odysseus' sight in the Underworld). Καὶ δή—mostly uttered by embedded narrators—has visual relevance at *Odyssey* 10.30 and 13.169, for example. Others have commented on the visual relevance of δή alone: see Denniston 1954:203 and 250 (the latter on καὶ δή); Ophuijsen (1993:141) on the visual value of δή in Plato's *Phaedo*; Bakker 1997:78–79 on δή in Homer. For more on καὶ δή, see Bonifazi, Drummen, and de Kreij 2016:III.4§§51–5; IV.2§101; IV.2§100; IV.3§80; IV.5§83.

This detail is not irrelevant: it provides a note of intense pathos in anticipation of the upcoming act of violence and so contributes directly to the emotional immediacy of the event. Even more striking is the expressive potential of the grammatically-acknowledged ambiguity in the frame of reference of the deictic markers αὐτοῦ, αὖθι, αὐτόθι, etc. Words of this class can have both proximal ("here," "now") and distal ("there," "then") reference. We posit a deliberate exploitation of this ambiguity in cases in which the "there and then" potentially merges with the "here and now" of the performance, as in the following passage:

> μνηστῆρες δ' ἀκάχοντο κατήφησάν τ' ἐνὶ θυμῷ,
> ἐκ δ' ἦλθον μεγάροιο παρὲκ μέγα τειχίον αὐλῆς,
> αὐτοῦ δὲ προπάροιθε θυράων ἑδριόωντο.
>
> *Odyssey* 16.342–344

> But the suitors felt distressed and confounded in their hearts,
> and they went out from the hall beyond the great wall of the courtyard,
> and there/here, before the gate, they sat in council.

In his translation of this passage, Richmond Lattimore renders the αὐτοῦ of the last line as "there."[29] His rendering reflects a very common (perhaps "default") tendency to distance narrated events from the *hic et nunc* of their telling. We suggest that the Greek is actually more elusive, and therefore more open to an immediacy-oriented reading.[30]

## 5. Divergences

This kind of studied ambiguity, however, is still a very far cry from the level of explicit involvement in the performance setting on display in Fjuljanin's text. Fjuljanin establishes a direct relationship between himself, the events of his narrative, and his audience, as we can see from his use of the full version of the "presentation formula":

> kad evo ti Arnautovića
>
> PN 662, l. 150

> When, here you are, the Albanian's son.

[29] Lattimore 1967: "And there in front of the palace gates they held an assembly" (249).

[30] On the visual and narrative functions of *au*- particles and adverbs in ancient Greek, see Bonifazi 2008 and 2012:185–292.

The address to the listener that is implicit in the deictic marker *evo* "here" becomes explicit when the formula is expanded to include the second-person pronoun *ti* (word for word, *kad evo ti* translates as "when here for you"). Fjuljanin also makes use of the functionally parallel formula *a da vidiš* (roughly, "you should have seen"), in which the second-person verb again makes explicit reference to the listener. These devices represent a widespread technique in Fjuljanin's tradition for foregrounding new visual steps in the narrative. Audience address is, in fact, a prominent feature of very many performance traditions, so that its complete absence from the Homeric poems is justly cause for surprise. Although Homeric narrative has a variety of techniques for singling out characters and details and otherwise directing the audience's mental vision, the poems do not make use of this most obvious and perhaps easiest way to achieve that goal.

A similar point may be made with regard to the metanarrative comments such as:

> e kako se zekan nagrdijo
>
> PN 662, l. 155
>
> Hey, how the horse had been disfigured!

The metanarrative comment in this case engages not only the audience's attention but also, more particularly, their mind's eye by introducing a visual description (of the horse's haggard appearance). The Homeric epics, by contrast, do not include comments like these. The question is: why? We might speculate that some explicit reference to the performer-audience relationship—some form of "back-channeling"—*was*, in fact, verbalized at a certain stage in the development of Homeric poetry, but that such references were screened out of the text in the process of textualization, as the written text gradually became more and more independent of a particular performance.[31] At the same time, it must be stressed that previously undetected aspects of the Homeric strategies for conveying vividness continue to be discovered, and that scholars' understanding of Homeric visuality will necessarily continue to evolve—perhaps so as to encompass precisely those features that appear on the surface to be absent. This paper is offered as a contribution to this evolving understanding.

31 Luka Marjanović, editor of an important collection of Bosniac epics, noted a suggestive phenomenon among his informants, who sometimes introduced into their sung verses a hypermetrical second-person pronoun (the dative *ti* "for you": see Marjanović 1898:liv). This form of listener address, essentially a highly compressed presentation formula, was not used when the performers were merely reciting their texts (presumably so that Marjanović could transcribe them).

## Bibliography

Andersson, T. M. 1976. *Early Epic Scenery: Homer, Virgil, and the Medieval Legacy.* Ithaca.

Bakker, E. J. 1993. "Discourse and Performance: Involvement, Visualization and 'Presence' in Homeric Poetry." *Classical Antiquity* 12:1–29.

———. 1997. *Poetry in Speech. Orality and Homeric Discourse.* Ithaca.

———. 2001. "Similes, Augment, and the Language of Immediacy." In *Speaking Volumes: Orality and Literacy in the Greek and Roman World*, ed. J. Watson, 1–24. Leiden.

———. 2005. *Pointing at the Past: From Formula to Performance in Homeric Poetics.* Hellenic Studies 12. Washington, DC.

Bonifazi, A. 2008. "Memory and Visualization in Homeric Discourse Markers." In Mackay 2008:35–64.

———. 2012. *Homer's Versicolored Fabric: The Evocative Power of Ancient Greek Epic Word-Making.* Hellenic Studies 50. Washington, DC.

———. 2016. "Particles as Cues to Structuring in South Slavic and Early Greek Epic." In Pagán Cánovas and Antović 2016:125–147.

Bonifazi, A., A. Drummen, and M. de Kreij. 2016. *Particles in Ancient Greek Discourse: Exploring Particle Use Across Genres.* Hellenic Studies 74. Washington, DC. https://chs.harvard.edu/book/bonifazi-drummen-de-kreij-eds-particles-in-ancient-greek-discourse/.

Canakis, C. 2011. "Teaching the Polysemous Connective *kai* to Balkan Learners of Modern Greek." *Studies in Greek Linguistics* 31:114–124.

Clay, J. S. 2011. *Homer's Trojan Theater: Space, Vision, and Memory in the Iliad.* Cambridge.

Denniston, J. D. 1954. *The Greek Particles.* 2nd ed. Oxford.

Elmer, D. F. 2009. "Presentation Formulas in South Slavic Epic Song." *Oral Tradition* 24:41–59.

———. 2010. "Kita and Kosmos: The Poetics of Ornamentation in Bosniac and Homeric Epic." *Journal of American Folklore* 123/489:276–303.

Erp Taalman Kip, A. M. van. 2009. "*Kai mēn, kai dē* and *ēdē* in Tragedy and Comedy." In *Discourse Cohesion in Ancient Greek*, ed. S. J. Bakker and G. C. Wakker, 111–133. Leiden.

Fleischman, S. 1990. *Tense and Narrativity: From Medieval Performance to Modern Fiction.* Austin.

Havelock, E. 1963. *Preface to Plato.* Cambridge, MA.

Jong, I. J. F. de. 2004. *Narrators and Focalizers.* 2nd ed. London.

Jong, I. J. F. de, and R. Nünlist. 2004. "From Bird's Eye View to Close-Up: The Standpoint of the Narrator in the Homeric Epics." In *Antike Literatur in neuer Deutung: Festschrift für Joachim Latacz anlässlich seines 70. Geburtstages*, ed. A. Bierl, A. Schmitt, and A. Willi, 63–84. Munich.

Lattimore, R., trans. 1967. *The* Odyssey *of Homer*. New York.

Lindahl, C. 2009. "Faces in the Fire: Images of Terror in Oral Märchen and in the Wake of September 11." *Western Folklore* 68:209–234.

Lord, A. B. 1953. *Serbocroatian Heroic Songs.* Vol. 2, *Novi Pazar: Serbocroatian Texts.* Introduction and notes, A. B. Lord. Preface, A. Belić. Belgrade.

———, ed. 1954. *Serbocroatian Heroic Songs.* Vol. 1, *Novi Pazar: English Translations.* With musical transcriptions by B. Bartók and prefaces by J. H. Finley, Jr. and R. Jakobson. Cambridge, MA. .

———. 2019. *The Singer of Tales.* 3rd ed. Ed. D. F. Elmer. Hellenic Studies 77. Publications of the Milman Parry Collection of Oral Literature 4. Washington, DC. Orig. pub. Cambridge, MA, 1960.

MacDonald, D. A. 1978. "A Visual Memory." *Scottish Studies* 22:1–26.

Mackay, E. A., ed. 2008. *Orality, Literacy, Memory in the Ancient Greek and Roman World.* Leiden.

Marjanović, L., ed. 1898. *Hrvatske narodne pjesme, odio prvi. Junačke pjesme (muhamedovske), knjiga treća.* Zagreb.

Minchin. E. 2001. *Homer and the Resources of Memory: Some Applications of Cognitive Theory to the* Iliad *and the* Odyssey. Oxford.

———. 2008. "Spatial memory and the composition of the *Iliad.*" In Mackay 2008:9–34.

Moulton, C. 1974. *Similes in the Homeric Poems.* Göttingen.

Nagy, G. 2009. *Homer the Classic.* Hellenic Studies 36. Washington, DC.

Ophuijsen, J. M. van. 1993. "OUN, ARA, DĒ, TOINUN: The Linguistic Articulation of Arguments in Plato's Phaedo." In *Two Studies in Attic Particle Usage: Lysias and Plato*, ed. J. M. van Ophuijsen and C. M. J. Sicking, 67–164. Leiden.

Pagán Cánovas, C., and M. Antović, eds. 2016. *Oral Poetics and Cognitive Science.* Berlin.

Purves, A. C. 2010. *Space and Time in Ancient Greek Narrative.* Cambridge.

Renoir, A. 1962. "Point of View and Design for Terror in 'Beowulf.'" *Neuphilologische Mitteilungen* 63:154–167.

Richardson, S. 1990. *The Homeric Narrator.* Nashville.

Rubin, D. C. 1995. *Memory in Oral Traditions: The Cognitive Psychology of Epic, Ballads, and Counting-Out Rhymes.* Oxford.

Schmaus, A. 1979. "Studije o krajinskoj epici." In *Gesammelte slavistische und balkanologische Abhandlungen, IV. Teil*, 77–235. Orig. pub. 1953 in *Rad Jugoslavenske Akademije nauke i umjetnosti* 297:89–247.

Scodel, R. 2002. "Homeric Signs and Flashbulb Memory." In *Epea and Grammata: Oral and Written Communication in Ancient Greece*, ed. I. Worthington and J. M. Foley, 99–116. Leiden.

Slatkin, L. 2007. "Notes on Tragic Visualizing in the *Iliad*." In *Visualizing the Tragic: Essays in Honour of Froma Zeitlin*, ed. C. Kraus, S. Goldhill, H. P. Foley, and J. Elsner, 19–34. Oxford.

Tannen, D. 1989. *Talking Voices: Repetition, Dialogue, and Imagery in Conversational Discourse*. Cambridge.

Tsagalis, C. 2012. *From Listeners to Viewers: Space in the* Iliad. Hellenic Series 53. Washington, DC.

Turkeltaub, D. 2005. "The Syntax and Semantics of Homeric Glowing Eyes: *Iliad* 1.200." *American Journal of Philology* 126:157–186.

Vermeule, E. T. 1965. "The Vengeance of Achilles." *Bulletin of the Museum of Fine Arts* 63:34–52.

Zeman, S. 2016. "Orality, Visualization, and the Historical Mind." In Pagán Cánovas and Antović 2016:168–195.

# 6

# Heroes and Their Snakes

JOSEPH FALAKY NAGY

IN THE *THE SINGER OF TALES*, Albert Lord mentions only briefly the famous traditional ballad of "Marko and Musa," the earliest printed version of which was collected by Vuk Karadžić from Tešan Podrugović of Gacko, Hercegovina, in 1815.[1] (Versions were collected by Milman Parry from various singers, including Salih Ugljanin in 1934 in Novi Pazar.[2]) There is, however, more discussion of this ballad to be found in Lord's 1966 contribution to the Roman Jakobson Festschrift, a piece titled "The Influence of a Fixed Text," and reprinted in Lord's *Epic Singers and Oral Tradition*.[3] In this study, he examines a variant of the ballad collected from Ilija Mandarić of Vrebac, Croatia, in 1934, a text housed in the Parry Collection. For Lord's purposes, this constitutes an example of a "Type B" text, that is, one heavily influenced by the published version of a song but also showing the impact of a literate singer's shaping it to his own performative standards. In the sequel to *The Singer of Tales*—*The Singer Resumes the Tale*—Lord cites "Marko and Musa" as an example of heroic "near-" or "almost-death," alongside the desperate fight of Beowulf with Grendel's mother and, in the *Song of Roland*, the combat of Charlemagne with the Saracen Baligant.[4]

In this study, I focus on a remarkable parallel between this "Marko" ballad and a story preserved in medieval Irish literature, centered on the motif of a snake (or snakes) inside the heart (or multiple hearts) of the hero's sinister,

1 Lord 2019:105. The Podrugović text is translated in Low 1922:124–131.

2 "Marko Kraljević and Musa the Highwayman," translated and annotated in Parry and Lord 1954:114-115, (358-366: commentary, including yet another version collected from Ugljanin and translated by Lord). On the Marko cycle of ballads, see Fisher 1990; a multiform of "Marko and Musa" is discussed on pp. 26–50.

3 Lord 1991:170–185 (174–181). In reference to the version collected from Podrugović, Lord, citing Karadžić, notes that the singer did not sing but *recited* his songs to the collector (175n3). Similarly, about the ballad of Marko and Musa collected from Ugljanin, the singer said, "It's not a regular song ... It's not sung to the gusle, but is told as a story" (Parry and Lord 1954:359).

4 Lord 1995:73. On this important narrative element, see also Lord 2019:208–209, 219–220.

supernaturally powerful opponent. I am not using "motif" here in the Stith Thompson (1955) sense. (In fact, the closest item to what we are considering here in the Motif-Index is not that close at all, though it bears a memorable designation: G328, "Rectum Snakes.") But I do recall that when I talked to Professor Lord about the Irish analogue to the remarkable denouement of the South Slavic ballad, it piqued his folkloristic curiosity, his fascination with the traditional accoutrements of heroic biography and their travels through time and space. So I have reason to hope that what follows may be a fitting tribute to my beloved teacher and the author of *The Singer of Tales*, which so deftly tracks both generic and genetic resemblances among hero tales and adumbrates the mythic strata underlying them.

The late John Miles Foley noted the peculiarity of the premise of the Marko narrative cycle,[5] centered on a scion of a conquered people in the service of the conquerors—an "unlikely hero" who undertakes the missions on which his masters send him often with something less than an eager spirit. The song of "Marko and Musa" features a figure very much like Marko, but a Marko turned bad and taking to dangerous extremes what Marko seems of a mind to do in many other ballads. Our song begins with a scene featuring the redoubtable mercenary named Musa in a reflective mood, drinking in a tavern, as he complains about how, despite his loyal service, the Sultan has never paid Musa properly. The erstwhile dependable soldier of the Sultan decides to become a big-time villain: he will make it impossible for anyone to reach the coast or embark on a sea voyage, he will intercept all shipments of imperial wealth and, building a house or tower, he will hang from it the bodies of the victims of his villainy. When the disruption brought about by Musa becomes intolerable, the Sultan sends his vizier and an army to address the grave problem, but these return defeated by Musa. The humiliated officer suggests that the Sultan summon Marko, but, as far as the Sultan knows, Marko died long ago, languishing in the Sultan's dungeon. Not so, it turns out; the vizier finds Marko, releases him from his imprisonment, where he has been dwelling among scorpions and snakes, and brings him to the court, albeit in terrible shape. The restoration of Marko in anticipation of his mission entails plenty of drink, a curious test involving a rod of dry dogwood from which Marko extracts fluid with his squeeze, and a visit to the smithy, where Marko obtains a new sword and lops off the arm of the smith after the latter gratuitously informs Marko that he had made an even better sword for Musa. Rehabilitated, recharged, and supplied with the (second-)best weapon in the world, the hero goes forth to fight with Musa the

5 Foley 1991:99–100.

"highwayman."[6] The two warriors engage in desperate combat, in which Musa clearly has the upper hand, pinning Marko down in a move reminiscent of what Grendel's mother does to Beowulf. Fortunately for the seemingly about-to-die Marko, his blood-sister, the *vila*, his supernatural benefactress and nemesis who appears in other Marko ballads as well, appears in response to Marko's reproachfully calling upon her. She reminds him of the two daggers he keeps in his boot.[7] With these, Marko underhandedly rips Musa apart. (This is where the story becomes strange.) Perhaps in search of the source of Musa's preternatural strength, Marko looks inside his opponent's corpse and discovers three hearts inside and a just-waking serpent perched on the third. Fully roused, the creature makes the dead body move across the ground. Even more remarkable, the serpent speaks. Had it woken in time, the snake says, Musa would be alive and Marko dead. Taken aback, Marko exclaims that he has slain a better man than himself. Returning to the sultan with Musa's head, Marko tosses it to him, and the Sultan springs in terror. Marko wonders aloud how much more frightened the Sultan would have been had he met Musa alive.

The medieval Irish analogue features no talking snake or any sense that the featured fight was as touch-and-go as that between Marko and Musa, but it sports its own notable details. The story exists in both prose and poetic forms, as is typical of the narrative lore contained in the *dindshenchas*, an anthology of tales and traditions, put together in Ireland sometime around AD 1000, that both records the legendary associations of famous locations in Ireland and purports to explain the etymologies of their placenames.[8] The extant versions of our story, as we shall see, are hardly displays of the storyteller's art, as is the South Slavic ballad. The prose merely presents the bare facts, while the poem alludes more than narrates. Moreover, the story as relayed in the two different media (prose and poetry) diverges in a key respect. This too is not untypical of the *dindshenchas* or for that matter of medieval Irish literary tradition in general, which could be said to *revel* in multiformity. The tale centers on the river Berba, or modern Anglicized Barrow, the second longest river in Ireland, which flows from the Slieve Bloom Mountains of County Laois down to the sea, close to the modern-day city of Waterford. The prose states that one Mac Cécht slew one Me(i)che, the son of the Morrígan, and found three hearts inside his opponent,

6 Lord's translation of *kesedžija* (Lord 1954:360; Lord 1995:73, where Lord also calls him a "road-blocker"). On the meaning and possible etymology of this word, see Low 1922:124n1.

7 As Foley observed, the *vila* metaphorically refers to the knives as *guje* "snakes," when she is reminding Marko of his still being armed, and asks where they are hiding. Thereby, she (or the singer Podrugović) anticipates the literal snake secreted in Musa's body (Foley 1986:215).

8 Stokes 1894:304 (see also Stokes 1892:483); Gwynn 1906:64–65, 104.

with the shape of a serpent through each ("co ndelbaib tri nathrach treithib").[9] Perhaps this expression implies that the snakes were still embryonic or not fully grown. (The word used for snake in all of these Irish texts, *nathair*, is cognate with English *adder*, originally *nadder*.) That they were real and dangerous snakes, and not just snake-like arteries or overgrown tapeworms, is confirmed by what follows in our text. Mac Cécht burns the snakes or the hearts themselves and disposes of them in a river. The ashes make the water boil, killing off every living thing in the stream, and give the river its name, *Berba*, supposedly from the verb *berbaid* 'boil'. (Whitley Stokes, the editor of the prose *dindshenchas* texts, drolly notes that this body of water named after deadly turbulence "is now the sluggish, silent river Barrow."[10]) Revealing the apocalyptic stakes that were actually involved in this fight between Mac Cécht and Meche, one prose version of the story ends with the statement that, "unless the latter's death had occurred, the adders would have grown in his breast till they would not have left an animal alive in Ireland,"[11] while another concludes: "Now if death had not befallen Meche the serpents in him would have grown, and what they left alive in Ireland would have wasted away."[12]

In agreement with the latter account, the poetic version of the *dindshenchas* of Berba hints at the nearly cosmic consequences that would have resulted had Meche been triumphant in the fight, implying that Ireland would have been laid waste had he not been slain. This account, however, features only one serpent and makes no mention of its having been found in Meche's heart. In fact, one could argue that the poem allows an interpretation according to which Meche *is* himself the *nathair*, the serpent. Mac Cécht's struggle, moreover, is described primarily in regard to this creature, which "made three turns [as] it approached the brigand (*berg*) to eat him."[13] Other ambiguities in the poem have to do with whether the remains of the serpent, referred to in the text as the "salchur serb na sen-nathrach" ("bitter filth of the ancient adder"), are the same as the "lúaithred Méchi" ("ashes of Meche") mentioned in the same quatrain, and whether it is these ashes and/or this filth that makes the river first grow silent ("rosbalb") and then boil ("rosberb"), or is it the river that, responding in its own preternatural way, silences, "cooks," and renders harmless the remains

9 Stokes 1894:394. Compare the image presented in the other prose version: "tri cenn natrach batar for[s]na tri cridib" ("three snakes' heads on the three hearts") (Stokes 1892:483).

10 Stokes 1894:394.

11 Stokes 1892:483.

12 Stokes 1894:394.

13 "Nathir fo thrí focheird cor / tathig in mbeirg dia bronnud" (Gwynn 1906:62). Gwynn suggests that the three "turns" are a reference to the snake's coils (104).

of the sinister warrior-cum-serpent.[14] Adding another sub-textual layer to the proceedings is the word used in the poem to describe the monster's opponent: *berg* 'brigand'—hardly the designation one would expect for a heroic savior of Ireland.[15]

Even further complicating the picture, the poem gives the *berg*'s name as Diancécht, not Mac Cécht, as in the prose.[16] If this is a record of an alternative tradition and not the product of scribal error, then the story takes on an even more "mythic" coloring. Diancécht belongs to the generation that medieval Irish literature describes as the magical and primeval settlers of Ireland, namely the Tuatha Dé Danann "Tribes of the Goddess Danu," among whom Diancécht figures as the healer par excellence.[17] If we view this charter member of what was most likely an archaic native pantheon as the serpent-slayer in our story, then we would be better able to account for the pointed repetition of *sen* 'ancient' in this poem of a mere twenty lines. The tribes of Leinster, the province through which the Barrow flows, are referred to in our text as "the people of ancient Ailbe" ("slúag sen-Ailbe"), a reference possibly to a mythical guard dog of Leinster named Ailbe.[18] The Irish in general, meanwhile, are dubbed the "peaceable host of ancient Ireland" ("slóg sádail na sen-Érend"). And, as we have already noted, the *nathair* itself is said to be *sen* 'ancient'.

Diancécht is not the only figure with mythological cachet who plays a role in the story of why the Berba is called the Berba. In the prose account, while his opponent Meche's father is not named, his mother is. This is highly unusual in medieval Irish tradition, where patronymics are much more common than metronymics. Meche's designated parent is the Morrígan "Spectral Queen" or "Great Queen," like Diancécht a member of the Tuatha Dé, and a figure especially associated with the battlefield and martial pursuits.[19] One of her most famous appearances in medieval Irish story set in the time after the coming of humans to Ireland and the receding of their magical predecessors has to do with her mocking the young hero Cú Chulainn when he is about to be over-

14 Compare the proactive Trojan river Scamander in *Iliad* XXI 136–384 and the equally lively Ulster river Cronn as discussed in Nagy 1996.

15 Could the slayer of Meche be of a kind with the notoriously brigand-like hero Finn mac Cumaill, a figure at the center of an extensive cycle of medieval and modern Irish tales, who is well known for his slaying of disruptive watery monsters (Nagy 1985:115–117)?

16 This Mac Cécht is presumably identical with the larger-than-life champion of the same name who serves the doomed high-king of Ireland in the medieval saga *Togail Bruidne Da Derga* (Knott 1936:8 and elsewhere).

17 Gray 1982:122–123.

18 Prominently featured in the early Irish heroic tale *Scéla Mucce Meic Dathó* (Thurneysen 1935:1 and elsewhere). According to this text, the placename Mag n-Ailbe, to which Gwynn says the Berba poem here refers (1906:104), was named after the dog (Thurneysen 1935:18, 66).

19 Gray 1982:129–130.

come by a spectral opponent in what is the hero's first combat experience.[20] The Morrígan's mocking, like the *vila*'s chiding of Marko for fighting with Musa on a Sunday,[21] marks a turnaround in the hero's fortunes, resulting in his triumph subsequent to his almost-death. Another parallel between the Morrígan of medieval Irish story and the *vila* of South Slavic heroic ballad is that these supernatural creatures alternate between singular and collective identities: it is not clear in the Marko ballads whether it is the same *vila* who keeps reappearing, just as the Morrígan or the Badb is sometimes described in the literature as a unique individual and at other times as a triad or even a type of supernatural being. In his commentary on the "Marko and Musa" ballad as recited by the *guslar* Podrugović for Karadžić, Svetozar Koljević observes that Musa resembles the slain warrior mentioned in Book 8 of the Aeneid, Erulus, who is said to have had three hearts.[22] This is not exactly the case: he is said (by the character Evander, reminiscing about how he slew Erulus) to have had three *animae*, all of which Evander took. He was, moreover, given these three lives, or chances to survive, by his goddess mother Foronia. Thus, while the analogy may not work in the case of Musa (of whose parentage we know nothing), it may have relevance in regard to the peculiarly endowed Meche and his mother, the otherworldly Morrígan.

How did the snake or snakes end up in the bodies of the seeming villains Musa and Meche? This question brings up a vast body of folklore (including the aforementioned Thompson motif) having to do with the ailments brought on by the introduction or insinuation of worms, serpents, or other parasitical creatures into the human body. Much of the folkloristic scholarship on internalized snakes has focused on a short story by the nineteenth-century New England author Nathaniel Hawthorne, "Egotism; or the Bosom Serpent," the tale of a man felled by depression and simultaneously invaded by a snake that, according to hearsay, had done the same to members of earlier generations of the protagonist's family.[23] What is especially relevant about Hawthorne's not-so-secret sharer (whose hiss can be heard in the background to anything the Byronic hero of this short story says) is that, as the title "Egotism" indicates, a person's having a snake inside him or her may create a deep sense of there being something wrong, but it also can give rise to an inflated sense of importance—after all, it *does* make the serpent's host "larger than life" in a dangerous way.

20 O'Rahilly 1976:16. The Morrígan here is referred to as "in bodb" ("the scald-crow"), her usual animal manifestation.

21 Low 1922:130.

22 Koljević 1980:196 [*Aeneid* VIII 562–567].

23 Hawthorne 2011:182–197; Barnes 1972; de Caro 1973. I thank my UCLA colleague Dr. Christine Goldberg for these references. See also Ermacora, Labanti, and Marcon 2016.

Hawthorne, of course, brings out the biblical resonances of this id-adder, which also ought to be taken into account in regard to the two heroic tales in question here and to the matter of their reception among members of their original or latter-day audiences. The above-mentioned phrase in the *dindshenchas* poem, "bitter filth of the ancient adder," certainly must have rung a Christian bell for medieval Irish *literati*, while the superfluity of hearts (symbolic of an excess of life, strength, or courage?) and the serpent's plucky defiance complicate the sinister connotations of both snakes and highwaymen.[24]

What if the snake or snakes in Musa and Meche did not come from the outside, whether welcomed or not; what if they had grown up within, as organic as any other aspects of these powerful figures with whom the snakes are so intimately associated? Doubtless relevant here is the Indo-European and Middle-Eastern complex of the dragon myth, as laid out by Joseph Fontenrose (1959), later developed by Calvert Watkins (1995),[25] and re-examined by John Shaw (2006) with particular reference to the mythological cast of characters in our Irish story.[26] The embargo-enforcing, serpent-harboring Musa is nothing if not a "blocker," like Vṛtra, the cosmic snake of Vedic tradition, underlying whose name are the concepts "resistance" and "obstacle,"[27] while Marko (paralleling Vṛtra's opponent, the god Indra), eliminates a hoarder and implacable enemy of the general distribution of goods when he slays Musa.[28] But in the Indo-European version of the myth as reflected in these two examples as well as in many from other, non-Indo-European traditions one could cite (including the ancient Akkadian account of the slaying of the dragon-like Tiamat by her descendant, the Babylonian supreme god Marduk[29]), there is something distinctly problematic and troubling about the slaying of the dragon. There is the intimation that "hero" and "dragon," as two not-unrelated figures brought together by tradition to engage in a predestined struggle, deep down are mirror images of one another, trapped as co-dependents in an ever-returning mythopoeic scenario—like Marko and Musa, whom I earlier characterized as a sinister multiform of Marko. (Or is it Marko who is a Musa "turned good," or at least

24 Of possibly marginal relevance, the state-sponsored Bosnia-Hercegovina tourism website describes the country as "The Heart-Shaped Land": https://www.tourismbih.com.

25 Watkins 1995:297–303 and elsewhere.

26 My thanks go to Dr. Jacqueline Borsje for bringing Shaw's article to my attention.

27 Watkins 1995:300, 304.

28 "It is the dragon's 'job', as Professor William Alfred has put it, to guard treasure. That is, the dragon keeps wealth from circulating: the ultimate evil in society in which gift-exchange and the lavish bestowal of riches institutionalized precisely that circulation" (Watkins 1995:300). On the other hand, Frashëri 1989 argues for a historical basis for the struggle between Marko and Musa. (I am grateful to the anonymous reader of this essay for the reference.) Of course, a mythological and a historical interpretation would not necessarily be incompatible.

29 Fontenrose 1959:148–153.

partially rehabilitated, after his time spent among the creeping-crawling denizens of the Sultan's dungeon?)

In conclusion, we should note that, in Plutarch's *Life of Cleomenes*, a serpent actually serves as the stand-in for a dead hero, not unlike the cardiac snake that outlives and speaks "for" Musa. The body of the exiled Spartan king Cleomenes, slain by his treacherous Egyptian hosts, was hoisted onto a cross for his friends and enemies to see. Then, says Plutarch:

> A few days afterwards those who were keeping watch upon the body of Cleomenes where it hung, saw a serpent of great size coiling itself about the head and hiding away the face so that no ravening bird of prey could light upon it. In consequence of this, the king was seized with superstitious fear, and thus gave the women occasion for various rites of purification, since they felt that a man had been taken off who was of a superior nature and beloved of the gods. And the Alexandrians actually worshipped him, coming frequently to the spot and addressing Cleomenes as a hero and a child of the gods; but at last the wiser men among them put a stop to this by explaining that, as putrefying oxen breed bees, and horses wasps, and as beetles are generated in asses which are in the like condition of decay, so human bodies, when the juices about the marrow collect together and coagulate, produce serpents. And it was because they observed this that the ancients associated the serpent more than any other animal with heroes.
>
> Perrin 1921:141; Plutarch *Cleomenes* 39[30]

I would argue that it is this same paradoxical linkage between the traditional images of hero and serpent that we see reflected in the stories of Meche and Musa; the same posthumous essence of the warrior that makes the River Barrow boil; and the same multivalent heroic sign that inspires Marko to say, after the death of Musa, whether apostrophically or in response to the still-alive and defiant serpent, that he slew a man better than himself.[31]

30 Daniel Ogden relates this story to the cult of the anguineal Agathos Daimon in Alexandria (2013:286–291). He also cites this story in his discussion of the intimate relationship between serpents and the "heroic dead" in Greco-Roman traditions (2013:247–270).

31 In the versions of the song collected from Salih Ugljanin, Marko's profoundly disturbing realization of his inferiority led to his death-like disappearance into the depths of a cave (Parry and Lord 1954:115, 364). Indeed, it says in one of Ugljanin's versions that, while Marko and his horse (after withdrawing into the cave) were never seen again, Musa's grave became a monument to the slain hero and a site for people to visit and pray for him (364).

# Bibliography

Barnes, D. R. 1972. "The Bosom Serpent: A Legend in American Literature and Culture." *Journal of American Folklore* 85/336:111–122.

Caro, R. J. de. 1973. "A Note about Folklore and Literature (The Bosom Serpent Revisited)." *Journal of American Folklore* 86/339:62–65.

Ermacora, D., R. Labanti, and A. Marcon. 2016. "Towards a Critical Anthology of Pre-Modern Bosom Serpent Folklore." *Folklore* 127:286–304.

Fisher, L. G. 1990. *Marko Songs from Hercegovina a Century after Karadžić*. New York.

Foley, J. M. 1986. "Tradition and the Collective Talent: Oral Epic, Textual Meaning, and Receptionalist Theory." *Cultural Anthropology* 1:203–222

———. 1991. *Immanent Art: From Structure to Meaning in Oral Traditional Epic*. Bloomington.

Fontenrose, J. E. 1959. *Python: A Study of Delphic Myth and its Origins*. Berkeley.

Frashëri, K. 1989. "Qui est Musa Arbanasi?" *Studia Albanica* 26:75–92.

Gray, E. A., ed. and trans. 1982. *Cath Maige Tuired: The Second Battle of Mag Tuired*. Irish Texts Society 52. Dublin.

Gwynn, E. J., ed. and trans. 1906. *The Metrical Dindshenchas* II. Royal Irish Academy Todd Lecture Series 9. Dublin.

Hawthorne, N. 2011. *Selected Stories*. Intro. B. Wineapple. John Harvard Library. Cambridge, MA.

Knott, E., ed. 1936. *Togail Bruidne Da Derga*. Mediaeval and Modern Irish Series 8. Dublin.

Koljević, S. 1980. *The Epic in the Making*. Oxford.

Lord, A. B. 1991. *Epic Singers and Oral Tradition*. Ithaca.

———. 1954. *Serbocroatian Heroic Songs*. Vol. 1, *Novi Pazar: English Translations*. With musical transcriptions by B. Bartók and prefaces by J. H. Finley, Jr. and R. Jakobson. Cambridge, MA.

———. 1995. *The Singer Resumes the Tale*. Ed. M. L. Lord. Ithaca.

———. 2019. *The Singer of Tales*. 3rd ed. Ed. D. F. Elmer. Hellenic Studies 77. Publications of the Milman Parry Collection of Oral Literature 4. Washington, DC. Orig. pub. Cambridge, MA, 1960.

Low, D. H., trans. 1922. *The Ballads of Marko Kraljević*. Cambridge.

Nagy, J. F. 1985. *The Wisdom of the Outlaw: The Boyhood Deeds of Finn in Gaelic Narrative Tradition*. Los Angeles.

———. 1996. "The Rising of the Cronn." In *Celtica Helsingiensia*, ed. A. Ahlqvist, 129–148. Commentationes Humanarum Litterarum 107. Helsinki.

Ogden, D. 2013. Drakōn: *Dragon Myth and Serpent Cult in the Greek and Roman Worlds*. Oxford.

O'Rahilly, C., ed. and trans. 1976. *Táin Bó Cúailnge: Recension 1*. Dublin.

Perrin, B., trans. 1921. *Plutarch's Lives* X. London.
Shaw, J. 2006. "Indo-European Dragon-Slayers and Healers, and the Irish Account of Dian Cécht and Méiche." *Journal of Indo-European Studies* 34:153–181.
Stokes, W., ed. and trans. 1892. "The Bodleian Dinnshenchas." *Folklore* 3:467–516.
———, ed. and trans. 1894–1895. "The Prose Tales in the Rennes Dindshenchas." *Revue celtique* 15:272–336, 418–484; 16:31–83, 135–167, 269–312.
Thompson, S. 1955. *Motif-Index of Folk-Literature*. Rev. ed. 6 vols. Bloomington.
Thurneysen, R., ed. 1935. *Scéla Mucce Meic Dathó*. Mediaeval and Modern Irish Series 6. Dublin.
Watkins, C. 1995. *How to Kill a Dragon: Aspects of Indo-European Poetics*. New York.

# 7

# Common Grief

## Weeping Over Hector and Rāma[1]

Nikolay P. Grintser

One of the main advantages of the line of inquiry opened by the path-breaking works of Milman Parry and Albert Lord is its comparative dimension. Formula and theme become not only distinct matrices for analyzing a given epic text or a given tradition; these notions also supply scholars with patterns for formal comparison between various texts and various traditions. The idea of formula underlies the present studies of the Indo-European poetic language,[2] while the category of theme provides a firm foundation not just for confronting at random disjointed elements of poetic content—motifs, characters, etc.—but for comparing clear-cut poetic structures parallel both in their subject and organization. I will try to give an example of this possibility of comparison, both on the level of formula and theme, between the Greek and Indic epic traditions. I argue that one of the main goals of such a comparison (and, at the same time, one of the most decisive proofs justifying it) is the elucidation through it of problematic aspects in each of the traditions compared. In my case, these would be problems concerning the Homeric text and its interpretation.

I have chosen for my case study the theme of lament over a hero's corpse in Greek and Sanskrit traditions because of the important role lament has played in the study of both Greek poetic culture and epic poetry more generally. In Greek tradition as such, the structure of ritual lament in Greek culture from Homer up to modern times has been thoroughly investigated in the classic work of Margaret Alexiou (2002). Since then, a number of works have appeared dealing

1 I would like to express my sincere gratitude to David Elmer and to the anonymous reader of this volume for many suggestive remarks that proved to be very useful in revising my paper. Certainly, all remaining faults and inconsistencies are my own.

2 See the foundational work of Schmitt 1967, with its continuation in Watkins 1995 and Costa 1998.

with Greek lament in both diachronic and synchronic perspectives.[3] Within studies of the latter type, several monographs have appeared containing detailed analyses of various types of ancient Greek literary, especially epic, lament.[4] In more general terms, the folk genre of lament has often been understood as the most important stage in the generic evolution of epic. It was marked as such already by Cecil Maurice Bowra in his *Heroic Poetry* (1952). Albert Lord himself took lament as one of the most vivid examples of a traditional ritual song and, again, he used Iliadic laments as an example of how folk songs could be transformed into epic form.[5] Recently, the complex interrelations between folk lament and epic have been investigated by several scholars, for example by Katharine Derderian (2001) and Reyes Bertolín Cebrián (2006). A comparative perspective might well cast some additional light upon this much-discussed topic.[6]

Indic tradition gives rich material for such a comparison: it is well known that in the *Mahābhārata* alone the entirety of Book 11—the *Stri Parva* (*Book of the Women*)—consists practically of laments only. I would like to say here that in my treatment of Indic material (and certainly not only in that) I am very much indebted to my late father, Pavel Grintser, a leading Russian Sanskritologist. In his study of Indic epic laments he distinguished between the narrative frame, describing the behavior and actions of the mourner, and the lament itself, which is divided into segments of praise, complaint, and reproach that alternate freely without any rigid structure.[7] As for Homeric laments, their compositional structure has been frequently analyzed, and already Dieter Lohmann showed that they are specifically marked by ring composition.[8] This is revealed, among other things, by symmetrical framing with formulaic beginnings and endings like τῇσιν δ' αὖθ' ... ἐξῆρχε γόοιο ("and among them (s)he started the lament") at the beginning and ὣς ἔφατο κλαίουσα, ἐπὶ δὲ στενάχοντο γυναῖκες ("so she said, groaning,

3 See especially, Holst-Wahrhaft 1992. On the contemporary Greek tradition, see Danforth and Tsiaras 1982, and Seremetakis 1991.

4 On epic laments, see Dué 2002, and especially the book of Tsagalis 2004, which tried to improve Alexiou's scheme of lament's structure by applying to it Albert Lord's category of "theme." Certainly, laments also remain in the focus of the analysis of Greek tragedy. See Loraux 2002, Schauer 2002, and Dué 2006.

5 See Lord 1991:110–111.

6 The interest in lament has been also stimulated by gender studies. As both in ancient and living folk traditions, laments are performed mostly by women (see e.g. Vidan 2003 on laments in Bosnian female songs); it has been argued that lament reflects some specific female world outlook contrasted to the traditionally "heroic" (and thus, male) epic perspective (on that, see Murnaghan 1999; Sourvinou-Inwood 2004:167–170; Perkell 2008). The article by B. Weinbaum (2001) claiming that female tradition based on lament shaped the entire body of classical Western literature could be cited as the most radical example of such an approach.

7 Grintser 1978.

8 Lohmann 1970:108–112.

and women cried in response") at the end. One might find similar formulas in the narrative framing of Indic laments; for instance, when Yudhisthira stops his mourning over Karna's corpse, "all men and women suddenly wailed in reply" (*tato vineduḥ sahasā strīpuṃsās* — 11.27.22).[9] This parallel may be traced back to the ancient ritual practice of antiphonal lament of the leader and the chorus.[10] In this ritual context, the aforementioned formula ἐπὶ δὲ στενάχοντο γυναῖκες—where γυναῖκες "women" may be replaced by πολῖται "citizens" or γέροντες "elders," as at *Iliad* 22.429 and 19.338—should be understood, as Deborah Beck has argued, as "cried, groaned in response," not just "groaned after him."[11] The same is true for the verb ἐξάρχω in the formula ἐξῆρχε γόοιο, where it certainly means not just "to begin," but as Christos Tsagalis supposes, also "to act as a leader" of the mourning chorus.[12] Here the sequence of the three laments of Andromache, Hecabe, and Helen over Hector's corpse in Book 24 of the *Iliad* is quite suggestive. Each of the three "solo parts" is introduced by ἐξάρχω, although all three of them are included within one and the same female lament defined by one and the same "term," γόος.[13] One might cite as a parallel the lament of the Muses over the corpse of Achilles in Book 24 of the *Odyssey*, when they grieve for nine days singing "in turn" (ἀμειβόμεναι).[14] As for the sequence of the Iliadic laments, it also turns out to be rather significant. When Hecabe replaces Andromache, taking from her the role of the main mourner (reflected

9 All quotations from Indic epics are given according to the following critical editions: *Mahābhārata, the Great Epic of India*, vv. 1–17 (Poona, 1927–1966); *The Vālmīki-Rāmāyaṇa*, vv. 1–7 (Baroda, 1960–1975).

10 Cf. Alexiou 2002:22.

11 Beck 2005:245–247.

12 Tsagalis 2004:69.

13 The terminology of lament has caused some discord among scholars. In *Iliad* 24 the sequence of three women's γόοι is preceded by the appearance of certain "singers" (ἀοιδοί) who are called "the beginners (ἔξαρχοι) of lament," where "lament" is denoted by a different term, θρῆνος (*Iliad* 24.720–722). Later on, this very word became the general term for ritual lament (cf., for instance, Sophocles *Electra* 88). The θρῆνος-γόος dichotomy is often treated as an opposition of funeral songs of male professionals to the extemporaneous shrieking and crying of female relatives (Alexiou 2002:12, Tsagalis 2004:6). The opposition is stressed by the fact that γόος is always given in direct speech, whereas θρῆνος is rendered indirectly (Nagy 1979:12). However, this dichotomy doesn't seem universal; for instance, Achilles in *Odyssey* 24.60–61 is wept over by quite professional female mourners, that is, the Muses, who perform θρῆνος. It seems that epic burial presumes the possible participation of some singers whose task might have been to sing the glory of the deceased. It is worth noting that the ἀοιδοί of *Iliad* 24 are also accompanied by the wailing of women (ἐπὶ δὲ στενάχοντο γυναῖκες, 24.722); the same formula recurs just a few lines later in the description of Andromache's "non-professional" lament (24.746). These considerations might lead to the conclusion that θρῆνος and γόος do not differ so much in their contents and manner of performance. In fact, it is only γόος that is described at any length in the Homeric poems; θρῆνος is usually only mentioned (Derderian 2001:33ff.).

14 Pucci 1993 argued also for the antiphonal nature of the laments of Briseis and Achilles over the corpse of Patroclus in *Iliad* 17.282–338.

in the use of ἐξάρχω), she appears to follow the ritual mentioned in the Sanskrit *Stri Parva*: "Reproaching you in such a way, the best of the ladies stopped, but the other wives pick up her lament as if she were their daughter-in-law" (*ty evaṃ garhayitvaiṣā tūṣṭīm āste varāṅganā / tām etām anuśocanti sapatnyaḥ svām iva snuṣām*, *Mahābhārata* 24.20). Here we seem to be dealing with a ritual rule according to which the dead man should be mourned by his widow, but if she for some reason stops or pauses in the course of the lament, it should be taken up and continued by her mother-in-law. As Hecabe in the *Iliad* also follows this rule, the Greek parallel may point at the possibility of reconstructing it already on the Indo-European level.

It is worth noting that both Andromache and Hecabe are mourning for Hector not for the first time in the *Iliad*. One might notice that Andromache's final lament is anticipated already in her speech to Hector (alive then) in Book 6;[15] it is interesting, therefore, that in Book 6 Hector meets with all three of his future mourners but in a different order: first with Hecabe, and then with Helen and Andromache.[16] Moreover, in Book 22, immediately after the hero's death, he is mourned first by Priam and then by Hecabe and Andromache. Priam's speech is not specified as a γόος, although he acts like other mourners performing a lament (not only using typical phraseology but, for instance, rolling in dust out of grief, as both Greek and Indic mourners do), and after his words we have a variant of the standard formula for concluding a lament: ὣς ἔφατο κλαίων, ἐπὶ δὲ στενάχοντο πολῖται ("So he spoke, grieving, and his fellow-citizens wailed in response," 22.429).[17] As for Hecabe, her speech starts with the usual formulaic qualification ἐξῆρχε γόοιο (22.430) and almost ends with the usual closural formula: the final line begins, as is regular, ὣς ἔφατο κλαίουσα (437). But instead of the expected ἐπὶ δὲ στενάχοντο γυναῖκες we have ἄλοχος δ' οὔ πώ τι πέπυστο ("but the spouse didn't know anything yet"). Anybody brought up upon oral-formulaic theory should know what a striking effect is achieved when a well-known part of a well-known formulaic line is replaced by unusual phrasing. The audience is immediately alerted to be most attentive to the contents of this "unforeseen" part of the verse.[18] Hence, we may assume that the singer

15 Cf. Tsagalis 2004:120ff. on Andromache's final lament as a sort of response to her own words during the meeting with Hector. On the generic proximity of Andromache's speech in Book 6 to lament, see Foley 1999:188–196. It is worth noting that, in general, a great majority of female speeches by Homer tend to be rather close to laments (Murnaghan 1999; Dué 2002:5).

16 On the symmetry of Books 6 and 24, see Macleod 1982:140.

17 Therefore, some of the scholars treat Priam's speech as a formal lament (see Pantelia 2002:24).

18 This might be true also for a single epithet implanted into a formulaic frame. So M. Edwards treats the epithet λευκώλενος "white-armed" in Andromache's lament in Book 24.723 (τῇσιν δ' Ἀνδρομάχη λευκώλενος ἦρχε γόοιο) as specifically aimed at creating a particularly tragic picture: "It is hard not to think that the change of the adjective is intended to evoke more vividly

here wished to draw attention to the fact that the ritual sequence of lament ("wife first") has been broken, and Hecabe has replaced Andromache as the first mourner.[19]

This supposition is confirmed by the following lament by Andromache herself, which is the most extensive one and ends with the proper concluding formula, ὣς ἔφατο κλαίουσα, ἐπὶ δὲ στενάχοντο γυναῖκες (22.515). Her speech, full of pain and sorrow, is defined as "lament" by the participle γοόωσα "lamenting," but her action is given a specific characteristic by the additional modifier ἀμβλήδην (ἀμβλήδην γοόωσα, 22.476). This adverb ἀμβλήδην is a Homeric hapax having a rather obvious morphological structure (ἀμβλήδην < ἀνά ,"up," + βάλλω "throw"). It is usually interpreted by commentators as something like "with deep sobs."[20] The semantic shift seems to be rather problematic. In later usage ἀμβλήδην presumes an action that is done anew (cf. Aratus *Phaenomena* 1069–1070: πάντα δέξαμεναι, πάλιν αὖτις ἀναβλήδην ὀχέωνται ["after mating with the male they mate again"], as opposed to the usual practice of mating only once). Moreover, in the *Iliad* itself we have the cognate noun ἀνάβλησις with the rather certain meaning of "delay," as at *Iliad* 24.655: ἀνάβλησις λύσιος νεκροῖο γένηται ("there is a delay with releasing the corpse"; cf. *Iliad* 2.380). In my view, the unique Homeric expression ἀμβλήδην γοόωσα bears the same semantics: Andromache mourns "with delay," both because she didn't know about her husband's death and because, after knowing about it, she fell down unconscious.[21] In the ritual context, it means that the first person to pronounce the γόος was not she but her mother-in-law, a fact

the picture of her bare arms around the corpse" (Edwards 1987:314). Tsagalis 2004:62 perceives in this case (in J. M. Foley's terms) "immediate referentiality combined with its traditional one."

19 In that case, the particle δέ in the second part of the line (ἄλοχος δ'οὔ πώ τι πέπυστο) should bear causative sense: "So she said wailing, *because* the wife didn't know yet." Cf. Chantraine 1981:357–358.

20 Tsagalis 2004:57. Understood in such a way, ἀμβλήδην turns out to be quite close to another, much more frequently signaled characteristic of lament: it is semantically similar to the epithet ἁδινός (sometimes translated as "sobbing") that is quite common in the opening lines of laments. Cf. *Iliad* 18.316 = 13.18: τοῖσι δὲ Πηλεΐδης ἁδινοῦ ἐξῆρχε γόοιο ("the son of Peleus began the sobbing lament among them"; cf. 22.430 = 24.747 of Hecabe). The adverbs ἁδινῶς and ἁδινόν, ἁδινά in an adverbial sense, are also used in the context of lamentation (*Iliad* 18.124, 19.314, *Odyssey* 24.317, etc.). But, in this case, the semantic development from "dense, thick" to something like "vehement, unceasing" seems more feasible.

21 In doing so, she behaves exactly like her Indic counterparts usually do (cf. *Mahābhārata* XI 17.1, 16.14–15, 21.10, 15.11; *Rāmāyaṇa* VI 32.6, 93.5 etc.). At that moment, she can't fall upon the body of the deceased and hold his head in her hands as she will do in *Iliad* 24.723–724. This ritual behavior also has parallels in Indic tradition (e.g. *Mahābhārata* XI 20. 4–18; *Rāmāyaṇa* VI 113.7, 114. 8). In the *Iliad*, Briseis also embraces the body of Patroclus (19.484). See Neumann 1965:89, 196 on this ritual gesture.

that has already been stressed by the variation of the formulaic line at the end of Hecabe's lament.

The sequence of laments in Book 22, having Andromache at the end, follows the rule once proposed by Johannes Kakridis, according to which, when a number of relatives or friends addresses a person, the closest and dearest (in our case, Andromache) is the last to speak.[22] The sequence of laments in Book 24, however, contradicts this principle: here Hector's widow speaks first, and the wailing at his funeral is finished by his sister-in-law, Helen.[23] But the parallels with Indic tradition show that, apart from literary considerations, we are dealing here with an ancient ritual scheme reproduced in the last book of the *Iliad* and (markedly) inverted in Book 22.

Together with its narrative frame (consisting of description of the mourner's actions and opening/closing formulas), the lament forms a tripartite structure. The same is true for the lament proper, which usually consists of 1) address to the deceased, 2) narrative, and 3) renewed address.[24] The direct addresses to the deceased at the beginning and the end of a lament are characteristic also for Indic epic. Compare, for example, in *Rāmāyaṇa* the brief lament of Ravana over his killed son beginning, "Alas! My child, the chief of the army of demons, having extraordinary might! Having conquered Indra, how have you

22 See Kakridis 1949:19–20 on this "ascending scale of affection." On the other hand, belatedness of Andromache's lament could be interpreted as a specific device making the audience intensely anticipate her appearance. Additionally, with such a sequence, the singer avoids exact duplication of the laments in Books 22 and 24. See Segal 1971b, Beck 2005:255.

23 Helen's lament (*Iliad* 24.761–776), being clearly opposed to those of Andromache and Hecabe (see Richardson 1993:350), emphasizes the symmetry existing between Book 6 and 24 (cf. Macleod 1982:149). On the one hand, the figure of Helen is specifically connected in the *Iliad* with the theme of war and, hence, with the posthumous glory of warriors established and proclaimed in songs. Thus, her lament, together with those of the other two, is the first song for the glory of Hector (Pantelia 2002). On the other hand, her taking part in the funerary rites may be interpreted as a sort of establishing of her own status that grows more and more important in the course of the poem (see Roisman 2006:28–32). Similarly, as Dué 2002:76 has argued, Briseis by her lamenting over the body of Patroclus (*Iliad* 19.282–301) also tries to maintain her role in Achilles' house. It is not by chance, therefore, that Helen constantly points at her family relations with Hector himself and his next of kin; her speech is permeated by kinship terminology: δαέρων φίλτατε ("dearest of brothers-in-law"); πόσις ("husband"); ἄλλος ... δαέρων ἢ γαλόων ἢ εἰνατέρων ("another of my brothers-in-law or sisters-in-law"); ... ἢ ἑκυρή, ἑκυρὸς δὲ πατὴρ ὣς ἤπιος αἰεί ("... or my mother-in-law—my father-in-law has always been like a tender father"). The importance of stressing within the lament family relations with the deceased was underlined already by A. Fingerle in his study of epic speeches (Fingerle 1939:167). See Suzuki 1989:21–29 and Taplin 1992:212–218 on the parallelism between Helen and Briseis in their role and functions.

24 Cf. Alexiou 2002:132–135, Holst-Warhaft 1992:112, Tsagalis 2004:15. This tripartite scheme could be related to the analogous structure of funerary ritual (Garland 1985:21) and, in a general ritual context, could be compared with the tripartite structure (invocation—narrative—supplication) of ancient hymns (Alexiou 2002:133–134, Tsagalis 2004:30).

been subjected to the power of Lakṣmaṇa now?" and concluding, "Deserting us without taking away my tormentation, while Sugrīva, Lakṣmaṇa and Rāghava are still alive, where have you gone?" (VI 92.6–7, 15, trans. K. M. Murthy). But one might notice that such addresses could be perceived throughout the entire lament, so that it is rather hard to draw the border between the narrative part and the final address (cf., for instance, the laments of Uttara over Abhimanyu in *Mahābhārata* XI 20.4–27 or that of Mandodari, the wife of Ravana in *Rāmāyaṇa* VI 113.3–86). Indeed, the same continuous addressing of the dead can be observed in Homer as well: in fact, this is true for all three laments for Hector in *Iliad* Book 24. One might say that the ring compositional scheme can be rather loose, but the direct addressing of the deceased with the words of grief, praise, complaint, or reproach is the indispensable crucial element of an epic lament.

In the *Mahābhārata* and the *Rāmāyaṇa* the beginning of the lament (or sometimes its narrative frame) usually contains the description of the corpse itself, often maintaining the contrast between its condition now and before: "Those illustrious heroes who used formerly to sleep on costly beds with their limbs smeared with sandal paste and powdered aloe, alas, now sleep on the dust!" (*Mahābhārata* XI 16.33); "He who was formerly encircled by kings vying with one another to give him pleasure, alas, he, slain and lying on the ground, is now encircled by vultures! He who was formerly fanned with beautiful fans by fair ladies is now fanned by (carnivorous) birds with flaps of their wings!" (17.12–13, trans. K. M. Ganguli). We find a similar picture in Andromache's first lament over Hector: "But now by beaked ships far from your parents will writhing worms devour you, when the dogs have had their fill, as you lie a naked corpse; yet in your halls lie clothes, finely woven and fair, fashioned by the hands of women" (*Iliad* 22.508–511). Along with forming the characteristic antinomy of wonderful past and painful present, living hero and dead corpse, we have here one more subordinate motif.[25] The dead hero's body is not just lying in dirt and dust,[26] it is being devoured by worms, birds, and (wild) beasts. In Sanskrit poems we have

25 On antithesis as the basic principle of lament's structure, see Alexiou 2002:165–171. Griffin 1980:2–3, following W. Schadewaldt, made these very words of Andromache a vivid example of Homer's individual technique. Indic parallels speak, rather, for a more universal, either typologically parallel or inherited, motif.

26 It is worth noting that sometimes it is not the dead one but the mourner who is described in such a way. For example, in the *Iliad* Achilles, "the great one, was lying in the dust, stretched far and wide" (αὐτὸς δ' ἐν κονίῃσι μέγας μεγαλωστὶ τανυσθεὶς κεῖτο, *Iliad* 18.26–27, cf. 16.775–776) when grieving over Patroclus. The same parallelism between mourner and mourned is a constant feature of Indic laments (see Grintser 1978:29–31). Therefore, this Iliadic scene need not be taken with Neo-Analysts as a specific borrowing from the actual scene of Achilles' death in the Cycle (*pace* Seaford 1995:170).

here mainly vultures and jackals (e.g. *Mahābhārata* XI 17.13–15) but also hawks, kites, and dogs and in Homer, as a rule, dogs and vultures (γῦπες).

Mutilation of Hector's corpse becomes the prominent theme in the final books of the *Iliad*, making not only the characters but also readers and commentators express some hard feelings about Achilles' treatment of his dead enemy or try to find some excuse for his cruelty. Comparative parallels could prompt us to look at the problem from a slightly different viewpoint. The motif of beasts devouring dead corpses on the battlefield naturally is not limited to Indic or Greek epic. For instance, Francis Magoun had identified it as one of the permanent themes of Anglo-Saxon epic poetry.[27] Certainly, in the *Iliad* it is not confined to Hector alone, as Charles Segal has shown.[28] Already in the famous proem to the poem, Achilles is said to make the heroes become "the spoil for dogs and birds of every kind." This is the usual threat that a hero may address to his opponent, as done by Agamemnon (2.393), Athena (8.379) and Hector himself (13.831–832; 15.351). This is the fate Hector promises for Patroclus' body after he kills Achilles' friend (17.125–127); it is from this outrageous abuse that Ajax, Menelaus, Athena, and Iris call on the Greeks to save the body of the dead hero (17.241, 255, 558; 18.179–180). It is worth noting that Priam, in his turn, just before his son's encounter with Achilles, longs for the hateful Greek to be torn apart by vultures and dogs (αἴθε θεοῖσι φίλος τοσσόνδε γένοιτο / ὅσσον ἐμοί· τάχα κέν ἑ κύνες καὶ γῦπες ἔδοιεν / κείμενον ["I wish that he were as much loved by the gods as he is by me! Then would the dogs and vultures speedily devour him as he lay unburied!"], 22.1–43), and at the same time draws a picture appropriate for his future lament over Hector, imagining that his own body will be devoured by dogs (22.66). To close the list, Hecabe foretells the gloomy fate of Hector himself: "by the ships of the Argives will swift dogs devour you" (Ἀργείων παρὰ νηυσὶ κύνες ταχέες κατέδονται, 22.89).

It is quite clear that this recurrent motif becomes a symbol of (pitiful, unworthy) death, and Achilles (22.335–336, 348, 354) just "picks up" an idea frequently expressed by other characters. Only, in his case, unlike all others, he transforms the symbolic metaphor, the potential wish, into actual deed. The death of a hero is the moment of culmination of his heroic achievements, the implementation of his heroic choice, like the one Achilles makes between a long happy life and posthumous glory. In fact, death *is* this "imperishable fame," κλέος ἄφθιτον, as the latter begins at the moment of death. At the same time, death is the moment of utmost grief, of the mighty hero's downfall. Lament transforms this two-sidedness of epic death into the contrasting images of the

27 Magoun 1955.

28 Segal 1971a.

hero's past beauty and power and his present miserable condition. The death of Hector is *the* death of the *Iliad*, anticipating both the future death of Achilles and the fall of Troy. As such, it is marked with a specially elaborated system of laments, making Hector's figure a personification of Trojan hope and Trojan might now lost forever. It may not be an accident, therefore, that the universally pitiful picture of a hero's body torn by beasts also becomes somewhat real in the case of Hector, so that the main death of the poem can receive the most impressive and "justified" mourning. In this respect, Achilles somehow "helps" his main enemy to get the top lamentation inside the *Iliad*. What initially was no more than a common formula of lament develops into a central image and a striking theme of the entire poem.

The idea of the hero's corpse being devoured by beasts can be traced back also to another motif typical of lament. That is the reproach addressed to the murderer—not just for the killing itself but for doing it in an unrighteous way or for some improper behavior before or after it. So Hecabe curses Achilles both for maltreating Hector's body and for selling her other sons into slavery (*Iliad* 24.751–756). In a similar way, in the *Mahābhārata* Gandhari blames Bhimasena for drinking blood from the corpse of her son Duhshasana, who has been killed by Bhima (XI 18.28). The reproaches may concern the way the killer performed the killing: so Gandhari blames Bhima for the illicit blow by which he killed her eldest son, Duryodhana (13.17–19, cf. 24.4–16). There are parallel cases also in Greek tradition—the most obvious is, however, not from the epic but the lament of Electra and Orestes in Aeschylus' *Choephori* (491ff.).[29]

The reproaches could be addressed not to the murderer but to the dead hero himself. They may be general, of the "Why did you desert me" type (Andromache to Hector in *Iliad* 22.481–484 or Uttara to Abhimanyu in *Mahābhārata* XI 20.14), or more specific, for example, "You promised something and didn't fulfill the promise" (Briseis to Patroclus in *Iliad* 18.295–300 or Sītā to Rāma in *Rāmāyaṇa* VI 32.21). One most remarkable instance of such an address is the question, "Why don't you talk to me?" which we come across already in Tablet VIII of the Akkadian *Epic of Gilgamesh*, when Gilgamesh grieves over Enkidu: "You are lost in the dark and cannot hear me!" (trans. N. K. Sandars). In Indic epic poems this thought is usually expressed by the formula, "Why don't you answer me? (*kiṃ māṃ na pratibhāṣase*: Sītā to Rāma in *Rāmāyaṇa* VI 32.21), with many variations, e.g. "Why don't you answer me, brother, when I am weeping over you?" (*vilapantaṃ ca māṃ bhrātaḥ kimarthaṃ nābhibhāṣase*: Rāma to Lakṣmaṇa in *Rāmāyaṇa* VI 102.21). In the *Iliad* (24.741–745), we have it in the lament of Andromache:

[29] On the tight links connecting tragic laments with epic and folklore, see Loraux 2002:47, 68, etc. and Dué 2006:50ff.

> ἀρητὸν δὲ τοκεῦσι γόον καὶ πένθος ἔθηκας
> Ἕκτορ· ἐμοὶ δὲ μάλιστα λελείψεται ἄλγεα λυγρά.
> οὐ γάρ μοι θνῄσκων λεχέων ἐκ χεῖρας ὄρεξας,
> οὐδέ τί μοι εἶπες πυκινὸν ἔπος, οὗ τέ κεν αἰεὶ
> μεμνῄμην νύκτάς τε καὶ ἤματα δάκρυ χέουσα.

> and accursed grief and sorrow have you brought upon your parents, Hector; and for me beyond all others will woeful sorrows be left. For at your death you did not stretch out your hands to me from your bed, nor speak to me any word full of meaning that I might have recalled night and day with shedding of tears.

It is worth noting here another motif that proves to be common to the Greek and Indic traditions. This is the comparison between the grief of a widow and that of the parents of the deceased, which Andromache makes here in claiming that her sorrow is much deeper. Interestingly enough, we have the same pattern present in the *Rāmāyaṇa* where the exemplary wife of India, Sītā, is twice mourning over her allegedly killed husband, Rāma. In both cases she is especially concerned about the hero's mother, Kausalya (*Rāmāyaṇa* VI 32.25–27, 48.20–21), but, comparing her pain to the mother's grief, she says, quite contrary to Andromache: "I do not repent so much for Rāma and Lakṣmaṇa or for myself or even my mother but for my unfortunate mother-in-law, Kausalya" (VI 48.20). Thus, we may assume such a comparison to be a universal motif for archaic lament, one that could be used differently on different occasions. Moreover, the difference between Greek and Indic usage may be treated as an additional hint at the various stages of epic development that those poems reflect, the Indic counterpart, with its emphasis on respect for parents and elders in general, reflecting a much more "ethicized" version of epic values. On the other hand, Andromache's preference of conjugal bonds over blood ties could seem rather suggestive in light of this opposition's further treatment in Greek tragedy, in particular (with the *Oresteia* as the most vivid example).

Among a lot of other thematic parallels that could be perceived in Greek and Indic epic laments, I would like to draw attention only to one more. That is the idea of early, premature death. In *Stri Parva* it permeates Gandhari's lament in its entirety and is stressed specifically when she is grieving about the younger generation of heroes, "the sons of the sons" (*Mahābhārata* XI 20.31–32, 25.26–27); Sītā weeps over the false image of the dead Rāma: "O, Rāma! It was mentioned even by soothsayers that your life span is lengthy. O, Rāma! Their words are wrong. You are short lived" (*Rāmāyaṇa* VI 32.12). Andromache starts her lament in Book 24 of the *Iliad* in a similar way: "Husband, perished out of your life you are, still in your youth" (725: ἆνερ ἀπ' αἰῶνος νέος ὤλεο). The same idea is maintained by Priam when he grieves over his sons whom Achilles killed in their prime (22.423: τόσσους γάρ μοι παῖδας ἀπέκτανε τηλεθάοντας), and by Thetis in her "prospective" lament[30] over destined-to-die Achilles, who "shot up like a sapling; when I had reared him like a tree in a rich orchard plot [I sent him off to fight]" (18.56–57 = 437–438: ὃ δ' ἀνέδραμεν ἔρνεϊ ἶσος· / τὸν μὲν ἐγὼ θρέψασα φυτὸν ὣς γουνῷ ἀλωῆς). Here we observe a metaphorical transformation, whereby the hero is described literally as a plant faded away. The same image can be perceived in Sanskrit texts, for instance, "two brothers of Avanti, Vinda and Anuvinda, lying there on the field, like two blossoming *shala* trees in the spring overthrown by the tempest" (*Mahābhārata* XI 25.26).

Following Gregory Nagy,[31] I would like to refer this common image to the vegetation imagery perceived in the already mentioned Indo-European formula "imperishable fame," as in the Sanskrit phrase *śrávaḥ ... ákṣitam* (*Rig-Veda* I 9.7 bc), which has a famous and much-discussed parallel in Greek, κλέος ἄφθιτον.[32] As Nagy has shown, the φθι- stem in the Greek epithet denotes exactly the idea of "fading away, wilting" of plants, and the notion of "imperishable fame" thus "conveys the *cultural* negation of a *natural* process, the growing and the wilting of plants, and also, by extension, the life and the death of mortals" (Nagy 1979:184). Moreover, we may think of the lamentation context as a possible place where this "negation" could have taken place, as the lament is both acknowledging the end of the hero's physical existence and proclaiming his past and future glory. Containing this imagery, it is not by chance that lament, on the whole, and Thetis' γόος, in particular, was linked by Nagy and then by others with the notion of immortality and κλέος as main themes of the epic.[33] The Indic parallels do nothing but support the idea that the formula itself could be hypothetically related to the genre of lamentation. "Imperishable fame" vs. a hero's "fading away" would be a

30 Thetis' speech addressed to the Nereids at the beginning of *Iliad* Book 18 is clearly anticipating her future lament over Achilles, which should take place, however, after the events of the *Iliad*; it is mentioned in *Odyssey* Book 24. The passage in *Iliad* 18 was for this reason treasured by the Neo-Analysts, beginning from Wilamowitz, and then by Schadewaldt, Kakridis (1949:65–75), and Kullmann (1960:38–39), who argued that it was borrowed from Cyclic tradition, either from the *Aethiopis* or from a putative *Achilleis* or *Memnonis*. However, Lohmann 1970:54 has shown how neatly this speech fits into the poetic structure of the Homeric text. Moreover, as the example of Hector (whom we have just shown to be also lamented "in advance" by Andromache, Priam, and Hecabe) proves, such an anticipation of a hero's death is characteristic of the *Iliad* (it is sufficient to mention here how often approaching death is foretold to Achilles by his mother Thetis, his enemy Hector, and even by his own horse).

31 See Nagy 1979:174–189.

32 Several scholars (see Floyd 1980, Finkelberg 1986 and 2007) have attacked the very idea of the Homeric phrase κλέος ἄφθιτον being an Indo-European inheritance. However, I find the arguments of Nagy 1990:122–127 and Watkins 1995:173–178 on that point most persuasive.

33 See e.g. Tsagalis 2004:150–151.

perfect antithesis, a compositional device that is, as Calvert Watkins (1995) has demonstrated,[34] so characteristic both of folklore and epic lament, as well as of Indo-European poetic language on the whole.

In connection with the lamentation theme, I would like to mention one lexical parallel that can also be traced back to the Indo-European level. In Sanskrit poems the description of a dead hero or an address to him often contains the formula *hataḥ śete* "he lies slain." We have here the collocation of two verbal roots, *han-* "to kill" (in participial form) and *śi-* "to lie" that can be reconstructed as Indo-European *$g^{u}$hen-* and **kei-*. Their mutual link and interchange was thoroughly analyzed by Calvert Watkins in his persuasive reconstruction of the formulaic structure of the Indo-European poetic description of a hero killing his enemy.[35] As a possible parallel he quoted a passage from Hecabe's lament where she describes Hector in the following way: νῦν δέ μοι ἑρσήεις καὶ πρόσφατος ἐν μεγάροισι / κεῖσαι, τῷ ἴκελος ὅν τ' ἀργυρότοξος Ἀπόλλων / οἷς ἀγανοῖσι βέλεσσιν ἐποιχόμενος κατέπεφνεν ("all dewy-fresh you lie in my halls as if you were newly slain, like one whom Apollo of the silver bow has assailed with his gentle shafts and slain," *Iliad* 24.757–759). Watkins convincingly argued that Greek πρόσφατος (the semantics of which are often debated by commentators[36]) should also be traced back to the Indo-European **$g^{u}$hen-*, meaning "newly slain." He also paid attention to some variations of the formula both in Homer and in later poetry. In *Iliad* 19.31–32 we have a cognate compound in the expression "men slain by Ares" (φῶτας ἀρηϊφάτους) in a strikingly similar context. The passage is not a lament, but here Thetis consoles Achilles and says that she will protect dead Patroclus (who "lies" [κεῖται] on the ground) from flies that are eager to devour the bodies of heroes "slain by Ares." So the situation described is akin to the lamentation motif analyzed before: a dead hero's body is devoured by birds, beasts, worms, and the like. Moreover, the examples Watkins drew from later sources come directly from laments. In Sophocles' *Ajax*, lines 898–899, Tekmessa uses a similar expression (changing one of the stems but not the meaning), at the very beginning of her mourning dialogue with the chorus: "Here lies Ajax newly slain" (Αἴας ὅδ' ἡμῖν ἀρτίως νεοσφαγὴς κεῖται). In Aeschylus' *Seven against Thebes,* Antigone and Ismene address their dead brothers with the expression πρόκεισαι κατακτάς, changing the meaning from passive into active: "you lie, having slain." One might add that corresponding Indic formulas are also frequently used in epic laments, mainly in their opening parts: for instance, Gandhari, in the opening of her lament for her son Vikarna,

34 Watkins 1995:176.

35 Watkins 1995:499–504.

36 In later sources it is usually understood as "fresh, recent." This meaning could be developed from "newly slain" (see Richardson 1993:357).

says that "he lies slain on the ground ... lies slain among the elephants" *(bhūmau vinihataḥ śete ... gajamadhyaṃ hataḥ śete, Mahābhārata* XI 19.1–2) and likewise when she weeps over Shalya: "here lies Shalya slain" (*eṣa śalyo hataḥ śete*, 23.1). Similar instances are numerous. A possible additional parallel to Hecabe's phrasing is that Sanskrit *śete* always occupies in these formulas the marked position at the end of the odd *padas*,[37] whereas Greek κεῖσαι in the Homeric hexameter (as well as κεῖται in tragic examples) occupies the marked position at the beginning of the verse. As for the 2nd person κεῖσαι vs. the Sanskrit 3rd person *śete*, in Indic poems we also have the 2nd person form when addressing the deceased directly: e.g. "Alas, o righteous one, you lie on the ground, slain unfairly by two foes" (*eko dvābhyāṃ hataḥ śeṣe tvam adharmeṇa dhārmikaḥ, Mahābhārata* XI 24.15). So we can tentatively restore the Indo-European poetic formula **gʷhen-to-* + **kei-* (+ personal ending) as a sort of opening for lament.[38]

So lament starts over the corpse of the hero who "lies slain" and aims (at least on a compositional and thematic, if not formulaic, level) at securing for him "imperishable fame" through praise, reproach, and blame.[39] Parallel imagery, motifs, and phrasing prove that the theme of epic lament bears in both traditions the same typology. Moreover, sometimes these parallels cast additional light on some controversial issues, like the sequence of laments within the *Iliad* or the disputed meaning of a single Greek word. On the other hand, the discrepancies can be even more telling than coincidences. The treatment of the parents/spouse opposition gave us one instance of this; I would like to end my paper with another. One idea that turns out to be quite popular with Homer is not attested in the epics of ancient India. That is the idea of getting pleasure or benefit from mourning. Achilles incites the Myrmidons to "enjoy the dire lamentation" (ὀλοοῖο τεταρπώμεσθα γόοιο, *Iliad* 23.10; cf. 23.98, 24.513), the mourners have "a yearning to wail" (ἵμερος γόοιο, 23.108, 24.507), they are satiated with lament (τώ κε κορεσσάμεθα κλαίοντέ τε μυρομένω τε, *Iliad* 22.427; cf. ἄσεσθε κλαυθμοῖο, 24.717) like they are with food or drink. One might argue that we are dealing here with remnants of ancient ritual or magic therapy[40] or

37 See Grintser 1978:29.

38 The parallels we have considered so far may certainly be regarded as typological. However, in the context of Indo-European "poetic language" theory, which traces such analogous formulas back to the proto-Indo-European language and culture, they could be interpreted as derived from this common genetic origin of Indo-European epic poetry.

39 As we have seen from both Indic and Greek examples, reproaches blaming a dead hero, e.g. for causing sorrow to his family or leaving his parents, wife, and children helpless, serve to stress additionally his premature death and his indispensability for his family, people, etc. In this respect, within epic lament, praise and blame are deeply interwoven.

40 Cf. "Priam tries to transform the bestial satiety of violence ... into the therapeutic satiety of lamentation" (Tsagalis 2004:175).

with the later process of epic aestheticization of ritual that makes lament akin to poetry with its main aim at τέρπειν "giving pleasure."[41] Be that as it may, we should assume that this idea is quite natural for the Homeric presentation of lament but proves to be totally alien to the moral values of the *Mahābhārata* and the *Rāmāyaṇa*.[42] The sages of ancient India persuaded their audience to lay the lament aside and turn to higher wisdom, like Vaishampayana does at the end of *Stri Parva*: "Dead or lost, the person that grieves for what has already occurred, obtains more grief. By indulging in grief, one increases it two-fold" (*Mahābhārata* XI 26.4). The heroes of the *Iliad* obtain such knowledge and inner comfort through the lament itself, and this difference tells us a lot not only about these two epic traditions but about the two cultures as such.

41 Derderian 2001:67–69.

42 One might argue, however, that the *Mahābhārata*, since it dedicates an entire book to the presentation of various laments, must also presume some sort of aesthetic pleasure that mourning brings along (I would like to thank David Elmer for drawing my attention to that point). It is worth noting, then, that whereas Homeric epic states "pleasure" explicitly as the utmost goal of lamentation, its Indic counterpart, if it implies it, never reveals such an implication *expressis verbis*. Once again, we may see here another sign of a more "ethicized" stage of epic development.

## Bibliography

Alexiou, M. 2002. *Ritual Lament in Greek Tradition.* 2nd rev. ed. Lanham, MD. Orig. pub. 1974, Cambridge.

Beck, D. 2005. *Homeric Conversation.* Hellenic Studies Series 14. Washington, DC.

Bertolín Cebrián, R. 2006. *Singing the Dead. A Model for Epic Evolution.* New York.

Bowra, C. M. 1952. *Heroic Poetry.* London.

Chantraine, P. 1981. *Grammaire homérique. T.II: Syntaxe.* Paris.

Costa, G. 1998. *Le origini della lingua poetica indoeuropea.* Florence.

Danforth, L., and A. Tsiaras. 1982. *The Death Rituals of Rural Greece.* Princeton.

Derderian, K. 2001. *Leaving Words to Remember: Greek Mourning and the Advent of Literacy.* Leiden.

Dué, C. 2002. *Homeric Variations on a Lament by Briseis.* Lanham, MD.

———. 2006. *The Captive Woman's Lament in Greek Tragedy.* Austin.

Edwards, M. 1987. *Homer: The Poet of the* Iliad. Baltimore.

Fingerle, A. 1939. *Typik der homerischen Reden.* Munich.

Finkelberg, M. 1986. "Is κλέος ἄφθιτον a Homeric Formula?" *Classical Quarterly* 36:1–5.

———. 2007. "More on κλέος ἄφθιτον." *Classical Quarterly* 57:341–350.

Floyd, E. D. 1980. "Κλέος ἄφθιτον: An Indo-European Perspective on Early Greek Poetry." *Glotta* 58:133–157.

Foley, J. M. 1999. *Homer's Traditional Art.* University Park, PA.

Garland, R. 1985. *The Greek Way of Death.* Ithaca.

Griffin, J. 1980. *Homer on Life and Death.* Oxford.

Grintser, P. A. 1978. "Stilisticheskoje razvertyvanije temu v sanskritskom epose" [The stylistic development of theme in Sanskrit epics]. In *Pamjatniki knizhnogo eposa*, ed. E. M. Meletinsky, 16–48. Moscow.

Holst-Warhaft, G. 1992. *Dangerous Voices: Women's Laments and Greek Literature.* New York.

Kakridis, J. 1949. *Homeric Researches.* Lund.

Kullmann, W. 1960. *Die Quellen der* Ilias. Wiesbaden.

Lohmann, D. 1970. *Die Komposition der Reden in der* Ilias. Berlin.

Loraux, N. 2002. *The Mourning Voice: An Essay on Greek Tragedy.* Ithaca.

Lord, A. B. 1991. *Epic Singers and Oral Tradition.* Ithaca.

Macleod, C. 1982. *Homer. Iliad: Book XXIV.* Cambridge.

Magoun, F. P. 1955. "The Theme of the Beasts of Battle in Anglo-Saxon Poetry." *Neuphilologische Mitteilungen* 56:81–90.

Mehta, J. M., et al., eds. 1960-1975. *The Vālmīki-Rāmāyaṇa.* 7 vols. Baroda.

Murnaghan, S. 1999. "The Poetics of Loss in Greek Epic." In *Epic Traditions in the Contemporary World: The Poetics of Community*, ed. M. Bessinger, J. Tylus, and S. Wofford, 213–220. Berkeley.

Nagy, G. 1979. *The Best of the Achaeans: Concepts of the Hero in Archaic Greek Poetry*. Baltimore. Repr. 1999.

———. 1990. *Greek Mythology and Poetics*. Ithaca.

Neumann, G. 1965. *Gesten und Gebärden in der griechischen Kunst*. Berlin.

Pantelia, M. 2002. "Helen and the Last Song for Hector." *Transactions of the American Philological Association* 132:21–27.

Perkell, C. 2008. "Reading the Laments in *Iliad* 24." In *Lament: Studies in the Ancient Mediterranean and Beyond*, ed. A. Suter, 93–117. Oxford.

Pucci, P. 1993. "Antiphonal Lament Between Achilles and Briseis." *Colby Quarterly* 29:258–272.

Richardson, N. 1993. *The Iliad: A Commentary* VI. Cambridge.

Roisman, H. 2006. "Helen in the *Iliad*; *Causa Belli* and Victim of War: From Silent Weaver to Public Speaker." *American Journal of Philology* 127:1–36.

Schauer, M. 2002. *Tragisches Klagen: Form und Funktion der Klagedarstellung bei Aischylos, Sophokles und Euripides*. Tübingen.

Schmitt, R. 1967. *Dichtung und Dichtersprache in indogermanischer Zeit*. Wiesbaden.

Seaford, R. 1995. *Reciprocity and Ritual: Homer and Tragedy in the Developing City-State*. Oxford.

Segal, C. P. 1971a. *The Theme of the Mutilation of Corpse in the* Iliad. Leiden.

———. 1971b. "Andromache's Anagnorisis: Formulaic Artistry in *Iliad* 22.437–476." *Harvard Studies in Classical Philology* 75:33–57.

Seremetakis, C. 1991. *The Last Word: Women, Death and Divination in Inner Mani*. Chicago.

Sourvinou-Inwood, C. 2004. "Gendering the Athenian Funeral: Ritual Reality and Tragic Manipulation." In *Greek Ritual Poetics*, ed. D. Yatromanolakis and P. Roilos, 161–188. Cambridge, MA.

Sukthankar, V. S., ed. 1927-1966. *Mahābhārata*. 17 vols. Poona.

Suzuki, M. 1989. *Metamorphoses of Helen: Authority, Difference, and the Epic*. Ithaca.

Taplin, O. 1992. *Homeric Soundings: The Shaping of the* Iliad. Oxford.

Tsagalis, C. 2004. *Epic Grief: Personal Laments in Homer's* Iliad. Berlin.

Vidan, A. 2003. *Embroidered with Gold, Strung with Pearls: The Traditional Ballads of Bosnian Women*. Milman Parry Collection of Oral Literature 1. Cambridge, MA.

Watkins, C. 1995. *How to Kill a Dragon. Aspects of Indo-European Poetics*. Oxford.

Weinbaum, B. 2001. "Lament Ritual Transformed into Literature: Positing Woman's Prayer as Cornerstone in Western Classical Literature." *The Journal of American Folklore* 114/451:20–39.

# PART III

# MULTIFORMITY

# 8

# The Homer Multitext and the System of Homeric Epic

CASEY DUÉ AND MARY EBBOTT

MILMAN PARRY AND ALBERT LORD'S WORK demonstrated that the oral tradition of the Homeric epics is a system that is good and useful for composition-in-performance and that also creates meaning for the audience in a special way.[1] While some oral traditions for which Parry and Lord's work has been illuminating can still be studied in performance, for the Homeric epics we rely on written texts to investigate and interpret this system. The question of how these texts should be understood, represented, and used is the inspiration for the Homer Multitext (HMT: http://www.homermultitext.org). This digital project, of which we are editors, builds upon the theory and fieldwork of Milman Parry and Albert Lord and expands their findings by presenting the surviving textual witnesses to the Homeric poems in a critical framework designed to account for and highlight the fact that they were composed and transmitted within an oral tradition of composition-in-performance. How can a digital scholarly edition provide easier access to these texts and help us to understand the system of Homeric epic better? In this essay we will give examples from two kinds of primary sources: (1) medieval manuscripts that contain not only the text of the poetry but also accompanying scholarly commentary on the poetry, called *scholia*; and (2) papyri, more fragmentary texts from a much earlier time period than the manuscripts. These examples illustrate the kinds of evidence that these texts provide for understanding and interpreting the system of Homeric poetry.

1 This paper has been revised since its presentation at the conference honoring Milman Parry in 2010 and its initial publication in *Classics@*14 in 2016. Please see the end of the essay for an update on the state of the Homer Multitext in 2020. For more on how meaning is created in performance through the interaction of the poet and audience, see especially Foley 1991, Bird 2010, and Ebbott 2020.

The Homer Multitext is a multi-dimensional, long-term, collaborative effort of many scholars that it is now starting to bear fruit, and we anticipate that it will continue to grow for years to come. We submit that our project embraces the full implications of the theory and fieldwork of Parry and Lord and extends them by taking advantage of the possibilities offered by digital editing, computational processing, and electronic publishing to present the Homeric texts in a way in which the oral, traditional nature of the epics can be better appreciated and investigated.[2] The Homer Multitext also seeks to present the textual transmission of the Homeric poems in a historical framework. As we have argued elsewhere (see especially Dué and Ebbott 2009 and 2010 and Dué 2019), such a framework is needed to account for the full reality of the complex medium of oral composition-in-performance in which these epics evolved over time and for the different historical contexts in which texts of these epics were produced. The Homer Multitext seeks to provide ways to explore these contexts both synchronically and diachronically. Using technology that takes advantage of the best available practices and open source standards that have been developed for digital publications in a variety of fields, the Homer Multitext offers free access to a library of texts and images that are licensed for scholarly re-use and to tools to allow readers to discover and engage with the Homeric tradition.

We and our principal collaborators on this project (which include the project architects, Christopher Blackwell and Neel Smith, and the associate editors, Douglas Frame, Leonard Muellner, and Gregory Nagy) assert that a multitext edition is a methodologically superior way of representing the transmission of an oral tradition, in that it does not seek to establish a single original from which all other surviving texts derive but rather endeavors to make accessible as many historical instantiations of the text as possible, together with their historical contexts.[3] In this belief we have been profoundly influenced by the fieldwork and scholarship of Albert Lord, who wrote that "the word *multiform* is more accurate than 'variant,' because it does not give preference or precedence

2 We want to thank our collaborators Christopher Blackwell and Neel Smith, who have created and continue to develop the technological infrastructure of the Homer Multitext and who also helped us in writing the portions of this paper that address that infrastructure.

3 See Nagy 1996a:113. Nagy was in fact the first to assert the need for a multitext edition of Homer, for which his evolutionary model (laid out most recently in Nagy 2020) forms a foundation: "The ultimate purpose in drawing up this scheme is to lay the groundwork for an eventual multitext edition of Homer, one that would be expected not only to report variant readings but also relate them wherever possible to different periods in the history of textual transmission." For more on the goals and theoretical underpinnings of the Homer Multitext, see the project website (http://www.homermultitext.org) as well as Dué and Ebbott 2010:153–165, Bierl 2015:193–194, and Dué 2019.

to any one word or set of words to express an idea; instead it acknowledges that the idea may exist in several forms" (Lord 1995:23; see also Lord 2019:106).

## How Do You Edit an Oral Tradition? Multiforms and Multitext

The question that inspired the creation of the Homer Multitext is this: "How do you make a critical edition of a now-past oral tradition, like that of the Homeric *Iliad* and *Odyssey*, that spanned a thousand years or more? What is the best way to represent the textual history of songs that were created in and for performance, but survive only in textual witnesses from later eras as oral-derived texts?" As we have noted in our previous work (see especially Dué and Ebbott 2009 and 2010), the practice of textual criticism, as applied to most humanistic texts, has conventionally had the goal of recovering the original composition of the author. The work of Albert Lord has made perfectly clear, however, that in an oral tradition there is no original composition to recover and that seeking one for a song within an oral tradition "simply makes no sense" (Lord 2019:106–107).[4] Thus, the fundamental goal of textual criticism must be different in the case of the Homeric epics. At the same time, we do not have the opportunity to witness or record performances within the tradition. Thus, our goal must differ also from those who collect records of living oral traditions. Our criticism must take into account both the shift from the oral medium to the written that happened over a long span of time and the fact that the surviving textual artifacts are from an even later period of time still.

We will begin this discussion of the goals for our project by addressing the multiformity of the Homeric epics, as first articulated by Lord. This multiformity, which is natural to an oral tradition in which poetry is composed in performance, calls for a different way to think about the textual witnesses that preserve evidence of that multiformity. A digital medium still does not allow us to "hear" directly the flourishing oral tradition in which the *Iliad* and *Odyssey* were composed. But the change from printed texts and conventional textual criticism to digital media and what we describe further below as a new critical approach to our texts does afford the opportunity to think about these oral-derived texts in new ways. That is, we are investigating what new ways of *seeing* a digital medium can provide and how those changes in visualization as well as access can enable new perspectives and new questions (see also Dué and Ebbott 2019). As we will be arguing here, this shift in medium opens up new paths for

4 Gregory Nagy's evolutionary model offers a model for the textualization of the oral tradition and the relative "fixity" in our textual sources (Nagy 2020). Such a model is in keeping with Lord's arguments against searching for, or positing, an "original."

discovering and new means for evaluating the evidence for the oral tradition preserved in the textual record.

Parry and Lord's foundational work demonstrated that the fluidity and multiformity of the Homeric textual tradition are a necessary product of the process of oral recomposition-in-performance.[5] One of the most important revelations of the fieldwork of Parry and Lord is that every time the song is performed in an oral composition-in-performance tradition, it is composed anew. Parry and Lord intentionally recorded the same singer composing and performing the notionally "same" song on multiple occasions and, likewise, the "same" song composed and performed by different singers. Lord's additional fieldwork in subsequent decades allowed him to go back and record those same singers again much later in their careers. The fieldwork of Parry and Lord therefore was inherently multitextual and provides a model for how to think about multiple texts of the "same" song.

The multitextual songs that Parry and Lord recorded revealed variation, or multiformity, to be a natural feature of the compositional process. Just as the idea of the "original" makes no sense in an oral tradition, the term "variant," as employed by textual critics when evaluating witnesses to a text, is not appropriate for an oral compositional process in which the singer composes as he performs. As we have already seen, Lord has explained the difference this way: "the word *multiform* is more accurate than 'variant,' because it does not give preference or precedence to any one word or set of words to express an idea; instead it acknowledges that the idea may exist in several forms" (Lord 1995:23). Our textual criticism of Homeric epic, then, needs to distinguish what may genuinely be copying mistakes from what are performance multiforms: that is, what variations we see are very likely to be part of the system and the tradition in which these epics were composed (Dué 2001a and 2019).

Parry and Lord's work, then, asks us to consider whether the variations we find in the textual record were valid parts of the system rather than mistakes or corruptions; doing so has meant changing the practices for textual criticism of the Homeric texts. Digital editing offers the opportunity for doing just that, for creating a new kind of textual criticism, one that we have called "digital criticism" (Dué and Ebbott 2009). One way in which a digital edition can change how we study and investigate the Homeric epics is by privileging our primary sources, while simultaneously preserving them and providing greater access to them. By providing access to primary sources—that is, the surviving medieval manuscripts and their scholia, the surviving papyri, and other texts that

5 See Parry 1971, Lord 1991, Lord 1995, and Lord 2019; see also Nagy 1996a, Nagy 2002, and Bird 2010.

quote or comment on the Homeric epics—"digital criticism" redefines a critical edition as one in which readers have the same access to these materials as the editors do, with each witness and its historical context accurately represented.

Once readers have access to the witnesses just as we editors do, the nature of criticism changes. Instead of choosing just one from among multiple attested readings or even emending texts in an attempt to return to the author's "original" composition, the editor creates a framework in which the textual witnesses are easily compared, placed within their historical contexts, and connected to yet further related witnesses. This new criticism still involves meaningful comparison of witnesses but with fundamentally different aims.[6] The goal is not to choose one multiform as "right" or "original" but to show the reader that both exist, while explaining what the witnesses are and pointing the reader to other witnesses that are related: for example, that contain a particular line, that contain the same formulaic expression, or that have some other relationship to the sources that the reader has chosen, so that she can further her investigation. One challenge that this new criticism presents for editors is that editors must take into account possible differing levels of expertise among readers. Such differences in expertise mean that we can no longer rely on a practice of reference to and abbreviation of primary sources that, although previously necessary in some ways because of the limitations of space in a print medium, serves mostly to obscure what the editor is reporting to have seen in the textual witnesses she has examined.

This fundamental editorial decision—that is, to make available each historical instantiation of the *Iliad* or *Odyssey* as a whole worthy of study (in

6 We may compare the so-called "new philology" of Bernard Cerquiglini (see especially Cerquiglini 1999) which calls for understanding individual manuscripts (of whatever genre of literature) within the context of their own historical communities. In Cerquiglini's model, the study of surviving manuscripts for the purposes of reconstructing a notional "Ur text" is a distortion of the way such manuscripts actually functioned. Although Cerquiglini's ideas are not focused primarily on the problems inherent in the textual criticism of oral-derived texts, they offer further justification for the inherent value in studying each historical document that transmits Homeric poetry on its own terms. We, as editors of the Homer Multitext, do not seek to deny the value of traditional textual criticism/philology for the investigation of the origin, transmission, and significance of particular multiforms; in fact, we argue that a multitextual approach *supports* these kinds of investigations while remaining true to the implications of the fieldwork of Parry and Lord. In this way we might be said to combine "old philology" with "material philology" or "new philology" (as advocated by Drout and Kleinman 2010). In seeking to present a critical framework for oral-derived texts, we have much in common with scholars of medieval (especially French) literature, who likewise grapple with how to represent texts that in their own time were in a constant state of flux. (See also Nagy 1996a:7–38 on the concept of *mouvance* as it applies to Homeric poetry.) For more on the theoretical underpinnings of the Homer Multitext and how our goals intersect with other projects (especially those that feature digitized manuscripts), see, in addition to Dué and Ebbott 2009, Dué, Blackwell, Ebbott, and Smith 2014, and Dué 2019.

comparison with other historical instantiations)—has been the subject of criticism in Massimo Magnani's recent (2018) analysis of the strengths and weaknesses of the Homer Multitext.[7] We have argued elsewhere about the problems inherent in a typical *apparatus criticus* (see, e.g. Dué and Ebbott 2009; 2010:153–159; 2019:252–253, and further below, as well as Dué 2019:160–161), and we aim to replace the practices that seek to reconstruct a hypothesized "original" (Dué and Ebbott 2019:252).[8]

Rather than devaluing the role of editors, however, this new concept of critical digital editions makes the role of editors even more important and necessary in representing precisely what each witness contains, creating the critical framework for presenting those witnesses, and putting the primary sources in historical context and in relation to one another in ways that users with different levels of expertise can understand. Further below we examine particular multiforms that appear in Homeric papyri and in the scholia of the Venetus A manuscript of the *Iliad*, and with those examples we explain in more detail how this criticism works in practice.

Of course, not every variation that survives in our medieval manuscripts, papyri, or ancient quotations is rightly called a "multiform" or "performance variant." Indeed, from these many types of witnesses, we find a number of different kinds of variation. It is easy to find in the textual transmission of the Homeric poems examples of multiforms in which different, but equally formulaic, words and phrases are used (see further below for detailed examples of these kinds of multiforms). But there are also cases of a single word change, differences in word division or accent, and other matters of orthography. We believe that these kinds of differences, which have not been traditionally of great interest to textual critics, are important for what they can reveal about the textual tradition and the editorial practices of earlier stages of transmission.

7 See also Dué 2019:160: "Magnani is careful to point out that the unusual choices we have made as editors are grounded in the *Iliad*'s special status as a poem composed in performance, and he notes that we rely on Albert Lord's formulation that for poetry composed in performance, there is no "original" that can be reconstructed. But he laments the absence of a single text to read (the establishment of which he calls "the final objective of every philological operation") as well as the absence of a traditional apparatus criticus. Magnani concludes, "There will certainly be a moment when the critical editor will be supported or even replaced by the AI, but the task of choosing the best possible text in a methodologically correct manner cannot but remain the essential purpose of the philological activity for most of the manuscript traditions handed down by a plurality of manuscripts" (2018:100). It is not clear why the Homer Multitext approach evokes the specter of AI replacing human efforts. As we make clear here and elsewhere, our practices are intended precisely to provide texts in a methodically correct manner (which a single text with apparatus would not be for the Homeric epics) and in a way that is also more inclusive and accessible than a single text with apparatus could ever be.

8 See also Reggiani 2019 for the usefulness of a multitext approach in digital editions of papyri and manuscripts related to ancient medicine.

We resist, therefore, the notion that by refusing to screen out even orthographical or other sorts of variation we might somehow be providing too much information, or we might not be critical enough. Even what might be considered outright scribal errors—an inevitable source of variation when dealing with handwritten material—might have something interesting to tell us about how these texts were assembled and their scholia compiled. For example, an accidentally omitted verse, later copied in the margin, might reveal something about the sources from which the scribe was drawing, especially in comparison with other manuscripts. Just such an example can be found in the Venetus A at *Iliad* 5.57. This verse is not present in the manuscript's main text, but it has been written in the margin. Closer study suggests that the omission is not an accident but a carryover from the exemplar on which this manuscript is based. If our interpretation is correct, the verse in the margin is most likely the result of collation against a second source.[9] Other types of "errors" can also be revealing. Holy Cross undergraduate researcher Christine Roughan noticed that in the Venetus A, a running count of the similes in the *Iliad* is kept in the margins, but for a significant section of the poem the numbering is abandoned, only to be resumed at a much later point with the correct count. Her further investigation showed that one long sequence of missing numbers corresponds to a particular quire. That quire happens to be the one that contains the Catalogue of Ships in book 2, for which the scribe has also noted in the margins the count of each contingent's number of ships (as reported in the poetry).[10] Such details about the construction of the manuscript will no doubt be of interest to codicologists and, indeed, to anyone interested in the possible exemplars of the Venetus A.

The ancient and medieval witnesses to the *Iliad* and *Odyssey* that survive are themselves quite multiform in their presentation of the Homeric text. The tenth-century Venetus A manuscript of the *Iliad* just mentioned is an excellent example. A typical folio in the Venetus A contains twenty-five lines of the Homeric text, surrounded on three sides by a body of marginal notes, all written in the same minuscule hand. Individual comments in the main body of scholia are generally but not always preceded by lemmata in semiuncial script. In the gutters of each page and in the margins between the text and scholia are written an additional set of scholia, in the same semiuncial script as the lemmata. Outside the main column of scholia in the far outside margins of each page are sometimes additional semiuncial scholia; on a few folios these scholia are extensive. These additional scholia may be written in the shape of a cross,

9 See the blog post by Amy Koenig and Annalisa Quinn on the Homer Multitext blog: http://homermultitext.blogspot.com/2011/07/notes-on-iliad-5.html.

10 For further details, see Roughan's own explanation on the Homer Multitext blog: http://homermultitext.blogspot.com/2011/09/composition-of-venetus-numbered-similes.html.

column, or another object. Still more semiuncial scholia may be found between lines and very near the text in various places around the page. At the far edge of many pages are the traces of (very likely) two correcting hands (see for example folio 24r and Allen 1899:172–176), and from the beginning of the poem up until verse 188 of book 2 an interlinear paraphrase appears in a later (thirteenth-century) hand. Throughout this commentary, which derives from the work of the Alexandrian editors of the Homeric poems, alternative readings are adduced and debated and thereby preserved (Nagy 2004:3–39).[11]

In the following sections, we will examine first some examples of multiformity from papyri, those much earlier witnesses that exhibit the greatest multiformity. Then, in a later section ("Homeric Scholia, a Window onto the Tradition"), we will provide an example from the scholia of the Venetus A manuscript. Within our discussions of these examples, we will continue to consider multiforms and scribal choices and errors. The digital diplomatic editions in the Homer Multitext report exactly what the witnesses contain because knowing precisely what each witness records has value for understanding the whole of the historical transmission of the epics and can provide the very evidence that is needed to continue to investigate these questions and many more. In addition to providing basic access to primary sources, then, the Homer Multitext seeks to make these sources more useful for research—research that then could ask questions of these sources that we have not been able to ask before. The Homer Multitext can also be used to understand better what Parry and Lord's work has already shown. Let us begin by examining examples of the general multiform nature of the oral tradition and the ways in which it shows up in our earliest textual sources.

## Homeric Papyri, Our Oldest Witnesses

In the earliest witnesses—papyri from the third century and second century BCE or quotations in Classical authors, such as Plato or Aeschines—we find differences on the level of entire lines of the poetry. There are numerous verses in the papyri that are seemingly intrusive from the standpoint of the medieval transmission. These additional verses, the so-called plus verses, are not present in the majority of the medieval manuscripts of the *Iliad*.[12] Other verses that are canonical in the medieval manuscripts are absent from the papyri—these may

[11] Some papyrus texts have also been preserved with scholia, though these are not as extensive as those in the medieval manuscripts. See McNamee 1981, 1992, and 2007.

[12] Nagy 2004:36–38 considers the plus verses as a "most valuable test case" for the multiformity of the Homeric system. He shows the profound value for recognizing the multiformity of the system in recovering "a significant portion of the Homeric repertoire."

be termed minus verses. Students of Parry and Lord know that composition-in-performance allows for the expansion or compression of the theme or episode that the singer is performing. These plus and minus verses are evidence of what any given performance might have included, the operation of the system underlying the performance, and what the epic tradition as a notional totality comprised (Dué 2001a). Far from being "banal"[13] or "inept"[14] (and therefore not worth our consideration), we assert that these examples of compression and expansion—coming late as they do in the performance tradition yet at the same time early from the standpoint of transmission of the textual tradition—provide unique insight into the system in which the Homeric poems were composed as well as the means by which they were transmitted.

We have been developing a collection of XML-encoded editions of Homeric papyri that users will be able to search and compare against other historical witnesses (https://github.com/homermultitext/homeric_papyri). The Homeric papyri are, with the exception of some ancient quotations, the oldest surviving witnesses to the text of Homer. Some papyrus fragments predate the medieval tradition by as many as 1200 years. They give us an otherwise irrecoverable picture of the *Iliad* and *Odyssey* as they were performed and recorded in ancient times. These fragments show that the poems were performed and recorded with a considerable amount of fluidity in antiquity, as indicated by the plus and minus verses. Also prevalent is variation in the formulaic phrasing within lines, such as the presence of one noun-epithet formula in place of another. It is not until about 150 BCE that the papyrus texts begin to present a relatively more uniform text.

*Iliad* p609 (Mertens-Pack 864.1; P. Mich. 6972) is one such early papyrus that displays these kinds of multiformity. It is a palimpsest and dates to the second century BCE, making it among the earliest of the witnesses to the text of *Iliad* 10.[15] The papyrus has two columns, containing 10.421–434 and 10.445–460, in which Diomedes and Odysseus interrogate and kill the Trojan spy Dolon. The papyrus exhibits both horizontal multiformity, on the level of individual words and even whole lines, and also vertical multiformity with a so-called plus verse

13 Pelliccia 1997:46. See also Finkelberg 2000, who cites Pelliccia as well as S. West 1967 and Powell 1991 in her argument that the known variants of the *Iliad* and *Odyssey* are too restricted to be considered multiforms. Further argumentation against this view of attested multiforms can be found in Dué 2019:55–104.

14 Kirk 1985: *ad* 1.1, on a variant *Iliad* proem. Cf. Janko's (1994) criticism of Van Thiel's decision not to bracket many verses considered by Apthorp to be interpolated: "This is not progress ... the removal of such lines almost always improves the poem's literary qualities" (293).

15 On this papyrus, see also Dué and Ebbott 2010:169–173.

between 10.432 and 10.434.[16] Many of these multiforms are not supported by any other extant manuscript or witness, and yet the variations themselves are demonstrably formulaic and, therefore, "Homeric."[17]

For example, at 10.423, the Venetus A has the formulaic speech introduction line τόν δ' ἀπαμειβόμενος προσέφη πολύμητις Ὀδυσσεύς ("Odysseus who is crafty in many ways answered him and said"). The papyrus clearly has πολύτλας δῖος Ὀδυσσεύς ("much-enduring radiant Odysseus") at line end and the first editor of this papyrus, Anthony Edwards, reconstructs the line as the equally formulaic [τὸν δ' ἠμείβετ'] ἔ[πει]ṭα πολύτλας δῖος Ὀδυσσεύς (Edwards 1984). Such multiformity often appears within the textual tradition at this level of formulaic, frequently-used lines. Both πολύμητις and πολύτλας are equally traditional and, indeed, distinctive epithets of Odysseus. Each formula also has a connection with ambush poetics, as we have explored in our book on *Iliad* 10.[18] Either is appropriate in this line, and so we need not reject either possibility. A multitextual approach to the Homeric poems allows both.

In our digital critical edition, then, whenever a reader indicates an interest in 10.423, she would be able to request all the witnesses that contain this line currently included in the HMT (with more being added as we continue to build it). She could then easily see on the screen and compare what each witness contains. The project's current infrastructure supports viewing options that include displaying just the text that a historical document like p609 contains (that is, a diplomatic edition) and also a display with the missing portions filled in with an editor's conjecture, clearly identified as such. For some expert readers, that alone will give them the information they are seeking as well as multiple pathways to follow for further investigation. For a less expert reader, however, the editor must give further context by providing easy access to the historical context, including such information as that the papyrus is second century BCE and a palimpsest as well as a guide to where more information can be found, such as the photographs of the papyrus available elsewhere online. Similarly for the Venetus A, we will need to specify that it is a tenth century CE Byzantine manuscript and to guide these less expert readers to our introduction

[16] For more on the concept of horizontal and vertical multiformity see Nagy 2001:115n25 and 2004:54–66.

[17] It is very often the case that the variations presented in the early papyri and quotations of the Homeric poems in other ancient texts are arguably as "Homeric" as those of the medieval manuscripts when examined, as we will do here, from the point of view of Homeric diction and formulaic language. See Dué 2001a and 2001b and Bird 2010 for other examples.

[18] See our interpretive commentary in Dué and Ebbott 2010 on lines 10.137, 10.148, 10.382 for πολύμητις and on 10.248 for πολύτλας. Both cunning and endurance of physical discomfort and fear are qualities associated with Odysseus as a master ambusher and with ambush in general (as described by Idomeneus in *Iliad* 13.269–287).

to the manuscript and other publications about it (see Dué and Ebbott 2014). Readers will also be able to search for other uses of the formula πολύτλας δῖος Ὀδυσσεύς in the Homeric corpus, and we will point them to commentary on the traditional meaning of the epithets (as we do in the footnote above). In sum, then, our edition is critical because it brings together multiple texts and offers tools for the meaningful evaluation of multiple witnesses and their multiform readings. As we continue to examine this papyrus for the kinds of multiformity it exhibits, the comparisons and commentaries we provide here give an idea of the kinds of context that the edition will make possible and, eventually, will make explicitly available.

If we look at 10.425 on the papyrus, we find further horizontal multiformity. The papyrus reads: ]ι νημερτὲς ἔνισπε. Edwards (1984) reads this line as [ μο]ι νημερτὲς ἔνισπε ("tell me and don't miss the mark"). There have been various suggestions for the restoration of the beginning of the line, based on what we find in other witnesses, but the metrical pattern of this text differs from the equivalent phrase we find in the Venetus A (δίειπέ μοι ὄφρα δαείω "tell me so that I may know"). Because of this difference, Edwards notes the possibility that the entire line was different (1984:13 *ad loc.*). We should not assume that we know what was on the papyrus based on what appears in much later witnesses. The phrasing and placement are similar to what we find at the end of *Iliad* 3.204: ὦ γύναι ἦ μάλα τοῦτο ἔπος νημερτὲς ἔειπες ("Woman, you have spoken this word without missing the mark"). For the imperative of ἐννέπω, we can compare also *Odyssey* 4.642, νημερτές μοι ἔνισπε, which is also in a context that leads to plotting an ambush. Finally, p609's version of the line matches the endings of lines such as *Iliad* 14.470, *Odyssey* 3.101, *Odyssey* 4.314, *Odyssey* 4.331, and *Odyssey* 22.166. δίειπέ μοι ὄφρα δαείω (the phrase attested in the Venetus A here) is not attested elsewhere in our *Iliad* or *Odyssey*, and ὄφρα δαείω appears only three times.[19]

Substitutions of one formula for another are typical of oral composition-in-performance, and we should not be surprised to find these kinds of multiforms preserved in the textual tradition. Other, more complex, kinds of performance variation are also attested in the papyri, however, as p609 demonstrates once again. At 10.432–434, the papyrus has a so-called plus verse. The Venetus A has the following sequence:

432 ἀλλὰ τίη με ταῦτα διεξερέεσθαι ἕκαστα;
433 εἰ γὰρ δὴ μέματον Τρώων καταδῦναι ὅμιλον
434 Θρήϊκες οἳ δ' ἀπάνευθε νεήλυδες ἔσχατοι ἄλλων·

[19] See Dué and Ebbott 2010:171, with thanks to William Duffy.

432 But why do you question me so precisely about each of these things?
433 For if you two are eager to enter into the crowd of Trojans,
434 here are the Thracians who have newly arrived, farthest apart from the others.

The lines on the papyrus have similar endings to the manuscript's lines 10.432 and 434,[20] but on this papyrus there are two lines between these:

433 ... ὁρμᾶται φίλον ἦτορ
433a ... δῦνα̣ι̣[ ̣]ι̣ στρατὸν ἐγγὺς [ἐόντ]ων

433 ... dear heart rouses
433a ... to enter the camp of those who are nearby

Edwards (1984:13) argues that "there can be no doubt that the sense ... is the same as that of K 433." If this is so, we can see here an example of expansion (or, conversely, of compression in the Venetus A version): the singer in performance can expand episodes, scenes, or speeches with more lines if he so chooses. Even a relatively short and simple expansion such as this one seems to be evidence of the performance tradition. The language of these lines is formulaic, and they are just as likely to have been generated by a traditional singer as those found in the majority of witnesses.

The antiquity of this papyrus fragment and the attestation of these particular multiforms elsewhere in Homeric epic should give these variations weight. We resist approaches that dismiss them (or similar multiformity) in the early Homeric papyri as "eccentric." P609 is no isolated example. The design of the Homer Multitext, then, provides access to these witnesses in full diplomatic editions and makes clear to readers both their early date and the formulaic nature of their language.

The Ptolemaic papyri as a group have been labeled "wild" and "eccentric" by papyrologists and editors of the Homeric poems alike. But as Dué has argued elsewhere, they are only "wild" from the perspective of the medieval transmission. The variations themselves present little that is surprising when considered from the viewpoint of the system as a whole (Dué 2001a and 2019:83–104). P40 (P. Hibeh 19) is another such "wild" papyrus, dating to the first half of the second century BCE (M. West 2001:90). It is a lengthy papyrus with quite a few

[20] The papyrus, however, seems to have the second person plural indicative form of the verb instead of the infinitive in 432.

plus verses as well as multiformity within individual lines. The following is an excerpt from fragment L of this papyrus:

302 <ὣς ἔφαν εὐχό>μενοι, μέγα δ' ἔκτυπε μητίετα Ζεὺ̣ς
302a [ca. 10 letters] φων ἐ̣π̣ὶ̣ δὲ στεροπὴν ἐφέηκεν·
302b <θησέμεναι γ>ὰρ̣ ἔμελλεν ἔτ' ἄλγεά τε στοναχάς τε
302c <Τρωσί τε καὶ> Δαναο̣ῖ̣<σι> διὰ κρατερὰς ὑ̣ς<μί>νας.
302d <αὐτὰρ ἐπεί ῥ' ὅ>μοσέν τε τελεύτησέν <τε> τὸν ὅρκον,
303 <Δαρδανί>δ<η>ς̣ Πρίαμος πρὸς μῦθον ἔειπ<ε·>
304 <κέκλυτέ μευ, Τ>ρῶες καὶ Δάρδανοι ἠδ' <ἐ>π̣ί̣κ̣<ουροι,>
304a <ὄφρ' εἴπω> τά μ̣<ε θυ>μὸς ἐνὶ στήθεσσιν ἀν<ώ>γε<ι.>
305 <ἤτοι ἐ>γὼν εἶμι πρ<ο>τὶ Ἴλιον ἠνεμόεσσαν·
306 <ο>ὐ̣ γάρ κεν τλαίην <ποτ' ἐν ὀφθα>λμοῖσιν ὁρᾶ<σθαι>
307 <μα>ρνάμ<ε>νον φίλο<ν υἱὸν ἀρηϊφίλῳ Μενελάῳ.>
308 <Ζεὺς μέν που> τ̣ό̣ <γ> ε̣ <οἶδε καὶ ἀθάνατοι θεοὶ ἄλλοι,>
309 <ὁπποτέρῳ θα>ν̣ά̣τοιο τέλ<ος πεπρωμένον ἐστίν.>
310 <ἦ ῥα, καὶ ἐς δίφρο> ν̣ ἄ̣ρ̣ <νας θέτο ἰσόθεος φώς>

*Iliad* 3.302–310 (fragment L, column I
of P. Hibeh 19 [= p40])[21]

302 So they spoke praying, and Zeus the deviser thundered loudly
302a and he let fly lightning.
302b For he was about to place still more sufferings and groans upon
302c the Trojans and the Danaans in powerful combat.
302d Next, once he [Agamemnon] had sworn the oath and completed the sacrifice,
303 To them Priam, descendant of Dardanos, spoke words,
304 "Hear from me, Trojans and Dardanians and allies,
304a let me say what my heart in my chest tells me to say:
305 I will go to wind-swept Ilion,

[21] The text and supplements are taken from the digital edition of this papyrus made by Joseph Miller, who follows the first edition of the papyrus by S. West (1967) in most respects. Note that text within angle brackets is not present on the fragmentary papyrus and has been supplied by the editor based on what is attested in the medieval manuscripts. Letters with dots underneath are visible but unclear on the papyrus. For 302a, M. West 1998 suggests [Ἴδης ἔκ κορυ]φῶν ἐ̣π̣ὶ̣ δὲ στεροπὴν ἐφέηκεν ("from the peaks of Ida he let fly lightning"). On this section of the papyrus, see also Bird 2010:86–89.

306 for I would never dare to watch with my own eyes
307 my dear son fighting with Menelaos, dear to Ares.
308 Zeus, I suppose, knows this, as well the rest of the immortal gods,
309 to which of the two the fulfillment of death has been allotted."
310 He spoke, and into the chariot he, a man equal to a god, placed the lambs ...

At verse 302, the papyrus seems to read ὣς ἔφαν εὐχόμενοι, μέγα δ' ἔκτυπε μητίετα Ζεὺ̣ς ("So they spoke praying, and Zeus the deviser thundered loudly") in contrast to the medieval manuscripts, which read ὣς ἔφαν, οὐδ' ἄρα πώ σφιν ἐπεκραίαινε Κρονίων ("So they spoke, but not yet did Zeus bring it to fulfillment for them"). Following that verse, there are four plus verses that are not attested in the medieval manuscripts. At verse 303, the papyrus reads πρὸς where the medieval manuscripts have μετὰ. At verse 304, the papyrus reads Δάρδανοι ἠδ' <ἐ>π̣ί̣κ̣<ουροι,> ("Dardanians and allies") where the manuscripts read ἐϋκνήμιδες Ἀχαιοί ("well-greaved Achaeans"). After 304 there is another plus verse. At verse 306, the papyrus appears to read <o>ὐ̣ γάρ κεν τλαίην <ποτ' ἐν ὀφθα>λμοῖσιν ὁρᾶ<σθαι> ("for I would never dare to watch with my own eyes") whereas the manuscripts have ἄψ, ἐπεὶ οὔ πω τλήσομ' ἐν ὀφθαλμοῖσιν ὁρᾶσθαι ("back, since I will not yet dare to watch with my own eyes").

As we can see in this small segment, this particular papyrus text differs from medieval texts of the *Iliad* in its number of lines and often within lines (with one verse almost entirely different at 302), but the variations are formulaic in nature, with the kind of compression and expansion and differences in choice of formula that we would expect of oral-derived texts. Verse 302 on the papyrus does not happen to survive in any other manuscript or papyrus in this particular location within the epic, but it *is* found at *Iliad* 15.377, indicating that it is a perfectly Homeric line. Verse 302 in the manuscripts (οὐδ' ἄρα πώ σφιν ἐπεκραίαινε Κρονίων) is also attested elsewhere in the poem (at *Iliad* 2.419). Here is another case where a multitextual approach can accommodate both without excluding one or the other.

There are five so-called plus verses in a span of fourteen lines, but four of these have close parallels elsewhere in the *Iliad*. 3.302b–302c on the papyrus resemble closely *Iliad* 2.39–40:

2.39 θήσειν γὰρ ἔτ' ἔμελλεν ἔπ' ἄλγεά τε στοναχάς τε
2.40 Τρωσί τε καὶ Δαναοῖσι διὰ κρατερὰς ὑσμίνας.

2.39 For he was about to place still more sufferings and groaning upon
2.40 the Trojans and the Danaans in powerful combat.

Verse 3.302d on the papyrus can be found at *Iliad* 14.280:

14.280 αὐτὰρ ἐπεί ῥ᾽ ὄμοσέν τε τελεύτησέν τε τὸν ὅρκον

14.280 Next, once he had sworn the oath and completed the sacrifice

And finally, verse 2.304a on the papyrus can be found at *Iliad* 19.102. In fact, this particular passage from *Iliad* 19, in which Zeus addresses the other gods, is contextually similar to the one we are exploring in *Iliad* 3:

19.100 ἤτοι ὅ γ᾽ εὐχόμενος μετέφη πάντεσσι θεοῖσι·
19.101 κέκλυτέ μευ πάντές τε θεοὶ πᾶσαί τε θέαιναι,
19.102 ὄφρ᾽ εἴπω τά με θυμὸς ἐνὶ στήθεσσιν ἀνώγει.

19.100 Making a solemn statement, he spoke among all the gods,
19.101 "Hear from me, all you gods and goddesses,
19.102 let me say what my heart in my chest tells me to say."

We can see that verse 3.304 on the papyrus is likewise parallel to 19.101, with the substitution of the contextually appropriate Τρῶες καὶ Δάρδανοι ἠδ᾽ ἐπίκουροι for πάντές τε θεοὶ πᾶσαί τε θέαιναι.

These differences are not a case of a rogue scribe inserting lines from elsewhere in the *Iliad* into *Iliad* 3. Rather, each of the variations presented by p40 are the kind of multiforms that are natural to oral poetry composed in performance. Milman Parry demonstrated the significance of this for the text of Homer:

> The formula thus is by no means the unit of the singer's poetry, but it nevertheless ever tends to become so, for no singer ever tells the same tale twice in the same words. His poem will always follow the same general pattern, but this verse or that will be left out, or replaced by another verse or part of a verse, and he will leave out and add whole passages as the time and mood of his hearers calls for a fuller or briefer telling of a tale or of a given part of a tale. Thus the oral poem even in the mouth of the same singer is ever in a state of change; and it is the same when his poetry is sung by others.
>
> Parry 1971:336

Following Parry, we, the editors of the Homer Multitext, view the early Homeric papyri as the vestiges of a once vibrant performance tradition of the *Iliad* and

*Odyssey*.[22] The variations preserved in the Homeric papyri are a unique channel into the oral tradition that we have lost. We are not seeking to privilege the papyri in any special way over the medieval transmission; rather, we seek simply to make the readings they contain readily available to scholars and anyone interested in the transmission of the Homeric poems and to suggest that they have great historical value in the picture they present of the state of the Homeric texts in the earliest stage at which we have it.

More than that, we believe that the more complete our evidence and, as a result of that more complete evidence, the better our understanding of the system in which the *Iliad* and *Odyssey* were composed, the better in turn we are able to understand the poetics of those compositions. Our multitextual edition and commentary on *Iliad* 10 (Dué and Ebbott 2010), from which we have taken some of the examples of multiformity discussed here, was intended as an extended application of the work of Parry and Lord to an episode of the *Iliad* whose authenticity as Homeric poetry has long been questioned. One of our central assumptions in that work is that the more evidence that we take into account, the more the theories of Milman Parry, who died quite early in his scholarly career, are borne out and the more illuminating they are as a result.

## Multitextual Evidence of Formulaic Diction

Parry's work on the Homeric epics famously examined noun-epithet formulas as a way to demonstrate and understand the oral-traditional nature of the Homeric epics. This aspect of Parry's work has been frequently challenged in subsequent scholarship and, we believe, misunderstood in important ways.[23] The Homer Multitext and a multitextual approach in general, can provide important

[22] See also Nagy 1996a, Dué 2001a, Bird 2010, and Dué 2019:83–104.

[23] For another example (besides the one discussed here) of the way that Parry's work on noun-epithet formulas has been misunderstood, see Dué and Ebbott 2010:254–256 and Dué 2011, with reference to the use of the seemingly interchangeable formulas νύκτα δι' ἀμβροσίην ("through the ambrosial night") and νύκτα δι' ὀρφναίην ("through the dark night") in *Iliad* 10. Although Parry described Homeric diction as being "free of phrases which, having the same metrical value and expressing the same idea, could replace one another" (Parry 1971:86), these two formulas for night occupy the same metrical space within the verse and so have been used to assert that Parry was wrong about the economy of Homeric diction. We have argued that, in fact, the two formulas are not conceptually the same and do not have the same thematic resonance. There is more than one way to say "night" in book 10 because night is not a monolithic concept. When a poet wanted to invoke night with its generic associations with relief and rest, νύκτα δι' ἀμβροσίην would be easily summoned. But the night of *Iliad* 10 is marked by anxiety, fear, and a raid on the enemy camp, hence we find νύκτα δι' ὀρφναίην in several places. In other words, each formula conveys a different "essential idea." (For Parry's definition of the formula as "a group of words regularly employed under the same metrical conditions to express a given essential idea," see Parry 1971:272.)

evidence for expanding our understanding of these and other formulas. In our commentary on *Iliad* 10 (Dué and Ebbott 2010:300–306), we examined Parry's work on fixed epithets in detail by focusing on the epithet βοὴν ἀγαθός in *Iliad* 10. βοὴν ἀγαθός is a fixed epithet. Fixed epithets, as Parry describes them, exhibit four interdependent characteristics: they are used in accordance with their metrical value and not in accordance with their signification; they are traditional; they are always ornamental; and they are often generic (Parry 1971:165–166). βοὴν ἀγαθός is fixed because it is always used in the same position in the line: it follows the weak caesura, a common placement within the line for epithets, but it can be (and is) used with more than one hero's name. Parry argues that these kinds of "rigorously" fixed epithets (which as a category can be seen as a subset of the more general kind of ornamental epithet), "clearly must have had, for the poets who used them, an existence independent of any particular type of noun-epithet formula" (1971:64–65). More controversial is Parry's contention that the poet uses these epithets for metrical reasons rather than their signification, and it is that point which is often targeted as the vulnerable underbelly of Parry's work.[24] For example, an argument has been put forward from a stated position sympathetic to Parry, that when this epithet is used at *Iliad* 10.283 it is actually contextually appropriate as the *final* appearance of it in *Iliad* 10 because once the Achaeans have departed on their mission, they will have to be quiet (Machacek 1994). In other words: no more shouting, we're on an ambush.

In our commentary, we go into greater detail about that argument and the multiple ways in which this particular challenge to Parry's work on epithets can be answered. But here we want simply to emphasize that a multitextual approach exposes a major methodological problem with such an argument, since it is predicated on this line containing the "final" instance of this epithet formula in the book. When we consult modern editions of *Iliad* 10, it can easily appear to be the case that βοὴν ἀγαθός is no longer used after verse 283. But when we consider the full range of evidence, including papyri and the scholia, and when we fully grasp what composition-in-performance means for the multiformity of the epic tradition, we see that such arguments about epithets in particular can be refuted on the basis of our textual evidence. On the papyrus that both Allen (1931) and M. West (1998) refer to as p90 (Oxyrhynchus 6.949, from the

24 As we assert in more detail in our commentary (Dué and Ebbott 2010:300–306), Parry's definition of the "essential idea" of epithets does not render them meaningless. Their ornamental nature means that we should not look for meaning in the immediate context but rather understand how the epithet signifies what Lord called its "traditionally intuitive meaning" (Lord 2019:69). Attacking the idea that singers use epithets for their metrical shape alone also ignores the scholarship in which followers of Parry and Lord have demonstrated that thought precedes meter in Homeric diction (see e.g. Nagy 1996b:22–25 and Foley 2002:133–134).

second–third century CE), there is a possible use of this epithet again at 10.446: [τον δ ημειβετ επειτα βοην αγα]θος Διομηδης, which would put it squarely in the middle of the mission, after Diomedes and Odysseus have captured Dolon. And from the scholia in both the Venetus A and Townley manuscripts, we have evidence of a version of 10.349, known to the Homeric critic Aristophanes of Byzantium, that also uses this epithet: ὣς ἔφατ', οὐδ' ἀπίθησε βοὴν ἀγαθὸς Διομήδης. The Homer Multitext allows easier access to such textual variation and thus changes the notion of what "the text" shows and does not show when it comes to the uses of these formulas.[25]

Since epithets like βοὴν ἀγαθός were so useful, flexible, and traditional—qualities that Parry himself identifies—it is difficult to prove the argument that the *absence* of one in a particular passage is significant: even with our limited evidence we can see that this epithet could indeed be used in more lines within this episode. Instead, a thorough understanding of the oral traditional poetics of these formulas requires us to take a larger view of their meaning, just as a true understanding of the textual tradition requires us to take into account all the evidence we have and to recognize that a singer might have sung this same episode with the multiformity natural to composition-in-performance. These are some of the differences between Homeric epic and modern poetry that Parry enjoined us to acknowledge and to appreciate with a different aesthetics. The Homer Multitext is being designed to allow us to see more easily the multiformity still present in the textual record.

## Homeric Scholia: A Window onto the Tradition

We saw in that last example how both papyri and scholia from medieval manuscripts offer important evidence for formulaic diction and therefore for the system of Homeric epic. Now we would like to take that one step further to look at how such evidence can also help us to understand the poetics of that system better. The multitextual manuscripts with scholia such as the Venetus A described earlier provide further evidence of multiformity of the system of Homeric epic. Easy access to and an accurate presentation of both the poetic texts and scholia of various manuscripts, then, also create an opportunity to consider what the multiforms in them can teach us about the poetry of the *Iliad*.

[25] An important component of the Homer Multitext will be the ability to search multiple texts, including papyri and scholia, for formulas. A great deal of progress has been made towards developing the infrastructure that will support that component of the project, but that type of search is not yet available as of the writing of this article.

To get a sense of this opportunity from just the briefest of examples, let us look at a scholion in the Venetus A on *Iliad* 3.100.[26] This line is part of Menelaos's reply to Hektor's proposal of a duel between Alexander and Menelaos over the woman both men claim, Helen. Menelaos agrees to the duel and explains why. The main text of the Venetus A—as well as those of other manuscripts in the Homer Multitext, namely, the Venetus B and the two Escorial manuscripts (Υ.1.1 and Ω.1.12, E3 and E4 in Allen's notation) and also most modern editions—reads: εἵνεκ' ἐμῆς ἔριδος καὶ Ἀλεξάνδρου ἕνεκ' ἀρχῆς· "because of my conflict and because of the way it started with Alexander." The line is marked in the Venetus A with a sign called a *diplē periestigmenē* (>:), or a dotted *diplē*, which Aristarchus used to indicate that he was disagreeing with a reading of Zenodotus on that line.[27] The note itself reads (we have represented it here as it appears in the manuscript, which at times omits accents or other details we might expect to see): ὅτι Ζηνόδοτος γράφει ἕνεκ' ἄτης. ἔσται δὲ ἀπολογούμενος Μενέλαος ὅτι ἄτη περιέπεσεν ὁ Ἀλέξανδρος. δια μέντοι τοῦ ἕνεκ' ἀρχῆς· ἐνδείκνυται ὅτι προκατῆρξεν:~ "[it is marked] because Zenodotus writes 'because of [his] error.' This would be Menelaos saying in his defense that Alexander [was the one who] had fallen into error. With 'because of his beginning' however, it reveals that he began the hostilities."

In the Homer Multitext, as we have seen above with the examples from the papyri, if a reader develops an interest in *Iliad* 3.100, or in folio 43v of the Venetus A, she can easily discover this scholion in a full diplomatic text. The names Zenodotus, Menelaos, and Alexander that appear in the scholion are also designated in the diplomatic edition with TEI-XML mark-up and unique identifiers, so that you know it is Alexander, the son of Priam, and not Alexander the Great or any other Alexander the scholia might mention. Searching for any one of those names within the HMT would also allow a reader to find this scholion. Connections to commentary on the line and scholion would then provide some of the information such as we offer below about comparable lines and what other witnesses read or offer as alternatives.

The disagreement between Aristarchus and his predecessor Zenodotus contained in the scholion at 3.100 provides valuable information about textual criticism in an earlier age, from which survives only partial written evidence. In terms of understanding the passage, however, our first reaction might be that the explanation about the difference between the two versions is not all that illuminating: is there an important distinction in meaning between saying it was

26 See Ebbott and Muellner 2012 for their discussion of the placement of scholia on the page and the multitextuality of this scholion as well as Dué 2019:151–153.

27 Pfeiffer 1968:218; McNamee 1981:247n3; Bird 2009:93. See Ebbott and Muellner 2012:131–132 for the succession of scholarly editing implied by the one scholion.

Alexander's error and saying that he started it? And so this brief note, similar to so many others about the choices that Aristarchus made in contrast to those Zenodotus had made, could be dismissed: such textual differences, modern scholars have said, are banal and unimportant, unworthy of consideration.

But to dismiss this different reading is to take a rather narrow view of this potential multiform. Why should we not consider Zenodotus' reading a true multiform or, we might also say, a performance variation, a potential end to a line in a performance when this was an oral poem? One piece of evidence in support of doing so is that the phrase Ἀλεξάνδρου ἕνεκ' ἄτης appears in this same position, after the weak caesura and completing the line, in at least two other lines: (1) *Iliad* 6.356, in which Helen says to Hektor that Hektor has had to take the brunt of the suffering caused by herself and Alexander's error, and (2) *Iliad* 24.28, where the narrator most famously alludes to the Judgement of Paris. For the latter line, the intermarginal scholion in the Venetus A records ἕνεκ' ἀρχῆς as an alternate reading. The line at *Iliad* 6.356 likewise reads ἀρχῆς in a papyrus and several manuscripts, according to Allen's (1931) apparatus. M. West (1998) adds two more papyri that contain the reading ἀρχῆς as either the main reading or an alternate one. So in each of these three lines, we have evidence for both multiforms, and that evidence tells us something about how oral composition-in-performance can work, when a singer, either by training or under the pressure of performance, might choose one or the other phrase in any of these places.

But this evidence should also make us pause before making any pronouncements about how often the Judgement of Paris is alluded to in the *Iliad*. Indeed, commentators often say that there is only this one reference to it in the whole epic, the one in book 24,[28] but if Menelaos could use that same phrase in book 3 that we see expanded on in 24 to indicate the Judgement and could in this way encapsulate that traditional sequence of events, our understanding of the frequency and thus our interpretation of that frequency, would have to change.[29] It cannot be denied that the multiforms in the scholia have much to teach us about the composition of the poetry. In turn, they also provide substantial food for thought about how we then interpret the poetry that has been transmitted. The profit to be gained from this particular scholion, and the many others like it, is not that it dramatically alters the sense of that one particular line, but that

[28] For a recent example, Mackie begins his discussion of *Iliad* 24 and the Judgement of Paris by stating, "Despite the importance of the Judgement of Paris in the story of the Trojan War, the *Iliad* has only one explicit reference to it" (Mackie 2013:1).

[29] The phrase Ἀλεξάνδρου ἕνεκ' ἄτης in *Iliad* 6.356 is followed by Helen's prediction that they will be a subject of song for future generations, suggesting that "Alexander's error" here, too, has a thematic connection to the Judgement and the epic tradition as a whole.

it makes a significant difference in our understanding of the system of Homeric epic as a whole.[30]

## The Homer Multitext: A Digital Means of Discovery

Our editorial rationale for the Homer Multitext as informed by the work of Parry and Lord underpins the creation of the digital editions of surviving witnesses to the *Iliad* and *Odyssey* within the Homer Multitext. These digital editions, in turn, allow for research into the texts in ways not possible before in terms of both natural language processing and data analysis of the poetic language. Even before our editions are complete, however, the Homer Multitext has published high-resolution digital images of five of the oldest multitextual manuscripts of the *Iliad*. These include the manuscripts in Venice known to scholars as the Venetus A (Marciana 822), the Venetus B (Marciana 821), and Marciana 841 (Allen's U4) as well as two manuscripts in the Escorial in Spain, Escorial Y.I.1 (294) and Ω.I.12 (513). Our collaboration with the e-Codices project of Switzerland (http://www.e-codices.unifr.ch/) has resulted in the publications of images of the *Iliad* manuscript with scholia known as Genavensis 44 that is similarly available for scholarly work under a Creative Commons License. The collaborators in the Homer Multitext are pursuing multiple lines of research simultaneously: historical, philological, and scientific research based on the content of the artifacts represented by this digital library and research into theories, techniques, and practices of massive, scalable, rigorous, and highly distributed digital scholarship.

The Homer Multitext has benefitted immeasurably from the technological infrastructure and assistance provided by the University of Houston's Research Computing Center. As we have noted, the project is a collaborative one, combining research in digital humanities with more traditional philology, and our work would not be possible without the support of the Research Computing Center. The project's information architects are Christopher Blackwell and Neel Smith, both Classicists who have acquired, in the course of their own research, considerable expertise in computational methods. Under their direction, the Homer Multitext has implemented a distributed, modular approach to integrating diverse digital objects into a research library. In broad terms, we deal with *texts*, *images*, and *data-objects*. Each example of each type of data has a unique, canonical identifier.

30 For more on how our understanding of the multiform nature of Homeric epic affects our interpretation of the poetics, see the sustained treatments in Dué 2002 and Dué and Ebbott 2010.

The amount of text and scholia contained in the five Homeric manuscripts already photographed is vast, and the project now publishes thousands of images that have not yet been fully transcribed or studied thoroughly. In 2017, we published a complete, web-based, digital scholarly edition of the entire contents of the Venetus A manuscript, the oldest complete witness to the *Iliad*, together with its scholia, which transmit scholarship about the poem from intellectuals who studied this poem in Alexandria, in Rome, and in Byzantium from the third century BCE until the Middle Ages. (For more on the contents of the Venetus A, see Dué 2009 and Dué and Ebbott 2014.) Prior to that publication, there did not yet exist a comprehensive edition of this manuscript and its scholia and thus no systematic way to evaluate the evidence offered in this manuscript. Our earliest work on the manuscript suggests that a significant portion of its scholia has not been published in the edition of Erbse.[31] We have therefore produced a complete scholarly edition of this special manuscript: its text, scholia, and all other elements on its 654 pages. The text and scholia have been transcribed (as a diplomatic edition, representing faithfully the text of the manuscript, including accents and spelling that are not "standard" from our point of view), and marked up with TEI-XML encoding for several key features. Each portion of the digital text, that is, each individual line of poetic text and each individual scholion, is then linked precisely to its location on the digital images we have published, by means of a procedure Blackwell and Smith have developed to inventory and map the scholia and all other markings or elements on the page. Thus, one significant feature of our edition is that any user can easily ("one-click") move from the transcription to the image of the primary source and see for herself what the manuscript says. The work, which has been funded by a National Endowment for the Humanities grant, was completed in 2017, but we continue to make improvements to our data and to the infrastructure designed to display it.

With the online publication of these images, freely accessible on-line and licensed for scholarly re-use, we expect scholars, from many areas of expertise, to contribute new discoveries about these manuscripts, their content and construction, and indeed the *Iliad* itself. The process of discovery began already when we were in Venice and Spain and Geneva, but it has never been our intention to limit the investigation of these pages to a select group of people. By making the manuscripts available in this way, we hope to encourage new and collaborative ways of exploring the *Iliad*, and new methods of scholarship. The *Iliad* has the ability to bring together scientists and historians and literary

31 Both the print and the electronic version of Erbse's edition of the scholia published by the *Thesaurus Linguae Graecae* frequently and by design excludes, emends, or abbreviates scholia from the Venetus A based on content, date, or placement. On this point see also Schironi 2018:9–14.

scholars: those interested in physical objects and the technology of creating them, preserving them, or capturing them digitally; those interested in the history of ideas; and those hoping to better understand the poetry and the tradition in which it was composed. Future research and publications on these manuscripts will further our own collaborative work on the Homeric poems, the system of oral poetry in which they were created, and the transmission of this oral tradition through time, but they will also allow us to learn from scholars from a wide variety of fields and thereby shed new light on a very ancient poem.

In a 2001 article (Dué 2001a), Dué argued that the multiformity of the Homeric texts, as evidenced by the earliest quotations of Homer and the Ptolemaic papyri, calls for a new approach to editing the texts of Homer. Building on the work of Gregory Nagy (especially Nagy 1996a), who was himself building on the insights of Parry and Lord into the oral traditional nature of Homeric poetry, she suggested that a web-based, multitext edition would be truer to the complexity of the transmission of the Homeric poems, which are oral-derived texts composed in performance. The texts as we now have them are the product of many singers over the course of many generations. What Milman Parry and Albert Lord's work shows us most essentially is that there is not one original text that we should try to reconstruct. Instead of reconstructing an "original text," the aim of the Homer Multitext, now at last becoming a reality after many years of planning, research, and the efforts of many collaborators, is to present a series of complete, historically contextualized texts, together with images of the artifacts that transmit them, and a variety of tools with which users can compare and analyze these historical documents.

The work of Parry and Lord is the inspiration for and foundation of the Homer Multitext, and we believe that the Homer Multitext as it continues to evolve will be useful for new research that will expand their findings and therefore also expand our understanding of the oral and textual traditions of the Homeric epics.

## Bibliography

Allen, T. W. 1899. "On the Composition of Some Greek Manuscripts: The Venetian Homer." *Journal of Philology* 26:161–181.

———. 1924. *Homer: The Origins and the Transmission*. Oxford.

———, ed. 1931. *Homeri Ilias*. Oxford.

Berti, M., ed. 2019. *Digital Classical Philology: Ancient Greek and Latin in the Digital Revolution*. Berlin.

Bierl, A. 2015. "New Trends in Homeric Scholarship." In Bierl and Latacz 2015:177–203.

Bierl, A., and J. Latacz, eds. 2015. *Homer's* Iliad*: The Basel Commentary. Prolegomena*. Berlin.

Bird, G. 2009. "Critical Signs—Drawing Attention to 'Special' Lines of Homer's *Iliad* in the Manuscript Venetus A." In Dué 2009:89–115.

———. 2010. *Multitextuality in the Homeric* Iliad*: The Witness of Ptolemaic Papyri*. Hellenic Studies 43. Washington, DC.

Brockmann, C., D. Deckers, L. Koch, and S. Valente, eds. 2014. *Teuchos: Handschriften- und Textforschung heute*. Wiesbaden.

Cerquiglini, B. 1999. *In Praise of the Variant: A Critical History of Philology*. Trans. B. Wing. Baltimore.

Clivaz, C., J. Meizoz, F. Vallotton, J. Verheyden, eds., with Benjamin Bertho. 2012. *Lire demain: Des manuscrits antiques à l'ère digitale/Reading Tomorrow: From Ancient Manuscripts to the Digital Era*. Lausanne.

Drout, M., and S. Kleinman. 2010. "Doing Philology 2: Something 'Old,' Something 'New': Material Philology and the Recovery of the Past." *The Heroic Age* 13: https://scholarworks.csun.edu/bitstream/handle/10211.2/2173/KleinmanScott201008.pdf?sequence=1.

Dué, C. 2001a. "Achilles' Golden Amphora in Aeschines' *Against Timarchus* and the Afterlife of Oral Tradition." *Classical Philology* 96:33–47.

———. 2001b. "*Sunt Aliquid Manes*: Homer, Plato, and Alexandrian Allusion in Propertius 4.7." *Classical Journal* 96:401–413.

———. 2002. *Homeric Variations on a Lament by Briseis*. Lanham, MD.

———, ed. 2009. *Recapturing a Homeric Legacy: Images and Insights from the Venetus A Manuscript of the* Iliad. Hellenic Studies Series 35. Washington, DC.

———. 2011. "Maneuvers in the Dark of Night: *Iliad* 10 in the Twenty-First Century." In Montanari, Rengakos, and Tsagalis 2011:165–173.

———. 2019. *Achilles Unbound: Multiformity and Tradition in the Homeric Epics*. Hellenic Studies Series 81. Washington, DC.

Dué, C., and M. Ebbott. 2009. "Digital Criticism: Editorial Standards for the Homer Multitext." *Digital Humanities Quarterly* 3: http://www.digitalhumanities.org/dhq/vol/003/1/000029.html.

———. 2010. Iliad *10 and the Poetics of Ambush: A Multitext Edition with Essays and Commentary.* Hellenic Studies Series 39. Washington, DC.

———. 2014. "An introduction to the Homer Multitext edition of the Venetus A manuscript of the *Iliad.*" The Homer Multitext: http://www.homermultitext.org/manuscripts/venetusA/VenA-Introduction-2014/.

———. 2016. "The Homer Multitext and the System of Homeric Epic." *Classics@*14: https://classics-at.chs.harvard.edu/classics14-due-ebbott/.

———. 2019. "The Homer Multitext within the History of Access to Homeric Epic." In Berti 2019:239–256.

Dué, C., C. Blackwell, M. Ebbott, and N. Smith. 2014. "Rediscovering Homer: Manuscript Digitization, the Homer Multitext project, and Two Eleventh-Century Manuscripts of the *Iliad* in the Escorial." In Brockmann, Deckers, Koch, and Valente 2014:2–10.

Ebbott, M. 2020. "Homeric Epic in Performance." In Pache 2020:9–20.

Ebbott, M., and L. Muellner. 2012. "Multitextual Reading in Manuscripts of the *Iliad* and the Future of the Homer Multitext." In Clivaz, Meizoz, Vallotton, Verheyden 2012:117–137.

Edwards, A. T. 1984. "P. Mich. 6972: An Eccentric Papyrus Text of *Iliad* K 421–34, 445–60." *Zeitschrift für Papyrologie und Epigraphik* 56:11–15.

Finkelberg, M. 2000. "The *Cypria*, the *Iliad*, and the Problem of Multiformity in Oral and Written Tradition." *Classical Philology* 95:1–11.

Foley, J. 1991. *Immanent Art: From Structure to Meaning in Traditional Oral Epic.* Bloomington.

———. 2002. *How to Read an Oral Poem.* Urbana.

Janko, R. 1994. "Homeri Odyssea." *Gnomon* 66:289–295.

Kirk, G. S., ed. 1985. *The* Iliad*: A Commentary.* Vol. 1, *Books 1–4.* Cambridge.

Lord, A. B. 1960. *The Singer of Tales.* Cambridge, MA.

———. 1991. *Epic Singers and Oral Tradition.* Ithaca.

———. 1995. *The Singer Resumes the Tale.* Ithaca.

———. 2019. *The Singer of Tales.* 3rd ed. Ed. D. F. Elmer. Hellenic Studies 77. Publications of the Milman Parry Collection of Oral Literature 4. Washington, DC. Orig. pub. Cambridge, MA, 1960.

Machacek, G. 1994. "The Occasional Contextual Appropriateness of Formulaic Diction in the Homeric Poems." *American Journal of Philology* 115:321–335.

Mackie, C. J. 2013. "*Iliad* 24 and the Judgement of Paris." *Classical Quarterly* 63:1–16.

Magnani, M. 2018. "The Other Side of the River: Digital Editions of Ancient Greek Texts Involving Papyrus Witnesses." In Reggiani 2018: 87–102.

McNamee, K. 1981. "Aristarchus and Everyman's Homer." *Greek, Roman and Byzantine Studies* 22:247–255.

———. 1992. *Sigla and Select Marginalia in Greek Literary Papyri*. Brussels.

———. 2007. *Annotations in Greek and Latin Texts from Egypt*. Oxford.

Montanari, F., A. Rengakos, and C. Tsagalis, eds. 2011. *Homeric Contexts: Neoanalysis and the Interpretation of Oral Poetry*. Berlin.

Nagy, G. 1996a. *Poetry as Performance: Homer and Beyond*. Cambridge.

———. 1996b. *Homeric Questions*. Austin.

———. 2001. "Homeric Poetry and Problems of Multiformity: The 'Panathenaic Bottleneck.'" *Classical Philology* 96:109–119.

———. 2002. *Plato's Rhapsody and Homer's Music: The Poetics of the Panathenaic Festival in Classical Athens*. Hellenic Studies 1. Washington, DC.

———. 2004. *Homer's Text and Language*. Urbana.

———. 2020. "From Song to Text." In Pache 2020:80–98.

Pache, C., ed. 2020. *The Cambridge Guide to Homer*. Cambridge.

Parry, M. 1971. *The Making of Homeric Verse: The Collected Papers of Milman Parry*. Ed. A. Parry. Oxford.

Pelliccia, H. N. 1997. "As Many Homers As You Please." *New York Review of Books* 44:44–48.

Pfeiffer, R. 1968. *History of Classical Scholarship: From the Beginnings to the End of the Hellenistic Age*. Oxford.

Powell, B. 1991. *Homer and the Origin of the Greek Alphabet*. Cambridge.

Reggiani, N., ed. 2018. *Digital Papyrology II: Case Studies on the Digital Edition of Ancient Greek Papyri*. Berlin.

———. 2019. "Ancient Doctors' Literacies and the Digital Edition of Papyri of Medical Content." *Classics@17*: http://nrs.harvard.edu/urn-3:hlnc.essay:ReggianiN.Ancient_Doctors_Literacies.2019.

Schironi, F. 2018. *The Best of the Grammarians: Aristarchus of Samothrace on the* Iliad. Ann Arbor.

West, M., ed. 1998–2000. *Homeri Ilias. Recensuit / testimonia congessit*. Stuttgart.

———. 2001. *Studies in the Text and Transmission of the* Iliad. Munich.

West, S. 1967. *The Ptolemaic Papyri of Homer*. Köln.

# 9

# The "Field of Song" and the Four-Legged Horse

## On the Dialogue of Genres in Kalevala-Meter Poetry

LOTTE TARKKA

IN 1922 HOURO KARPPO, a refugee from Viena Karelia, performed a set of yoiks and laments for the Finnish ethnomusicologist Armas Väisänen. The performance was interrupted by a mistake. In her defense, the woman quoted a proverb: "The horse has four legs, but it stumbles. Man has only one tongue to cry, laugh, yoik, and sing with—no wonder he falters."[1] The human capacity to process oral performances is indeed limited: human beings possess one single tongue, and because of this limitation, the many genres of expression are easily blurred. Even a horse could fail, though far better equipped. In Viena Karelia, the proverb was commonly used to point out linguistic incompetence: mixing up one's words or the conventions of performance.[2] The types of expression singled out by Houro are, in fact, folklore genres in the Viena area: laments (crying), mocking songs (laughing), yoiks, and Kalevala-meter poems (singing). Houro herself was an acclaimed ritual lamenter whose recorded performances moved the listeners to tears even when mediated by the phonograph.[3]

Karppo's parable is one of the rare documented metapoetic statements to describe a vernacular understanding of genres in the Finnish-Karelian culture area. It assesses the challenge of mastering a wealth of genres and the ever-present possibility of mixing them either by accident or for a specific purpose. The dialogue of folklore genres, or generic intertextuality, represents a creative use—or misuse—of tradition and language. Its dynamics show the ways in which people actually use oral tradition,[4] for example, by commenting on generic ideals by using a proverb, a genre orchestrated by ideals of its own. In some

1 SKS KRA Väisänen 1922 AA IV 1.
2 SKS KRA Paulaharju 1913 c7411.
3 Kallberg 2011a:141.
4 See Bauman 2004:31.

contexts, the dialogue of genres thwarts the goal of finalizing a performance; yet in others, it maximizes the expressive power of the traditional idiom.

In the following, I will discuss concepts and methodological tools based on an intertextual reading of genres. The main argument rests on my empirical study of Kalevala-meter oral poetry collected in the parish of Vuokkiniemi, Viena Karelia, near the Finnish-Russian border during the period 1821–1921.[5] The aim of the study was to analyze the system of genres as an expressive and communicative system or, in Kenneth Burke's words, "equipment for living."[6] The method and the underlying theoretical understanding of genre is influenced by the work of linguistic anthropologists and folklorists such as Richard Bauman and Charles Briggs but conditioned by the specificity of archival materials. The texts were collected without much contextual data for purposes that had little to do with the interpretation of the poems in their local context. The corpus is relatively large, consisting of nearly 3,000 poems in the Kalevala-meter, and it can be contextualized with the help of ethnographic accounts and other genres of folklore collected from the area.

In the analysis of regional corpora made up of a large number of genres, the most striking aspect of intertextuality is its capacity to traverse the boundaries of genre. In Karelian oral tradition, the density of the intertextual network is brought about by the use of one common poetic language, coined as the Kalevala-meter, in almost all genres of poetry as well as in idiomatic speech. The elasticity and wide scope of application of this poetic language renders it exceptional.[7] Various criteria of form, content, age, function, and performance style have been used in the classification of Kalevala-meter poetry, but few scholars have sought to account for the system as a whole. There is a consensus on four major categories: epic or narrative poetry, incantations or charms, ritual songs, and lyric poetry. In my examination of the Vuokkiniemi corpus, I detected thirty genres of poetry, complemented by minor folklore genres such as proverbs and riddles and poetic lines in prose tales in the Kalevala meter.[8]

In his prologue to the *Kanteletar*, a collection of edited folk poems in the Kalevala meter published in 1840, Lönnrot expressed his concern for the boundaries between the genres of oral poetry. He had built the epic *Kalevala*[9] on

5 A revised edition of the dissertation (Tarkka 2005) appeared in 2013 (Tarkka 2013). Several articles based on the work in progress have been published in English (e.g. Tarkka 1993; 1994; 1996).

6 Burke 1957.

7 Kuusi 1994:41.

8 The technical classification was based on multiple criteria typically used in detecting sub-groups of Kalevala-meter poetry, such as narrativity, context of use, and function. On the deconstruction of this initial genre analysis, see Tarkka 2013:93–97; Tarkka 2016.

9 Lönnrot 1835, 1849.

narrative poems but, in the *Kanteletar*, the range of genres was far greater, and their relations intrigued the editor. The boundaries did not hold:

> Separating these songs and poems into distinct groups has not been an easy task; indeed, at times it has been downright onerous. Now and again, epic poems cross the borderline to incantations, and so do lyric songs ... From the other side, lyric songs merge with contemporary songs, and even there the boundary is often blurred. But every man does the best job he can within his understanding, and so have I. I am not to blame if patches in the field of song have at times been left secluded or if at other times the borders have been transgressed.[10]

The spatial metaphor used by Lönnrot to designate the poems he was working with—a *field of song*—encapsulates his Romanticist notion of poetry. One of Lönnrot's aims in editing and publishing folk poetry was to promote the nascent Finnish literary culture by providing it with aesthetic ideals based on folklore. This project of cultivating and domesticating "natural" poetry into an ordered "garden of song" and for the purposes of the elite was indeed comparable to the task of a farmer designing his field into separate patches.[11] For Lönnrot, the problem of genre was not only a technical one. The theoretical discussion in the prologue reveals his anxiety about a literate audience's competence to appreciate and understand oral poetry and its system of genres. Oral poetry seemed to miss the primary guiding line for interpretation—namely, a set of clearly defined genres and an understanding of how to read them. Paradoxically, the aesthetic advantage of oral poems over literary ones was this very same disorderly, natural, and spontaneous quality.

In the classification and analysis of oral corpora, typological or academic systems of genre are clearly inadequate:[12] any single text can often be classified into several categories, and it may contain elements and episodes referring to several genres. The borders between vernacular, or emic, genres of oral poetry are more akin to interfaces than to boundaries: instead of dissecting they mediate. Methodologically, one way of alleviating the friction between typological and vernacular concepts of genre is to take generic interfaces and interactions as the starting point.[13] Rather than contesting the idea of genre analysis, the notion of generic intertextuality complements it. Focusing on the interplay of genres, we can use typological concepts of genre without being constrained

10 Lönnrot 1840:xlvi–xlvii.

11 Lönnrot 1840:iii–iv, xxxiii.

12 On the debate on emic versus etic folklore genres, see Honko 1976, 1989; Ben-Amos 1976, 1992.

13 See Briggs and Bauman 1992:145.

by their false rigidity; we can describe vernacular or local systems of genre more accurately and, finally, we can gain a deeper understanding of oral poetry as a system of communication.

In the actual use of the vernacular or emic generic systems, the genres gain their expressive power and significance only in relation to each other.[14] Each song sung and word uttered acquires meaning in the interpretative frame of the tradition as a whole. Even if the genres can be—and even have to be—separated for analytical purposes, a richer appreciation of their meaning requires a shift in the opposite direction: a synthesis provided by the notion of generic intertextuality. Generic intertextuality, or the dialogue of genres, involves the interaction of principles of composition and interpretative frames specific to genres of oral tradition.[15]

My definition of genres corresponds to that of William Hanks: genres are frames that guide the production and reception of discourse and that consist of historically specific conventions and ideals. Hanks develops Richard Bauman's idea of genre with the assertion that genres "consist of orienting frameworks, interpretive procedures, and sets of expectations that are not part of the discourse structure but of the ways actors relate to and use language."[16] The analysis of large corpora of oral poetry and the challenges of archival data with little or no contextual information call for a multi-dimensional approach to genre. As Peter Seitel writes:

> The interpretive powers of genre grow from its ability to name and provide a perspective on four conceptual spheres: categorization of texts, intertextual reference, performance in a social field, and "form-shaping ideology"—a framework for creating and understanding kinds of speech. ... [D]efinition and description of a corpus are not the end but the beginning of interpretation; they provide a focus for analysis, a rich topic for critical dialogue.[17]

Any given genre has interpretive powers not only for those who use it for communicative purposes but also for the scholar, and these aspects are compatible. However, the tension between natural, emic categories of genre and scholarly concepts makes the analysis of generic combinations open to debate. The

14 E.g. Briggs and Bauman 1992:132, 138; Tarkka 1993:172, 176.

15 Bakhtin 1986:60–102; Bauman 2004; Briggs and Bauman 1992:145–146; Dorst 1983.

16 Hanks (1987:670) refers to a paper originally presented by Bauman in 1986 at the annual meeting of the American Anthropological Association, published first in 1992 and reprinted in Bauman 2004 as "And the Verse is Thus: Icelandic Stories About Magical Poems"; see also Briggs and Bauman 1992:14–143.

17 Seitel 1999:14–15.

genres in dialogue are recognized, categorized, and named by the researcher who is an outsider to the culture he or she is studying. Although intergeneric strategies of meaning had been acknowledged by the singers, we have—due to the biases of the nineteenth-century collectors[18]—little data to verify it. As factual, formal, stylistic, thematic, or functional characteristics discernible from texts, even archived artifacts, these strategies do, however, indicate the ways in which the singers used the material and conventions at their disposal—either consciously or unconsciously. Incompetence and unsuccessful performances often bring the implicit assumptions about generic conventions to the surface, as demonstrated by the documentation of Karppo's performance.

## Intertextuality in Oral Expressive Forms

Repetition, formulaicity, and stereotypicality permeate the life of oral tradition, from the level of texture to pragmatics. After all, a traditional speech act is recognized as traditional only if reiterated and thus linked to a series of previous performances[19] and the "pool of tradition," or "*everything that is institutionally implied in the act of performance.*"[20] The scale of the element reiterated varies from concise traditional formulae to entire texts, and the redundancy and fixity of form affect the production, reception, and interpretation of oral tradition. The creation of intertextual associations is based on such repetition: recognizability (of a text, a genre, a motif) is a prerequisite for any transformation of meaning. Both John Miles Foley and Paul Zumthor argue that meaning in oral poetry is based on formulaic composition, which is essentially a set of intertextual strategies that enables the presence of the previous performances in the present one.[21]

Like generic instability, redundancy in oral poetry troubled Elias Lönnrot. He assumed it to be displeasing to a literate audience and apologized in the prologue to the *Kanteletar*:

> The same phrases appear now and then in two, or even in many more, different songs. Readers should not censure us for this, or think that we could have tossed these and those words out of the song because they have already appeared in a previous song. We had no right to do so. If, in one song, we find the words *on these wretched borderlands, the*

18 The individual, local, and contemporary uses of poetry were not on the agenda: folklore collection focused on those texts and genres that were conceived as the purest reflections of antiquity and a heroic past.

19 E.g. Bauman 2004:146–147.

20 Foley 2002:107–108.

21 Foley 1991:7–13; Zumthor 1990:89–89; see also Haring 1988:365.

> *poor Northern country*, or *in these bad times, the waning age*, or *woe is me, the poor boy, woe the boy of poor fate*, it does not mean that they cannot reappear in other places. Such phrases, like other old saws, must have lived among the people from times immemorial and, as such, they were mixed unaltered into songs. Such things are nothing out of the ordinary in folksongs; indeed, even in educated circles people may use words once uttered by others as if they were their own.[22]

In this first account of formulaic elements in Finnish-Karelian folk poetry, Lönnrot did not dismiss repetition as senseless reiteration, for the appearance of an expression in one context did not preclude its rightful appearance in another. Such "phrases" or parallelistic couplets in the Kalevala meter were essential to both the poetic idiom and colloquial speech. Even for Lönnrot, recurring phrases were authentic expressions of the singer or speaker's subjectivity: they were used as if they were one's "own," even if they had been used "before" and by others—in a word, they were traditional.

In the interpretation of a traditional text or texts, the repetitive and formulaic elements manifest the unique strategies for creating meaning particular to the poetic tradition. As Albert Lord put it, meaning clings to the recurring elements, for example, themes or formulae, from one context of use to another as an "echo" or "fragrance," a connotative meaning: "Each theme, small or large—one might even say, each formula—has around it an aura of meaning which has been put there by all the contexts in which it has occurred in the past."[23] Meaning is grounded in all the situations in which the poet or singer has used the elements, and the audience's manner of interpretation conforms to the interpretation of the performer: it is also based on previous experiences of usages of the repeated element. This kind of synthesizing interpretive strategy is possible because the poet and audience share the same experiences of textual production and reception.[24]

In his theory of traditional referentiality, John Miles Foley worked on Lord's basic notions and created an outline of a specifically oral aesthetics.[25] Structural, repetitive, and conventional elements do more than simply facilitate oral composition. Their possible domains of significance extend to individual lines and passages and also to entities larger than any individual text, the whole tradition: "Traditional referentiality, then, entails the invoking of a context that is enormously larger and more echoic than the text or work itself,

22 Lönnrot 1840:xlix.
23 Lord 2019:158; see also 68, 100.
24 Lord 2019:158.
25 Foley 1991; 1995.

that brings the lifeblood of generations of poems and performances to the individual performance or text."[26] These metonymic relationships to the whole of tradition are based on allusion: each instance of a textual unit alludes to past and potential instances of its use within the traditional idiom. Tradition is "the enabling referent" that makes interpretation possible and performance "the enabling event" in which and through which an interpretation can be made.[27]

If all the recurrent elements (e.g. formulae, epithets, etc.) were merely clichés with automaticized meanings, using them would fail to generate new semantic contents. A rich and allusive expressive economy emerges from a sufficiently—but not excessively—versatile use of texts. Intertextual signification in oral literature is constructed upon a tension between an individual's creative freedom and the power of convention. The formulae mentioned by Lönnrot are common and versatile until the point where they echo no particular contextual meaning. Still, they evoke the essential ideas expressed in these contexts and enriched and substantiated by multiple uses. If the repeated element has one dominant context of use, however, this context affects the interpretation of the element in all its subsequent uses. If the dominant context is linked to central ideas and values of the community, this effect is particularly strong. For example, mythic images and motifs gain their meaning from the slowly changing mental templates of mythology, and they have the power to channel these meanings to new contexts of use and simultaneously charge them with mythic and ritual resonance.

In the following, I will discuss kinds of intertextuality that enable such traditional referentiality. For the purposes of this discussion, intertextuality will be defined as the dynamic production of meanings in expressive culture through an ongoing dialogue of references and cross references to previous discourses: texts, songs, and performances. Texts and genres have no fixed and stable identities, nor autonomy. Instead they are emergent and relational, produced and reproduced in communicative praxis.[28] In the production and interpretation of a text—for example, a Kalevala-meter poem—the singers and their audiences related the present performance to their repertoire of related performances. The interpretive task of the scholar is analogous: he or she has to trace down all the possible texts and performances that might affect interpretation and then argue for their applicability. The intertextual relations are conditioned by the community's social and historical circumstances and channeled according to the tendencies of tradition, fixity of texture, and conventionality. Far from free and infinite, signification in oral poetry is thus drawn towards what is typical

26 Foley 1991:7.
27 Foley 1992:278; Foley 1995:xiv, 1, 7, 27–28.
28 See e.g. Titon 2003:73–74.

and traditional. Despite—or indeed because of—these centripetal forces of traditional interpretation, atypical combinations create a remarkable potential for new meanings.[29]

The meanings that extend as "auras" from one performance (or text) to another are based on frames of interpretation interacting within the system of genres. The text (motif, or formula) typically appearing in one generic context carries with it the conventional, genre-specific meanings and expectations even when used in another generic context. The consequent clash of interpretations (the typical or expected one and the one implied by the present context) challenges the old meanings and fuels the generation of new ones. The performer and the audience both master the traditional generic system even if their competence may vary both in quality and quantity; in each performance, the cultural code enables them to grasp the generically determined meanings or challenge them. As Briggs and Bauman argue,[30] generic intertextuality links elements of discourse (or texts) to generic ideals, that is, to "generalized or abstracted models of discourse production and reception"—not to other, previous elements of discourse. As no rendering of a text ever fully matches those models, there is always an "intertextual gap" between generic ideals and actual performances.[31]

The dialogue of genres is a central intertextual strategy for generating meaning in and across expressive forms. Within the poetic tradition it is possible to differentiate between several strategies for establishing such dialogues. Like genres themselves, these strategies coordinate principles of composition, performance, and interpretation and are thus a joint effort of performers and their audiences. They overlap conceptually and they can be applied simultaneously. Generic intertextuality is a variable, rather than a homogenous phenomenon, and regional differences in, e.g., the social function, performance context, and style of Kalevala-meter poetry determine the dominant type of generic intertextuality.[32] Furthermore, the inclination of any given genre to generic combination and dialogical structures, or its degree of "polylogicality," varies, and it is possible to analyze quantitatively some strategies of generic intertextuality.[33] Here, I will present a preliminary examination of some of the most obvious strategies: hybridization of genres, intergeneric translation, multi-generic performances, and sequential combination of genres. To conclude, I will discuss the implicit interpretive tension in texts or textual elements that are seemingly standard

[29] For a review of the notion of intertextuality in folklore studies, see Tarkka 2013:88–103; Tarkka 1993:172–177; for intertextuality as a "poetics of quotation," see Tarkka 2016.

[30] Briggs and Bauman 1992:147.

[31] Briggs and Bauman 1992:149.

[32] Tarkka 1996:53.

[33] Tarkka 2013:97–100. A polylogical genre typically combines with other genres—in Bakhtinian terminology, it constitutes a complex or secondary genre (Bakhtin 1986:61–62).

representatives of generic ideals but are open to various context-specific interpretations that radically alter those ideals and the expectations bound to them.

## Hybridization and Intergeneric Translation

The combination of genres within one single text rarely hinders our recognition of the genres in question. However, there are texts whose genre escapes definition—texts in which generic dialogue is dense enough to produce hybrid forms. Such texts are often marginalized in research and archival classification by being labeled as mistakes, idiosyncrasies, or exceptions.

Hybrids can be defined as texts displaying several generic markers with no genre dominating the other. In 1834, one of Lönnrot's most influential informants, Arhippa Perttunen, performed a peculiar text. Beginning in verse form, with words from lyric songs and aphoristic poems, the text alludes to courting epics and then evolves into a neck riddle, which offers a prose account of the use of minor genres and their folk interpretation. Arhippa's performance fuses Kalevala-meter poetry, versified speech, riddles, and folktale, leaving none of the genres untouched by this fusion: the rhetorical structures and interpretative frames associated with all genres involved clash and change in the process. To tell a tale and to contemplate central values in his community, the performer sets in motion the entire system of folklore genres. In his radical combination of traditional elements, Arhippa maximizes the intertextual gap between his performance and the generic ideals connected to many genres of prose and poetry; in doing so, he claims authority as an innovative and creative singer.[34] The hybrid text puzzled Lönnrot for years, and in the process of compiling the *Kanteletar*, he gradually versified the whole tale, finally classifying it as a "narrative song blended with mythical elements."[35] This act of bringing the text closer to generic ideals and expectations not only made it understandable for a wider audience but also portrayed it as a traditional representative of one, albeit invented, genre.

Groups of multi-generic texts can form a hybrid genre, if they recur frequently and are recognized within the community. The most widely known and discussed hybrid genre is the pervasive lyric-epic tradition in the southernmost area of Kalevala-meter rune-singing.[36] The Viena Karelian yoik is another obvious case. The northern Viena yoik was closely related to the Sámi yoik and strongly influenced by the alliterative style of laments; it was non-metrical and improvised. In the Vuokkiniemi parish, however, only the village of Vuonninen belonged to this culture area. The rest of the parish cherished the yoik style

34 SKVR $I_3$ 2008; Tarkka 2013:302–323; see Briggs and Bauman 1992:149.

35 Lönnrot 1840 III 59; Tarkka 2004:254–259.

36 Harvilahti 1994:97–98; Siikala 1994:27–29.

of southern Viena. These hybrid yoiks are cast in the Kalevala meter and share the thematic focus of Kalevala-meter lyric poetry but are locally identified and named as yoiks on the basis of performance style and melody. Identical poetic lines could be used in lyric songs and yoiks of the southern style, but their tone and meaning changed according to the melody and performance style specific to these genres.[37] Thus, in the core region of Kalevala-meter rune-singing, the yoik tradition was absorbed within the register of the dominant poetic idiom.[38] As in the case of the Kalevala-meter hybrid yoik, hybrid genres often indicate border zones between culture areas. Similarly, they often arise at times of radical cultural change: they are genres in transition.

One of the conventional hybrid genres in Kalevala-meter poetry is the proverbial poem or aphorism. The aphorism typically consists of several proverbial couplets, and it presents advice and parables elucidating moral and aesthetic ideas. The themes and even the lines used may also appear in lyric poetry. The difference lies in the performance style and finite form of the texts: as opposed to the aphorism, the lyric uses the first person and is ideally sung, not uttered or recited. According to Thomas DuBois,[39] proverbialization is a native hermeneutic tradition in lyric that describes typical feelings and collective modes of understanding. The ambiguous distinction between lyric poems and aphorisms can be made on the degree of proverbialization realized in the text.[40] In accordance with this emphasis, the messages conveyed and the tone differ: the lyric poem is subjective and affective; the aphorism is assertive, generalizing, even normative. A singer from the Vuonninen village, Anni Lehtonen, was renowned for her ability to improvise serial aphoristic couplets, such as this one:

> Ota oppi otsahas,
> neuvo nenävartehes,
> kun lähet moalla vierahalla,
> uusilla asuin mailla.
>
> Take your learning onto your forehead,
> the advice onto the bridge of your nose,
> when you leave for foreign lands,
> new lands to dwell in.
>
> (SKS KRA Paulaharju 1915 c9232)

37 SKS KiA Väisänen 3119:16–45, SKS KRA Paulaharju 1911:26. On the qualities of the poetic meter in the southern Viena yoiks, see Kallberg 2011b:84–85.

38 Väisänen 1990:141.

39 DuBois 1996.

40 See Tarkka 2016.

Lehtonen explained that the first parallelistic couplet was used as an independent proverb, and its meaning could be summed up as a request: "Listen, when you are taught!"[41] Typically, the couplet appears in songs or long epic poems in which parents—human or animal—teach their offspring strategies for survival.[42] In the aphorism, Lehtonen gives the didactic gesture a new focus: knowledge is an asset in unfamiliar circumstances. The latter couplet commonly occurs in lyric poetry, and its appearance activates the interpretative frame of the songs of homesickness and nostalgia especially important in the songs sung by young wives. With this frame in mind, the whole could be interpreted as an opening to a didactic poem for the bride, a well-established genre performed at the wedding ritual.

The aphorism illustrates the role of the couplet and parallelism in the composition of Kalevala-meter poetry: the parallelistic proverbial couplets are joined together to produce thematically motivated associations. The longer the poem, the clearer its poetic and "entextualized" quality, that is, its detachability from everyday discourse that guarantees the significance of the text even outside the original context of performance.[43] The fusion of the proverb and the sung lyric poem brings about a change in the mode of performance: uttered and contextualized in the flow of speech, the aphorism pierces the boundary between the poetic universe and everyday discourse.[44]

When considered in the context of proverbs, the genesis of the aphorism is a case of generic transformation by amplification. In a set of proverbs joined together in an aphorism, there is no necessary change in interpretative frame—unless the contents of the couplets are contrasted.[45] However, in the Kalevala-meter yoik from southern Viena, the ethos of the genres combined (lyric poetry and yoik proper) contrast sharply. In the yoiks, which are typically sung by young women, desirable partners are extolled with sensual images, whereas unwanted ones are ridiculed with sharp, often erotic, overtones. The lyric poems center on the emotional aspect of courting and marriage, expressing the expectations, fears, and hopes of the poetic ego.[46] Together, the genres produce a dynamic universe of meanings—and thus, an apt outlet for ambivalent emotions.

Cultural change and contacts encourage not only the hybridization of genres but also intergeneric translation of a text from one poetic language to another.

41 SKS KRA Paulaharju 1912–1913 c4713.

42 E.g. SKVR $I_3$ 1062.

43 Bauman and Briggs 1990:73–74.

44 Tarkka 2016.

45 Contrasting contents of parallel couplets represent the stylistic feature called negative parallelism: an affirmative statement is followed by its negation. Such stylistic features challenge the obvious interpretations of the whole set.

46 Tarkka 2013:283–287.

During transitional periods, the same textual contents could thus be cast in more than one poetic meter. In the late nineteenth century, Kalevala-meter poetry coexisted in Viena Karelia with rhymed folksongs, and able singers could choose the poetic meter at will. One such singer was Miihkali Perttunen, the son of the abovementioned Arhippa. In the eyes of Romanticist folklore collectors, Miihkali had become an iconic figure, "the blind Homer of the North," and he received a small pension from the Finnish Literature Society. On August 29, 1894, he performed two versions of a song of thanks dedicated to his patrons, the "good gentlemen of Helsinki."[47] The collectors—or Miihkali himself—named both poems *Miihkali's Song*, indicating a presumption that the two performances were identical as instances of the same song. This identity clearly concerns the levels of theme and communicative function only: the singer depicts his ability to sing, the reactions of the collectors, and the generosity of the "gentlemen." The first version, cast in the Kalevala meter, climaxes in a generic amplification, a prayer to protect the patrons and their economic pursuits.[48] The second is structured in parallelistic rhyming quatrains, and it also refers to God as the protector and provider of the "gentlemen of Helsinki." It is clear that Miihkali was a master in the Kalevala meter but a novice in rhyming couplets.

The choice of genre determines the tone of the text and also hints at an ideological conflict. As Briggs and Bauman have noted,[49] generic intertextuality orders discourse in historical and social terms: genres are associated with different times (e.g. the past vs. modernity), ethnic groups (e.g. Finns, Karelians, and Russians), and social classes (e.g. the rural peasants vs. the urban elite). Invoking a genre or playing with that invocation thus foregrounds the tension between the opposing categories in question. Many Viena Karelians considered rhyming songs modern, mundane, and "foreign," either Finnish or Russian, whereas Kalevala-meter songs were "our songs," or "the old songs of Karelia."[50] Performing the "same" song in these two poetic languages in succession also hints at the problematic intercultural communication in the recording situation: the song performed by a poor, rural Karelian to thank the rich, urban, and Finnish-speaking elite maximizes its effect by translating the message from the "old" language to the "new" one. In this particular case, intergeneric translation aimed at creating a consensual atmosphere and thus relativizing the radical cultural chasm between the speaker and the addressee. In the clumsy rhyming stanzas, Miihkali is creating a common ground for intercultural exchange.

47 SKS KRA Karjalainen 1894 b144, b146.
48 Tarkka 2013:143–146.
49 Briggs and Bauman 1992:147–148.
50 Tarkka 2013:499.

## Genres in Performance

For those studying archived oral tradition, the most challenging aspect of generic intertextuality is the dialogue of genres within the performance. The evidence for multi-generic performances is obscured by the procedures involved in textualization and archiving. Most of the documented Kalevala-meter poems were written down in situations specifically arranged for this purpose. Initiated and controlled by the collector and without audience participation or other factors contributing to the performance arena,[51] rune-collecting sessions were performances out of the ordinary. The resulting written representations of oral poetry were consequently a far cry from the local ideals and experiences of finalized performances. Furthermore, written documents tend necessarily to cut the flow of performance into segments, resulting in textual objects that may easily be subjected to generic classification. Decontextualization gives an impression not only of atomistic texts but of genres with categorical boundaries and exclusive identities. If the text is defined more broadly, however, the situation changes: the meaningful unit is the performance as a whole, and the interpretation of any single textual item has to take into account all the genres put into play.

Intergeneric maneuvering has been the rule in heightened, full-fledged performances of Kalevala-meter poetry. During the wedding ritual, the points of view of the parties were expressed and juxtaposed through ritual songs, songs of mockery, laments, incantations and spells, proverbs, and allegorical ceremonial speech.[52] Ritual wedding songs structured the ritual whole and put forth the values and expectations of the two kin groups. Songs of mockery and didactic poems explicitly addressed the groom and the bride's abilities to fulfill those expectations. Laments functioned as an outlet for the emotions of the bride, who faced final separation from her childhood home. Incantations and spells secured the couple and those present from the social malevolence and envy that could magically harm the whole community undergoing a reorganization of social statuses. Proverbs and ceremonial speech articulated central notions and values in an indirect, metaphorical fashion. The expression and reformulation of communal and individual values, expectations, and emotions could only be accomplished by the dialogical orchestration of genres.

Ritual performances, such as weddings and bear-killing rituals, formed a favorable setting for extensive and varied use of folklore genres, and it seems that the formality of the performance in general tended to enhance dialogical

51 See Foley 1995:47–49; Tarkka 2013:141.

52 Tarkka 2013:70, 278.

use of genres. In public gatherings and festive singing contests, the competing singers challenged each other with mocking songs and raised their spirits with boasting words and magical formulae—a practice portrayed in epic poems such as *The Singing Contest*.[53] As markers of significant performances the singer's opening and closing formulae that frame epic poems are, however, the most obvious proof of the performative efficacy of generic combinations. Especially the long narrative poems were typically performed in public and with a high degree of formality. The performance arena remained incomplete without the use of the singer's formulae, a genre dedicated to marking a performance. Although seamlessly bound to the epic narrative, they often were documented and published as independent texts and classified as lyric poetry.[54]

What happens to these contextually determined generic dialogues when the texts are performed and transmitted out of context—or the context locally acknowledged as an appropriate one? It was already mentioned that the decontextualization inherent in the act of documentation produces atomistic texts and represents genres as solid entities—as in the case of the singer's opening and closing formulae. This is, however, not always the case. As a performance, the rune-collecting session was a collaborative event in which the singer and the collector often aimed at producing a text that would approximate the ideals and expectations of both parties. To fill in the missing frame provided by the context, the singer sometimes included descriptions of a typical performance setting in his text. This is often pronounced in ritual texts recorded outside the ritual context. As a rule, the contextual information was given in a prose statement, but sometimes it was woven into the poetic text; for example, the performer's role and identity could be disclosed by simply telling who is uttering a particular text in the ritual, or by presenting this text as words uttered by a protagonist in the poem.[55]

Such narrative contextualization of ritual poetry relies on the prime strategy of generic intertextuality employed widely in Kalevala-meter poetry: the sequential combination of genres. This most conspicuous form of generic intertextuality manifests itself in two ways: embedded insertions and serial combinations. The generic tensions appear explicitly in the text, which unfolds as a sequence of elements drawn from many genres.

53 Tarkka 2013:226–230.
54 Tarkka 2013:69, 99, 129.
55 Tarkka 2013:349–350.

## The Multi-Generic Epic

The move from a multi-generic performance to a multi-generic text is gradual and largely dependent on the recording situation with its techniques, aims, and underlying notions concerning performance and textuality. Traditional referentiality, or the consciousness of all the genres and texts in the culture relevant to the theme, was the grounds for both building and understanding fictive or mythic universes of meaning and narration and for verbalizing them in any particular performance. Emic notions of genre were elementary to the organization of these meanings and narratives.

The epic is the quintessentially multivocal platform for sequential combinations of genre.[56] In the Vuokkiniemi corpus, epic poems contain episodes of incantation, lyric poetry, aphorisms, prayers, proverbs, riddles, and yoiks. Scholars of the *Kalevala* have paid special attention to incantations, lyric poetry, and ritual songs embedded in the epic.[57] One reason for this complexity and narrative depth is the alternation of narration, descriptive passages, and reported speech in dialogues, in both the *Kalevala* and its oral sources.[58]

A generic insertion or interpolation is a passage embedded within the text but representing a genre distinct from its textual context. Such embedded insertions are usually presented within dialogues by the protagonists, as lines uttered by the heroes, or in passages evaluating the narrative. They broaden the fictive universe by giving voice to protagonists and by portraying traditional speech acts.

Viena Karelian epic poetry was characterized by metapoetic themes and plot types that centered around poetry itself: the poets made poetry about people performing poetry. This reflexive assessment of the rune-singing culture necessitated representation of traditional performances within the narrative universe. Singing is effectively described by making the protagonist of the epic sing. These embedded performances within the epic result in intergeneric combinations.[59]

As a metapoetic strategy, singing about singing has a performative function: it has an impact on the context. As the singers sang about themselves and their own cultural competence, they reflected upon tradition in situations in which tradition was being constructed. In his studies on Eddic poetry, Lars Lönnroth underscores the prevalence of the phenomenon in oral poetry.[60] The

56 DuBois 1995:149, 161; Tarkka 1993:183, 187n18; Tarkka 1994:265; Tarkka 1996:53–54.

57 E.g. Kaukonen 1990:169, 172, 174.

58 Tarkka 1996.

59 Tarkka 2013:168–206.

60 Lönnroth 1979:95.

double scene, as he terms it, refers to the connection between the situation of performance and the fictive universe: it is "something that happens during the course of an oral performance whenever the narrative appears to be enacted by the performer or his audience on the very spot where the entertainment takes place."[61] Here, narrated event and narrating event merge, providing a possibility for the fusion of the heroes' and the performers' identities.[62] In Kalevala-meter poetry, the double scene is closely connected to generic intertextuality, as its realization requires not only the use of singers' formulae, whereby a favorable performance reality is created but also the representation of the protagonists' dialogues and the embedded generic discourse connected to them.

Comparative parallels for double scenes in Eddic and Kalevala-meter poetry have been presented by Richard Martin, Dwight Reynolds, and Richard Bauman. According to Martin, who has studied representations of speech and performance in the Homeric epics, the *Iliad* is largely based on vernacular "speaking culture," a mode of speech employed in the epic in the heightened and authoritative speech acts of the heroes.[63] The epic accounts of the speech acts represent the purest form of mimesis. Reynolds's research on the northern Egyptian epic tradition *Sīrat Banī Hilāl* points at the affinity between the performers of epic and the heroes whose exploits they recount: both are singers. The double scene, that is, a scene in which the hero performs a poem, is a recurrent feature in these poems.[64] In his study of the Icelandic *kraftaskáld* legends, Bauman examines representations of magical performances as generic intertextuality.[65] The interplay between the Viena epic and its performers corresponds to the situation presented by Reynolds: epic heroes, like rune-singers, use incantations to solve problems. The relationship between the Viena Karelian singer and Väinämöinen, the main epic protagonist, was predominantly one of collegial affinity.

The significance of embedded performances is highlighted in the formulae that frame them—such as "he spoke thus, uttered a word."[66] Frames for signaling the lines uttered by the heroes are among the most widely used stock formulae in Kalevala-meter poetry.[67] They may be short, comprising only half a line, or they may take up one entire line or two parallel lines. Sometimes the frame can be emphasized by referring to traditional singers' opening words and

61 Lönnroth 1979:95

62 Bauman 1986:112; DuBois 1995:150, 156; Tarkka 1993:181, 2013:177.

63 Martin 1989:xiv.

64 Reynolds 1995:72–73, 79, 87, 90, 100. See also Reynolds in this volume.

65 Bauman 2004:15–33.

66 SKVR $I_4$ 1095.

67 Saarinen 1994:191.

thus evoking an image of an actual performance.[68] The transition to a line of dialogue is often obvious, even without a frame. Yet the lack of frame to introduce a generic interpolation may also indicate that the shift to reported speech signals an evaluation by the performer or the speaker of the poem, expressed in a generic idiom best suited for this task. The identity of the speaker within the poem is crucial because it determines the rhetorical function of the insertion.

I shall give three examples from the Sampo-cycle that forms the core of the *Kalevala*.[69] Väinämöinen, the epic hero and sage,[70] has just created the world but is now drifting in the primal sea, agonized and fearing death. The reactions of the hero are portrayed by three kinds of embedded performances. First, he resorts to a lyric song to express his agony:

> Itkie tihustelouve,
> voia vuopahattelouve:
> "Jouvuin pois omilta mailta
> mailla muilla vierahilla,
> äkki ouvoilla ovilla,
> en tunne tupia näitä,
> osoa en ovissa käyvä."
>
> He cries and whimpers,
> groans and growls:
> "I had to leave the lands of my own
> for other, strange lands,
> for doors so odd,
> I don't know these rooms,
> I can't find my way through the doors."
>
> (SKVR $I_1$ 58a)

As in the case of Väinämöinen's cosmic nostalgia, the embedded lyric poems typically describe the emotions and motives of the protagonists. Significantly, identical lyrical lines were used by the singers in songs of homesickness.[71] Väinämöinen's lament is framed as a line of dialogue in which the conventional

68 E.g. SKVR $I_1$ 299.

69 Kuusi 1990.

70 There is no adequate translation of the Finnish-Karelian term for the ritual specialist known as *tietäjä*; here, the term sage is used because of its emphasis on the ideal of wisdom, signaled by the term's etymological basis, *tieto* "knowledge." The *tietäjä* mastered incantations and various ritual techniques such as divination, and his main task was to heal disease; see Siikala 2002:79–84; Tarkka 2005:82–95, 131–133, 138–152.

71 E.g. SKVR $I_3$ 1377; Tarkka 2013:405–412.

words to represent a speech act are replaced with varying depictions of crying: this is a song of sorrow. Väinämöinen's "hissing cry" brings tears "plumper" than hazel hen eggs and heavier than cranberries in his eyes.[72]

Second, Väinämöinen evaluates the situation in a more sober manner, by uttering a proverb:

> Siitä kulki Väinämöinen,
> kulki kuusissa hakona,
> petäjässä päänä pölkyn.
> Itsche nuin sanoksi virkko:
> "Haittan' on hako vesillä,
> köyhät eellä rikkahalla."
>
> And so Väinämöinen was cast adrift,
> drifted as a trunk among spruces,
> as a log among pines.
> He himself put into words:
> "Driftwood troubles the waterways,
> the poor bother the rich."
>
> (SKVR $I_1$ 79)

Väinämöinen's comment is a common proverb in Viena Karelia. The basis for its inclusion in the scene is vague—an uncertain link is established between Väinämöinen's drifting and the general notion of the harmfulness of driftwood. In itself, the proverb expresses a profound sense of injustice: for the rich, the poor are reduced to harmful obstacles in the process of gaining wealth. In this context, the insertion focuses on the portrayal of Väinämöinen's repertoire of tradition, words, and poetry. His acts are repeatedly authorized by displays of his wisdom and a disposition coined in the formulaic epithet "old and steadfast" (*vaka vanha*).

The formulaic speech acts and epithets identifying the speaker as Väinämöinen, the authoritative sage and singer, discernibly shape the interpretative frame—even of lines that are not explicit generic interpolations. Väinämöinen's weighty speech generally takes the form of proverbial language, even if the words he uses are not always established proverbs. This proverbial way of speaking is a special characteristic enhanced by the traditional image of Väinämöinen. As noted by Iivo Marttinen, an ethnographer from Vuokkiniemi, the poignancy of proverbs made them sound as though "they had been spoken

[72] SKVR $I_1$ 95.

by Väinämöinen himself."[73] By internalizing this characteristic, the listener learned not only to differentiate between a saying or proverb and other speech genres but also to elaborate on expressive form and content.

Later, when the heroes are raiding for the fantastic wealth-producing object, the *sampo*, more proverbs, such as "Anything spare won't capsize a boat," are performed.[74] All the proverbs mentioned, mostly uttered by Väinämöinen, are identifiable and traditional performances for those socialized into the rune-singing culture and idioms of spoken language. As the listener identifies a familiar performance taking place within the fictive or mythic universe, this imaginary realm is drawn closer: it is enriched with detail, made perspicuous, topical, and familiar. The talk of the heroes was immediately recognized—after all, the listeners used the same expressions themselves. Väinämöinen not only authorized traditional performances: traditional performances were a proof of Väinämöinen's wisdom.

The last and ultimate strategy used by Väinämöinen is magical. Uttering an incantation, he raises a rainstorm to carry him to the shore:

"Oi Ukko ylijumala,
yli toatto taivahańi,
taivahallińi Jumala.
Luo sie pilvi luotehelta,
toini on lännestä lähätä,
kolmas on koko terältä,
lomatusta loukahuta,
kassa potkalta porohkat."
Sekä nousi, jotta joutu,
kasto potkalta porohkat ...
kantopa vanhan Väinämöisen
paikoilla papittomilla ...

"Oh, Ukko, god supreme,
highest father in the heavens,
heavenly God.
Conceive a cloud from the northwest,
cast another from the west,
a third one from all around,
clap them all together,

73 SKS KRA Marttinen 1893, preface to c1-904.

74 SKVR $I_1$ 79a. The idiomatic translation is "Better safe than sorry." On the *sampo* in the Vuokkiniemi corpus, see Tarkka 2013:209–225.

wet the flintlock's powder."
And it rose, and it rushed,
and it wet the flintlock's powder ...
carried old Väinämöinen,
to the priestless places ...

(SKVR $I_1$ 78)

The portrayal of the singing of magical charms is especially salient in the narrative universe of Kalevala-meter epics.[75] In his analysis of the *kraftaskáld* legends, Richard Bauman has noted that in many epics, the heroes accomplish things with magical means, verbal or otherwise. As an example, Bauman presents a passage from the *Kalevala*.[76] Embedded performances are justified by the narrative and, especially in the case of incantation, often lead to solving a problem and moving the plot forward. They also lend emotional depth to the characters' actions. In *The Singing Contest*, for example, the hero expresses his anger by singing a song endowed with magical power.[77]

The embedded incantation brings with it an implicit theory about the power of the word and the efficacy of the incantation. In the words of Greg Urban, "any narrative text containing instances of reported speech embodies a kind of 'theory' about the relationship between speech and action"[78]—in this case, the conceived causal and intentional link between Väinämöinen's words and the storm. The evidence provided by the embedded incantation is strong: as Bauman notes, the incantation and the account of its effectiveness follow each other in a tight parallelistic construction.[79] Bauman emphasizes that quoted speech "not merely recounts, but re-presents the quoted discourse."[80] Unlike in the legends studied by Bauman, I argue that reported speech and embedded ritual performances maintain a trace of the illocutionary power of incantations.[81] Similar quotations appear in ritual texts imbued with magical power, and the embedded text itself could be used in real life rituals by the same performers. The same applies to lyric poetry: through an embedded lyric performance, some of the genre's expressive and emotional power is transferred to the epic.

Within the poetics of traditional referentiality, overt illustration of the efficacy of the incantation was entirely optional. Even though the embedded

75 DuBois 1995:149–157; Tarkka 1994:272–273; Tarkka 1996:53–54.

76 Bauman 2004:29–30. Bauman's example is an incantation for producing rain, with which Väinämöinen waters his field in the *Kalevala*'s second canto (Lönnrot 1963:12–13).

77 E.g. SKVR $I_1$ 183; see also Reynolds 1995:156–157.

78 Urban 1984:310.

79 Bauman 2004:30.

80 Bauman 2004:21.

81 See Bauman 2004:22; DuBois 1995:150.

incantations did serve to legitimate both the incantation tradition and Väinämöinen's authority, the cultural standing of incantations and the mythical sage was sufficiently established, thus making explicit demonstration needless. The mere recognition of Väinämöinen's figure and the incantatory register ensured that the audience understood the plot.

An embedded incantation in an epic poem has a reciprocal signifying relation to the epic: while it authorizes the epic through the performative power of the incantation, it also authorizes the tradition of incantations through the mythical epic universe. In addition to authorization, embedded elements can also bring forth parody and humor, as the combination of genres activates two incongruent frames of interpretation.[82]

Another strategy of sequential combination is the serial development of the poem by linking passages from various genres into lengthy sequences or chains. Here, the generic insertion is not framed within the host text; rather, it typically produces a permanent change of genre. Such serial texts are often highly stable combinations of an epic introduction and an incantation.

In the epic poem *The Knee Wound*, Väinämöinen suffers an injury to his knee and undertakes a journey to the upper and lower worlds in search of a mythical healer. Only the third attempt is successful, and the wound is healed with an incantation. Although the poem is firmly linked with the sage's role as a healer and has an established connection with incantations, it does not necessarily continue with an incantation. Sometimes closure is achieved with a laconic statement of Väinämöinen's cure ("He was cured then"); sometimes the poem continues with other plot types (SKVR $I_4$ 2145, SKVR $I_1$ 89). Typically, however, *The Knee Wound* appears as a narrative introduction to blood-stopping words, as an alternative to *The Birth of Iron*, an incantatory narrative of origins that describes the birth of the substance causing the wound. *The Knee Wound* operates as a *historiola* for the words for blood-stopping: during the course of the ritual, the healer sketches a prototypical healing event in order to replicate its success in the present of the ritual.[83]

The ritual context endowed *The Knee Wound* with magical power. In the mythical account, both the power to heal and the propensity to be healed were traced back to the beginning of time, from which they emanated to the present. In some cases, however, the combination of *The Knee Wound* and the incantation is finalized by returning to the fictive universe, for example, by describing Väinämöinen's deeds after the cure.[84] The return to the fictive universe is redundant in the ritual context, and it disrupts the transposition

82 Tarkka 2013:265–301.

83 See e.g. Siikala 2002:89, 91.

84 SKVR $I_1$ 304.

of magical power from the mythical world to the present situation. The whole turns into a representation of a magical act, lacking the ritual efficacy of such acts.[85]

Even in the case of an established and typical combination of the epic with incantations, such as *The Knee Wound* and the words for blood-stopping, the incantation can be embedded in the narrative poem as the sage-hero's utterance, which is framed with opening formulae (e.g. "thus [he] spoke to his knee" SKVR $I_1$ 317). As the incantation sequence begins, the singer's position vis-à-vis the epic protagonists is altered. No longer is he simply a narrator describing Väinämöinen's wound; instead, he now assumes the role of healer. Because the words of the incantation are often framed as lines uttered by the eternal sage himself, Väinämöinen appears to be speaking through the mouth of the performer. Identification with a powerful mythic figure authorizes the ritual and guarantees its efficacy.[86]

Incantations for blood-stopping detached from the narrative episode may draw upon the plot of *The Knee Wound* and its pattern of three repetitions used in describing the quest for a healer. The opportunity provided by the narrative *historiola* for the performer to identify with the mythical healer is not always used, but simply knowing the narrative pattern guarantees that the healer's authority will be acknowledged. Anni Lehtonen frames her incantation for blood-stopping as a description of a healing ritual, as something "the men say, when they staunch blood":

Astua lekuttelen
ylimmäistä tietä myöten
ylimmäisehen talohon.
Jo kysyn kynnykseltä,
anun alta ikkunoijen:
"Oisiko talossa tässä
uron tuskan tuntijoo,
salpoajaa verisatijen?"

I waggle my way
along the highest road
to the highest house.
Right at the threshold, I ask,
beneath the windows, I utter my pleas:
"Can anybody in this house

[85] See also DuBois 1995:150.
[86] Tarkka 2013:116–118, 192.

grasp the hero's pain,
stop the rain of blood?"

(SKVR $I_4$ 196)

The performer of the incantation, a male blood-stopper, occupies the place of the poem's speaker: he recounts the journey he is taking to the otherworld. After the third attempt, he arrives at the "lowest house" and meets the god Ukko, "the keeper of the clouds." The divine healer "himself puts into words":

"Nyt tulkoh Jumalan tunti,
apu Herran astukkoo
tämän tuskan tuntijaksi …."

"Now let the hour of God arise,
the aid of the Lord come forth
to grasp this pain …."

(SKVR $I_4$ 196)

According to Lehtonen, the healer now "begins to recite similar spells" to those uttered by Ukko. At this stage, the double scene is fully realized. As Lehtonen states, the performer's words are similar to those used by the mythical healers at the beginning of the text. The text clearly shows the positions available to the hero of the poem; the singer (or performer of an incantation) can assume these positions during a performance even to the point that the poem acquires a first-person narrator—an atypical feature in Viena Karelian narrative poems. The speaker's connection to the epic's heroes remains implicit but recognizable for those acquainted with the traditional poem types.[87] The imposition of the rhetorical structure of an incantation onto an epic plot—or the epic plot onto the incantation— is one form of the implicit dialogue of genres.

Even if generic embedding is most common in epic poems, it also appears in incantations and lyric poetry. Hunting incantations described the hunter's frustration with lyric verses: the ritual intervention realized in the performance was motivated by the experiences of want and hunger. Lyric songs that focused on the anxieties of social life often turned into magic formulae that fought malevolent or envious fellow humans interpreted as witches.[88] The hybrid potential of lyric songs and proverbs hints at the possibility of their sequential combination. A lyric song recorded in Ingria from an unknown singer starts with conventional motifs from songs sung by young unmarried women. The girl is waiting

87 See also DuBois 1995:192–193.

88 Tarkka 2013:340, 124–125.

to be courted, perhaps by a boy she loves. The passage describes the frustration of waiting and the passing of time, crystallizing the mood of the speaker into an idiomatic expression: "Ain't nothing from nowhere!" After the abrupt evaluation, the tone changes:

> Sananlaskuss' on sanottu,
> niin on ennen ennustettu:
> Yö pitkä ukotta maata,
> päivä pitkä lounahitta.
>
> It's been said in a proverb,
> thus was once foretold:
> The night is long if you lie without a man,
> the day is long without a meal.
>
> (SKVR $XIII_1$ 2465)

What is unusual here is the naming of the embedded genre. The proverb itself describes the same situation as the lyrical prologue but now with a new tone typical of the genre. The short statement provides solace by pointing up the shared nature of the speaker's experience: she is not the first one to suffer; many like her have felt the same. The shift in tone is temporary, however, and the singer continues with a lyric song. The incorporation of a new lyrical motif is signaled with a frame that indicates a return to the dominant genre of the song:

> Niin se ennen neito lauloi
> mataroan mennessänsä:
> "Kuin mä saisin suuren sulhon,
> sulhon suuren ja sorian ..."
>
> And so the maiden used to sing
> as she went to gather bedstraw:
> "If only I could get a tall bridegroom,
> a bridegroom tall and slender ..."
>
> (SKVR $XIII_1$ 2465)

The frame implies that songs like this were sung by young women as they did their chores. The song itself is traditional and well known; it has been sung before.[89] The ensuing lyrical passage reformulates the theme of an endless

[89] E.g. SKVR $XIII_2$ 4174, 4175.

night of waiting, now with upbeat defiance and renewed hope. As pointed out by Senni Timonen,[90] those lyric poems that consist of several traditional motifs are especially likely to tell a tale, often an autobiography, simultaneously evaluating it and linking the subjective experience to collective emotions and ways of expressing them. The dialogue of genres is an effective means for accomplishing such contrasting and complementary foci. Distinctions of grammatical person in verbal forms indicate genre-specific points of view: the poetic speaker of the lyric poem foregrounds the subjective experience whereas the proverb grounds that subjectivity in a collective stance. The Ingrian case of an amplified and multi-generic lyric performance also illustrates the regional variation in generic intertextuality. Ingrian Kalevala-meter poetry is characterized by lyric-epic narrative songs in which narration proceeds in the first person singular.[91] This hybrid form of the epic genre contributes to the hybridization of the lyric genre and makes it susceptible to narrative elaboration and dialogical amplification by non-narrative genres as well.

## Implicit Dialogues

Knowledge of the fictive or mythic universe of the poems and competence in diverse generic practices served as what Foley has called the "enabling referents": as singers performed and audiences interpreted their performances, traditional referentiality made even incomplete messages understandable.[92] The singer may or may not choose to amplify his epic performance with generic insertions. According to Lönnrot, Viena Karelian singers clearly articulated the tendency to leave some generic combinations implicit. Ritual songs and magic incantations, Lönnrot asserted, were mainly sung separately but when a narrative poem reached a scene that depicted the use of these genres, the singers told the collector: "Here starts the common incantation for iron" or "Here one should sing wedding songs, and you will get them from the women."[93] The expressions "here starts" and "here one should sing" refer to the option of extensive and explicit generic combination. The singers could leave them implicit in the performance because the local audience could fill in the allusion. Lönnrot, however, was an outsider who needed instruction. Further, while writing the *Kalevala* for an amateur literate audience, he decided to bring

90 Timonen 2004:81, 161, 166.

91 Harvilahti 1994:96–97.

92 See Foley 1995:1, 7, 28.

93 Lönnrot 1849:ii-iii; cf. Magoun's translation in Lönnrot 1963:375–376.

the generic allusions to the surface and amplify the epic text with extensive passages of ritual poetry.[94]

In archival research, explicit demonstrations of generic intertextuality are to be found on the textual level, for example in sequential combinations of genres within one single text. Also, the hybridization of genres is often evident in the analysis of larger corpora of oral poetry. As genres are determined by thematic, stylistic, structural, and performative characteristics, the intergeneric manipulation may be accomplished at any of these levels. Such intertextual cues remain largely implicit in archival records but have been elementary in the lives of oral poetries. In her analysis of the musical structures and performative styles in Ingrian Kalevala-meter poetry, Kati Kallio has referred to generic intertextuality (or "interperformativity") triggered by other-than-textual aspects of the poem: a single poem could be interpreted as representing various genres depending on the use of genre-specific minor formulae, themes, patterns of repetition, refrains, song structures, and melodies.[95] Typical "ways of singing," which included textual, musical, and performative aspects, were characteristic of specific situations (e.g. weddings), and their use in other situations still referred to the typical, culturally acknowledged contexts.[96] Such interperformative cues are evident in the hybrid genres discussed above. If the performance mode (singing vs. speaking) differentiated lyric poems from aphorisms and the melody type from southern yoiks, a transformation on the musical level transformed the whole interpretive framework bound to the genre.

An identical text—a line, a couplet, a poem—may thus have various meanings and generic attachments in different performance situations: the use to which it is put makes the difference. As pointed out by Lönnrot, the same elements could be used in numerous contexts and genres, and they have no single original meaning. Such multi-purpose elements used in many genres create associations as well as differences within the system of genres. Choosing an expression with an identifiable and conventional context of performance—for example, one defined by ritual regulation and alleged magical efficacy—may create radically new meanings, commenting on and evaluating persons or circumstances. The same applies to finalized texts.

The shorter the text, the more flexible were its possible uses in communicative practices: even a two-line poetic utterance may contain the possibility of many genres within it. This implicit generic dialogue is usually impossible to detect in archival materials. Yet a short performance by one of the most famous singers of Kalevala-meter poetry, Paraske Nikitin from Ingria, is a case in point.

94 Tarkka 1996:53–55; Tarkka 2013:96–97.
95 Kallio 2011:419.
96 Kallio 2011:404; see also Lord 2019:158, 68, 100; Tarkka 2013:85–86.

Her use of two lines used commonly in a snake charm shows that a novel context of use, or recontextualization, inverts the interpretative expectations bound to genre. According to the collector, "Paraske said this whenever her husband grimaced: 'Dribble dripped from the villain's mouth, slobber from the scoundrel's jaws!'"[97]

Paraske had learned the couplet from the very husband to whom it was directed, and it typically appears in a mythical account of the origin of the snake or the frog, used in a healing charm for a snake bite: the devil (or Judas) runs until exhausted and begins to slobber. The snake is born from this potent excretion.[98] In a marital repartee, Paraske thus made an intertextual reference to the supranormal realm and a myth describing the origin of evil. Tradition was employed in exchanges of words when what was said was to be given special emphasis, effect, and cultural resonance. The emotional content and intention of this performance for those involved ranges from aggression and disgust to a joking relationship of sorts: the husband is the devil. The performance is a generic hybrid: on the basis of the textual content alone, the couplet can be classified as a charm but as far as the context of performance and communicational function are concerned, a nagging proverbial phrase.

As generic ideals guided the use of a particular genre, its performance in an unexpected situation affected the meanings communicated. Elements of both proverbial poems and yoiks—generic hybrids in themselves—belonged to the sphere of artistic and marked performance, but they could be incorporated in everyday conversation. In Viena Karelia, proverbial poems, proverbs, and proverbial expressions were constantly used in conversation. All of them could be cast in the Kalevala meter and all of them were referred to with the emic term *poverkka*.[99] Armas Väisänen noted that his informants commented upon the collecting situation and answered questions with "yoik words,"[100] that is, strongly alliterative phrases that used special vocabulary characteristic of yoiks. Such poetic and performative interventions in conversation have several communicative impacts that derive from the activation of generic traditional referentiality. References to proverbs authorize messages and give them an aura of traditional wisdom whereas "yoik words" change the tone of conversation into one that is playful and even abusive.

97 SKVR $V_3$ 1290.
98 E.g. SKVR $V_2$ 2555, 2576.
99 Tarkka 2016.
100 Väisänen 1990:139–140.

## Conclusion

Characteristics bound to any genre are put into use, organized, and manipulated in performances in various ways, maximizing or minimizing the fit between the generic ideal and the actual performance, that is, managing the intertextual gap.[101] An analysis of these calibrations affects the way we perceive and conceptualize folklore performances and traditionality. Fidelity to generic ideals and adherence to previous performance practices foregrounds the traditional authority inherent in the idea of folklore as an embodiment of cultural continuity and textual stability. Transmutation of those ideals and practices involves a move in the opposite direction: performance becomes the nexus of individual creativity and innovation.[102] Generic intertextuality (or the maneuvering of generic ideals and their realizations within the system of genres) thus reflects the tension between subjectivity and collective tradition or instability and stability. Even if the production of meaning requires some stability and recognizability within the system of genres, instability is ever present in creative decisions, fortunate mistakes, and the ever-changing and ideologically torn contextual sphere. Even such innovation can only be articulated against the background of tradition.

The use and interpretation of folklore genres is associated with social, ideological, and historical factors;[103] crying, laughing, yoiking, and singing (or performing a lament, a mocking song, a yoik, or a lyric or epic poem) index particular groups of performers and audiences (or addressees), underlying assumptions about the order of things (religious or social), and specific timeframes of use and origin of the discourse (past vs. present, mythic vs. the here-and-now). Simultaneously, genres are characterized by semantic content, thematic emphasis, and a point of view.[104] They evoke universes of meaning that can be identified but never separated. Through this capacity of genres, generic interaction affects the ways in which people create both coherence and contrastive reasoning in the social universe, allowing them to consider a given theme in terms of several generic realities. The dialogue between modes of knowledge, expression, and understanding enables the relativization and contestation of values, the elaboration of ambiguous emotions, and reconciliation with social conflict and change as well as ritual transitions.

[101] See Briggs and Bauman 1992:149.
[102] See Briggs and Bauman 1992:149.
[103] See Briggs and Bauman 1992:147.
[104] See e.g. Siikala and Siikala 2005:88.

## Abbreviations

SKS KiA Finnish Literature Society Literature Archives
SKS KRA Finnish Literature Society Folklore Archives
SKVR Niemi, A. R., and V. Saminen, eds. 1908-1937. *Suomen Kansan Vanhat Runot*. 5 vols. Helsinki.

## Bibliography

Anttonen, P., and R. Kvideland, eds. 1993. *Nordic Frontiers: Recent Issues in the Study of Modern and Traditional Culture in the Nordic Cultures*. NIF Publications 27. Turku.

Bakhtin, M. 1986. "The Problem of Speech Genres." In *Speech Genres and Other Late Essays*, ed. C. Emerson and M. Holquist, 60–102. Austin.

Bauman, R. 1986. *Story, Performance, and Event: Contextual Studies of Oral Narrative*. Cambridge.

———. 2004. *A World of Others' Words: Cross-Cultural Perspectives on Intertextuality*. Oxford.

Bauman, R., and C. Briggs. 1990. "Poetics and Performance as Critical Perspectives on Language and Social Life." *Annual Review of Anthropology* 19:59–88.

Becker-Nielsen, H., et al., eds. 1979. *Medieval Narrative. A Symposium*. Odense.

Ben-Amos, D. 1976. "The Concepts of Genre in Folklore." In Pentikäinen and Juurikka 1976:30–43.

———. 1992. *Do We Need Ideal Types (in Folklore)? An Address to Lauri Honko*. NIF Papers 2. Turku.

Briggs, C., and R. Bauman. 1992. "Genre, Intertextuality, and Social Power." *Journal of Linguistic Anthropology* 2:131–172.

Burke, K. 1957. "Literature as Equipment for Living." In *Perspectives by Incongruity*, ed. S. E. Hyman, 100–109. Bloomington.

Dorst, J. 1983. "Neck-Riddle as a Dialogue of Genres: Applying Bakhtin's Genre Theory." *Journal of American Folklore* 96/382:413–433.

DuBois, T. 1995. *Finnish Folk Poetry and the Kalevala*. New York.

———. 1996. "Native Hermeneutics: Traditional Means of Interpreting Lyric Songs in Northern Europe." *Journal of American Folklore* 109/433:235–266.

Feintuch, B., ed. 2003. *Eight Words for the Study of Expressive Culture*. Urbana.

Foley, J. M. 1991. *Immanent Art: From Structure to Meaning in Traditional Oral Epic*. Bloomington.

———. 1992. "Word-Power, Performance, and Tradition." *Journal of American Folklore* 105/417:275–301.

———. 1995. *The Singer of Tales in Performance*. Bloomington.

———. 2002. "Selection as Pars Pro Toto: The Role of Metonymy in Epic Performance and Tradition." In Honko 2002:106–127.

Hanks, W. 1987. "Discourse Genres in a Theory of Practice." *American Ethnologist* 14:666–692.

Haring, L. 1988. "Interperformance." *Fabula* 29:365–372.

Harvilahti, L. 1994. "The Ingrian Epic Poem and its Models." In Siikala and Vakimo 1994:91–112.

Honko, L. 1976. "Genre Theory Revisited." In Pentikäinen and Juurikka 1976:20-25.

———. 1989. "Folkloristic Theories of Genre." In Siikala 1989:13–28.

———, ed. 1990. *Religion, Myth, and Folklore in the World's Epics: The Kalevala and its Predecessors*. Berlin.

———, ed. 2002. *The Kalevala and the World's Traditional Epics*. Studia Fennica Folkloristica 12. Helsinki.

Honko, L. and V. Voigt, eds. 1981. *Adaptation, Change, and Decline in Oral Literature*. Studia Fennica 26. Helsinki.

Huttu-Hiltunen, P., et al., eds. 2011. *Laulu kulttuurisena kommunikaationa. Proceedings from the Runosong Academy Jubilee Seminar, 8–10 October 2010. Runolaulu-Akatemian julkaisuja* 16. Kuhmo.

Kallberg, M. 2011a. "A. O. Väisänen Vienan Karjalassa 1915." In Piela, Knuuttila, and Blomster 2011:136–149.

———. 2011b. "Vienanjoiku vuoden 1915 valossa." In Huttu-Hiltunen et al. 2011:77–88.

Kallio, K. 2011. "Interperformative Relationships in Ingrian Oral Poetry." *Oral Tradition* 25:391–427.

Kaukonen, V. 1990. "The Kalevala as Epic." In Honko 1990:157–179.

Koski, K., Frog, and U. Savolainen, eds. 2016. *Genre, Text, Interpretation*. Studia Fennica Folkloristica 22. Helsinki.

Kuusi, M. 1990. "Epic Cycles as the Basis for the Kalevala." In Honko 1990:133–155.

———. 1994. "Questions of Kalevala Metre: What exactly did Kalevala language signify to its users?" In Siikala and Vakimo 1994:41–55.

Lord, A. B. 2019. *The Singer of Tales*. 3rd ed. Ed. D. F. Elmer. Hellenic Studies 77. Publications of the Milman Parry Collection of Oral Literature 4. Washington, DC. Orig. pub. Cambridge, MA, 1960.

Lönnrot, E. 1835. *Kalevala taikka vanhoja Karjalan runoja Suomen kansan muinosista ajoista*. Helsinki.

———. 1840. *Kanteletar elikkä Suomen kansan vanhoja lauluja ja virsiä*. Helsinki.

———. 1849. *Kalevala*. Helsinki.

———. 1963. *The Kalevala or Poems of the Kaleva District*. Trans. F. B. Magoun. Cambridge, MA.

Lönnroth, L. 1979. "The Double-Scene of Arrow-Odd's Drinking Contest." In Becker-Nielsen et al. 1979:94–119.

Martin, R. 1989. *The Language of Heroes: Speech and Performance in the* Iliad. Ithaca.

Pekkilä, E., ed. 1990. *Hiljainen haltioituminen. A.O. Väisäsen tutkielmia kansanmusiikista.* Helsinki.

Pentikäinen, J., and T. Juurikka, eds. 1976. *Folk Narrative Research.* Studia Fennica 20. Helsinki.

Piela, U., S. Knuuttila, and R. Blomster, eds. 2011. *Taide, tiede, tulkinta. Kirjoituksia A.O. Väisäsestä.* Kalevalaseuran vuosikirja 90. Helsinki.

Reynolds, D. 1995. *Heroic Poets, Poetic Heroes: The Ethnography of Perfomance in an Arabic Oral Tradition.* Ithaca.

Saarinen, J. 1994. "The Päivölä Song of Miihkali Perttunen." In Siikala and Vakimo 1994:180–196.

Seitel, P. 1999. *The Powers of Genre: Interpreting Haya Oral Literature.* New York.

Siikala, A-L., ed. 1989. *Studies in Oral Narrative.* Studia Fennica 33. Helsinki.

———. 1994. "Transformations of the Kalevala Epic." In Siikala and Vakimo 1994:15–38.

———. 2002. *Mythic Images and Shamanism: A Perspective on Kalevala Poetry.* Folklore Fellows' Communications 280. Helsinki.

Siikala, A-L., L. Harvilahti, and S. Timonen, eds. 2004. *Kalevala ja laulettu runo.* Helsinki.

Siikala, A-L., and J. Siikala. 2005. *Return to Culture: Oral Tradition and Society in the Southern Cook Islands.* Folklore Fellows' Communications 287. Helsinki.

Siikala, A-L., and S. Vakimo, eds. 1994. *Songs Beyond the Kalevala: Transformations of Oral Poetry.* Studia Fennica Folkloristica 2. Helsinki.

Tarkka, L. 1993. "Intertextuality, Rhetorics and the Interpretation of Oral Poetry: The Case of Archived Orality." In Anttonen and Kvideland 1993:165–193.

———. 1994. "Other Worlds: Symbolism, Dialogue and Gender in Karelian Oral Poetry." In Siikala and Vakimo 1994:250–298.

———. 1996. "Transformations of Epic Time and Space: Creating the World's Creation in Kalevala-Metric Poetry." *Oral Tradition* 11:50–84.

———. 2004. "Viisaampansa vieressä maannut. Genrejen välinen vuorovaikutus kalevalamittaisessa runossa." In Siikala, Harvilahti, and Timonen, 2004:215–269.

———. 2005. *Rajarahvaan laulu. Tutkimus Vuokkiniemen kalevalamittaisesta runokulttuurista 1821–1921.* Helsinki.

———. 2013. *Songs of the Border People: Genre, Reflexivity, and Performance in Karelian Oral Poetry.* Folklore Fellows' Communications 305. Helsinki.

———. 2016. "The Poetics of Quotation: Proverbial Speech, Entextualization and the Emergence of Oral Poems." In Koski, Frog, and Savolainen 2016: 175–199.
Timonen, S. 2004. *Minä, tila, tunne. Näkökulmia kalevalamittaiseen kansanlyriikkaan.* Helsinki.
Titon, J. T. 2003. "Text." In Feintuch 2003:69–98.
Urban, G. 1984. "Speech about Speech and Speech about Action." *Journal of American Folklore* 97/385:310–328.
Väisänen, A. O. 1990. "Karjalan joiku." In Pekkilä 1990:138–146.
Zumthor, P. 1990. *Oral Poetry: An Introduction.* Theory and History of Literature 70. Minneapolis.

# 10

# The Many Deaths of Mustaj Beg of Lika

MIRSAD KUNIĆ

TRANSLATED BY PETER MCMURRAY

## Introduction

IN HIS SEMINAL TEXT, *Studije o krajinskoj epici* (Studies on Epic Song of the Krajina),[1] Alois Schmaus points out the importance of tales or stories (*priče)* in Bosniak epic in order to show that the tale is, in fact, the element by which that epic tradition differentiates itself from other epic traditions. Moreover, he refers to other authors—like Gesemann, for example[2]—who had noted this particular characteristic in Bosniak epic before him so that he could devote the central chapters of his study—Chapters VII and VIII, entitled "The Structure of the Song," in two parts—to this problem. However, having mentioned Schmaus, I must point out another direction in his argumentation in order to justify my own from the outset. Namely, this renowned expert of Bosniak epic claims that the themes and heroes *of the Krajina* are the structural core that makes this epic tradition worthy of attention. The most common themes in these songs are connected with life in the Krajina along the frontier or border, including themes

1 The term *krajina* generally means "frontier" or "borderland" but was also more technically used as *Vojna krajina*, the "military border," referring specifically to the region along the border between the Ottoman and Austro-Hungarian Empires, often called the *Bosanska krajina*, spanning much of northwestern Bosnia-Herzegovina today. The term was revived during the wars of the 1990s by Serbian secessionists in present-day Croatia. In this text, the term "Krajina" is left untranslated when it refers to the geographical region. For consistency and intelligibility in translation, the adjectival form (*krajiški*) is usually rendered by the use of "Krajina" as a modifier, as in,"Krajina epic songs." I am grateful to Mirsad Kunić, Kristijan Lepešić, David Elmer, and Aida Vidan for their thoughtful comments on this translation. Any mistakes that remain are my own. –Trans.

2 "In his study of the motif of the duke (*vojvoda*) Prijezda, Gerhard Gesemann points out the 'expansions' typical of Muslim epic" (Schmaus 1953:108).

of raiding, captivity, and liberating from captivity; campaigns and conquest of cities and castles; abduction and ransoming; and so on. They also include heroes who live and act along the border: Mustaj Beg of Lika, Mujo and Halil Hrnjica, Tale of Lika, Alija Bojičić, Ibro Durutagić, and others. The repertoire of thematic 'expansions' typical of Muslim epic would also include the deaths of certain heroes, which would certainly be the case for the death of the hero Mustaj Beg of Lika. This essay focuses specifically on the theme of the death of this hero in a number of different songs both within and outside of the Milman Parry Collection, drawing primarily on the findings of Schmaus's study.

## Krajina Identity

The term *krajiški*, the adjectival derivative of "Krajina," connotes the existence of a special identity which designates life along the border and which, as an identity, does not correspond to an existing religious, national, or cultural identity. If I were to try to distill all the possible actions of an epic hero from the Krajina into one, it would be the act of crossing the border, which is always repeated anew. Behind all the themes and all the reasons and causes for crossing the border, a complex desire *for the other*—and ultimately for knowing oneself in the other's image—is inscribed somewhere in the depths of the narrative structure of Krajina epic songs.

Another important characteristic of the Krajina hero is that he does not love acting alone, and there is an almost inconsequentially small number of such songs in which he does act alone. Above all, that means that the "singer of tales" could not have imagined singing a song only about Tale or Halil because such a song would be *incomplete* without Mujo and Mustaj Beg of Lika, and thus that song and its performer would very likely be rejected by the audience. This collectivism in Krajina epics connotes an entire, ordered world, a community with all its own norms and value systems. Mustaj Beg of Lika, whom Schmaus calls the King Arthur of Bosniak epic, is the supreme authority whose voice is heeded all the way to Istanbul. He is the upright ruler of the Krajina community as well as the guardian of its legal system. Mustaj Beg subordinates his own need to prove himself as an individual to the need of the collective, which only he with his authority can cultivate.

Udbina, a town in the Krbava region of present-day Croatia, was the political (and thus narrative) center of Bosniak activity in the Krajina during the Ottoman period. This community of heroes and their associates in and around Udbina functions perfectly: everyone knows his place and his role. It is not solely a community of heroes; rather, their frontier space is made complete by many other objects and figures without which the average person cannot function. They all have their own home and hearth (*odžak*), their own families, mothers, faithful wives, sisters, blood-brothers and helpers. Yet not one of them has a father: they are heroes without fathers, a circumstance that is firmly based in the realism of the epic world, for it would be difficult for two generations of males, father and son, to live side by side in those harsh conditions. As such, this epic tradition abounds with scenes of families drinking coffee, of motherly and sisterly concern and love, of relaxing and socializing in Mustaj Beg's tavern, and of working in the fields—here life is present in all its varieties.

There are no disagreements among the heroes of Udbina, and since each of them carries out his duties in their entirety, a perfect division of labor prevails among them. Mujo and Halil are responsible for duels/single combat: one wins them by means of wisdom, the other by his youthful vigor and strength. Mustaj Beg serves as the tactical leader for major campaigns and group battles, and Budalina Tale (or Tale the Fool) entertains them all. They all know one another's strengths, and could not achieve anything individually. Only when they join together is their full might on display. It is almost impossible to imagine Mustaj Beg without his comrades-in-arms from Lika; Mujo without his wife, his mother, and numerous blood sisters (who regularly appear as innkeepers);[3] Budalina Tale without his blood brother Rade and without the "audience" he entertains with his antics; or Alija Bojičić without his "own" border.

In this way, a fundamental expansion of epic action takes place in the spatial and temporal dimensions of the Krajina epic tradition. In its spatial dimensions, the subject of epic interest ceases to be solely the battlefield but also includes the surrounding space and figures like Mustaj Beg of Lika who typically observe battle from the sidelines. In its temporal dimensions, it encompasses periods before and after combat proper as well as periods of preparation for combat. These periods not only entail the arming of the hero, scenes the Krajina epic tradition cultivates to perfection, but also the entire ceremonial elaboration of their tactics, whether for a direct encounter with an enemy or for knightly competition. The spatial and temporal expansion of epic action results from the qualitative development of epic to the point of recognizing the importance of *environment* and *context*.

Budalina Tale is a particularly interesting and complex figure in Bosniak epic, especially Krajina epic. By virtue of his many attributes, he is in fact an exceptionally important representative of the Krajina hero. Through him, a closed and harmonious world is brought into contact with something external (outsiderly) and dissonant, lighthearted, and different. He shatters the

3 The practice of becoming blood brothers or sisters plays an important role in forging community in South Slavic epic, creating a layered kinship network that can motivate a variety of decisions and actions within a given tale. – Trans.

monotony of epic stability, he grounds and demystifies the pathos of the epic *agon*, and he introduces elements of play into the world of knightly competition. For Mikhail Bakhtin, Tale would be a carnivalesque hero, directed with his entire being *downward*, toward the earth, within an epic environment directed *upward*, toward heaven. This lowered gaze toward the earth is a symbolic projection of an urge that identifies itself with mundane and worldly, rather than with eternal and heavenly, values. But Tale was only able to adopt this lighthearted persona through contact with a *different*, lighthearted spirit of the Mediterranean Renaissance in his frequent excursions *across the border* to the coastal cities of Zadar and Šibenik.

## The Epic Biography of a Hero

In addition to this established, collective representation of heroes as part of a Krajina identity, however, I would also highlight the image of the individual in these epics—that is, the personal profile of the character of the hero. This individualization of the hero's character is yet another of the distinguishing traits of Bosniak epic, a process by which the exalted image of the epic hero is partially deconstructed and brought down to the level of a realistic literary figure. Mustaj Beg was the greatest authority figure of Lika and the Krajina, a frontiersman and commander who resided at Udbina. He was an authority figure who led, planned, and made decisions—and an authority figure people believed in and listened to unquestioningly. Once he charged at the head of an army to help Ibro Durutagić, but his soldiers admonished him that it was not his place to lead from the front ("Lika, rise up at Golub valley / but it is not given to you to strike first," Hörmann II, 60.1111–1112).[4] Mustaj Beg generally stayed back because he was the commander-in-chief and strategist who should watch the battle from a safe distance. Typically, the first to charge were the standard-bearers (*bajraktari*), then the rest of the army from Lika, and only then Mustaj Beg. He ruled from Udbina, where he had his own tavern. When he would enter the tavern, everyone jumped to their feet; he would typically sit and look out the window,

[4] Two major published collections are used throughout this essay, each of which is referred to by the name of its collector/editor. The first is the collection of Kosta Hörmann (abbreviated here as "Hörmann"), *Narodne Pjesme Muslimana u Bosni i Hercegovini*, published in two volumes (1888 and 1889). The second is that of Luka Marjanović (abbreviated as "Marjanović"), also published in two volumes a decade later (1898 and 1899) as volumes III and IV of Matica Hrvatska's series, *Hrvatske Narodne Pjesme*. (Marjanović's volumes are specifically entitled, *Junačke pjesme* [*muhamedovske*], or "Heroic Songs [Muhammadan]," highlighting the particular focus on Muslim epic songs.) Quotations from these volumes are cited by collector's name, volume number, song number, and line number(s) (for songs), or by collector's name, volume number, and page number (in the case of editorial comments or front matter). –Trans.

watching for messengers and listening to conversation, only to join in with it later. The appearance of a messenger at Udbina or a brawl in the tavern are just two of the many ways the plot commences; in both cases, Mustaj Beg is compelled to get involved and set the plot in motion.

For both military actions and bridal processions, it was necessary to seek permission from Mustaj Beg. If battle was decided upon, the firing of a cannon informed the entire Krajina that they should make their preparations and gather at an agreed-upon location.

> Beže viče Eminića svoga:
> "Opali topa, moje dite drago,
> Mog zelenka gradu na bedenu,
> Nek se svija Lika i Krbava!"
>
> Marjanović IV, 26.735–738

> The Beg commands his dear Eminić:
> "Fire the cannon, my dear child,
> my green canon on the city walls,
> let Lika and Krbava gather together!"

Captive maidens were given the freedom to choose for themselves whether to stay or return to their own homes, which rightly enhanced Mustaj Beg's stature as the guardian and "personification of the legal system."[5] As the "grand old man" of heroic song, he did not rush recklessly into battle at any cost but rather behaved as a leader who showed concern for the lives of his soldiers.[6] In one situation, he refused to give in to the extortion of his adversary, devising a way to avoid battle ("This steed will not go to the wedding festivities, / and no maiden will ride this steed either, / all our wedding guests will perish," Hörmann I, 36.364–366). In another, when the Ban of Zadar posted guards in the Kotar region and prohibited raiding, he ordered his own men from Lika to give up raiding and accept working their fields.

Mustaj Beg is the hero from start to finish. Songs start and end with him, yet no one holds this against him. That is his role in the administration of the Krajina, a role that Rašid Durić summarizes as follows (Durić 2000:68):

5 "In contrast to the traitor stands Mustaj Beg, who acts as the personification of the legal system" (Schmaus 1953:179).

6 "The experienced hero is the *grand old man* of heroic song: an old warrior decorated with a garland of glory, wise and wary, one who warns and gives counsel, he typically leaves the fighting to the younger generation and gets involved himself only when the younger warriors fail or get themselves into a hopeless situation" (Braun 2004:34).

> As an epic hero, Mustaj Beg of Lika is most often sung about at the beginning and end of epic songs, in the notable role of gathering the heroic world together at his court in Udbina. Mustaj Beg is often involved in the armed defense of the people of Lika, who are persecuted at the hands of Christians at the Ottoman-Venetian border. In direct conflicts, Mustaj Beg typically participates only at the beginning to initiate the skirmish. He then retreats to some vantage point, where he follows its course with the aim of justly rewarding warriors according to the bravery and acumen they demonstrated. Since he is a famous hero in his own right, enemies challenge him to duels as well, but Mustaj Beg does not personally respond; in his place, as a rule, he sends a *bedel*—a deputy, to which, according to unwritten law, every hero is entitled.

He first shouts from his horse, Golub, with the call to battle, "Lambs for Allah, tributes on St. George's Feast Day / The armies of Kotor are rushing to Mosor!" This cry invigorates the armies of Lika: "Push on, brother, there's Mustaj Beg!" (Hörmann II, 65.809–812). But having rallied them, he does not charge into battle with the standard-bearers and armies of Lika. At the close of battle, he is the primary speaker, he gathers information about the wounded and the dead, and he equitably shares the spoils they seize. Sometimes, however, he is unable even to observe the battle, either because of a thick fog on the battlefield or excessive distance from the battle proper. To overcome the first of these obstacles, the Beg turns to God directly, praying that he dispel the fog on the field so he may see who wins:

Tad Mustaj-beg istjera Goluba,
Pa udari abdest turski na se,
Pa on klanja četiri rećata,
Pa on Bogu obje diže ruke:
"Daj mi, Bože, vihar sa Palije,
Da rastjera maglu u krajeve
Da ja vidim čija gine vojska,
Čija gine, čija li dobiva!"

Hörmann II, 75.713–720

Then Mustaj Beg drove his horse Golub on,
and he performed Turkish ablutions,
and he prostrated himself four times,
and raising both hands to God, said:

"God, send me a gale from Palija
to dispel this fog to the other regions,
so I may see which army perishes,
which perishes, and which prevails!"

For following a battle from great distances, a spyglass (*durbin*) is necessary:

Jer beg silnu sakupio vojsku,
Kod bega se bile čadorovi,
U njeg vavik durbin u desnici,
Jer on gleda svojih uhodnika.

Marjanović III, 11.413–416

For the Beg had gathered a mighty army.
The tents were near the Beg,
who always had a spyglass in his right hand,
for he was watching his troops.

When a spyglass is not sufficient, he then calls an intermediary, Omer Blažević, to climb the highest fir tree and relate (transmit!) to him how things unfold at a race at Tihovo. Omer Blažević appears here as a kind of *commentator* or medium that relays information from the site of events.[7]

Mustaj Beg thus became a privileged member of the epic community who alone has the right to be absent from battle and yet, at the same time, to be informed about its results. As a privileged member of this community, the Beg must not be forgotten so long as battle is waged on the battlefield, and therefore the cited examples are ideal ways to keep him in the tale. Again, Mustaj Beg takes time to perform ablutions and pray (see above), after which the action continues:

U boga mu kabul dova bila,
Dok mu vihar sa Palije puhne,
A rastjera maglu u krajeve.
Kad pogleda niz duge poljane,
Trave nema gdje ne ima glave,
Busa nema gdje ne ima trupa,
Doline se krvi nadolije.

Hörmann I, 75.721–727

[7] The term "transmit" (*prenosi)* and the "medium that relays" information (*prenosnik informacija*) are key terms for communication generally but especially so for oral literature. These are idiomatic Bosnian terms for the transmission of a poem or legend from one singer/generation to the next. –Trans.

> His prayer to God was accepted,
> and the wind from Palija blew,
> and dispelled the fog to other regions.
> When he looked along the long meadow,
> no patch of grass was without a head,
> no clump of dirt was without a body,
> blood poured through the valley.

Retaining Mustaj Beg in the tale is motivated by the rupture of the epic/agonic essence of the song and by the desire to preserve a complete image of all that is unfolding. And, thus, even this retention adds further still to the foregoing list of characteristics of the spatialization of the song.[8] In this way, Mustaj Beg is bound up in the process of characterization and psychologizing, as well. He acts as a holistic figure, a persona who makes plans and determines tactics in battle and not just as a hero who goes from battle to battle. He is a persona who shows feeling, grieves, and cries, a persona who wants to authenticate his own existence—but in his own way, without weapons. A figure who ultimately *wants to be* present in the tale even when not in battle.

On the other hand, the epic singer makes clear that it is no longer just the battlefield that matters for the story but also what happens around it. He becomes conscious of the fact that the battlefield is just one location in that space and that not everyone participates. In other words, the singer becomes conscious of the space in which he places his characters, which marks an important shift in the development of epic song. From the primeval plot that unfolds only in time, a plot emerges that unfolds both in time and in space.[9] The gap between narrative time and real time diminishes: the space of the epic song grows closer, fuller, and more concrete. Schmaus characterizes this spatial unfolding as follows (Schmaus 1953:151):

> Instead of a concentration of plot, achieved through the dominance of time and certain processes of isolation, one finds a greater concentration of events characterized by proximity and vividness. But the more the spatial component takes hold, the less dynamic the plot becomes.

8 Schmaus recognized these characteristics primarily in parallelisms of plot, detailed descriptions, character development (especially in terms of psychology), the development of a middle-ground narrative (what Schmaus calls the "*srednji plan*" that connects a literary "foreground" of main characters and locations with a kind of "background" cultural setting), and so forth.

9 "In Christian songs the spatial component is completely subordinated to the temporal. Space is demarcated, so to speak, with few points to allow the plot to unfold; it is therefore abstract and remote. The gap between narrative time and real time is greater; thus epic action moves forward in large steps [*velikim koracima*]" (Schmaus 1953:151).

I would like to believe that such an oral epic poet—aware of real time and space as well as of space that expands and time that lasts beyond the epic at hand—becomes conscious of the traditional context that gave rise to his song and the broader song tradition. In other words, the cultivation of this broader awareness of space and spatialization in Krajina epic can be understood as a site of singers' reflexivity about the tradition as a whole and their place within that tradition. I am mindful of David Bynum's warning that the knowledge of the researcher and of the singer are not the same,[10] but I would, nevertheless, like to believe that some fundamental connection exists between these phenomena of spatialized narration (within a song) and the tradition-at-large, inscribed in the deep structures of singers' consciousness—a kind of *unconscious knowledge*, similar to the way in which the epic singer's movements and rhythm in playing the *gusle* are connected with the tale itself, as discussed in this volume by Scaldaferri and Neziri. We might think of this as the same kind of knowledge that enabled Avdo Međedović to sing his epic song, *The Wedding of Smailagić Meho*, with its similarities in construction to the *Iliad* and *Odyssey*. This theme of the epic knowledge singers within a tradition possess has important potential for future scholarly discussion.

## The Death of the Hero

The hero constantly lives with the specter of death, a fate he awaits—or even hopes for—as the final act of a heroic existence. Where possible, it stands at the heart of the warrior's ideals to further garland him with the glory of eternal life. The Krajina hero, however, has his own reasons to live and not die: the space along the border makes his existence purposeful and full to the extent that a hero stops being an artist of war and becomes an artist of living (*življenje*) or perhaps more precisely stated, an artist of living-another-day, of surviving (*preživljenje*). The principle "be ready to die at any moment" turns into "survive at all costs." The *raison d'être* shifts from an exalted heavenly perspective to that of earthly everyday life. All Krajina heroes behave accordingly, especially Budalina Tale, which once again resonates with Bakhtin's key theses about the importance and genesis of comedic culture. So it comes as no surprise that in Bosniak epic, only a small number of songs are sung about the death of Krajina heroes. This argument relates directly to the aforementioned claims about the *unconscious knowledge* of the Krajina epic singer. The difference between him and some other singer lies in the fact that the Krajina singer *becomes conscious*

10 "In this way too the radical difference between the collectors' knowledge and the traditional oral epic singers' knowledge is apparent" (Bynum 1986:303).

of the fact that he requires a living hero, not a dead one, while other singers *do not know it.*

A few songs about the death of Mustaj Beg of Lika, the commander of all the Krajina heroes, exist in other collections, including five such songs in the Milman Parry Collection. Luka Marjanović included a song of 334 verses from Salko Vojniković (no. 35) in his collection. In that version, a certain Jana Uzolačka (sometimes instead called "Janja") brings about the death of the Beg by gathering "60 Hungarian women," who, "to the disgrace of Mustaj Beg of Lika [and] every nobleman," join their party in order to call him to action (i.e. elicit a response) while the Bans of Zadar and Šibenik are lying in wait for him. Two *harambaše* ("bandit-chiefs"), Tutek and Trivun, wound the Beg and his horse, Golub, then an unnamed goatherd cuts off his head and carries it first to Jana and then to the Bans of Šibenik and Zadar. The bans rebuke the poor goatherd for having taken the head of such a great hero in that way, and they punish him for it with death. The song concludes with an explicit pronouncement of the consequence of the killing of Mustaj Beg of Lika: "The Beg is no more, raiding is no more" *(Nesta bega nesta četovanja),* and then, in turn, Lika is no more, easily conquered by its enemies from the coast (*Primorci*). Marjanović informs us that the same singer had announced the coming death of the Beg in the previous song, confirming once again the thesis that the singer has a complete view of the epic world that extends beyond the confines of a single performance or song.

At the same time, Salko Vojniković apparently found it necessary to further authenticate his own version by returning Mustaj Beg back to the place he was taken from: reality. He recounted to Marjanović that he learned the song about Mustaj Beg's death from a certain Dželil Šabić. But not just the song: he also learned an account of an interesting event related to it. This Šabić had once found himself at the marketplace in Šibenik, where people quickly learned that he was a good singer and requested that he sing something. When Šabić sang the song of the death of Mustaj Beg of Lika, an elderly woman called out and through tears told him that she was, in fact, that Jana Uzolačka who had caused the Beg's death (Marjanović IV:639). The singer Alija Prošić, however, had his own, different version of the factual confirmation of heroic characters from a story about his grandfather who, while living among Christians, "found a Hungarian woman in a tavern, all white like a dumpling (or milk), with white arms all the way to the bicep, and he asked how old she was, and she answered that she was Janja Uzolačka herself" (Marjanović IV:639). Marjanović also includes variations in the song texts themselves about the death of Mustaj Beg, as seen in one variant taken down in writing from Bećir Islamović. According to this version, three *harambaše* kill the Beg and a fourth, Tutek *harambaša,* cuts off his head. His comrades from Lika find the Beg headless and carry his body away to Udbina to bury him. Tutek *harambaša*, in turn, carries the head as a gift for the Austrian emperor, expecting a great reward, but the emperor berates him for killing such a hero. Young women take the head and dance a *kolo* around it. Eventually the Beg's companion Rade gathers the courage to set out in pursuit of his severed head; he finds Tutek *harambaša* first and exacts punishment, then finds the head as well, takes it back to Lika, and restores it to the body.

Hörmann's collection contains a song (vol. I, song 30, 349 verses long, written down in Avtovac) in which the aged Ćejvan Aga, with a feeling of guilt, reflects on the death of Mustaj Beg:

A znate li, a bezobraznici,
Evo puno sedam godin' dana
Kako nam je bego poginuo
Nijeste se more potežili
Da siđete na begovu luku,
Da vidite oburvane kule
I begovu sirotinju tešku
I Bećira, Mustaj-Bega sina.

Hörmann I, 30.16–22

Do you realize, you insolent ones,
look, a full seven years have passed
since our Beg was killed.
Ah, you haven't rushed out
to go down to the Beg's valley
to see the fallen towers
and the Beg's poor people
and Bećir, Mustaj Beg's son.

Mujo and Tale then undertake a campaign for revenge and enslave the Beg's killer, Jovan of Uzavlje, sparing his life because he expresses a desire to convert to Islam.

## The Death of Mustaj Beg in the Parry Collection

It is interesting that Vojniković's short song about Mustaj Beg's death is narrated on a somewhat different narrative matrix than are the songs of the Parry Collection. In particular, in Vojniković's version, Jana Uzolačka consciously defies and challenges the Beg, which was a part of the plan of the Bans of Zadar and Šibenik to get their hands on the Beg. Not even such an imagined conspiracy could have ensured success; it was necessary to find a way by which weapons and bullets of some kind could be used to shoot the Beg for no conventional bullet could hit the Beg (see Marjanović IV, 35.34). They must be bullets cast from gold. All this could only be ensured by a traitor in the Beg's immediate circle—in this case, Huremaga Kozličić. The songs about Mustaj Beg's death in the Parry Collection, in contrast with those in Marjanović's collection, for example, diverge from the foregoing matrix, thereby offering new resolutions with a whole series of elaborated details, which offer further confirmation of the strategy of intensifying the whole narrative.

In the Milman Parry Collection, five songs[11] have been preserved that narrate Mustaj Beg's death:

1. Suljo Tunović, *Smrt Ličkog Mustajbega* (The Death of Mustaj Beg of Lika), PN 921, 526 verses (January 3, 1935, Gacko)
2. Hajro Ferizović (about 90 years old), *Smrt Ličkog Mustajbega* (The Death of Mustaj Beg of Lika), PN 12393, 1611 verses (June 17, 1935, Bijelo Polje)
3. Avdo Međedović (63 years old), *Smrt Ličkog Mustaj-bega* (The Death of Mustaj Beg of Lika), PN 6807, 2393 verses (June 28, 1935, Bijelo Polje)
4. Šećo Kolić, *Smrt Ličkog Mustajbega* (The Death of Mustaj Beg of Lika), PN 6832, 1458 verses (July 2, 1935, Bijelo Polje)
5. Avdo Međedović, *Smrt Ličkog Mustaj-bega* (The Death of Mustaj Beg of Lika), LN 203, 1356 verses (August 16, 1951, Bijelo Polje)

The longest song on this theme was taken down by dictation by Parry from Avdo Međedović, a singer who knew how to develop this and other themes more quantitatively but also in more qualitative and creative ways than other oral singers. It would seem that in Avdo's performance (PN 6807), Parry received not only the longest but also the highest-quality song about Mustaj Beg's death. The song of Šećo Kolić, Avdo's fellow resident of Bijelo Polje, taken down on July 2, four days after Avdo's, is second in length but not in the quality of its epic narrative. Because of this, when Albert Lord

[11] Two songs of Murat Žunić have titles that suggest that they also deal with the death of Mustaj Beg, both entitled *Osudita smrt Ličkog Mustaj-bega* (The Death Sentence of Mustaj Beg of Lika), PN 1919 and 1958. However, these songs, in fact, recount his captivity and freeing. In general, the practice of giving titles to songs, brought about by written literary conventions, most often resulted from the side of the collector/scribe and not from the singers themselves, since performers do not call songs by titles but rather by their contents and especially by their central theme. I was also unable to find one other related song listed in the Milman Parry Collection: *Hrnjica Mujo osvećuje Ličkog Mustajbega* (Mujo Hrnjica Avenges Mustaj Beg of Lika), PN 6810, 6291 verses (recorded by Milman Parry on June 29, 1935, in Bijelo Polje).

came sixteen years later, continuing the search for secrets of epic composition, he wanted to record Avdo Međedović a second time on the same theme. The result was such that he received a song roughly 1,000 verses shorter and, more importantly, inconsistent and confusing in its epic narration. If, on previous occasions, he had been able to figure out the secret of expansion, in this case he found solutions to the question of the reduction or compression of epic plots.

The abstract system of all formulas, themes, and processes inevitably calls for a capable singer (and it inevitably finds such a singer to the degree one exists). Such a system remains a possibility in all performed songs, yet one that is apparently never (fully) present in a single place. To say this is nothing new, and thus I run the risk of reinventing the proverbial wheel. But having introduced this problem, allow me to attempt to orient it in a fruitful direction. What is my position in all of this? How can I situate myself relative to all songs (an imaginary construct!) and an individual song or toward an imagined singer of all possible songs and a specific singer of a specific song? The question arguably takes on more importance when I pose it in parallel with the question of the relationship of Parry and Lord to the same issues. They were, after all, outsiders, yet they experienced these songs directly in performance. By contrast, I simultaneously have the privilege of belonging to that tradition, which attests to its own existence in all possible and impossible songs and singers, but also the disadvantage that I approach this tradition exclusively through recorded texts (a disadvantage shared by essentially all scholars of South Slavic epic today).

However, I attempt to overcome this handicap by creating the illusion that, through the whole corpus of collections of oral literature up to the present, *nearly* all possible songs have become available to me, at least in a recorded/dictated form. A new kind of virtual archive has been created, a meta-archive encompassing hundreds of songs across time and space—more than any single singer could have known. Another illusion, then, necessarily follows the first: that this imagined singer-of-all-tales, on account of the availability of nearly all songs, has become at least slightly more possible, closer, and more real. Imagining such an archivally-generated singer, we might productively recombine different versions of a given song or episode from a hero's life (what Lord has called a "multiform") and try to raise questions about that underlying narrative. Again, I necessarily situate my own position, simultaneously confirmed and displaced by tradition, in a speculative sphere, and I contrast the rather speculative conclusions I suggest here with the empirical conclusions of Parry and Lord.

As such, the plot of the five songs from the Milman Parry Collection can be pulled together and represented as the plot of a single hypothetical song. The *common elements* of the songs about Mustaj Beg's death[12] would then be:

1. Mustaj Beg's decision to take Jana/Janja as a lover/wife
2. Sending a patrol to Uzolac/Uzo to confirm Jana's beauty
3. Failed opposition by the Beg's current wife
4. Summoning and gathering of armies/wedding guests
5. Departure of the army for Uzolac, scouting and taking of the city
6. Abduction of Jana and Mustaj Beg's enjoying of her charms
7. Jovan's escape from Italy and return with a powerful army
8. Defeat of the Krajina armies and the death of Mustaj Beg
9. Reward from the Christian kings to Jovan for the Beg's head

The song by Suljo Tunović (PN 921, 526 verses) belongs to the group of songs that sing about avenging the death of Mustaj Beg. The plot takes place in Kanidža, an important site for Bosniak epic, located in "Unđurovina" (i.e. Ottoman Hungary),[13] in the tavern where old Ćejvan Aga reminds those heroes present of the Beg's death and of the need for revenge. The song has two interesting scenes: the first tells of Halil's wandering through wooded dells while the second tells, with a dose of humor, about Halil's attempts to join in the *kolo* of some young women.[14] It is tempting to (mis)use the first scene and interpret it as an entirely coincidental symbol for the singer's inability to find his way as he

[12] "If we take all the extant texts of the song of Smailagić Meho and from them extract all the common elements, we have constructed something that never existed in reality or even in the mind of any of the singers of that song. We have simply then the common elements in this restricted number of texts, nothing more, nothing less" (Lord 2019:107).

[13] This was the reason Luka Marjanović called these "Unđur songs" (unđurske pjesme). Within the broader framework of Krajina epic, Marjanović distinguishes between Lika and Unđur songs: "I have divided these songs into two major groupings (or cycles): based on the locations and regions where the events of the songs take place, since that is the designation used by singers themselves and those who know the songs well. ... The Lika songs, of which we have about 150, fall into the first, much larger grouping. Unđur or Ungjur songs (Hungaria, Ungjurska, Ungjurovina), of which we have about 40, fall in the second. The events of both groupings begin in their respective regions, but they also extend into neighboring lands" (Marjanović III:xxxiv).

[14] A useful contrast can be seen in the song from the Hörmann Collection published as number 30 in his book, which also recounts the avenging of Mustaj Beg's death, and which was also written down in the Gacko region (in the town of Avtovac) only about 50 years earlier. It includes two key differences: the gathering of heroes is not in Kanidža but rather in Udbina, and Mujo and Tale, rather than Halil, lead the campaign for vengeance.

wanders through the dells of epic narrative. But, for now, I will hew more closely to traditional philology.

By all appearances, the singer Hajro Ferizović brought together two major themes about Mustaj Beg of Lika in his lengthy, 1,611-verse performance: the theme of death and the theme of revenge. This song could even be taken as evidence for the hypothesis that newer and larger epic creations come into existence through the merging of smaller ones, with the suture that testifies to this stitching together still fresh and visible. It appears at the boundary between verses 294 and 295:

"Ja ne žalim Mustaj-bega Ličkog
No obraza cijele Krajine
I namuza cara Sulejmana."

Sade ode na Krajinu vojska.
Sade prođe vakta nekoliko ...

PN 12393, ll. 292–296

"I do not mourn Mustaj Beg of Lika
but rather the honor of all Krajina
and the prayers of Sultan Suleiman."

Now the army sets out for Krajina.
Now a few prayer times pass ...

The first theme is developed according to the standard pattern:

1. At Eid, Mustaj Beg informs his wife of his intention to carry away Janja Uzolačka; his wife protests on account of Janja's being a Christian Vlach
2. He sends his standard-bearer Mejrić as scout to confirm Janja's beauty
3. The gathering of the army, departure, and abduction of Janja
4. The Beg's decision to surrender himself to Janja's charms in his tent
5. The motif of betrayal: the Kozilić and Huremović families keep watch at Kozara
6. Jovan flees to Italy
7. He returns with an army and attacks
8. Mujo and Tale caution the Beg to abstain from romance and depart for home because danger is lurking

9. They lead the Beg to the mountains and they return to battle
10. The Beg once again stops and succumbs to Janja's charms
11. Jovan comes, kills him, cuts off his head, and carries it to Italy

However, the reason the theme is sung in just 293 verses can be seen from individual parts: in fact, Ferizović has "fallen short" at those sections which have the potential for ornamentation, such as the subtheme of sending the summons and gathering heroes as well as the subtheme of sending a scout to the fortress-city Uzor. For this reason, moments of ornamentation are notably more extensive in the second theme:

1. The gathering at Eid at the home of the Beg's wife: she was distraught that no one had avenged her Beg; she denounces Mujo, who says that he already went out to scout but concluded that the city was so well fortified it could not be conquered
2. The decision to go seek revenge
3. Writing a letter to the heroes (lines 403–775)
4. Logistical preparations and gathering the heroes (to line 1039)
5. Halil's scouting (verse 1450); encounter with the barmaid Pava and Janja; Janja's readiness to help in seeking revenge
6. Siege and conquest of the city; the death of Jovan

Ferizović spends around 370 verses (lines 443–775) on the summoning of heroes alone, more than the entire preceding theme, and more than 200 verses (lines 815–1039) on the gathering of new heroes, a total of slightly fewer than 700 verses. The following heroes are summoned:

1. The Vezir of Buda with 30,000 Janissaries and 30 cannons
2. The Vezir of Travnik with 20,000 Janissaries and 20 cannons
3. Osman Beg Šestokrilović from Osijek with 30,000 Janissaries and 30 cannons
4. Two begs from Sarajevo, Fetibegović and Rustem Beg
5. Beg Ljubović from Nevesinje
6. Alibeg Dadić from Mostar
7. Alija Novljanin from Novi Grad
8. Beg Zatović and Ograščić with 40 soldiers
9. Beg Alajbeg from Klis

10. Hadži Kapetan from Udbina
11. Baba Ahmetović Dedo from Cetinje
12. Smajil Beg
13. Murat Beg Kapetanović from Bosnia
14. Tuzla Alibeg
15. Hivzi Beg from Banja Luka
16. Bešir Buljubaša from Stijena
17. Omer Blažević from Otoka
18. Tale Orašović (only Tale is summoned personally by the herald Osman Bajraktar and not by a letter, "because Tale does not know how to read letters")
19. Prince Najaš and Serf Matijaš

The theme of Halil's scouting the fortified city of Uzor extends all the way to l. 1450, such that the battles at the siege and the taking of the city span all of 161 verses.

## Avdo's Performance

Avdo Međedović drew attention to himself with his performances of lengthy epic songs, with a skill for narrating in verse that earned him the title "our Yugoslav Homer" (see Lord 2019:xvii). As the only epic singer who sang two songs about Mustaj Beg's death, he opens for us the possibility of comparing two performances on the same theme at different points in time.

Međedović's first performance (PN 6807, 2393 verses), recorded on June 28, 1935, in Bijelo Polje, deals solely with the theme of the Beg's death but was nevertheless 792 verses longer than that of Ferizović. If I were to limit myself only to his first section and only to the first theme in Ferizović's performance, the difference would be even more drastic. Indeed, Hajro Ferizović's section on the death of Mustaj Beg is reduced to the level of a news bulletin or report which, again, can be treated in its entirety as a kind of introduction to the main tale: the tale of revenge.

Most likely while seeking ever-longer performances of this song, Parry came upon Avdo Međedović and received a 2,393-verse song with all the elements of epic narrative that made Avdo a superior perfomer.[15] Avdo showed

15 *Smrt Ličkog Mustaj-bega* was the first song Parry recorded from Avdo on June 28, 1935.

his refined skill in describing or developing existing scenes to an unprecedented level. The description of Jana's beauty, which comes immediately after the five-verse prelude (*pripjev*) is, in fact, a hymn to her beauty and does not exist in any other version. Spanning some sixty verses, it speaks of her birth and years growing up as well as the pride that caused her to reject suitors of the highest rank from all sides.

Otkako je postala Krajina,
Nije bolja podrasla devojka,
Nego što je Uzovlje ravno,
Mila sestra Uzovca Jovana,
E gospođa Jana Jovanova.
Koliko je u stasu visoka
I u pasu tanka i lijepa!
Tud đevojka lica gosposkoga,
Jal je vila ja li je rodila,
Jal joj vila na babine bila
Mulćim nije što joj svoje nije.
Jana ruse kose odgojila,
Bi se s rusom kosom opasala.

PN 6807, ll. 6–18

Since the Krajina was established
no better maiden had grown up
than from the plain of Uzovlje
the charming sister of Jovan Uzovac.
O, my lady Jana, sister of Jovan,
how tall she stands in stature
and how thin at the waist, and beautiful!
The maiden has a divine face,
is she a *vila* fairy, or the child of a *vila*,
or was a *vila* among her forebears?
No worldy possession compared to her [beauty].
Jana let her strawberry locks grow
She could wrap her strawberry locks around her waist.

Such an introduction has another function as well: to lay the groundwork for what follows; to give reason for the Beg's desire to take Jana to wife along with his first; but also, on some level, as in the *Iliad*, to foreshadow the wholesale tragedy of the events.

Avdo made use of a second opportunity for expansion with the subtheme of sending letters/summonses to the heroes/wedding guests. His list extends the number of heroes to be summoned to twenty-six. However, it is not merely the calling and listing of all the names that might come to the singer's mind in that moment—in the act of what Lord called "composition in performance," the in-the-moment creative process of performing epic (see Lord 2019:5). It is true skill to invoke all these names and, in addition, to respect the order which must reflect the hierarchy, status, and renown of the heroes:

1. the Vezir of Travnik
2. Fetibegović from Banja Luka
3. Čelebić from Jajce
4. Ljevak Omeraga from Lijevno
5. Husejin Tuzlić from Tuzla
6. Beg Hašinić from Brčko
7. twelve begs from across the Una
8. Mehmed Zenković and Babahmetović
9. Ibro Hamajlić and Alem Kadunić
10. Ramo from Glamoč and Tale Oraški
11. seven brothers-in-law from Bišće
12. Mujo Hrnjićki
13. Huremaga Kozličić
14. Hadži Kapetan
15. Kahriman, the *ćehaja* of Udbina
16. Alibeg Gavrić and Selim Velagić
17. Ramo from Glamoč[16]
18. Alajbeg of Klis
19. Nušin Kurtagić
20. Hasan Kunić
21. Zuko *buljukbaša*
22. Šarac Mahmutaga

16 Our Homer has dozed off a bit here, so he summons Ramo from Glamoč a second time. (Ramo is first summoned as part of action 10 in this sequence, as numbered here.)

23. Šabanaga Zorić
24. Mehmedaga the Arab
25. the *dizdar* of Udbina

Although Ferizović's list is somewhat shorter, it must be noted that it is more precise and believable: namely, Ferizović includes alongside the names of some of the heroes the number of soldiers and cannons the heroes will bring which, again, must accord with the status and reputation they have. There is no lapse in concentration or correcting mistakes, as happens with Avdo, such as when Ramo from Glamoč is summoned twice or later when Avdo lists his hero Tale somewhere in the middle, even though he should be called at the end, as a rule, just as he appears last in the gathering of heroes. And one final detail in the summoning of Tale more generally: he is not summoned by letter but, rather, in person by a herald, which serves as a reminder of the vigilance necessitated by his mercurial temperament.

In general, introducing Budalina Tale into the song takes place in the moment when the summoned heroes gather where, again, as a rule, he appears last. In fact, Međedović developed this scene into an entire episode of 175 verses in total, in which smaller units can be discerned in their entirety:

1. awaiting and the announcement of the heroes' arrival
2. the arrival
3. description of the dun horse
4. clothing and weaponry
5. the ill-omened standard-bearer
6. Hodža Šuvajlija
7. the heroes from Orašac
8. the Pasha's suspicion and the Beg's reassurances
9. Tale's dissatisfaction with the Beg
10. enticing Tale with wine

The episode is further enlivened with the Beg's announcements of Tale's arrival and the Pasha's skepticism while awaiting the indispensable hero. With his own arrival, the hero Tale breaks the monotony of enumerating each hero's arrival. He shatters the atmosphere of expectation with his own buffoonery, which clashes with the stern, serious environment. Tale's second scene follows when those heroes who had already arrived prepare to depart with their armies for the city of Uzor, where Tale is given the task of *tertib* or forming them into ranks and arranging them. In this scene, as well, Tale demonstrates in a few dozen verses the splendor of his appearance, and he amuses those around him.

Sixteen years later, on August 16, 1951, Albert Lord intentionally asked Avdo to repeat his performance of the same song, receiving in return a performance shorter by 1,037 verses. This performance follows the basic points in the development of plot, but it also shows the weakness of the singer, who at that time was seventy-nine years old. A side-by-side comparison would look as follows:

## Avdo Međedović

| June 28, 1935 | August 16, 1951 |
|---|---|
| - five-verse prelude | - prelude of just one verse |
| - hymn in praise of Jana's beauty | - missing |
| - fame of Jana's beauty reaches the Beg | - missing |
| - Mejrić and Vrcić sent to scout | - Desnić and Nemić sent |
| - Beg's wife asks the standard-bearers not to tell the truth | - same |
| - description of travel to Uzovlje | - missing |
| - description of Jana's beauty | - same |
| - return and false testimony | - same |
| - again, fame of Jana's beauty reaches the Beg | - same |
| - Beg sends Mejrić | - same |
| - at Eid, Beg tells his wife his intentions | - Beg sends Nemić |
| - Mustaj Beg's rage at his wife | - Beg's wife surmises that Beg in fact found out about Janja's beauty |
| - announcing the campaign | - same |
| - writing a letter to the heroes | - same |
| - arrival of the summoned heroes | - missing |
| - special episode upon Tale's arrival | - missing |
| - scene of *tertib* arrangements | - missing |
| - missing | - Halil goes to scout |
| - conquest of Uzovlje and kidnapping of Janja | - same |
| - Jovan's flight to Italy | - same |

| | |
|---|---|
| - Mustaj Beg's succumbing to charms of Janja's beauty | - same |
| - Jovan's attack | - same |
| - Tale's warning | - same |
| - Mustaj Beg's death | - same |

It is known that Parry conducted experiments with singers, encouraging them to perform:

1. The same song from the same singer within a short period of time
2. The same song from different singers within a short period of time
3. The same song from the same singer after a longer period of time

An obvious difference in the two performances of Avdo Međedović, separated by a period of sixteen years, is the impact of the age of the singer and the shifting requirements of maintaining the tradition of epic singing. That it happened in this way serves as evidence of the following hypothesis: had Avdo been encouraged, within a short period of time, to sing on this same theme, it is certain that we would have received a song of similar or even greater length and of similar quality. It is interesting that Međedović has also "fallen short" at almost the same places and with the same details as did Hajro Ferizović: the prelude, summoning the heroes, arrival of the heroes, and the scenes with Tale Ličanin. As a result of the two aforementioned reasons (aging, changes in tradition), we ultimately see a good performer becoming an average one.

The song of Šećo Kolić (PN 6832), like that of Ferizović, brings together two themes: the Beg's death and its avenging. The first section most likely[17] begins in the same way as most of the previous ones: with Mustaj Beg's decision to send his standard-bearer (in this song, Nuko) to Uzorje to scout. In his version, all plot elements are present without any special lingering on individual details but with nearly twice as many verses (518) as in Ferizović's. However, points of more extensively developed themes coincide with the same such points in Avdo's performance from 1935: summoning and gathering heroes and the second of Halil's departures to scout. At the same time, this was the final song on the theme of Mustaj Beg's death that Milman Parry encountered.

[17] Again, I am not entirely certain because I was unable to consult the notebook containing the beginning of the song.

## On the Hero's Death

The question posed above, "What does the death of an epic hero mean?" might be reformulated: "What does the death of a *Krajina* hero mean?" For it can be concluded from everything I have discussed thus far that the Krajina possesses a special epic tradition with different characters and special themes, so that the treatment of this final event in the biography of a Krajina hero demands a different approach. If I have concluded that a Krajina hero is no longer "an artist of war," ready to die at any moment, then that means that death itself takes on different contours. Specifically, for such a hero death becomes not a metaphysical but a purely physical phenomenon, which no longer means passage to a world of glorious beings but, rather, the cessation of further existence: the loss of the possibility, for example, to enjoy the charms of such a beauty as Jana Uzolačka (Mustaj Beg), or the loss of the possibility to abandon oneself to youthful follies (Halil), or the loss of the possibility to take care of one's home, wife, mother, sister, and younger brother (Mujo). Death is conceived of from this side and not the other, as an experience of this world and not the other, with everything oriented definitively toward the earth and the problems of everyday existence.

The prehistory of Mustaj Beg's death is also intriguing. In the song by Salko Vojnović from the Marjanović collection, the cause of the Beg's death is Jana's provocative behavior in the maiden's *kolo* dance, supported by Huremaga Kozličić's betrayal. In the songs of the Parry collection, however, the cause of his death is found in the Beg's wife's opposition and curse, in the treachery of certain subjects, and in the Beg's succumbing to the charms of Jana's beauty at critical moments of the battle with Jovan. The Beg's wife accepts the decision for him to take a second wife but only on the condition that she not be "Vlach" (Christian) by birth. When she finds out that Jana in fact is, she opposes his decision or sends the Beg off with a curse.[18]

1. Hajro Ferizović (PN 12393, ll. 34–43):

> "Zašto, beže, sve ti jazuk bilo?
> Jer je Janju rodila Latinka,
> Zadojila vinom i rakijom,
> A mene je rodila Turkinja,

[18] Traditional folk song, especially in women's genres like *sevdalinka* and balladry, maintains the belief that a woman's cursing comes to fruition and always strikes its intended target. From a psychological perspective, such a belief may be attributed to the subordinate position of women in society and especially in a patriarchal culture, which substitutes the power of the curse for a woman's actual power to defend herself.

Zadojila medom i šećerom.
Slušaj mene, beg Mustaj-beg Lički!
Ako diga na Uzorje vojsku,
Zarobijo Jovanovu Janju,
Stigao te Jovan u planinu,
Tebe, beže, pošjeko glavu!"

"Why, Beg, are you behaving so disgracefully?
For Janja was born to a Christian woman,
and was nursed[19] on wine and brandy,
but I was born to a Turkish (Muslim) mother,
and was nursed on honey and sugar.
Listen to me, Mustaj Beg of Lika!
If you raise an army at Uzorje,
and capture Janja, the sister of Jovan,
then may Jovan catch you at the mountain,
and may he cut off your head, my Beg!"

2. Avdo Međedović (1935 version, PN 6807, ll. 703–716): Mustaj Beg's wife, Hanka, agrees only on the condition that she (the Beg's second wife) is of good birth and Muslim, but she won't hear of Jana [*sic*]:

"Svaki šeher ima poglavice,
I u svakog po dobra devojka;
Neko sestru, neko ćerku rani,
Neko, beže, od brata devojku.
Svakoga ću tebe dozvoliti,
Begeniši, ja ću je prositi,
I ja ću joj jenđikada biti,
A sal Janu neću posuliti,
Jer je Jana sestra Jovanova,
I Janu je rodila Latinka,
Krmećijem mesom podhranila,
Da s vrh mene bide gospodarka,
To ti nikad halaliti neću,
Niti reći, niti dozvoliti!"

[19] The verb is a play on words, meaning both "to nurse" or "to breastfeed" but also "to indoctrinate." –Trans.

"Every city has its leader,
and each of them has a fine maiden;
some have a sister, some are raising a daughter,
some, my Beg, a niece.
I would allow you to take any one of them,
choose one you like, I will ask for her hand,
and I will stand as her bridesmaid,
but I can't make peace with Jana,
for Jana is Jovan's sister,
and Jana was born to a Christian woman,
she was brought up eating pork.
To rule over me as lady of the house,
I will never give that my blessing.[20]
I won't speak of it nor allow it!"

And when the Beg grows angry and begins to take his wrath out on her, she curses him (ll. 730–738):

"Ne udri se, osušile ti se!
Da Bog da i Muhammed svetac,
Pošo, beže, i digo krajinu,
I otišo zdravo u Uzovlje,
Porobijo Janu Jovanovu,
Sve to zdravo došla iz Uzovlja,
A ti osto izgubijo glavu,
Ostala ti udovica Jana,
Da se priča dok j' ovog džihana!"

"Don't lash out, may (your hands) wither away on you!
May God and his saint Muhammad grant
that you go, my Beg, and raise up the Kraijna,
that you depart safely to Uzovlje
and take Jana, the sister of Jovan, as a slave,
and that she come safely from Uzovlje.
But may you lose your head,
and may Jana be left your widow,
that it may be told as long as this world remains!"

20 The root of the word *halaliti,* translated here as "to give one's blessing," is the word *halal*, referring to legally permissible action in Islam but also especially with regards to food. The term builds poetically on the fact that Jana was brought up eating pork. –Trans.

3. Avdo Međedović (1951 version, LN 203, ll. 98–113):

> "Vala beže i tako mi Boga
> Ovo ću ti istinito kazat'
> Sve ću jade moje oprostiti
> Bosne grada sedamdeset ravno
> A kol'ko je u te grade aga
> Kol'ko aga i kol'ko begova
> Svaku ću ti curu o.. ovlaziti[21]
> Dvorove toga gospodara i u njega sestru zaiskati
> Ilji sestru ili mi milu šćerku
> I njojzi ću biti jenđe-kada
> Oprostiti Janju nikad neću
> Jeli je Ja.. Janju rodila Srpkinja
> I svinjskim je mesom podranila
> Da mi Janja u dvorove sudi
> Boga mi je ukabulit' neću
> Pa ću se nazvat pušćenica"
>
> "By God, my Beg, so that's how it is.
> I will tell you in truth,
> I will forgive you for all my sorrows.
> Bosnia, with its 70 cities—
> and how many agas are there in those cities,
> how many agas, and how many begs?
> I would visit any of their daughters for you,
> going to the courts of a lord to inquire about his sister,
> either his sister or his dear daughter,
> and I'll be her bridesmaid.
> [But] I will never forgive you for [taking] Janja.
> Wasn't she born to a Serbian woman?
> And brought up eating pork?
> If Janja orders me around in these halls,
> by God, I would never accept her
> and I would pronounce myself divorced."

21 Probably *ob(i)laziti.*

4. Šećo Kolić (PN 6832, ll. 167–183):

"O beg lički direk od Krajine
Đe si beže vojsku potkupijo
I spremijo Kopiljana tvoga
Kopiljana Nuka bajraktara
Te je tebe Janju uhodio
Silovitu vojsku potkupijo
Da ti tražiš Uzoračku Janu
Da pogaziš bijelu Kadunu
E Kadunu Mustaj begovicu
Jeli vakat četeres godina
Kako samti kuću pohodila
Od valjane kuće Atlagića
Nijesam ti hatar ištetila
Ni sjedenjem tebe iščekala
Nisam beže namaz propušćila
Pa moj beže direk od Krajine
Hajde beže ni donijo glavu"

"O Mustaj Beg of Lika, pillar of Krajina,
how could you dare to gather the army, my Beg,
and send your bastard son,
the bastard Nuko, the standard-bearer
who found Janja for you?
You gathered that violent army
so you could seek after Jana of Uzovlje,
so you could trample on the fair woman,
yes, the wife of Mustaj Beg.
Has it been forty years
since I came to your house
from the noble house of Atlagić?
I have never betrayed your love
nor sat idly as I waited for you.
I have never missed namaz prayers.
So my Beg, pillar of Krajina,
go now, my Beg, and may [Jovan] bring us your head."

The motif of betrayal, as in the aforementioned song from the Marjanović collection, is connected to:

1. Hajro Ferizović – the two Kozlić's and three Huremović's
2. Avdo Međedović (1935) – the seven Atlagić brothers-in-law from Bišće
3. Avdo Međedović (1951) – the seven Atlagić brothers-in-law from Bišće
4. Šećo Kolić – the insulted wife of Mustaj Beg

In all four songs, the Beg fails to resist Janja's beauty and his decision to enjoy her charms leads to his death. All the causes enumerated here confirm the hypothesis about the primarily human—rather than lofty ethical—reasons for Mustaj Beg's death.

## Conclusion

Alois Schmaus noticed the specificity of Krajina epic songs, especially in their development of epic plot. The plot and its heroes are bound up to such a degree that one can accordingly speak of the specificities of Krajina heroes. That specificity is reflected, above all, in the complexity of those heroes and the need to motivate their actions, all of which necessarily brings to mind what scholars of literary realism call "characterization."

In the gallery of complex and, above all, intriguing heroes, Mustaj Beg occupies a special place as the "King Arthur" of Krajina epic, as an authority and strategist whom all unquestioningly heed. In this essay, I have tried to focus on one concrete theme—that of Mustaj Beg of Lika's death—and to explore in what ways this theme is handled in epic poetry. Although an epic singer needs, first and foremost, a living hero, not a dead one, the theme of the Beg's death was bound to "have its turn" and be sung. A survey of the songs suggests that a relatively small number of songs were sung about the Beg's death. This most likely results from the fact that, while death for the epic hero is just as important as life itself, a living hero is much more valuable for a singer. The death of a hero means the end of singing! (That remains true, despite the paradox of Mustaj Beg's wife's curse in the 1935 Međedović version that the story of the Beg's infidelity would be told as long as this world exists.)

In addition to a few of Marjanović's songs, five songs from the Parry Collection have been identified with this theme. I have sought what Lord called *common elements* in all the songs with the theme of the Beg's death and arrived at a plot of the song unlike anything an actual singer had sung in his performance. Sometimes the theme of death is accompanied with that of revenge (Kolić and Ferizović), without any particular motivation for the killing of the Beg, while in other versions, everything is coherently motivated: from the Beg's desire for a new wife and his wife's curse on him to his fateful death in the attempt to abduct the beautiful Vlach (Christian) woman. In cases where the actions of Mustaj Beg of Lika have such motivations, emphasis is placed on the need for the pleasure of mortal life, and death comes as a moment of rupture within this pleasure, a theme on which Avdo, in particular, elaborates in his performances. This great hero of the Bosniak and Krajina epic traditions dies because the curse of his wife overtakes him and because he transgresses religious norms (Jana is a Vlach!), but also—and this is particularly important in this context—because he subordinates the ethics of the heroic deed to the aesthetics of hedonistic pleasure. That was the *border* or boundary within which the hero Mustaj Beg of Lika could exist as the supreme authority of the orderly community of Udbina and which he transgressed when he allowed himself to succumb to the everyday pleasures of the beautiful Jana.

## Abbreviations

| | |
|---|---|
| Marjanović | Marjanović, Luka, coll. and ed. 1898–1899. *Hrvatske Narodne Pjesme. Junačke pjesme (muhamedovske).* Vols. III and IV. Zagreb. |
| Hörmann | Hörmann, Kosta, ed. 1990. *Narodne pjesme Muslimana u Bosni i Hercegovini.* Vols. I and II. Sarajevo. |
| LN | Lord Number, prefixed to item numbers of materials in the Milman Parry Collection of Oral Literature collected by Albert Lord. |
| PN | Parry Number, prefixed to item numbers of materials in the Milman Parry Collection of Oral Literature collected by Milman Parry. |

## Bibliography

Bakhtin, M. 1968. *Rabelais and His World.* Trans. H. Iswolsky. Cambridge, MA.

Bošković-Stulli, M, ed. 1971. *Usmena književnost.* Zagreb.

———. 1977. *Usmena književnost kao umjetnost riječi.* Zagreb.

Braun, M. 2004. *Srpskohrvatska junačka pesma.* Trans. T. Bekić. Belgrade. Orig. pub. 1961.

Buturović, Đ. 1976. *Studija o Hörmanovoj zbirci muslimanskih narodnih pjesama.* Sarajevo.

———. 1992. *Bosanskomuslimanska usmena epika.* Sarajevo.

Buturović, Đ., and M. Maglajlić, eds. 1998. *Bošnjačka književnost u književnoj kritici. II, Usmena književnost.* Sarajevo.

Bynum, D. 1986. "The Collection and Analysis of Oral Epic Tradition in South Slavic: An Instance." *Oral Tradition* 1:302–343.

Čolaković, Z. 2004. *Mrtva glava jezik progovara.* Podgorica.

Durić, R. 1998. "Epski junak Budalina Tale." In Buturović and Maglajlić 1998:418–429.

———. 2000. *Junaci epske pjesme Bošnjaka.* Tuzla.

Gesemann, G.. 2002. *Studije o južnoslovenskoj epici.* Trans. and ed. Tomislav Bekić. Belgrade. Orig. pub. 1926.

Jakobson, R., and P. Bogatirjov. 1971. "Folklor kao naročit oblik stvaralaštva." . Trans. M. Bošković-Stulli. In *Usmena književnost. Izbor studija i ogleda,* , ed. M. Bošković-Stulli, 17–31. Zagreb. Orig. pub. as "Die Folklore als besondere Form des Schaffens," 1966.

Kunić, M. 2012. *Usmeno pamćenje i zaborav: Krajiška epika i njeni junaci*. Tešanj.

Krnjević, H. 1998. "Tale Ličanin—epski junak i vedri antijunak." In Buturović and Maglajlić 1998:403–417.

Lord, A. B. 2019. *The Singer of Tales*. 3rd ed. Ed. D. F. Elmer. Hellenic Studies 77. Publications of the Milman Parry Collection of Oral Literature 4. Washington, DC. Orig. pub. Cambridge, MA, 1960.

Maglajlić, M. 2004. "Mustaj-beg Lički—od krajišničkog junaka do epskog zapovjednika." *Radovi Filozofskog fakulteta u Sarajevu* 13:145–165.

Murko, M. 1951. *Tragom srpsko-hrvatske narodne epike: Putovanja u godinama 1930–1932*. Trans. J. Arneri and J. Ljudevit. Zagreb.

Šamić, M., et al., eds. 1972–1981. *Bibliografija radova o narodnoj književnosti I–VI*. Sarajevo.

Schmaus, A. 1953. *Studije o krajinskoj epici*. Zagreb.

Karadžić, V. 1972. *Srpske narodne pjesme III. Pjesme junačke srednjijeh vremena*. Belgrade.

Zanini, P. 2002. *Značenja granice: Prirodna, istorijska i duhovna određenja*. Trans. S. Slatinac. Belgrade. Orig. pub. 1997.

# 11
# Oral Epic in Stolac
## Collective Tradition and Individual Art

John Miles Foley†

*This essay is dedicated to the memory of Albert Bates Lord.*

LET ME START BY ESTABLISHING a thumbnail itinerary for the discussion to follow. We begin by posing a central question that has generated a great deal of exchange and controversy: in the (re)creation and performance of oral epic, do we assign greater weight to the larger, implicit tradition or to the single, idiosyncratic performer who is realizing one instance of that tradition? To offer a response to this longstanding conundrum from the arena of verifiable, recorded oral epic, I turn to the South Slavic tradition as collected by Milman Parry, Albert Lord, and Nikola Vujnović, principally in the 1930s and specifically in the region known as Stolac.[1] The Muslim (i.e. Bosniak) songs from this area were assigned to me by Albert Lord for editing and translating in 1976, and I have been working with them ever since, particularly with the performances of four *guslari*: Halil Bajgorić, Ibro Bašić, Mujo Kukuruzović, and Salko Morić.[2] In examining their compositional art, I will be employing concepts developed in my earlier work, including the notion of "register" or way of speaking from anthropological linguistics,[3] the nature of "words" in oral traditions (including

1 On background for the Parry-Lord theory and fieldwork, see Foley 1988 and Mitchell and Nagy 2000. Translations from South Slavic, ancient Greek, and Anglo-Saxon are my own.

2 On the singers and their songs, see Lord 1954; Kay 1995; Foley 2004; and the website of the Milman Parry Collection of Oral Literature (https://mpc.chs.harvard.edu). Let me express my gratitude to David Elmer and Matthew Kay for their assistance in accessing the Stolac materials, and to Stephen Mitchell and Gregory Nagy for permission to use them in this and other publications.

3 I explicitly adopt here Dell Hymes's definition of registers as "major speech styles associated with recurrent types of situations" (1989:440), based ultimately on the work of M. A. K. Halliday. For a discussion of registers in oral tradition, see Foley 1995:49–53 (theory), 82–92 (in oral-derived

formulaic phraseology, themes or type-scenes, and story-patterns), and, more generally, the singers' ethnic or emic poetics.[4] We will also borrow a term from digital media studies—"distributed authorship"—to gain some perspective on the role of individual practice within a collective tradition.[5] At every juncture, I will be suggesting that we shrug off the textual ideology that has crippled our apprehension of traditional oral art and, instead, focus on songs as existing within an expressive ecology or ecosystem, a far more realistic model for untextualized oral epic.[6]

## Stolac as a Micro-Tradition

As Lord explained in the introduction to the first volume of *Serbocroatian Heroic Songs* (hereafter *SCHS*), the fieldwork team, which included Parry, Vujnović, and himself, identified and collected from *guslari* within six geographically defined centers. These were Novi Pazar, Bijelo Polje, Kolašin, Gacko, Stolac, and Bihać.[7] The Stolac region is interesting for several reasons. Historically, it was the first of the six areas in which the research team collected and consisted of a broad mixture of Muslim, Orthodox, and Catholic singers, with the first of these groups most important to Parry because their song-performances were of greater length and thus more parallel to Homer's epics. In all, they recorded twenty-eight *guslari* during the 1933–1935 expeditions, with Lord adding seven new singers during his 1950–1951 trip. Secondly, Stolac was the home of Vujnović, who served as translator, interviewer, and colleague. Very importantly for both his work in the field and later as transcriber of acoustically-recorded performances that he remade even as he "wrote them down,"[8] Vujnović was, to an extent, himself a singer of tales who gave his employers fifteen songs during the period 1933–1935.

Ibro Bašić, sixty-eight years old and illiterate, contributed twelve songs in various media during the same period as well as his avowed repertoire, a conversation about songs and singing, and several *probe* (test recordings), a strategy by which the research team elicited multiple beginnings to a given performance

texts), 110–115 (in Serbian charms), and 150–175 (in the Homeric Hymns). Applications to Homer and to South Slavic epic are available in Foley 1999:65–88.

4 On South Slavic epic poetics, see Foley 1990:158–200, 278–328, and 359–387 (structure), 1991:61–134 (traditional meaning in Muslim and Christian epic), and 2002:188–218 (epic in the context of other genres).

5 See also Foley 2012:74–76 for application of this concept to oral tradition.

6 See further Foley 2012:117–125.

7 For selected publications of the epic song-performances collected in these areas, see *SCHS* 1–2 (various singers from Novi Pazar), *SCHS* 3–4 and 6 (Avdo Međedović from Bijelo Polje), *SCHS* 14 (various singers from Bihać), and Foley 2004 (Halil Bajgorić from Stolac).

8 See "Nikola Vujnović's Resinging," in Foley 2004:145–191.

for later comparison. Mujo Kukuruzović, forty-three and also illiterate, likewise recorded a dozen songs in various formats as well as the same ancillary items. Halil Bajgorić, the *guslar* I have studied most closely, provided seven song-performances in 1933–1935 and another three during Lord's later visit, with the same complement of supporting items. It is necessary to add that, just as with the songs themselves, these three singers' stated repertoires varied within limits; both the narratives (often with kinetic, story-line designations rather than conventional bookish titles) and their sources varied from one interview to the next. For these masters of oral epic, what they performed wasn't an inventory of static things but rather a series of dynamic explorations of pathways.[9]

The register employed by the Stolac singers was both shared and personal. Like other species of language, it exhibits different levels of structure, morphology, and lexicon. We can identify *pan-traditional language*, which shows similarities from singer to singer across all six collecting areas; a *dialectal level* typical of the particular area (here Stolac); and an *idiolectal level* attributable to the individual poet. As Lord showed, not only does all epic language vary within limits (I would say "follow traditional rules"[10]), but it also contains a tiered lexicon of traditional modes of expression: story-patterns, themes or typical scenes, and formulaic phraseology. Following the *guslari* themselves, I have discussed each of these rule-governed bytes of composition and reception as "words" or *reči*.[11] Instead of making or construing their performances in textually defined, fixed units, singers deploy a pattern-driven register that promotes a fluent experience for both performer and audience.

Besides characteristic structure and morphology, these traditional units show both diachronic and synchronic variation.[12] Crucially, this adaptability and recurrence form the basis of their idiomatic, often proleptic signification. That is, along with the tectonic function of story-patterns, themes or typical scenes, and formulaic phraseology, these traditional "words" index more-than-literal meanings that they evoke *pars pro toto* for the fluent *guslar* and his audience or even latter-day readers (those who learn the traditional lexicon). In effect,

9 As Homer himself puts the matter at *Odyssey* 8.480–81, "the Muse has taught them the pathways [*oimas*], for she loves the singers' tribe"; and as Demodocus explains at *Odyssey* 22.347–48: "the god implanted all sorts of pathways [*oimas*] in my mind." See further Foley 2012, which explores the homology between oral tradition and the Internet as technologies for navigating pathways.

10 On traditional rules, see Foley 1990; from structure to meaning, Foley 1991; with applications to various traditions, Foley 1995 and 1999.

11 On the South Slavic singers' own explanation of *reči*, see Foley 2002:11–21.

12 For the classic demonstration of diachronic structure in traditional phraseology, see Nagy 1974, with important analyses and demonstrations in 1979, 1990, and 2004. On synchronic structure, Lord 2019 remains the fundamental investigation, although Lord also showed his awareness of the diachronic background throughout his work.

the singers' *reči* act not like warehoused textual integers but as lemmata to the implied epic tradition.

Two very common story-patterns in Stolac are the Wedding Song and the Return Song. In the former type a fiancée, kidnapped by an enemy Christian *ban*, is sought by her betrothed (often seconded by a companion). There ensues a major battle between Turkish and Christian forces and a rescue that culminates in the long-delayed wedding. This is from one perspective a coming-of-age story, and it is brilliantly exemplified by the famous performance by Avdo Međedović of the Bijelo Polje region, "The Wedding of Smailagić Meho" (*SCHS* 3 and 4). Another popular story-pattern, the Return Song, is essentially the tale of Odysseus, complete with a hero's long absence and its consequences at home, followed by his return in disguise, an athletic and/or actual battle with suitors, and the winning of his wife or fiancée (or not, as things may turn out).[13]

Story-pattern morphology allows for rule-governed variation not only in character, geographical context, and length or elaboration, but also on other levels. The Return Song may involve two heroes, for example, who together constitute a double-cycle narrative. Or, quite commonly, the female with whom the hero seeks to reunite has in fact already capitulated to one of the suitors, so categorically that when her disguised mate tests her by falsely reporting his own death she outright laughs in unrestrained delight. In such Clytaemnestra-like cases, the song does not end but veers off into a second story that relates how the hero turned traitorous and joined enemy forces before coming to his senses and realigning himself with his Turkish comrades. The Parry Collection houses hundreds of both Wedding and Return tales from the six collecting regions, and we find a number of examples—with expectable variations—within the Stolac micro-tradition.

## Traditional Morphology and the Individual

Within the Stolac region, we can identify dimensions of variability at the levels of story-pattern, theme or typical scene, and formulaic phraseology. Reviewing some of this flexibility in "words" will help provide a background for shared compositional reflexes versus versions attributable to individual *guslari*. It is well to keep in mind that we will be encountering differences, both among regions and among singers within any given area, alongside a more general, pan-traditional similarity across the larger macro-tradition that Parry, Lord,

13 On the Return Song in its Indo-European context, see Foley 1999:115–167.

and Vujnović investigated and recorded either acoustically or by oral dictation to an amanuensis.[14]

## Story-patterns

Within the epic subgenres of Wedding and Return, the two basic tale-types persist. Structurally, each one follows a recognizable latticework of events, with early narrative signals suggesting a story-map that will guide both performer and audience (and readers, if they know the tradition). For instance, whereas the prologue or *pripjev* to a song usually divulges nothing of the action to come (acting instead as a ritual "breakthrough into performance"[15]), the very first four-syllable increment of the main narrative can by itself subtend the particular subgenre of epic to follow. If a performance starts the main story with *i pocmili*, or "And he cried out,"[16] for example, the listener knows beyond doubt that a Return Song is in the offing. Why? Because that story-pattern conventionally begins with a captive shouting in prison, loudly enough to wake the *ban's* infant son and sole heir and keep him from nursing. For that threatening situation, the only possible relief is to send the captor's wife, the *banica*, to strike a bargain for release of the offending prisoner. Thus signaled, and via an expressive economy that only the dedicated traditional register can support, the *Odyssey*-like tale begins.

In brief, both story-patterns can accommodate the presence or lack of a prologue; a broad *dramatis personae* of heroes, heroines, allies, and adversaries; various interstitial events (told expansively or telegraphically, if at all); and a broad geographical domain with numerous cities and other landmarks. Return Songs can be either single- or double-cycle song-types, as mentioned above, and the composite story that results from the returning hero finding an unfaithful mate awaiting him is a viable pathway. These built-in options foster the ready telling of a great many epic tales in multiple song-performances, which are best thought of not as a tidy anthology or cycle but rather as a constellation of possible instances that collectively figure forth the implied epic tradition. At every point, the actions and events of these story-patterns are idiomatic and proleptic; because of their necessary and enriching connection to the implicit

14 The research team made two different kinds of acoustic recordings: sung performances at full speed to the accompaniment of the *gusle*, and recited performances without instrumental accompaniment. They also wrote down songs in textual format at a much more deliberate pace. On the collecting expeditions, see further Mitchell and Nagy 2000.

15 This term is taken from Hymes 1975, reprinted with "Appendix" and "Postscript" in Hymes 1981:79–141.

16 I translate these and other parallel instances as historical present tenses.

"wordhoard" (to borrow a term from Old English oral-derived poetry[17]), they stand as metonymic of—as lemmata for—the epic tradition as a whole. Audiences and performers are immersed in a real-time exchange, communicating within the same expressive register or code.

## Themes or typical scenes

Just as there is a natural morphology among "word"-instances at the level of the entire story, so there are pan-traditional, dialectal, and idiolectal levels of composition (and therefore of reception) at the middle level of what Albert Lord called the "theme."[18] One singer's version of Arming for Battle or Readying the Hero's Horse, two typical scenes that tend to appear together in a variety of song-types, can establish this point. The Stolac singers overlap in their inventory of armor, weapons, and equine finery, sometimes mentioning many of the very same items and practices (e.g. for the warrior, shirts of spun gold, elaborate pants with braided seams, high boots with magnificent spurs, a lance, a sword, a mace, even a headpiece with revolving decorative feathers; for the horse, a thorough washing and grooming followed by a blanket and a saddle with five cinctures, a braided mane interwoven with precious metals, and golden reins). All of these features (and more) are indexical of heroic preparation of the warrior and his faithful mount and, as such, indicative of an adventure to ensue. At the same time, no one of them is by itself necessary; the larger traditional idea invoked through such codes is larger and richer than any single element or combination of elements. From a complementary perspective, none of the features should ever be considered "missing" or left out; instead, each of them participates in summoning an implied, idiomatic whole.[19]

17 A few references to the Anglo-Saxon concept will make the point: (1) at *Andreas* 316, God is testing Andreas who, eager for help with his sea-passage, *wis on gewitte, wordhord onleac* ("wise in his mind, unlocked his wordhoard"); (2) at line 601 of the same poem, God continues the testing: *Đa gen weges weard wordhord onleac* ("Then still the guardian of the wave unlocked his wordhoard"); (3) at *Widsith* 1, the title character begins his "historical" recitation of courts and peoples he has putatively visited with the following line: *Widsiþ maþolade, wordhord onleac* ("Widsith spoke, unlocked his wordhoard"); and (4) at line 258–259 of *Beowulf*, the title hero's answer to the coastguard's challenge to identify himself and his men begins with this indexed introduction: *Him se yldesta andswarode / werodes wisa, wordhord onleac* ("The chief answered him, / leader of the troop, unlocked his wordhoard"). Two further examples with similar import may be found at line 3 of *Vainglory* and line 1 of *Meters of Boethius* 5; a final example, at line 19 of *The Order of the World*, involves (at least metaphorically) the concept of writing within a mix of riddling and homiletic language. All citations are taken from *The Anglo-Saxon Poetic Records* (Krapp and Dobbie 1961).

18 For the classic exposition, see Lord 2019:71-104; overview at Foley 2011.

19 For evidence of this expressive algorithm in South Slavic oral epic, see Foley 1991:61–134; in Homer, Foley 1999:169–199. The core concept here is that traditional oral performances—and

As illustration of how one of the Stolac singers handles (we might say "personalizes") the Arming/Readying sequence, consider Halil Bajgorić's coda to the two themes. In consonance with the traditional idea that hero and horse are comrades-in-arms, each with his own set of responsibilities during the expedition to come, the *guslar* chooses to close his presentation of the double-scene with an extended, Homeric-style simile. It is worth remarking that such lengthy similes are relatively rare in the South Slavic epic tradition, with most such figures not exceeding a single decasyllable line. But for whatever performative reason, Bajgorić here turns to a quite elegant extended comparison that aligns the admirable independence of the hero's horse to the quotidian experience of a young shepherdess alone on a mountain (40–49):[20]

Sam se šede dorat okretati,
Po avliji *ji* tamo *vi* jamo,
Prez kandžije *hi* prez binjadžije.
Kako dorat potkočijo glavu!
K'o *vu* brdu piški čobanica
*v*U kukulju, *vu* šarenu gunju,
Još kojoj je *v*osamn'es' godina,
Još koja je jedina *vu* mame;
Pa joj mama meće *v*užinicu
Da joj nje bi šćerka *v*ogladnila.

Alone the bay horse began to prance,
Through the courtyard back and forth,
Without a whip and without a rider.
How proudly the bay horse bore his head!
Like a careless young shepherdess up on a mountain,
Clothed in her hood and motley jacket,
Only eighteen years of age,
And her mother's only daughter;
Her mother put up a small snack for her
So her little girl wouldn't go hungry.

Juxtaposing the horse's ability to stride riderless around the courtyard to the young girl's carefree day tending her sheep, the singer conjures the same sort of nature-warfare or nature-heroism interface that informs so many of Homer's

the "words" that make them up (see note 11 above)—do not "repeat"; instead, they *recur*. See further the discussion of this concept in Foley 2012:208–212.

[20] Foley 2004:51.

similes, especially in the *Iliad*. Using an idiolectal strategy, Bajgorić has further explicated a traditional idea associated with the hero-horse interaction.

## Formulaic phraseology

As a caveat, it is well to recall that formulaic phraseology—like the higher-level traditional units we call story-patterns and themes—is an emergent product of a rule-governed process. We will understand formulaic verses best by keeping in mind the forces that shape the overall idiom: the decasyllabic framework, to be sure,[21] as well as optional, occasional devices such as end-colon, leonine rhyme, and acoustic patterning in the form of alliteration and assonance. Most fundamentally, however, singers in Stolac and elsewhere in the South Slavic epic tradition depend upon *traditional rules* that involve metrical word-placement and a tiered series of constraints.[22] Performers work within this flexible set of directives, which foster variation within limits rather than either fixed, static increments or wholesale instability. Such rule-governed flexibility is the platform for individual expression within the traditional register, for personal creativity that embraces and, in fact, depends upon the traditional phraseological heritage.

The formulaic repertoires of the Stolac *guslari* illustrate this dynamic interaction of individual and tradition, consisting as they do of regional or dialectal phrases alongside personal or idiolectal equivalents. For example, consider the various avatars of an idea we could summarize as "for a long time," a prominent adverbial phrase that appears very frequently in a wide variety of songs and song-types. An analysis of 14,000 lines from the recorded Stolac epic tradition uncovers a dialectal formula, *za nedjelju dana* ("for a week of days"), that is employed by all three singers sampled: Bajgorić, Bašić, and Kukuruzović. But each of them has other options as well to express the same idea, options that are not shared with their comrades but that seem, on available evidence, to be

21 An interesting aspect of the decasyllabic symbiosis with phraseology in performance is the frequent accommodation of "short" or "long" verses with vocal rests or extrametrical syllables, respectively. This kind of accommodation suggests that more study needs to be undertaken on the non-verbal aspects of performance. See further Foley 2004:80; more generally, Foster 2004 on the music accompanying Bajgorić's performance; Erdely 1995 on the music associated with song-recordings from the Bihać region; and Reichl 2000 on performance and music in oral epic.

22 See note 10 above. As a simple example, in the second (six-syllable) colon of the decasyllable the syllabically shorter word conventionally takes initial position, whatever the customary prose word order might otherwise be. The only exception to this rule, which amounts to a tiered exclusion, is for an initially accented disyllable, which migrates toward the line-ending zeugma begun by the strongly stressed ninth syllable. Cf. the shorter-before-longer order of *reče lakrdiju* (spoke a word) with the exclusion prompted by the long rising tone in *lakrdiju víknu* (shouted a word). For more rules and examples, see Foley 1990:176f.

idiolectal. For instance, Bajgorić alone uses the formula *dva bijela dana* ("two white days"), while only Kukuruzović deploys the "word"-synonyms *sedam godin' dana* ("seven years of days") and *cijo mjesec dana* ("a whole month of days").[23] Parsed into their component lexical units, these formulas obviously diverge. But in terms of the South Slavic epic register, which yields actual articulated phrases only as products deriving from a rule-governed process, they are equivalent. The point is that all of these variants are pathways to the same traditional idea, generated in performance through the natural morphology of the register and empowered by the indexical force of traditional referentiality. The singers simply navigate these pathways in different ways.

As one further example of the referential value of formulaic phraseology, I summon a proleptic "word" used by all three singers—Bajgorić, Bašić, and Kukuruzović—across their performance repertoires and over a variety of narrative situations. The phrase in question takes two forms, both of them dialectal in distribution: *[X] skoči na noge od tala* ("[X] jumped to his/her feet from the ground") and *Pa on(a) skoči na noge lagane* ("Then he/she jumped to his/her light feet"). On the surface, the thrust of these verses appears to be clear enough: some character jumps either from the ground or to his/her feet, apparently a preliminary to an undefined subsequent action for which no motive is explicitly supplied. But at even that general literal level, the act can appear oblique, awkward, or even nonsensical; in one case, a woman "jumps to her feet from the ground" on the second story of a household when she hears a messenger knock on the gate down below. Instead of imputing clumsiness or error to the singer, however, we should look beyond the literal, fragmented sense of the phrase (a composite "word" in its own right) to the idiomatic meaning of the action, which research has established as "a heroic or honorable response to an unexpected turn of events that demands the principal's immediate attention."[24] With this information in hand, we can see that the woman on the second floor is idiomatically cast in the mold of a heroic figure about to embark, and indeed the message from her captive fiancé—which the messenger will soon deliver—amounts to an unforeseen call to action leading to his rescue.

## Emic versus Etic Perspectives

The Stolac singers use this traditional register, this special way of speaking, both to compose their epic narratives in performance and to foster ready reception among fluent audiences and latter-day readers. Because their "words" are

23 See Foley 1990:191–192. For more on South Slavic epic phraseology, see Elmer 2009, 2010.

24 Cf. Foley 1991:83–87; definition on p. 86.

emergent products of a rule-governed process, they are best understood not as repetition but rather as recurrence.[25] That is, formulas, themes, and story-patterns are deployed not merely to answer tectonic needs but to achieve expressive goals, and they operate not just structurally but idiomatically. The register through which the *guslari* realize their tales is powerful precisely because it morphs according to traditional rules and because it reaches beyond literal signification to encoded connotations that enrich the song-making and song-receiving experience for all concerned. We can sum up this heightened, more-than-textual semiotics in proverbial fashion by observing that "Oral traditions work like language, only more so."[26]

Framing these realities in the common dialectic of emic (ethnic) versus etic (analytic) points of view can help to lay bare some of the inapposite assumptions we tend to make about oral epic composition, both in the South Slavic and in other oral traditions.[27] From our external or etic perspective, we often unthinkingly apply text-centric criteria to non-textual situations, puzzling over "inaccuracies" and "omissions" we identify in a series of performances of the same story by the same singer, for example. This attitude once led an eminent Homerist to castigate the South Slavic *guslari* for not managing their performances more carefully (read: according to his preferred textual standard).[28] It was, in particular, the frequent claim by these singers that they compose *rečima po rečima*, or "words for words," that so disappointed this and other scholars. On the face of it, and on the basis of the analyses carried out by Parry and Lord, the singers seemed to fall short.

[25] See note 19 above.

[26] This represents a slight variation on the first of the pseudo-proverbs invented to explain key characteristics of oral traditions; see further Foley 2002:125–145.

[27] Of course, this premise could be extended beyond epic to myriad other genres of oral tradition and related forms. Of special interest are living clusters of oral traditions that exist in interactive ecologies; see, e.g., the multi-generic South Slavic ecology (Foley 2002:188–218) and the evidence of "leakage" across generic boundaries in oral-derived traditional poetry (Foley 2003). On the related issues of truth and history in South Slavic oral epic, see Foley 2010.

[28] In speaking of the art of the Novi Pazar *guslari* whose song-performances were recorded by the Parry-Lord-Vujnović team—songs he was entirely unable to read or understand in the original language—G. S. Kirk nonetheless arrogantly pronounced as follows (1962:100): "These particular poets pay lip-service to the ideal of complete accuracy in reproduction and are under the impression that they come very close to it. They are, in fact, far too optimistic; and their very confidence and lack of self-criticism prevents them from trying to achieve a higher standard of accuracy, which certainly lies within their power. The truth remains that even within their simple and unsophisticated oral tradition, with its incomplete formular technique, poems—not merely 'substance' or 'technique'—*are* transmitted, though with some variation and contamination." Many of these misapprehensions persist in Kirk 2010 (e.g. 69–85), along with ignorance of an enormous amount of pertinent scholarship on Homer and South Slavic epic from the 1970s onward.

But did they? Were the *guslari*, in any possible sense, correct? If we substitute the singers' internal or emic definition of a "word"—that is, a flexible, coded thought-byte deployed for the purpose of telling traditional tales in the performance arena—then there can be no doubt: they are absolutely correct in their *rečima po rečima* claim. As we have seen, each of their "words" derives from a process that yields many different products. Story-patterns provide a recognizable map or latticework at the same time that they license broad variations in characters, events, and so forth. Themes are multiforms that accommodate different levels of detail and inventories of material culture, in response to the exigencies of the performance underway and the individual singer's proclivities. Formulaic phraseology, also composed of traditional "words," rather than textual or lexical increments, exists to morph within limits and thus will dependably exhibit what some have wrongly labeled "instability" among instances.[29] To put the matter most straightforwardly (without interposing an etic lens), *guslari* are claiming not word-for-word but rather "word"-for-"word" fidelity. They are not speaking about printed or memorized creations to be compared by manuscript collation but about in-process, emergent performances that can be realized only through a flexible, powerful idiom.

## Distributed Authorship

In order to move toward an answer to the question that began this inquiry—namely, whether South Slavic epic is more of a collectively- or individually-driven phenomenon—let us borrow a term and concept from the lexicon of digital technology. By the phrase "distributed authorship," software engineers designate a continuous process of rule-governed creation and innovation, a process that involves multiple "authors" who contribute to an application that, strictly speaking, belongs to no one person. Under such conditions, no single person is wholly in charge of developing what amounts to an ever-changing collection of parallel, non-hierarchical products, each of which amounts to a tailored (and further tailorable) instance of the software rather than a downstream, dead-end artifact. To focus on any one person's or group's version as

29 Even in the case of noun-epithet formulas for named heroes, there are always alternative indexes or pathways that identify the character in question. And when that inventory of possible products is small, we are still confronting a recurrence rather than a repetition; in such cases, a singer or some larger group has found a few possibilities to be ideal solutions to the ongoing process of navigating the tradition's network of pathways. As a caveat, it is well to remember (1) that, unlike Homer, the South Slavic *guslari* utilize noun-epithet formulas that are identical in length (exactly filling the six-syllable second colon of the ten-syllable line); and (2), more generally, that South Slavic epic is not uniform in flexibility throughout the "words" that make up its register.

terminal or epitomized is to misunderstand the dynamics of distributed authorship, whose essence is its ongoingness.

Open-source software, as opposed to proprietary, bought-and-sold, commercial products, provides the clearest example of this contributory dynamics. According to the widely observed policy, open-source software is shared freely among its user- and developer-base, with not only the process and products but also, and crucially, the generative code that underlies them made freely available to others. Instead of purchasing a boxed set of disks or an internet download, and instead of pledging to observe the strict, anti-piracy licensing terms, open-source software presents itself as a learning and innovating opportunity from the ground up. Average users may choose merely to deploy it "as is," free of charge of course, while IT specialists may decide to rework its code to create something unique for their own unique purposes, again free of charge. No legal or financial barrier stands in the way of "appropriating someone else's work" because the open-source community understands the ever-evolving work as belonging to everyone—past, present, and future.

Now consider the application of this concept to oral tradition, and in particular the South Slavic epic, with special attention to the dimensions of sharing, rule-governed innovation, and performance. To take the last item first in *hysteron-proteron* style, I begin by citing Lawrence Lessig's pithy observation (made of digital composition but translatable to oral composition) that "code is performative; what it says, it does."[30] Lessig is emphasizing the ability of code to actually *do something*, to cause something to happen, by virtue of what one might call its linguistic power. Oral tradition (OT) also depends upon code—the story-patterns, themes, and formulas discussed above—to accomplish its expressive ends via traditional structure and referentiality. Because OT code is a special language or register, it can access worlds of implication and meaning that non-coded language by definition cannot access. Also like digital code, the OT register is shared among its community of performers and audiences, morphing according to the traditional rules that govern its shapeshifting.

To draw out the homology,[31] the Stolac epic tradition can be understood as a small study in distributed authorship. Ibro Bašić, Mujo Kukuruzović, and Halil Bajgorić share a generative code, a system of expression that allows them to access the implied tradition and to formulate parallel, non-hierarchical performances. No one of them is the "author" of a given story (much less its story-pattern), any more than we can attribute either formulaic or thematic code to a single *guslar*. The register they jointly use, and compose within, supports an

[30] Lessig 2002:57.

[31] Cf. other aspects of the homology as described in Foley 2012:55–60.

infinite variety of individual realizations—at all levels of composition and across the spectrum from pan-traditional language through dialectal and on to idiolectal elements. In sum, we can say that authorship of South Slavic epic from Stolac is distributed across the Stolac region rather than assignable to any single person. Furthermore, that distribution also includes, to varying extents, both other geographical regions and other singers that preceded those recorded by Parry, Lord, and Vujnović, not to mention those *guslari* who succeeded them in the years following. Counter-intuitively for text-trained scholars, the genius of the South Slavic oral epic tradition lies precisely in its shared, rule-governed, idiomatic code. And that code is the personal possession of no one singer, but rather the dynamic lingua franca spoken fluently by all of them.

## Coda

In conclusion, then, let us return to our opening question—whether South Slavic oral epic is more of a collectively or individually driven phenomenon—and offer the simplest, most accurate answer we can muster: "Yes." With this response we affirm that neither side of the equation is primary or determinative; in fact, the relationship between tradition and performer is always and necessarily symbiotic. Based on the morphology and idiomatic meaning of the shared epic register, construed as "words" rather than words, the Stolac *guslari* (and *a fortiori* oral performers in many other epic and non-epic traditions) make and remake songs and song-types whose "authorship" is distributed rather than singular. In fact, we can avoid the false binary that stems from textual ideology by citing another homemade proverb: *without a tradition there is no language; without a performer there is only silence.*[32]

[32] Foley 2002:185.

## Abbreviations

*SCHS* = Lord, A. B., and D. E. Bynum, eds. 1953-1980. *Serbocroatian Heroic Songs*. 6 vols. Cambridge, MA.

## Bibliography

Elmer, D. F. 2009. "Presentation Formulas in South Slavic Epic Song." *Oral Tradition* 24:41–59. http://journal.oraltradition.org/issues/24i/elmer.

———. 2010. "Kita and Kosmos: The Poetics of Ornamentation in Bosniac and Homeric Epic." *Journal of American Folklore* 123/489:276–303.

Erdely, S. 1995. *Music of Southslavic Epics from the Bihać Region of Bosnia*. New York.

Foley, J. M. 1988. *The Theory of Oral Composition: History and Methodology*. Bloomington.

———. 1990. *Traditional Oral Epic: The Odyssey, Beowulf, and the Serbo-Croatian Return Song*. Berkeley.

———. 1991. *Immanent Art: From Structure to Meaning in Traditional Oral Epic*. Bloomington.

———. 1995. *The Singer of Tales in Performance*. Bloomington.

———. 1999. *Homer's Traditional Art*. University Park, PA.

———. 2002. *How to Read an Oral Poem*. Urbana.

———. 2003. "How Genres Leak in Traditional Verse." In *Unlocking the Wordhord: Anglo-Saxon Studies in Memory of Edward B. Irving, Jr.*, ed. M. C. Amodio and K. O'B. O'Keeffe, 76–108. Toronto.

———, ed. and trans. 2004. *The Wedding of Mustajbey's Son Bećirbey as Performed by Halil Bajgorić*. Folklore Fellows Communications 283. Helsinki.

———. 2010. "Traditional History in South Slavic Oral Epic." In *Epic and History*, ed. D. Konstan and K. Raaflaub, 347–361. Oxford.

———. 2011. "Theme." In *The Homer Encyclopedia*, ed. M. Finkelberg, 3:862–864. Oxford.

———. 2012. *Oral Tradition and the Internet: Pathways of the Mind*. Urbana.

Foster, H. W. 2004. "The Role of Music." In Foley 2004:223–60.

Hymes, D. 1975. "Breakthrough into Performance." In *Folklore: Performance and Communication*, ed. D. Ben-Amos and K. Goldstein, 11–74. The Hague.

———. 1981. *"In Vain I Tried to Tell You": Essays in Native American Ethnopoetics*. Philadelphia.

———. 1989. "Ways of Speaking." In *Explorations in the Ethnography of Speaking*, ed. R. Bauman and J. Sherzer, 433–451, 473–474. 2nd ed. Cambridge.

Kay, M. W. 1995. *The Index of the Milman Parry Collection, 1933–1935: Heroic Songs, Conversations, and Stories*. New York.

Kirk, G. S. 1962. *The Songs of Homer*. Cambridge.

———. 2010. *Homer and the Oral Tradition*. Cambridge. Orig. pub. 1976.

Krapp, G. P., and E. V. K. Dobbie, eds. 1961. *The Anglo-Saxon Poetic Records: A Collective Edition*. 6 vols. New York.

Lessig, L. 2002. *The Future of Ideas: The Fate of the Commons in a Connected World*. New York.

Lord, A. B. 1954. "General Introduction." In Lord and Bynum 1953-1980:1.3–20.

———. 2019. *The Singer of Tales*. 3rd ed. Ed. D. F. Elmer. Hellenic Studies 77. Publications of the Milman Parry Collection of Oral Literature 4. Washington, DC. Orig. pub. Cambridge, MA, 1960.

Mitchell, S., and G. Nagy. 2000. "Introduction to the Second Edition." In Lord 2019:xi–xxxviii.

Nagy, G. 1974. *Comparative Studies in Greek and Indic Meter.* Cambridge, MA. Repr. 2001.

———. 1979. *The Best of the Achaeans: Concepts of the Hero in Archaic Greek Poetry*. Baltimore. Rev. ed. 1999.

———. 1990. *Pindar's Homer: The Lyric Possession of an Ancient Past*. Baltimore.

———. 2004. *Homer's Text and Language*. Urbana.

Reichl, K., ed. 2000. *The Oral Epic: Performance and Music*. Berlin.

# PART IV

# ORALITY AND TEXTUALITY

# 12

# The Written Text as a Metaphor for the Integrity of Oral Composition in Classical Persian Traditions and Beyond

Olga M. Davidson

## Introduction

The centerpiece of this essay is a brief narrative found in the classical Persian text of the *Shāhnāma* or "Book of Kings," a monumental poem composed in the early eleventh century CE by a poet named Ferdowsi, literally "the man of paradise." In this narrative, the poet tells the story of the genesis of an archetypal "Book of Kings" celebrating the kings and heroes of the Iranian Empire. This book, says the poet, became the ultimate source of his own classical Persian poem:

> There was a book [*nāma*] from ancient times | in which there was an abundance of stories.
> It was dispersed into the hands of every *mōbad*. | Every wise one [of the *mōbads*] possessed a portion of it.
> There was a nobleman [*pahlavān*], born of the *dehqāns*, | brave, powerful, wise, and noble,
> one who inquired into the earliest days. | He sought to retrieve all the past stories.
> From every region an aged *mōbad* | he brought, who would remember this book [*nāma*].
> He asked them about kings of the world | and about the famed and glorious heroes,
> when and how they held the world in the beginning | that they should have passed it down to us in such a wretched state,

> how, with a lucky star, | every day completed a heroic exploit for them.
> The great ones, one by one, recited before him | the stories [*sokhanhā*] about kings and the turnings of the world.
> When the lord heard their words from them | he set the foundations for a renowned book [*nāma*].
> Thus it became his memorial in the world. | The small and the great praise him.
>
> *Shāhnāma* I 21.126–136[1]

According to this story, an archetypal book had once been disintegrated—only to become reintegrated many years later at the initiative of a wise nobleman who put together the fragments of the disintegrated book. This nobleman, described as a descendant of elite Zoroastrian landowners (*dehqāns*), proceeded to gather experts (*mōbads*) from all over the Iranian Empire.[2] Each one of these experts brought with him a fragment of the original book. Then, lining up the experts in order, the nobleman invited each one of the experts to recite, in proper order, what was contained in each fragment. This way, the archetypal book was reintegrated, and it was this book that became the primal source of Ferdowsi's own *Shāhnāma*. As I have argued in earlier work, "Ferdowsi's description of this genesis amounts to a myth-made stylization of oral poetry."[3]

This is not to say that Ferdowsi's *Shāhnāma* is oral poetry in and of itself. Ferdowsi's poem acknowledges that it was written down, and to that extent, it cannot be described as oral poetry in the sense of a composition-in-performance. Nevertheless, this poem also acknowledges its own derivation from poetry as performed by oral poets.

In the present work, I will argue that the picturing of a disintegrated and then reintegrated book is a metaphor for oral poetry, and that we find this metaphor attested in a wide variety of oral traditions that have evolved independently of each other. As we will see, such a metaphor can serve a variety of purposes in a variety of cultures that differ widely with regard to their use of written texts.

To get a better sense of such a metaphor, I will consider:

1 Citations of passages from the *Shāhnāma* follow the volume- and section- and line-numberings of Bertels 1960–1971. The translations are mine.

2 Further analysis in Davidson 2013a:29. *Mōbad* means "priest" or "wise man" and *dehqān* means "landowner." The latter meaning, however, masks the actual function of the *dehqān*: as a chief owner of property in a particular locale, he is the "authority" not only in the narrow sense that he has administrative powers but also in the broader sense that he actually validates the traditions of that given locale.

3 Davidson 2005:268.

- other classical Persian narratives that feature variations on the theme of a disintegrated and then reintegrated Book of Kings
- other Iranian narratives about other kinds of books
- non-Iranian narratives found in other Indo-European traditions.

## Other Classical Persian Narratives Featuring Themes Relating to the Book of Kings

### Two narratives from the Bāysonghori Preface

I start with a classical Persian prose text featuring two further narratives that are most similar in content to the poetic narrative I quoted from the *Shāhnāma* of Ferdowsi. These two narratives are embedded within the framing narrative of the preface of a book stemming from a recension of Ferdowsi's *Shāhnāma*, commissioned in 1426 CE by the Timurid prince Ghiāth-al-Din Bāysonghor.[4] The book, known as the Bāysonghori *Shāhnāma*, is now housed at the Golestan Museum in Tehran, and I will be quoting here from the text of the preface to this book. From here on, I will refer to this text as the Bāysonghori Preface, abbreviated BP.[5] Near the very beginning of the text (BP 368), the framing narrative says that there were numerous copies of the *Shāhnāma* in the imperial library of Prince Bāysonghor. But none of them "agreed with his delicate constitution and elegant disposition." So, that was the impetus, according to the logic of the framing narrative here, for a new recension. And the circumstances were right: "when in the time of his imperial rule—may this period of peace be doubled—works of art dominated and well-measured speech held immeasurable value, dried up shoots of wisdom and knowledge were refreshed day by day with the subsidizing drops of rain from his learning." So, when the prince called for a collation of texts, the production of "a more complete and accurate copy" was acted upon, and the text highlights all the editorial work that went into the production of an enhanced text for this book. The framing narrative now

4 Bāysonghor was ruler of the city of Herat from 1416/1417 until 1433, the year of his death. This prince was the son of the king Shāhrokh and grandson of Timur, that is, of Tamerlane himself. The production of the book was completed in 1430, on January 30, by Mowlanā Jaʿfar Bāysonghori, a Tabrizi calligrapher who appears to have also served as librarian to the prince in Herat.

5 The text of the preface to the Bāysonghori *Shāhnāma* has been edited by Mohammad Amin Riyāhi 1993:364–418. My citations of relevant passages in the Bāysonghori Preface (BP) will follow the convention: BP + the page-number in the Riyāhi edition. In my citations, I will make paraphrases of the relevant passages, occasionally highlighting the specific words being used; also, I will occasionally offer loose translations, enclosed within quotation marks. In a forthcoming project, Mohsen Ashtiany and I will produce a literal translation of the whole Bāysonghori Preface.

proceeds to aetiologize this editorial work in the form of two embedded narratives that tell about the genesis of an archetypal book of kings:

> [1] The just king Anōshirvān loved collecting accounts of the past generations and having them shorn of their anomalies. And he habitually sent messengers to research throughout the world and gather stories of the rulers of different regions along with other noteworthy accounts and to deliver a copy of their research to the [royal] library.
>
> [2] When it came to Yazdgerd's reign, all those historical accounts had been preserved in his library but in no particular order. He ordered Dāneshvar the Dehqān—a senior figure at the royal court [*madā'in*], who combined courage with learning and wisdom—to organize a list of chapters and arrange them in order from the beginning of the rule of Kayomarth to the end of the reign of Khosrow Parviz. And whatever lacunae he found there he filled and appended by asking information from the learned and from the Zoroastrian *mōbads*. And so a chronicle of sheer perfection and comprehensiveness was created.
>
> BP 369

In terms of these two embedded narratives, the archetypal book of kings that each one of the two shahs had commissioned seems to be the same text that Ferdowsi supposedly turned into Persian poetry around 1010 CE. At least that is how this archetypal book of kings is imagined in the embedded narratives.

In effect, these two embedded narratives about two earlier shahs serve the purpose of *prefiguring* the recension undertaken by the would-be shah Bāysonghor (this prince died before he ever became shah), which is the main topic of the framing narrative. In the second of the two embedded narratives I have just quoted, it is made explicit that the textual recension involves not only earlier texts but also performances stemming from oral traditions. By implication, the variations found in the texts of the *Shāhnāma* that were housed in the library of Bāysonghor were understood to be derived from not only textual but also performative variations in the transmission of lore about kings and heroes.

But this gesture of *prefiguration* glosses over a major complication concerning the transmission of this lore. The texts commissioned by the two shahs who are figured here as prototypes of Prince Bāysonghor would have been composed not in Persian but in Pahlavi, the imperial language of the Sasanian Dynasty. The shah Khosrow I Anōshirvān was ruler of the Sasanian Empire from 531 to 579 CE, while the shah Yazdgerd III, the very last king of the Sasanian Empire, ruled from 632 to 651 CE. And there is a further complication concerning the transmission: as we read from the words of Ferdowsi himself, the prototype for his poetic version of the Book of Kings is envisaged as a text written in Pahlavi prose, and it is up to the poet to turn the prose of the Pahlavi book into Persian poetry. Here is how the poet speaks about this Pahlavi prototype:

> In my city I had a congenial friend [*mehrbān*]. | You might say that he and I were in one skin.
> He said to me: "This idea of yours is good. | Your steps indeed tend to goodness.
> This book [*nāma*] written down in Pahlavi, | I will present to you so that you may not slumber!
> You have lucid language and youth. | You have the words for heroic composition.
> Go, render anew this book [*nāma*] of kings! | With it seek honor among the great!"
> When he brought this book [*nāma*] to me, | it inflamed my dark soul.
>
> I 23.156–161[6]

## Narrative from the so-called Older Preface[7]

A still further complication concerning the transmission of lore about Iranian kings presents itself in the so-called Older Preface to the *Shāhnāma*, hereafter abbreviated OP, attested in the London manuscript of the *Shāhnāma* (L, British Museum), dated 1276 CE, as also in other manuscripts.[8] The content of the OP is dated all the way back to the middle of the tenth century.[9] According to the narrative of the OP, a Book of Kings composed in Persian prose was commissioned by a certain Ibn ʿAbd al-Razzāq, a local potentate of Tus (which was the native city of Ferdowsi), in concert with his administrator, Abū Manṣūr al-Maʿmarī (OP §6). The resulting work, finished in 957 CE (OP §7), was based on a "compilation" of older books (OP §6). The narrative relates that Ibn ʿAbd al-Razzāq had been inspired to commission this book after hearing the story

6 For this and other examples of references to a prototypical book written in Pahlavi prose and then supposedly turned into Persian poetry, see Davidson 2013a:27–29.

7 This section is an epitome of arguments already presented in Davidson 2001 and 2008.

8 In Davidson 2013a:60, I list some other medieval manuscripts of the *Shāhnāma* that contain this Older Preface. The text of the Older Preface has been edited by Riyāhi 1993:170–180.

9 In what follows, numbers preceded by the sign § refer to the divisions of the text of the OP in the translation by Minorsky 1964. Besides the Older Preface and the Bāysonghori Preface, another comparable text is the preface to the Florence manuscript of the *Shāhnāma*, dated 1217/1218 CE, supplemented by the preface to the Topkapi manuscript (Riyāhi 1993:264–287); still another comparable text is the "intermediate" preface (see Riyāhi 1993:326–338).

of the genesis of the book *Kalīla and Dimna*, which is a celebrated collection of fables stemming ultimately from India (OP §6).

As we are about to see, the events that are adduced in the Older Preface to explain how the book *Kalīla and Dimna* attained its supposedly perfect form are presented as a prefiguration of the events that explain how the *Shāhnāma* supposedly reached its own perfection—once it was turned into poetry by Ferdowsi.

According to the Older Preface, the Sasanian shah Khosrow I Anōshirvān commissioned a translation of the *Kalīla and Dimna* from the "Indian" language into Pahlavi (OP §4). It was this same shah, as we already noted in the Bāysonghori Preface, who commissioned the reintegration of a supposedly disintegrated Book of Kings, likewise written in Pahlavi (BP 369). Having noted this detail once again, I return to the narrative of the Older Preface: so, many years after the translation of the *Kalīla and Dimna* into Pahlavi, the Caliph al-Maʾmūn (who ruled from 813 to 833 CE) ordered a translation of this book from Pahlavi into Arabic, through the agency of his administrator Ibn al-Muqaffaʿ (OP §4).[10] Then the Samanid Amir Naṣr II b. Aḥmad (who ruled from 914 to 943), through the agency of his secretary Balʿami, commissioned a translation from Arabic into Persian prose (OP §5). And, finally, Balʿami's prose version was transposed into Persian verse by the poet Rudaki, who flourished in the late ninth and early tenth century CE (OP §5). It is said of the Persian prose version that "the book fell into men's hands and every man turned its pages" and of the poetic version that from then on, *Kalīla and Dimna* "was on the tongues of the great and the lowly" (OP §5).[11] Ferdowsi himself draws a parallel between his own *Shāhnāma* and Rudaki's *Kalīla and Dimna*, stressing that the uniqueness of both compositions depends on what is described as the turning of prose into poetry (*Shāhnāma* VIII 655.3460–3464).[12]

The rhetoric of the narrative I just analyzed in the Older Preface operates on a principle that I describe as an ascending scale of prestige. At the climax of the narrative, the Persian prose version of the *Kalīla and Dimna* is capped by the Persian poetic version. And now we are about to see that the same kind of rhetoric is at work in the "happy ending" built into the narrative of the Older Preface about the genesis of the *Shāhnāma*. In this instance, just before the climax of the narrative is reached, the Book of Kings has been translated from Pahlavi prose into Persian prose (OP §15–§16). Then, in a final and perfect culmination of the process of composition, the Persian prose text is superseded

10 The narrative here is anachronistic: Ibn al-Muqaffaʿ had been executed in approximately 759 CE, well before the reign of al-Maʾmūn.

11 Translations from Minorsky 1964:266.

12 Davidson 2013a:38.

by the Persian poetic version. This time, it is Ferdowsi who converts the prose into poetry, and his patron is specified as Maḥmud of Ghazna, who ruled from 998–1030 CE (OP §16). In this narrative, there is no explicit time-gap between the compilation of the Persian prose version and its subsequent conversion into Persian poetry: "And after they had compiled it in prose, Sulṭān Maḥmud, son of Sebüg-tegin, ordered the sage Abu'l-Qāsim Manṣur Ferdowsi to turn it into the *dari* ['court'] language in verse, and the circumstances of it will be mentioned at their proper place" (OP §16).[13]

According to one influential theory, this crucial part of the narrative, the climax, is an "interpolation."[14] But the advocates of this theory overlook the rhetorical integrity of the Older Preface when they proceed to excise the supposedly interpolated part of the text. With the excision in place, the truncated text is then "archaeologized" as having had a completely different purpose from that which the OP itself announces as its *raison d'être*, namely, to introduce the poetry of the *Shāhnāma*. Instead, in terms of the theory, the text was intended to introduce a hypothetical "prose *Shāhnāma*," which, although no longer extant, supposedly corresponded to the original text commissioned by Ibn ʿAbd al-Razzāq.

Opposing this theory, I argue that the narrative of the Older Preface requires the text that preceded the poetic *Shāhnāma* to serve as a foil, marking the penultimate stage in the process that led to the perfection of the final product. Narrative precedents provide a clear model for the construction of such a foil: at least in terms of the rhetoric of the narrative, it is evident that the predecessor-text must have been written in prose, just as Balʿami's prose Persian *Kalīla and Dimna* constituted the predecessor-text for the poetic Persian *Kalīla and Dimna* of Rudaki. Similarly, in terms of the logic that takes shape in the narrative of the Older Preface, the *Shāhnāma* must have existed in a prose version that functioned as a predecessor-text to the poetic *Shāhnāma* of Ferdowsi. Such a rhetorical crescendo, in which a prose *Shāhnāma* commissioned by Ibn ʿAbd al-Razzāq becomes a stepping-stone to a grander and more perfect work, articulates a point of view marked by a poetic *Shāhnāma* commissioned by Maḥmud of Ghazna.

The purpose of the preceding discussion is not to suggest that a prose *Shāhnāma* commissioned by Ibn ʿAbd al-Razzāq, the potentate of Tus, never existed. Rather, it is to demonstrate that the narrative in the Older Preface about the commissioning of such a prose *Shāhnāma* is inextricably tied to its narrative concerning the conversion of this prose into poetry by Ferdowsi, the poet of

13 Translation from Minorsky 1964:271 (his transliterations have been modified here).

14 Minorsky 1964:271n2. For the most influential exposition of this theory, see Qazvini 1944 and Minorsky 1964, and the critique in Davidson 2001.

Tus. In other words, the narrative of the Older Preface rhetorically motivates the *Shāhnāma* of Ferdowsi instead of the earlier "prose *Shāhnāma*" that serves as its foil.

### Another narrative from the Bāysonghori Preface

There is a comparable narrative in the Bāysonghori Preface concerning the same Sultan Maḥmud, would-be patron of Ferdowsi in the eleventh century CE: this king showed a keen interest in locating texts of the *Shāhnāma* stemming from western Iran (in this case, Fars, at BP 371) and from eastern Iran (in this case, Sistān, at BP 373). In this case, the activity of gathering regional variants of the *Shāhnāma* in the era of Maḥmud is presented as a prototype for the interest of Prince Bāysonghor himself in attempting to enhance the text of the *Shāhnāma* by way of augmenting it with regional variants.

A result of such attempts at enhancement by augmenting the actual text of the poetic composition by way of regional variants is the enormous size of the Bāysonghori *Shāhnāma*. This fifteenth-century book contains over 58,000 verses. It has 346 folios (with six columns and thirty-one lines per page) and only twenty illustrations, by comparison with most books of the *Shāhnāma* in the fourteenth century, which typically have around 300 folios and many more illustrations.[15]

## Iranian Narratives about Other Kinds of Books

At the beginning of a thirteenth-century narrative poem about the early life of Zoroaster and the beginning of his public life as a prophet, the poet speaks of his source in the following words:

> I saw a notebook [*daftar*] from the time of the empire | in a script
> which is called Pahlavi.
>
> *Zardoshtnāma* line 14[16]

Later on in the poem, the poet says that a *mōbad* urged him to translate the book into Persian verse. Here is what the *mōbad* tells the poet:

> You see these ancient stories | of which no one recalls the origins,
> foundation, and root.
> No one understands this script. | I fear it will disappear altogether.

[15] The relevant statistics are gathered by Hillenbrand 2010:105.
[16] This poem is edited by Rosenberg 1904 (re-edited by Dabir-Siyāqi 1959).

> It is better that you put it in verse, | in beautiful language and in *dari*
> [Persian] script.
>
> *Zardoshtnāma* lines 23–25[17]

Such medieval Persian narratives about the rescuing of books written in Pahlavi can be traced back to still earlier Iranian narratives. Already in the ancient Avestan tradition, a book could be seen as the foundation of performance. A case in point is a narrative that we find in the *Dēnkard*, which is a tenth-century Pahlavi compendium of Zoroastrian beliefs and customs (in Pahlavi, the word *Dēnkard* or *Dēnkart* means "Acts of Religion"). In the *Dēnkard*, we find a story about the transmission of archetypal Avestan texts—texts that date back ultimately to the second millennium BCE. According to this story, three pivotal moments in the transmission happened in three successive eras of Iranian imperial kingship. The three eras are represented by three kings who stem from three successive Iranian dynasties, which are [1] the Achaemenid, [2] the Parthian, and [3] the Sasanian. Here is the relevant text, as translated by the noted Iranist Mary Boyce:

> [1] Daray [Darius III], son of Daray, commanded that two written copies of all Avesta and Zand, even as Zardusht [Zoroaster] had received them from Ohrmazd [Ahura Mazda], be preserved … [2] Valakhsh the Ashkanian [Vologases I] commanded that a memorandum be sent to the provinces (instructing them) to preserve, in the state in which they had come down in (each) province, whatever had survived in purity of the Avesta and Zand as well as every teaching derived from it which, scattered through the land of Iran by the havoc and disruption of Alexander, and by the pillage and plundering of the Macedonians, had remained authoritative, whether written or in oral transmission. [3] His Majesty Ardashir [Ardashir I], King of kings, son of Pāpak, acting on the just judgment of Tansār, demanded that all those scattered teachings should be brought to the court. Tansār assumed command, and selected those that were trustworthy, and left the rest out of the canon.
>
> Boyce 1984:114[18]

So we see a spanning of three consecutive dynasties in this narrative:

[17] The translation is mine. For further commentary and bibliography, see Davidson 2013a:37–38.

[18] See also Skjærvø 2012:41.

- [earliest phase 1] The Achaemenid dynasty is represented here by the king Darius III, who ruled the Persian Empire from 336 to 330 BCE. In the Dēnkard, Darius III is known simply as Daray son of Daray.
- [later phase 2] The Parthian dynasty is represented here by the king Vologases I, who ruled the Parthian Empire from about 51 to 78 CE. In the Dēnkard, Vologases I is known simply as Valakhsh.
- [still later phase 3] The Sasanian dynasty is represented here by the king Ardashir I, founder and first ruler of the Sasanian Empire, whose kingship extends from 208 to 242 CE. In the *Dēnkard*, Ardashir I is known as Ardashir son of Pāpak.[19]

On the basis of such comparative evidence, I argue that the medieval Persian narrative of Ferdowsi's *Shāhnāma* about a disintegrated and then reintegrated book can be traced back to earlier Iranian traditions. I especially note, in phase two of the narrative in the *Dēnkard*, the reference to the scattering of the texts of the Avesta: to quote again from the translation of Boyce, the texts were "scattered through the land of Iran." In brief, then, the ancient Avestan tradition is seen in terms of a book that serves as the foundation of performance. So there is a deep prehistory to be found in the linkage of book and performance.

## Comparable Non-Iranian Narratives Found in Other Indo-European Traditions

Over a century and a half ago, Jules Mohl had already interpreted the passage I quoted from Ferdowsi's *Shāhnāma* at the beginning of this chapter as an example of a well-known type of myth that serves to explain the genesis of a national epic poetic tradition.[20] Following my analysis of this passage from the *Shāhnāma*, Gregory Nagy interprets it as evidence for the kind of culture "where written text and oral tradition coexist."[21] In such cultures, as Nagy argues, "the idea of a written text can even become a primary metaphor for the authority of recomposition-in-performance."[22] The consequences are enormous:

> The intrinsic applicability of text as metaphor for recomposition-in-performance helps explain a type of myth, attested in a wide variety of cultural contexts, where the evolution of a poetic tradition, moving

19 Davidson 2013b:110–111.

20 Mohl 1838:xi; see also Davidson 2013a:43.

21 Nagy 1996:70; see also his pp. 7–38, supporting the view of Lord 1991 and 1995; also Davidson 2013b:21.

22 Nagy 1996:70.

> slowly ahead in time until it reaches a relatively static phase, is reinterpreted by the myth as if it resulted from a single incident, pictured as the instantaneous recovery or even regeneration of a lost text, an archetype.[23]

For Nagy, the most striking comparative parallel with the Persian model is a set of ancient Greek myths that tell of the disintegration and subsequent reintegration of the Homeric corpus itself, culminating in the historicized narrative of the "Peisistratean Recension."[24] Other comparable parallels include the medieval Irish aetiology of the "lost" book of the *Cattle Raid of Cúailgne*.[25] Another parallel adduced by Nagy is the medieval French narrative of *Guiron le courtois*, which "lays the foundation for its authority by telling of the many French books that were produced from what is pictured as an archetypal translation of a mythical Latin book of the Holy Grail."[26] Just as the whole tradition of medieval French romance presents itself as an overall corpus that derives its individual parts from translations of a mythical Ur-text written in Latin, I argue that the whole of Ferdowsi's *Shāhnāma* derives itself from a comparable Ur-text written in Pahlavi.[27] Yet another parallel comes from ethnographic fieldwork on the oral epic tradition of an illiterate society, the untouchable Malas of India: "The epic, it is claimed [by the performers], was first written by a Brahmin poet, torn into shreds, discarded, and then picked up by the present performers."[28]

## Conclusion

I started with Iranian traditions as I examined the theme of the disintegrated and then reintegrated book. And I concluded by surveying parallel themes in non-Iranian traditions, both cognate (as in the case of Greek, Irish, and other Indo-European traditions) and non-cognate (as in the case of substrate traditions in India). On the basis of these parallel themes, I argue in general that oral traditions can compare themselves metaphorically to written traditions.

23 Nagy 1996:70.

24 Nagy 1996:71–72.

25 Nagy 1996:70, following J. F. Nagy 1985:292–293 (also 1986 and 1997); see also Davidson 2015.

26 Nagy 1996:71; see also Davidson 2013a:38n43.

27 Davidson 2013b:33, with reference to Davidson 2013a:35–39.

28 Blackburn 1989:32n25; see also Nagy 1996:71. Further parallels are adduced by Davis 1996, which I analyze in Davidson 2013b:34–35 in conjunction with the parallels that I adduced in Davidson 1994 (first edition of Davidson 2013a).

# Bibliography

Bertels, Y. E., et al., eds. 1960–1971. *Ferdowsi: Shāhnāma* I–IX. Moscow.

Blackburn, S. H. 1989. "Patterns of Development for Indian Oral Epics." In *Oral Epics in India*, ed. S. H. Blackburn, P. J. Claus, J. B. Flueckiger, and S. S. Wadley, 15–32. Berkeley.

Boyce, M. 1984. *Textual Sources for the Study of Zoroastrianism*. Manchester.

Davidson, O. M. 2001. "Some Iranian Poetic Tropes as Reflected in the 'Life of Ferdowsi' Traditions." In *Philologica et Linguistica: Festschrift für Helmut Humbach*, ed. M. G. Schmidt and W. Bisang, supplement, 1–12. Trier.

———. 2002. "Haft K̠ᵛān." *Encyclopaedia Iranica* 11:516–519.

———. 2005. "Persian/Iranian Epic." In *A Companion to Ancient Epic*, ed. J. M. Foley, 264–276. Oxford.

———. 2008. "The Testing of the *Shāhnāma* in the 'Life of Ferdowsi' Narratives." In *The Rhetoric of Biography: Narrating Lives in Persianate Societies*, ed. L. Marlow, 11–20. Cambridge, MA.

———. 2013a. *Poet and Hero in the Persian Book of Kings*. 3rd ed. Cambridge, MA. Orig. pub. Ithaca. 1994.

———. 2013b. *Comparative Literature and Classical Persian Poetics*. 2nd ed. Cambridge, MA. Orig. pub. Costa Mesa, 2000.

———. 2015. "Parallel Heroic Themes in the Medieval Irish *Cattle Raid of Cooley* and the Medieval Persian *Book of Kings*." In *Erin and Iran: Cultural Encounters between the Irish and the Iranians*, ed. H. E. Chehabi and G. Neville, 36–44. Cambridge, MA.

Davis, D. 1996. "The Problem of Ferdowsi's Sources." *Journal of the American Oriental Society* 116:48–57.

Hillenbrand, R. 2010. "Exploring a Neglected Masterpiece: The Gulistan Shāhnāma of Bāysunghur." *Iranian Studies* 43:97–126.

Lord, A. B. 1991. *Epic Singers and Oral Tradition*. Ithaca.

———. 1995. *The Singer Resumes the Tale*. Ed. M. L. Lord. Ithaca.

Minorsky, V. 1964. "The Older Preface to the Shāh-nāma." *Iranica, Twenty Articles*, 260–274. Publications of the University of Tehran 755. Tehran.

Mohl, J., ed. 1838–1878. *Le livre des rois* I–VII. Paris.

Nagy, G. 1996. *Homeric Questions*. Austin.

Nagy, J. F. 1985. *The Wisdom of the Outlaw: The Boyhood Deeds of Finn in Gaelic Narrative Tradition*. Berkeley.

———. 1986. "Orality in Medieval Irish Narrative." *Oral Tradition* 1:272–301.

———. 1997. "How the *Táin* Was Lost." *Zeitschrift für Celtische Philologie* 49–50:603–609.

Qazvini, M. 1944. "Muqaddama-ye qadim-e Shāhnāma." In *Hazāra-ye Ferdowsi*, 123–148. Tehran.

Riyāhi, M.A., ed. 1993. *Sar-chashma-hā-ye Ferdowsi shenāsi*. Tehran.

Rosenberg, F., ed. and trans. 1904. *Le livre de Zoroastre (Zartusht Nāma) de Zartusht-i Bahram ben Pajdu*. St. Petersburg. Repr. 1959, ed. M. Dabir-Siyāqi, Tehran.

Skjærvø, P. O., ed. and trans. 2012. *The Spirit of Zoroastrianism*. New Haven.

# 13

# The Oral Background of the Eddas and Sagas

Gísli Sigurðsson

More than fifty years after the publication of *The Singer of Tales*, the book and the ideas therein still serve as a fresh wind in the textually-oriented field of Old Norse Studies where very few have taken up the issue of how an oral background for medieval texts can possibly affect the modern appreciation of them. It should be noted, however, that a notoriously high percentage of the exemptions to that general rule are contributing to this volume.

The lack of interest in the oral background is most deplorable, and it may perhaps be explained by the fact that the majority of medievalists naturally focus their attention on religious and learned texts as these are a considerable part of the medieval textual production in continental Europe. Such texts have a much stronger background in booklearning than the orally-derived poetry and secular narratives that make up the bulk of the Old Norse material. The approach of medievalists who are analyzing learned products of clerics has influenced scholars of Old Norse, who have in recent decades shown that the texts from the Old Norse world also show clear influence of Latin learning, theology, and the Christian book culture of the time, thus making them a part of the European scene. We now appreciate that this is what should be expected from cultural products of the time as opposed to regarding them as more or less purely oral and secular products of a nationally-defined Icelandic culture—as was perhaps an acceptable approach in the nineteenth century. The more interesting, from the present point of view, and the more problematic aspect of this Europeanization of the culture is how the texts also reflect the indigenous oral culture by which they were ultimately inspired (Sigurðsson 2004:21–48).

When we take the oral approach, everything which has previously been accepted as the received wisdom must be reevaluated: we must both focus on each manuscript version of a given text and give it full credit in every respect as the unique product which it is (both looking at the age of the manuscript and every meaningful variation in its social and personal context, in the manner of New Philology—an exciting example of which is to be found in the *Homer Multitext Project*, described in this volume), but at the same time we have to read the manuscripts as the products of a continuous oral tradition that can go far back in time. Thus, we are dealing with texts that are young and old at the same time, reflecting contemporary interests and learning as well as some memory of old. And we cannot be certain which is which.

We have acquired this knowledge and awareness from the study of living oral cultures rather than from academic speculation about how such a culture could have been, speculation necessarily involving inference from incomplete written evidence and ideas about memory from within the medieval church, as opposed to using concrete evidence about living oral cultures as a point of reference. And this new knowledge should alter our approach to the texts, that is if we lived in an ideal world of learning where scholars can change their minds and methods when new evidence is presented to them—as we are all told we should do in our scholarly quest for the truth (the *veritas* which we see in the Harvard emblem). But rather than meeting the challenge of this new knowledge, many either choose to ignore it and continue with their old editing ways (McGann 1991:15), or at the best reinvent some literary terms to be able to claim that they actually allow for all this within the framework of written texts and written traditions.

I have tried in various publications to apply the learning derived from oral studies to the Old Norse corpus: the Eddic poetry, the mythology as it is presented in Snorri's *Edda*, and to the secular family sagas. I have not found it fruitful to focus on the formulaic language as such but, rather, to apply the comparative approach and use the idea of variation in an oral and manuscript culture. The variation reflects the interests, knowledge and talent of all involved in a performance—and, as a result, the problems associated with the textualization of a primarily oral text.

In the case of Eddic poetry, the scholarship has been based on the idea that these poems, which all agree were written down from oral tradition in the thirteenth century, can and should be dated to different centuries from the ninth century onwards, based more or less on circular arguments and differences in language, style, form, and content. Even though the difficulties, if not impossibilities, of dating are dawning on more and more scholars, many have been reluctant to take the full oral comparative approach which would suggest that all these differences could be much better explained with different individual preferences of the singers and their audiences, based on their gender, social status, geographical surroundings, and other factors. When applying the oral approach, we can thus explain the differences in the poems in terms of oral variation as a result of the conditions around their performance and writing, rather than as the product of a Darwinian literary development of taste in static and fixed poetic texts that were composed by an individual at some point in time and then committed to the imperfect memory of preservers until the time of writing. If we read the written poems from the thirteenth century as the products of an oral culture (as opposed to separate works of authors in different ages that were memorized verbatim), we see before us variation of the main heroic stories or themes based on different perspectives that can be attributed to the differing interests of women and men, as I have demonstrated earlier (Sigurðsson 1990, 1998), some focusing on the heroines and their emotions and others thinking more about the male heroes and their physical activities in a male dominated warrior context, still others reflecting special interests in the lower social classes, even showing some geographical preferences, and so on. From that oral perspective, we can classify and understand the similarities and differences between the poems in light of a multivoiced variation that is likely to have been alive at the time when these texts were written—rather than as the product of many different but singlevoiced time periods, each with their stylistic and thematic preferences.

When it comes to the mythology, as it was recorded by Snorri Sturluson (1178/1179–1241) in his *Edda* in the early thirteenth century, more than 200 years after the official acceptance of Christianity in Iceland, it has been a constant source of bafflement how all these seemingly pagan ideas could possibly be recorded so long after paganism as a religious system was abandoned in the north. It is an achievement in itself to have this learning recorded in book form by a professionally trained, secular insider in the culture, rather than by an outside field worker or a cleric; recorded, that is, by an individual who realizes the potential of the book which he is the first to entrust with his oral learning. Scholarship has shown, as might have been expected, that Snorri's ideas are not purely pagan by any means but heavily influenced by ideas and book learning of his time, and his text is not strictly oral either but presented in a very bookish way. Given that, the most interesting part of this achievement escapes us if we do not add the thinking of the oral background to our toolkit. Snorri was not a folklore collector, rounding up stories from informants, and he was not a scholar using scattered and poorly preserved poetry to reconstruct a system out of fragmentary information or sources, as a modern scholar would do. Rather, Snorri was brought up and professionally trained orally to become a politician, lawman, and skaldic poet, a profession which required the mythological background to compose and understand the images and metaphors used in skaldic poetry (Sigurðsson 2004:6–17). Snorri reached the highest level in all of his professions, not just as a poet, story-teller, and writer. He was a chieftain (*goði*) and lawspeaker in 1215–1218 and again in 1222–1231. A son of a minor chieftain, Snorri was fostered by the most influential man in the country at the time, Jón Loftsson in Oddi, who had direct contacts with the Royal House in Norway. In connection with Snorri's climbing up the social ladder, he spent time in Norway and Sweden in 1218–1220 and became a friend of King Hákon and Earl Skúli in Norway. When Snorri returned to Norway in 1237–1239, he was drawn into a conflict between Hákon and Skúli, who was revolting against Hákon and was killed in 1240. Snorri had backed Skúli in this confrontation and left for Iceland without Hákon's consent. This was interpreted as treason, so the King had his men in Iceland execute Snorri at his home in Reykholt on September 23, 1241. Besides the *Edda*, Snorri is regarded as the author of *Ólafs saga helga hin sérstaka* (a separate saga about St. Ólaf), *Heimskringla* (assembled sagas about the Kings of Norway from a mythological beginning down almost to Snorri's time), and often promoted as the author of *Egils saga*, possibly the first family saga about the tenth century poet, farmer, and viking Egill Skallagrímsson—in addition to several skaldic poems attributed to him. But how could Snorri and all the professional skaldic poets like him keep track of the background mythological information required for their exceptionally complicated verbal art form?

Again, the idea of using fieldwork in cultures who still keep their mythologies alive orally comes to our rescue. The stories and the systematic presentation of them may have been held together by the world itself, the earth, and the dome above, which the stories propose to describe in mythological terms: Snorri's illusion in the *Gylfaginning* (lit. *Gylfi's Illusion*) of the *Edda* turns the sky into the abode of the gods in front of the recipient of the wisdom within the written text. The mythological phenomena which the text explains are constantly referred to as being in the sky (seventy-seven obvious references). For example, the gods' dwellings are in the sky (*á himni*), the world tree stands above the sky (*yfir himni*) and Gylfi (who calls himself Gangleri) claims that the three instructors, Hár, Jafnhár and Þriðji, tell great tidings about the sky (*mikil tíðindi ... af himninum*). In the end, when the lesson is over and the illusion thus vanishes, the pupil Gylfi/Gangleri is left alone in the open. He is surrounded by the world around him as we usually see it with our bare eyes and with none of the mythological illusions visible any longer. Rather than to see a palace and a city as before, Gangleri is in the middle of a field, probably with the ordinary sun and the moon, stars, and planets above him where the story-telling magic had previously made him see the dwellings of the gods and the world tree above. Snorri's *Edda*, as a presentation of his knowledge, was no doubt intended and written for an exclusive audience, that is a literary/poetic elite intent on seriously studying the art of skaldic poetry. The *Edda* thus becomes understandable as the written product of an oral culture that did not let go of its cosmological knowledge and terminolgy, even though the religious aspect of it had to yield to Christianity. The mythology therein would then be similar to mythologies around the globe, which all have an astronomical aspect to them, as becomes apparent when they are studied as a part of a living culture.[1]

A short, almost in passing, explanatory note in the nineteenth century Icelandic folklore collection of Jón Árnason might contain the confirmation needed in order for us to be able to actually prove that people in Iceland spoke of real and visible phenomena in the sky with mythological vocabulary in the nineteenth century. In the chapter on nature legends in the first volume of *Íslenzkar þjóðsögur og Æfintýri* (1862), it says on pp. 658–659, under the heading "Airvisions and Moontales" (*Loptsjónir og Túnglsögur*):

> Sun-dogs or extra suns are points of light around the sun, not uncommon in the South. If two sun-dogs are seen at the same time, on each side of the sun, one in front and the other behind, it is said that the sun is "í úlfakreppu," or that "it runs both in front and behind the sun" and both sayings are derived from the wolves Sköll, who was thought to swallow the Sun, and Hati, who was to take the Moon. Sometimes this is called "gílaferð," and the sun-dog in front of the sun "gíll." He is thought of as a bad omen for weather, if one is not running behind too, but that sun-dog is called wolf too, and from that the saying is derived: "Seldom a 'gíll' means good unless a wolf comes running after."[2]

In a footnote, Jón himself refers to Chapter 12 of *Gylfaginning* in *Snorri's Edda* and stanza 39 of the Eddic poem *Grímnismál* in order to explain these wolves. *Snorri's Edda* says of the sun and the wolves:

> Then High replied: "It is not surprising that she [i.e. the sun] goes at great speed, he comes close who is after her. And she has no escape except to run away." Then spoke Gangleri: "Who is it that inflicts this unpleasantness on her?" High said: "It is two wolves, and the one that is going after her is called Skoll. She is afraid of him and he will catch her,

1 Selin 2000.

2 "Hjásólir eða aukasólir, það eru ljósdílar í kríngum sólina, eru ekki sjaldsénar á Suðurlandi. Ef tvær hjásólir sjást í einu, sín hvoru megin sólarinnar, önnur á undan sól, en hin á eptir, er það kallað, að 'sólin sé í úlfakreppu,' eða að 'það fari bæði á undan og eptir sól,' og er hvorttveggja orðatiltækið dregið af úlfunum Sköll, sem átti að gleipa sólina og Hata, sem átti að taka túnglið. Stundum er þetta kallað 'gílaferð,' og hjásólin, sem fer á undan sól 'gíll.' Hann þykir ílls viti með veður, ef ekki fer einnig á eptir sólu, en sú hjásól er enn kölluð úlfur, og er þaðan dreginn talshátturinn: 'Sjaldan er gíll fyrir góðu, nema úlfur á eptir renni.'"

> and the one that is running ahead of her is called Hati Hrodvitnisson, and he is trying to catch the moon, and that will happen."[3]
>
> Faulkes 1987:14–15

If it were not for the chapter in the *Þjóðsögur* of Jón Árnason, no one would ever contemplate the possibility that this episode in *Snorri's Edda* was explaining sun-dogs sometimes observed on either side of the halo that surrounds the sun in such conditions. The same can be said about the moon-halo which Björn Jónsson ([1994?]:185–188) thinks is being referred to in the previous chapter in *Snorri's Edda*, where the characters Bil and Hiuki are said to be "carrying between them on their shoulders a tub called Sæg; their carrying-pole was called Simul. Their father's name is Vidfinn. These children go with Moon, as can be seen from earth" (Faulkes 1987:14).[4] Björn suggests that the carrying-pole should be understood as the light beam that stretches between the moon-dogs—and the tub itself must then be the moon—"as can be seen from earth," which is a very straightforward statement in the text itself encouraging this kind of interpretation. Before Björn, Richard Allen (1899:267) had come up with this interpretation and suggested a parallel in Jack and Jill (i.e. Hiuki and Bil), whom native speakers of English know from the nursery rhyme: "Jack and Jill went up the hill / to fetch a pail of water, / Jack fell down and broke his crown / and Jill came tumbling after." This little verse, according to Björn ([1994?]:186), describes how the moon-halo dissolves—as seen from earth, of course.

The vocabulary used by Jón Árnason about the sun-dogs on the halo around the sun can hardly be understood as anything but evidence for a continuous tradition from much earlier times about how myths are used to describe real phenomena in the sky. If that were not the case, we would have to conclude that Jón Árnason or someone else before him had come up with this interpretation of the mythology—and thus preceded both Richard Allen and Björn Jónsson in putting forth the mythological explanation of celestial phenomena. Of these two possibilities, the former is much more likely, to say the least. It is not easy to come up with any alternative explanation. So, for once, it looks as if we have something in our field that amounts to a scientific proof; thus we can state with full confidence that the mythology of the Edda has an astronomical dimension that has largely gone unnoticed.

3 "Þá svarar Hár: 'Eigi er það undarlegt að hún fari ákaflega. Nær gengur sá er hana sækir, og engan útveg á hún nema renna undan.' Þá mælti Gangleri: 'Hver er sá er henni gerir þann ómaka?' Hár segir: 'Það eru tveir úlfar, og heitir sá er eftir henni fer Skoll. Hann hræðist hún og hann mun taka hana. En sá heitir Hati Hróðvitnisson er fyrir henni hleypur og vill hann taka tunglið, og svo mun verða' " (Pálsson 1988:24–25).

4 "á öxlum sér sá er heitir Sægur, en stöngin Símul. Viðfinnur er nefndur faðir þeirra. Þessi börn fylgja Mána, svo sem sjá má af jörðu" (Pálsson 1988:24).

A parallel development can be observed in how the classical pagan perception of the heavens has survived through the ages. It has not yet yielded to attempts to Christianize the sky above us. We still apply the names of classical gods to the planets and the constellations. The entire system is "written" in the sky and thus memorized through naming phenomena in front of us. As such, Snorri cannot be wrong about the tradition, because he is a living part of it. Snorri is an authentic source, as is every other informant—which is not the same as claiming that what Snorri writes is the same as another individual would express, either in his own time or 100, 200, or 300 years earlier (Sigurðsson 2014).

When it comes to the sagas themselves, we have, since the dawn of saga studies, been debating how oral and historical the sagas are, as opposed to authorial works of fiction—with every possibility in between as an argued option. These oppositions are, of course, no longer valid, as we have realized that orality and traditional continuity is no evidence for historicity, and oral story-tellers and poets can be equally creative and inventive as any author who operates in writing. In the process of the scholarly debate, however, the generally assumed pattern of one written work influencing another has entangled us in a web of hypothesis about written connections between sagas and debate about hypothetical dates of hypothetical written originals. Rather than going along with this ever more complicated fabrication of lost written works, it comes as a fresh start to be able to allow for orality behind the written texts and thus begin our analysis afresh from the manuscripts as they are, allowing for circulating oral stories about the same characters and events that we read about in the written works. It should, of course, not be downplayed or forgotten that these written works are structured and composed utilizing the medium through which they are presented: the Book, with a beginning, middle, and end, and lots of intertwined stories woven in, in between.

Even though we acknowledge the general role of writing as an artform in the structuring of the sagas, we can see that the written sagas are still operating with the esthetic principles of oral story-telling. Characters can be abruptly brought into the text, with their traditional background from outside that particular written text assumed; well-known events can be referred to on the assumption that the audience is familiar with them, even though nothing is told of them in that particular saga; and so on (Sigurðsson 2004:123–250).

We can even see this oral allowance, if that is what we can call the possibility in an oral performance of referring to information outside the text, being used to its full potential in the highly literary construction of *Njáls saga*—to finally single out an actual saga (see Sigurðsson 2018) on the general advice to take the most simple example and then evaluate its complexity.

*Njáls saga* is preserved in numerous manuscripts, the oldest dated to around 1300, and it is generally assumed that the saga was first written shortly before that time. The saga is set in the Southern quarter of Iceland in the late tenth and early eleventh centuries, that is, in the period when the old paganism was being replaced by Christianity (which was officially accepted as the religion of the country at the legal assembly, the Alþingi, in the year 1000). *Njáls saga* is often claimed to be the very best saga, carefully constructed with every minor detail playing a role in its complicated web of meaning. The main characters are the friends Gunnar of Hlíðarendi in Fljótshlíð, physically strong but not very intellectual, and Njáll of Bergþórshvoll, a man of law and wisdom. Their wives, Hallgerður and Bergþóra, get into a trivial conflict over seating at a feast; the conflict escalates until they start having each other's workmen (*húskarlar*) killed. Gunnar and Njáll fail to make peace between them and, as a result, the marriage of Gunnar and Hallgerður suffers—she even steals some cheese and thereby arouses Gunnar's anger. Later, Gunnar does not follow Njáll's advice, is found guilty of murder, and sentenced to exile abroad. He does not leave the country, however, and his enemies gather their forces and eventually kill him at home—after a renowned defence. Skarphéðinn, son of Njáll, takes revenge but spares a certain Mörður Valgarðsson who had played an active role in the killing of Gunnar. The sons of Njáll get into a feud with Þráinn Sigfússon, Gunnar's cousin and the son-in-law of Hallgerður. Skarphéðinn kills Þráinn and Njáll then offers to foster his son, Höskuldur. Höskuldur grows up as one of Njáll's sons and Njáll arranges to set up him up as a chieftain, *goði*, while his sons receive no social status. Mörður plants lies that encourage hatred and envy between the sons of Njáll and Höskuldur, resulting in an undeserved killing of Höskuldur, much deplored by Njáll. Höskuldur's widow, Hildigunnur, asks her cousin Flosi to take revenge. He gathers a force and burns down the farm at Bergþórshvoll, with Njáll and his entire family inside. Only one male escapes, Njáll's son-in-law, Kári Sölmundarson from the Hebrides. After legal dealings at the Alþingi, in which Mörður Valgarðsson plays an active part, Kári takes up revenge and kills one burning-participant after another, a mission that even takes him out of the country. The revenge culminates when some of the "burners" fall in the Battle of Clontarf near Dublin in 1014. Finally, Flosi and Kári go on a pilgrimage to Rome and eventually make peace between them when Hildigunnur marries Kári.

For many the idea of an oral background for this saga (as demonstrated by Lars Lönnroth [1976]) can still be waved away as a reasonable general theory but of no importance for a modern reading. It has long been appreciated that *Njáls saga* is an exceptionally well-composed saga from a literary point of view, so well that many have agreed with Bååth (1885:159) that the author had such good command over his material that he wrote "den första linjen [...] med blicken fäst på den sista" ("the first line with his eyes fixed on the last"). Many have also seconded Lars Lönnroth's observation that *Njáls saga* differs from other sagas in not providing a thematic prelude about the ancestors—as do *Egils saga* and others, in a well-known medieval fashion.

If, however, we read the oral traditional background into the first two sentences in *Njáls saga* ("Mörður hét maður er kallaður var gígja. Hann var sonur Sighvats hins rauða." "There was a man named Mord, whose nickname was *gígja* [a violin-like stringed instrument]. He was the son of Sighvat the Red."), we realize that previous emphasis on *written textual links* and failure to take the oral traditional background of *Njáls saga* into account has led scholars to overlook that this is one of the most thematic openings of any prose narrative, thematic in the sense that it evokes all the major themes of the saga through what Foley (1991:6–8) called "traditional referentiality." The opening includes a pointed reference to the oral traditional background, as we can deduce from an unrelated written source, *The Book of Settlements*, which provides the knowledgeable listener (as the written *Book of Settlements* would not have been widely available to the audience of *Njáls saga* for private reading) with the key themes of the saga told about the forefathers and mothers of the main hero of *Njáls saga*, Gunnar of Hlíðarendi: conflict of *húskarlar* ("male servants") over seating that leads to a killing near a ferry of the son of Sighvat the Red (rather than of Sighvat himself, as *Njáls saga* later indicates in passing without elaborating further), a lamenting woman craving revenge by fire, and reconciliation (involving Mörður *gígja*, the first person mentioned in the *Njáls saga*) by marriage of members of the feuding parties (the parents of Gunnar of Hlíðarendi).[5] By a pointed reference that immediately evokes what must have been a well-known story about a serial killing in the family of Sighvat the Red, a version of which has only been preserved for us to read in *The Book of Settlements*, the audience of *Njáls saga* is immediately tuned into all the major themes of the magnificent saga that is about to begin: a trivial matter of honor and seating (in a ferry—rather than at a feast as in the saga—involving *húskarlar* in both works) that leads to the killing of a significant character; outlawry (from Fljótshlíð in both stories); a woman goading male members of her family to take revenge; houseburning; and reconciliation (involving Mörður *gígja* rather than his namesake Valgarðsson in the saga) by marriage of members of the feuding parties (the parents of Gunnar of Hlíðarendi in *The Book of Settlements* rather than the parents of Flosi [i.e. son of Kári and Hildigunnur], father of Kolbeinn, the very last characters mentioned and introduced in *Njáls saga*).

5 Cf. Pálsson and Edwards 1972:130–132.

The opening of *Njáls saga* can thus be read as the first of its many forebodings, preceding by several lines the more famous one about Hallgerður's thief's eyes when she is first introduced as a child—as is later developed when she steals the cheese as a married woman.[6] The foreboding effect of the allusion in the first line stretches all the way to the last line of the saga about the ultimate reconciliation with the marriage of Kári and Hildigunnur, whose grandson is Kolbeinn, "er *ágætastur* maður hefir verið einnhver í þeirri ætt. Og lúkum vér þar Brennu-Njáls sögu" ("who was *the most distinguished* man in that line. And here I end the Saga of the burning of Njal"). To tie all this perfectly together and make sure that no one has missed the parallel with Gunnar and his parents—whose background story was evoked in the first line of the saga – it may be observed that the only other instance of the word *ágætastur* in *Njáls saga* is when Gunnar is advised towards the end of Chapter 70 to take precautions because of all his envious enemies, "þar er þú þykir nú *ágætastur* maður um allt land" ("since you are thought to be the *most distinguished* man in the whole land")—thus grouping these two "products" of the reconciliations, Gunnar and Kolbeinn, together with the same attributive word. Even though many have agreed in general with the previously quoted conclusion by Bååth (1885:159) about the author of *Njáls saga* having had such good command over his material that he wrote "the first line with his eyes fixed on the last," I do not think that anyone has taken it quite as literally as this pattern seems to suggest.

It does not do justice to the marvelous opening of *Njáls saga*, which brings to mind the entire "prelude recounting the settlement in Iceland of an ancestral clan" (Andersson 2006:183) that scholars have found missing in the written *Njáls saga*, to think of it as evidence of the author of *Njáls saga* having borrowed these themes and names from a lost version of *The Book of Settlements* in order to get some ideas for his fictive saga—as Baldur Hafstað has suggested (2001). Baldur is an adherent of the literary reading of the sagas and was the first to comment on these parallels. Rather, the opening should be read in view of the oral background, as a reference to the tradition from which *Njáls saga* is derived and with which its audience was familiar—to a greater or lesser degree, of course, depending on the individuals. This reference is a fine example of the poetics of oral tradition, carried on into the written world of *Njáls saga*—poetics that will remain obscure and unappreciated as long as scholars continue to read the sagas with only the methods of contemporary literary analysis and without fully incorporating the notion of the sagas' oral traditional background.

To conclude: more than half a century after its publication, *The Singer of Tales* can still be regarded as the ultimate inspiration to new approaches and

6 See Sveinsson 1971:50–61.

fresh readings of the medieval texts that take up most of our time in Old Norse Studies. The insights into oral poetry, storytelling, performances, reception, textualization, and cultural contexts that it has evoked are still far from being fully explored. The examples I have taken from the Eddic poems, *Snorri's Edda* and *Njáls saga,* should be sufficient to demonstrate that the oral approach leads to no trivial findings but generates results and ideas that redefine the field as we know it, if they are taken up and used by more scholars than just those of us who have added the oral aspect to our eyesight.

## Bibliography

Allen, R. 1899. *Star-Names: Their Lore and Meaning.* New York. Repr. 1963.

Andersson, T. M. 2006. *The Growth of the Medieval Icelandic Sagas (1180–1280).* Ithaca.

Bååth, A. U. 1885. *Studier öfver kompositionen i några isländska ättsagor.* Lund.

*Brennu-Njáls saga.* In Torfason et al. 1987:134–345 and in Hreinsson 1997 III:1–220, trans. R. Cook.

Egilsdóttir, Á., and R. Simek, eds. 2001. *Sagnaheimur: Studies in Honour of Hermann Pálsson on his 80th birthday, 26th May 2001.* Vienna.

Faulkes, A. trans. 1987. *Snorri Sturluson: Edda.* London.

Foley, J. M. 1991. *Immanent Art: From Structure to Meaning in Traditional Oral Epic.* Bloomington.

Hafstað, B. 2001. "Egils saga, Njáls saga and the Shadow of Landnáma: The Work Methods of the Saga Writers." In Egilsdóttir and Simek 2001:21–37.

Hreinsson, V., ed. 1997. *The Complete Sagas of Icelanders.* Reykjavík.

*Íslenzkar þjóðsögur og Æfintýri* [Icelandic folktales and fairy tales]. 1862. Vol. 1. Coll. J. Árnason. Leipzig.

Jónsson, B. [1994?]. *Star Myths of the Vikings.* Swan River, Manitoba.

Lönnroth, L. 1976. *Njáls Saga: A Critical Introduction.* Berkeley.

McGann, J. J. 1991. *The Textual Condition.* Princeton.

Pálsson, H., ed. 1988. *Edda Snorra Sturlusonar.* Reykjavík.

Pálsson, H., and P. Edwards, eds. and trans. 1972. *The Book of Settlements. Landnámabók.* Winnipeg.

Selin, H., ed. 2000. *Astronomy across Cultures: The History of Non-Western Astronomy.* Dordrecht.

Sigurðsson, G. 1990. "On the Classification of Eddic Heroic Poetry in View of the Oral Theory." In *Poetry in the Scandinavian Middle Ages*, ed. T. Pàroli, 245–255. Spoleto.

———, ed. 1998. *Eddukvæði.* Reykjavík.

———. 2004. *The Medieval Icelandic Saga and Oral Tradition: A Discourse on Method.* Cambridge, MA.

———. 2014. "Snorri's Edda: The Sky Described in Mythological Terms." In *Nordic Mythologies: Interpretations, Intersections, and Institutions*, ed. T. R. Tangherlini, 184–198. Berkeley.

———. 2018. "*Njáls saga* and Its Listeners' Assumed Knowledge: Applying Notions of Mediality to a Medieval Text." In *RE:writing: Medial Perspectives on Textual Culture in the Icelandic Middle Ages*, ed. K. Heslop and J. Glauser, 285-294. Zürich.

Sveinsson, E. Ó. 1971. *Njáls Saga: A Literary Masterpiece.* Trans. P. Schach. Lincoln, NE.

Torfason, J., B. Halldórsson, S. Tómasson, and Ö. Thorssson. 1987. *Íslendinga sögur og þættir.* Reykjavík.

# 14

# Držić's Magician and Lucić's Captive Maiden

## Oral Sources and the Croatian Renaissance Drama

Aida Vidan

Croatian Renaissance literature has long been considered a cultural pinnacle, as relevant in the context of its own time as it was in the subsequent centuries. Comprising a range of diverse authors and original works, it reflected an awareness of both contemporary Western sources and local folklore heritage. The former influences have been thoroughly researched in particular by Croatian and Italian scholars, while the latter have remained more difficult to document. Aware of the abundant ties between oral tradition and the South Slavic literary output, Albert Lord devoted significant attention to the hallmark achievements of the baroque and national-revival era already in his seminal *The Singer of Tales* (Lord 2019).[1] It is in this line of inquiry that the present chapter seeks to examine the earlier, hitherto less explored Renaissance period. Connections between some of the most prominent texts of the Croatian Renaissance and traditional heritage are illuminating not only for the purpose of providing an additional line of interpretation to these works but also as a path towards uncovering their hidden political messages.

I argue that traditional oral heritage supplies a key to understanding the principal works by the two central figures of the Croatian Renaissance: *Robinja* (*The Slave Girl*, ca. 1526) by Hanibal Lucić (c. 1485–1553) from the island of Hvar and *Dundo Maroje* (*Uncle Maroje*, 1551) by Marin Držić (1508–1567) from Dubrovnik. Both pieces belong to the dramatic corpus performed during the carnival season, but at the same time possess a politically provocative layer hiding in plain view and delivered at the locus of contested political power. In

1 In particular, writers such as Ivan Gundulić (1589–1638), Andrija Kačić Miošić (1704–1760), Ivan Mažuranić (1814–1890) from Croatia and Petar Petrović Njegoš (1813–1851) from Montenegro, who all drew their inspiration from the local oral tradition both in terms of the subject matter and versification, have been a focus of numerous studies.

other words, they can be interpreted on two levels: in addition to the public text meant to offer an inoffensive narrative within literary frameworks, there also exists an underlying covert script that comments on the abysmal political situation in which the Croatian territories were engulfed. These plays push the literary frontiers while being cognizant of the previous practices—in Lucić's case a rich history of love poetry written on the Croatian coast and in Držić's the vibrant resonances of *commedia erudita* from the neighboring Italian shores—but, at the same time, they draw on motifs and linguistic wealth preserved in the oral traditional corpus.

The staging of these works during the carnival season stemmed from older customs as various "forms of protocol and ritual based on laughter and consecrated by tradition existed in all the countries of medieval Europe; they were sharply distinct from the serious official, ecclesiastical, feudal, and political cult forms and ceremonials" (Bakhtin 1984:6–7). Mikhail Bakhtin claims that these practices offered an entirely different vision of the world which was highly divergent from the official discourse and essentially created "a second world and a second life outside officialdom" (Bakhtin 1984:6–7). Particularly important for the current discussion is the notion of duality harbored in the works of Renaissance writers, including Lucić's and Držić's contemporary Rabelais, on whom Bakhtin focuses in his analysis of the carnivalesque. Similarly, Bakhtin correlates laughter and the concept of freedom and locates the roots of the comical in folkloric communal experience, which are all conclusions highly relevant for understanding Lucić's and Držić's works. Temporarily discarding the established order and hierarchies, carnival, with its permission for laughter, destabilizes any closed, completed system and advocates for freedom, if not in absolute, then in relative terms (Bakhtin 1984:10).

In Bakhtin's view, Rabelais, Cervantes, and Shakespeare represent a radical shift in the history of laughter and import into it a profound philosophical meaning that uncovers essential forms of truth, history, and man's existence in the world (Bakhtin 1984:66). Coming on the heels of rigid medieval visions, which in their official discourses discounted laughter and called for timeless stability, the Renaissance literary corpus is additionally marked by the introduction of historical time and the questioning of "absolute truths." While "[i]n the Renaissance, laughter in its most radical, universal, and at the same time gay form emerged from the depths of folk culture," allowing for "shifting from top to bottom, casting the high and the old, the finished and completed into the material bodily lower stratum for death and rebirth" (Bakhtin 1984:72, 81–82), it also entered into dialogue with social and historical change. Again, as will be demonstrated below, both Lucić and Držić capitalize on this development and indirectly reflect on the specific historical moment.

By insisting on the relativity of all values, carnival of the Renaissance period questioned the immobile social order and introduced historicity and specificity that engaged the audience on a different level. Thus, from behind the carnival mask and its communal rowdiness, other voices also spoke that undermined a static picture of the world and celebrated not only its physical renewal rooted in pagan rituals but also called for social and political reordering. As Bakhtin points out, the specific circumstances at which these verbal acts aimed were different in various corners of Renaissance Europe, but their common denominator is the communal inclusiveness of laughter and its renewing, re-birthing effect: "The cyclical character is superseded by the sense of historic time. The grotesque images with their relations to changing time and their ambivalence become the means for the artistic and ideological expression of a mighty awareness of history and of historic change which appeared during the Renaissance" (Bakhtin 1984:25). Upholding Bakhtin's approach and insisting on adhering to concrete social reality, Bristol points out that "Renaissance drama is important in that it invites consideration of forms of collective life and of subjectivity other than those proposed and legitimated by a hegemonic culture" (Bristol 1985:5).

Similarly, Ivan Lozica discusses carnival's subversive aspects and the broad divide that developed between the theater of the industrialized era and "primitive" forms of folk theater linked to carnival festivities. Echoing Bakhtin, he further stresses that carnival commentary on society, especially criticism of it, stems directly from folk culture, which is characterized by ambivalence and humor (Lozica 2007:201). In the Croatian theater of the Renaissance period, this relation enters a complex stage, but the path of influence is still open from the traditional into the institutional and vice versa, which will be of particular interest with regard to Držić's comedy. In some cases, as in Lucić's play, scholars have been divided, with one camp emphasizing the precedence of the literary tradition, the other foregrounding the oral heritage. Given that Držić's and Lucić's most renowned pieces were both performed during the carnival season, the timing places them in a direct relation to the folklore tradition of the region and calls for an interpretation from this particular viewpoint.[2]

Moreover, it is possible to argue that these authors employ elements from oral tradition as a palimpsest which allows them, on the one hand, to entertain with festive content and, on the other, to provide a commentary on the state of political affairs in the *reliquiae reliquiarum* of what was once a prominent Croatian state. This palimpsestuous reading (Dillon's term, 2007:4) weds the older ritual

2 The timing of both Držić's *Uncle Maroje* and Lucić's *The Slave Girl* is based on the information provided in the plays themselves. For more details on Držić's plays, see the relevant entries in Novak et al. 2009; for discussion of the carnival components in Lucić's *The Slave Girl*, see Tomasović 1988 and Mrdeža 1987.

layer with the already institutionalized theater and its highly elaborate forms. However, rather than perceiving various cultural imprints as unrelated and mechanically superimposed on one another, the organic approach advocated by Gérard Genette is more suitable in this case. In his interpretation, no text exists in its singularity but only as a transtextual entity since all literary works evoke one another in some way (Genette 1997:1–9). Given the proximity of the Renaissance theater to earlier folkloric practices built on the formulaic principles and fluidity of forms that belong to a vast body of communally remembered and transmitted materials (Foley 1991), it is only appropriate to extend this approach to the area in which traditional and written literatures cross-pollinate so effectively. Orality implies a coexistence of mutually interwoven motifs which, if perceived on a timeline, behave as palimpsests whose layers are directly related to and built on one another. It is thus possible to argue that the notion of transtextuality is first and foremost characteristic of oral forms and still intrinsic to the early modern theater to which both Lucić and Držić belonged.

Turning to the political-historical subtext of the plays, it is necessary to outline the circumstances in which Croatia (or rather, what remained of it) found itself in the sixteenth century. The rapid advancement of the Ottomans was swiftly engulfing most of the Croatian territory. One of the decisive clashes was the battle of Krbava (near Udbina) in 1493 led by the Croatian viceroy of Hungarian descent, Emerik Derenčin (Imre Derencsényi), and the noble family of Frankopan, in which the Croatian army suffered a major defeat and lost some 13,000 combatants (Kekez 2009).[3] The Ottomans soon expanded their control to most of the Dalmatian hinterland and were endangering navigation in the Adriatic, clashing there continually with Venetian ships (Novak 2009:447–452). In 1537, the Croatian stronghold of Klis succumbed to the Ottomans after several decades of resistance. This opened the path for pillaging the middle Dalmatian region. Ottoman forces were in close proximity to the Venetian-ruled Zadar and Split, as well as the area surrounding Dubrovnik, which remained a free city-republic with tributary obligations first to the Hungarian court (from 1358 to 1526) and subsequently also to the Ottoman Empire (from 1442 to 1804).[4] As Novak puts it, "[i]n the Renaissance Croats lived under three rulers, under the

3 Recent research points to the fact that viceroy Derenčin and Bernardin Frankapan (Frankopan) had opposing views on the military strategy in battling the Ottomans. The viceroy's tactics were used at the battle of Krbava, which resulted in a complete defeat of the Croatian side. In the months prior to the battle, Derenčin and Frankapan clashed over other issues such as the ownership of the port of Senj, and it was only the looming danger of the Ottoman conquerors that brought them to the same side (Kekez 2009).

4 For a detailed account of the political and cultural circumstances in Renaissance Dubrovnik, see Foretić 1969, Mitić 1988, and Harris 2003.

Venetian Doge in Dalmatia and Istria, under the Turkish Sultan in Slavonia and Bosnia and Herzegovina, and after the disappearance of the Hungarian Jagiellonians, under the Habsburg Empire in the continental area around Zagreb, Karlovac, and Varaždin" (Novak 2009:469).[5] The neighboring area suffered a similar fate. In 1521, Belgrade fell to the Ottomans, while in 1526, the battle of Mohács effectively obliterated Hungary. The islands and the narrow Dalmatian coastline continued to be under Venetian control from 1420 until 1797.

Despite the fragmentation of the Croatian territories and an abysmal political situation, this was one of the golden eras for literary activity. In fact, it was exactly this period that marked the beginning of the literary canon, which during the nineteenth-century National Revival served as one of the principal components for the process of language standardization. Most of the literary activity in this period took place along the Dalmatian coast, which had strong cultural and economic ties with Italy but resented its political presence. The intellectual elites, including writers, were commonly educated at Italian universities. One might therefore expect that in literature many influences would stem directly from Italian Renaissance models, but the picture would be significantly distorted if only these elements were emphasized.

In Italy, after Nicholas Cusanus's rediscovery in 1429 of twelve previously unknown comedies of Plautus, and Giovanni Aurispa's uncovering of Donatus's commentaries on Terence, the Cinquecento saw a blossoming of theatrical activity, in particular the rise of *commedia erudita* (Brand 1995:xxx). Although resonances were strong enough across the Adriatic to gradually expel the *sacre rappresentazioni* for the sake of populist drama,[6] a process parallel to the one in Italy, the rise of drama in Croatia had its own circumstances and path of development. A close examination of the language of Renaissance Croatian plays, as well as written lyric poetry of the time, reveals a heavy reliance on oral sources and the incorporation of numerous formulas in the written texts. Frequently, the themes transposed from oral sources into written texts acquired not only a different aesthetic function but also additional layers of meaning, some of which clearly had political connotations.

Although this chapter is not primarily concerned with the linguistic features of the two plays, it is relevant to mention that Lucić, for instance, draws on the oral tradition in his descriptions of the maiden slave but at the same time uses

5 Unless otherwise noted in the bibliography, all translations of sources published in languages other than English are my own.

6 It is indicative that early printed editions of Plautus circulated both in Dubrovnik (from 1482 and 1499) and in Hvar (from 1499): Švelec 1976:6.

a highly stylized form of expression and complex versification.[7] Držić, on the other hand, exploits not only some of the folkloric motifs recurring throughout the Western literary canon but also in many of his plays adopts phrasing from oral poetry as a part of his expression (Vidan 2010:65–71). In *Dundo Maroje* and likely in his earlier lost play *Pomet*, he ventures into prose thereby opening the gate for heteroglossia with his characters of versatile backgrounds and dialects. This choice reflects one of the central linguistic preoccupations of *commedia erudita*—the inability of commonly used versification patterns to convey comic dialogue (Brand 1995:xxxv)—and Držić, well aware of the demands of comedy, opts for a type of expression that allows him to bring the living language onto the stage (Čale 1978:197-198). Bakhtin underscores the importance of linguistic democratization brought about by the Renaissance on the example of Rabelais's flamboyant expression: "Such an active plurality of languages and the ability to see one's own media from the outside, that is, through the eyes of other idioms, led to exceptional linguistic freedom" (Bahktin 1984:471). The same can be said for Marin Držić. It is thus evident even from these passing remarks that the language of the discussed plays has palimpsestuous features which go hand in hand with their complex artistic message.

Lucić's *Robinja* (*The Slave Girl*, written ca. 1526 [Lucić 1988]) focuses on the motif of an abducted maiden, which is abundant both in the oral poetry of the region and in Renaissance literary writings: there are at least five other sixteenth-century texts, in addition to Lucić's, which in their titles refer to a captive maiden, and many others which exploit this subject matter in some part of their narrative, so that the motif serves to define a genre subcategory (Novak 1976; Fališevac 2007:10). Relying on Vodnik's earlier research (Vodnik 1909), Novak brings to attention several literary precursors to Lucić's play: Džore Držić's poem *Čudni san* (*A Strange Dream*), Mavro Vetranović's mascherata *Dvije robinjice* (*Two Slave Girls*), and two brief pastoral pieces by the same author (Novak 1976).[8] Džore Držić's poem was included in the *Kanconijer*, a collection of Renaissance poetry, assembled by Nikša Ranjina in 1507 (Vodnik 1909:91). Novak further develops Vodnik's interpretation of the motif of a captive maiden as a correlative to "the long-standing Croatian obsession with freedom and the impossibility of its realization in the given circumstances" (Novak 1976:190). He also cites Petković, who recognized in this subject matter the imported

7 Vončina examines the linguistic characteristics of Lucić's poetic expression in *The Slave Girl* and points out that, although Lucić's doubly-rhymed, dodecasyllabic verse is not imported from oral tradition, which favors the decasyllable, there are many stylistic elements clearly derived from oral tradition (Vončina 1976:172–173).

8 Both Džore Držić (1461–1501) and Mavro Vetranović (1483–1576) were born and lived in Dubrovnik.

Mediterranean theme of Moreška (discussed below), an elaborately choreographed sword dance in which two opposing armies, typically the Blacks and the Whites, fight over a captive maiden. Novak, too, underscores this component, but he rejects the focus on the origin of the motif and sets forth an important question: why, unlike any other European literature, is the Croatian corpus saturated with this motif? He perceives it as a logical development within the local tradition and explains its frequency as having a political motivation, showing a gradual shift from allegorical theme towards incorporation of specific circumstances in later texts (Novak 1976:186–194). In addition, he points out that the dramatic corpus built around the motif of a captive maiden is, along with Držić's opus, the most important achievement of early Croatian theater. Analyzing the interplay between oral and written literatures in the Renaissance period, Ben-Amos similarly concludes that "[a]ny attempt to establish a cause-and-effect relationship between society and literature requires, first and foremost, the identification of the social trends that might have been the contributing factor for the emergence of a particular literary form" (Ben-Amos 2010:441).

Although Novak is correct in his assessment that the sources will remain inconclusive, for the purpose of the current argument it is helpful to recall Vodnik's findings with regard to the oral background of Lucić's *The Slave Girl*. Vodnik's close comparative reading of Lucić's text and Džore Držić's *A Strange Dream* reveals ties to the troubadour tradition and provides evidence that Lucić was likely familiar with Držić's poem. Furthermore, Vodnik holds that the motif of a captive maiden was not an invention of Džore Držić's but had already become a convention by his time (Vodnik 1909:94), especially in light of the fact that much of the troubadour poetry is marked by the employment of ready-made motifs ("thus we have to point to folk poetry as the original source of the captive maiden motif"); nevertheless, he concedes that it is impossible to know if this motif entered traditional poetry through a real event or whether it could be of international origin (Vodnik 1909:107). By contrast, he is less convinced of the connection between Lucić's piece and Vetranović's *Two Slave Girls*, citing narrative differences (primarily the appearance of the two slave girls captured by the pirates) as the main argument. Vodnik does not indicate that he was aware of Vetranović's two pastorals, which Novak dates to before 1509, when Vetranović entered a Benedictine monastery—thus early enough for Lucić to have read them before writing *The Slave Girl* (Novak 1976:195; Novak et al. 2009:857). On the other hand, Vodnik dates *The Slave Girl* to around 1520 and definitely after the peasant uprisings of 1510 and 1514 on Hvar (Vodnik 1909:97).[9] Given the strong literary and economic connections between Dalmatian cities, it is likely

9 For futher details on the peasant uprisings, see Kasandrić (1977) and Raukar (1987).

that Lucić was familiar with the works of his Croatian literary predecessors and also attuned to the local oral songs. After all, his contemporary from Hvar, Petar Hektorović (1487–1572), in his *ecloga piscatoria* entitled *Ribanje i ribarsko prigovaranje* (*Fishing and Fishermen's Conversation*, 1556) included two *bugarštice* (oral songs) by local peasants. Although the stylistic features of Lucić's *The Slave Girl* are much more elaborate than those found in oral poetry (its 1038 verses are doubly-rhymed dodecasyllables) and his language is a sophisticated literary idiom (Vončina 1976:154–176), in many instances the influx of oral elements is easily recognizable, especially, as already stated, with regard to descriptions of the maiden.

The play's three acts unfold the story of a maiden of noble background captured by the Turks (also referred to in the play as *gusari* 'pirates'), who is brought to the Dubrovnik market where she is recognized by her former admirer. Unbeknownst to her, he pays a ransom for her to the Turks and tests her by not revealing his identity in order to learn why she had never shown any fondness towards him while living at the court. The most substantive part of the drama consists of the girl's lament about her captivity and her explanation of how it was up to the young man to ask for her hand from the king (in whose care she lived after her father had been killed by the Turks). It all ends well, and the young man takes the maiden to his house where, as we later learn from the servants, the recognition takes place, the relationship is consummated, and preparations are under way for the wedding.

Both Radić (1899) and Vodnik (1909) insisted on the existence of ties between Lucić's play and several traditional Dalmatian songs. Vodnik cites three examples: an oral song from the island of Hvar, one from the nineteenth-century song collection by Baltazar Bogišić (Bogišić 1878), and another from the collection by Baldo Glavić (1889). Despite these sources, the question of influence remains open: did the motif originate in oral traditional poetry and move to written literature or vice versa? A century later and with a trove of oral materials from the region—including not only the *Matica hrvatska* corpus on which Vodnik relied (composed largely of songs from Dalmatia) but also more than eleven thousand ballads and lyric songs collected in Herzegovina by Milman Parry and Albert Lord—we have a much larger basis for comparison, but a definitive answer is equally elusive. Still, it is of prime interest that the thematic category involving various forms of abduction of a maiden is one of the most popular in this corpus. For example, multiforms from the Parry Collection provide narratives that vary from the kidnapping of one girl to kidnapping a shipload of girls, such as in the song PN 2467a ("Zarobio beže Alibeže," Notebook no. 13, written down by Hamdija Šaković in 1935) by Stoja Bjeloglav from Gacko. Similarly, the song *Senjanin Ivo and Božo Rajković*, recorded in 1886 from Kate Murat, from the island of Šipan near Dubrovnik, by her son, is a narrative about a double abduction of a girl and her female servants (Murat 1996:50–60). Hasnija Hrustanović from Gacko provided a song (PN 2611, Vidan 2003:171–173) in which a maiden is captured by the Christians and given to their viceroy, who treats her like his own daughter (thus we have some similarities to Lucić's maiden, who lives under the auspices of a king, although she is captured only afterwards). The viceroy hopes to get a ransom for her and prompts her to ask her family for help, but in the end only her former admirer responds and gets her back. Recalling that Croatia was then divided between Venice, Hungary (later the Habsburgs), and the Ottomans, it is hardly surprising that local authors were preoccupied with the topics of captivity and freedom and that this was reflected in both the oral and literary corpus alike.

Lucić's play, however, has much stronger ties to historical circumstances than any of the oral songs, and it is worth looking into specific details in order to reach its hidden subtext. The principal character of his *The Slave Girl*, the rescuer-fiancé, bears the historical name Derenčin, and it is explicitly stated that he is related to the Croatian viceroy Derenčin who was, as already noted, the leader of the Croatian army against the Ottomans at the battle of Krbava in 1493, where he perished along with most of his soldiers. In addition to Vodnik's analysis of the characters' links to historical personages (Vodnik 1909), the most relevant discussion to date is that by Vončina who, on the basis of historical clues given in the play, suggests 1527 as the year when it was written, after the fall of Belgrade and the battle of Mohács. He further offers a chronology demonstrating that the captive girl, named Danica in the play, is modeled on Benigna, the daughter of Majer Blaž (Blaž Podmanicki), who was Matthias Corvinus' military leader and who defended Belgrade against the Ottomans after he became viceroy in 1470. Although Majer Blaž is mentioned elsewhere, in *The Slave Girl* he becomes the grandfather. Danica/Benigna is given an imaginary father called Vlasko who apparently perished at the hands of Turks (Vončina 1976:140–150). In her exchange with Derenčin, Danica reveals that she comes from the area of "Savah i Dravah" (the Sava and Drava rivers), and Vončina points out that the latter was reached by the Ottomans only during the Mohács operation (Vončina 1976:137). It should be mentioned here that Derenčin, Majer Blaž, and many other historical names from this period, such as Matthias Corvinus's father János Hunyadi (Sibinjanin Janko) and Vuk Grgurević (Zmaj Ognjeni Vuk) also entered the regional oral tradition.

Utilizing a historical family name, whose significance was certainly known to Lucić, and appending it to a fictional figure was a firm signal to his audience that the play had political ramifications. Viceroy Derenčin is remembered in cultural memory as a defender of his homeland, and in the play his fictional relative appears as a defender of a captive maiden. Since the female element often stands as a metaphor for the country, the motif of an abducted maiden served Lucić well to carry the weight of both an inoffensive literary narrative and a disguised political metaphor for a land yearning for liberation (Tatarin 2003:13). What is more, the play is situated in Dubrovnik, which, unlike the author's home island, was unoccupied at the time, and this gesture is Lucić's nod to the *libertas* so arduously celebrated by this city-state. His and Vetranović's resentment towards the threat the Ottomans posed for Dubrovnik, the only free zone in the region, is very much in line with that of Marin Držić as demonstrated below.[10]

Given the carnival spirit, it is not surprising that the plays of both Lucić and Držić revolve around feasts: the former concludes with the captive maiden's and her rescuer's wedding party, and the latter includes numerous scenes in which food and feasting represent the essence of happy living. Držić's principal character is named "Table Sweeper," and it is not by chance that he subsumes the author's *Weltanschauung.* "In the act of eating ... the confines between the body and the world are overstepped by the body; it triumphs over the world, over its enemy, celebrates its victory, grows at the world's expense. This element of victory and triumph is inherent in all banquet images. No meal can be sad," concludes Bakhtin (Bakhtin 1984:282). Additionally, he stresses that "the ritual of the feast tended to project the play of time itself, which kills and gives birth at the same time, recasting the old into the new, allowing nothing to perpetuate itself" (Bakhtin 1984:82). By making the feast one of the central narrative junctions, Lucić and Držić underscore the material and the bodily principle which is inclusive of all people and functionally re-generative in nature. In the same vein, both plays are brimming with sexual connotations: in Lucić's, characters discuss the stained sheets after the consummated marriage,[11] while in Držić's, the prodigal son succumbs to the charms of a courtesan while the others keep plotting how to win her attention. This focus on fertility and the life of "the belly and the reproductive organs" (Bakhtin 1984:19) is yet another act of defiance, which was in line with the carnivalesque spirit, subversive laughter, and the insistence on the rejuvenation of physical and social order.

Related to the motif of a captive maiden in literature is the traditional mock battle Moreška, which was recorded already in the seventeenth century on the island of Korčula and is still performed there. Wherever Spanish dominance

10 Vončina points to an ambiguous passage in Lucić's *The Slave Girl*, which may be hinting at Dubrovnik's reluctance to oppose the Turks (Vončina 1976:151–152), while Vetranović's *Pjesanca slavi carevoj* ("A Poem in the Emperor's Honor") explicitly discusses the question of Dubrovnik's tribute to the Ottomans and the fear that the city may be taken by them.

11 For discussion of the juncture between ideology and the body in Lucić's play see Novak 1987.

reached (owing to Charles V, this included a great deal of the Mediterranean basin), these types of performances took root. Since Dubrovnik had strong ties with the Spanish-held Naples in the sixteenth century, it is conceivable that the Moreška could have reached Croatia from Naples or possibly some other Italian city. In a series of complicated choreographies, the Korčula Moreška depicts a fight between the army of the Black (Moorish) King, who abducts a *bula* (Muslim lady), and that of the White King (typically dressed in red for enhanced effect), who in the end wins the maiden. Since Greek antiquity, Korčula has been known as Korkyra Melaina (Black Korčula), owing to its dense pine woods. Harris and Čale Feldman demonstrate that "a hidden transcript of resistance to external rule was insinuated into the imported narrative of Turks, Moors, and Christians" (Harris and Čale Feldman 2003–2004:299). In their interpretation "the Blacks were not Muslims but Korčulans, representatives of Black Korčula" (Harris and Čale Feldman 2003:312), which is evident from poetic imagery that is highly sympathetic to the Black King: "the young woman's opening speech pointedly undermines the ethical values with which 'black' and 'white' have traditionally been imbued in Europe" (Harris and Čale Feldman 2003–2004:311). Repossession of the maiden by the White King is viewed as a true abduction, and the White King with his soldiers is recognized as a guise for the Venetian invaders who had held the island of Korčula for several centuries. The maiden is thus possibly a metaphorical embodiment of the violated island of Korčula. What was on the surface a simple evocation of the clash between Christians and Muslims could be also read, in Harris and Čale Feldman's words, as a "hidden transcript" of the fate of the island of Korčula itself. Discussing the Korčula Moreška in the context of the rise of dramatic genres in Croatia not only illuminates further the political ramifications of this custom but also links it to an older layer of folklore tradition and to the Croatian secular theater.

If Lucić's political protest is only implied and Moreška's is embedded in a centuries old ritual, Držić's attempts at subversion are much more robust and palpable—not only through his most important play *Uncle Maroje* (1551) but also his secret letters to Cosimo I de' Medici, in which he openly calls for the overthrow of Dubrovnik's government.[12] The comedy itself is a rich fabric of linguistic textures and nuances and an assembly of vivid and intricately related characters (Stankiewicz 1990). It relies on the well-known narrative pattern of "the prodigal son," who escapes from Dubrovnik to Rome on business but falls victim to his hedonistic impulses. While courting a lady of questionable morals, he also competes with her other suitor, who happens to be of German origin.

[12] For discussion of the dating of *Uncle Maroje* see Tatarin 2011:85–96. A detailed account of manuscripts containing Držić's works, including *Uncle Maroje*, is found in Rešetar 1930: xix-xl.

Having heard about his son's profligate conduct, old Maroje comes to Rome to salvage what he can, as does the son's fiancée with her escort. Typically for a Renaissance play, the principal characters have servants who are often the ones not only propelling the action forward but also offering wisdom to the world. Many critics have commented on the seminal role that Pomet Trpeza (roughly translated, "Table Sweeper," the German suitor's servant modeled on the classical "hungry slave") has both as a character and as the meta-textual encapsulation of the author's own views. He is the one who rules over both the geographic and communicative spaces, and it is thus with good reason that he pronounces himself "the king of men." He is the measure of wisdom and the one best able to understand and adjust to different situations. Arguably, Pomet's most important statement in the play is: *Ma se je trijeba s brjemenom akomodavat; trijeba je bit vjertuozu tko hoće renjat na svijetu* (Držić 1964:223; "One needs to adjust to the times and be a virtuoso if he wants to rule the world").[13]

While most of the comedy concerns money and the pleasures it can buy, the character of Pomet additionally occupies himself with philosophical questions, central among which is how to survive in volatile times and persuade fickle Fortune to stay on one's side. Adjusting to circumstances is essential, and it implies assessing one's allies and enemies in order to be able to come up with the right strategy. Pomet's ability to perceive the situation from someone else's point of view and to direct events to his advantage not only makes him the supreme character but also ties his role to that of both the ruler (of the theatrical world) and writer (of the play itself). And indeed, the question of how to rule was weighing heavily on the minds of many kings and statesmen during the Renaissance. Držić's text suggests his familiarity with Machiavelli's *Il Principe* (Čale 1990, Tatarin 2007), but his obsession with the concept of ruling, the malaise called avarice, political alliances, and more specifically, the position of his native Dubrovnik on the turbulent map of sixteenth-century Europe comes forth with full force in *Uncle Maroje*'s first Prologue.

As others have demonstrated, this prologue serves as a literary overture to an actual political conspiracy that occurred fifteen years after the play's premiere and involved the Duke of Tuscany, Cosimo I de' Medici, who, Držić hoped, would help him in bringing down Dubrovnik's government (Kadić 1962:80; Jeličić 1976;

[13] The continuation of Pomet's monologue is as follows: "The King is his people's man if he knows how to rule. It's not about riches because I see many miserable ones with riches; it's not about learnedness because I see many strange ones in this company; it's not about being a hero with a sword in one's hand because many times these are killed or fill the dungeons; it's not about being a poet or being able to write comedies because these are harassed by everyone and made to work like porters at every wedding, and instead of thankfulness they are told 'Wasn't good at all' and gain enemies; it's not about being a peasant because others make these sing when they'd rather cry. One has to be patient and give the bad times their due in order to enjoy the good times."

Čale 1978:200).[14] Although Dubrovnik was the only free Croatian territory at the time and its government was successfully navigating the political scene, the situation was precarious. The Ottomans' looming presence, thought Držić, called for a strengthening of Dubrovnik's ties with Western rulers, rather than succumbing to the Ottomans' ever-increasing tributes and taxation. He believed that the governing policy of subservience was not so much rooted in Dubrovnik's political interests as it was a source of easy profit for the members of the ruling caste. Kunčević discusses in detail Dubrovnik's relations with the Porte and its tributary obligation which the city-state insisted was an economic rather than political arrangement (Kunčević 2015:99–111). Despite an ostensible image of political harmony, there existed a bifurcation of interests between the common citizens and the closed circle of Dubrovnik patricians from whose ranks Držić's family fell out, a fact he deeply resented. Moreover, political discord arose even among some of the ruling members themselves (Senker 2009:151–154; Kunčević 2015:51–52, 151–155). Having lived in Siena as a young man between 1538 and 1545, where he enjoyed the high status of Rector of the Domus Sapientiae and thus had access to the social elite,[15] and having traveled in the service of the Austrian count Christoph von Rogendorf to Istanbul in 1546, Držić experienced firsthand both the West and the East; but he likely also had access to information available in diplomatic and espionage circles.

However, not being able to voice his thoughts openly, Držić used literature as a vehicle for alerting his fellow citizens. He begins his comedy with a prologue in which a magician named Long Nose tells a narrative, very much in the vein of tale-tellers, about his travels in the faraway lands of the Great and Small Indies, of New and Old Indies.[16] The Old India was a utopian place of noble-looking, ethically superior people, but as creatures from the other Indies began mixing with them, the good "real" people (*ljudi nazbilj*) began to perish and the disfigured animal-like creatures, the "unreal, naught" people (*ljudi nahvao*) took over. It was avarice that triggered this situation because the strange creatures were brought to the bucolic Old India for the purpose of trading. Money and greed are thus the source of many evils. In the concluding part of the prologue, it is also stated that the play will reveal who the good real people and who the "naught" people are, the latter clearly referring to the nobility populating Dubrovnik's governmental structures and presumably sitting in the audience.

14 A survey of interpretations of the Prologue to *Dundo Maroje* is offered in Tatarin 2009, while Držić's subversive activities are detailed in Kunčević 2007 and 2009.

15 For analysis of Držić's time in Siena, in particular the years 1541 and 1542, his involvement in a forbidden comedy production, and on Italian theatrical influences, see Košuta 1961.

16 A detailed discussion of allegorical journeys in the Western literary output as well as the impact of Renaissance maritime discoveries on the magician's role is found in Košuta 1964.

Through the words of his Indian magician, Držić is evidently criticizing the fact that the Dubrovnik government was greedy first and foremost for its own profit. And what is more, the comedy was staged in the City Hall,[17] Dubrovnik's central locus of power, but the criticism was mitigated by the exotic cloak of an Indian tale and the time of carnival.[18]

And why India of all places? Using a hidden narrative stemming from the fourth-century Indian oral collection *Pañćatantra*, which was supposedly designed as a manual for rulers, Držić condemns tongue-in-cheek Dubrovnik's government from its own throne.[19] As mentioned previously, his stay in Siena exposed him to Italian literary currents and it is quite likely that he became acquainted with some of the works that were structurally and thematically modeled on *Pañćatantra*. In the course of the early- to mid-sixteenth century there appeared a remarkable number of collections which were influenced by Giovanni di Capua's *Liber Kalilae et Dimnae: Directorium vitae humanae* (ca. 1270), a version of *Pañćatantra* based on Abdullah ibn al-Moqaffa's Arabic version entitled *Kalila wa Dimna*, which di Capua in Italy began translating into Latin from Rabbi Joel's twelfth century Hebrew rendition and completed from the Arabic (Beecher et al. 2003:14–27). Di Capua's translation served as the basis for the Spanish version called *Exemplario contra los engaños y peligros del mundo*, which was also the first one to be published in 1493 with nine successive editions (Beecher et al. 2003:26). Not surprisingly, its moralistic tales, which often served as a model for prescribing certain types of behavior, easily entered the works of Renaissance writers as attested in Agnolo Firenzuola's *La prima veste de' discorsi degli animali*, written in 1540 (thus around the time of Držić's stay in Siena) and published posthumously in 1548 (A. Seroni in Firenzuola 1958:441–443). Similarly, in 1552, the Florentine Anton Francesco Doni published in Venice his *La filosofia morale del Doni: Tratta da molti degni Scrittori Antichi prudenti*, which in its opening recalls India as the tales' source.[20] Another author drawn to animal and magic tales stemming from oral tradition is Giovanni Francesco Straparola, who published

17 Novak provides an insightful examination of the dynamics between political structures and theater in Renaissance Dubrovnik, with a particular focus on *Uncle Maroje* (Novak 1984:62-77).

18 As noted by Košuta, a resonance of India in European literary imagination of the time is reflected also in Rabelais' *Fourth Book*. The first incomplete edition was published in Lyon in 1548, just three years before *Uncle Maroje* was staged; its first full edition was published in 1552, a year after Držić's play (Košuta 1964: 271).

19 The *Pañćatantra* ("five books"), comprising didactic tales featuring animals, is presumed to be of folk origin and is among the most widely disseminated folktale collections.

20 In Doni's words: "Il presente Libro honorati lettori, su ritrouato scritto ne la India, con titolo di SAPIENZA MORALE: & di quella lingua su tradotto ne la Persica, chiamandolo ESSEMPIO DEL BEN VIVERE " (1567:1).

his *Le piacevole notti* in the period from 1550 to 1553.[21] It is, I believe, beyond any doubt that Držić was familiar with either di Capua's translation, Firenzuola's manuscript, or some other work relying on the Indian collection of oral tales. However, Držić utilized its basic narrative to depict a local political situation, in the process giving the oral narrative a double functionality: public and hidden.

Fifteen years after the Prologue was written, Držić traveled to Florence with the goal of overturning the Dubrovnik government; there he sought the help of Cosimo I de' Medici. In his six letters to Medici written in summer 1566 (five of which survive, while one is referred to in a subsequent letter), he chastises Dubrovnik's ruling nobles and reveals his hope for intensification of the city-state's Western orientation.[22] The link between the Prologue and Držić's later political activities in Italy is essential, as first suggested by Živko Jeličić (Novak et al. 2009:850). However, the Prologue can be fully understood only if read in the context of the Indian oral collection that found such wide dissemination in Italy (and elsewhere) and which provided Držić with sophisticated tools of political activism.

This context of transtextuality opens up a question of reception which looms large because of insufficient data pertaining to the earlier period. It is reasonable to ask which layers of these palimpsestuous texts the audiences addressed by Lucić and Držić were able to discern, as well as to what degree they could relate to the potentially subversive political messages. As Senker underscores, the performance of *Uncle Maroje* (and this is true for *The Slave Girl* as well) was open to the general public and set in the main square, although it was noted that it was eventually moved to the City Hall because of the bad weather (Senker 2009:148). The profile of Držić's audience is discernible from his inclusive gesture in the play's two prologues: the first in which Magician Long Nose addresses not only Dubrovnik nobles but also "the old folks, women, the old and the young, the tall and the tiny, the folks with whom peace resides and who stay away from warfare" and the second which mentions "the gentle and good-natured assembly, folk old and wise." The author was thus aware of the broadest spectrum of spectators but aimed his central message at those who did not have power in their hands. What is more, Držić concludes Long Nose's

21 Straparola's case is particularly revealing as it generated a heated scholarly debate on interactions between oral and written literature. Prompted by Ruth B. Bottigheimer's perception of Straparola as the "fairy godfather" who invented the "rise tale" in the 1550s, scholars such as Dan Ben-Amos, Jan Ziolkowski and Francisco Vaz da Silva argue quite the opposite: that Straparola, having lived at the point of convergence of oral and written, drew on preexisting oral sources and in essence built on these as any gifted oral storyteller would have, with the difference that in the sixteenth century the transmission channel became a printed book (Ben-Amos 2010:430; Ziolkowski 2010:394; da Silva 2010:401).

22 For more on Držić's conspiracy, see Dayre 1938; Delić-Gozze 2007; Kunčević 2007, 2009.

speech by saying that, for the audience, the origin of the evil people disturbing the world should be more important than the comedy they are about to see. Although the question of reception cannot be answered in a satisfying way, the context of the plays, as well as their timing, indicate that "by entering carnival and becoming public, theater symbolically returned to all Dubrovnik citizens the rights which political changes of the late Middle age took away" (Senker 2009:160). Despite different circumstances, much of the same could be said for Lucić's Hvar.

The interplay between the oral and the written in these examples renders a complex dialogic exchange of the public and hidden narratives which presented audiences with differing sets of communicative codes. A written text that assimilates oral components as a part of its narrative spectrum can superimpose an intention to convey different layers of reality in a more intricate fashion than is evident in the oral narratives it relies upon. However, as the example of the Moreška illustrates, the true polyphonic nature of traditional materials is set forth when the oldest layers are resurrected to accommodate new patterns of reality. What is at play here is a strong sense of collective memory in which oral and written emerge as cultural palimpsests, as different manifestations of the same experiences, and share the type of multi-functionality that allows for preservation of both aesthetic values and collective identity.

## Bibliography


Bakhtin, M. M. 1984. *Rabelais and His World*. Trans. H. Iswolsky. Bloomington.

Batušić, N., ed. 1987. *Hanibal Lucić*. Dani hvarskog kazališta 13. Split.

Beecher, D., J. Butler, and C. Di Biase, eds. 2003. *Sir Thomas North: The Moral Philosophy of Doni popularly known as The Fables of Bidpai*. Ottawa.

Ben-Amos, D. 2010. "Straparola: The Revolution That Was Not." *Journal of American Folklore* 123/490:426–446.

Bogišić, B. 1878. *Narodne pjesme iz starijih, najviše primorskih zapisa*. Belgrade.

Brand, C. P. 1995. "The Renaissance of Comedy: The Achievement of Italian 'Commedia Erudita.'" *Modern Language Review* 90:xxix–xlii.

Bristol, M. D. 1985. *Carnival and Theater: Plebeian Culture and the Structure of Authority in Renaissance England*. New York.

Čale, F. 1978. "Marin Držić između filozofije i politike." In *Hrvatska književnost u evropskom kontekstu*, ed. A. Flaker and K. Pranjić, 193–221. Zagreb.

———. 1990. "Pomet's Machiavellism. From Artistic Vision to Conspiratory Reality." *Most/The Bridge* 1–2:129–154.

Dayre, J. 1938. "Marin Držić, urotnik u Firenci." In *Dubrovačke studije*, 19–23. Zagreb.

Delić-Gozze, V., ed. 2007. *Conspiracy Letters of Marin Držić to Cosimo I de' Medici*. Zagreb.

Dillon, S. 2007. *The Palimpsest. Literature, Criticism, Theory*. London.

Doni, A. F. 1567. *La filosofia morale del Doni. Tratta da molti degni Scrittori Antichi prudenti*. 2nd ed. Venice.

Držić, M. 1964. *Novela od Stanca. Tirena. Skup. Dundo Maroje*. Ed. I. Dončević. Zagreb.

Fališevac, D. 2007. *Dubrovnik—otvoreni i zatvoreni grad: studije o dubrovačkoj književnoj kulturi*. Zagreb.

Firenzuola, A. 1958. *Opere*. Ed. A. Seroni. Florence.

Foley, J. M. 1991. *Immanent Art: From Structure to Meaning in Traditional Oral Epic*. Bloomington.

Foretić, V. 1969. "Dubrovnik u doba Marina Držića." In *Marin Držić: Zbornik radova*, ed. J. Ravlić, 7–27. Zagreb.

Fotez, M., ed. 1976. *Renesansa*. Dani hvarskog kazališta 3. Split.

Genette, G. 1997. *Palimpsests: Literature in the Second Degree*. Lincoln, NE.

Glavić, B. M. 1889. *Narodne pjesme. Zbirka I*. Dubrovnik.

Grčić, M., ed. 1988. *Ribanje i ribarsko prigovaranje/Robinja*. Zagreb.

Harris, M., and L. Čale Feldman. 2003–2004. "Blackened Faces and a Veiled Woman: The Early Korčula Moreška." *Comparative Drama* 37:297–320.

Harris, R. 2003. *Dubrovnik. A History*. London.

Jeličić, Ž. 1976. "Ponovo o prologu Dugog Nosa." In Fotez 1976:360–369.

Kadić, A. 1962. "The Croatian Renaissance." *Slavic Review* 21:65-88.

Kasandrić, I. 1977. "Društveno-politički uzroci sukoba pučana s vlastelom na Hvaru." *Radovi* 10:93–102.

Kekez, H. 2009. "Bernardin Frankapan i Krbavska bitka: je li spasio sebe i malobrojne ili je pobjegao iz boja?" *Modruški zbornik* 3:65–101. http://bib.irb.hr/datoteka/438224.Hrvoje_Kekez-Bernardin_Frankapan_i_Krbavska_bitka.pdf.

Košuta, L. 1961. "Siena nella vita e nell'opera di Marino Darsa (Marin Držić)." *Ricerche Slavistiche* 9:67–121. Repr. as "Siena u životu i djelu Marina Držića," in *Putovima kanonizacije: Zbornik radova o Marinu Držiću (1508-2008)*, ed. N. Batušić and D. Fališevac, 220-262. Zagreb.

———. 1964. "Il mondo vero e il mondo a Rovescio in 'Dundo Maroje' di Marino Darsa (Marin Držić)." *Ricerche Slavistiche* 12:65-122. Repr. as "Pravi i obrnuti svijet u Držićevu *Dundu Maroju*." In *Putovima kanonizacije: Zbornik radova o Marinu Držiću (1508-2008)*, ed. N. Batušić and D. Fališevac, 263-306. Zagreb.

Kunčević, L. 2007. "'Ipak nije na odmet sve čuti': Medičejski pogled na urotničke namjere Marina Držića." *Anali Zavoda za povijesne znanosti Hrvatske akademije znanosti i umjetnosti u Dubrovniku* 45:9–45.

———. 2009. "Urota, Urotnička pisma." In *Leksikon Marina Držića*, ed. S. P. Novak, M. Tatarin, M. Mataija, and L. Rafolt, 837–846. Zagreb.

———. 2015. *Mit o Dubrovniku: Diskursi o identitetu renesansnoga grada*. Zagreb.

Lord, A. B. 2019. *The Singer of Tales*. 3rd ed. Ed. D. F. Elmer. Hellenic Studies 77. Publications of the Milman Parry Collection of Oral Literature 4. Washington, DC. Orig. pub. Cambridge, MA, 1960.

Lozica, I. 2007. "O karnevalu: diverzija, kohezija, opsceno i mitsko." In *Prešućeno, zabranjeno, izazovno u hrvatskoj književnosti i kazalištu*, Dani hvarskoga kazališta 36, ed. N. Batušić, 190–207. Zagreb.

Lucić, H. 1988. *Robinja*. In Grčić 1988:133–196.

Mitić, I. 1988. *Dubrovačka država u međunarodnoj zajednici (Od 1358. do 1815)*. Zagreb.

Mrdeža, D. 1987. "Lucićeva 'Robinja' kao renesansna drama." In Batušić 1987:149–158.

Murat, A., coll. 1996. *Narodne pjesme iz Luke na Šipanu*. Ed. T. Perić-Polonijo. Zagreb.

Novak, S. P. 1976. "Hrvatske dramske robinje." In Fotez 1976:185–204.

———. 1984. *Planeta Držić: Držić i rukopis vlasti*. Zagreb.

———. 1987. "Posteljni i ženidbeni obredi u Lucićevoj 'Robinji'." In Batušić 1987:159–166.

———. 2009. *Slaveni u renesansi*. Zagreb.

Novak, S. P., M. Tatarin, M. Mataija, L. Rafolt, eds. 2009. *Leksikon Marina Držića.* Zagreb.

Radić, A. 1899. "Narodni izvor Lucićevoj 'Robinji'." *Zbornik za narodni život i običaje* 4:34–45.

Raukar, T. 1987. "Hvarsko društvo u XVI stoljeću." In Batušić 1987:42–53.

Rešetar, M., ed. 1930. *Djela Marina Držića*. Zagreb.

Senker, B. 2009. "Karnevalsko u Dundu Maroju." In *Marin Držić - svjetionik dubrovačke renesanse. Zbornik radova s međunarodnoga znastvenog skupa (Pariz, 23.-25. listopada 2008)*, ed. S. Anđelković and P.-L. Thomas, 147–173. Zagreb.

Silva, F. V. da. 2010. "The Invention of Fairy Tales." *Journal of American Folklore* 123/490:398–425.

Stankiewicz, E. 1990. "The Thematic Conflicts in Držić's Dundo Maroje." *Most/ The Bridge* 1–2:155–174.

Švelec, F. 1976. "Hrvatska renesansna drama." In Fotez 1976:5–22.

Tatarin, M. 2003. "O ženskim mukama, robinjama, ljudima nazbilj i nahvao, grabancijaškim čarolijama i još koječemu." In *Stara hrvatska drama*, ed. M. Tatarin, 5–31. Zagreb.

———. 2007. "Držić i Machiavelli (Nacrt za jedno čitanje Držićeva makijavelizma)." In *Jezik književnosti i književni ideologemi: Zbornik radova 35. seminara Zagrebačke slavističke škole*, ed. K. Bagić, 63-85. Zagreb.

———. 2009. "Nazbilj-nahvao." In *Leksikon Marina Držića*, ed. S. P. Novak, M. Tatarin, M. Mataija, and L. Rafolt, 534–536. Zagreb.

———. 2011. *Čudan ti je animao čovjek. Rasprave o Marinu Držiću*. Zagreb.

Tomasović, M. 1988. "'Robinja,' dramska igra Hanibala Lucića." In Grčić 1988:197–203.

Vidan, A. 2003. *Embroidered with Gold, Strung with Pearls: The Traditional Ballads of Bosnian Women.* Milman Parry Collection of Oral Literature 1. Cambridge, MA.

———. 2010. "Marin Držić i usmena riječ: tragom formule, teme i mita." *Dubrovnik* 21:65–83.

Vodnik, B. 1909. "Postanje Lucićeve 'Robinje.' Literarno-historička studija." *Rad Jugoslavenske akademije znanosti i umjetnosti* 176:83–134.

Vončina, J. 1976. "O izvorima i jezičnim slojevima Lucićeve 'Robinje'." In Fotez 1976:135–184.

Ziolkowski, J. M. 2010. "Straparola and the Fairy Tale: Between Literary and Oral Traditions." *Journal of American Folklore* 123/490:377–397.

# PART V

# PERFORMANCE AND CONTEXT

# 15

# Performances, Texts, and Contexts

## Olaus Sirma, Johan Turi, and the Dilemma of Reifying a Context-Dependent Oral Tradition

Thomas A. DuBois

UNDERSTANDABLY, PERHAPS NECESSARILY, the earliest scholarly and artistic attempts at collecting and representing oral traditions tended to gravitate to genres with a marked, even emphatic *breakthrough* into performance.[1] A genre in which the performer could be said to take the stage, perform, receive approval and/or censure and then yield the stage to the next performer was appealing to both medieval scribes and nineteenth-century folklorists, for it allowed them to recognize performances as "items" of oral tradition that could be profitably recorded and shared with a later reading audience. Such items needed to possess enough verbal cues that a later audience would be able to understand what they were about and why the scribe or scholar had decided to record them.

What happens, however, when a genre of oral tradition does not display such easily discernible boundaries? And what happens when, as in the case of Sámi *joik*, this tendency toward conversational embeddedness is accompanied by an understanding of the genre as wholly reliant on the context and interpersonal situation in which it is performed? In this paper, I revisit two texts of great importance to Sámi literary and cultural history: Johan Scheffer's *Lapponia* (1673) and Johan Turi's *Muitalus Sámiid birra* (1910).[2] The first of these contains

1 For discussion of this important term in folklore research and the "performance school" that employed it in particular, see Hymes 1975, 2004; Bauman 1975, 1986; Rudy 2002.

2 I quote the prose text of *Lapponia* using its 1674 English translation, *The History of Lapland* (Scheffer 1674). Translations of Sirma's poems, however, are my own, based on the original Kemi Sámi texts. Quotations from *Muitalus* are taken from the 2010 edition of the text, edited by Mikael Svonni (Turi 2010). Translations of the Turi texts are my own as they appear in my translation *An Account of the Sámi* (Turi 2011).

the texts of the first two Sámi songs ever committed to writing, songs which Scheffer received—along with a detailed explanation of how they were used—from a young Kemi Sámi minister-in-training, Olaus Matthias Sirma (Čearbmá Ovllá). The second, *Muitalus Sámiid birra* ("An Account of the Sámi"), was authored by Johan Turi in collaboration with the Danish artist and ethnographer Emilie Demant. Turi's *Muitalus*, written in 1908, appeared in print for the first time in 1910 and is thus now more than a century old. It is considered the first secular book written in Sámi, and I had the good fortune to work with Sámi linguist Mikael Svonni to produce a new translation of that work, a translation which appeared in 2011 (Turi 2011). What I hope to show in this paper is how Sirma and Turi endeavored in the texts they wrote to present *joik* not as discrete songs to be notated and catalogued or set apart as reified works of art but rather as implements in an ongoing social relation between singers, audiences, and the circumstances of life. I argue that Sirma and Turi were searching for a framework to present *joik* as an embedded, context-dependent ethnographic event, and because they found willing listeners in Johann Scheffer and Emilie Demant, they were able to include contextual information as a central element of their presentations of Sámi singing. I posit that these two men—the first contributors to the study of Sámi folklore—found ways to resist the atomizing or itemizing tendencies of folksong collection of their day in a manner that has much to teach us in our work as students of oral culture in the twenty-first century.

## Sámi Song

The Sámi (formerly called "Lapps") are an indigenous people of the Nordic region, living today in Finland, Norway, the Russian Federation, and Sweden. Traditionally, they lived off a variety of different hunter-gatherer and herding activities, adapted to the differing local environments and resources of the region. Many Sámi today, as in the past, speak one or more of a set of roughly twelve closely related Finno-Ugric languages referred to by linguists according to geographic locations or Sámi ethnonyms (e.g. Northern Sámi, South Sámi, Lule Sámi, Inari Sámi, Skolt Sámi). Varieties of Northern Sámi are today the most widely spoken surviving Sámi language, with more than twenty thousand active speakers. Many of the other Sámi languages have dwindled to a few hundred speakers or are entirely extinct. Roughly half of the population of c. 80,000 that considers itself ethnically Sámi speak no Sámi language whatsoever. Likewise, many Sámi today no longer practice traditional livelihoods to any great extent. Nonetheless, Sámi ethnic identity has strengthened over the past century, in part through the valorization of distinctive traditional genres such as *joik*, and

Sámi status as a unique people living within the Nordic region has been recognized by the governments of Finland, Norway, and Sweden.

The emphatic breakthrough associated with many genres of folklore cross-culturally is far from the norm in the often conversationally embedded, context-dependent Sámi musical genre known as *joik*. The North Sámi *luohti,* South Sámi *vuolle,* and Skolt Sámi *levdd*—all classified by musicologists and Sámi studies scholars as part of a single, overarching *joik* genre—share a tendency toward fairly brief musical motifs, crooned or sung full-throated, with lyrics that consist of a short poetic text, a name and epithets, or simply a string of vocables.[3] In some *joik* performances, such as Nils Mattias Andersson's great South Sámi *vuolle* about difficulties on the mountain Oulavuolie, recorded by a Swedish radio team in 1953, the singer moves seamlessly between a speaking and singing voice throughout his nearly ten minutes of vocal performance, blurring the line between what a non-Sámi listener might recognize as a "song" and what might be regarded simply as commentary or conversation.[4] This same characteristic blurring of boundaries can be noted in the Forest Sámi Jonas Edvard Steggo's bear *vuolle,* in which the singer seemingly interrupts his song to comment on the nature of the bear, only to be urged by the somewhat perplexed sound crew recording the performance to resume his singing.[5] One can recognize within such moments intermittent characteristics of voice and manner that folklorists would describe as "breakthrough," but to focus on such performative boundaries without attention to the overarching mechanisms that tie the *joik* performance integrally to its ambient ordinary conversation, or to related narratives,[6] or even to silence, is to miss part of the elusive essence of the genre from a Sámi perspective.

As noted above, the "blurry edges" of *joik* coincide with a related tendency to perform *joik* as an adjunct of ordinary conversation or other daily activities. In their introduction to the genre, Kjellström, Ternhag, and Rydving recount instances of *joik* performance that reflect the seemingly spontaneous, emotionally charged situations in which individuals choose to *joik.*[7] Song performances could occur when a person was alone, in reaction to animals or landscape in one's vicinity, or as a response to something now far away. A young Sámi named Torkel Tomasson, returning to his home tracts in the 1940s after his first studies at the University of Uppsala, far to the south, recounted his surprise at the

3 Graff 1993, Jones-Bamman 1993, Ruong 1997, Gaski 1999.

4 Arnberg et al. 1997:158–162, CD 1, track 16.

5 Arnberg et al. 1997:28, 213, CD 2, track 54.

6 Stoor 2007.

7 Kjellström, Ternhag, and Rydving 1988:12–15.

intensity with which he began to *joik* his home landscape when first seeing it again.[8] In another account of roughly the same period, a distraught father burst into *joik* when coming upon the body of his son and the wreckage of the car in which he had died.[9] Nor has this tendency to burst into song at emotionally fraught moments diminished over time: a contemporary teenaged North Sámi *joik* performer, Johan Máhtte Skum, created a stirring *luohti* in honor of a winning goal in an important soccer championship game.[10] *Joik* can equally be used to contemplate absence: singers recount using *joik* to envision friends or places otherwise lost to them, keeping them alive in their memories through a musical portrait meaningful to any person conversant in the tradition but tinged with deep personal and emotional significance.

Scholars of the twentieth century have been able to analyze *joik* in a manner that recognizes these important characteristics of the genre. Sirma and Turi wrote their accounts long before the advent of ethnographic contextualization, however, when genres of oral tradition were standardly approached from the point of view of established literary forms and when the need for information beyond that provided in the text was often regarded as a failing. Facing the very real possibility of audience incomprehension or disapproval of *joik* in the absence of further contextualizing information, Sirma and Turi chose to present their songs in a manner that emphasized and spelled out their broader cultural meanings.

## Olaus Sirma

Olaus Sirma enrolled at the University of Uppsala in the late seventeenth century, having traveled to the south of Sweden to receive training for the ministry. There, he came in contact with Johann Scheffer, a German scholar who had been charged with the task of writing a book about the Sámi.[11] Scheffer drew on past published works about the Sámi as well as extensive notes and accounts from Lutheran ministers who had been posted in the north and wrote a book in Latin, which became a sensation in seventeenth-century Europe. Olaus Sirma's songs and explanations were part of the materials Scheffer used to write his book.

Scheffer does not include Olaus's songs in any section devoted to music or entertainment. Instead, he embeds them in a chapter focusing on courtship and wedding traditions. As Scheffer explicitly states in his chapter, he relies upon

8 Kjellström, Ternhag, and Rydving 1988:14.

9 Kjellström, Ternhag, and Rydving 1988:15.

10 Skum 2006.

11 For a full account of this relation, see DuBois 2006:5–13; DuBois 2008.

the accounts of Samuel Leem and Olaus Magnus for much of his material about Sámi courtship and marriage. His information regarding the place of *joik* in these proceedings, however, is drawn entirely from Olaus Sirma.

According to Scheffer, courtship begins with a young man sizing up the reindeer wealth of the woman he hopes to marry. If a young woman is sufficiently wealthy, and the suitor has formed a good opinion of her at "publick Meetings, at Fairs, or when they [i.e. the Sámi] pay their usual Tribute," the suitor visits the bride's father to make a formal suit. Scheffer details the ceremonial receipt of the wedding suit in the drinking of brandy and then the kissing of future bride and groom. If the bride accepts the groom's attentions, Scheffer notes, the "Marriage is as good as concluded."[12] The wedding, however, does not occur immediately but only after a long series of preparations, including the groom's giving of gifts to all the bride's extended family and obtaining their blessings on the marriage and the groom's gift of both goods and labor to the bride's father in anticipation of his eventual receipt of the bride and her reindeer. Writes Scheffer:

> Nevertheless, the Consummation of the Marriage, after the Consent of the Parents is obtained, is sometimes deferred for a long time, nay for Two or Three Years ... The Reason for this long Courtship is, because the Suitor lies under an Obligation of getting the consent, not only of her Parents, but of all the Kindred and Relations, before he can enjoy her, which must be done by Presents ...[13]

It is in this protracted engagement period that Scheffer embeds the two *joik* songs he obtained from Sirma. Sirma's original manuscript account is preserved at the Uppsala University library. In it, Sirma describes Sámi *joiking* in this way:

> Dhesze wijsor begynna dhe, på dhetta, och annadt sätt: Siungandes somblige mehra, sombl. mindre, effter som hwar och een inbillar sigh dhem bäst kunna fatta och componera. Stundom repetera dhe samma sångh åfftare. Icke häller hafwa de någon wisz thon, uthan siunga, eller Joiga, denna wiisan, hwilken de kalla Morse Faurog, eller Brude wijsa, effter dheras wahna och som dhem bäst tyckes liuda.

> These songs begin in this and other ways. Some sing more, others less, according to their own inclinations to create and compose. At times they repeat the same song over and over. Nor do they have any set tune

[12] Scheffer 1674:285.
[13] Scheffer 1674:285.

> but sing and *joik* this song, which is called *Moarsi fávrrot,* the bride's song, according to their custom and as it seems best to them to sing.[14]

Although this passage comments on the performance mode in particular, Sirma also describes proper contexts and conduct for the songs' use in his broader text. As apparent above, he refuses to consider *joik* as a functional equivalent of song or music-making as he understands these from Swedish culture, instead opting to import the verb *joik* (based on the Sámi *juoigat*—to perform a *joik*), underscoring the essential differences between the Sámi genre and any seemingly comparable variety of music-making among the Swedes. One of the presented *joik* texts, he notes, is sung in the winter, when journeying to a fair to see one's bride-to-be. The second *joik* encapsulates the musings of a man thinking about the Lake Oarrejávri and his bride-to-be living by its shores and is described as a "summer song." The opening of this latter *joik* begins in this way:

> Pastos päivä kiufwrasist jawra Orrejaura!
> Jos koasa kirrakeid kornagadzim
> Ja tiedadzim man oinämam jaufre Orrejawre
> Man tangaszlomest lie sun lie,
> Kaika taidä mooraid dzim soopadzim
> Mak taben sadde sist uddasist,
> Ja poaka taidä ousid dzim karsadzin,
> Mack qwodde roannaid poorid ronaidh.
>
> Shine bright, oh Sun on the lake, Oarre Lake!
> If I climbed up on a spruce tree
> And knew that I saw the lake, Oarra Lake,
> In the heather where she'd be waiting.
> All those trees I'd chop away
> Which have started growing there lately,
> And all those branches I would prune
> Which have sprouts, good sprouts.[15]

Over the course of the song, the lyric speaker expresses his yearning for his bride-to-be as well as his indecision about what actions to take. In the end, he resolves to take the road leading back to his bride: *Oucta lie miela oudas waldäman / nute tiedäm pooreponne oudastan man kauneman* ("one alone I need to choose now / that I may better find my way").[16] Scheffer's chapter, shaped by Sirma's firsthand input,

[14] Kjellström et al. 1988:11.
[15] DuBois 2006:5–6.
[16] DuBois 2006:6.

describes the protracted courtship situation that makes sense of his *joik* texts: the endless longing of an extended engagement, the periodic absences due to differing work responsibilities, the insecurity about whether the long-anticipated marriage will ever take place. The chapter thus offers readers a key to understanding the songs as implements in a complex social interaction between groom and bride, amidst a monitoring community and environment.

To Scheffer, acquainted with the *joik* tradition from Olaus's description and examples, *joik* is emphatically *not* a type of musical entertainment in itself but rather a form of ritual communication within the fraught and delicate matter of courtship. Indeed, later in his chapter, when describing wedding ceremonies, Scheffer remarks pointedly: "They don't know what a Fidler or Musick is, and Laugh at Dancing as a foolish Thing ... as I have been credibly informed by Olaus Matthias, a young Student, and a Native of Lapland."[17] Olaus seems to have made the function of *joik* clear to the professor and to have led him to underscore its embeddedness in the communicative/ritual framework of the courtship.

On publication, of course, the careful contextual framework suggested by Sirma and Scheffer seems to have had little effect. Readers were captivated by Sirma's songs but read them in isolation from all the social details provided in the text. The songs became, in classic literary terms, "transcendent"—i.e. decontextualized—and as such, they were to be experienced for what they could express to a reader of any cultural background. As Wretö shows,[18] the newly emergent independent songs became compared to the ancient lyrics of Greece and Rome and were used to illustrate the universality of human aesthetic sentiment. Scheffer's Latin rendering found further translation by literary greats of the eighteenth and nineteenth centuries such as Herder, Goethe, and Runeberg, and in this way became frequently anthologized elements of various collections. Responding to this decontextualizing move, the Scottish scholar Hugh Blair writes in 1765 in admiration of the songs:

> Surely among the wild Laplanders, if any where, barbarity is in its most perfect state. Yet their love songs which Scheffer has given us in his *Lapponia* are proof that natural tenderness of sentiment may be found in a country, into which the least glimmering of science has never penetrated.[19]

Within the English-speaking world, Sirma's songs are perhaps best known through a single couplet incorporated into Longfellow's 1855 poem *My Lost*

17 Scheffer 1674:295.
18 Wretö 1984:49.
19 DuBois 2006:12.

*Youth.* Longfellow's lyric speaker, apparently a man in his waning years, reflects wistfully on his childhood haunts. At the end of each stanza, he alludes to Sirma's lines *parne miela piägga miela / Noara jorda kockes jorda* ("a boy's will, the wind's will / a young man's thoughts, long thoughts") with the lines: "And the fragment of a Lapland song runs in my memory still: / A boy's will is the wind's will / and the thoughts of youth are long, long thoughts." James Taft Hatfield shows how Longfellow came upon Sirma's poems as anthologized in Herder's *Volkslieder* and even locates Longfellow's personal volume of Herder with a check alongside the poem in "an obscure corner of Craigie House."[20] With no real familiarity with Sámi culture and only the decontextualized song as his guide, Hatfield argues:

> *My Lost Youth*, in its original content, and in all the applications which have been made of it, exhibits a misinterpretation of the Lapland song. The original argument is "The will of boys is the will of the wind"—fluctuating and unable to reach a clear decision on a matter of urgent importance; "the thoughts of youth are long thoughts"—that is, hesitating and uncertain—while to Longfellow, and ourselves, the significance is: "a boy's mind is full of vague prophecies and longings; he has outreaching visions and dreams."[21]

Of course, as Hatfield might have known if he had had greater access to Sirma's notes and Scheffer's chapter, the situation depicted in Sirma's song has less to do with "urgent importance" than "vague prophecies and longings"—it is the direct result of a protracted and uncertain engagement. Hatfield's study, although exemplary in its literary sleuthing of Longfellow's sources and subsequent reception, fails to embrace the contextual information that Sirma and Scheffer provided. One could even argue that Longfellow's adaptation of the lines from Sirma depict well the way in which *joik* works for Sámi people: becoming a musical motif running in one's memory that finds its present meaning not so much in its verbal content but in its social context. In this way, Longfellow's poem is perhaps a better cultural translation of Sirma's song than any of the more literal translations that preceded it, in that it embraces rather than eschews the idea of contextualization.

[20] Hatfield 1930:1189.
[21] Hatfield 1930:1190.

# Johan Turi

The story of Johan Turi's literary career is an important one for Sámi cultural history. Turi wished to create an authoritative account of Sámi culture—a kind of Sámi updating of Scheffer's *Lapponia*—with the explicit intent of helping improve the situation of Sámi people at the beginning of the twentieth century. Turi believed that if the Swedish government authorities and others in power were to understand the hardships, travails, and beauty of Sámi culture, they would work to preserve rather than stamp out the culture. In planning his book, he received decisive help from Emilie Demant, a young Danish artist who had come to the north of Sweden to experience Sámi life firsthand. Turi and Demant met on the Kiruna-Narvik train line that was used to transport ore from Hjalmar Lundbohm's newly established mine at Kiruna to the Norwegian coast. It was Demant who obtained financial assistance from Lundbohm to publish Turi's book, along with the loan of a cabin on a mountain alongside Torneträsk, where Demant and Turi spent an autumn writing and discussing the material that eventually became *Muitalus.*[22] One of the last chapters in that work is entitled *Sápmelaš lávlluid birra* ("On Sámi Songs") and is meant to explain the nature and function of *joik* in Turi's North Sámi culture. Turi begins his account in this way:

> Sápmelaš lávluma dadjá juoigamin. Dat lea okta muitingoansta nuppiid olbmuid. Muhtumat muitet vášis ja muitet ráhkisvuođain, ja muhtumat muitet moraštemiin. Ja adnojit dat lávllut muhtun eatnamiin ja ealibiin—návddis ja bohccos—gottis. Dat lávllu málle lea ná—got dás vuollelis álgá.[23]

> Sámi singing is called *joiking.* It is a practice for recalling other people. Some are recalled with hate, and some with love, and some are recalled with sorrow. And sometimes such songs concern lands or animals: the wolf, and the reindeer, or wild reindeer. The following is an example of this sort of song.[24]

From here, Turi launches into a long and elaborate story which many later readers have regarded as a digression but which, I believe, is an elaborate and careful attempt to illustrate the meanings of *joik* in context. The account begins with one young woman (who we later learn is named Elle) urging another

22 Kuutma 2006:83–102.

23 Turi 2010:167.

24 Turi 2011:161

woman (Anne) to *joik* Niillas, a rich and handsome man in the vicinity whom everyone wants to marry. Writes Turi:

> Dál dadjá nubbi nieida nuppi niidii:
>
> —Juoiggas dan du irggát Niillasa.
>
> Niilas lea čáppat juohke nieidda mielas, ja juohke nieida háliidii oažžut alccesis boadnjin, ja dainna juige su olu. Ja dan lávllu namma lea *luohti*. Ja de dál alga juoigat Niillasa luođi:
>
> > Voja voja nana nana,
> > stuora hága, stuora geamppa,
> > stuora fávrru, stuora leambada,
> > voja voja nana nana,
> > go dat juo viekhalii,
> > de manai dego loddi,
> > voja voja nana nana.[25]
>
> One girl says to another girl:
>
> "*Joik* your boyfriend Niillas."
>
> All the girls find Niillas attractive, and they all want him as their husband, and so they *joik* him often. And this sort of song is called a *luohti*. And so the girl begins to *joik* her Niillas-*luohti*:
>
> > Voya voya nana nana
> > He is so vigorous, he is so splendid,
> > He is so handsome, he is so warm
> > When he ran away, he was like a bird in flight
> > Voya voya nana nana.[26]

As Turi explains, this is Elle's cunning way of surreptitiously testing how serious Anne's feelings are for Niillas, the man with whom Elle wishes to establish her own romantic relation. As Elle knows, and as the narrative shows us, *joik* gives voice to interior emotions and also puts them on display for others to observe.

The second occasion of *joik* performance in Turi's narrative is actually a case of *non*-performance. Anne challenges Elle in turn to *joik* the man that she thinks Elle is serious about, another wealthy (but less attractive and less intelligent)

25 Turi 2010:167.
26 Turi 2011:161.

man named Máhtte. Elle and Máhtte have already become engaged, but Elle is no longer enthusiastic about the match. When invited to *joik* her fiancé, Elle refuses, making the excuse: *Ii Máhtte fuola mus, sus leat buorebut go mon*[27] ("No, Máhtte isn't interested in me. He has someone better in mind"[28]). Such is emphatically not the case, but the statement allows Elle to avoid depicting herself as a hard-hearted woman spurning her fiancé's love. Turi's plot thickens, but it also calls attention to a crucial contextual reality of *joik*: such singing is not only potentially significant when performed but also when a singer refrains from doing so.

From here, the narrative turns to Niillas, who performs a *luohti* of his own in praise of Elle. Niillas does so when alone, however, knowing that Elle is already spoken for and thus not available as a potential wife. Interestingly, the *luohti* which Turi attributes to Niillas is very similar in form and wording to that performed by Anne:

> Voja voja nana nana,
> stuora leambada, stuora geamppa,
> ja stuora čeahpi,
> voja voja nana nana,
> stuora ja fávrru,
> dat leai suohkana buoremus nieida,
> voja voja nana nana.[29]

> Voya voya nana nana,
> She is so warm, she is so splendid,
> She has such skill,
> voya voya nana nana,
> She is so great and handsome,
> She's the best girl in the parish,
> voya voya nana nana.[30]

The repetition of lines and form may imply a certain stock vocabulary for songs of love or, alternatively, a rhetorical aim of accentuating the similarities between the use of such songs in general. The difference between two similar *luohti* texts lies not in their wording, perhaps, but in their contextual details, particularly the questions of who *joiks* whom and in what circumstances. Of course, it is a mystery how Turi knows the words of a *luohti* which was supposedly performed

27 Turi 2010:167.
28 Turi 2011:161.
29 Turi 2010:167.
30 Turi 2011:162.

while Niillas was alone. By implication, the *luohti* must have been performed again in later occasions, after Elle and Niillas had established themselves as a couple. At this point, the *luohti* would take on a different meaning, one of confirmation rather than of longing, as in this first narrated instance.

At this point, Elle takes matters into her own hands, *joiking* a message that expresses her interest in Niillas and pointedly suggesting that Niillas could steal her away from Máhtte if he cared to try. Characterizing Niillas at first as Anne's catch, she then describes Niillas as making Máhtte cry, an act which could only come about if Niillas were to steal Elle away:

> Anne fillestii suohkana buoremus bártni,
> Voja voja nana nana
> Suohkana buoremus bártni,
> Voja voja nana nana
> Go válddii nuppi bártni moarsi
> Voja voja nana nana
> Ja guđii Máhte čirodit[31]
>
> Anne bagged herself the best guy in the parish through trickery
> Voya voya nana nana
> The best guy in the parish
> Voya voya nana nana
> He took another guy's bride
> And made Máhtte cry.[32]

Niillas hears the *joik* and takes the hint, forming a romantic relation with Elle after all. Ever the artful storyteller, Turi lets us hear one more *joik* from the guileless and hoodwinked Máhtte before he discovers the truth, echoing in its warmth and wording the affectionate *joik* performances of Anne, Elle, and Niillas. In the end, however, Máhtte discovers the truth, allowing Turi to depict the performance of *joik* in anger:

> Ja go Máhtte gulai, ahte Niillas lea Ellii addán gihliid, de son juoiggai ja čierui:
>
> > Voja voja nana nana
> > Stuora behtolačča.

31 Turi 2010:168.
32 Turi 2011:162.

> Ja čierui ja morašii nu ahte goase jierbmi seahkana, ja suhtai Niillasii ja gottii bohccuid Niillasis. Ja go jugai gárremiidda, de juoiggai ja garrudii ná:
>
> Voja voja nana nana
> Biro, beargalat,
> Mon gottán visot Niillasa herggiid,
> Voja voja nana nana
> Sáhtána behtolaš Elle
> Mieska bittu
> Gal dat dakkárat leat olu,
> Voja voja nana nana.
>
> Ja de ain veahaš čirodii ja juoiggadii.[33]
>
> And when Máhtte heard that Niillas had given engagement gifts to Elle, he *joiked* and wept:
>
> Voya voya nana nana
> The great deceiver.
>
> He cried and was so sad that he nearly lost his mind. And he began to hate Niillas and killed some of his reindeer. And when he had gotten himself drunk, he *joiked* and cursed in this way:
>
> *Biro* demons, *beargalat* devils,
> I'll kill all Niillas's geldings,
> Voya voya nana nana
> And that damned deceiving Elle, rotten slut!
> There are many of her kind
> Voya voya nana nana.
>
> And then he cried some more and kept *joiking*.[34]

Depicting the intense emotion of a hate-filled *joik,* Turi also provides a clear example of the seamless alternation between speech and song that later song recordings of Sámi *joik* documented. *Joik* can serve as a vehicle for aggression, performed alongside physical acts like killing a rival's reindeer and in accompaniment with antisocial acts like excessive drinking. Turi is intent on showing

[33] Turi 2010:168.
[34] Turi 2011:163.

the genre in all its facets, not just in its most positive or productive ones, and his narrative helps illustrate and underscore this range of functions.

From here, however, the situation shifts, as Máhtte's sister Ingir convinces him to court another wealthy girl named Márjá instead. Máhtte does so, and a wedding feast is planned for the coming Easter. Turi depicts the details of the engagement, the journey of the wedding party to the church village, libations of alcohol dispensed to spirits of the land, wedding *joik*s performed by guests, and blessing *joik*s performed by family members. Illustrating the religious use of *joik* to entreat localized female spirits (*háldi*) for their continued benevolence, Turi writes:

> Ja dan báikkis láveje juoiggadit veaháš eatnama háldiid ná:
>
> Háldi spanu
> Čáppa nieiddaide lehkos giitu,
> Voja voja nana nana,
> Go ledje nu buorit,
> Ahte leat várjalan min girkovuojániid,
> Nu ahte eai leat fierran alla riiddiin,
> Voja voja voja voja
> Nana nana nana
> Giitu lehkos ráhkis háldeáhkuide,
> Voja nana nana
> Ja várjal ain,
> Voja voja nana nana
> Min bohccuid
> Voja voja nana nana nana.[35]
>
> And in this place they used to *joik* a little the *háldi* spirits of the land as follows:
>
> Thanks be
> to the slender beautiful *háldi* girls,
> Voya voya nana nana
> Who have been so kind,
> As to guard our church-going driving reindeer,
> So that they were not injured going down the steep slope,
> Voya voya voya voya
> nana nana nana

[35] Turi 2010:172–173.

Thanks be to the beloved *háldi* women
Voya nana nana
Continue to guard them,
Voya voya nana nana
Our reindeer
Voya voya nana nana nana.[36]

*Joiks* can be directed at beings on the supernatural plane who will understand and appreciate the communications. The *joik* above both acknowledges ongoing or recent supernatural protection and helps secure continued support for the singer and community in the future.

Turi also recounts the later wedding of Niillas and Elle, providing details of the customs associated with weddings in general and providing a stark contrast between the wedding of Máhtte and Márjá—full of blunders and a lack of knowledge of how things work—and that of Niillas and Elle, favorites of the district. In this account, *joik* is depicted as a means for local men to express their frustrations in not getting Elle for themselves and for others to confer praise and blessings on the new couple. As the wedding draws to a close, Turi depicts the celebration devolving into a cacophony of competing *joiks*, as each participant expresses personal views aloud: *Ja de dál juige ovtta jitnii nu ahte ii gullon ii mihkege*[37] ("And now they all *joiked* at the same time so that one couldn't hear a thing"[38]). *Joik* is public, but it is also private: a personal expression performed out loud for all to hear but felt within the heart. In a sense, all experience of *joik* is an overhearing of a private enunciation of values and opinions made audible through sung performance.

Turi goes on to describe the subsequent marriages of both Máhtte and Márjá and Niillas and Elle, telling of their ups and downs in married life and the ways in which other community members felt about them. After many turns of plot and character, Turi closes with the telling statement:

> Juoigamuš lea dakkár go lea rievttes čeahpes juoigi, de lea nu hávski gullat, goase čirrosat bohtet guldaleddjiide. Muhto go dakkár juoigit leat, guđet garrudit ja bániid gasket ja uhkidit goddit bohccuid ja vela isida nai, ja de dat leat ahkidat gullat.[39]
>
> *Joiking* is such that if it is really artful, it is very pleasant to listen to: tears nearly come to one's eyes while listening. But if it is that kind of

36 Turi 2011:168.
37 Turi 2010:179.
38 Turi 2011:174.
39 Turi 2010:183.

> *joiking* that includes swearing and gnashing of teeth and threats to kill reindeer or even their owners, then it is terrible to hear.[40]

After so many turns of the story, it would be easy to assume that Turi had lost track of his tale or his original purpose for writing it. Yet this statement—clearly a reference to Máhtte's *joiking* in anger at the beginning of the account—brings us back to the beginning of the story and sums up the varied uses and understandings of *joik* as a communicative act, always performed in context and with clear reference to the situation at hand.

It is interesting to wonder why Turi worked so hard to present *joik* as this sort of deeply context-dependent, elusive genre, the meaning of which had to be sought in community dynamics and personal viewpoint rather than in some externally apparent framework of form and meaning. Perhaps, in keeping with his book's overall agenda, Turi sought to remind his readers of the fact that the key to understanding Sámi people and Sámi culture lay in listening to the words of Sámi people themselves rather than in appraising their situation and way of life from the outside. Without inside information, the *joik* is nearly meaningless; when Sámi views are taken into account, however, the *joik*, like other aspects of Sámi culture, comes to make sense as meaningful, intentional, and of enduring value. Perhaps in placing this account of *joik* near the end of his book, and just before an account of the tragic events of the Kautokeino Uprising, Turi meant to suggest that listening to what the Sámi have to say about Sámi life can greatly enrich, or even alter altogether, the ways in which the broader public as well as government authorities regard Sámi livelihoods, society, and culture.

What we can learn as folklorists from both Sirma's accounts of courtship *joiking* and Turi's more extended depiction of the same sort of context more than two centuries later is that *joik* never occurs as an isolated, context-independent act. It is never separable from its context. Perhaps *joik* resists performative isolation because it is inherently a device to stave off isolation—it is a means of linking persons and things to one another, a means of contextualizing people and of commenting on the situations in which people find themselves, despite the vagaries of time and space or the strains of interpersonal relations. Although enacted almost always by a single person, it is not a solo performance but, rather, a collaborative one—created not only by the singer but also by the audience, the figures being *joiked*, and the particular context in terms of time and place. Both Olaus Sirma and Johan Turi understood this essential aspect of *joiking*, and they presented the tradition as integrally context-dependent in their accounts.

[40] Turi 2011:178.

It falls to those of us who describe ourselves as scholars of oral tradition today to consider how well we have listened to the words of Sirma and Turi. Do we accept *joik* and other highly context-dependent folkloric genres as necessarily embedded in communicative and social webs, or do we seek to isolate the songs and re-situate them as somehow "transcendent" works independent of their place and performance, much in the manner of the eighteenth- and nineteenth-century literati who first read and interpreted Sirma's songs? My question is not meant to be rhetorical: even if many folklorists would immediately say that they value contextualization as an integral part of their study and presentation of oral performances, it is nonetheless a reality that anthologies of folklore come out every year in formats that confine contextualization to headnotes or footnotes and that present songs as isolated verbal texts. Modern technologies of filming and sound recording seem to offer a greater incorporation of contextual detail by their very nature, but choices of editing, camera angle, and annotation can still be marshaled so as to present performances as discrete nuggets rather than as enmeshed moments. The filmmaker looks for "good quotes" to pull out of a longer recorded (and discarded) interview or edits a scene so that it presents a sharper notion of beginning, middle, and end. Pacing is altered by B-roll insertions or editorial reworking of the order or nature of the materials performed. The vast array of YouTube videos uploaded and watched every day by hundreds of thousands of viewers amply illustrate these tendencies: often their form, and perhaps also their appeal, lies in a kind of isolation, the sense that the video is a discrete work that contains within itself all the clues necessary for its proper interpretation and appreciation. The methodological, and ultimately aesthetic, question before us is whether we will use the frameworks of representation and analysis available to us in the twenty-first century—elaborate technology for the recording, preservation, presentation, and annotation of oral performances—to convey better the rich networks of association and emergent meaning that surround the performance of folklore, i.e. its blurry edges and provisional, evolving meanings. Or, failing that, will we fall back on itemizing and isolating tendencies of representation to reify and make static the songs we seek to understand? If we strive for representational schemes that maximize contextualization, then Sirma and Turi suggest valuable models for how to do so, even within the simple and seemingly confining technical parameters of the published text. It is perhaps in their complex narratives—as well as in the interjections that sometimes seem to crowd or interrupt a song performance in sound recordings—that the keys to the value and meaning of *joik* and to our understanding of our work as scholars of oral tradition may ultimately reside.

## Bibliography

Arnberg, M., I. Ruong, and H. Unsgaard. 1997. *Jojk*. Kristianstad. Orig. pub. Stockholm, 1969.

Bauman, R. 1975. "Verbal Art as Performance." *American Anthropologist*, New Series 77:290–311.

———. 1986. *Story, Performance, and Event: Contextual Studies of Oral Narrative*. Cambridge.

DuBois, T. A. 2006. *Lyric, Meaning, and Audience in the Oral Tradition of Northern Europe*. South Bend.

———. 2008. "Un chanteur devenu poète: Sirma Ovllá et le début de la littérature samie." In *L'Image du Sápmi*, ed. K. Andersson, 307–319. Örebro.

Gaski, H. 1999. "The Secretive Text: Yoik Lyrics in Literature and Tradition." *Nordlit* 5:3-27.

Graff, O. 1993. "Den samiske musikktradisjonen." In *Fanitullen: Innføring i norsk og samisk folkemusikk*, ed. B. Aksdal and S. Nyhus, 384–441. Oslo.

Hatfield, J. T. 1930. "Longfellow's 'Lapland Song'." *PMLA* 45:1188–1192.

Hymes, D. 1975. "Folklore's Nature and the Sun's Myth." *Journal of American Folklore* 88/350:345–369.

———. 2004. *"In Vain I Tried to Tell You": Essays in Native American Ethnopoetics*. Lincoln, NE. Orig. pub. Philadelphia, 1981.

Jones-Bamman, R. 1993. *"As Long as We Continue to Joik, We'll Remember Who We Are." Negotiating Identity and the Performance of Culture: The Saami Joik*. PhD. diss., University of Washington.

Kjellström, R., G. Ternhag, and H. Rydving. 1988. *Om jojk*. Hedemora.

Kuutma, K. 2006. *Collaborative Representations: Interpreting the Creation of a Sámi Ethnography and a Seto Epic*. Folklore Fellows Communications no. 289. Helsinki.

Rudy, J. T. 2002. "Toward an Assessment of Verbal Art as Performance: A Cross-Disciplinary Citation Study with Rhetorical Analysis." *Journal of American Folklore* 115/455:5–27.

Ruong, I. 1997. "Remembering, Feeling and Yoiking." In Arnberg, Ruong, and Unsgaard 1997:7–39.

Scheffer, J. 1674. *The History of Lapland*. Oxford. Orig. pub. 1673.

Skum, J. M. 2006. *Nilut Cup*. https://urort.p3.no/track/JohanMahtteSkum/nilut-cup.

Stoor, K. 2007. *Juoiganmuitalusat—Jojkberättelser: En studie av jojkens narrativa egenskaper*. Sami Studies 4. Umeå.

Turi, J. 2010. *Muitalus sámiid birra*. Ed. M. Svonni. Karasjok. Orig. pub. 1910.

———. 2011. *An Account of the Sámi*. Trans. T. A. DuBois. Chicago.

Wretö, T. 1984. *Folkvisans uptäckare: Receptionsstudier från Montaigne och Schefferus till Herder*. Upsaliensis Historia litterarum 14. Stockholm.

# 16

# The Poetics of Immanence in the American Mountain *Märchen*

Carl Lindahl

Most who pause to commemorate the history of *The Singer of Tales* will remember vividly how they first made its acquaintance. The publication of the present volume marks fifty-seven years since I was introduced to Albert Lord, from the distance of the back row of a Harvard lecture hall where he orchestrated the appearances of other great scholars—Theodore Andersson, David Bynum, Charles W. Dunn, Einar Haugen, Thorkild Jacobsen, B. J. Whiting, Evon Vogt—under the arc of a course titled "Oral and Early Literature," my single most career-shaping college experience. The others spoke about what they knew best—*Gísla saga*, *Enuma Elish*, the Middle English *King Horn*, Turkish and Norwegian folktales, the Ulster Cycle, the Tsimshian story of Asdiwal. All spoke from great expertise, and all spoke more dramatically than Lord. Lord spoke in an almost whispery voice that nonetheless commanded engagement. Even from the back of the hall, I clearly heard his every word on the *Odyssey*, on the South Slavic heroic *pjesme*, for which he assigned his translation of the songs from Novi Pazar[1] and, of course, on *The Singer of Tales.*

The man and the book shared the same soft-spoken boldness. More than five decades later, I still start at the calm audacity of the book's opening line: "This book is about Homer."[2] I marvel at how the text follows the South Slavic songs everywhere the singer goes, even when he is not singing. Lord's take on performance was both braver and more balanced than anything the yet unborn performance school of folkloristics would put forth.[3] Lord's phrase, "composition in performance"[4] was as powerfully compact as the opening sentence of *The*

1 Lord 1954.
2 Lord 2019:xxxix.
3 Kapchan 1995.
4 Lord 2019:5.

*Singer of Tales*, and the assertion that the traditional singer effected "the preservation of tradition by the constant re-creation of it"[5] upended my preconception of an impassable gulf between tradition and creativity. Within two decades of Lord's book, the performance school, in promoting itself, would make the dialectical overstatement—perhaps the necessary dialectical overstatement, but damaging nonetheless—of dismissing historical and comparative narrative studies to secure their emphasis on the moment of performance and, in the process, effectively erasing generations of painstaking and still important scholarship. Lord did no such thing. The singer and his song did not have to abandon their historical context to emerge from it. Indeed, how can something emerge from a thing that does not itself exist for the listener? How can we identify what is emergent if we do not truly know what it emerges from? Lord knew the absurdity of scholarship built on such a feint. What he did instead, I believe, was create an analogue, and the most nearly complete statement to its time, of what German narrative scholars were then calling *Märchenbiologie*: a thoroughly contextualized, holistic study of how the tale and the performance and the audience live with their shared art and lives.[6]

Among the many treasures of *The Singer of Tales*, the part that struck me most strongly at first reading was the second chapter, "Singers: Performance and Training," which introduces the performers both en masse and individually by describing, largely in their own words, how they live with a song. "It has to come to one," says Sulejman Makić: "One has to think ... how it goes, and then little by little it comes to him."[7] If the singer hears a new song, says Makić, he must live alone with it for a day before singing it in public, "so he won't leave anything out. It would be possible" for a singer to sing a new song immediately upon hearing it, "but one couldn't sing it like that all the way through right away."[8] A second singer, Šećo Kolić, would be alone when he tended sheep on the mountainside, and it was in that isolation, as much as in the village, that he lived with his song:

> When I was a shepherd boy, they used to come for an evening to my house, or sometimes we would go to someone else's for the evening,

5 Lord 2019:29.

6 *Märchenbiologie*, or *Biologie des Erzählguts* (best rendered in English as "biology of storytelling"), traces its roots as a term and concept to Olrik's "Biologie des Märchens" (Olrik 1909:3) but came of age with the work of Asadowskij (1926), Henssen (1939), Ortutay (1972b), and their contemporaries. Lüthi (1982:120) defines the purview of *Märchenbiologie* as "the personality of the ... narrator and the role of the folktale and the act of narration in the life of the individual and the community." The best summaries of the contributions of the *Märchenbiologen* are by Dégh (1977, 1995).

7 Lord 2019:27.

8 Lord 2019:27; Lord 1954:266.

> somewhere in the village. Then the singer would pick up the gusle, and I would listen to the song. The next day when I was with the flock, I would put the song together, word for word, without the gusle, but I would sing it from memory, word for word, just as the singer had sung it ... I didn't sing among men until I had perfected the song.[9]

In the singers' descriptions, the time lived alone with the songs often assumed an importance that equaled, or even outweighed, that of the time spent singing in public. Some of the greatest singers seemed to prefer a private rather than a public life with songs and, like Sulejman Fortić's mentor, "lived withdrawn from the rest."[10] When, in preparation for this essay, I re-read Lord's chapter on the singers for the first time in decades, it immediately struck me that their words had been the prime shapers of my personal path toward a folklorist's future, which has been to explore the private dimensions of public performance. What happens in the minds of listeners and narrators as a tale unfolds? What does the tale do to them, and how do they live with it when it is not being told?

The performances I've come to know best are folktales told in the eastern Kentucky mountains, particularly in one family, the Farmer-Muncy-Lewis family, with a relatively rich textual history, including more than eighty performances recorded between 1949 and 2010.[11] Tales told by living narrators are remembered in connection with earlier narrators—a human chain stretching back about 170 years to the childhoods of the great-grandparents of the women who dominate the family's art today. The Parry-Lord definitions of formula and formula system cannot apply without a pyrrhic struggle to the oral prose fiction of the Southern Appalachians. Yet Lord's performance biology helps us construct a "poetics of immanence" for mountain storytelling. Every telling embeds three types of "immanent art" (to use the phrase that John Foley [1991] has gracefully given us): the forestory, the telling itself, and the understory.

9 Lord 2019:21. By "word for word," the singers do not mean to say that they memorize the epic texts; Lord immediately steers readers away from such a conclusion by inserting a note in the text quoted here (Lord 2019:21, 305).

10 Parry 1954:225.

11 The performances include eleven tape-recorded by Leonard Roberts from Jane Muncy (1949, 1955); more than forty (some tales existing in as many as three versions) written by Jane's aunt, Nora Morgan Lewis (1955); eight audio recorded by Carl Lindahl from Jane's aunt, Glen Muncy Anderson (1997, 2003); twenty-two audio recorded by Lindahl from Jane (2000, 2001, 2003, 2008); and one digitally recorded by Lindahl from Glen's daughter, Peggy Cummins (2010). All of the recordings made by Roberts and written by Nora Morgan Lewis as well as most of those recorded by Lindahl are on deposit in the library of Berea College, Kentucky. Previously published versions include nine tales told by Jane in her childhood (Roberts 1955; Roberts 1969), ten told by the adult Jane (Lindahl 2001a and 2004), two told by Glen (Lindahl 2001a and 2004), and three written by Nora (Lindahl 2006 and 2010).

> The forestory is the flow of past souls and stories that precede and frame the telling. The performance is the present, audible, oral creation. The understory is the tale as visualized within the listener during ... performance and held in memory long afterwards. The performance is the rainbow arc above the horizon, but it is only part of a wide and largely hidden narrative circle, from which it emerges and into which it descends.[12]

The three stories converge invisibly during the performance, but the forestory and the understory live on from one telling to another *and* beyond the confines of the tale itself.

First, through the forestory, the Kentucky narrators live with the textual immanence of the numberless stories they have heard before, and those texts are bound together with the *contextual* immanence of the people who told them and the places in which they were told. For those listeners who do not themselves go on to gain recognition as storytellers, the context lingers longer in memory and plays at least as great a role in spurring performance as does the remembered text. Whether or not family members now remember much about a story that they once heard, all of them remember in extraordinary detail exactly who told it and where they were when they heard it. The teller and the site of the telling were inseparable from the tale. For Jane Muncy, the major living narrator, the story sprang from a context artfully controlled by the family's all-time master narrator, her grandmother, Sydney Farmer Muncy. It was 1942, Sydney was sixty-seven years old and Jane, the daughter of a marine off at war in the Pacific, was four. On the day Jane and I first met, she described to me in minute detail how her grandmother taught her to love the family tales, in the context of a family ritual enacted every night and beginning with an effort to discover where the war had taken Jane's father and uncle Gill:

> [O]ur life together alone took on a pattern of creativity [, with my grandmother] ... teaching me how to listen to stories, and ... how to read the censored letters that came from my father and my Uncle Gill. Uncle Gill was a straightforward kind of guy, who liked to drink a lot, and he would write on and on and on and ... say things that ... the war effort people didn't want him to disclose. So his letters would be one or two sentences, and then a whole lot of cut-outs, and one or two sentences, and a whole lot of cut-outs. It was very frustrating to us, as we were trying to figure out where he was, because he couldn't tell us. My dad, however, was more cunning, and he would say things ... like,

12 Lindahl 2010:257.

> "Mom, you know that [shell] necklace that I sent to Jane? Well, that necklace came from Uncle Sol's store. Remember Uncle Sol? You can remember him, where he lived out on that little place all by himself?" And she would go get the map ... and she would say, "Ah, okay, it means he's on the Solomon Islands, it's an island all by itself, and that's the Sol he's talking about, and they have shells." And so ... we had like a little war map and flags and his picture nearby. And he was my hero.
>
> And *she* was my comfort ... [T]he comforting thing we did at night was, we looked at the map one more time, we listened to the war news, we got into our nightgowns—I don't remember what *mine* looked like, but I remember hers was white and cotton and it had tiny bits of lace around the neck and around the sleeves. And then we wound up the clock ... we banked the fire, and we went to bed. But that wasn't the end of the day, because the end of the day usually involved her telling me at least a couple of stories that she had heard as a child—and then drifting off to sleep. I would always drift off to sleep with my ear at her back, because I liked to hear her heart beat.
>
> And then she would talk about *all* her ancestors: "and so-and-so had so-and-so and so-and-so and so-and-so, and then *they* had so-and-so and ..." Kind of like reading the chapter of the Bible called Kings, when you just heard who descended from whom and not much else about them.
>
> So we were bedtime buddies and bedtime storytellers, and I would [name] a *favorite* story I wanted to hear, and she would usually tell that, and then she would tell me the favorite story she wanted to tell me ...[13]

In the absence of Jane's parents, Sydney's ritual brought the entire family, living and dead, into the bedroom. Just before lights out, uncle Gill and father Mark were traced on the map; then the line of previous lives that had flowed over centuries into hers were chanted to her in the dark, giving way to a tale that was about all of those lives and somehow also about Jane. Here, all of the absences were bound together and made palpably present to the rhythm of a heartbeat, the primal wordless story we all hear first, pre-born. Grandmother Sydney created the greater audience—through words and gestures that summoned the generations into Jane's presence.

[13] Lindahl 2004:1.284–286.

In the fifty-eight years between Jane's first hearing her grandmother's tales and the account that she shared with me, the texts of Sydney's tales have never, in Jane's mind, separated themselves from the circumstances of their telling. But, in daily life, there are some verbal shards that break free from memory to create a sort of forestory chorus. Whether or not family members, thinking back, can reconstruct the story's plot, they remember floating phrases, especially phrases that name magical objects or supernatural beings, and these few words wander freely in the world beyond the tale, functioning as proverbial expressions to bestow names upon objects and people encountered in daily life. "Puddin-tuddin bag" was the name for a magic sack that a witch used to capture her victims in the tale of "Merrywise"—but it was used constantly by the extended family to name any outsize container: a purse, a basket, a shopping cart.[14] "Dirtybeard" was the name of a fairy tale villain who stole food from the hero Jack and his brothers. The name was applied to a long-bearded, itinerant moocher in the neighborhood, and that man in turn, along with his name, then became a central figure in a tall tale often told in the community.

As the example of Dirtybeard attests, the immanence of the forestory flowed both ways: phrases became means by which the story could live on in the outside world or through which the outside world could penetrate the story. Similarly, "Rawhead and Bloodybones," the widespread name of a bogeyman who hunted down misbehaving children at night, was imported into a family fairy tale to name a different kind of creature who made his eponymous folktale one of the most popular in the neighborhood. With such phrases, rendered as concrete nouns within the tale and applied as metaphors beyond it, the metonymy between the audience's world and the world of the tale persisted in the times between performances. In the course of a given day, a teller might utter the name of a figure from a story told last night or to be told tomorrow. The forestory was everywhere. Its immanence assured that the story itself was always on the verge of being realized.

The relationship between the daily world and the storyworld was constant, omnipresent, and deeply personal. It was also visual. Recalling performances long past, listeners would visualize not just the tales' contexts but, even more vividly, their characters and storyscapes. In 1997, Glen Muncy Anderson, the daughter of master narrator Sydney Farmer Muncy, recalled for me how, eighty-three years before, she had first experienced the context and telling of "Rawhead and Bloodybones":

14 Lindahl 2005:193.

> I was four; it was total dark and I'd be in bed in the corner, with my two brothers in other beds and my mother in the big bed, all in the same room. The boys would clamor and clamor to hear "Rawhead and Bloodybones"—and I'd think, "Oh, no, here we go again. Scare me to death." I'd be awake all night.[15]

> I had a pull-out bed ... and I would sleep on that for a while, and then I'd get so scared that ... [I'd] get up and crawl across the floor and get in bed with [my mother].[16]

> I'm all right now. But at the time I thought they were real. You know, children—things are real to them ... Do you see how that might scare a little four-year-old girl sleeping off in the corner by herself? I could picture just a bloody mass of bones, and it would scare me bad.[17]

In the tale, the Rawhead and Bloodybones creatures are, like the Grimms's Frau Holle, figures of justice who mete out rewards to the good and punishment to the bad. They may be terrifying in appearance, but they are predictably fair in deed.

The images evoked by Sydney's phrases formed the foundation of the understory, the untold tale engraved on the listeners' minds in pictorial form. Glen saw the Rawhead and Bloodybones, but she never described them. She simply lived alone with the visualized tale in an isolation parallel to that she had felt when lying in the darkened room apart from her mother. Glen did not tell this tale aloud or even to herself, yet she interacted with it intensely and made it her own. She even bestowed private names on the characters: the wicked stepsister who tried to ruin the heroine's life became "Susie" after a classmate that constantly bullied Glen. Glen grew up to become an accomplished narrator herself, but she found the images spawned by her mother's performances so unsettling that she avoided telling stories centered on such figures as Rawhead and Bloodybones. Jane, in contrast, savored the same stories, told by the same teller—and cherished the images that they instilled.

As the time for performance approaches, the forestory triggers the tale. Each performance is understood and greeted on the basis of its prior contexts. When Jane Muncy remembers the performances of her aunt Nora, she visualizes a scene vastly different from that in which her grandmother Sydney's stories emerged.

15 Lindahl 2001b:85.
16 Lindahl 2004:2.546.
17 Anderson 1997.

> At Aunt Nora's house the dark would fall and the fire would be there, and we would sit around in rocking chairs. The little kids would come in and out of the shadows and sometimes we would, at the end of the evening, end up in our ... parents' laps, and listening to the stories, particularly if there was a scary one. And the scary ones would come toward the end of the day when they wanted us to come out of the shadows and ... get into the cuddling down period ... And the fire would flicker, there was always looking in the fire.[18]

Details of the family's remembered forestories reveal how various narrators at various times laid the ground not merely for a performance but for a contrapuntal understory.

To open up the understory it is necessary to obscure the immediate surroundings and erase everything extraneous to the forestory. Cultivating the understory is an act of progressive, selective sensory deprivation. To open the mind's eye, it is crucial to curtail the listener's ability to see the world before her. The darkened bedroom, where Jane and Glen heard their earliest tales—and the fireside, where flames blinded them to their other surroundings: these were two sites that spurred a listener's power to visualize. As the visible world melts into darkness or fireglow, the teller speaks in slowly rhythmic, almost whispered tones.[19] Through this combination of darkness and rhythm, the listener begins to see the story, which she absorbs primarily not as a memorized plot, nor as a string of words, but through visual images. The less the light, the better the screen upon which to project the self-made images suggested by the teller but processed by the listener herself. This one-two combination of diminishing visual, and subtly emerging aural, stimuli bears a not irrelevant resemblance to the stereotypical hypnotist's technique of using a watch as a pendulum to deaden the eyes while intensifying the suggestive power of whispered words. Then the listener, now focused on the muted textures of the narrator's voice, is freed to project powerful, internally generated images against a backdrop of darkness.[20]

Jane's family's tales are so spare of visual detail that any semi-descriptive name or phrase will leave its listeners with a strong internal image. And it was

18 Lindahl 2004:1.326.

19 It seems to me that the venerable and widespread image of the blind bard, of which Homer is the greatest example, functions as a metaphor for the power of oral art to dissolve the visible world and create a sort of second sight through the suggestive imagery that emerges through the process of selective sensory deprivation.

20 This and the following two paragraphs closely follow the published descriptions in Lindahl 2009:217–219.

largely through the persistent visual effects of these self-created images that Jane and other family members recalled their stories. Grandmother Sydney

> would go into more detail with the story, and sometimes less detail, but *my* picture from my head—and I think in pictures very vividly—my pictures were filling in all the details that she didn't tell me.[21]

Two types of self-created images prevailed: the explicitly personal and the overtly otherworldly. Jane pictured protagonists that were essentially self-portraits and monsters so real she could touch them. Her favorite folktale character was a boy that her grandmother dubbed "Merrywise," a name that seems to have been made up by her grandmother expressly for Jane.[22] This is the picture that Jane created from the name:

> He was small, smaller than the other boys of course, maybe up to their shoulders. And he wore sort of a knickers kind of clothing, like little boys would wear. He had a little boy haircut that maybe came down over his ears. It was sort of round, and he had freckles. I had freckles too. [I started out ashamed of them. But my grandmother] always told me that *she* had freckles as a child. "And freckles ... made you beautiful." And so, when I pictured Merrywise, I pictured Merrywise as sandy blond hair and freckles—sort of like me. *Surprise. Surprise.*
>
> Lindahl 2001b:88

The second group of images that strongly struck Jane were the central symbols of the magic landscape, figures not seen anywhere in this world but powerfully present within her mind. One such figure was Rawhead and Bloodybones, whose tale Jane has heard and then told continuously for seventy years. This creature, aside from the female protagonist, was the only consistent character in the tale. Yet tellers rarely described him. By far the most elaborate description of Rawhead and Bloodybones to appear in any of the family performances is eleven-year-old Jane's fifteen-word characterization in the oldest surviving recording: "it looked like a skull. And it was bloody and it had bones on it."[23] The second-longest description is "funny-looking thing" applied by Jane at age sixty-two in her performance of 2000;[24] other recorded performances reveal

21 Lindahl 2009:213.

22 "Merrywise" seems to have been a name used only in stories told to Jane by her grandmother Sydney or by her youngest aunt, Hope. Tales with the same plots, when told by Jane's older aunts Nora and Glen, identified the lead character by the name of Jack instead of Merrywise.

23 Roberts 1955:56.

24 Lindahl 2001a:62.

nothing of how the creature looked. Yet the internal images created by listeners and re-seen by them every time they heard or told the tales, were indelible and dramatic. Thinking back, Glen recalled that she saw "a bloody mass of bones" when listening to others tell the tale, though she never used such dramatic imagery when she herself told it. Even when Rawhead and Bloodybones did not instill terror in the listener, they left a lasting visual impression. For Jane, the internal goodness of these creatures outweighed the horror of their faces:

> I didn't find the Rawhead and Bloodybones scary at all. I thought of them as benevolent, even though I could picture them ... as a skull, with bones underneath them like crosses, sort of like the kind you might see on a poison medicine bottle—with some bloody, gory stuff coming on them, but they were so good to ... the heroine that, that they had to be pretty good critters. And I think that ... that's true, no matter what it looks like, or how you describe it, if it's good on the inside, it's good. If it does good, it's good.[25]

In the forestory, the folktale phrases spoken in everyday life brought together the most magical and the most mundane; similarly, in the understory, the listeners' everyday human world (Glen's nemesis, Susie, or Jane's own, freckled face) inhabited the magic landscape.

The term "formula" is not inapt for describing three of the building blocks of the tale. Each of these three devices corresponds to one of the three arcs in the narrative cycle. First, the proverbial names and phrases of the forestory (like "Rawhead and Bloodybones") live in family discourse beyond the boundaries of the tale, available to invest future tales with referents and meanings derived from daily life.

The second type of formula is that body of brief memorized phrases pointedly repeated during performance to help structure the tale. These fixed phrases were often chanted or whispered in mantra-like fashion. As many as eight times in the story of "Rawhead and Bloodybones," the title creature commands characters, "Wash me and dry me and lay me down easy."[26] At least six times in every telling, the witch in "Merrywise" would chant, "I'll get up and whet my knife."[27] Eight times the ghostly child in "Flannel Mouth" calls out "cold in the snow, Mother."[28]

25 Lindahl 2001b:87.
26 Lindahl 2004:1.315–321.
27 Lindahl 2004:1.287–293.
28 Lewis 1955.

The third formula type inhabits the understory and therefore exists in a realm beyond words: this is the stock of striking visual images fashioned privately by each listener in response to the narrator. In the second chapter of *The Singer of Tales*, Lord describes how certain South Slavic epic singers lived alone with their poems, putting together the songs in their minds as they pursued isolated tasks like the herding of sheep. Lord did not extend his definition of formula from the oral to the visual plane, and the South Slavic singers who spoke to him offered only the vaguest hints that visual imaging may have constituted part of their creative process. Sulejman Makić, for instance, pronounces enigmatically that the song "has to come to one"; "One has to think ... how it goes, and then little by little it comes."[29] Yet the current work of Anna Bonifazi and David Elmer strongly suggests that epic singers are guided in their telling by what they "see" in their minds' eyes.[30] While the role of visualization in the composition of South Slavic epic is just now being explored, Jane Muncy and other master narrators from Appalachia have spoken at length on how visual images have influenced the ways in which they have remembered and retold their tales.[31]

In Appalachia, all three story realms—forestory, performance, understory—possess their characteristic formulas, which are demonstrably more influential in shaping the story than any memorized plot. In Farmer-Muncy-Lewis narrative tradition, the plots are significantly less stable than the formulas. I have listened to nine different recorded and live performances of "Rawhead and Bloodybones" as rendered by Jane and her aunts over a period of sixty-one years, and I have read three manuscript versions of the tale set down by Jane's aunt, Nora Morgan Lewis, in 1955.[32] The family treats the plot with remarkable fluidity. Some villains change names and identities; the heroine might have one or two stepsisters. The heroine's helpers could be, by turns, old men, old ladies, hungry dogs, horses, or inanimate objects. The heroine could end the tale living alone with her money or married to a prince. But the forestory proverbs, the shaping mantra that emerges in each performance—"Wash me and dry me and lay me down easy"—and the visual imagery implanted in each listener's understory are constant from telling to telling. These formulas merge the everyday

29 Lord 2019:27.

30 See Bonifazi and Elmer in this volume.

31 See, for example, Lindahl 2009:217–219.

32 The earliest of these performances is Jane Muncy's of 1949, later published by Roberts (1955:54–58); two of Jane's five later performances (recorded in 2000, 2001 [twice], 2003, and 2008) have been published (Lindahl 2001a:60–67, 2004:1.315–321); one of two by Jane's aunt Glen (recorded in 1997 and 2004) has also been published (Lindahl 2001a:57–60). Three unpublished versions were written by Jane's aunt Nora (Lewis 1955), and an unpublished version was recorded from Jane's cousin Peggy Anderson Cummins in 2010.

and the otherworldly so thoroughly that the presumably fictional storyworld fills each house where the tellings unfold.

The formulaic utterances that permeate everyday speech, and the privately cultivated images that those utterances conjure in each hearer's mind, create threads that tie fantasy to reality and serve as pathways along which the magic world and the daily world meet. The verbal and imagistic intersections of the everyday and the otherworldly are reflected in the tale plots as well. The immanence of the forestory and understory fosters porosity: in Kentucky mountain houses—small containers for larger families—the story, like the family, is omnipresent. The firelight and the darkness are everywhere within as surely as the shadows of the mountains are everywhere without. Through storytelling, the outer shadows and the spirits that they harbor are ushered inside. Reflecting this environment, the two most commonly narrated plot clusters in the Kentucky mountains feature porous houses, houses that however sturdily built and well locked, are eternally open to predators from another realm.[33] The contexts of most family performances, and the images created in response to most, have rubbed off on the *content* of the most popular tales.

The family repertoire contains no fewer than six similar, if distinctly different, plots based on the theme of the porous house.[34] The best known, "Grown-Toe," is also the most popular Appalachian tale. As Sadie Stidham, a storyteller and local historian who grew up a few miles from Jane's aunt Nora, once told me, "Every child in the mountains knows that story."[35] We recognize it as a variant of the "Golden Arm," featured in Mark Twain's essay, "How To Tell a Story."[36] The outline is very simple: Someone, often unknowingly, takes a body part from a corpse or a monster; the violated being comes to the house of the thief to retrieve the missing part; in most versions, the story ends as the creature tears the thief apart.[37]

33 The two most common plot clusters are related, respectively, to tale types ATU 366 and ATU 326 in *The Types of International Folktales* (Uther 2004); all of the six family tales described below belong to one cluster or the other.

34 The six plots include two subtypes of *The Man from the Gallows*, ATU 366 in Uther's *Types of International Folktales* (2004; see note 9), and four additional unique manuscript tales by Nora Morgan Lewis: "Flannel Mouth" (published in Lindahl 2010:268–269; motifs E234.3, *Return from dead to avenge death (murder)*; Q554, *Mysterious visitation as punishment*; Q211.4 *Murder of children punished* [Thompson 1955–1958]); "The Rich Woman" (Lewis 1955; published for the first time below; motifs N271, *Murder will out*; Q554; Q211.4), and two still unpublished tales: "It Came from the Loft" (Lewis 1955; motifs N271; Q211.4; Q554) and "Jack Sees the Headless Man" (ATU 326, *The Youth Who Wanted to Learn What Fear Is*, the second-most commonly collected Appalachian tale type).

35 Stidham 2004.

36 Twain 1897:13–15.

37 The tale type is ATU 366 (Uther 2004). "Grown-Toe" represents the most common mountain subtype; Nora Morgan Lewis's manuscript version (1955) is reproduced in part here. A less popular subtype is

In Nora's version, a poor family—father, mother, boy, and girl—makes a spare living digging potatoes: "They were the tater digginest people in the whole country around."[38] One day, the man finds a big toe among the potatoes. The family may be fed up with potatoes, for the father orders the wife to cook the toe for dinner. Late that night, a voice emanating from some unknown place in the house cries out for its big toe. The woman sends, by turns, the boy, the girl, and the husband to search for it; they cannot find it, so the woman goes herself and finally stares up the cabin chimney. In Nora's words,

> And there it sat.
>
> [The old woman] sure was scared by now, and she said, "Come on, old man, quick," but he could not hear one word she said, as he was covered up head and ears. Well, the old woman kept looking at it; she had never seen anything so mean looking.
>
> "What have you got that long nose for?"
>
> "To smell you up."
>
> "What have you got those big scaly ears for?"
>
> "To hear what you have to say about me."
>
> "What have you got those ... long black claws for?"
>
> "To tear you all to pieces as you did my grown toe."
>
> Saying that it jumped down the chimney and began scratching and biting the old woman. She called to the old man, "Help! Help!" but he could not hear her as he had fainted. She grabbed the broom and began to wallop it over the head, and punch it in the eyes. Finally, she knocked it out the door. When she dared to look out it was right smack dab in her garden hiding another toe. Some thought this thing was a varmint, some thought it was a booger, some thought it was a gruesome grudge, but the old woman knew it was a grown toe.[39]

---

represented by Jane Muncy's "Tailipoe" (two performances, dating from 1955 and 2001, published in Lindahl 2004:1.329–333). Four of the Farmer-Muncy-Lewis recordings represent a hybrid of the two subtypes: two told by Glen Anderson (in 1997 and 2004; the former published in Lindahl 2004:2.545–547) and two told by Glen's daughter Peggy Cummins in 2004 and 2010 in unpublished recordings.

38 Lewis 1955.

39 Lewis 1955. I have standardized the spellings of a number of words in this passage. Nora Morgan Lewis was a teacher by profession, but the tales that she commits to writing are filled with "oral-isms" that were not typically part of her written English: for example, "ever one" instead of

Although "Grown-Toe" contains its opportunities for terror—a terror instantly recalled by Nora's many childhood listeners decades after they last heard her performances—it is one of her few openly comic stories. Even so, it possesses special wrinkles reflecting the immanence of the performance situation. In the Farmer-Muncy-Lewis households, the women owned the magic. The stories were told almost exclusively by females, and grown men were typically missing from the audience. The forestory that Jane's grandmother shared with her invoked absent males, but those males lived largely in the imagination: they came home late, if they came home at all. In the understory as well, females tended to supplant males, as when Jane re-imaged the boy hero Merrywise as an androgynous creature who looked exactly like herself.

The female narrators have ways of marking the absence of their men. "Grown-Toe," like the family's other porous house tales, stresses themes of female responsibility and female power. Although the husband is the one who orders the toe to be cooked and eaten, it is the wife who faces up to the creature and runs it off. The husband becomes a figure of ridicule when his wife takes on the monster while he lies unconscious from fear. This telling bears the marks of a household in which the women did indeed run the families when the men were off at war. Nora Lewis's tale of "The Rich Woman" presents these same themes, but in a somber manner. Here, the woman seems to live utterly alone. She also kills alone, and then suffers alone as her home becomes her torture chamber. A woman forced into heading a household becomes a hero, but a woman who embraces her aloneness and her power can become at least as monstrous as the thing that stalks her. The Rich Woman is a brutal slaveowner thoroughly repellent both to Nora's mountain community and to twenty-first century readers:[40]

> Once there was a very rich woman. She owned a fine white house and a lot of Negro slaves, a fine carriage to ride in and a beautiful purple dress, and she had biscuits every morning. She just about had ever thing, but nothing pleased her at all.
>
> Spring came and she called all her Negro slaves to her. She gave one a task to do. "Now there will be no loafing this spring like there was

"everyone" and "sot" for "sat." I think it important to note that Sydney Farmer Muncy, her daughters Nora and Hope, and her granddaughter Jane all enjoyed and excelled in both oral and written artistic expression; as a rule, they cultivated written styles that varied substantially from their oral styles.

40 The storyscape of "The Rich Woman" represents the antithesis of Nora's world view. Her grandfather was an anti-slavery Union veteran whose descendants considered slave-owning equivalent to murder. They expected brutality from slaveowners and would look upon the Rich Woman's conversion as a miracle affirming the potential for goodness in all souls.

last spring." Every one hurried away to do as she said for she whipped Negroes right and left for no cause at all.

She called a small Negro girl who waited on her and did odd jobs in the kitchen. "What do you want, Missie?" the child said.

"I want you to make a lettuce bed; it must be done right or no telling what will happen to you." The girl picked up the mattock and began to dig. She dug and dug and smoothed the lettuce bed so good. It was a good lettuce bed. She called her mistress to come and see if the lettuce bed would do. She came and did not speak, just picked up the mattock and dug the slave in the head until she was dead, rolled her over in the shade, and called to a Negro boy to "come here and make that lettuce bed right." Well, the boy dug and dug and had the bed just right. Then he called to the mistress to come and see how she liked it. When she came she did not say one word, just picked up the mattock and dug the boy in the head until he was dead, rolled him over in the shade and called to a Negro man to "Come and do this lettuce bed right." Well he came and dug and dug until it seemed perfect, called his mistress to come and see how she liked it. When she came she killed him too.

An old Negro slave that had been with her for a long time came out and said, "Missie, I can make the lettuce bed just like I've always done." So the old Negro slave began to dig. She dug and dug, and sifted the dirt three times a pint at the time; when it was done she called her mistress to "come and see." The woman came and grabbed the mattock to kill the Negro slave. There! She had killed four of her slaves.

Soon the Negro woman's baby began to cry—she could not stand to hear it cry. It cried all night. The next morning she had the Negros buried. She told one of the Negro women to take the baby some place so she couldn't hear it cry.

"Now I'll try to sleep," she said. "I should not have killed them; they were mine though." She lay a long time then all at once something got real hot above her. She looked up at the loft; there was a hand white with heat. She got into another bed but the hand just followed her. It was hotter all the time! What could she do? Or where could she go to get away from it? Finally she told them to bring the Negro baby and put it beside her. While the baby was there she did not seem so hot, but she could not keep the baby with her always. When the baby was taken

> away for one minute the white-hot hand got very close to her, and she could not bear it. She sent for all the preachers to come and pray until it left. A crowd of preachers came and began to pray for the hand to be removed, but the hand stayed right there. Then they went to praying that she might be forgiven. All at once the hand left her, going through the roof, setting the house afire, and burning it to the ground.
>
> The woman raised the Negro baby and loved her very much.
>
> She went ever night to the graves of the four Negroes she had killed and prayed that she might be forgiven until she felt her soul was saved.
>
> From that time on until she died, she was known for her kindness to her slaves. When she died and her will was read she had left all her plantation and money to her slaves.[41]

"The Rich Woman," like all of the family's other porous house tales, climaxes in the same readily recognized, sparsely staged setting: the dwelling's darkened interior. The house—ideally, the family's ultimate bastion against the worst that nature, or human nature, may send against it—is suddenly rendered hopelessly vulnerable. Something uninvited, or unintentionally invited, has worked its way inside, and it will not be expelled unless or until the woman of the house controls it.

All six of the family's porous house tales stress isolation and interdependence. As the creature closes in, there is no hope for help from beyond the house. Only one person is responsible for the supernatural attack, but all will suffer if someone does not face down the demon. Both tales project a strong sense of social responsibility, even when the family or the group is divided: to mend the social fabric, one person, nearly always a woman, must shoulder responsibility for all. This is a fundamental understanding of life as shared by the mountain families I know best. The tales that impart this understanding are as porous as the houses they present. The house in which the tales are told, through its immanence, moves inside the tale—as the imagined house, normally hidden within each listener, expands to become immanently public and shared. The forestory, performance, and understory become one.

I did not plan that this essay take its present shape. Rather, it was created inadvertently by the same process it describes because I could not sit down to work on it without first literally seeing its forestory: the distant figure of Albert Lord, viewed from the back row of a lecture hall, humbly, quietly, audaciously—and immanently—explaining how Homer was composed in performance.

41 Lewis 1955. I have standardized some spellings and punctuation of Nora's text (see note 39 above).

## Bibliography

Anderson, G. Muncy. 1997. Unpublished interview. Rec. C. Lindahl. May 4, 1997. Danville, KY.

Asadowskij, M. 1926. *Eine sibirische Märchenerzählerin.* Folklore Fellows Communications 68. Helsinki.

Dégh, L. 1977. "Biologie des Erzählguts." In *Enzyklopädie des Märchens* 2:386–406. Göttingen.

———. 1995. "Biology of Storytelling." In *Narratives in Society: A Performer-Centered Study of Narration*, Folklore Fellows Communications 255, 47–61. Helsinki.

Foley, J. M. 1991. *Immanent Art: From Structure to Meaning in Traditional Oral Epic.* Bloomington.

Henssen, G. 1939. "Stand und Aufgaben der deutschen Erzählforschung." In *Volkskundliche Beiträge: Richard Wossidlo am 26 Januar 1939 zum Dank dargebracht von Freunden und Verehrern und dem Verlag*, ed. H. Teuchert, 133–137. Neumünster.

Kapchan, D. A. 1995. "Performance." *Journal of American Folklore* 108/430:479–508.

Lewis, N. M. 1955. Folktales. Forty-seven handwritten and typescript copies of forty-one different tales. About five of the tales are likely to be Ms. Lewis's original creations. The texts appear variously in unpaginated notebooks, loose-leaf manuscripts, and typescripts. All of the dated items (about one-third of the total) are assigned to 1955. Berea College Special Collections. SAA 96. Berea, KY.

Lindahl, C. 1997. "The Oral Aesthetic and the Bicameral Mind." In *Gilgamesh: A Reader*, ed. G. Maier, 328–336. Wauconda, IL.

———, ed. 2001a. *Perspectives on the Jack Tales and Other North American Märchen.* Special Publications of the Folklore Institute 6. Bloomington.

———. 2001b. "Sounding a Shy Tradition: Oral and Written Styles of American Mountain Märchen." In Lindahl 2001a:68–98.

———, ed. 2004. *American Folktales from the Collections of the Library of Congress.* 2 vols. Armonk, NY.

———. 2005. "Proverbs Ever After: Proverbial Links between the Märchen Diction and the Everyday Conversation of a Kentucky Mountain Family." In *Res Humanae: Proverbiorum et sententiarum ad honorem Wolfgangi Mieder*, ed. C. Földes, 187–196. Tübingen.

———. 2006. "The Uses of Terror: Appalachian Märchen-telling, Folklore Methodology, and Narrator's Truth." *Fabula* 47:264–276.

———. 2009. "Faces in the Fire: Images of Terror in Oral Märchen and in the Wake of September 11." *Western Folklore* 68:209–234.

———. 2010. “Leonard Roberts, The Farmer-Muncy-Lewis Family, and the Magic Circle of the Mountain Märchen.” *Journal of American Folklore* 123/489:251–275.

Lord, A. B., ed. 1954. *Serbocroatian Heroic Songs.* Vol. 1, *Novi Pazar: English Translations.* With musical transcriptions by B. Bartók and prefaces by J. H. Finley, Jr. and R. Jakobson. Cambridge, MA.

———. 2019. *The Singer of Tales.* 3rd ed. Ed. D. F. Elmer. Hellenic Studies 77. Publications of the Milman Parry Collection of Oral Literature 4. Washington, DC. Orig. pub. Cambridge, MA, 1960.

Lüthi, M. 1982. *The European Folktale: Form and Nature.* Trans. J. D. Niles. Philadelphia.

Olrik, A. 1909. “Epische Gesetze der Volksdichtung.” *Zeitschrift für deutsches Altertum und deutsche Literatur* 51:1-12.

Ortutay, G. 1972a. *Hungarian Folklore: Essays.* Trans. I. Butykai. Budapest.

———. 1972b. “Mihály Fedics Relates Tales.” In Ortutay 1972a:225–285.

Roberts, L. W., ed. 1955. *South from Hell-fer-Sartin: Kentucky Mountain Folk Tales.* Lexington.

———, ed. 1969. *Old Greasybeard: Tales from the Cumberland Gap.* Detroit.

Stidham, S. W. 2004. Unpublished interview. Rec. C. Lindahl, June 2, 2004. Berea College, Special Collections.

Thompson, S. 1955–1958. *Motif-Index of Folk-Literature: A Classification of Narrative Elements in Folktales, Ballads, Myths, Fables, Mediaeval Romances, Exempla, Fabliaux, Jest-Books, and Local Legends.* Revised ed. 6 volumes. Bloomington.

Twain, M. 1897. *How to Tell a Story and Other Essays.* New York.

Uther, H.-J., ed. 2004. *The Types of International Folktales: A Classification and Bibliography.* 3 vols. Folklore Fellows Communications 284–286. Helsinki.

# 17
# Indigenized Applications of the Oral-Formulaic Theory in China

GEJIN CHAO

THE ORAL-FORMULAIC THEORY, developed from the seminal theories of Milman Parry and Albert Lord, was first introduced in Chinese to mainland China in the 1990s.[1] Since then, it has not only wielded considerable influence on the contemporary development of China's folkloristics but has also led to a "paradigm shift" in its theories and methodologies. Epic studies enjoy particular privilege in China. Meanwhile, the Oral-Formulaic Theory itself has been "indigenized" in a country full of living oral creativities and cultural diversity. The present paper intends to draw a rough sketch of the relationship between the Oral-Formulaic Theory (hereafter referred to as "the Theory") and current trends in China's folkloristics under three headings: first, from epic studies toward oral poetics; second, from oral poetics toward a paradigm shift in folkloristics; and, finally, reflections on indigenized applications of the Parry-Lord legacies.[2]

## From Epic Studies toward Oral Poetics

Large-scale epic surveys were not initiated in China until the 1950s. They have since gone through ups and downs, but they have presented a general picture of epic traditions with diverse texts and dynamic diffusion in multi-ethnic China. Systematic studies on epics began to take shape in the 1980s and consequently brought about a batch of in-depth monographs and comprehensive resources

1 See Nagy 1996:19–20 for the necessity of distinguishing between "the oral theory" and the "theories" of Parry and Lord concerning the relationship between Homeric poetry and other oral poetries. The Oral-Formulaic Theory can be regarded as the most popular and significant approach applied by Chinese folklorists in the past twenty-five years. For a bibliography of Chinese applications of the Theory, see Qubumo Bamo's chapter in this volume.

2 The present chapter is somewhat related to one of my Chinese monographs (Chao 2008).

drawing on specific expertise. The book series, Epic Studies in China, written and edited by scholars of the Institute of Ethnic Literature (IEL), can be regarded as a guide to the approaches and achievements in this period.[3] To illustrate the contributions to the scholarship in epic studies since the 1980s, I would like to give some examples.

In conceptualizing and defining epic, Chinese scholars have responded to the diversity of epic traditions existing in China. Extending their classifications beyond the working assumptions and theoretical frame of Western scholars, they have divided epic songs into three types: creation epics, origination epics, and heroic epics.[4] With regard to the transmission of epics, scholars are no longer fettered by textual models taken from classical works or written epic; instead, they pay close attention to the oral transmission of living epics that are deeply rooted in folklife and traditional expressive culture. With respect to epic singers and storytellers, scholars attach great importance to observing training, inheritance, and apprenticeship within their socio-cultural contexts. For instance, Tibetan epic singers can be divided into at least five different types according to the way in which they learned and mastered their own epic performances.[5]

Epic studies in China underwent a "revolution," to some extent, from the late twentieth century to the early twenty-first century. In brief, the focal points of Chinese epic studies shifted toward interactive explorations along the following dimensions, each of which has a dual aspect I discuss below: (1) textual research and field study; (2) local tradition and intergenerational continuity; (3) collective transmission and individual creativity; (4) tradition-bearers and face-to-face audiences in oral textual communities; (5) the etic and the emic; and (6) "text-reading oriented" and "voice-listening oriented" approaches.

1. *The dual concern with textual research and field study* means replacing the literary frame of reference that was once dominant in folk literature studies in China. We can see a gradual shifting of attention from textual interpretations of epic texts in socio-historical and literary-critical perspectives to on-the-spot investigations of cultural factors in living oral epic as folk narrative tradition. By the same token, there has been a shift from explorations of the position of the epic genre in literary history to an emphasis on situated observations of

3 For example, see Rinchindorji 1994 (Mongolian epic Jangar); Vjam-dpal-rgya-mtsho 1999 (Tibetan epic Gesar); Y. Lang 1999 (Kirgiz epic Manas); Y. Liu 1999 (the Southern epics); Sechinbatu 1999 (the Jangar epic and Mongolian religious culture); Rinchindorji 2001 (Mongolian heroic epic cycles); as well as Zhumaturdu and Yisak 2002 (Jusup Mamay, a master of Manas). For a very pertinent evaluation of the series, see Zhong 2000:iv–x.

4 See Zhong and Bamo 2002. See further the overview with descriptions of living oral epics in Chao, Yin, and Bamo 2010 as well as thirteen case studies of both the northern and the southern epics in Chao and Bamo 2010.

5 See E. Yang 2007 and 2017.

epic performance in oral communication and on collective memories within a given community. It is fair to say that both Chinese folkloristics and the field of folk literature and art more generally have in recent years responded to the profound change that has occurred within epic studies, a change that has definitely produced a positive turn in collective reflections and debates on the interrelation between "text" and "field."[6]

2. With regard to *the dual emphasis on local tradition and intergenerational continuity*, Chinese scholars are giving more and more attention to the diffusion and transmission of traditional epic performance, tracking in successive studies the evolution of different epic traditions and the cultural practices that drive it. For instance, long-term field observation shows that *Hnewo*, or Nuosu epic performance, always takes place in conversational, dialogic discourse between hosts and guests in three ritualized contexts, each of which has a competitive aspect: wedding ceremonies, cremation rites, and rituals for sending the dead to their ancestral holy land. These performances, more so than other related traditions, are continuously changing in a process of "emergent shift." *Kenre*, or verbal dueling, stimulates the oral transmission of the epics and involves the active acceptance of the audience.[7]

3. *The double dimension of collective transmission and individual creativity* supplements and modifies an earlier axiom in the study of folk literature, according to which folk narrative was exclusively considered "collective" or "anonymous." Numerous field studies have shown that talented traditional singers and storytellers in contemporary China have made substantial contributions to the evolution of oral traditions with their distinctive styles and repertoires. Examples include Grags-pa and Bsam-grub (Tibetan); Jusup Mamay (Kirgiz); Pajai, Jimbajamsu, Javiin Juunai, and P. Arimpil (Mongolian); and Qomo Yynuo (Yi). Meanwhile, scholars continue to carry out fieldwork in local areas in order to experience folk life and to observe traditions at various scales, from individual epic singers to groups of singers, families, clans and communities.[8]

4. As for *the dual approach to tradition-bearers and face-to-face audiences in oral textual communities*, more and more scholars prioritize examining the epic performance as an overall structure understood as an integrated process of message-delivering and message-receiving. Audiences are thus no longer

6 For more information about relevant debates, see Y. Chen 2004, L. Yang 2006, and Shi 2010.

7 See Bamo 2003a. See also Bamo 2005, which explains and illustrates each of these narrative contexts at length and identifies their shared basis in dialogic discourse.

8 For fieldnotes and life histories based on field studies of tradition bearers and their communities, see for instance E. Yang 1995, G. Chen 2002, Zhumaturdu and Yisak 2002, Chao 2004a, Zhumaturdu 2006, E. Yang 2007, and Z. Huang 2009. In addition, Bamo's field study reports and articles on Yi epic singers and verbal dueling contribute relevant insights: see further discussion in Bamo 2003a and Bamo 2008.

considered passive "receivers" with ears. Instead, they are seen as active participants in the performative process and indispensable partners with whom the singers create a "meaning" that is generated and transmitted in the course of their interaction.[9]

5. Thanks to a unique fusion of horizons, Chinese epic scholars, who mostly come from ethnic minority groups, possess *a dual position that is both etic and emic* in dealing with their own epic traditions. This methodological combination is directly related to their own cultural consciousness and self-awareness. For instance, minority scholars have discovered more intricate types of epic texts by studying up close indigenous traditional cultures in their mother tongues. Besides texts belonging to common categories, others have been found and classified according to local folk taxonomies, for example: the *gter-ma* (excavated texts) in Tibetan epic tradition,[10] and, among the Nuosu Yi people, the *Hnewo Abu* (male epic text) and *Hnewo Amo* (female epic text), and the *Hnewo Anuo* (black epic narratives) and *Hnewo Aqu* (white epic narratives).[11] And thus a consensus has been built across generations of epic scholars, that an examination of a given oral tradition would not be an in-depth one unless it takes into account the perspectives of both "the insider" (from a local perspective) and "the outsider" (from the scholarly point of view).

6. Lastly, *the dual analytical method of muzhi (目治 or "text-reading oriented") and erzhi (耳治 or "voice-listening oriented")*, summarized by the late folklorist Jingwen Zhong,[12] does not simply stress that the "reading" of folk narratives, or textual analysis, should give way to listening to on-the-spot singing and storytelling. Nevertheless, efforts to set forth rules of oral poetics[13] have led scholars to realize that a large number of oral traditional phenomena require the formulation of further cultural interpretations in light of new critical methods, so that diverse oral traditions may be observed and appreciated fully.

## From Oral Poetics toward a Paradigm Shift in Folkloristics

As a modern discipline, Chinese folkloristics has traditionally included studies of folk literature and art, tracing its origin to the New Culture Movement (around the time of the May Fourth Movement of 1919, with the foundation of the

9 Zhumaturdu 2009.
10 Nor-bu-wang-dan 2001.
11 Bamo 2004a and 2004b.
12 I refer to Jingwen Zhong's remarks in his seminar at the School of Chinese Language and Literature, Beijing Normal University, 1998.
13 See Chao 2000b and 2002a.

Folksong Studies Society at Peking University in January 1918 as its "first sound"). But after a century in existence, it is in a new period of "transformation."[14] The contribution of epic studies to Chinese folkloristics provides, to some extent, a special opportunity for the development of folklore research itself. Within the framework of Chinese epic studies—as a traditional domain of folk literature and art in China—a theoretical path has gradually come to be well-defined, as indicated by the successive publication of numerous works devoted to living epic traditions largely based on case studies and carried out within the framework of the Theory, which has achieved a wider recognition and acceptance in terms of oral poetics.[15]

As the old Chinese saying goes, "When water flows, a channel is formed." The new findings of empirical research in ethnography and textual analysis within epic studies, especially among IEL oral tradition researchers who form a visible working team (hereafter referred to as "IELOTeam"), have brought about a "paradigm shift" in China's contemporary folkloristics. This paradigm shift includes a better understanding, derived from Western folklore research, of how to explore oral narrative traditions through fieldwork and ethnographic interpretation; a thorough acquaintance with the conceptual tools and theories applied to Chinese epics in Western epic studies; and an ongoing effort to balance the tension between literary critique focusing on written texts and doing fieldwork centering on collecting oral texts.[16]

Research results are beginning to reflect the shift as well, through a more detailed inquiry into issues surrounding "orality" and "literacy,"[17] a broader focus on specific epic traditions rather than individual epic texts, analysis of formulaic diction and oral poetics rather than structural or functional elements, and greater interest in the "meta-narrative" statements of performers/practitioners and communities as well as the field experiences of local researchers.

In addition, Chinese academics—who used to be, by and large, "consumers" of Western learning—have become "producers" of indigenized theories, introducing

[14] Since it is impossible to cover the entire history of the discipline within one paper, I will simply give a broad overview, making use of a telegraphic "economy" or "thrift" (to recall Milman Parry) of the recent decades around the turn of the century, focusing on the specific domain of research on oral traditions.

[15] To take a few examples illustrating the team-structure (IELOTeam) and the major work of scholars at IEL: Chao 2000a, Nor-bu-wang-dan 2001, Yin 2002 and 2003, Bamo 2003a, Sechinbatu 2006, Damrinjab 2006b, Z. Huang 2007, Li 2008, and Zhumaturdu 2009. Dawataya 2006 on Mongolian epics in Orait traditional culture and G. Chen 2003 on manggus stories and storytelling in east Inner Mongolia are closely related to the above-mentioned direction; Nachin 2004, on oral narrative and folk belief, and G. Wang 2010, on Gesar epic performance and singers among the Tuzus, are also influenced by the new trend of studies on epics and oral traditions.

[16] Chao and Liao 1999, Bender 2002, and Bamo 2003b.

[17] Z. Liu 2004.

theoretical concerns into their own practices. For example, Chinese folklorists have translated and transformed basic concepts of western Oral poetics, developing new terminologies and concepts for epic studies in China through folk taxonomies, oral glossaries, and traditional expressions of folk narrative traditions. They have also begun applying Western theories in localized studies.[18] The IELOTeam has also provided practical methodologies for field study, transcribing, documenting and digitizing traditional cultural expressions.[19]

Explorations into oral poetics in China, which have benefited enormously from the field study of epic traditions, have enabled the drawing of illuminating analogies with other oral genres and have in turn provided critical nourishment for the theoretical construction of contemporary Chinese folkloristics. Chinese research on oral traditions of every geographical region and chronological period has improved markedly in recent years. The diachronic approaches and comprehensive method that characterized Chinese folkloristics in the past are gradually being replaced by synchronic analysis and a holistic perspective, combining empirical research and theoretical reflection, as one American scholar has indicated:

> Though the bulk of published materials are "text-based" (sometimes with little or no description of the performance process and context), in recent years a small number of younger, well-positioned Chinese scholars have turned a critical eye to developments in folklore studies in Europe and the United States and have begun experimenting with a bundle of approaches that, if considered from a distance, might be called the "oral pragmatics" school of Western folklore/folk narrative studies. The body of theory constituting this syncretizing approach (which seems pragmatic both in the sense of descriptive methodology and ethnopoetic politics) wields a theoretical tool-kit that includes Parry-Lord oral-formulaic theory, a performance/contextual/ethnography of communication approach, Lauri Honko's ideas on the "folklore process" and the "process of textualization," reception aesthetics, John Miles Foley's ideas on "traditional referentiality" (and his syncretic approach), and research on the psychophysical implications of performance... It will be interesting to see where this oral pragmatics approach goes in China, given the large number of local

18 See Chao 2000a, 2000b, and 2000c; Yin 2003 and 2015; Bamo 2003a, 2003–2004, and 2004b.

19 For the IEL's manifold practices, especially the Threefold Solution refined by IELOTeam, see Bamo's essay in the present volume.

oral traditions still available for study, despite the increasing waves of modernization.[20]

The statistics in the China National Knowledge Infrastructure (CNKI), though incomplete, provide a rough picture of the frequency with which "the Theory" or the notion of "oral poetics" has been employed in Chinese folkloristics and its parallel disciplines between 1999 and 2010: 62 PhD dissertations, 75 MA theses, and 416 papers are recorded there. These statistics do not include compositions published in minority languages; there have been some dissertations and theses written in Mongolian, Uygur, Tibetan, and other minority languages. Nevertheless, these results permit multiple observations:

First, Chinese folklore research explores a broad spectrum of the genres and expressivity of oral or oral-connected traditions, which allows for a range of analytical approaches. In addition to a rich, multiethnic variety of epics, there are numerous local genres, including folk song, ballad, lyrics, chant, tale, legend, proverb, aphorism, riddle, storytelling, song fair, elegy, sacred song, traditional opera, localized drama, shadow puppetry, clapper talk, cross-talk, ritual, dance, music, *baojuan* or Precious Scrolls, *bianwen* or Buddhist Preachments, romance, vernacular novel, and classical novel (just to name a few).[21]

Second, studies of tradition-bearers and practitioners focus not only on contemporary epic singers and ancient narrators but also on individual storytellers, troupes or accompanists in groups, and even audiences.

Third, with regard to the sub-disciplines of folklore studies, the Theory and the notion of oral poetics have clearly found wide application in various interrelated fields, such as epic studies, mythology, and the studies of folktales, ballads, storytelling, traditional opera, folk belief, rites of passage, ceremonial festivals, etc.

Fourth, the ideas of Parry and Lord have been applied to numerous ethnic groups and communities, such as the Han, Mongolian, Tibetan, Monba, Kirgiz, Uygur, Kazak, Hezhen, Hui, Manchu, Bonan, Tu, Dongxiang, Yugur, Yi (including the Nuosu, Sani, and Luowu branches), Bai, Hani, Mulao, Zhuang, Dai, Miao, Yao

20 Bender 2003:236–237.

21 In order to specify local and traditional genres clearly, I give some examples in Chinese: 吴语叙事山歌、信阳民歌、黑衣壮民歌、莲花山花儿、洮岷花儿、伞头秧歌、祁太秧歌、小章跑竹马、鲁南五大调、苏州弹词、扬州平话、广州讲古、河北宝卷、河湟皮影、灵宝道情、拉魂腔、全州孝歌、壮族歌圩、白族歌会、萨满神歌、包公故事、蒙古族魔法故事、壮族吟诗、楚剧、吕剧、粤剧、评剧、孟戏、元杂剧、乐府与乐府史、佛曲、佛教广律套语、六朝唱导文、敦煌变文、唐代变文、汉代奏仪、蒙古族安代仪式、藏戏、门巴戏、鄂州牌子锣、巴东堂戏、朝阳社火、丧仪结构、台湾庙会演剧、土家族毛古斯舞、蒙古族箴言、苗族"萨滚"祭词、苗族古歌、兰州鼓子、关汉卿戏剧、东北二人转、徽州目连戏、扬州清曲、董永遇仙传说、唐五代白话小说、《聊斋志异》、古典小说。For more information, see CNKI at: https://www.cnki.net/.

(in the Hua, Bunu and Pan), and other minority peoples, covering dozens of languages and dialects.

Fifth, in the realm of higher education, graduate students at dozens of universities throughout China, especially those studying folkloristics, are keen to utilize the Theory and its methods in their MA theses and PhD dissertations.[22] Some examples of topics, taken from recent PhD dissertations at Beijing Normal University alone, include: story-pattern and narrative sequence in the textual analysis of folktale morphology (Kang 2003); folk beliefs and oral narrative (Yin 2003 and 2015); traditional/everyday performative practices of local genres (J. Wang 2004, X. Huang 2006, Nishimura 2011); folk narrative tradition and storytelling transmission (Zhu 2002, Lin 2007); running bamboo-horse as ceremonial performance (Zhang 2004); and singing traditions among ethnic groups (Lu 2005, Zheng 2009).

Finally, a far-reaching impact on related disciplines can be observed, including ethnomusicology, traditional opera studies, Chinese classics, ancient literary theory, ancient poetics, communication (e.g. oral transmission in the pre-Qin period), anthropology, history and oral history, cultural ecology, oriental studies, English teaching and bilingual education, translation studies, literacy studies (e.g. Jiangyong Nushu 江永女书 or "female scripts" in Jiangyong County), studies on ancient documents (e.g. *Hongfan*《洪范》, *Yizhoushu*《逸周书》, *The Analects of Confucius*《论语》, *Shangshu*《尚书》), the protection of the intellectual property of folk cultures, and the study of Western classics in China (for instance, studies on Plato's dialogues, Aristotle's *Poetics,* or Cedric Whitman's studies on Homeric poetry).[23]

Meanwhile, the proliferation of theoretical debates within the discipline indicates that a kind of open-ended discourse has taken shape in China, marking a milestone in the indigenization of the legacies of Parry and Lord. Heated disputes in discussions focusing on "field, text, and context" have in turn initiated critical reflections on the history of scholarship, intergenerational dialogue, and a veritable paradigm shift in Chinese folkloristics. For example: Gejin Chao and Lianshan Chen reflect upon "orality" and "textuality"; Wei Lyu and Jianzhong Wan propose a rethinking of the ontological characteristics of folk literature; Hubin Yin discusses ties between ancient classics and oral traditions; Aidong Shi criticizes "conceptualized thoughts and conceptualized education" in editing textbooks of folklore studies; Qubumo Bamo thinks critically about "the formatted approach to folk narrative traditions"; Mark Bender raises questions concerning trans-linguistic strategies; Ganglong

[22] For a statistical analysis of 133 theses and dissertations that applied the Theory from 2000 to 2017 in mainland China, see C. Guo 2018.

[23] Three influential works of this kind are M. Zhao 2005, Boteletu 2007, and Dawataya 2014.

Chen reinterprets local genres and folk storytellers; Deming An articulates the formulation of "folkloristics at home"; Lihui Yang questions "the sacred nature" of myths; Wei Lyu gives his analysis of inter-subjectivity and academic ethics; Bingzhong Gao, Xiaohui Hu, and Jinwen Chen define "folk" and "lore," situating these terms between different traditions of scholarship both in the West and in China; the debate between Aidong Shi and Jianxian Chen culminates in an intensive discussion of whether to "depart from the field and return to the text" or to "go into the field then resume textual analysis"; Bingzhong Gao, Tieliang Liu, and Mashiba Nishimura offer different propositions about "how to write folklore"; Gejin Chao, Qubumo Bamo, Wei Lyu, and Xiaohui Hu summarize keywords in folkloristics and terminologies for handling local knowledge; Bingzhong Gao, Wei Lyu, and Xiaohui Hu articulate the notions of "life-world" and "folklife" in their discussions; and, finally, many other scholars are engaged in resolving the tension between researching and safeguarding intangible cultural heritage.[24] This wide range of topics indicates that an unprecedented degree of interaction, reflection, and criticism is currently taking place in the circle of folklore research in China.

Additionally, the Forum of Folk Culture Studies (FFCS), an important online platform for Chinese folkloristics created by a group of young folklorists in 2002, has held a regular series of symposiums and has facilitated a channel for communication and discussion among teachers and students throughout the country and beyond. The Forum has contributed notably to the introduction of foreign theories and methods, including those associated with Parry and Lord, to Chinese folkloristics, in particular, by fostering an intergenerational dialogue among different viewpoints in the field.

The above-mentioned factors and dynamics have reinforced the trend of indigenizing the theories of Parry, Lord, and others, and the consequent paradigm shift in Chinese folkloristics. Here I would like to cite the pertinent remarks of two scholars whose summary evaluations, though different, are worth reproducing:

> Folk literature is classified as oral literature in traditional scholarship on folk literature and art, however, folk literature has never really been treated as oral literature; instead, oral literature has been turned into written texts at the outset, and then studied under the conceptual frame and scientific paradigm of written literature. That is why the long-standing practice putting much emphasis on the written

[24] In the interest of economy, though I omit a longer list of relevant references, I would like to mention a few works: Lyu 2001, G. Chen 2003, Dong 2003, Y. Chen 2004 and 2005, Hu 2004 and 2010, Bender 2005, Lyu and An 2006, Wan 2006, B. Gao 2010, and Shi 2010.

paradigm leads to the loss of independence of folk literature and art as a specific discipline. Although many folklorists devote themselves to field study and manage to get rid of the written-text-centered paradigm that used to be dominant in studies of folk literature and art, the disciplinary independence of folkloristics is still vague due to the trend for more and more scholars to follow the routes of anthropology and sociology at the price of giving up textual analysis and the quest for meanings.[25]

Ever since the mid-to-late 1990s, Chinese folklorists, who used to focus primarily on meta-folklore, have begun to study folklore in context. They not only pay attention to fieldwork but also place a great emphasis on the participatory observation of various aspects of on-the-spot fieldwork, such as folk life, the concrete situation of folk performance, interpersonal interactions in the whole process of performance, and the intricate connections with social life, relationships, cultural traditions occurring in performance, and so on. All of which demonstrates an ethnography-orientated holistic approach, enhanced by a series of key concepts, such as space and time, individual, society, performance, transition, everyday life, etc. It reveals that scholars who study folklore in context have developed common interests, sharing objects of research, methods, and academic orientations, and thus a "paradigm shift" in folklore research has begun to take shape.[26]

## Reflections and Prospects

To conclude, I would like to return to the topic of the indigenization of Western theories and methodologies in order to outline a new perspective in modeling international co-operation and partnerships in the development of oral traditions research in China. What I want to emphasize here is that the problem of methodology is actually a problem of epistemology as well. In the light of the sociology of knowledge, we have been reflecting soberly on the extent to which we—participating in both interdisciplinary dialogues and international scholarship—have been aware of different academic traditions, different cognitive systems, and methods for sharing knowledge, so as really to turn from "consumers" of foreign theories to "producers" of China's own theories.[27]

25 Z. Liu 2004.

26 X. Liu 2009.

27 Jinwen Zhong, one of the founders of modern Chinese folkloristics, once seriously staked a claim for making appropriate applications of foreign folklore theories. His argument serves as

Briefly, problems of theories and methodologies, including concepts and terminologies, not only invite us to rethink principles of "pursuing dialogues" in the production of knowledge but also challenge us to reflect on our roles, with multiple identities as creators, receivers, communicators, and participators in cultural transmission and academic exchanges.[28]

In sum, multiple domains connecting to oral tradition are priorities for the IEL: cultural diversity, identity, pluralism, and local knowledge of the different ethnic groups of China as well as other subjects that are basic elements for the sustainable development of Chinese ethnic and world cultures during a period of globalization. Ethnic minorities in China boast of an amazing richness of oral traditions. With diverse languages, age-old chains of transmission, typological diversity, and wide geographic diffusion, most of these forms of living verbal art have been handed down for centuries, allowing us to carry out close-up studies within specific cultural contexts, to explore the countless facets of expressive forms among different cultures, and to appreciate the fascinating matrix of human creativity. Given that many of the issues arising from the cultural diversity of multi-ethnic China parallel those in other countries, living oral traditions, for example, should be especially relevant to international scholars of verbal art, as indicated by the following comments of the late John M. Foley:

> This is precisely the place where colleagues in China, with its great richness of living oral traditions among minority populations, can assume leadership. Chinese colleagues are in a position to do what no one else in the world can do: to experience, record, and study oral traditions of remarkable diversity on an unmatched scale. If in the coming years the Oral Theory can be tested across the enormous variety of traditions found in multi-ethnic China, the scholarly world will benefit significantly.[29]

These encouraging remarks suggest that recent trends in China may point to possibilities for building a Chinese School in oral traditions research. We would like to try our best to do so.

---

a warning that China should not merely become a testing-ground for Western assumptions but should strive to be a source of innovative thinking in the creation of theories and methodologies with Chinese characteristics; see further Zhong 1998 and 2000.

28 For further discussion of challenges in the comparative study of oral epic, see Chao and Foley 2003.

29 See Foley 2000:10–11. This Chinese edition of Foley's *The Theory of Oral Composition: History and Methodology* (1988) includes a new preface by the author, a translator's foreword, and extra notes.

Finally, I would like to conclude by citing one of my favorite Chinese aphorisms: "海纳百川，有容乃大" (The ocean is vast because it is fed by hundreds of rivers). The proverb means that one should be as inclusive as the vast ocean, which admits hundreds of rivers and should draw on the strengths of others. The conference and this volume on the legacies of Milman Parry and Albert Lord have come at a welcome time since they have permitted us to take a step back and to observe our position and our handling of the crucial issues concerning the past, the present, and the future of oral traditions research as an interdisciplinary endeavor. I am sure that the legacies of Parry and Lord will not only continue to benefit scholars across the humanities but all of us, today and in the future.[30]

[30] See Chao 2013, 2016, and 2018; Feng 2016 and 2019; for a discussion on the latest developments in scholarship on oral epic traditions over the past seventy years in China, see Bamo 2019.

# Bibliography

Bamo, Q. 巴莫曲布嫫. 2003a. *Shishi Chuantong de Tianye Yanjiu: Yi Nuosu Yizu Shishi Lewo wei Ge'an* 《史诗传统的田野研究：以诺苏彝族史诗"勒俄"为个案》 [A field study of epic tradition: Nuosu epic Hnewo as a case study]. PhD diss., Beijing Normal University.

———. 2003b. "Koutou Chuantong/Shuxie Wenhua/Dianzichuanmei: Jiantan Wenhua Duoyangxing Taolun zhong de Minsuxue Shijie"口头传统・书写文化・电子传媒—兼谈文化多样性讨论中的民俗学视界 [Oral tradition, literacy, and electronic media: The fusion of horizons in folkloristic studies and discussion about cultural diversity]. *Minsu Xuekan* [Journal of folklore research] 5:40–56.

———. 2003–2004. "'Minjian Xushi Chuantong Geshihua' zhi Piping: Yi Yizu Shishi Lewo Teyi de 'Wenben Yilu' Weili" '民间叙事传统格式化'之批评—以彝族史诗《勒俄特依》的'文本迻录'为例[上、中、下] [A critique of the "formatted approach to traditional oral narratives": The case of the problematic textualization of the Yi epic Hnewo Teyy; a monograph serialized as parts I, II, and III]. *Minzu Yishu* [Ethnic art] 2003(4):39–45; 2004(1):18–26; and 2004(2):32–40.

———. 2004a. "Xushi Yujing yu Yanshu Changyu: Yi Nuosu Yizu de Koutou Lunbian he Shishi Chuantong Weili" 叙事语境与演述场域—以诺苏彝族的口头论辩和史诗传统为例 [Narrative context and performative field: Nuosu verbal dueling and epic tradition as a case study]. *Wenxue Pinglun* [Literary reviews] 1:147–155.

———. 2004b. "Xushi Xinggou/Wenben Jiexian/Xushi Jieyu: Chuantong Zhishexing de Faxian" 叙事型构・文本界限・叙事界域：传统指涉性的发现 [Narrative configuration/textual boundary/narrative distinction: Discovering traditional referentiality]. *Minsu Yanjiu* [Folklore studies] 3:112–132.

———. 2005. "Kezhi yu Lewo: Koutou Lunbian zhong de Shishi Yanshu" 克智与勒俄：口头论辩中的史诗演述[上、中、下] [Kenre and Hnewo: Epic performance in verbal dueling, A monograph serialized as parts I, II, and III]. *Minjian Wenhua Luntan* [Folk culture forum] 1:20–25; 2:15–22; and 3:21–28.

———. 2008. "Zai Koutou Chuantong yu Shuxie Wenhua Zhijian de Shishi Yanshuren: Jiyu Ge'an Yanjiu de Minzuzhi Xiezuo" 在口头传统与书写文化之间的史诗演述人—基于个案研究的民族志写作 [Epic performers between orality and literacy: A case study on ethnographic writings] *Journal of Beijing Normal University (Social Sciences Edition)* 1:74–84.

———. 2019. "Yi Koutou Chuantong Zuowei Fangfa: Zhongguo Shishixue Qishinian" 以口头传统作为方法：中国史诗学七十年及其实践进路 [Oral tradition as methodology: Epic studies and practical approaches over the past seventy years in China]. *Minzu Yishu* [Ethnic art], 6:29–37.

Bamo, Q., and M. Liao 廖明君. 2004. "Tianye Yanjiu de Wuge Zaichang" 田野研究的"五个在场—巴莫曲布嫫访谈录 [Five basic factors in co-presence for field study: An interview]. *Minzu Yishu* [Ethnic arts] 3:14-27, 100.

Bender, M. 2001. Review of Chao 2000a. *Asian Folklore Studies* 60:360–362.

———. 2002. "Zenyang Kan Meige: 'Yi Chuantong wei Daoxiang' de Chuxiong Yizu Wenxue Wenben" 怎样看《梅葛》：'以传统为取向'的楚雄彝族文学文本 [How to read Miggu: Tradition-oriented texts in Chuxiong Yi's literature]. Trans. W. Fu. *Minsu Yanjiu* [Folklore studies] 4:34–41.

———. 2003. "Oral Narrative Studies in China." *Oral Tradition* 18:236–238.

———. 2005. "Luelun Zhongguo Shaoshu Minzu Koutou Wenxue de Fanyi" 略论中国少数民族口头文学的翻译 [Some thoughts on translating Chinese ethnic oral literature]. Trans. S. Wu, rev. Q. Bamo. *Minzu Wenxue Yanjiu* [Studies of ethnic literature] 2:141–144.

Boteletu 博特勒图. 2007. *Hu'erqi: Ke'erqin Difang Chuantong zhong de Shuochang Yiren jiqi Yinyue* 《胡尔奇：科尔沁地方传统中的说唱艺人及其音乐》 [Huurchi: The storytellers and their music in the local Horchin tradition]. PhD diss., Chinese National Academy of Arts, 2005. Beijing.

Chao, G. 朝戈金. 2000a. *Kouchuan Shishi Shixue: Ranpile Jiangge'er Chengshi Jufa Yanjiu* 《口传史诗诗学：冉皮勒〈江格尔〉程式句法研究》 [Oral poetics of oral epic: Formulaic diction of Arimpil's Jangar singing]. PhD diss., Beijing Normal University. Nanning.

———. 2000b. "Kouchuan Shishi Shixue de Jige Jiben Gainian" 口传史诗诗学的几个基本概念 [Some basic concepts in poetics of oral epic]. *Minzu Yishu* [Ethnic art] 4:71–79.

———. 2000c. "Kouchuan Shishi Wenben de Leixing: Yi Menggu Shishi Weili" 口传史诗文本的类型—以蒙古史诗为例 [On types of oral epic texts: Mongolian epic as a case study]. *Minzu Wenxue Yanjiu* [Studies of ethnic literature] 4:58–62.

———, ed. 2001. *Chinese Oral Traditions*, special issue, *Oral Tradition* 16. https://journal.oraltradition.org/issues/16ii/volume-16-issue-2-chinese-oral-traditions/.

———. 2002a. "Guanyu Koutou Chuanchang Shige de Yanjiu: Koutou Shixue Wenti" 关于口头传唱诗歌的研究：口头诗学问题 [Studies on verbally-transmitted song-poems: Issues in oral poetics]. *Wenyi Yanjiu* [Studies of literature and art] 4:99–101.

———. 2002b. "Trich Dich Mot So Thuat Ngu Lien Quan Den Su Thi Trong Cuon Sach Cua" [An excerpted translation from Gejin Chao's *Glossaries and terminologies for epic studies*]. Trans. Nguyen Thuy Loan. *Thong Bao Van Hoa Dan Gian 2002* [Annual of folk culture 2002]: 701–706. Hanoi.

———. 2003. "Minsuxue Shijiao xia de Koutou Chuantong" 民俗学视角下的口头传统 [Oral tradition in the folklore studies perspective]. *Guangxi Minzu Xueyuan Xuebao* [Journal of Guangxi Minzu College] 3:10–11, 18.

———. 2004a. *Qiannian Juechang Yingxiongge: Weilate Menggu Shishi Chuantong Tianye Sanji* 《千年绝唱英雄歌—卫拉特蒙古史诗传统田野散记》 [The heroic songs of the past: Fieldnotes on the Oirat Mongolian epic tradition]. Nanning.

———. 2004b. "Mongolian Epic Identity: Formulaic Approach to Janggar Epic Singing." In *Reflections on Asian-European Epics*, ed. G.-S. Yousof, 149–162. Kuala Lumpur.

———. 2008. "Cong Hema dao Ranpile: Fansi Guoji Shishi Xueshu de Fanshi Zhuanhuan" 从荷马到冉皮勒：反思国际史诗学术的范式转换 [From Homer to Arimpil: Reflections on the paradigm shift in international epic studies]. *Zhongguo Shehui Kexueyuan Wenxue Yanjiusuo Xuekan* [Annals of the Institute of Literature, Chinese Academy of Social Sciences]:1–39.

———, ed. 2013. *Zhongguo Shishixue Duben* 《中国史诗学读本》 [A reader of epic studies in China]. Beijing.

———. 2016. *Shishixue Lunji* 《史诗学论集》 [Oral epic traditions in China and beyond]. Beijing.

———. 2018. "Koutou Shixue" 口头诗学 [Oral poetics]. *Minjian Wenhua Luntan* [Folk culture forum] 6:120–125.

Chao, G., and Q. Bamo, eds. 2010. *Guoji Bowuguan: Zhongguo Koutou Shishi Chuantong Zhuanhao*《〈国际博物馆〉：中国口头史诗传统专号》 [Living epic traditions in China]. *Museum International* (Chinese edition) 62/245.

Chao, G., and J. M Foley. 2003. "Koutou Shixue Wuti: Sida Chuantong de Bijiao Yanjiu" 口头诗学五题：四大传统的比较研究 [Five topics in oral poetics: Challenges in comparative oral epic]. *Dongfang Wenxue Yanjiu Jikan di yi ji* [Bulletin of Oriental literature] 1:33–97.

Chao, G., and M. Liao. 1999. "Kouchuan Shishi de Wudu: Chao Gejin Fangtan Lu" 口传史诗的误读：朝戈金访谈录 [On the misreading of oral epic: An interview with Chao Gejin]. *Minzu Yishu* [Ethnic art] 1:8–18.

Chao, G., H. Yin 尹虎彬, and Q. Bamo. 2010. "Zhongguo Shishi Chuantong: Wenhua Duoyangxing yu Minzu Jingshen de 'Bowuguan'" 中国史诗传统：文化多样性与民族精神的'博物馆 [Living oral epic traditions in China: Celebrating cultural diversity and ethos]. In Chao and Bamo 2010:5–27.

Chen, G. 陈岗龙. 2002. *Pajie Yanjiu* 《琶杰研究（蒙古文）》 [A study of Mongolian epic singer Pajai, in Mongolian]. Hohhot.

———. 2003. *Manggusi Gushi Lun* 《蟒古思故事论》 [A treatise of manggus stories]. Beijing.

Chen, Y. 陈泳超, ed. 2004. *Zhongguo Minjian Wenhua de Xueshushi Guanzhao* 《中国民间文化的学术史观照：民间文化青年论坛第一届会议论文集》 [A contemplation of the history of scholarship in Chinese folk cultures: Proceedings of the first symposium organized by forum of folk culture studies]. Harbin.

———. 2005. *Zhongguo Minjian Wenxue Yanjiu de Xiandai Guizhe* 《中国民间文学研究的现代轨辙》 [Tracing the history of scholarship in folk literature in modern China]. Beijing.

Damrinjab 旦布尔加甫, trans. and ed. 2002. *Ka'ermeike Jiangge'er Jiaozhuben* 《卡尔梅克〈江格尔〉校注本》 [An annotated edition of Kalmyk Jangar]. Beijing.

———, trans. and ed. 2006a. *Hanharangui: Weilate Yingxiong Shishi Wenben ji Jiaozhu* 《汗哈冉贵—卫拉特英雄史诗文本及校注》 [Haan Harangui: Texts and annotations of heroic epics in Oirat]. Beijing.

———, trans. and ed. 2006b. *Weilate Yingxiong Gushi Yanjiu* 《卫拉特英雄故事研究》 [A study of heroic storytelling in Oirat]. Beijing.

Dawataya 塔亚. 2006. *Weilate Mengguzu Wenhua Yanjiu* 《卫拉特蒙古族文化研究》 [Studies of Oirat Mongolian culture]. Hohhot.

———. 2014. *Jiangge'er Shuochang Yiren Yanjiu* 《江格尔说唱艺人研究》 [A study of Jangarchi]. Hohhot.

Dong, X. 董晓萍. 2003. *Tianye Minsuzhi* 《田野民俗志》 [Folklore fieldwork]. Beijing.

Feng, W. 冯文开. 2016. *Zhongguo Shishixue Shilun* 《中国史诗学史论（1840–2010）》 [On the history of the scholarship in epic studies in China, 1840–2010]. Beijing.

———. 2019. *Zhongguo Shaoshu Minzu Shishi Yanjiu de Fansi yu Jiangou* 《中国少数民族史诗研究的反思与建构》 [Reflection and construction: Ethnic minority epic studies in China]. Beijing.

Foley, J. M. 1988. *The Theory of Oral Composition: History and Methodology*. Bloomington.

———. 2000. *Koutou Shixue: Pali-Luode Lilun*《口头诗学：帕里－洛德理论》. Trans. G. Chao from Foley 1988. Beijing.

Gao, B. 高丙中. 2010. *Zhongguoren de Shenghuo Shijie: Minsuxue de Lujing* 《中国人的生活世界：民俗学的路径》 [Chinese life-world: Approaches of folkloristics]. Beijing.

Guo, C. 郭翠潇. 2018. "Koutou Chengshi Lilun zai Zhongguo Yanjiusheng Xuewei Jiaoyu Lingyu de Yingyong (2000–2017): Jiyu 133pian Shuoshi he Boshi Xuewei Lunwen de Jiliang Fenxi" 口头程式理论在中国研究生学位教育领域的应用. (2000–2017) —基于133篇硕士、博士学位论文的计量分析 [The application of oral formulaic theory in the field of graduate degree education in China, 2000–2017: Based on the statistical analysis of 133 theses and dissertations]. *Minzu Wenxue Yanjiu* [Studies of ethnic literature]: 119–125.

Hu, X. 户晓辉. 2004. *Xiandaixing yu Minjian Wenxue* 《现代性与民间文学》 [Modernity and folk literature]. Beijing.

———. 2010. *Fanhui 'Ai yu Ziyou de Shenghuo Shijie: Chuncui Minjian Wenxue Guanjianci de Zhexue Chanshi* 《返回爱与自由的生活世界：纯粹民间文学关键词的哲学阐释》 [Returning to the life-world of love and freedom: A purely philosophical interpretation of keywords in folk literature]. Nanjing.

Huang, X. 黄旭涛. 2006. *Qitai Yangge Biaoyan Chuantong de Tianye Kaocha* 《祁太秧歌表演传统的田野考察》 [A field study on qitai yange and its traditional performance]. PhD diss., Beijing Normal University.

Huang, Z. 黄中祥. 2007. *Hasake Yingxiong Shishi yu Caoyuan Wenhua* 《哈萨克英雄史诗与草原文化》 [Kazak heroic epics and grasslands culture]. Beijing.

———. 2009. *Chuancheng Fangshi yu Yanchang Chuantong: Hasakezu Minjian Yanchang Yiren Diaocha Yanjiu* 《传承方式与演唱传统：哈萨克族民间演唱艺人调查研究》 [Mode of transmission and singing tradition: An investigation of Kazak folk singers]. Beijing.

IELOTeam. 2006. "Gouzhu Zhongguo Shaoshu Minzu Wenhua Yichan de Shengmingxian" 构筑中国少数民族文化遗产的生命线 [Constructing a lifeline for cultural heritage of Chinese ethnic minority groups, IEL scholars' conversations in writing]. *Zhongguo Minzu Bao* [China ethnic news], April 11, 2006.

Jin, D. 今旦, and X. Ma 马学良, trans. and eds. 1984. *Miaozu Shishi* 《苗族史诗》 [Epics of the Miao people]. Beijing.

———. 2006. *Butterfly Mother: Miao (Hmong) Creation Epics from Guizhou, China*. Trans. M. Bender from Jin and Ma 1984. Indianapolis.

Kang, L. 康丽. 2003. *Zhongguo Qiaonyu Gushi Xushi Xingtai Yanjiu* 《中国巧女故事叙事形态研究》 [A study of narrative morphology of Qiaonyu folktales]. PhD diss., Beijing Normal University.

Lang, Y. 郎樱. 1999. *Manasi Lun* 《玛纳斯论》 [A treatise of Kirgiz epic Manas]. Hohhot.

Lang, Y., Tse-wang-Gyur-me 次旺俊美, and E. Yang 杨恩洪, eds. 2001. *Gesa'er Yiren Sang Zhu Shuochang Ben* 《格萨尔艺人桑珠说唱本》[The transcribed collection from Tibetan epic master singer Bsam-grub's oral performances]. Lhasa.

Li, L. 李连荣. 2008. *Zangzu Shishi Gesa'er Xueshushi* 《藏族史诗〈格萨尔〉学术史》 [The history of scholarship in studies on the Tibetan Gesar epic]. PhD diss., the Graduate School of the Chinese Academy of Social Sciences, 2000.

Lin, J. 林继富. 2007. *Minjian Xushi Chuantong yu Gushi Chuancheng: Yi Hubei Changyang Duzhenwan Tujiazu Gushi Chuanchengren Weili* 《民间叙事传统与故事传承—以湖北长阳都镇湾土家族故事传承人为例》 [Folk narrative tradition and storytelling transmission: A case study on tradition bearers of the Tujia ethnic group in Duzhenwan township in Changyang of Hubei Province], PhD diss. Beijing Normal University, 2005.

Liu, X. 刘晓春. 2009. "Cong 'Minsu' dao 'Yujing zhong de Minsu': Zhongguo Minsuxue Yanjiu de Fanshi Zhuanhuan" 从'民俗'到'语境中的民俗'—中国民俗学研究的范式转换 [From 'folklore' to 'folklore in contexts': The paradigm shift in Chinese folklore research]. *Minsu Yanjiu* [Folklore studies] 2:5–35.

Liu, Y. 刘亚虎. 1999. *Nanfang Shishi Lun* 《南方史诗论》 [A treatise on the Southern epics]. Hohhot.

Liu, Z. 刘宗迪. 2004. "Cong Shumian Fanshi dao Koutou Fanshi: Lun Minjian Wenyixue de Fanshi Zhuanhuan yu Xueke Duli" 从书面范式到口头范式：论民间文艺学的范式转换与学科独立 [From written paradigm to oral paradigm: On the paradigm shift and disciplinary independence of the studies of folk literature and art.] *Minzu Wenxue Yanjiu* [Studies of ethnic literature] 2:57–64.

Lord. A. B. 2000. *The Singer of Tales*. 2nd ed. Ed. S. Mitchell and G. Nagy. Cambridge, MA. Orig. pub. 1960.

———. 2004. *Gushi de Geshou*《故事的歌手》. Trans. H. Yin from Lord 2000. Beijing.

Lu, X. 陆晓芹. 2005. *Xiangtu zhong de Gechang Chuantong: Guangxi Xibu Dejing Yidai Zhuangzu Shehui de Yinshi yu Nuan* 《乡土中的歌唱传统：广西西部德靖一带壮族社会的"吟诗"与"暖"》 [Singing traditions in rural society: A case study on the chanting "nam[22] θei[11]" and "thua" among the Zhuang people in Dejing county]. PhD diss., Beijing Normal University.

Lyu, W. 吕微. 2001. *Shenhua Hewei: Shensheng Xushi de Chuancheng yu Chanshi* 《神话何为—神圣叙事的传承与阐释》 [What is myth: Transmission and interpretation of sacred narratives]. Beijing.

Lyu, W., and D. An, eds. 2006. *Minjian Xushi de Duoyangxing* 《民间叙事的多样性：民间文化青年论坛论文集》[The diversity of folk narratives: Proceedings of the second symposium organized by The Forum of Folk Culture Studies, selected papers]. Beijing.

Mair, V., and M. Bender, eds. 2011. *The Columbia Anthology of Chinese Folk and Popular Literature*. New York.

Nachin 纳钦. 2004. *Koutou Xushi yu Cunluo Chuantong—Gongzhu Chuanshuo yu Zhulaqincun Xinyang Minsu Shehui Yanjiu* 《口头叙事与村落统—公主传说与珠腊沁村信仰民俗社会研究》 [Oral narrative and legends among villages: The legend of the princess and studies on the belief and social customs of Zhulachin village]. PhD diss., Central Minzu University of China, 2003. Beijing.

Nagy, G. 1996. *Homeric Questions*. Austin.

———. 2008. *Hema zhu Wenti* 《荷马诸问题》. Trans. Q. Bamo from G. Nagy 1996, with translator's preface and extra notes. Guilin.

Nishimura, M. 西村真志叶. 2011. *Richang Xushi de Ticai Yanjiu: Yi Jingxi Yanjiataicun de "Lajia" wei Ge'an* 《日常叙事的体裁研究：以京西燕家台村的"拉家"为个案》[A genre study on everyday narratives: The "lajia" in Yanjiatai village in western Beijing as a case study]. PhD diss., Beijing Normal University, 2007. CASS Series of Folkloristic Studies, ed. G. Chao.

Nor-bu-wang-dan 诺布旺丹. 2001. *Fuzang Shishi Lun* 《伏藏史诗论》[A study on gter-ma texts of the Gesar epic: Discovering a hidden treasure in Tibetan Buddhism]. PhD diss., the Graduate School of the Chinese Academy of Social Sciences.

Rinchindorji 仁钦道尔吉. 1994. *Jiangge'er Lun* 《〈江格尔〉论》 [A treatise on the Mongolian epic Jangar]. Hohhot.

———. 2001. *Menggu Yingxiong Shishi Yuanliu* 《蒙古英雄史诗源流》 [On the origin and development of Mongolian heroic epics]. Hohhot.

Rinchindorji, G. Chao, Sechinbatu 斯钦巴图, and Damrinjab, eds. 2007–2009. *Menggu Yingxiong Shishi Daxi* (4 juanben) 《蒙古英雄史诗大系（4卷本）》 [Collection of Mongolian heroic epics, 4 volumes]. Beijing.

Sechinbatu 斯钦巴图. 1999. *Jiangge'er yu Mengguzu Zongjiao Wenhua* 《〈江格尔〉与蒙古族宗教文化》 [The Jangar epic and Mongolian religious culture], PhD diss., the Graduate School of the Chinese Academy of Social Sciences, 1998. Hohhot.

———. 2006. *Menggu Shishi: Cong Chengshi dao Yinyu* 《蒙古史诗：从程式到隐喻》 [Mongolian epic: From formula to metaphor]. Beijing.

Sechinmenghe 斯钦孟和, ed. 2002–2019. *Gesi'er Quanshu*《格斯尔全书（12卷本）》[The complete collections of the Mongolian Geser epic, 12 volumes]. Beijing.

Schipper, M., S. Ye 叶舒宪, and H. Yin 尹虎彬, eds. 2011. *China's Creation and Origin Myths: Cross-Cultural Explorations in Oral and Written Traditions*. Boston.

Shi, A. 施爱东. 2010. *Zhongguo Xiandai Minsuxue Jiantao* 《中国现代民俗学检讨》 [Reflections on disciplining folkloristics in modern China]. Beijing.

Vjam-dpal-rgya-mtsho 降边嘉措. 1999. *Gesa'er Lun* 《〈格萨尔〉论》 [A treatise on the Tibetan Gesar epic]. Hohhot.

———, ed. 2002. *Gesa'er Jingxuan Ben*《格萨尔精选本》[The selected collection of the Tibetan Gesar epic]. Beijing.

Wan, J. 万建中. 2006. *Minjian Wenxue Yinlun* 《民间文学引论》 [An introduction to folk literature]. Beijing.

Wang, G. 王国明. 2010. "The Tuzu Gesar Epic: Performance and Singers." *Oral Tradition* 25: 381–390.

Wang, J. 王杰文. 2004. *Shanbei Jinxi de Santou Yangge: Minzhong de Huixie yu Xiangtu Shehui de Zhixu* 《陕北、晋西的"伞头秧歌"—民众的诙谐与乡土社会的秩序》 [Santou yangko in the north of Shaanxi Province and the west of Shanxi Province: Folk humor and the order of rural society]. PhD diss., Beijing Normal University.

Yang, E. 杨恩洪. 1995. *Minjian Shishen: Gesa'er Yiren Yanjiu* 《民间诗神—格萨尔艺人研究》[Folk muse: Studies on Gesar epic singers]. Beijing.

———. 2007. *Ren zai Lyutu: Zangzu Gesa'erwang Zhuan Shuochang Yiren Xunfang Sanji* 《人在旅途——藏族〈格萨尔王传〉说唱艺人寻访散记》 [A traveler is en route: Fieldnotes on searching for Tibetan epic storytellers and singers]. Nanning.

———. 2017. *Minjian Shishen: Gesa'er Yiren Yanjiu (Zengdingben)* 《民间诗神—格萨尔艺人研究(增订本)》 [Singer and storyteller in Gesar epic tradition: A follow-up study]. Beijing. Orig. pub. 1995.

Yang, L. 杨利慧. 2006. "Cong 'Ziran Yujing' dao 'Shiji Yujing': Fansi Minsuxue de Tianye Zuoye Zhuiqiu" 从'自然语境'到'实际语境'—反思民俗学的田野作业追求 [From 'natural context' to 'realistic context': Reflections on fieldwork aspirations in folklore research]. *Minsu Yanjiu* [Folklore studies] 2:5–20.

Yin, H. 尹虎彬. 2002. *Gudai Jingdian yu Koutou Chuantong* 《古代经典与口头传统》 [Classical canon and oral tradition]. Beijing.

———. 2003. *Hebei Minjian Houtu Xinyang yu Koutou Xushi Chuantong* 《河北民间后土信仰与口头叙事传统》 [Houtu-worship and traditional oral narrative within local communities in Hebei Province]. PhD diss., Beijing Normal University.

———. 2015. *Hebei Minjian Houtu Diqi Congbai* 《河北民间后土地祇崇拜》 [Folk belief in Houtu goddess of the local land in Hebei Province]. An extended edition of Yin 2003. Beijing.

Yin, H., and M. Schipper, eds. 2004. *Zhongguo Shaoshu Minzu Wenhua zhong de Shishi yu Yingxiong* 《中国少数民族文化中的史诗与英雄》 [Epic and hero in China's minority cultures]. Guilin.

Zhang, S. 张士闪. 2004. *Xiangtu Shehui yu Xiangmin de Yishu Biaoyan: Yi Shandong Changyi Diqu Xixiaozhangcun Zhuma Biaoyan wei Ge'an* 《乡土社会与乡民的艺术表演—以山东昌邑地区西小章村竹马表演为个案》 [Rural society and villagers' artistic performance: A case study on running bamboo horse in Xixiaozhang village located in Changyi area of Shandong Province]. PhD diss., Beijing Normal University.

Zhao, M. 赵敏俐等. 2005. *Zhongguo Gudai Geshi Yanjiu: Cong Shijing dao Yuanqu de Yishu Shengchanshi* 《中国古代歌诗研究—从〈诗经〉到元曲的艺术生产史》 [Studies on Chinese song-poems: The history of art production from the Book of Songs to Yuan opera]. Beijing.

Zheng, C. 郑长天. 2009. *Yaozu Zuogetang de Jiegou yu Gongneng: Xiangnan Panyao Gangjie HuodongYanjiu* 《瑶族"坐歌堂"的结构与功能—湘南盘瑶"冈介"活动研究》 [Structure and function of sitting-in-singing-house: Research on gangjie of the Pan Yao people in South Hunan Province]. PhD diss., Beijing Normal University, 2007.

Zhong, J. 钟敬文. 1998. "Dui Zhongguo Dangqian Minsuxue Yixie Wenti de Yijian" 对中国当前民俗学一些问题的意见 [Suggestions for some problematic issues in China's current folkloristics]. In *Zhongguo Minjian Wenxue Jiangyanji* [Lectures on Chinese folk literature], 108–145. Beijing.

———. 2000. "Introduction." In Chao 2000a:i–xvi.

Zhong, J., and Q. Bamo. 2002. "Nanfang Shishi Chuantong yu Zhongguo Shishixue Jianshe" 南方史诗传统与中国史诗学建设—钟敬文先生访谈录 [Southern epic traditions and disciplining epic studies in China: An interview with Zhong Jinwen]. *Minzu Yishu* [Ethnic arts] 4:41–48.

Zhu, X. 祝秀丽. 2002. *Liaoningsheng Zhongbu Xiangcun Gushi Jiangshuren Huodong Yanjiu* 《辽宁省中部乡村故事讲述人活动研究》 [A field study of storytellers and their practices in rural areas situated in the center of Liaoning Province]. PhD diss., Beijing Normal University.

Zhumaturdu, A. 阿地里・居玛吐尔地. 2006. *Manasi Shishi Geshou Yanjiu* 《〈玛纳斯〉史诗歌手研究》 [Studies on singers of epic Manas]. PhD diss., the Graduate School of the Chinese Academy of Social Sciences, 2004. Beijing.

———. 2009. *Koutou Chuantong Yu Yingxiong Shishi* 《口头传统与英雄史诗》 [Oral tradition and heroic epic]. Beijing.

Zhumaturdu, A., and T. Yisak 托汗·依莎克. 2002. *Dangdai Hema: Manasi Yanchang Dashi Jusupu Mamayi Pingzhuan* 《当代荷马:〈玛纳斯〉演唱大师居素普·玛玛依评传》 [The critical biography of Jusup Mamay: A master of Manas singing]. Hohhot.

# 18

# The Institute of Ethnic Literature's Institutionalized Approaches to Living Oral Traditions

QUBUMO BAMO

MORE AND MORE CHINESE SCHOLARS, institutions, organizations, and centers of expertise are applying the legacies of Milman Parry and Albert Lord to contextualized studies of living oral traditions. I would like to describe and discuss the work of the Institute of Ethnic Literature (IEL), an affiliate of the Chinese Academy of Social Sciences (CASS), as a specific case illustrating this trend. IEL is a community of scholars, teachers, graduate students, and staff dedicated to understanding literature and literary processes across local languages and cultures. The Institute has been at the forefront of promoting the various theories, methodologies, and practices that have contributed to establishing research on oral traditions as a "renewed" field of academic study in China. Earlier, but significant, applications of the Oral Formulaic Theory have been in large part reshaped, especially in connection with the study of oral epic, by taking into account the wealth of ethnic minorities' diverse traditions. A step-by-step analysis of institutionalized strategies for conceptualizing and developing oral traditions research as a new emerging field will provide a close-up illustration of the dynamics that have arisen from the interaction between internationalized discourse and indigenized research. In focusing on IEL, in no way do I mean to diminish the accomplishments of other institutions that have made important contributions to this body of research.

## The Oral Formulaic Theory Applied to Living Traditions in China: A Brief Retrospection

I begin with the principal applications of the Oral Formulaic Theory (hereafter referred to as "the Theory") within diverse living traditions in China.

The Theory was originally formulated in the English-speaking world, which accounts for the fact that Chinese scholars have had to develop strategies for dealing with a twofold "absence": neither the original contributors nor the original objects of study belonged to the Chinese sphere. These "absences" were compounded by the fact that China was, at the time, suffering all kinds of disruption from the Cultural Revolution, including with regard to academic exchanges.

As early as 1969, the German-American Sinologist Hans H. Frankel (傅汉思) applied the Theory to classical Chinese *epos* collected in the South and North Dynasties in his article, "The Formulaic Language of the Chinese Ballad 'Southeast Fly the Peacocks'" (《孔雀东南飞》).[1] To my knowledge, this is the earliest application of the Theory to material in Chinese. Two years later, Alsace Chun-chiang Yen/Ping-chiu Yen (晏君强/晏平秋) submitted a Harvard doctoral dissertation, directed by Albert Lord and Francis Cleaves, that applied the Theory to Chinese demon tales (the dissertation was published in 1990).[2] Ching-Hsien Wang (王靖献/杨牧) drew more attention from Western scholars with the publication of his PhD dissertation, *The Bell and the Drum: Shih Ching as Formulaic Poetry in an Oral Tradition*, in 1974.[3] Since then, the Theory has been applied by scholars outside China to Chinese classical poetry, vernacular novels, and other ancient Chinese genres. For instance, Marsha L. Wagner, with reference both to Gregory Nagy and Ruth Finnegan, explored the folk origins of *ci* (词), a representative lyric genre that originated in the Tang Dynasty and flourished in the Song Dynasty.[4] Unfortunately, however, Chinese scholars still know relatively little about the efforts of foreign scholars to connect the legacies of Parry and Lord to Chinese traditions. Various well-known political, academic, and linguistic barriers—and especially China's previous isolation—made it difficult for Chinese researchers to appreciate the far-reaching potential of the Theory in application to so many different languages until the 1990s. Only *belatedly* have Western folklorists examined living traditions in China in light of the Theory: Vibeke Børdahl (易德波) and her collaborators, as well as Mark Bender, have applied the Theory to *shuoshu* (说书), or storytelling in oral traditions in China, and have made significant progress in exploring contemporary living oral traditions. These English-language works, however, had not yet been systematically translated and disseminated among academics

1 See further Frankel 1969.
2 See Yen 1990; see his further applications of the Theory in Yen 1975 and 1997.
3 See C. H. Wang 1974. For book reviews, see Fusek 1979, Bynum 1979, and Lord 1986.
4 See Wagner 1984, especially the Introduction.

in mainland China until 2016, though some IEL scholars use them as teaching materials.[5]

The Chinese translation of Ching-Hsien Wang's *The Bell and the Drum*,[6] which finally appeared in mainland China in 1990, was once mistaken for the "first case" applying the Theory to ancient Chinese poetry. The book did not, however, draw much attention until Karl Reichl's article "Parallelism in South Slavic and Turkic Epic Poetry: Towards a Poetics of Formulaic Diction" was translated by G. Chao and published in the journal *Studies of Ethnic Literature*, an IEL publication.[7] Thanks to the links made in this study between the findings of Parry and Lord and the living epic traditions of Turkic ethnic groups in both central Asia and China, a new window on western scholarship on oral epic was opened, which has had significant consequences for scholarship on oral traditions at IEL.

## About IEL and Its Strategic Framing

For forty years, since its inception in 1980, the IEL has contributed much to the study of ethnic literature in China. Its research program focuses on the following areas: (1) the literature of ancient and contemporary ethnic groups, oral and written; (2) theoretical concerns relating to issues of literary evolution; (3) literary relations among various ethnic groups, with an emphasis on comparative approaches; (4) expressive cultures in combination with oral tradition and verbal art; (5) literary theory and contemporary criticism; and (6) collecting, recording, transcribing, translating, digitizing, and publishing oral texts and written works. Eighteen ethnic groups are represented among the scholars, administrators, and emeriti of the IEL, including: Mongol, Zang (Tibetan), Uygur, Kirgiz (Kyrghyz), Russ (Russian), Man (Manchu), Xibe, Chosen (Korean), Daur, Hui, Yi, Miao (Hmong), Bai, Zhuang, Dong, Dai, Naxi (Nakhi), and Han[8]; eighty percent of the scholars have native language-level command of one or more ethnic minority languages.

5 See Børdahl 1996, 1997, 1999; Børdahl and Wan 2010, Børdahl, Li, and Ying 2004; Børdahl and Ross 2002; Olivová and Børdahl 2009; Bender 1998, 2003a.

6 Wang 1989.

7 Reichl 1990. Founded in November 1983, *Studies of Ethnic Literature* (SEL) focuses on ethnic folk literature and oral traditions, ancient ethnic minority written literature and writers, reviews of modern and contemporary ethnic minority writers and their works, theoretical and methodological reflections, comparative approaches to ethnic minority literature and culture, recommendations and comments on new works, related foreign research, tendencies and developments in the field, and more. SEL also provides an international venue for research on the world's ethnic literatures and oral tradition. To date, SEL has published 183 issues in total, covering 4217 papers and articles.

8 All the name spellings of ethnic groups in China in the present article are adopted by "A Roman Alphabet Spelling of Name and Code for All Ethnic Minorities in China," or The National Standard GB3304–91.

As of October 2020, IEL scholars have undertaken the completion of 42 national-level projects and 111 provincial and ministerial-level projects; published 175 books and monographs, 2461 papers, essays and articles, 205 kinds of research materials, 14 reference books, and 36 collections of essays, as well as 27 books and 196 papers through translations both from ethnic minority languages and foreign languages. They have also trained 120 graduate students from multi-ethnic groups in both PhD and MA programs.[9]

Because of the many subdisciplines of East and Central Asian Studies with which IEL scholars are engaged—including Tibetan Studies, Mongolian Studies, Turkic Studies, Man (Manchu) Studies, Naxi (Nakhi) Studies, Yi Studies, and Miao (Hmong) Studies—the work of the Institute is necessarily international in character. The IEL has links with institutions and scholars in many countries throughout the world and boasts expertise that can be of value for any international scholar or institution whose work addresses cultural diversity, local knowledge, or regional and international cooperation in the social sciences and humanities. So far, the IEL has held 108 international and domestic symposiums along with 8 sessions of the IEL International Seminar Series on Epic Studies and Oral Tradition Research, and has sponsored 564 international exchanges and visits by individuals.

Framing a strategic planning scheme is crucial to the long-term success of an institution such as the IEL. The Institute's sustainable development strategies were at the forefront of the heated debate centered on *text* and *field* in 2003, when Chinese folkloristics recognized the ideas of Parry and Lord as an important frame of reference for the advancement of folklore research at the national level.[10] In 2004, the various divisions and centers based at the IEL committed themselves to a long-range plan for expanding research on ethnic literature with emphasis on the study of oral traditions. The IEL Working Group for Epic Studies supported these efforts by articulating and enacting strategic principles. In particular, the Group set out the guiding slogans "steadily ongoing" and "not rushing out everywhere," which fostered great progress in the development of oral traditions research; helped individuals, groups, and divisions to transition from their previous comprehensive approaches to a specific focus on their own specialties; and strove to create a distinctive institution with specific academic strengths and its own cultural character on a grander, more institutionalized scale. In what follows, I wish to explore this process of institutionalization with specific reference to applications of the ideas of Parry and Lord.

9 For a general review of these multiple outcomes, see Chao in this volume.
10 See. Y. Chen 2004.

## A "Prelude" to the Expertise of Oral Traditions Research in China

The 1950s and 1980s saw two large-scale general surveys of folk literature at the national, provincial, and local levels: the so-called "Movements of Collecting and Collating Folk Literature." Across the nation and over several generations, folklorists, historians, ethnologists, ethnomusicologists, socio-cultural workers, and government surveyors collected and recorded the cultural legacies of minority groups in different ways. Many of these efforts have become the foundation for academic research among professionals, universities, and institutions.

Since the turn of the twenty-first century, the two "Movements" have been subjected to critical scrutiny by folklorists and experts in ethnic literature, resulting in serious reflection on nationwide collections of folk literature and arts. Scholars discovered that, almost without exception, these projects were carried out by administrative directives from the central government to local governments, with political intervention in scholarly approaches. Folk literature of different kinds was collected in various problematic formats and treated more as written than as oral literature. Epics, lyric songs, myths, tales, and other local genres were published with little reference to how they were originally presented and represented. Indeed, the question of how best to grasp the meaning of folk literature, which had previously been posed in terms of models taken over from written literature, only produced positive results with the transformation of assumptions (and ideologies) brought about by the importation of the notion of "oral tradition"—the new term became a real concept to replace "folk literature." Subsequently, the Oral Formulaic Theory and its methods provided a promising basis for responses to the complex issues involved. A review of what has happened at the IEL reveals this shift to be more a consequence of exchange between Chinese and foreign academics than something that arose spontaneously.

Since the mid-1990s, Chinese epic scholars—mostly from the IEL—have traveled abroad as visiting scholars at universities and institutions in Europe (e.g. the Folklore Fellows' Summer School in Finland) and North America (e.g. Harvard University, the University of Missouri, and Indiana University). These scholars introduced selected works concerning the Oral Formulaic Theory to China. In doing so, they put the spotlight on the two main traditions of Western scholarship on oral tradition—what we might call the "Finnish School" and the "Harvard School"— broadening scholars' notion of epic poetry (from classical epic to folk and oral epic, for example), while articulating a new vision of the relation between orality and literacy that better reflects empirical reality and the life-world itself.

Hubin Yin, Gejin Chao, and other epic scholars at IEL played crucial roles in this regard. They not only provided a systematic introduction to the Theory but also laid a new emphasis on oral poetics based upon their overviews and in-depth interpretations of influential works.[11] There was a certain amount of serendipity in these early years: Yin attended Gregory Nagy's seminar at Harvard between 1994 and 1995, with the result that he paid much attention to introducing the Harvard School to Chinese scholars, focusing on a study of the history of scholarship on oral tradition that synthesized that history as a whole. Within a few years, Yin had not only embarked on a close reading of Lord's *Singer of Tales* but had also absorbed many of Nagy's works and had published multiple papers, ranging from conceptual interpretation to ethnographic methodology, forming a clear picture of the Theory and its history. In 1995, Chao participated in an epic workshop, led by John Miles Foley and Lauri Harvilahti, at the Folklore Fellows Summer School in Finland and then spent the following academic year at Harvard. Two years later, Foley delivered his illuminating lecture on the Theory in Beijing at the official invitation of IEL. Foley's 1997 article, "The Oral Theory: An Approach to Studies in Oral Tradition," written specifically for *Studies of Ethnic Literature* and translated by Chao, presented for the first time to Chinese readers the study of oral tradition as a new discipline.[12] Chao concentrated on the history and methodology of the Theory and later, in both field studies and theoretical works, applied the approaches of Parry and Lord to Mongolian epic tradition by creating a new analytical model for textual analysis. Together, Chao and Yin, who have successively held leadership positions in the IEL, have made indispensable contributions to the institutionalization of research on oral traditions.

Along with dozens of papers, translations of several seminal books have been published in Chinese in the past two decades, including Foley's *The Theory of Oral Composition: History and Methodology*, Lord's *The Singer of the Tales*, Nagy's *Homeric Questions*, Richard Bauman's *Verbal Art as Performance*, Walter Ong's *Orality and Literacy: The Technologizing of the Word*, Reichl's *Turkic Oral Epic Poetry: Traditions, Forms, Poetic Structure*, Børdahl's *The Oral Tradition of Yangzhou Storytelling*, and Bender's *Plum and Bamboo: China's Suzhou Chantefable Tradition*.[13] In the meantime, Chinese scholars have

11 See Chao 1997, 1999a, 1999b, 2000b, and 2000c; Chao and Liao 1999; Yin 1996a, 1996b, 1998, 2002b, and 2002c; and Bamo 2003.

12 Foley 1997.

13 Their Chinese editions are listed here in chronological order: Foley 2000, Lord 2004, Nagy 2008, Bauman 2008, Ong 2008, Reichl 2011, Børdahl 2016 and 2018, and Bender 2019. Other translation projects are underway with the support of the IEL.

been developing multiple ways to further interpretations of oral theories. Furthermore, performance-centered field study has now become a common practice in Chinese folkloristics and has attracted attention from other disciplines, especially as a result of debates over the relation between *text* and *field*, resulting in a continually deeper engagement with the legacies of Parry and Lord and the further application and indigenization of Western theories and methodologies.[14]

## Institutional Strategies for Oral Traditions Research

Since 2000, folklorists in China have become increasingly mindful of a major methodological issue complicating the study of oral heritage, namely, that the study of oral traditions necessarily rests upon the recording of verbal art, that is, the creation of texts. IEL scholars, as interpreters of Parry, Lord, and other Western scholars, have helped to articulate the role of the academic community in reconceptualizing oral tradition in a way that places greater demands on situated observation and field study of living verbal arts. The IEL has made great progress in indigenizing applications of the legacies of Parry and Lord—including their methods for fieldwork and documentation, their theoretical and interpretive frameworks, their analytical procedures, and their comparative methods—through its institutional innovations.[15]

### The first research center of oral traditions in China

In order to promote scholarship on oral traditions, IEL established the Oral Traditions Research Center (OTRC) on September 16, 2003. The OTRC is the first center of expertise on oral traditions in China.

China enjoys remarkable cultural diversity. Among minority groups there is an extraordinary amount of intangible culture in the form of oral traditions, local oral genres, ways of speaking, or other living forms of cultural expression that is almost unknown to the dominant Han Chinese culture and undocumented in an ethnographically rigorous form. Much of this intangible culture is in danger of extinction. Accordingly, the Center seeks to foster cooperation between interregional and international institutions and researchers to safeguard intangible cultural heritage by promoting cultural diversity in oral traditions; to provide advice and expertise in support of professional research on oral traditions and policy-making by national and regional governments, especially with respect

14 For a general review, see Bender 2003b.

15 See Zhu 2018.

to intellectual property rights in folklore; to raise awareness at the local, regional, and national levels of the significance of oral traditions in intangible cultural heritage, and to ensure respect for the cultural creativity of the local communities, minority groups, and individuals concerned; to assist local communities and minority groups in understanding cultural diversity, creativity, and the value of intercultural discourses between different languages and civilizations; and to learn from past experience and to speak with a collective voice in support of future projects advancing the same interests.

Furthermore, the Center has worked to provide researchers with methodological guidance in accordance with the following objectives: to promote the fundamental working model adopted by IEL, which includes a definition of oral heritage along with strategies for safeguarding intangible cultural heritage and to make good use of interregional and international resources; to provide guidelines for fieldwork, including ethnographic interviews, questionnaires, recordings of folklore, research reports, and archival practices; to develop a sustainable database system for ethnographic surveys that accounts for cultural diversity and ethnic identity; to conduct a survey to help researchers understand the current situation of oral traditions in danger of disappearing, and to devote case studies to some representative minority communities and individual tradition bearers; and to produce an analytical report summarizing statistical data, field records, site reports, case studies, and collections of audio-visual materials and still photography.

## Archive/base/network: A threefold solution

Building on domestic practices and international experiences in safeguarding oral and intangible cultural heritage, the IEL has instituted a three-part solution to the challenges posed by the study of living oral traditions in a diverse and rapidly modernizing environment. The three parallel projects that make up this solution are first, "The China Ethnic Literature Research Archives," which integrates resources and digital documentation; second, "Oral Tradition Field Study Bases," which seek to provide in-depth and long-term documentation of traditions; and third, "The China Ethnic Literature Network," an information-sharing platform. Collectively, these projects aim to advance theoretical research on minority oral traditions, to aid in maintaining the cultural diversity of minority groups in China, and to safeguard oral and intangible cultural heritage at local, national, and international levels.

## Archives

Development and modernization represent serious threats to oral traditions, especially in the western regions of China where many oral traditions are in danger of disappearing altogether. Accordingly, we have sought to bring the attention of government authorities to the need for a nationwide database for the protection of the diversity of local culture, such as oral epics, ways of speaking, forms of ethnic narratives, and native expressions of local knowledge. In the late 1990s, the academic committee of CASS decided to launch two new projects under the executive guidance of IEL—the "Database of Oral Epics in China" and the "Archive of Oral Traditional Texts of Ethnic Groups in China." In order to provide a long-term framework for developing these resources, IEL created the China Ethnic Literature Research Archives, a unique folklore database that focuses on the systematic collecting, processing, cataloguing, classifying, and preserving of oral traditions among ethnic minorities in the country.

To give some sense of their scope, by the early 2010s, the archives had collected a large amount of research data, encompassing 2,885 different recordings totaling 6,884 hours of audio and video, 19,735 photographs, 8,369 volumes of texts (including manuscripts, block-printed editions, transcriptions, and fieldwork reports as well as modern publications), 332 data sets, and three digitizing documentation projects. The digital archives total twenty-five terabytes of storage units to date. This data, which covers more than twenty local genres, has been collected from forty-five ethnic groups, including the Mongolian, Tibetan, Tu, Monba, Lhoba, Uygur, Kazak, Kirgiz, Xibe, Tajik, Man (Manchu), Ewenki, Daur, Hezhen, Zhuang, Buyei, Dong, Dai, Sui, De'ang, Jingpo, Achang, Miao (Hmong), Yao, Yi , Bai, Naxi (Nakhi), Hani (Akha), Lisu, Lahu, Derung, Jino, Nu, Qiang, Pumi, Va, Tujia, and Li, to give a partial list. The fieldwork areas include Inner Mongolia, Xinjiang, Tibet, Qinghai, Gansu, Sichuan, Guangxi, Yunnan, Guizhou, Heilongjiang, Jilin, Liaoning, and Beijing. Additional data has been collected from the neighboring countries and districts such as Pakistan, Japan, Korea, Mongolia, the Kyrgyz Republic as well as the Russian Federation (including the Buryatia, Kalmykia, and Tuva). Data and recordings document folk religious and ritual practices, rites of passage and traditional festivals, and folklife experiences and personal life histories of folk artists and epic performers. Well represented are documentations of the "Three Heroic Epic Cycles"—the Tibetan-Mongolian epic *Gesar/Geser*, the Mongolian epic *Jangar*, and the Kirgiz epic *Manas*—that are still performed and transmitted orally by epic singers and storytellers amongst various ethnic groups in remote areas of China. Apart from these three great epics, the Epic Collection in the archives covers forty-three different epic traditions pertaining to ethnic minorities in Southern and Northern China.

### Field study bases

In order to document and to revitalize minority oral traditions, the IEL set up thirteen Field Study Bases for Ethnic Oral Traditions in western China between 2003 and 2016: Jaruud Base for Mongolian Bensen Ülger Storytelling in Inner Mongolia (2003), Liping Base for Grand Song of the Dong (2004) in Guizhou, Tianyang Base for Boutodo Culture and Oral Narrative of the Zhuang in Guangxi (2004), Mgo-lok Base for Tibetan Tribal Epic Tradition in Qinghai (2004), Mdzod-dge Base for Tibetan Epic Singing in Sichuan (2004), Moggu Base for Nuosu Yi Verbal Dueling and Epic Performance in Sichuan (2005), Akqi Base for the Kirgiz Epic *Manas in* Xinjiang (2005), Rma-chu Base for the Tibetan Epic *Gesar* in Gansu (2006), Hoboksai Base for Oirat Mongolian Oral Tradition in Xinjiang (2006), Ziyun Base for the Miao King Yalu Epic in Guizhou (2012), Baarin Right Banner Base for Safeguarding Geser Epic Culture in Inner Mongolia (2012), Yul-hrul Base for the Tibetan Gesar Epic Tradition in Qinghai (2014), and Nileke Base for Safeguarding and Research of Geser Culture in Xinjiang (2016). Having been partly inspired by the pioneering fieldwork methods of Parry and Lord, as well as Honko's formulation of "Thick Corpus" (Honko 2000), our scholars go to great efforts to formulate and improve working models for conducting field study; we carry out long-term observations, research, preservation, conservation, and promotion of oral tradition in its living cultural context and social situation. A major goal of these efforts is to ensure the sustainable development of oral traditions over time. To that end, we seek not only to gain a deeper understanding of the currently emergent situation of oral traditions through a regional/intercultural assessment and examination but also to encourage participation of individuals, groups, institutions, and communities in the management, preservation, protection, and promotion of oral heritage. As the IEL continues efforts to textualize and translate epic and other folk narrative texts from situated oral performances, more bases will be constructed in the relevant communities in order to ensure that these projects are carried out in the cultural ecosystem of traditional knowledge.

### Network

The China Ethnic Literature Network (CELN, http://iel.cass.cn/) is an information-sharing platform created by the Digital Studio of the IEL at CASS in 1999, the predecessor of IEL's Documentation and Information Center for Studies in China's Ethnic Literature. Our goal is to promote China's minority literature and scholarly practice in a variety of interactive media formats and to make them accessible to scholars and students desiring new information concerning oral cultural heritage and literary creativity. We hope, by our work, to be able to foster a new notion of "partners in knowledge" and to build a "digital community" for enhancing research and education at local, national, and international levels. The CELN aims to be the national portal website for ethnic minority literature and folklore documentation and research. There are currently over 14,000 entries on research papers, articles, book reviews, field reports, news, and events accumulated in 282 channels and sub-channels. As IEL's official website, the CELN has already had a wide influence on the study of ethnic minority literature, folk literature and art studies, folkloristics, and on those working with oral and intangible cultural heritage. Furthermore, the IEL has entered into agreements with partner institutions in the US, Finland, Korea, and Japan to collaborate on the improvement of a database system. And in September 2011, IEL launched the "Cross-Media Archives for Ethnic Oral Traditions," a long-range project aiming at a sustainable information infrastructure in light of the Institute's threefold approach. Since then, we have multiple test cases, both domestically and internationally, that we are monitoring.

With regard to studies on oral traditions, there is a significant history of collaboration between researchers in technologies and humanities to address methodological challenges. For example, David F. Elmer has led ongoing efforts with the Milman Parry Collection of Oral Literature at Harvard University to develop best practices for the digital documentation of oral epic traditions and potential applications in interdisciplinary studies.[16] A project, "The Construction of Thematic Databases for Ethnic Oral Traditions in China: Developing Discipline-Based Metadata Standards on Oral Traditions," received five years of funding (2017–2021) as one of the major projects supported by the National Social Science Fund of China. It is jointly executed by the IEL and the Computer Network Information Center, Chinese Academy of Sciences (CNIC, CAS). As an interdisciplinary project for the research and development of standards specifically for use in academic research, it can be considered a definitive source for the development of thematic databases on oral traditions. Following the concept and principle of "first standards, then establishment of archives," it covers metadata standards, rules for collection and documentation, and methods for data descriptions. Indeed, the ongoing project marks the first cooperation between two subsidiary and specialized institutions under the CASS and the CAS respectively. Such cooperation demonstrates a kind of interdisciplinary "boundary work" with each institution's functions complementing the other's.

[16] See Elmer 2018.

What attracts our analytic attention and challenges our imagination, as an institution in these efforts to create a sustainable electronic infrastructure, is the conceptualization of "digital communities" for shaping innovation and disseminating cultural legacies, for creating a new model of partnership-in-knowledge production, and for facing up to a new and historic opportunity for multilateral cooperation between academic institutions, governmental departments, public societies, and local communities, including the bearers and practitioners of oral tradition and living heritage.[17]

The IEL's epistemological practices, professional expertise, and careful steps toward creating its working model of "Archive/Base/Network" has not only produced a number of promising possibilities but has also cultivated an institutional space to practice reflexive sociologies of local knowledge with a view to developing new perspectives for sustaining cultural diversity, creativity, and freedom.[18]

## Conclusion

The IEL has sought to provide an institutional framework for the study, collection, and documentation of oral traditions in many other ways as well, for example, by training graduate students (as part of the Department of Ethnic Literature within the School of Chinese Language and Literature at the University of CASS), convening professional training programs (notably the International Seminar Series on Epic Studies and Oral Tradition Research), and working with organizations and institutions such as UNESCO, the International Council for Philosophy and Human Sciences, and China National Center for Safeguarding Intangible Cultural Heritage, to promote living oral traditions and humanities.

In all of these efforts, especially those outlined in detail above, IEL scholars have sought to apply the legacies of Milman Parry and Albert Lord. These various projects demonstrate the successful combination of Chinese practices and experiences with foreign theories and methodologies, giving impetus to research programs, projects, and activities on various aspects of oral tradition. Focusing on their own research subjects, scholars at the IEL absorb new academic thoughts and emphasize case studies from which they refine working models and methodologies for doing fieldwork, in order to explore the past, present and future of the oral traditions and intangible cultural heritage of ethnic minorities in China. IEL scholars go into the field one after another, building up a conceptual frame to deepen the understanding of oral texts and attempting to bring

17 See Bamo, Guo, Gao, and Zhang 2018.
18 See Bamo and Chao, with Niles 2016.

about a "paradigm shift" away from the written criteria that have been used to approach oral traditions in the past.[19] As one folklorist has indicated, thanks to the contributions of IEL scholars to research on oral traditions, a profound change has taken place in contemporary folkloristics in China.[20] Today, more institutionalized approaches to living oral traditions adopted by the IEL and beyond are resulting in more localized practices for conducting field study on ethnic oral traditions amongst a rising generation of promising scholars educated at the IEL.[21]

In the long term, moreover, safeguarding the diversity of oral traditions in China must be a systematic endeavor, one that can only be achieved by means of active promotion, multifaceted collaboration, and greater institutional management. The ideas of Parry and Lord have been seminal in the study of oral poetics, and they have had a pervasive influence not only on generations of scholars in China but also on diverse institutions in related fields throughout the world. The Institute of Ethnic Literature provides a good example of how these ideas have shaped an institution that continues to contribute to international scholarship on oral traditions.[22]

19 For discussion of achievements in this regard, see Chao in the present volume.

20 Cited from Tieliang Liu's speech at the foundation ceremony of the IEL's Center for Oral Traditions Research, September 16, 2003.

21 To take four case studies as a contribution made by young scholars, see H. Gao 2011, Zhu 2015, Liu 2018, and Luo 2018.

22 The author thanks Aaron P. Tate for proofreading and editing portions of this essay, parts of which are adapted from the IEL Bulletin "A Brief Introduction to IEL, CASS," printed for the celebration of the thirtieth anniversary of IEL in 2010.

## Bibliography

Bamo, Q. 巴莫曲布嫫. 2003. *Shishi Chuantong de Tianye Yanjiu: Yi Nuosu Yizu Shishi Lewo wei Ge'an* 《史诗传统的田野研究：以诺苏彝族史诗"勒俄"为个案》 [A field study of epic tradition: Nuosu epic Hnewo as a case study]. PhD diss., Beijing Normal University.

Bamo, Q., and G. Chao. 朝戈金, with J. D. Niles. 2016. "Documenting Living Oral Traditions: China's Institute of Ethnic Literature as Case Study." *Journal of American Folklore* 129/513:270–287.

Bamo, Q., C. Guo 郭翠潇, Y. Gao 高瑜蔚, and J. Zhang 张建军. 2018. "Koutou Chuantong Zhuanye Yuanshuju Biaozhun Dingzhi: Bianjie Zuoye yu Shuzi Gongtongti"口头传统专业元数据标准定制：边界作业与数字共同体 [Developing discipline-based metadata standards on oral traditions: Boundary work and digital community]. *Minjian Wenhua Luntan* [Folk culture forum] 6:56–67.

Bauman, R. 1977. *Verbal Art as Performance.* Prospect Heights, IL. Repr. 1984.

———. 2008. *Zuowei Biaoyan de Koutou Yishu* 《作为表演的口头艺术》. Trans. L. Yang and D. An, from Bauman 1977. Guilin.

Bender, M. 1998. "Suzhou Tanci Storytelling in China: Contexts of Performance." *Oral Tradition* 13:330–376.

———. 2003a. *Plum and Bamboo: China's Suzhou Chantefable Tradition*. Urbana.

———. 2003b. "Oral Narrative Studies in China." *Oral Tradition* 18:236–238.

———. 2019. *Mei yu Zhu: Zhongguo Chuantong Suzhou Pingtan*《梅与竹：中国传统苏州评弹》. Trans. D. Li 李东鹏 with Q. He 何其亮, from Bender 2003a. Beijing.

Børdahl, V. 易德波. 1996. *The Oral Tradition of Yangzhou Storytelling*. Richmond.

———. 1997. "Professional Storytelling in Modern China: A Case Study of the Yangzhou Pinghua Tradition." *Asian Folklore Studies* 56:7–32.

———, ed. 1999. *The Eternal Storyteller: Oral Literature in Modern China* (with photos by J. Ross). Richmond.

———. 2016. *Yangzhou Pinghua Tantao* 《扬州评话探讨》. Trans. V. Børdahl and F. Mi 米锋 with J. Li 李今芸, from Børdahl 1996. Nanjing.

———, ed. 2018. *Shuoshu: Yangzhou Pinghua de Kouchuan Yishu*《说书：扬州评话的口传艺术》. Trans. H. Li 李含冰, from Børdahl 1999. With photos by J. Ross 罗爱德. Yangzhou.

Børdahl, V., and J. Ross. 2002. *Chinese Storytellers: Life and Art in the Yangzhou Tradition* (textbook with VCD). Boston.

Børdahl, V., F. Li, and H. Ying, eds. 2004. *Four Masters of Chinese Storytelling: Full-length Repertoires of Yangzhou Storytelling on Video*. Copenhagen.

Børdahl, V., and M. B. Wan, eds. 2010. *The Interplay of the Oral and the Written in Chinese Popular Culture*. Copenhagen.

Bynum, D. E. 1979. "The Bell, the Drum, Milman Parry, and the Time Machine." *Chinese Literature: Essays, Articles, Reviews* (CLEAR) 1:241–253.

Chao, G. 朝戈金. 1997. "Mongolian Oral Epic Poetry: An Overview." *Oral Tradition* 2:322–336.

———. 1999a. "Koutou Chengshi Lilun yu Shishi Chuangbian Wenti" 口头程式理论与史诗创编问题 [On the oral formulaic theory and issues in epic compositions]. *Zhongguo Minsuxue Niankan 1999* [Annals of Chinese folklore research 1999]:176–189. Shanghai.

———. 1999b. "Kouchuan Shishi de Tianye Zuoye Wenti: Nansilafu he Menggu Shishi Tianye Zuoye Shuping" 口传史诗的田野作业问题—南斯拉夫和蒙古史诗田野作业述评 [Theoretical concerns on doing fieldwork in epic studies: An analogy to fieldworks in Yugoslavia and Inner Mongolia]. *Minzu Wenxue Yanjiu* [Studies of ethnic literature] 3:39–43.

———. 2000a. *Kouchuan Shishi Shixue: Ranpile Jiangge'er Chengshi Jufa Yanjiu* 《口传史诗诗学：冉皮勒〈江格尔〉程式句法研究》 [Oral poetics of oral epic: Formulaic diction of Arimpil's Jangar singing]. Nanning.

———. 2000b. "Kouchuan Shishi Shixue de Jige Jiben Gainian" 口传史诗诗学的几个基本概念 [Some basic concepts in poetics of oral epic]. *Minzu Yishu* [Ethnic art] 4:71–79.

———. 2000c. "Kouchuan Shishi Wenben de Leixing: Yi Menggu Shishi Weili" 口传史诗文本的类型—以蒙古史诗为例 [On types of oral epic texts: Mongolian epic as a case study]. *Minzu Wenxue Yanjiu* [Studies of ethnic literature] 4:58–62.

———, ed. 2001. *Chinese Oral Traditions*, special issue, *Oral Tradition* 16. https://journal.oraltradition.org/issues/16ii.

———. 2001. "The Oirat Epic Cycle Jangaar." *Oral Tradition* 16:402–435.

———. 2002. "Guanyu Koutou Chuanchang Shige de Yanjiu: Koutou Shixue Wenti" 关于口头传唱诗歌的研究：口头诗学问题 [Studies on verbally-transmitted song-poems: Issues in oral poetics]. *Wenyi Yanjiu* [Studies of literature and art] 2002:99–101.

———. 2003a. "Minsuxue Shijiao xia de Koutou Chuantong" 民俗学视角下的口头传统 [Oral tradition from the perspective of folklore studies]. *Guangxi Minzu Xueyuan Xuebao* [Journal of Guangxi Minzu College] 3:10–11, 18.

———. 2003b. "Guowai Koutou Chuantong Yanjiu he Jiaoxue Shijian" 国外"口头传统"研究和教学实践 [Teaching oral traditions overseas]. In *Jiaoliu yu Xiezuo: Zhongguo Gaodeng Yuanxiao Shoujie Feiwuzhi Wenhua Yichan Jiaoyu Jiaoxue Yantaohui Wenji* [Proceedings of national conference on higher education in teaching intangible cultural heritage], 54–57. Beijing.

———, ed. 2008. *Zhongguo Xibu de Wenhua Duoyangxing yu Zuqun Rentong: Yan Sichou Zhilu de Shaoshu Minzu Koutou Chuantong Xianzhuang Baogao* 《中国西部的文化多样性与族群认同：沿丝绸之路的少数民族口头传统现状报告》 [A critical survey of cultural diversity and identity of ethnic groups in West China and beyond: How to safeguard oral traditions along the Silk Roads]. Beijing.

Chao, G., and M. Liao 廖明君. 1999. "Kouchuan Shishi de Wudu: Chao Gejin Fangtan Lu" 口传史诗的误读：朝戈金访谈录 [On the misreading of oral epic: An interview with Chao Gejin]. *Minzu Yishu* [Ethnic art] 1:8–18.

Chen, Y. 陈泳超, ed. 2004. *Zhongguo Minjian Wenhua de Xhueshushi Guanzhao* 《中国民间文化的学术史观照： 民间文化青年论坛第一届会议论文集》 [A contemplation of the history of scholarship in Chinese folk cultures: Proceedings of the first symposium held by the Forum of Folk Culture Studies]. Harbin.

Elmer, D. F. 2013. "Digitalization of The Milman Parry Collection of Oral Literature: Achievements, Challenges, and Visions." Lecture at the Fifth IEL International Seminar Series on Epic Studies and Oral Tradition Research, Beijing, November 29, 2013, .

———. 2018. "Mi'erman Pali Koutou Wenxue Tecang de Shuzihua: Chengjiu, Taozhan ji Yuanjing" 米尔曼·帕里口头文学特藏的数字化:成就、挑战及愿景. Trans. S. Li 李斯颖 and Q. Bamo, from Elmer 2013. *Minzu Wenxue Yanjiu* [Studies of ethnic literature] 2: 114–120.

Foley, J. M. 1988. *The Theory of Oral Composition: History and Methodology*. Bloomington.

———. 1997. "Koutou Chengshi Lilun: Koutou Chuangtong Yanjiu Gaishu" 口头程式理论：口头传统研究概述 [The oral theory: An approach to studies in oral tradition]. Trans. G. Chao. *Minzu Wenxue Yanjiu* [Studies of ethnic literature] 1: 86–90.

———. 2000. *Koutou Shixue: Pali-Luode Lilun* 《口头诗学：帕里—洛德理论》. Trans. G. Chao, from Foley 1988, with author's new preface to Chinese edition, translator's foreword, and extra notes. Beijing.

Frankel, H. H. 傅汉思. 1969. "The Formulaic Language of the Chinese Ballad 'Southeast Fly the Peacocks.'" In *Bulletin of the Institute of History and Philology* (BIHP) 39:219–241. Taipei: Academia Sinica. Reprinted in *Harvard Journal of Asiatic Studies* 34(1974): 248–271.

Fusek, L. M. 1979. Review of *The Bell and the Drum* by C. H. Wang. *Chinese Literature: Essays, Articles, Reviews* (CLEAR) 1:99–103.

Gao, H. 高荷红. 2011. *Manzhu Shuobu Chuancheng Yanjiu* 《满族说部传承研究》 [Transmission of Manchu traditional storytelling]. PhD diss., Graduate School of the Chinese Academy of Social Sciences, 2008.

Honko, L. 2000. "Thick Corpus and Organic Variation: An Introduction." In *Thick Corpus, Organic Variation and Textuality in Oral Tradition*, 3–28. Helsinki.

Liu, J. 刘镜净. 2018. *Koutou Chuantong Wenlei de Jieding: Yi Yunnan Yuanjiang Hanizu Haba wei Ge'an*《口头传统文类的界定：以云南元江哈尼族哈巴为个案》[Defining oral traditional genre: Xapa amongst the Hani people as a case study]. MA thesis, the Graduate School of Chinese Academy of Social Sciences, 2007. Beijing.

Lord, A. B. 1986. "Perspectives on Recent Work on the Oral Traditional Formula." *Oral Tradition* 1:467–503.

———. 2000. *The Singer of Tales*, 2nd ed. Ed. S. Mitchell and G. Nagy. Cambridge, MA. Orig. pub. 1960.

———. 2004. *Gushi de Geshou* 《故事的歌手》. Trans. H. Yin, from Lord 2000. Beijing.

Luo, D. 罗丹阳. 2018. *Miaozu Guge Gangsenai Chuancheng Yanjiu* 《苗族古歌<瑟岗奈>传承研究》[A study on the transmission of the Miao epic song "seib gangx neel"]. MA thesis, the Graduate School of the Chinese Academy of Social Sciences, 2007; PhD diss., Minzu University of China, 2011. Beijing.

Nagy, G. 1996. *Homeric Questions*. Austin.

———. 2008. *Hema zhu Wenti* 《荷马诸问题》. Trans. Q. Bamo, from G. Nagy 1996, with translator's preface and extra notes. Guilin.

Olivová, L., and V. Børdahl, eds. 2009. *Lifestyle and Entertainment in Yangzhou*. Copenhagen.

Ong, W. J. 1988. *Orality and Literacy: The Technologizing of the Word*. London.

———. 2008. *Kouyu Wenhua yu Shumian Wenhua: Yuci de Jishuhua* 口语文化与书面文化：语词的技术化. Trans. D. He, from Ong 1988. Beijing.

Reichl, K. J. 1989. "Parallelism in South Slavic and Turkic Epic Poetry: Towards a Poetics of Formulaic Diction." *Oral Tradition*, 4:360–381.

———. 1990. "Nansilafu he Tujue Yinxiong Shishi zhong de Pingxingshi: Chengshihua Jufa de Shixue Tansuo" 南斯拉夫和突厥英雄史诗中的平行式：程式化句法的诗学探索. Trans. G. Chao, from Reichl 1989. *Minzu Wenxue Yanjiu* [Studies of ethnic literature] 2:85–91.

———. 1992. *Turkic Oral Epic Poetry: Traditions, Forms, Poetic Structure*. The Albert Bates Lord Studies in Oral Tradition 7. New York.

———. 2011. *Tujueyu Minzu de Koutou Shishi: Chuantong, Xingshi yu Shige Jiegou* 《突厥语民族的口头史诗：传统、形式与诗歌结构》. Trans. A. Zhumaturdu, from Reichl 1992. Beijing.

Sanders, T. T. 1976. Review of C. H. Wang *The Bell and the Drum: Shih Ching as Formulaic Poetry in an Oral Tradition*. *Bulletin of the School of Oriental and African Studies* 39:256–256.

Wagner, M. L. 1984. *The Lotus Boat: The Origins of Chinese Tz'u Poetry in T'ang Popular Culture*. New York.

Wang, C. H. 王靖献/杨牧. 1974. *The Bell and the Drum: Shih Ching as Formulaic Poetry in an Oral Tradition*. Berkeley.

———. 1975. "Towards Defining a Chinese Heroism." *Journal of the American Oriental Society* 95:25–35.

———. 1989. *Zhong yu Gu: Shijing de Taoyu jiqi Chuangzuo Fangshi* 《〈诗经〉的套语及其创作方式》. Trans. Q. Xie 谢谦, from Wang 1974. Chengdu.

Yen, A. (Yen, P. C.) 晏君强/晏平秋. 1975. "The Parry-Lord Theory Applied to Vernacular Chinese Stories." *Journal of the American Oriental Society*, 95: 403–416.

———. 1990. *Chinese Demon Tales: Meanings and Parallels in Oral Tradition*. Harvard Dissertations in Folklore and Oral Tradition. Ed. A. B. Lord. PhD diss, 1971, Harvard University. New York.

———. 1997. *Proverbs, Songs, Epic Narratives, Folktales of East Asia: Selected Texts, Parallel Analysis and Comparative Approach*. New York.

Yin, H. 尹虎彬. 1996a. "Shishi de Shixue: Koutou Chengshi Lilun Yanjiu" 史诗的诗学：口头程式理论研究 [Poetics of epic: Studies in oral formulaic theory]. *Minzu Wenxue Yanjiu* [Studies of ethnic literature] 3:86–94.

———. 1996b. "Koutou Wenxue Yanjiu zhong de Chengshi Gainian." 口头文学研究中的程式概念 [The concept of formula in oral literature research]. *Minjian Wenxue Luntan* [Tribune of folk literature] 3:57–64, 29.

———. 1998. "Koutou Shixue de Benwen Gainian." 口头诗学的本文概念 [The concept of text in oral poetics]. *Minzu Wenxue Yanjiu* [Studies of ethnic literature] 3:89–93.

———. 1999. "Koutou Shixue guanyu Ge de Gainian." 口头诗学关于歌的概念 [The concept of song in oral poetics]. *Minzu Wenxue Yanjiu* [Studies of ethnic literature] 4:83–87.

———. 2002a. *Gudai Jingdian yu Koutou Chuantong* 《古代经典与口头传统》 [Classical canon and oral tradition]. Beijing.

———. 2002b. "Pali Luode Koutou Shixue Shilun." 帕里、洛德口头诗学试论 [On Parry-Lord oral poetics]. *Zhongguo Minsuxue Niankan 2000–2001* [Annals of Chinese folklore research 2001–2002]:157–173.

———. 2002c. "Koutou Shixue yu Minzuzhi." 口头诗学与民族志 [Oral poetics and ethnography]. In *Minsu Yanjiu* [Folklore studies] 2:19–30.

Zhu, G. 朱刚. 2015. *Zuowei Jiaoliu de Koutou Yishu Shijian: Jianchuan Baizu Shibaoshan Gehui Yanjiu*《作为交流的口头艺术实践—剑川白族石宝山歌会研究》 [Verbal art as communication: The study on Shibaoshan song-fair of the Bai people in Jianchuan]. MA thesis, the Graduate School of Chinese Academy of Social Sciences, 2007; PhD diss., Minzu University of China, 2013. Beijing.

———. 2018. "Hafu Daxue Yanjing Xueshe yu Zhongguo Koutou Chuantong Yanjiu de Lanshang: Yi Zhongguo Shehui Kexueyuan Minzu Wenxue Yanjiusuo weili." 哈佛大学燕京学社与中国口头传统研究的滥觞—以中国社会科学院民族文学研究所为例 [Harvard-Yenching institute and the inception of Oral Traditions Research in China: The Institute of Ethnic Literature of the Chinese Academy of Social Sciences as case study]. *Minzu Wenxue Yanjiu* [Studies of ethnic literature] 6:69–80.

## Online References

*Chinese Oral Traditions*, special issue, *Oral Tradition* 16(2) 2001. https://journal.oraltradition.org/issues/16ii

China Ethnic Literature Network (IEL website): http://iel.cass.cn

China Folklore Network: http://www.chinafolklore.org/

*Epic Traditions in China* (a special column): http://cel.cssn.cn/ztpd/zgss/

Web articles and forums:
http://cel.cssn.cn/ztpd/ktctyj/
http://www.chinafolklore.org/web/index.php?ChannelID=176
http://www.chinafolklore.org/forum/forumdisplay.php?fid=227

UNESCO Intangible Cultural Heritage: https://ich.unesco.org/en
Gesar epic tradition: https://ich.unesco.org/en/RL/gesar-epic-tradition-00204
Manas: https://ich.unesco.org/en/RL/manas-00209
Hezhen Yimakan storytelling: https://ich.unesco.org/en/USL/hezhen-yimakan-storytelling-00530

China National Inventory of Representative Elements of Intangible Cultural Heritage:
http://www.ihchina.cn/project#target1

# PART VI

# AUDIBLE ARCHIVES

# 19

# The Singing of Tales

## The Role of Music in the Performance of Oral Epics in Turkey and Central Asia

Karl Reichl

When Albert Lord published his ground-breaking study of South Slavic oral epic poetry in 1960, he entitled his book *The Singer of Tales*: the *singer* of tales, not the narrator of tales. With this title, Lord acknowledged the fact that the South Slavic *pjevač* is literally a singer, who accompanies his *song*—appropriately termed *pjesma*—with a musical instrument. Although music is not discussed in Lord's book, he was, of course, aware of the importance of the musical aspect of performance. In the first volume of *Serbocroatian Heroic Songs*, he included Béla Bartók's transcription of one of the songs (*The Captivity of Đulić Ibrahim*).[1] Lord collaborated with Béla Bartók on their *Serbo-Croatian Folk Songs*[2] and encouraged Stephen Erdely to transcribe more songs from the Parry collection, a collaborative effort that resulted in the full transcription of three South Slavic epics from the Bihać region of Bosnia.[3] As the epics are sung in performance, the analysis of music can be helpful for a correct transcription, at least when the texts are transcribed from the recordings rather than taken down from the singer's dictation. Lord notes this in his preface to the first volume of *Serbocroatian Heroic Songs*:

> The musical transcriptions in this volume were done by the eminent musicologist, composer, and pianist, the late Béla Bartók. In 1941 Professor George Herzog, then of Columbia University and now of Indiana University, yielded his position as musicologist for the Parry

1 Lord 1954:437–467.
2 Bartók and Lord 1951.
3 Erdely 1995.

> Collection to Professor Bartók, who had been his teacher in Budapest. As these scholars worked on the music, they made valuable suggestions about the text, and for both their musical skill and their linguistic sense I am indebted to them.[4]

When we look at editions and translations of oral epics worldwide, we find that even if the importance of music is acknowledged, it is generally ignored in practice. This is so even in cases where a living tradition furnishes material for a study of the music. Lauri Honko, who edited, together with his local collaborators Chinnappa Gowda and Viveka Rai, the Tulu epic of *Siri*,[5] gives some information on the differences between the dictated and the sung versions of the epic in the accompanying textualization volume[6] as well as on the singing of the epic in the paddyfields.[7] In Daniel Biebuyck and Kahombo Mateene's edition and translation of the Banyanga *Mwindo* epic (from the Democratic Republic of the Congo), the performance of the epic is characterized as "music, rhythm, song, dance, movement, dramatic entertainment,"[8] but the music is neither discussed nor illustrated. In some cases, the musical aspect is somewhat better described. John Smith's edition, translation and study of the Rajasthani epic of *Pābūjī* contains a section on "The words and music of Pābūjī's epic."[9] Similarly Gordon Innes's edition and translation of three Mandinka versions of the epic of *Sunjata* gives some information on music, also with some musical examples.[10] The volumes in the excellent Russian series *Èpos narodov SSSR* ("Epics of the Peoples of the Soviet Union"), now entitled *Èpos narodov Evrazii* (Epics of the Peoples of Eurasia), generally have an appendix on the music of the epics edited and translated, often with musical notations. Only rarely do editions and translations of epics contain musical illustrations in sound. A notable exception are the volumes of the series *Pamyatniki fol'klora narodov Sibiri i Dal'nego Vostoka* (Monuments of the Folklore of the Peoples of Siberia and the Far East), published by the Russian Academy of Sciences in Novosibirsk. In the early volumes, small records—and in later publications CDs—are added to the various editions and translations. The second edition of Lord's *The Singer of Tales*, prepared by Stephen Mitchell and Gregory Nagy (2000), did just that: added a CD with a video clip and all the examples of the book as audio files. In my edition of the Karakalpak epic of *Edige*

4 Lord 1954:xiv–xv.
5 Honko 1998b.
6 Honko 1998a:81–88, 276–321.
7 Honko 1998a:548–557.
8 Biebuyck and Mateene 1969:14.
9 Smith 1991:14–53, with musical notations.
10 Innes 1974:17–24.

in the Finnish Folklore Fellows Communications series, I have followed this practice by including a CD with audio and video clips.[11]

The widespread use of the internet has changed this picture in recent years. A number of epic performances, at least in snippets, can be watched on YouTube. A particularly rich mine is the UNESCO Intangible Heritage site. Audio files are also available for a number of epics in the Parry collection; the electronic version of John Foley's edition and translation of *The Wedding of Mustajbey's Son Bećirbey* from the Parry collection (2004) has links to these audio files.[12]

This is not to say that the music of epic is not discussed, but these discussions are generally restricted to musicological audiences and only occasionally found in works aimed at a nonspecialist readership. Some examples of works on the music of oral epic are Ruth Stone's books on the epic performances of the Kpelle of Liberia,[13] the in-depth study of Persian and Turkic epic singers in Iranian Khorasan by Ameneh Youssefzadeh, with illustrations on a CD,[14] and a collection of articles on the performance and music of oral epics edited by me.[15] Although scholars are aware of the importance of music, in particular when they concentrate on oral epics in performance, in their discussions and interpretations musical analysis is clearly accorded a minor role, if found at all.[16] Understandably, scholars equipped to work on the texts of oral epics will only rarely also be specialists for the study of their music, while for ethnomusicologists the necessity to deal with sometimes sizable texts might be a reason for preferring to study instrumental music and the music of songs rather than the music of epics. As the example of Lord and Bartók shows, however, cooperation across disciplines is possible and desirable.

It is typical of a great number of epic traditions that the melodies to which an epic is sung are both repetitive and of a fairly simple structure. This creates an effect of monotony, certainly on the listener who is not familiar with the musical culture of the epic tradition in question. A certain monotony will probably be the first impression also of the music of South Slavic oral epics. Looking at the transcriptions Bartók provided, one can see, however, that the melodies are anything but simple. The sung melodic line is incessantly varied as the singer is reciting the epic;

11 Reichl 2007.

12 UNESCO: http://www.unesco.org/culture/ich/index.php?lg=en&pg=00001; Parry Collection: https://mpc.chs.harvard.edu; Foley's edition: http://archive.oraltradition.org/zbm. For Reichl 2022, five audio and three video samples are available on the publisher's website (http://www.routledge.com/9780367761318).

13 Stone 1982, 1988.

14 Youssefzadeh 2002.

15 Reichl 2000.

16 On the music of epic, see also the collection of articles edited by Zemtsovskiy 1989 and the entries on epic in the two major music encyclopedias, *The New Grove* (Pegg and Porter 2001) and *Die Musik in Geschichte und Gegenwart* (Suppan 1979).

it is enriched by melismas and entertains a subtle dialogue with the music of the accompanying instrument. It has been repeatedly stated that the music of the recitation of oral epics is simple—"unbelievably simple" in the words of the ethnomusicologist Curt Sachs—and hence a sign of "the domination of poetry over music." [17] Whether this view is justifiable is a question difficult to answer. Performance traditions whose music is composed along the lines of repetitive, "stichic" melodies, with a fairly restricted ambitus and small intervals, would have to be studied in detail before a conclusion regarding the position of music vis-à-vis the text can be reached. My own observations with regard to this type of melodic and musical structuring in the recitation of the Karakalpak singer (*jıraw*) Jumabay Bazarov have led me to think that even the simplest type of recitation has a musical significance of its own in addition to being a vehicle for the projection of the singer's voice.[18]

There are, however, also epic traditions where music is clearly in the foreground. In *The Korean Singer of Tales*, a title modeled on Lord's seminal study, Marshall R. Pihl explains:

> The Korean singer of tales is called a *kwangdae*. His oral narrative is known as *p'ansori*, a long form of vocal music in which he sings a work of narrative literature with appropriate dramatic gesture. ... [T]he four essential characteristics of *p'ansori* [are]: it is a solo oral technique, it is dramatic, it is musical, and it is in verse.[19]

When one listens to *p'ansori* narratives or watches the video of various *p'ansori* performances on UNESCO's Intangible Heritage website, one is certainly struck by the theatrical dimensions of this type of epic performance, where both singing and acting seem to play an important part.

It would be a worthwhile task to study the role of music in various types of epic performance and to develop some kind of taxonomy. Clearly, this is the subject of a book-length study. In the present context a choice has to be made. Given that Âşık Şeref Taşlıova, one of the singers who performed at the conference on "Singers and Tales in the 21st Century: The Legacies of Milman Parry and Albert Lord," came from a tradition where music is an important element of epic, I will focus on this type of epic. My examples will come from the world of the Turks, from both Turkey and, due to my own research, the Turkic-speaking areas of Central Asia. Linking the oral epic tradition of Turkey with those of Uzbekistan, Turkmenistan, or Karakalpakistan is done in a spirit of comparative

17 Sachs 1962:8.
18 See Reichl 2007:163–178.
19 Pihl 1994:3.

analysis and not, I would like to emphasize, from a pan-Turkic stance. As in other language families, the speakers of these (on the whole fairly closely) related languages share first of all a linguistic heritage. This heritage does, however, extend into the cultural realm, and a case can be made for interpreting some of the common features in their oral traditions as inherited. This, however, is not the goal of the remarks that follow. It should also be noted that these traditions are geographically contiguous and that they share traits with other oral traditions of the area, most notably with that of the Iranian Tajiks.[20]

## Prosimetrum: The Form of *hikâye* and *dāstān*

Albert Lord entitled his book the singer of *tales*, not of epics. This is helpful when it comes to Turkic traditions. Much Turkic oral epic poetry conforms to the genre expectations of "epic" which, as is well known, are based on the Homeric epics and the later European tradition, from Virgil to Milton and beyond. Oral works like the Kirghiz *Manas* or the Kazakh *Qoblandı* are narratives in verse, of heroic nature, of epic proportions (some versions of *Manas* are considerably longer than the *Iliad*), and also, in style and narrative structure, of "epic grandeur." But there are also other kinds of oral narrative. Some of these are heroic in nature and differ from epics like *Manas* or *Qoblandı* only by their form: they are composed in a mixture of verse and prose. *Prosimetrum*, as the mixture of verse and prose is termed in literary criticism, is known from many traditions. It is characterized in the *Princeton Encyclopedia of Poetry and Poetics* as "[a] text composed in alternating segments of prose and verse. The *prosimetrum* is widely attested in both Western and Eastern lit[erature]s and apparently appears worldwide. Typically, the verse portions serve as lyric, emotive, or personal insets within a philosophical or narrative frame, often with connectives between prose and verse sections ..."[21] As a rule, the verse portions predominate while the prose portions

20 For a general survey of Turkic oral epics, see Boratav 1964a, Chadwick and Zhirmunsky 1969, and Reichl 1992. In the following discussion, words in Turkish and Azeri are written according to the current Latin orthography used in Turkey and Azerbaijan. Uzbek, Karakalpak, and Turkmen are today written in Latin script but according to different rules and with different conventions. In order to avoid too much heterogeneity, for the transliteration of the Turkic languages other than Turkish and Azeri, a system adapted from the recommendations of the *International Journal of Middle Eastern Studies* for the transliteration of Persian has been used: sh = Turkish ş, ch = Turkish ç, j = Turkish c, gh = Turkish ğ, q = velar k; ā, ō, ū for long vowels; I have retained Turkish ö and ü for umlauts and ı for the unrounded velar i-sound. Open e I have noted by the phonetic schwa-sign as in the Azeri script (ə). Arabic loanwords are written as in the respective Turkic language (*hikâye* instead of *ḥikāya* etc.).

21 Greene et al. 2012:1115–1116, at 1115. For a survey of prosimetric narrative in world literature, see Harris and Reichl 1997; in this volume, there is also a chapter on the mixture of verse and prose in Turkic oral epic poetry (pp. 321–348).

serve as narrative links between them. This implies that these narratives can be viewed as epics in verse with interspersed prose (rather than prose narratives with interspersed verse). While some Turkic traditions favor verse epics, others prefer prosimetric oral narratives. Sometimes the same epic might be sung by one singer in verse only, by another in a mixture of verse and prose. To give only one example, the various Uzbek versions of the epic of *Alpamish* are in a mixture of verse and prose, while most Kazakh versions of the same epic are in verse; among the Karakalpaks, versions both in verse and in *prosimetrum* are found.[22]

In addition to heroic epics, there is also a different type of orally performed narrative among the traditions discussed here. These narratives are composed in a mixture of verse and prose and their reciters are, as in the case of the heroic epic, singers of tales, sometimes the same singers who recite heroic epics. However, these narratives differ from the heroic epic in content and style: their plot centers on adventure and love, and the verse portions in these prosimetric narratives are often monologues and dialogues of the protagonists, typically lovers whose love has been thwarted by some misfortune and who express their feelings in lyrical songs. As with the heroic epics, the prose is recited, while the verse portions are sung. On account of their orientation and style, it seems appropriate to call these oral narratives "romances." There is no space here for a discussion of genre; suffice it to say that the distinction between "epic" and "romance" which W. P. Ker (1908) has drawn with regard to medieval literature, can also be applied to these two types of oral narratives of the Turkic world: heroic epics (in verse or in a mixture of verse and prose) on the one hand and (generally prosimetric) "lyrical epics" on the other.[23]

In native terminology, the *tales* the epic singers perform are called *dāstān* in many Central Asian Turkic traditions and *hikâye* in Turkey. Both terms are loanwords (from Persian and Arabic, respectively) and they are overgeneralized insofar as they comprise heroic songs, adventure narratives, and love tales—in other words, both "epic" and "romance." Other terms are also used; in Kazakh, heroic epics are generally denoted by the word *jır*, but the terms *dāstān* and *qissa* (from Arabic) are also used and not always clearly distinguished.[24] The singers' repertoire might comprise representatives of different genres.

[22] On *Alpamish* as a heroic epic (with close parallels to the return of Odysseus), see Chadwick and Zhirmunsky 1969:292–296, Reichl 1992:160–170, West 2012, and Levaniouk (2022).

[23] There is also a further type of oral epic among the Turkic-speaking peoples which might be called "shamanistic." It is found, for instance, among the Altaians and the Yakuts; Bowra explicitly excluded this type of epic from his *Heroic Poetry* (1952:5–9). All these types have, of course, subtypes and overlapping subgenres. On genre, see Reichl 1992:119–141.

[24] The basic meaning of Persian *dāstān* is "tale, story." The Arabic noun *ḥikāya*, "tale, story," is derived from the verb *ḥakā* "to speak, narrate"; the noun *qiṣṣa*, meaning both "cut" and "tale," is derived from the verb *qaṣṣa* "to cut."

Not in all traditions are generic borders drawn identically; in some, a singer's repertoire might be more specialized with respect to genre (or subgenre). Prosimetric romances are found in a wide area of Eurasia: in Turkey, Azerbaijan, Turkmenistan, Uzbekistan, Karakalpakistan (a part of Uzbekistan), Kazakhstan, and in Northwestern China among the Uighurs. Not only the genre but also specific romances are shared by all these Turkic peoples. To give an example, *Ashıq Gharib and Shah-Sanam* is one of these "lyrical epics." It is the story of a young man, Gharib, and a young woman, Sanam, who were promised to one another when they were born but who became separated through the evil intentions of the girl's father. When the girl, Sanam, is about to be married to another man, Gharib, who had become a love-sick singer (*âşık*), appears in disguise. In most versions, he comes just in time and Sanam, who had remained faithful to him, can become his wife. The plot will sound familiar: this romance is one of the most widely disseminated representatives of the motif of the "Return of the Husband in Disguise."[25] There are Turkish, Azerbaijanian, Turkmen, Crimean Tatar, Uzbek, Karakalpak, and Uighur versions of this romance. In Turkey, the romance is also found as a "folk book" (chap book, *halk kitabı*).

## Turkish *âşık* and Central Asian *bakhshi*

The singer of tales is in most of the traditions I have enumerated called *bakhshi*, a word which in Old Uighur means "teacher" and was later used to denote the shaman. Although the latter meaning persists in a number of Turkic languages, the modern Uzbek, Turkmen, or Uighur *bakhshi* is an epic singer only.[26] In Turkey the word *âşık* (Azeri *aşıq*) is used for the singer of tales and the traditional folk singer. This word, an Arabic loan, seems to have come into use at the beginning of the sixteenth century; it literally means "lover" and, according to P. N. Boratav, expresses the belief that a singer received his poetic gift in a dream, when a *pir* (saint) made him drink from the *aşk bâdesi*, the cup of love.[27] M. Fuad Köprülü and others have shown that there is also an intimate connection between some Turkish *âşık*s and dervish monasteries.[28] As with the term *bakhshi*, the term *âşık* has various shades of meaning, which depend on place and time, on local tradition and milieu. Although the very general idea of an *âşık* as a performer of "folk" lyrics to the accompaniment of the *saz* (a plucked instrument of the lute

25 Holzapfel 1990. On this romance and its music, see Reichl 2022:209-216.

26 On the term *bakhshi*, see Köprülü 1966:145–164 (originally published in the Turkish version of the *Encyclopedia of Islam*, 1942).

27 Boratav 1964c:129–131.

28 See Köprülü 1966:184–187; see also Reinhard and de Oliveira Pinto 1989:64–82 (on the relationship of the *âşık*s to different religious groups).

family) finds wide acceptance among speakers of Turkish, the precise form of the poetry (and music) performed and the role of the performer as composer can be meaningfully discussed only when one focuses on individual singers or more narrowly defined traditions.[29]

Âşık Şeref Taşlıova was one of the last Turkish folk singers who acquired his repertoire in the traditional way and who still, as of 2010, performed *hikâyes*.[30] He was born in 1938 in a village in the vicinity of Kars in northeastern Turkey (Çıldır province). His ancestors on his father's side came from the Caucasus, from a Turkic ethnic group called Karapapak or Terekeme, a group closely related to other Oghuz Turks, i.e. the Turks of Turkey, the Azerbaijanians and the Turkmens. Like other folk singers, Şeref Taşlıova started to learn and sing songs early. As a youngster of fifteen, he became apprenticed to Âşık Kasım, the son of a famous singer, Âşık Şenlik (1850–1913). He stayed with Âşık Kasım for a year and then went to learn with two other singers, Âşık Gülistan (1900–1972) and Âşık Müdâmî (1914–1968). From these three singers, Şeref Taşlıova learned to play the *saz*, to sing songs, and to narrate *hikâyes*. In addition, he was in contact with many other singers, some as his masters in younger years and many as his colleagues and competitors in various singer festivals and competitions. He, in turn, had five pupils who have become masters on their own (Şah İsmail, Korkmaz İkan, Nuri Şahinoğlu, Hikmet Arifi Ataman, Sadrettin Ulu). Âşık Şeref Taşlıova performed in many countries and on many occasions. I met Âşık Şeref first in Turkmenistan in 2006 on the occasion of the celebration of the four hundredth birthday of the seventeenth-century folk singer Karacaoğlan. In 2009, the Turkish *âşıklık* (minstrelsy) tradition, of which Âşık Şeref was an important representative, was inscribed on UNESCO's "Representative List of the Intangible Cultural Heritage of Humanity." In June 2010, Ardahan University awarded him an honorary doctorate.[31]

Âşık Şeref Taşlıova's œuvre was fairly large. A comprehensive edition of his poems or songs was published in 2010, prepared by his son Muammar Mete Taşlıova, lecturer of Turkish Folklore at Hitit University in Çorum (on the Black Sea). The book contains ca. 450 poems, classified as eight-syllable, eleven-syllable, and *divan(i)*-poems (fifteen-syllable verse lines, modeled on the *aruz* [quantitative] meter of classical poetry). The folksong genres represented are *koşma* (four-line stanzas, with an identical rhyme in the fourth line),

[29] On the various terms for singers (including the denotations *jıraw*, *aqın*, *jomoqchu*, *manaschı* and others), see Reichl 1992:57–91. On the Turkish *âşık* and his *epic* repertoire, see Çobanoğlu 2000, Başgöz 2008. For a discussion of the Azerbaijanian *aşıq*, see Blum 1972, Èldarova 1984, Oldfield 2008 (on women *aşıq*s with a predominantly lyric repertoire).

[30] Âşık Şeref Taşlıova died in 2014, four years after the conference.

[31] For his biography, see Taşlıova 2010:4–45.

*türkü* (folksong), and *destan* (narrative songs).[32] In addition, there are almost fifty contest poems (*karşılaşmalar*), comparable to the medieval *tenso/tenzone* or, nearer home to Turkish poetry, the Kazakh *aytıs*.

Some of his epic repertoire has also been published.[33] The singer distinguished four kinds of narrative: (1) *hikâyes* of tradition, which he learned from other singers (*usta malı hikâyeler*); (2) *hikâyes* of his own composition (*kendi tasnifi hikâyeler*); (3) traditional short narratives, often of an anecdotal character (*usta malı serencamlar*); and (4) short narratives of his own composition (*kendi tasnifi serencamlar*).[34] The first category comprises fourteen *hikâyes*, of which six have been edited (among them *Kirman Şah* and a branch from the *Köroğlu* cycle). The second category comprises six *hikâyes*, all of which are included in the recent edition. Of the third and fourth categories, comprising ten and two narratives, respectively, eight of category (3) and all two of category (4) are found in the edition of 2008.

To give an idea of the proportions of these tales, I will briefly describe one of the traditional *hikâyes* and one of his own composition. *Kirman Şah Hikâyesi* is a traditional *hikâye* and, like all of the singer's narratives, composed in a mixture of verse and prose. In print it comprises fifty-five pages; there is no indication of how long the original performance was. Judging from other texts in the collection where the performance time is given, it must have taken the singer at least four hours, probably longer, to tell and sing the tale. *Kirman Şah Hikâyesi* has about thirty verse passages, ranging from one to six four-line stanzas; in most cases, the verse passages have three four-line strophes (amounting to a total of 364 lines). The plot of this *hikâye* conforms to the adventure and love tale pattern of Turkish romance. The shah of Horasan, Ahmet Şah, marries the beautiful Mahbup Hanım. On false grounds he banishes his wife, who is pregnant and gives birth to a son, Kirman, in faraway Tiflis. When grown into a young man, Kirman is given a love potion by three dervishes in his dream. He departs to find "the girl of his dreams," Mahperî, but before he can marry her, he must first deliver her from the clutches of an ogre (*dev*). After the wedding, Kirman is betrayed and wounded by his two stepbrothers, the sons of his father's second marriage. He reaches Tiflis and is finally healed and reunited with his wife by the help of his faithful horse, Karakaytaz, but also his faithful friend the mighty Reyhan Arap (a figure from the *Köroğlu*-cycle). The narrative pace is swift. Moments of rest are the songs interspersed into the tale. Âşık Şeref's style is characterized by lively dialogue, narrator's comments on words and expressions, manners and

32 On the genres of folk poetry, see Boratav 1964b. Turkish *destan* denotes a genre of folksong, while Uzbek (Uighur, Karakalpak etc.) *dāstān* denotes the oral epic (heroic epic and romance).

33 Türkmen, Taşlıova, and Tan 2008.

34 The word *serencam* means "a noteworthy event."

customs, appeals to the audience, and formulas of narrative transition. One of these is actually taken from the fourteenth-century *Book of Dede Korkut* (*"At ayağı külüng olur, âşık dili yürük olur" demiş eski üstatlarımız*).[35]

The second *hikâye* I would like to briefly summarize is of his own composition and was performed by Âşık Şeref at the conference in 2010. It is entitled *Bağdat Hanım ile Hafiz Hikâyesi* (The Tale of Lady Bağdat and Hafız).[36] In the vicinity of Kars, on the western shore of Lake Çıldır, are the ruins of the town of Kalaça. In former times a man by the name of Reşit Bey lived in Kalaça. He had a beautiful daughter called Bağdat. On the eastern shore of Lake Çıldır, in a place named Albız, lived at the same time Mahmut Ağa; he had a son by the name of Hafız as well as two daughters. One night, three dervishes appear in Bağdat's dream and give her a love potion to drink. They also serve Hafız a love potion in his dream. The young people fall in love with one another, their "366 veins and 144 bones burn with the fire of love." Hafız has a rival, but his courtship is, in the end, successful, and Bağdat's father is ready to consent to his daughter's marriage to him. Bağdat lights an oil lamp every night on a tower balcony of her house. The unsuccessful suitor's family, however, hasn't given up and engages a wily crone to break the engagement. She suspects that the light is there to help Hafız swim across the lake every night to see his beloved. On the seventh night, Hafız does indeed cross the lake, but it is the night his foes have managed to extinguish the light. Hafız drowns. When Bağdat hears what has happened, she dies of grief. The two lovers are buried side by side.

This *hikâye* comprises eleven pages in print. The printed version took three hours to record (in 1998); it contains a total of 220 verse lines, generally arranged in four-line stanzas, including an introductory poem of 32 lines (called *döşeme*). Looking at the printed edition, it might seem that the prose predominates; in actual performance, however, the singing of the lyric insertions fills most of the time.[37] The singer took the plot of his *hikâye* from a legend, which he published under the title "Çıldır Gölü Efsaneleri" (Legends of Lake Çıldır) in a local journal (*Kars Eli*) in 1966–1967.[38] What is interesting about this *hikâye* is, of course, that it is a modern version of a very old tale, the story of Hero and Leander, a story

[35] Türkmen, Taşlıova, and Tan 2008:20. ("'The horse's leg is fast, the *âşık*'s tongue presses forward,' said our old masters.") In the *Book of Dede Korkut*, the formula is *At ayağı külüg ozan dili çevük olur* ("The horse's leg is fast, the *ozan*'s tongue is swift"); for an English translation of the *Book*, see Sümer, Uysal, and Walker 1972.

[36] Türkmen, Taşlıova, and Tan 2008:245–275.

[37] When Âşık Şeref performed at the conference, he was asked to shorten the *hikâye*. He understood this as telling the whole story and leaving out some of the lyric passages. This led to a predominance of the spoken over the sung word.

[38] Türkmen, Taşlıova, and Tan 2008:275.

which has been retold in innumerable versions, from Ovid and Musaeus to Franz Grillparzer.[39]

Âşık Şeref was a creative artist and, at the same time, a traditional singer. Among his songs, there are many topical lyrics, which express his ideas about contemporary events and social values. In his artistic expression, he was both individual and traditional: individual in his views, traditional in his style. He was a representative of Turkish folk music and *âşık* art; but he was also a representative of a type of art which is found in a wider area. There are many parallels between the way Âşık Şeref acquired his repertoire, transmitted the epic heritage of his culture, and composed within the traditional mould of Turkish folk poetry, and the way Uzbek, Turkmen, or Uighur *bakhshis* become epic singers and performers, transmit traditional poetry, and shape their native verbal and musical art with their own compositions. Central Asian epic singers have generally learned their art from a master singer, sometimes their father or uncle. From the affiliations of a singer to his master or masters and a master to his pupils, "genealogies" of singers can be plotted; groups of singers "descending" from a common "ancestor" have been called "singer schools" (Uzbek *bakhshi maktablari*). Local centers of such singer schools have been identified, in Uzbekistan, Kyrgyzstan, and other areas. By their training, the singers acquire a repertoire of *dāstāns*. At the same time, they learn shorter poems (Uzbek *terma*) and begin to compose poems of their own (on topical subjects or on their lives). The first Uzbek *bakhshi* I recorded (in 1981), Chāri Shāir Khojamberdi-oghli, sang in addition to excerpts from various *dāstāns* (*Rawshan*, *Goroghli*, *Alpāmish*, *Avazkhān*, *Rustamkhān*), *terma* on the following topics: "My *dombra*" (the singer's musical instrument), "On the Party," "On the Party Congress," "On Tashkent," "On Boka" (the name of the place where his collective farm was), "On Lenin," and "On Our Newspaper." In these songs, general reflections were mixed with reminiscences of autobiographical events. The *terma* are traditional in style but, at the same time, individual compositions. Among the Kazakhs, the favorite improvised genre of the singers (called *aqıns* rather than *bakhshis*) is the *aytıs*, a contest poem.[40] Sometimes real contests with other poets take place—such as the contest festivals in which Âşık Şeref often took part in Turkey—and sometimes a singer performs the songs exchanged in a contest between famous singers as one poem. The singer's song is then, as it were, a reenactment of a past *aytıs*.

39 For a detailed discussion of the "Hero-and-Leander" story in folklore and medieval literature, see Reichl 2015.

40 See Winner 1958:29–34; compare Erdener 1995. Two types of *aytıs* are generally distinguished: *aytıs* between singers/poets and *aytıs* between a *jigit* (young man) and a *qız* (young woman). This kind of contest poetry is also found in other traditions as, for instance, among the Kirghiz and Karakalpaks.

## The Role of Music in *hikâye* and *dāstān*

The verse parts of prosimetric epics and romances are sung by the singers to the accompaniment of a string instrument, often a plucked lute (*dombra*, *dutar*, *rabab*, *saz*), sometimes also a bowed lute (*qobuz*). In Turkey, the *saz* is used, which comes in different sizes (*divan sazı*, *meydan sazı*, *bağlama*, *cura*). In some traditions there is an additional musician accompanying the singer, as, for instance, a *ghijjak* (or *ghirjek*) player among the Turkmens and the Karakalpaks (the *ghijjak* is a type of spike fiddle). In Khorezm in Uzbekistan (Urgench, Khiva), the singer is accompanied by a small ensemble. There are various words to designate the melodies used to accompany the sung portions of *dāstān* and *hikâye*, such as *navā* (Uzbek), *nama* (Karakalpak), *hava* (Azeri, Turkish), and *makam* (Turkish). The latter is the term favored by Turkish *âşıks*. This is a somewhat confusing use of the word *makam*, as in Turkish classical music a *makam* is, on the one hand, a scale with a specific sequence of intervals and, on the other, a set of "melodic formulas" typical of each *makam* (somewhat similar to a mode in Gregorian chant). This is a legacy from Arab music (Arabic *maqām*); Turkish music theorists distinguish more than 300 *makams* in classical music.[41] In the music of the *âşıks*, however, the term *makam* is basically equivalent to *hava*. In the Kars region of Turkey, i.e. the region from which Âşık Şeref came, over 150 *makams* are in use among *âşıks*. For the performance of the verse passages in the *hikâyes*, Âşık Şeref used a total of sixty *makams*. A similarly rich corpus of melodies is found in other traditions. One of the last traditional Karakalpak *bakhshi*s (Karakalpak *baqsı*), Genjebay Tilewmuratov (1929–1997) used, according to his own information, about eighty *nama*. He learned the art of performance from his father, Tilewmurat-baqsı Atamurat-ulı. He began playing the *dutar* at the age of seven and by the age of twelve had mastered three epics, *Yusup and Akhmet*, *Sayatkhan and Həmra* and *Qırman-dəli* (of the *Göroghli* cycle).[42] He worked as a teacher and later as an artist on local radio and television stations.[43]

There are a number of tasks and problems that await solution in connection with the musical aspects of an *âşık*'s or *bakhshi*'s performance. Some are of a technical, others of an interpretative, nature. It is an unfortunate fact that most editions of Turkic heroic epics and romances are without musical illustrations either in sound or in notated form. This is also true of Âşık Şeref's œuvre. The transcription of non-Western music is a general problem of ethnomusicological research and need not be discussed here. The problem is also familiar

41 See Reinhard and Stokes 2001.

42 Turkish and Azeri *Köroğlu* corresponds to Uzbek and Uyghur *Göroghli*, Türkmen *Görogli* and Karakalpak *Görughlı*.

43 On this singer, see Maqsetov 1983:188–196. Some of his music is edited in Allanazarov 2002.

from the various transcriptions of South Slavic epic melodies (Béla Bartók, Stephen Erdely, George Herzog, and others).[44] Then there is the problem of analyzing the music, of finding a descriptive framework that does justice to the subtlety of the music and yet is accessible to a wider musically interested readership. Some of these problems have been discussed with regard to the Turkish *âşık* tradition by Ursula Reinhard and Tiago de Oliveira Pinto,[45] often, incidentally, citing Âşık Şeref as their informant. Reinhard and de Oliveira Pinto distinguish eight types of *makam* from the region of Kars according to a number of criteria: (1) *makams* associated with a particular singer as their composer (i.e. *Şeref makamı*); (2) *makams* referring to ethnic origin (e.g. *Türkmen makamı*); (3) *makams* typical of a particular epic (e.g. *Köroğlu makamı*); (4) praise poetry *makams* (*Güzelleme makamı*); (5) *makams* with a special type of singing mode (e.g. *hoş dımak* "with a sweet voice"); (6) *makams* classified according to musical criteria; (7) *makams* for religious and meditative poetry; and (8) *divan makams*, which they explain as follows: "According to Âşık Şeref there are twenty-one *divani*. They are often sung in Bektaşi monasteries. Their topics are the transitoriness of the world, the powerlessness of man, God's might, and the burden of human existence."[46] Clearly these are very diverse criteria, which are only marginally helpful for a better understanding of the musical quality and structure of these melodies. Musical analysis is, however, possible, and Reinhard and de Oliveira Pinto do, in fact, provide a number of suggestions for a musical characterization of these *makam*.

Although there is variation in the use of melodies among different *âşıks* and *bakhshis*, there is yet a traditionally prescribed relationship between particular verse parts of a *dāstān* or *hikâye* and its music. The various melodies a singer masters have names, and these names are associated with specific verse passages. In a study of the way Azerbaijanian *aşıqs* sing the epic of *Köroğlu*, Tariel' Mamedov distinguishes and illustrates various melodies, such as *Deli Köroğlu*, *Meydan Köroğlu*, *Misri Köroğlu*, *Jangi Köroğlu*.[47] Ferruh Arsunar, in her edition of a Turkish version of *Köroğlu*, adds musical notations to the various verse passages, with names such as *Cengi meydan havası*, *Nikâh havası*, *Göç havası*, and *Hasret havası*.[48] The Turkish *âşık* Orhan Bahçıvan maintains that there are forty *Köroğlu* melodies, among them *Deli Köroğlu makamı*, *Meydan Köroğlu*, *Misri*

44 On musical transcription, see the survey by Ellingson 1992.

45 Reinhard and de Oliveira Pinto 1989.

46 Reinhard and de Oliveira Pinto 1989:89, my translation.

47 Crazy (or brave) Köroğlu, Köroğlu on the battle-field, Köroğlu with his Egyptian sabre, Köroğlu's fight. See Mamedov 1984.

48 Melody of the battlefield, wedding melody, (nomadic) migration melody, nostalgic melody. See Arsunar 1963.

*(kılıç) havası*, and *Cengi makamı*.[49] In his performance of *The Tale of Lady Bağdat and Hafiz* at Harvard University in 2010, Âşık Şeref sang three songs as part of the tale; in the first song, Bağdat tells her mother about the visit of the dervishes in her dream; in the second, Hafız tells his mother that he had seen a beautiful girl "whose eyes are like those of a gazelle" (*Ana, ben bir güzel gördüm, / Gözleri ceylana benzer*); in the third, Bağdat begs her parents not to separate her from her lover (*Ana [Baba], beni sevdiğimden ayırma*). According to the singer's information, he sang the first song in the Local Praise-Poem melody (*Yerli Güzellemesi havası*), the second in the Köroğlu Praise-Poem melody (*Köroğlu Güzellemesi*), and the third in the Erzurum-Hasankale regional melody (*Erzurum-Hasankale ağzı*). None of the songs the *âşık* sang on that occasion are found in the edited text, but there are poems (with different words) in the places where the singer sang the first and the third song.

What has been said about lyrical epics also applies to heroic epics. In 1956, excerpts from the epic *Alpamysh* (*Alpamıs*) in the Karakalpak version of the singer (*jıraw*) Qıyas Qayratdinov (1903–1974) were tape-recorded, and in 1999 edited with their melodies. This edition contains thirty melodies with descriptive names such as *Alpamıs naması*, *Noghaylı naması* or *Ullı ziban naması*.[50] In addition to such descriptive names there are, both for Turkish and Central Asian oral epics, also names referring to various types of song or poem, such as *Köroğlu koşması* or *Deyiş* in Turkish and, in Karakalpak, *Kelte tolghaw naması*.[51] Some of the verse passages are more closely linked to particular melodies than others. In the Karakalpak versions of *Ashıq Gharib and Shah-Sanam*, for instance, the melody *Aruwkhan* (Beauty) is used for a famous passage at the end of the *dāstān* when Sanam, at the sight of her lover, who is standing at the foot of her pavilion, is ready to throw herself into his arms. Some of these songs have also been transmitted separately and can be heard performed by singers who are unable to tell a tale.

There is no space here for musical analysis. Nevertheless, I would like to give one musical example to illustrate the way a poem can be musically shaped in the performance of a *hikâye* or *dastan*. My example comes from the *dastan Qırman-dəli* from the cycle of adventure romances linked to their central hero Köroğlu or Göroghlı. This was one of the *dastans* in Genjebay Tilewmuratov's repertoire, as mentioned above. Unfortunately, his version has not been recorded. In 1995, I was able to record a complete version of this *dastan* from a Turkmen singer in Törtkul, southern Karakalpakistan, Gulum-bakhshi Ilmetop (1939–1999). In Turkmen the *dastan* is called *Kharman-dəli* (Crazy Kharman). This is the name of

49 https://web.archive.org/web/20081121033711/http://www.minidev.com/turku/turku7.asp.
50 Alpamysh melody, Noghay melody, Long speech melody. See Karāmatli and Mirza 1999.
51 Short *tolghaw* melody. *Koşma*, *deyiş* and *tolghaw* are types of song.

the main heroine: she announces that she will give her hand in marriage only to the man who will defeat her in a wrestling match and in a singing contest. Göroghlı (Göroglı) also enters the lists but is not successful. In the end, only Ashıq Aydın, the patron saint of singers, is able to defeat Kharman-dəli in the singing contest. The *dastan* begins with Kharman-dəli sending an old woman—called *mama-jan* "dear granny" by her—to Göroghlı to invite him to the contest. The following is the first song:[52]

Chandıbile *geler yarım ey-jan-ey* Görogliga,
Bar mama-jan, *ey-vaey*, khabarıng ber,
Bar mama-jan, *ey*, khabarıng ber!
Aslı gerchek beg oglın(a)-*ey*,
Bar mama-jan-*ey*, khabarıng ber!

Dilegim, *yar-ey dad-ey*, bersin alla,
Chünki ıgtıkadım, valley,
Chünki ıgtıkadım, valley!
*Akh*, Yene berey yüz müng tılla!
Bar, mama-jan-*ey*, khabarıng ber!

Görogli beg, *yar-ey*, gelip görsün!
Mama-jan, *ey-vaey*, ömür bersin,
Mama sang(a)-*ey* ömür bersin!
*A*, Mening bilen-*ey* dövran sürsin!
Bar mama-jan-*ey*, khabarıng ber!

Kharman-dəli, *yar-ey*, diyirler manga,
Igtıyarım diydim sang(a)-*eı*.
*Ey*, Igtıyarym diydim sang(a)-*eı*,
Bar, mama-jan-*ey*, khabarıng ber.

To Görogli in Chandıbel
Go, *mama-jan*, deliver your message,
Go, *mama-jan*, deliver your message!
To the brave son of a beg
Go, *mama-jan*, deliver your message!

52 Transcribed here according to the transliteration system used in this article; note that the transcribers of the music prefer the older Cyrillic orthography of Turkmen.

May God grant my wish,
Because of my faith, by God,
Because of my faith, by God!
I will give another hundred thousand pieces of gold.
Go, *mama-jan*, deliver your message!

May Görogli-beg come and see,
May he give his life, *mama-jan*,
May he give you his life!
May he live in happiness with me!
Go, *mama-jan*, deliver your message!

I am called Kharman-dəli,
I have given you my permission (to leave),
I have given you my permission.
Go, *mama-jan*, deliver your message!

The poem is in stanzas of five or four lines. The text of this poem in other Turkmen versions, as far as they are published, is very similar to Gulum-bakhshi's text. They are, however, all in stanzas of four lines. The five-line stanza results from a repetition of the second line; in the fourth stanza, however, a line seems to be missing (when compared to other versions).[53] The poem is composed in octosyllabic verse lines; in singing the lines, the *bakhshi* frequently inserts extra syllables, some meaningless (*ey*), some meaningful words (*yar* "beloved"). These extra syllables are printed in italics. In addition to extra syllables in the line, there are also extra syllables between the lines and between stanzas (as shown in the musical transcription below). In some words the case ending *–a* (dative) is elided when an *ey* is added.

Like the Karakalpak *baqsıs*, Türkmen singers of the Tashauz (Dashoguz) tradition, to which Gulum-bakhshi belongs, play the *dutar* and are accompanied by a *ghijjak*-player. In the following notation of this song, only the voice and the dutar accompaniment is given. The *ghijjak* adds a further melodic line, which embroiders the *dutar* part and supports the voice. The transcription of words and music has been prepared by Djamilya Qurbanova and Murad Qurbanov of the Turkmen National Conservatory in Ashkhabad.

This example shows that the poem as text and the poem as song are almost entirely different entities. The poem is fairly simple; its content is straightforward: Kharman-dəli asks the old woman to take an invitation asking Göroghlı to

53 It is the line *Enem, yashıng yetsin yüze* (My mother, may our life reach a hundred years!) in Pelwan-baxshi's version; Karryev 1983:324.

Figure 1a. Transcription of *Qırman-dəli* as performed by Gulum-bakhshi Ilmetop, p. 1. Transcribed by Djamilya Qurbanova and Murad Qurbanov.

Figure 1b. Transcription of *Qırman-dəli* as performed by Gulum-bakhshi Ilmetop, p. 2. Transcribed by Djamilya Qurbanova and Murad Qurbanov.

Figure 1c. Transcription of *Qırman-dəli* as performed by Gulum-bakhshi Ilmetop, p. 3. Transcribed by Djamilya Qurbanova and Murad Qurbanov.

Figure 1d. Transcription of *Qırman-dəli* as performed by Gulum-bakhshi Ilmetop, p. 4. Transcribed by Djamilya Qurbanova and Murad Qurbanov.

come to her. There is little embroidering on this, and, unlike some of the lyrical passages later in the *dastan*, the poem is in a fairly plain style, without images or metaphors. The rhyme-words are also simple; there are no poetic words or onomatopoetic words, as often in these songs. The musical performance, on the other hand, is highly dramatic, full of energy, varied, ornamental, and skillful.

The drama of the musical performance is further enhanced by the use of different melodies for different verse passages. This offers the singer the possibility of expressing different moods in music. This is particularly noticeable in lyrical epics or love romances. The adaptation of the music to the content is, however, also found in heroic epics which are traditionally performed with a comparatively small set of melodies. In these epics, wedding songs (*yār-yār*), contest songs (*aytıs*), or elegies (*armān*) can be inserted, such as the wedding songs in *Alpamysh* or "Qanıkey's lament" in *Manas*. While there is a traditional link between verse-passage and music, the singer is also free to adapt his performance to the situation. No two performances are identical, either textually or musically. Ameneh Youssefzadeh translates a Persian-speaking *bakhshi*'s answer to the question of which melody he uses as follows:

> [...] The performer has hundreds of *maqâms* at his disposal. Depending on the mood of the audience and the choice of poems he can choose cheerful (*shâd*), burning (*suznâk*), martial (*razmi*) or melancholy (*hoznâvar*) tunes. In the *dastans*, however, melancholy melodies are preferred, since they treat of distant love.[54]

These observations make it clear, I think, that music plays an important role in the performance of Turkic oral epics, in particular in the case of lyric epics. They further suggest that there is a relationship between words and music that is conventional and, with all individual variation, of a traditionally prescribed kind. From an aesthetic point of view, we would like to know more about this relationship. When we read an oral epic as a text only, is this like reading the libretto of an opera? In other words, are we missing the really important part? No doubt, some literary works are legitimately appreciated in their own right and not only when set to music. Beaumarchais' *Le Mariage de Figaro* is a successful play, as is Synge's *Riders to the Sea*; the one does not need Mozart's music nor the other Vaughan Williams' setting. Mozart's opera buffa and Vaughan Williams' music-drama exist in *addition,* not in place of their libretti. For other operatic works, however, the text is more truly a libretto only, a collection of words set to music. We can read the text of *Fidelio*, but what we appreciate aesthetically is Beethoven's opera, the dramatization and setting to music of the text.

54 Youssefzadeh 2002:198 (my translation).

Or is reading the text of an oral epic like reading the text of a folksong or a ballad? We know that folksongs and ballads are sung and, depending on our traditional knowledge, we might even "hear" the sound of a folksong or ballad while reading it. On the other hand, we can analyze and interpret the literary qualities of folksongs and ballads independently of their music; in fact, this is what most non-musicological studies do. It seems to me that with lyrical epics, the situation lies somewhere between opera and folksong or ballad. For the audience, the performer is both narrator and musician, and the impression of a performance is not unlike that of a singspiel (without the acting on stage): the narrative alternates between spoken prose and sung verse, it progresses from aria to aria with spoken passages in between. It is a musico-poetic entity, which is appreciated as a whole, as a unity of telling, reciting, singing, and playing.

Saying that music is an indispensable part of an epic performance does not say anything about the specific relationship between words and music. Ballads can have a fairly loose relationship to the tunes to which they are sung. The idea that music "expresses" the meaning of a text is of comparatively modern date and is a misleading concept when looking at a traditional song. However charming and however "right" one might find the melody of a folksong or ballad, the relationship between words and music has not the same intensity as, for instance, in a Romantic *lied*. Composers like Schumann or Schubert strove to translate the meaning and mood of a poem into the language of music with a conscious attention to poetic and musical detail, which is quite uncharacteristic of traditional song, however rich the musical and poetic texture. "Expression" in the music of oral epics is couched in terms of the traditional music of the local culture. There are some programmatic elements in the music of *âşık*s and *bakhshi*s—as for instance an imitation of a horse's gallop by the strokes of the *dombra*—but on the whole the relationship between words and music can be seen as dependent on the musical system. In the course of singing a verse passage, the Uzbek *bakhshi* progresses from lower voice registers to higher registers till he reaches a culmination point. There is a great amount of tension in his musical performance. This musical progression (also found in other traditions; it is very marked in the performance of Turkmen *bakhshi*s) is part of the system of Uzbek (or Turkmen) music, in this case linked to the ascent to a culmination point (Uzbek *awj*) in classical *maqām* music. Such musical structuring is appreciated by the audience. It is system-dependent and can only be understood from within, just as modulation from a major to a minor key in the development of a sonata movement only makes "sense" in the context of Western classical music.

The world of the Turkic-speaking peoples is vast and variegated. In their oral traditions, a rich heritage of tales, poetry, and music has been transmitted and cultivated. Just looking at the repertoire of a single singer of tales, we find poetry of many different genres and subgenres. Âşık Şeref's œuvre comprises a surprising variety of songs and prosimetric tales, and he mastered a wide range of *makams* and *âşık* melodies. To do justice to his poetic and musical art, a detailed study would be necessary, which would have to enter also into the minutiae of musical analysis. The same can be said of the epic singers from Central Asia. Given this variety and diversity, no generally true characterization of the role of music in the performance of oral epics in Turkey and Central Asia can be made, except one: that music is an integral part of the singers' performance and that a disregard for this aspect of their art reduces their works—perhaps not to libretti but certainly to "Words without Song."

## Bibliography


Allanazarov, D. 2002. *Qaraqalpaq xalıq sazları* [Karakalpak folk melodies]. Nukus.

Arsunar, F., ed. 1963. *Köroğlu*. Ankara.

Bartók, B., and A. B. Lord. 1951. *Serbo-Croatian Folk Songs: Texts and Translations of Seventy-Five Folks Songs from the Milman Parry Collection and a Morphology of Serbo-Croatian Folk Melodies.* With a foreword by G. Herzog. New York.

Başgöz, İ. 2008. *Hikâye: Turkish Folk Romance as Performance Art*. Bloomington.

Bazin, L., A. Bombaci, and P. N. Boratav, eds. 1965. *Philologiae Turcicae Fundamenta* II. Wiesbaden.

Biebuyck, D., and K. C. Mateene, eds. and trans. 1969. *The Mwindo Epic from the Banjynga (Congo Republic)*. Berkeley.

Blum, S. 1972. "The Concept of the ʿĀsheq in Northern Khorasan." *Asian Music* 4:27–47.

Boratav, P. N. 1964a. "L'épopée et la 'ḥikāye.'" In Bazin, Bombaci, and Boratav 1964:11–44.

———. 1964b. "La poésie folklorique." In Bazin, Bombaci, and Boratav 1964:90–128.

———. 1964c. "La littérature des ʿāšïq." In Bazin, Bombaci, and Boratav 1964:129–147.

Bowra, C. M. 1952. *Heroic Poetry*. London.

Chadwick, N. K., and V. Zhirmunsky. 1969. *Oral Epics of Central Asia*. Cambridge.

Çobanoğlu, Ö. 2000. *Âşık Tarzı Kültur Geleneği ve Destan Türü* [The cultural tradition of the *âşık* style and the genre of *destan*]. Ankara.

Èldarova, È. 1984. *Iskusstvo ashygov Azerbaydzhana* [The art of the *ashıq* of Azerbaijan]. Baku.

Ellingson, T. 1992. "Transcription." In *Ethnomusicology: An Introduction*, ed. H. Myers, 110–152. New York.

Erdely, S. 1995. *Music of Southslavic Epics from the Bihać Region of Bosnia*. New York.

Erdener, Y. 1995. *The Song Contests of Turkish Minstrels: Improvised Poetry Sung to Traditional Music*. New York.

Foley, J. M., ed. and tr. 2004. *The Wedding of Mustajbey's Son Bećirbey as Performed by Halil Bajgorić*. Folklore Fellows Communications 283. Helsinki.

Greene, R., S. Cushman, S. Cavanagh, J. Ramazani, and P. Rouzer, eds. 2012. *The Princeton Encyclopedia of Poetry and Poetics*. 4th ed. Princeton.

Harris, J., and K. Reichl, eds. 1997. *Prosimetrum: Crosscultural Perspectives on Narrative in Prose and Verse*. Cambridge.

Holzapfel, O. 1990. "Heimkehr des Gatten (AaTh 974)." *Enzyklopädie des Märchens* VI. Cols. 702–707. Berlin.

Honko, L. 1998a. *Textualizing the Siri Epic*. Folklore Fellows Communications 264. Helsinki.

———, ed., in collaboration with C. Gowda, A. Honko, and V. Rai. 1998b. *The Siri Epic as Performed by Gopala Naika*. 2 vols. Folklore Fellows Communications 265, 266. Helsinki.

Innes, G., ed. and tr. 1974. *Sunjata: Three Mandinka Versions*. London.

Karāmatli, F. M., and T. Mirza, eds. 1999. *Alpamıs*. Tashkent.

Karryev, B. A., ed. and trans. 1983. *Gör-ogly. Turkmenskiy geroicheskiy èpos* [Göroghly. A Turkmen heroic epic]. Moscow.

Ker, W. P. 1908. *Epic and Romance: Essays on Medieval Literature*. 2nd ed. London.

Köprülü, M. F. 1966. *Edebiyat Araştırmaları* I [Studies in literature I]. Istanbul.

Levaniouk, O. 2022. "The Dreams of Barčin and Penelope." *Harvard Studies in Classical Philology* 112:1–34.

Lord, A. B., ed. 1954. *Serbocroatian Heroic Songs*. Vol. 1, *Novi Pazar: English Translations*. With musical transcriptions by B. Bartók and prefaces by J. H. Finley, Jr. and R. Jakobson. Cambridge, MA.

———. 2019. *The Singer of Tales*. 3rd ed. Ed. D. F. Elmer. Hellenic Studies 77. Publications of the Milman Parry Collection of Oral Literature 4. Washington, DC. Orig. pub. Cambridge, MA, 1960.

Mamedov, T. 1984. *Pesni Këroglu* [The songs of Köroğlu]. Baku.

Maqsetov, Q. 1983. *Qaraqalpaq jıraw baqsıları* [Karakalpak *jıraws* and *baqsıs*]. Nukus.

Oldfield, A. C. 2008. *Azerbaijani Women Poet-Minstrels: Women* Ashiqs *from the Eighteenth Century to the Present*. Lewiston.

Pegg, C., and J. Porter. 2001. "Epics." In *The New Grove Dictionary of Music and Musicians*. 2nd ed. London. Vol. 8:265–269.

Pihl, M. R. 1994. *The Korean Singer of Tales*. Cambridge, MA.

Reichl, K. 1992. *Turkic Oral Epic Poetry: Traditions, Forms, Poetic Structure*. Albert Bates Lord Studies in Oral Tradition 7. New York. Repr. Abingdon, 2018.

———, ed. 2000. *The Oral Epic: Performance and Music*. Intercultural Music Studies 12. Berlin.

———, ed. and tr. 2007. *Edige: A Karakalpak Oral Epic as Performed by Jumabay Bazarov*. Folklore Fellows Communications 293. Helsinki.

———. 2015. "Hero and Leander: Medieval and Folkloristic Variations on a Classical Theme." In *Dall' Antico al Moderno. Imagini del Classico nelle Letterature Europee*, ed. P. Boitani and E. De Rocco, 87–119. Rome.

———. 2022. *The Oral Epic: From Performance to Interpretation*. New York.

Reinhard, K., and M. Stokes. 2001. "Turkey. IV. Art Music." In *The New Grove Dictionary of Music and Musicians*. 2nd ed. Vol. 25:913–918. London.

Reinhard, U., and T. de Oliveira Pinto. 1989. *Sänger und Poeten mit der Laute*. Berlin.

Sachs, C. 1962. *The Wellsprings of Music*. Ed. J. Kunst. The Hague.

Smith, J. D., ed. and tr. 1991. *The Epic of Pābūjī: A Study, Transcription and Translation.* University of Cambridge Oriental Publications 44. Cambridge.

Stone, R. M. 1982. *Let the Inside be Sweet: The Interpretation of Music Event among the Kpelle of Liberia.* Bloomington.

———. 1988. *Dried Millet Breaking: Time, Words, and Song in the Wọi Epic of the Kpelle.* Bloomington.

Sümer, F., A. E. Uysal, and W. S. Walker, trans. 1972. *The Book of Dede Korkut: A Turkish Epic.* Austin.

Suppan, W., with H. Helgason. 1979. "Epos." In *Die Musik in Geschichte und Gegenwart. 16. Supplement: Earsden-Zweibrücken.* Cols. 101–114. Basel.

Taşlıova, M., ed. 2010. *Âşık Şeref Taşlıova. Hayatı ve Şiirleri* [Âşık Şeref Taşlıova. His life and his songs]. Ankara.

Türkmen, F., M. Taşlıova, and N. Tan, eds. 2008. *Âşık Şeref Taşlıova'dan Derlenen Halk Hikâyeleri* [Folk *hikâyes* collected from Âşık Şeref Taşlıova]. Türk Dil Kurumu Yayınları 931. Ankara.

West, S. 2012. "Some Reflections on Alpamysh." In *Homeric Contexts: Neoanalysis and the Interpretation of Oral Poetry*, ed. F. Montani, A. Rengakos, and C. C. Tsagalis, 531–542. Berlin.

Winner, T. G. 1958. *The Oral Art and Literature of the Kazakhs of Russian Central Asia.* Durham, NC.

Youssefzadeh, A. 2002. *Les bardes du Khorassan iranien. Le bakhshi et son répertoire.* Travaux et mémoires de l'institut d'études iraniennes. Paris.

Zemtsovskiy, I. I., ed. 1989. *Muzyka èposa. Stat'i i materialy* [The music of epic. Articles and materials]. Yoshkar-Ola.

# 20

# From the Archive to the Field

## New Research on Albanian Epic Songs

Zymer U. Neziri and Nicola Scaldaferri[1]

THIS ESSAY AIMS primarily to point out some new directions in research on Albanian epic song. Starting from archival materials and the issues they raise for further investigation in the field, it will focus in particular on certain structural elements of the songs related to their performance. The Albanian-language archival materials of the Milman Parry Collection of Oral Literature (henceforth MPCOL), collected in the 1930s by Milman Parry and Albert Lord, provide significant insight into the tradition. The first section offers an overview of the major collections and scholarly research on Albanian epics through the twentieth century, a rich body of work that includes local fieldwork-based studies as well as important foreign contributions that document the geographical scope and contents of the Albanian epic tradition, which constitutes an important part of the oral heritage still alive in Europe today. The second section focuses more narrowly on the materials collected by Milman Parry and Albert Lord in the 1930s, exploring the ways in which those songs as well as the singers' biographies—which have often been neglected in discussion of the MPCOL—still hold valuable insights for the study of oral poetry more broadly. In particular, this essay explores the implications of the collection process itself, as embedded in recordings and texts from the MPCOL. Finally, the third section summarizes some recent research conducted by the authors focusing on the singer Isa Elezi-Lekëgjekaj, one of the most important living practitioners of this epic tradition. His performances highlight some of the demands placed on the body and the resulting bodily techniques that emerge as part of this performative tradition.

1 The first section of this essay grows out of the research of Zymer Neziri; the others reflect the field-based research of Nicola Scaldaferri, carried out in collaboration with Neziri.

## 1. Old and New Scholarly Perspectives

Epic songs are a fundamental part of Albanian cultural identity. Albanian culture includes two linguistic areas: the Tosk dialect area covers the Southern part of Albania, while the Geg dialects are spoken in Northern Albania, Kosova, and the areas inhabited by Albanians in North Macedonia and Montenegro. The practice of epic singing persists most actively in the Geg area, in Northern Albania and Kosova, and especially in specific regions, such as Rugova in Kosova at the border with Albania and Montenegro. The main repertoire of epics songs is called *Këngë* (or *Kânge*, in the Geg dialect) *Kreshnike*, usually translated as "songs of the frontier warriors"; it is also called *këngë trimash* "songs of the heroes" or *këngë të moçme* "ancient songs." Both textually and in their performance, *Këngë Kreshnike* have their own particular traits that distinguish them from other poetic repertoires.[2] They are usually performed by a singer who accompanies himself with a one-string bowed instrument called *lahuta* in Albanian. The poems feature legendary characters, dealing most often with the deeds of two brothers, Muji and Halil, their friends and relatives, or other heroes like Gjergj Elez Alia, as they struggle against their enemies and encounter the presence of supernatural elements. The songs are performed during holiday gatherings, social visits to people's homes, and family celebrations.

Research and publications on *Këngë Kreshnike* date back to the end of the nineteenth century.[3] Besides local collectors, sometimes supported by local institutions, some foreign scholars have also played an important role in the study of the Albanian epics. Indeed, an early fifteen-line fragment, clearly recognizable as belonging to the *Këngë Kreshnike*, was published by the Austrian linguist Gustav Meyer in 1897. At the beginning of the twentieth century, complete versions of Albanian epic songs were published thanks to local collectors like Hasan Fejzullahu and Gasper Jakova-Merturi. The establishment of a large corpus of Albanian epic songs is mainly due to the work of the Franciscan friars and Jesuits based in the city of Shkodër. The town served as the old capital of a *vilayet* during the Ottoman Empire; it was an important cultural center with historical connections to Western culture and Venice and a strong presence of the Catholic church. In Shkodër, thanks to the initiative of the friar Bernardin Palaj, songs identified as *Këngë Kreshnike* started to appear in the journal *Hylli i Dritës* (The Star of Light). This journal, founded by Father Gjergj Fishta in 1913, was an important forum for bringing together cultural and political ideas; from

[2] Among others, see Pipa 1978:102–137 and Ahmedaja 2012. Similar songs are also present in the epic repertories of the neighboring Slavic populations.

[3] A wide account of the Albanian collection on legendary epics can be found in the different papers included in Neziri 2006 and Neziri 2008.

the outset, it focused primarily on Albanian history, literature, and folklore, including excerpts of Fishta's poem *Lahuta e Malcís* (The Highland Lute). A collection of a substantial number of *Këngë Kreshnike*, edited by the friars Bernardin Palaj and Donat Kurti, appears in the series *Visaret e Kombit* (The Treasure of the Nation) published in 1937, the twenty-fifth anniversary of Albanian independence from the Ottoman empire; the volume has the title *Kânge kreshnikësh dhe legjenda* (Songs of the Frontier Warriors and Legends), and includes thirty-four songs about Muji and Halil. Additionally, important research was carried out by foreign scholars, including (among others) the Austrian scholar Maximilian Lambertz, the Italian friar Fulvio Cordignano, and especially Milman Parry and Albert Lord in the 1930s, whose landmark research is discussed below.

After World War II and the establishment of Enver Hoxha's regime in Albania, local scholars based in Tirana and Prishtina carried out research on epics with the support of various institutions like the *Instituti i Shkencavet* (Institute of Sciences) and the *Instituti i Folklorit* (Institute of Folklore), which would later become the *Instituti i Kulturës Popullore* (Institute of Folk Culture). This institute created a framework for the study of traditional Albanian folklore, with the aim of building a national culture. The research focused primarily on the collection of texts, published in volumes edited by Qemal Haxhihasani in 1955 and 1966. Later, scholars began focusing on the study of musical melodies too, with a book edited in 1983 by Ferial Daja. In parallel to these local developments, foreign scholars, such as Stavro Skendi and Agniya Desnitskaya, also made authoritative contributions that deal, in turn, with the controversial issue of the relationship between the repertoire of *Këngë Kreshnike* and that of neighboring Slavic traditions.[4]

Meanwhile, research conducted in Kosova is of particular importance in the field of epic. Inhabited by a large majority of Albanians yet remaining outside the national borders of the state of Albania when it was formed, Kosova was for decades—both before and after the breakup of Yugoslavia—an autonomous province of Serbia, with moments of tension with Belgrade, until its unilateral declaration of independence in 2008. Despite this sensitive situation (which has sometimes hindered the study of aspects of Albanian culture), scholars in Kosova have been able to promote and publish important work. While the *Këngë Kreshnike* in Albania represents only a portion of the local oral traditional corpus, in Kosova—where the Geg dialect is widely present—the epic is at the center of scholarly research. The institutional base for research on oral heritage in Kosova, including the epic tradition, has been the *Instituti Albanologjik*

4 See especially Desnickaja [Desnitskaya] 1975 and 2007. About this complex point, see, among others, the contributions published in A. N. Berisha 1998 and Neziri 2006.

*i Prishtinës* (The Institute of Albanology, Prishtina), which played an important role for decades in the cultural and political consciousness of the Albanians of Kosova. After a pioneering period in the 1950s, the institute began its full range of activities in 1967. Led for many years by the distinguished scholar Anton Çetta, the institute supported the publication of multiple volumes on epic, with research carried out by scholars like Rrustem Berisha, Anton Nikë Berisha, and Zymer Ujkan Neziri. As early as 1952, they began publishing texts of epic songs in the volume of folk songs, *Këngë popullore shqiptare të Kosovës dhe Metohisë* (Dançetoviq 1952), with subsequent contributions made by several volumes of *Këngë Kreshnike* published in 1974, 1991, and 1993. More recently, Neziri has been editing the most ambitious project supported by the Institute, a multivolume study of the epics of the area of Rugova, which remains the principal repository of living tradition to the present. Three volumes have already been published, with two of those devoted to the repertories of individual singers.[5]

For decades following World War II, the international isolation of Tirana and Prishtina hindered the circulation of these materials and scholarly discussion internationally. In Albania more recently, important changes have started to emerge in the realm of cultural politics and the activities of local scholars, while scholarly contact with Western countries has also increased. In Kosova, too, from the fall of Yugoslavia to its declaration of independence in 2008, an important process of opening and increasing contact with foreign scholars is underway. Local research projects of note, in addition to Neziri's long-term project, include the publication of other collections of epics and reprints of older collections that are no longer available: in 2008, Anton Nikë Berisha reprinted fifty-one texts from older collections, and in 2009 Nimon Alimusai republished twenty canonical texts. In addition, books devoted to folk songs and oral tradition (e.g. Krasniqi and Krasniqi 2007) or textbooks for school (e.g. Neziri 1999) include significant parts of epics. The reprinting of the work of the friars of Shkodër, especially the landmark volume *Visaret e Kombit*, unavailable for decades, is especially important. Published in 2007 to mark the 70th anniversary of the first edition, the reprint grew out of an initiative of the Franciscan community, still present today in Shkodër, with their important library.

A key step in fostering deeper contacts and communication between scholars in Albania and abroad has been the translation of important studies and collections into and from Albanian, such as Stavro Skendi's book (1954; transl. 2007), which includes in an appendix an especially important article by Russian scholar Agniya Desnitskaya. Translations of key collections and texts

[5] Vol. 1 (Neziri 2009) includes the songs collected from Adem Salihi-Shala, Adem Syla-Kurtaj, and Çelë Sokoli-Demëbogaj; vol. 2 (Neziri 2011) is devoted to the songs of Isuf Selman-Kuklecaj; and vol. 5 (Neziri 1997) to those of Haxhi Meta-Nilaj. All these singers died in the 1990s.

from Albanian into Russian, Serbo-Croatian, and French date back to the mid-twentieth century. And since the first English publication of *Këngë Kreshnike* (Elsie 1994), the work of Robert Elsie has been of particular importance in translating, disseminating, and popularizing Albanian language and literary culture. For instance, his 2004 book of translations with Janice Mathie-Heck, *Songs of the Frontier Warriors: Këngë Kreshnikësh*, is a bilingual edition of a selection of epic songs with texts taken from the old collection of *Visaret e Kombit*, republished in a modernized orthography. The book marks an important milestone in making these texts accessible to a much wider audience.

A recurring theme in recent scholarly discussion on Albanian epic is the UNESCO Intangible Heritage List, especially since 2005 when UNESCO declared polyphonic vocal music from southern Albania a Masterpiece of the Oral and Intangible Heritage of Humanity.[6] A subsequent discussion arose about the possibility of petitioning UNESCO to include the *Këngë Kreshnike* on the Intangible Heritage List as well. On the one hand, there is clear consensus that some areas, especially the region of Rugova in Kosova, have great relevance for oral epic tradition; on the other hand, the complex political situation in Kosova makes a formal nomination for the Intangible Heritage List very unlikely, since it requires the support of a country with direct interest in preserving that tradition. The topic has been very popular in recent years at conferences and festivals, such as the festival of Gjirokastër, Albania, in September 2009, where musical performances and a scholarly conference were held jointly.[7] The issue was raised again at an August 2010 conference organized in Prishtina by the two main cultural institutions of Albania and Kosova working on epic tradition, the Institute of Albanology, Prishtina, and the Center for Albanian Studies, Tirana (*Qendra e Studimeve Albanologjike, Tiranë*), with an international academic board chaired by Zymer Neziri.[8] The conference brought together a sizable number of Albanian scholars from Tirana, Prishtina, and Skopje along with international scholars from across Europe, the United States, and Japan, fostering a transnational conversation about the importance of Albanian epic and the current state of scholarly research on the topic.

6 For further background about the iso-polyphony, see Tole 2007.

7 Established in 1968 and held every five years, the festival of Gjirokastër was one of the most important musical events during the regime of Enver Hoxha. After a hiatus of a few years, the festival was revived and today represents an important showcase for traditional Albanian cultural performances and practices.

8 The conference was convened under the title, "Epos of the Frontier Warriors: A Monument of the Albanian Cultural Heritage" (*Eposi i Kreshnikëve: monument i trashëgimisë kulturore shqiptare*). Two volumes of proceedings appeared in 2016 (Neziri and Sinani 2016).

## 2. Albanian Material from Parry and Lord: New Directions

Another key corpus for the documentation of and research on Albanian oral poetry is the Albanian-language holdings of the Milman Parry Collection of Oral Literature (MPCOL) at Harvard University.[9] Despite being collected more than eighty years ago, these materials still point to new directions in the study of oral literature. There are two main groups of materials in the MPCOL collected by Parry and Lord as part of their broader research on South Slavic epics. The first group comprises recordings of epics, performed by bilingual singers from Novi Pazar—especially Salih Ugljanin in November 1934—as well as lyric songs and other fragments, most notably featuring the polyglot singer Fatima Biberović, originally from Prizren but living in Gacko when Parry and Lord recorded her in April and May 1935. The second group includes transcribed texts collected by Albert Lord in a set of notebooks during his 1937 trip to northern Albania.

This Albanian corpus from the MPCOL is revealing, both in terms of the study of the *Këngë Kreshnike* and in relation to epic repertoire and performance more generally. The use of recording technology, especially the special apparatus used by the researchers, allowed them to document these Albanian performances in full and to produce the first uninterrupted recording of a complete epic in Albanian. Lord's notebooks from Albania include a body of texts exceeding 22,000 lines, collected from about forty singers. Its texts are comparable to other collections made in Albania and Kosova, while also featuring the longest Albanian oral poem ever collected.[10]

The collection of these materials by Lord coincides with some of the most relevant publications of *Këngë Kreshnike* by local collectors. In 1937, the year of Lord's Albanian trip, the landmark volume *Visaret e Kombit* was also published. While Lord was in Shkodër, the point of departure for his collecting journey, he was in touch with Franciscan friars and other local collectors who helped him in his research. In a notebook in the MPCOL entitled *Adresser*, which Lord used as a diary for his journey, he mentions the Franciscan press of Shkodër (p. 8) as well as the friar Bernardin Palaj (p. 12), present in some of Lord's photos. He also collaborated with Murat Paci, a teacher at the local *gymnasium* (high school),

9 Scaldaferri et al. 2021 provides a catalogue of the Albanian texts and recordings in the MPCOL, a selection of the most significant texts, and related photographs and documents. On the bilingual singer Salih Ugljanin, see Kolsti 1990. See also Neziri 2006, Neziri 2008, and Scaldaferri 2012.

10 The recorded song, 236 lines long, is *Muja e Gavran Kapetani*, PN 672, recorded November 24, 1934, and performed by Salih Ugljanin; the longest transcribed epic text is *Kanga e Sirotin Alis* (2,163 lines), dictated by the singer Adem Brahimi, included in Notebook 5 (Dorëshkrim 60). Both texts are printed in Scaldaferri et al. 2021: 131–141, 237–329..

who sent Lord a notebook with transcribed texts after his return to Cambridge, which is also preserved in the MPCOL.

While in Albania, Lord worked with some of the same singers as local collectors, who deemed certain of these singers the best of their generation. Following Parry's methodology from a few years earlier, Lord provides essential details about the singers and their lives, in addition to the song transcriptions. He typically notes biographical data for the singers (including age, religion, writing ability, training, languages spoken, travels, and contact with other singers), song titles for the singer's entire repertoire, and the complete transcription of the text of one or more representative songs. We rarely find this kind of information in other epic collections of the time. A singular case is that of Gjergj Pllumbi, a famous singer from Shala, whose poetic repertoire was documented by other leading scholars like Ernest Koliqi, Fulvio Cordignano, and Anton Çetta. In Lord's manuscript, we find arguably the most reliable information about Pllumbi's activity and background, otherwise depicted in a romantic and often unrealistic manner by other scholars at the time. For example, Koliqi (1959–1960) drafted a kind of heroic portrait of Pllumbi (like the heroes of his songs), stressing his role as a local chief, while highlighting the complete isolation that surrounded him as a rhapsodist living in the mountains. In contrast, Lord notes key details like his teacher's name (Mark Kolesh from Theth), the trips he took to many parts of Yugoslavia, and the complete list of songs in his repertoire.

All these elements are certainly important in terms of documentation, ethnographic data, the cultural history of the collection, and the expansion of the songs of the repertoire of the *Këngë Kreshnike* itself. However, even more significantly, these archival materials return our attention to the field, encouraging us to pay particular attention to aspects of performance. Such a shift in focus, made possible by the existence of audio recordings, is especially crucial for the performance of Albanian epics, with consequences for the question of their versification.

The Albanian recordings by Ugljanin, which include both sung lines and rhythmically-recited songs, offer a useful point of departure. The presence of recited, rather than sung, texts—a phenomenon occurring in the Slavic materials too—is due to the period of mourning after the assassination of the Yugoslav King Alexander I in Marseille on October 9, 1934. For several weeks after his death, singing was restricted. In the Albanian epics, the method of performing lines—whether sung or recited—results in corresponding changes in the meter of versification. This shift can be seen in one of the most unique recordings of Ugljanin, the song *Mark e Musa* (PN 659, 154 lines long). Here, Ugljanin begins the song by singing the first six lines. Then, without any interruption, he shifts to rhythmic recitation of the texts.

In the performance of this song, the presence or absence of sung melody corresponds to changes in the metrical structure. The verses presented in the sung performance (1–6) are similar to the decasyllabic (with two long stresses on the final syllables), while those of the recited texts (7–154) are similar to the octosyllabic, with two isochronous stresses (usually on the 3rd and penultimate or final syllables). This change in the verse results from the switch from singing to recitation, all within the performance of a single song. Here is the transcription of the text performed by Ugljanin with stressed syllables underlined (numbers enclosed in parentheses indicate stressed syllables in the recited version):

sung:

| | |
|---|---|
| E lum për ty-o, moro, j-lumi Zo-jo-te | 12 |
| konka çua Kraleviçu Ma-rka | 10 |
| edhe Marku n'kôm-o çi o çu-a | 10 |
| me Sharanin n'shpid-o m'i kish ra-me | 10 |
| e n'shpid Sharanit Marku çi i ka shku-a | 11 |
| e n'Stamboll-o Marku kish pa shku-a | 10 |

recited:

| | |
|---|---|
| kur po shkon Marku n'Stamboll | 7 (3,7) |
| bash tu mbreti konka dal | 7 (3,7) |
| bash tu mbreti konka dal | 7 (3,7) |
| tri taborr i kan rrethua | 8 (3,7) |
| tri taborr i kan rrethua | 8 (3,7) |
| edhe Markun e kan ngujua | 9 (3,8) |

sung:

Glory to the Lord, the blessed Lord / Kraljevic Marko arose / and Marko rose to his feet / he mounted onto the back of Sharan / and Marko set out mounted on Sharan / Marko went toward Stambol

recited:

when Marko was on his way to Stambol / to appear before the Emperor / to appear before the Emperor / three battalions surrounded him / three battalions surrounded him / and they besieged Marko

In fact, this example suggests a kind of expansion/compression system of the line, depending on the presence or absence of repetitions and filler words, which allows a shift from a sung, decasyllabic mode of performance to a recited, octosyllabic one. Such changes appear in many other examples of songs from Albanian and Arbëresh oral tradition.[11] However, in the case of epics, this point has particular significance because it is also bound up with the very method of collecting songs.

Recording a song while it is sung, recording its recited text, or transcribing it in a recited version under dictation are all different ways of collecting a song with different performance conditions. All three forms were used in collecting the MPCOL materials, as explained by Lord.[12] Indeed, Parry began collecting texts by dictation, much as earlier collectors had done for their published collections of epics. However, even when he was using sound recording devices, Parry did not stop collecting dictated texts. His conceptualization of a Homeric scholar (or scholar of epic, more generally) mirrors the hypothesis of the Homeric text as a written transcription of a dictated performance.[13]

With regard to the difference between dictating and singing, Lord's essay, "Homer's Originality: Oral Dictated Texts," goes further still, articulating a qualitative difference, referred to by singers themselves, between a text dictated with the aim of making a written transcription and a sung performance.[14] The singers seem perfectly aware of this difference between a sung performance of a text and a dictation for transcription, as evidenced by a conversation between Nikola Vujnović and the bilingual singer Sulejman Makić:

> NV: Which do you think makes the better song, when it is dictated and written down, or when it is sung?
>
> SM: It can be written more correctly, but it can be sung more exactly.
>
> NV: So, then, do you think that it is finer when it is sung and better when it is written?
>
> SM: Yes, I think it is finer.

11 For a focus on a similar rhythmical mechanism, analyzing especially *arbëresh* lines, see Scaldaferri 2008 and 2009.

12 See Lord 1954:18.

13 This is revealed by Parry's own words in *Ćor Huso: A Study of Southslavic Songs*: "I even figure to myself, just now, the moment when the author of the *Odyssey* sat and dictated his song, while another, with writing materials, wrote it down verse by verse even in the way that our singers sit in the immobility of their thought, watching the motion of Nikola's hand across the empty page, when it will tell them it is the instant for them to speak the next verse" (Parry 1971:451).

14 Lord 1991:38.

NV: ... Why is it better when it is written? ...

SM: Because you speak more slowly, more leisurely, but you can't write as exactly as you can sing.[15]

For Parry and Lord, the moment of transcribing a recited text, dictated line by line, becomes a relevant form of performance, even if it is not the usual one for singers.[16] In the case of the Albanian epics, the difference between sung and recited performance goes even further because, as we have seen, it entails a change in meter. This change raises new questions about Albanian epics, which are commonly thought to be characterized by a decasyllabic line. Although the most common Albanian folk verse is the octosyllabic line, in all the major collections, legendary epics mainly employ decasyllabic lines and have been consequently defined in this way by the most authoritative scholars.[17] Moreover, the case of Ugljanin is particularly striking because this change occurs during a single performance. Performance emerges as a kind of Procrustean bed in which lines can be stretched or shortened with repetition and filler words as they are adapted to the structure created by the presence of melody or the rhythm of recitation.[18]

## 3. From Archival Discs to New Video Field Recordings

The song of *Mark e Musa* serves as the starting point for a research project that shifts from the geographies documented in the MPCOL to the border area of Rugova, mentioned above as the center of Albanian-language epic performance today, focusing on different ways of performing epic songs. Ugljanin's method of singing a song in decasyllabic lines while reciting it in octosyllabic lines is

15 Lord 1954:263.

16 Significantly, some of the most sophisticated poems of the MPCOL, such as the celebrated *Wedding of Smailagić Meho* by Avdo Međedović, were collected in this manner.

17 This happens, for example, in a major contribution on oral Albanian versification, Pipa 1978. Namely, the repertory of *Këngë Kreshnike*, in his opinion, is based on the decasyllabic line, and is distinct from other Albanian epics, which are in octosyllabic lines. His analysis is mainly based on the epic texts published in *Visaret e Kombit* and never on recorded material. See Pipa 1978:126–137; see also Skendi 1953 and 1954.

18 A study of a similar mechanism is discussed in Scaldaferri 2008, in which an improvised poetic text in octosyllabic lines is dictated line-by-line to a group of women who "transform" and sing it in decasyllabic lines. Albanologist Francesco Altimari has recently re-examined the *Songs of Milosao* by the Arbëresh poet Girolamo De Rada; this landmark masterpiece of Albanian literature, at the crossroads between orality and literacy, is famous for the difficulty it presents in understanding its metrical structure, which is supposed to be octosyllabic. Altimari argues convincingly for a metrical system based on rhythmic principles that have been modeled upon the rhythmic versification of oral tradition; see Altimari 2017.

confirmed by research conducted with many other singers, especially one of the most acclaimed singers active today in Rugova, Isa Elezi-Lekëgjekaj.[19] Isa Elezi is perfectly aware, like other singers, that singing and reciting are different modes of performing a text. For example, a group of researchers asked Isa to perform the same song, *Kanga e marteses se Halilit* (The Song of the Wedding of Halil), on different occasions. These occasions were filmed in order to document variations of wording between one performance and another.[20] In the first performance (Version A, singing mode), Isa sang the text while accompanying himself on the *lahuta*, according to the "normal, sung" performance method. The lines are about 11–12 syllables (with repetitions and filler words) and the rhythm is set by the melody as well as by the movements of the singer's hands while bowing the instrument:

| | |
|---|---|
| [An-ë] O lum-e për ty-e Zot oi lumi Zot | 11 |
| e po hiç s'jem kjenë po ti na ke dhan' | 11 |
| eu hiç eu pa shybe po çaren na e ban | 11 |
| e tridhet' agë-o po n'llanxhe janë dalë | 12 |
| e sa kanë marrë lafin e kan fol | 11 |
| e sa kanë marrë pijen e po pin' | 11 |

Glory to the Lord, the blessed Lord / He gave us everything / from nothing He created us / the thirty Agas assembled in the place of council / they started to talk / they started to drink

In the second performance (Version B, reciting mode), Isa rhythmically recited the text without singing. The results reveal precisely the same performance practice as that of Ugljanin's recitation: the rhythmically-recited verse has eight syllables (plus or minus one) and the rhythm is set by the regular presence of two isochronous accents (underlined):

| | |
|---|---|
| Lum për ty oj lumi Zot | 7 (3, 7) |
| hiç s'jem kan' e na ke dhan' | 7 (3, 7) |

19 In civil records, Isa Muriqi (born 1947). About this singer and his importance, see Neziri 2006:149–182.

20 This research trip to Rugova in November 2006 included Nicola Scaldaferri, Zymer Neziri, and the photographer Stefano Vaja. Some elements and photographs were previously published in Scaldaferri 2011. For the video documents see: http://leavlab.com/portfolio/epic-songs-balkans. A second fieldtrip in Rugova, supported by LEAV-University of Milan, was undertaken in June 2018 by Nicola Scaldaferri and Giovanni Cestino in order to investigate more deeply the different performances of Isa Elezi. The materials, including other walking performances, have also been presented at the seminar "L'epica leggendaria del Kosovo," followed by a concert with epic songs hosted by the Giorgio Cini Foundation in Venice, November 13, 2018. The proceedings of the seminar are in preparation.

hiç pa çare çaren na' ban 8 (3, 8)
ish çu Muja n'nate n'saba' 8 (3, 8)
avdes t'paç burri ki marr' 7 (3, 7)
Zot i madhi kabull ja past' ba 9 (3, 9)
Halil ag's po i ban za 7 (3, 7)
çou Halil vlla me u shtërgu-a 8 (3, 7)
pse n' llanxhe po duem me shkua 8 (2, 7)

Glory to you, the blessed Lord / He gave us everything / from nothing He created us / Muji arose in the morning / he washed up before praying / the Lord blessed him / Muji told Aga Halil / get up, brother Halil, dress yourself / we must go to the place of council

At this point, Isa was asked to do a third performance: to dictate the text line-by-line in order to allow a listener to transcribe it without the help of a recording. The aim was to recreate the mode of collection of many texts before the advent of sound recording, a mode that remained in use even after the introduction of recording technologies, including in Lord's 1937 collection of Albanian materials. In this third performance (Version C, dictating mode), the timing of Isa's recitation depended on the speed of the scribe taking dictation. Even though the number of syllables resembles the previous recited performance (Version B), now the rhythm is broken by the pauses required by the dictation—indicated approximately in seconds in square brackets—and the regularity of isochronous accents is totally lost:

Lum për ty oj lumi Zot [..3"..] 7
hiç s'jem kan' [..2"..] e na ke dhan' [..5"..] 7
pa shybe çaren n'e ban [..7"..] 7
ish çu Muja n'nate n'saba' [..9"..] 7
po pin kafe me sheqer [..8"..] 7
çou Halil, v'lla, i ki than' [..8"] 7
dy en llanxhe tek janë dalë [..8"..] 7
Bashk' me ag' llaf kan' ba [..9"..] 6
ven' e kuqe n'faqe u ka dal' [..11"..] 8
sa raki-a n'llaf i ka hap' [..10"..] 8
Jan' dredh' shok't Muj's i kan' than' [..10"..] 7

Glory to you, the blessed Lord / He gave us everything / from nothing He created us / Muji arose in the morning / he drank coffee with sugar / wake up, Halil told him / they both went to the place of council /

> they start to talk with the Agas / their face was red like the wine / they enjoyed the raki / the friends started to criticize Muji

The poem *Kanga e marteses se Halilit* is performed by Isa Elezi differently each time, each with a rhythmic specificity that affects the meter of the verse. These results problematize the presumed ideal of a decasyllabic line. Moreover, even the categories of octosyllabic and decasyllabic verses, as most scholarship describes them, prove to be inadequate since the rhythm of the isochronous stresses (especially in the recited version) appears to be much more important than the number and length of syllables, which in these examples is subject to slight variation.

Ultimately, the variations in "performances" of the same song suggest a disconnect between the reality of performance and the fixity of lines typically found in the published corpus of epic texts. At a minimum, this raises the question of the role scholars play in collecting—or more precisely in some cases, in establishing, or even co-creating—the texts of epic songs. Scholars as early as Skendi have acknowledged this point, highlighting how collectors often justified their interventions in editing and rearranging texts according to romantic ideals in order to mold them according to certain artistic and literary values.[21] Such methods made it possible to coherently analyze printed verses of oral poetry by existing literary and metrical standards. At the same time, it meant that these texts were not necessarily representative of real performance practice, especially with regard to rhythm and meter. This gap makes recordings like Ugljanin's *Mark e Musa* even more precious, since we find in it a real performance of a singer—from a period when epic performances still took place—without such intensive mediation by scholars.

As so often happens with fieldwork, surprises also lead to new research questions beyond those being addressed. Such was the case with our research with Isa Elezi, which went beyond simply verifying the existence of different ways to perform a text with regard to rhythm. During a recording session in August 2008, Isa Elezi seemed frustrated by our requests for long sessions of recitations without singing or playing the *lahuta* for accompaniment as he sat in front of listeners armed with a video camera and an audio recorder. Suddenly, he arose and started to recite while pacing around the room. He was reciting the text as he had in the second version (Version B, reciting mode), but now he was marking the two stresses of each recited line with his footsteps. He explained his rationale clearly:

21 See Skendi 1954:20–21.

> Ma mirë e thom fjalorin, se me kjenë unxhë, pa lahutë, pse unë e thom me kamë, me hap:
>
> Lum për ty ei lumi Zot 7 (3, 7)
> hiç s'jem kjen Zoti na ka dhan' 8 (3, 8)
> ai pa shybe çaren na e ban' 8 (3, 8)
> m'ish çu Muja n'nate n'saba' 8 (3, 8)
> adet Mu-ja e ki pas' 7 (3, 7)
> pa le dielli sabain m'e fal 8 (3, 8)
> i madhi Zot kabull ja baft' 8 (4, 8)
> n'ball' t'oxhakut Muja m'ish dredh' 8 (3, 8)
> m'i ka shti ibrikat n'oxhak 8 (3, 8)
> pike Muja kafe me shiqer 9 (3, 9)
> po-i ki ra Mujs qef për bjeshk' 8 (4, 8)
>
> Pse i bie n'hapje, mua ma kollaj, m'vjen se unxhun, e tash ajo n'varet prej njerëzve.

> I can tell it much better it this way, sitting without *lahuta* it is difficult; I tell it standing, with footsteps:
>
> Glory to you, the blessed Lord / He gave us everything / from nothing He created us / Muji arose in the morning / as was Muji's habit / he greeted the sun of the morning / the Lord blessed him / Muji was at the fireplace / he put the pot in the fireplace / he drank coffee with sugar / Muji went out in the mountains
>
> Because I mark [the stress] with the footstep, for me it is better than sitting, it depends on the person.

As pointed out above, singers find themselves in an unusual situation when called on to dictate a text without singing or to perform without an instrument that is otherwise always used. Such discomfort has been documented with singers from many musical cultures around the world. However, the element most sorely missed by singers in the recited version would seem not to be melody per se but, rather, body movement, which helps the singer maintain rhythm. For example, other scholars have noted how certain singers, when asked to perform without *lahuta*, use sticks of wood to imitate its bowing movement. A striking case took place during the Gjirokastër festival in September 2009. A singer was performing a newly composed song with his grandchildren: while the grandfather played the *lahuta*, his grandson sang, moving his hands rhythmically to simulate the actions of playing, imitating the rhythmic bowing movements of his grandfather.[22] As many theories of embodied performance would suggest, corporeal movement plays a crucial role in rhythmically framing the performance and in reinforcing the technique of memorizing and composing using formulas. As one such example, a well-known passage in Eric Havelock's *Preface to Plato* connects mnemonic mechanisms with bodily performance by way of rhythmic movement. Moreover, for Havelock, this aspect is critical for constructing the Greek concept of the *Mousikē*, a multisensory, multiaesthetic phenomenon that would later be split into different performing arts: poetry, music and dance.[23]

Demonstrating a certain continuity of performance methods and concepts across time and space, the living epic forms of the Western Balkans today show traces of the importance of body movement in epic performance. The "walking performance" of Isa Elezi is relevant, not only because it demonstrates how the body becomes involved in rhythmic movement but also because of the singer's conscious use of footsteps as a rhythmic marker in versification. In the case of this walking performance, the regular movement of his rhythmic footsteps establishes a rhythmic frame that "pulls" the words of each line or formula. This approach suggests that we might think of the footstep—a recurring trope in poetry since ancient time—not only in a theoretical and metaphorical way but perhaps also more concretely in connection with actual physical performance. More broadly, it reminds us once again of the salient connection between poetry, song, and the rhythmic movement of the body, present since the performing arts of antiquity.

22 The text of that song was composed by Shaban Lajci, a singer from Gucinje who now resides in the United States. He was present at the conference in Cambridge in December 2010. For video of this performance as well as other videos of Isa Elezi's performance, see: http://leavlab.com/portfolio/epic-songs-balkans.

23 Havelock 1963:148–152. For other aspects that link body, voice, memory, and technologies, see Scaldaferri 2014.

## Bibliography

Ahmedaja, A. 2012. "Songs with Lahutë and Their Music." In *Balkan Epic: Song, History, Modernity*, ed. P. V. Bohlman and N. Petković-Djordjević, 101–132. Lanham, MD.

Alimusaj, N. 2009. *Nga lahuta e Dukagjinit (këngë kreshnike dhe balada)*. Prishtina.

Altimari, F., ed. 2017. *'Canti di Milosao,' by Girolamo De Rada*. Rubbettino.

Berisha, A. N. 1998. *Qasje Poetikës së letërsisë gojore shqipe*. Prishtina.

———. 2008. *Antologji e kangëve kreshnike shqiptare*. Prishtina.

Berisha, Rr., S. Fetiu, and A. Zejnullahu, eds. 1991. *Këngë kreshnike* II. Prishtina.

Bllaca, R. 1997. *Këngë popullore* I. Prishtina.

Çetta, A., ed. 1974. *Këngë kreshnike* I. Prishtina.

Çetta, A., F. Syla, M. Mustafa, and A. N. Berisha, eds. 1993. *Këngë kreshnike* III. Prishtina.

Cordignano, F. 1943. *La poesia epica di confine nell'Albanian del Nord*. 2 vols. Venice.

Daja, F., ed. 1983. *Rapsodi kreshnike: tekste e melodi*. Tirana.

Dançetoviq, V. 1952. *Këngë popullore shqiptare të Kosovës dhe Metohisë*. Prishtina.

Desnickaja [Desnitskaya], A. V. 1975. "Mbi lidhjet boshnjake-shqiptare në lëmin e poezisë epike." *Gjurmime Albanologjike: Folklor dhe etnologji* 5:41–61.

———. 1988. "Mbi formulat e gjuhës dhe formulat e poezisë epike shqiptare." *Gjurmime Albanologjike: Folklor dhe etnologji* 18:65–82.

———. 2007. "Për studimi e traditave epike të ballkanit. Ngjashmëritë dhe dallimet e ciklit epik shqiptar 'Muji e Halili' me eposin e Bosnjës." *Skendi Stavro. Poezia epika gojore e shqiptareve dhe e sllaveve të jugut, Bota shqiptare*, 307–342. Tirana.

Elsie, R. 1994. *Albanian Folktales and Legends: Selected and Translated from the Albanian*. Tirana.

Elsie, R., and J. Mathie-Heck, eds. 2004. *Songs of the frontier Warriors / Këngë Kreshnikësh: Albanian Epic Verse in a Bilingual English-Albanian Edition*. Wauconda, IL.

Havelock, E. A. 1963. *Preface to Plato*. Cambridge, MA.

Haxhihasani, Q. 1955. *Këngë popullore legjendare*. Tirana.

———. 1966. *Epika legjendare. (Cikli i kreshnikëve)*. Vol. 1, *Folklori shqiptar* II. Tirana.

Koliqi, E. 1959–1960. "Rapsodi e rapsodie delle Alpi Albanesi." *Shêjzat* 3:350–355, 4:113–119, 168–170, 320–329.

Kolsti, J. 1990. *The Bilingual Singer: A Study in Albanian and Serbo-Croatian Oral Epic Traditions*. New York.

Krasniqi, F., and S. Krasniqi. 2007. *Këngë popullore* I. Prishtina.

Lambertz, M. 1917. *Die volkspoesie der Albaner: Eine einführende Studie*. Sarajevo.

———. 1958. *Die Volksepik der Albaner*. Halle (Saale).

Lord, A. B., ed. 1954. *Serbocroatian Heroic Songs*. Vol. 1, *Novi Pazar: English Translations*. With musical transcriptions by B. Bartók and prefaces by J. H. Finley, Jr. and R. Jakobson. Cambridge, MA.

———. 1984. "The Battle of Kosovo in Albanian and Serbocroatian Tradition." In *Studies on Kosova*, ed. A. Pipa and S. Repishti, 65–83. Boulder.

———. 1991. *Epic Singers and Oral Tradition*. Ithaca.

———. 2019. *The Singer of Tales*. 3rd ed. Ed. D. F. Elmer. Hellenic Studies 77. Publications of the Milman Parry Collection of Oral Literature 4. Washington, DC. Orig. pub. Cambridge, MA, 1960.

Meyer, G. 1897. *Albanesische Studien: Beiträge zur Kenntniss verschiedener albanesischer Mundarten* VI. Vienna.

Neziri, Z. U. 1997. *Epika Legjendare e Rugovës* V. Prishtina.

———. 1999. *Këngë të kreshnikeve*. Prishtina.

———. 2006. *Studime për folklorin*. Vol. 1, *Eposi i kreshnikëve dhe epika historike*. Prishtina.

———. 2008. *Studime për folklorin*. Vol. 2, *Epika gojore dhe etnokultura*. Prishtina.

———. 2009. *Epika Legjendare e Rugovës* I. Prishtina.

———. 2011. *Epika Legjendare e Rugovës* II. Prishtina.

Neziri, Z. U., and S. Sinani, eds. 2016. *Epos of the Frontier Warriors: A Monument of the Albanian Cultural Heritage* (*Eposi i Kreshnikëve: monument i trashëgimisë kulturore shqiptare*) I–II. Prishtina.

Palaj, B., and D. Kurti, eds. 1937. *Visaret e Kombit*. Vol. 2, *Kânge Kreshnikësh dhe Legjenda*. Tirana. Repr. 2007, Shkodër.

Parry, M. 1971. *The Making of Homeric Verse: The Collected Papers of Milman Parry*. Ed. A. Parry. Oxford.

Pipa, A. 1978. *Albanian Folk Verse: Structure and Genre*. Munich.

Scaldaferri, N. 2008. "Appunti per un'analisi della versificazione tradizionale arbëreshe." In *Omaggio a Gerolamo De Rada / Homazh për Jeronim De Radën. Proceedings of the International Conference*, ed. F. Altimari and E. Conforti, 351–382. Rende.

———. 2009. "Vargu arbëresh i traditës gojore." *Gjurmime Albanologjike: Folklor dhe etnologji* 39:9–26.

———. 2011. "Voce, memoria, ritmo, movimento corporeo. Esempi di performance dei canti epici dei Balcani." In *L'esperienza del corpo*, ed. L. Ferrarini, 145–163. Milan.

———. 2012. "Remapping Songs in the Balkans: Bilingual Albanian Singers in the Milman Parry Collection." In *Balkan Epic: Song, History, Modernity*, ed. P. V. Bohlman and N. Petkovic, 203–223. Lanham, MD.

———. 2014. "Voice, Body, Technologies: Tales from an Arbëresh Village." *TRANS-Revista Transcultural de Música/Transcultural*

*Music Review* 18. http://www.sibetrans.com/trans/articulo/475/voice-body-technologies-tales-from-an-arberesh-village.

Scaldaferri, N., ed., with V. Friedman, J. Kolsti, and Z. U. Neziri. 2021. *Wild Songs, Sweet Songs: The Albanian Epic in the Collections of Milman Parry and Albert B. Lord*. Publications of the Milman Parry Collection of Oral Literature 5. Cambridge, MA.

Skendi, S. 1953. "The South Slavic Decasyllable in Albanian Oral Epic Poetry." *Word* 9 / *Slavic Word* 2:339–348.

———. 1954. *Albanian and South Slavic Oral Epic Poetry*. Philadelphia.

———. 2007. *Poezia epika gojore e shqiptareve dhe e sllaveve të jugut*. Tirana.

Sokoli, R. 1954. "Prozodia dhe metrika jonë popullore." *Nëntori* 8:177–227.

———. 1984. "Lahuta dhe kënget e kreshnikëve." *Nëntori* 1:186–205.

Tole, V. S. 2007. *Enciklopedia e Iso-polifonisë popullore shqiptare / Encyclopedia of Albanian Folk Iso-Polyphony*. Tirana.

# 21

# Tracking the South Slavic Epic Register

Ronelle Alexander

The Milman Parry Collection of Oral Literature, housed in Harvard University's Widener Library, offers a unique window into the past and specifically into the world of Yugoslav oral epic as it existed in the 1930s among a non-literate population. Thanks to Milman Parry's foresight, scholarly rigor, and perseverance, the materials allow scholars working nearly a century later to experience this no-longer-living oral tradition almost at first hand. Central to the collection are continuous audio recordings (on aluminum discs), and notebooks with transcriptions made by a team member who was present at (and took part in) the recording process. Furthermore, the recordings include not only lengthy song texts (sung to the *gusle* as well as recited) but also conversations with the singers. We can thus analyze the language of the songs in detail and also compare the language of song with the language used by the same individuals in a more neutral, non-singing situation.

Indeed, one of Parry's primary goals in his Yugoslav field research was to find an analogue to the Homeric *Kunstsprache* within a living tradition and to develop an empirical understanding of its inner workings. Could a single individual create and remember songs of the length and complexity of the *Iliad* and the *Odyssey*? If so, by what methods? Parry's great achievement was to demonstrate that singers are able to compose in performance because they have internalized a specific set of rules which allows (and requires) elements of speech to be combined in just the right ways to achieve the desired communication. Albert Lord, who took on Parry's mantle after the latter's untimely death in late 1935, called this set of rules a "specialized poetic grammar," or "a special grammar within the grammar of the language."[1]

Lord's description of this "poetic grammar," in terms of theme and formula, falls roughly within the framework of the Chomskyan linguistic theory

1 Lord 2019:37.

prevalent at the time, according to which the role of grammar was to describe the competence of a speaker of a particular language. Chomsky's focus, and that of linguists who have followed in this vein, was on the idealized grammar which represented this "competence"; they referred to instances of actual speech production as "performance."[2] For them, the opposition between competence and performance was more or less that between a consistent overall system vs. the often imperfect actual realizations of this system; their primary focus was (and still is) on achieving a full description of the idealized underlying system.

Other linguists felt that the idea of "linguistic competence" should not be restricted to the confines of an idealized grammar, but that the context of speech must also be taken into account. To right the balance, the anthropological linguist Dell Hymes introduced the term "communicative competence,"[3] and the notion that competence in a language meant not only the ability to recognize and produce grammatically correct utterances but also the ability to recognize and produce utterances appropriate to the particular speech situation. The study of these different "ways of speaking," and the fact that they were frequently associated with particular groups or communities, evolved into the discipline known as the ethnography of speaking.

Linguists outside the Chomskyan sphere also began to focus more attention on the context of speech. The discipline of sociolinguistics, which studies varieties of language that are correlated with (and affected by) socially-determined factors of language use, came to the forefront in the 1960s and has continued to grow. Within sociolinguistics, the concept that correlates most closely with communicative competence is that of register. The term itself was first coined in 1956 by T. B. W. Reid, and the concept was popularized by M. A. K. Halliday, who defined it as "the configuration of semantic resources that a member of a culture typically associates with a situation type."[4] As in the case of "ways of speaking," registers do not exist in isolation. Rather, as Jean Ure notes, "the register range of a language comprises the range of social situations recognized and controlled by its speakers—situations for which appropriate patterns are available."[5] Each register is tied to a particular recurring social situation and functions both to signal the speakers' recognition of that situation (as opposed to some other situation) and to allow the communication appropriate to that particular situation to take place more effectively. Nearly every community recognizes something akin to a "formal" register and a "casual" register, but other registers are more specialized.

2 Chomsky 1965.
3 Hymes 1966.
4 Halliday 1978:111.
5 Ure 1982:5.

The fact of performance itself, in the sense of poetic performance, also came to be the focus of separate sub-disciplines. Anthropologists began to focus on performance in the sense of verbal artistry and "an understanding of performance as socially constitutive and efficacious,"[6] while folklorists began to view their objects of study not just as cultural items but also as communicative acts.[7] Within the ethnography of speaking, anthropologists studied "ethnopoetics" or the different ways in which oral performance could be structured and the necessity for textual transcripts to take this into account.[8]

How do these new theoretical advances relate to the work of Parry and Lord? Which of the above tools is most relevant to our study of the materials of the Parry collection? To address this question, let us first return to Chomsky's opposition of competence and performance (idealized grammar vs. individual and often imperfect implementations in actual speech), an opposition frequently compared to the Saussurian dichotomy of *langue* and *parole*. One fairly obvious interpretation of Lord's "specialized poetic grammar" that exists "within the grammar of the language" would be that it corresponds to the "competence" of Chomsky's idealized "speaker-hearer"—in which the latter concept would correspond to Parry and Lord's idealized "singer of tales."

Yet even in 1960, Lord recorded his hesitation that the dichotomy of *langue* and *parole* would apply to the language of oral performance. "It might be worth suggesting," he wrote, "that we have in the case of oral epic performance something that is neither *langue* nor *parole*, but some third form," or even "something that is both *langue* and *parole* at the same time under different aspects, thus making a third form of communication, or of relationship, peculiar to oral verbal art."[9] This observation would indicate that Lord already realized (as did Parry before him) that an analysis of the language of epic song must make reference not only to "competence" in both the senses outlined above but to "performance" as well. In other words, an appropriate framework would be one that would include all of the perspectives mentioned above.

Such a framework has in fact been proposed by John Foley. Making reference not only to Halliday's definition of register but also to performance theory, ethnopoetics, and the ethnography of speaking broadly defined, he has spoken in some detail of the "epic register" with reference to verbal art of different sorts in different cultures.[10] This is a very productive move, in that it allows us

6 Bauman and Briggs 1991:79.

7 Bauman 1977.

8 Hymes 1994.

9 Lord 2019:303-304.

10 Foley 1992, 1995, 1996, 1999. The self-contained article printed in 1996, "*Guslar* and *Aoidos*: Traditional Register in South Slavic and Homeric Epic," was reprinted with only minimal

to refer to all the different elements of this very complex phenomenon under the umbrella of a single term. Indeed, by the inclusion of the word "epic," this conceptual framework introduces yet another element, that of genre. If one views genre in the more traditional sense, that of established literary canons, then the term "epic register"—part conventionalized and static and part situational and dynamic—might seem something of an oxymoron.

More recent views of genre, however, see it in much more fluid terms. Sociolinguists now view register, genre, and style as three distinct but overlapping concepts. Biber and Conrad, for instance, note that both genre and register make reference to the intended purpose of a particular instance of a "text variety" (which can be either spoken or written) as well as to its situational context, and that they differ only with reference to the actual linguistic features, which are "functional" in the case of register and "conventional" in the case of genre.[11] Linguistic anthropologists go even further in pointing out not only the "porousness" of each of the two categories but also the fact that each is continually renegotiated in practice.[12] In the case of the epic singers studied by Parry and Lord, therefore, where each song is composed anew in performance, which in essence meant that each instance recreates the genre, such a multifaced approach holds a great deal of promise.

Of course, as with any powerful conceptual approach, there will be things that still need working out "on the ground." In the hopes that this method will become practicable, I should like to make two cautionary notes, each having to do with the obvious fact that registers do not exist in isolation. The first is related to the fact that any one register must be defined with reference to a specific community and the second to the fact that it must be defined in relation to other registers available to that particular community. In what follows I speak only of the Parry-Lord material; however, the cautions are general ones which may be applicable in other instances as well.

As is well known, Parry and Lord carried out their extensive fieldwork in the Yugoslavia of the 1930s, and Lord did additional fieldwork in the Yugoslavia of the 1950s. The series in which portions of the materials have been published bears the title *Serbocroatian Heroic Songs*, where the adjective identifies the language in which the songs were sung. Clearly, therefore, the speech community to which the songs "belonged" was seen as unified by language. Of course, even then the language was pluricentric—a single language with recognizably different norms serving populations in different regions—and anyone familiar

changes as chapter 3 (entitled "Homer and the South Slavic Guslar: Traditional Register") of the 1999 book *Homer's Traditional Art*. See also Foley's contribution to the present volume.

11 Biber and Conrad 2009:2.

12 See Bauman and Briggs 1991 on genre and Agha 2006 on register.

with the material knew that the singing tradition they described was native only within part of the language area covered under the rubric "Serbo-Croatian." Still, because the language was generally recognized as a single entity, this term was sufficient as a rough identification of the type of tradition being discussed.

When Yugoslavia broke up in 1991, however, the language formerly known as Serbo-Croatian split into Bosnian, Croatian, and Serbian, a division formally recognized by the Dayton agreement of 1995 (the independent state of Montenegro, established in 2006, has proclaimed Montenegrin as its official language, and although codification of that language is underway, it does not yet have the generational time-depth of recognition, either among its speakers or within the world at large, as the other three). This of course places scholars of the epic tradition in a quandary: how is one to refer to the unified tradition studied extensively by Parry and Lord? The choice made by Foley is to call it "South Slavic epic tradition," and it is clear when he states that he uses this term "to designate genres of verbal art that ... can occur, for example, among either ethnic Serbs or ethnic Croats,"[13] that he intends it as a substitute for the term "Serbo-Croatian."

But this is misleading: the term South Slavic clearly includes not only the former Serbo-Croatian but also Slovenian, Bulgarian, and Macedonian. It is true that Parry himself consistently used the adjective "Southslavic" but always with the more general meaning in mind, even mentioning once in this context the hope that "the Macedonian and Bulgarian regions may furnish more definite evidence."[14] Now that the evidence is in, however, the use of this adjective to modify the noun "epic" is seen to be highly misleading, since Slovenian does not have an epic tradition at all whereas the Bulgarian epic tradition, now much better known outside Bulgaria, is clearly so different from that studied by Parry and Lord that no one who knows them both would ever group them together. Thus, whereas until quite recently one could reasonably speak of a modern-day group unified by the fact of speaking "Serbo-Croatian," one can in no way speak of a modern-day group unified by the fact of speaking "South Slavic." Thus, the phrase "a particular version of *the South Slavic language* devoted solely to the performance of epic poetry" simply has no meaning.[15]

The problem becomes even more acute when one uses the phrase "South Slavic epic" to modify the noun "register." The name of a language used as a cover term can reasonably apply to all speakers of a language or, with express qualification, to a subset of them; and the name of a register used as a cover term (such as "baby talk" or "legalese") can also apply to the traits common to

13 Foley 1995:xii, n3.

14 Parry 1971:445.

15 Foley 1996:25; 1999:74, my emphasis.

such registers in different languages. But, as nearly all definitions of "register" make clear, any one register is defined by the fact of functioning within (and at the service of) a particular well-defined social unit. The fact that there is no such unit definable as "South Slavic" deprives this term of practical functional meaning.

The breakup of what used to be Serbo-Croatian has created many a dilemma for which there is no easy solution, and this instance is no exception. One possible choice would be to speak of the "Bosniak epic register," where the adjective refers to what is now a clearly defined social unit—Muslims who speak what used to be called Serbo-Croatian. Another would be to speak directly of a particular set of singers and texts and speak of the "Herzegovinian Stolac epic tradition," a choice which might seem apt in this instance, since Foley has clearly identified all his examples as deriving from his close and thorough study of singers from this specific area. A third would be to use an ad hoc term such as "P-L epic tradition," referring to the specific singing register that functioned in the 1930s in the regions where Parry and Lord worked. But if one is to reap the full benefits of the concept "register," there must be a clearer and more concretely grounded identification of the social group within which it functions.

The second caution has to do with the fact that a register is, by definition, relative. One can only identify "formal" speech in relation to speech that is less formal, "baby talk" in relation to the kind of talk which occurs outside the presence of babies, "academic jargon" in relation to more neutral prose, and the like. Indeed, the attractiveness, as well as the explanatory power, of the idea "epic register" is that it points not just to a type of language but also to a particular situation, one in which that language is not only appropriate and expected but one which has also contributed to the formation of the register itself (for still living traditions, one may add "... and which continues to contribute to its ongoing definition"). To arrive at a thorough and nuanced understanding of this complex phenomenon, therefore, it is clearly necessary to define the distinctive traits of the register; and this, in turn, can only be done by assuming that those who command the register (either actively or passively) have the competence which allows them to differentiate it from the other registers which they also command.

Which other registers should these be? Should one contrast the register appropriate to the specific performance arena of epic song with that of other specific performance arenas and speak of the folktale, or the proverb, or the charm, register? Or should one think more broadly and contrast the overall performance arena (and the register with which it is most commonly associated, the epic) with that of speech outside the performance arena? The second choice seems to make the most sense, and this is what Foley has done. Thus, he has stated his intention to contrast the language of epic song of the singers of Stolac with that of "the unmarked conversational standard" of these same singers,[16] specifying further that this should be the singers' "own conversational registers."[17] Not only is this the correct choice, but it is also a particularly apposite one, in light of the fact that the Parry Collection includes audio recordings not only of extended stretches of epic singing but also of extended stretches of conversation between Parry, his field assistant Nikola Vujnović, and the same individuals who did the singing. Thus, although the tradition is no longer living in the form in which Parry and Lord encountered it, one has the next best thing in the ability to contrast extensive recorded samples of these two speech styles.

But the problem that arises here is that the "conversational register" represented by the recordings of these particular conversations is far from neutral, everyday speech. One might counter that there is no such thing as absolutely neutral speech, and this is of course true. Still, most people have a rough sense of the neutral and unmarked, and the fact that they do is what allows us to identify conventional genres as marked in some specific way or common registers as defined in some specific way. In the case of the unlettered population of a small provincial town such as Stolac in the 1930s, the best approximation of the "unmarked conversational standard" would be that of the local dialect as it is described by ethnographers and dialectologists: here, the description made by Asim Peco on the basis of work with elderly and highly traditional speakers gives the best approximation.[18]

In Parry's case, although the speech he recorded was clearly conversational, the social context was far from neutral. Neither the physical environment in which the conversations took place nor the social situation of which each of the participants was highly aware could be regarded as ordinary or unmarked. One must, therefore, take these factors of "unnaturalness" into account if one uses this speech style as the standard against which to define the epic register. Of course, Parry was not a sociolinguist or a dialectologist, and he was much less concerned with providing a natural speech environment than he was with making maximal amounts of durable quality audio recordings of continuous singing or speech performance. He accomplished this latter feat by creating an ad hoc recording studio out of two adjoining hotel rooms, placing himself, Nikola, and the singer before a microphone in one room and the recording apparatus (managed by his student assistant, Albert Lord) in the other room. Using the apparatus specially designed by Parry, Lord was able to manipulate the different aluminum discs in a way that allowed recording to proceed without interruption.

16 Foley 1996:25, 1999:74.

17 Foley 1996:25n32, 1999:293.

18 Peco 1964.

From the singer's point of view, this was a highly marked situation. First, the conversation took place not in the comfortable and familiar environment where relaxed chatting would normally take place, such as the village square or the yard of someone's home, but in the hotel room of a foreign visitor. Not only that, the singer was placed directly in front of a large mechanical device and expected to speak straight into it in the knowledge that what he said would be recorded onto discs that were being manipulated in a neighboring room. Second, the social differences between the interlocutors could not go unnoticed. In most instances (and in all instances of Stolac singers), the singer was a Muslim who was being questioned by a countryman of a different religion (Nikola was Catholic) who, in turn, was clearly taking directions from a foreigner of yet a different religion (Parry was Protestant). Furthermore, the singer, an individual of some stature and consequence in his own community (both in terms of prestige and chronological age), was answering questions put to him by a Catholic compatriot in his late 20s, himself in the employ of an American who also had stature in his own faraway community but was nevertheless only in his early 30s. Finally, the singer was speaking in the knowledge that he would be judged by what he said and sang, and paid accordingly, by a young man who was himself receiving pay from the ultimate instigator of the entire situation, the youthful American professor representing a distant university.

No interview situation is completely neutral, of course, and one must always contend with the observer's paradox. Still, the characteristics of this particular situation are much more marked than might be the case were these recordings to have been made by linguists, ethnographers, or folklorists working today. Furthermore, in interpreting the material of these conversations, we must take into account not only this highly marked contextual background but also the fact that, in most cases, our source is limited to a written transcription, and that the majority of these transcriptions (including all those relevant for the current analysis) were made several years after the fact. It is also relevant that the transcriber was Nikola Vujnović himself, working at that point in the US, where he had been brought specifically for this purpose. Nikola thus had the advantage (as well as the possible disadvantage) of his own recollections of the recording situation.

To demonstrate the possible action of all these factors, I will quote from the transcript of a section of the conversation with the Stolac singer Ibro Bašić and then analyze the conversation not only on the basis of the written transcript but also the audio discs from which the transcription was made.[19] In the

[19] Both the full transcript (PN 6598) and the audio files of one portion of it (discs 4405–4406) were made available to me courtesy of the Milman Parry Collection of Oral Literature housed in

excerpt below, I have transcribed the text exactly as Nikola wrote it. Portions spoken by Nikola are given in italics; portions spoken by Ibro are in roman type. For purposes of analysis, I have broken the text up into lines and sub-sections, added line numbers, and provided an English translation.

## A. "Word for Word" Fidelity (1–13)

1 ***Pjevaš li to Ibro, jednu pjesmu uvjek isto svaki put? Recimo riječ za riječ?***

1a *Ibro, when you sing a song, is it always the same each time? Word for word, so to speak?*

2 **Ma, ja, ja, pjevam brte ono kako, pa je zgodnije ono znaš**

2a Well, I, I, when I sing, you know, it's like, well it goes better, you know,

3 **kad čojek uz gusle pjeva ono ode, sve redom oni pjeva onako,**

3a when you sing it to the gusle. Then everything goes fine the way it should when you sing.

4 **kad kaziva riječ po riječ muka je to, neku zaboravi, neku prebaci, neku tako.**

4a But when you recite it word for word that's hard. You forget something, you omit something, stuff like that.

5 **A onako kad pjeva uz gusle ono ide sve ono jedan za drugijem tako.**

5a But when you sing to the gusle everything goes in order just right.

6 ***A znaš li ti šta je to kazat riječ za riječ kad pjevaš?***

6a *So do you know what it means to sing something "word for word"?*

7 **To je rećemo besjeda, ko benzir to je reć taman ko ja i ti sad se razgovaramo,**

7a That's like talking, like, well, to say, just like you and I are talking now.

8 **ono pa govorimo eto tako i pjesma ono govorimo biva.**

8a Well, we talk, and that's what a song is, it's like talking.

---

Harvard's Widener Library. I am particularly grateful to David Elmer and Peter McMurray for facilitating my access to audio recordings.

9 ***A nepreskočiš nikada ništa kad pjevaš jedan put i dva put jednu pjesmu?***

9a *And you never skip anything when you sing a song once, and then the same song again?*

10 **Pa jok.**

10a Oh, no.

11 ***Nikad ništa?***

11a *Never ever?*

12 **Jok nesmije se preskočit. Ono što zna i što čuje ono mora onako pjevat**

12a No, you musn't skip [anything]. You have to sing it just the way you know it and hear it,

13 **i ono mora gonit onako.**

13a and you have to push it through like that.

## B. Learning Songs as a Youth (14–31)

14 ***Ibro.***

14a *Ibro.*

15 **Ja.**

15a Yes?

16 ***Kad si bijo mlad koliko ti je puta trebalo da čuješ jednu pjesmu pa da je naučiš?***

16a *When you were young, how many times did you need to hear a song in order to learn it?*

17 **Baš kad sam mlad bijo mogo sam je odjednom primit,**

17a Well when I was young, I could pick it up right away [= in one hearing],

18 **a Bogami sad Nikola nemogu. Nemogu je primit Bogami**

18a but by God, Nikola, I can't do that now. I can't pick it up

19 **i što primi zaboravi, ono iz glave odma izađi.**

19a and what I do pick up I forget. It just goes right out of my head.

20 ***I veliš ti samo jedan put da je čuješ?***

20a *So you say you only had to hear it once?*

21 **Ja kad sam bijo mlad, nek bi je čuo od pjevača jednom**
21a When I was young, all I had to do was hear it once from a singer,
22 **odma bi je primijo. A sad Bogami nemogu.**
22a and I picked it up immediately. But now, by God, I can't.

23 ***Ma kako to Ibro?***
23a *Well, how is that, Ibro?*

24 **Ama eto tako.**
24a Well, it just is.

25 ***Kako se može tako dugačka pjesma primit.***
25a *How can someone pick up such a long song?*

26 **More se primit ono sluša čojek ono i drago mu [4406] kako oni pjevač pjeva**
26a It's possible to do. It's like you listen, and you like the way the singer sings it,
27 **pa sluša i drago mu. Jer to kako iđe, taman ko škola i učenje.**
27a and you listen and you like it. That's how it goes, just like school and learning.
28 **Samo mu kaži rećemo jednom onu zadaću i ono uvrti u glavu.**
28a You just say once what the task is, and it goes straight into one's head.
29 **Jergo sad neiđe nikakav u školu nemore primit više**
29a And if you never went to school, you can't get it anymore;
30 **vet u đetinjstvu primi, i mora primiti tako pa ono mu ište srce znaš, pa da primi.**
30a you [have to] learn it in childhood. And when your heart wants it, you know,
31 **Pa ondak teža pretegni, teža pretegni, i ono zaboravi.**
31a then you get it. But then it gets harder and harder, and you forget.

## C. In Search of Variants (32–50)

32 ***A vidiš Ibro. Ti si pjevo jednu pjesmu o Đerđelez Aliji***
32a *Look now, Ibro. You sang a song about Đerđelez Alija,*

33 ***i jednu pjesmu o begu Ljuboviću.***
33a *and one about Beg Ljubović.*

34 **Ja.**
34a Yeah.

35 ***I jednu pjesmu o Alagić Aliji.***
35a *And one about Alagić Alija.*

36 **Jes.**
36a Yes.

37 ***A bili ti znao koju drugu pjesmu da ima naprimjer još jedna o Alagiću***
37a *So would you know of any other songs, for instance another one about Alagić*
38 ***ili jedna još o Đerđelezu, ili još jedna ili dvije o Ljuboviću, bili znao ti?***
38a *or another one about Đerđelez, or one or two more about Ljubović? Would you know [some of these]?*

39 **Nebi, nebi Bogami Nikola.**
39a No I wouldn't, by God, Nikola. I wouldn't.

40 ***Nebi znao?***
40a *You wouldn't know [any more]?*

41 **Neznam brte Bogami, nema fajde jer ono čojeku što treba,**
41a I don't know any, by God. There's no point. If what somebody wants is
42 **i ono tačno, ja bi pjevo, rećemo i pjevo, a koju neznam Bogami**
42a something I know well, then I'd sing it. But by God, if I didn't know it
43 **brate nebi, jeli? Sad ono kad je ono u redu znaš,**
43a I wouldn't sing it, would I? If you know it, then it all goes in order, but [if not]
44 **pa prebaci onu otud, pa onu otud, pa nekud neiđe.**
44a you mix this thing in here, and that thing in there, and it ends up not working.

45 ***A jesili ti čuo kada druge pjesme o njima da pjevaju?***
45a *Well, have you ever heard other [singers] sing some different songs about them?*

46 **Ko? Ja?**
46a Who, me?

47 ***E.***
47a *You.*

48 **Jesam slušavo ove pjesme a ja drugije slušavo sam i druge pjesme**
48a Yes, I've heard these songs, and I've heard others, other songs,
49 **pa Bogami zaboravijo, ama slušavo ima nazad rećemo dvajest godin**
49a but by God, I've forgotten them. It was some twenty years ago that I heard them,
50 **pa ono čojek zaboravi odma. Zaboravi.**
50a and that's the sort of thing you forget right off. You forget.

## D. "Word for Word" Reprise (51–69)

51 ***Što ono znači riječ za riječ pjevati u pjesmi?***
51a *What does it mean to sing a song "word for word"?*

52 **Kako što znači?**
52a What do you mean, what does it mean?

53 ***Kažeš, ja sam pjevo Bogami sve riječ za riječ,***
53a *When you say, "By God, I sang that song completely word for word,"*
54 ***što je ono riječ za riječ?***
54a *what does that "word for word" mean?*

55 **Ono ti je ko ono rećemo što se zove besjede, riječ,**
55a That's, you know, well, it's like what they call speech, a word.
56 **ono besjede rećemo, ono jeli taman ko što ja tebi sad kazivam,**
56a It's like speech, you know? It's just like how I'm talking to you right now.
57 **to je kaže to je riječ to je naš jezik, sve ono.**
57a That's, you know, that's a word. It's our language. A word, you know, it's speech, all that.

58 ***Ali što je riječ? Što je riječ kažimi?***
58a *But what's a word? Tell me what a word is.*

59 **Besjeda.**
59a Speech.

60 ***Besjeda.***
60a *Speech?*

61 **Ja besjeda, to je reć to je reć riječ taman ko što ja tebi kažem sada,**
61a Yes, speech. It's like, like, a word is just like I [would] say to you now,
62 **jeli to knjiga Nikola? Jeli to ibrik Nikola. E tako je to je reć.**
62a "Is that a book, Nikola? Is that an *ibrik* [coffeepot], Nikola?" There, that's how to say—how to say a word.

63 ***Što je recimo jedna riječ u pjesmi. Kažimi jednu riječ iz pjesme?***
63a *Well, then, what's a word—a word in a song? Tell me a word, tell me, from a song.*

64 **Ovo ti je ovako rećemo to je reć riječ,**
64a Here, then, let's say, here's [how you] say a word:
65 **"Podranijo od Kladuše Mujo, na vrh tanke načinjene kule."**
65a "Mujo of Kladuša arose early atop his fine well-made tower."

66 ***A to su stihovi.***
66a *But those are verses.*

67 **E pa ja to je kod nas, to jes kod vas, a kod nas reče se to.**
67a Ah—well, that's how it is with us—I mean with you. Us, that's how we say it.

68 ***Ahaha!***
68a *Aha!*

69 **Ja tako je to.**
69a Yes, that's how it is.

## E. Pinning down "a Word" (70–87)

70 ***A na primjer kada kaže ono podranijo što je ono?***
70a *So for instance, when you say this "arose early," what is that?*

71 **To je reć uranijo ili usto hoćeš, pa ono podranijo.**
71a Well, that is to say "got up early," or if you want, also "arose early."

72 ***A što je ono?***
72a *And what is that?*

73 **Ja neznam što je ono vet ovo ti je ovako rećemo, šta je ono.**
73a I don't know what that is. It's, you know, just the way we say it, that's all.
74 **Podranijo od Kladuše Mujo ili rećemo, to je reć podranijo,**
74a "Mujo of Kladuša arose early," or you could say maybe "arose early,
75 **prije zore, ogranka sunca. To je reć podranijo, uranijo, podranijo, tako.**
75a before dawn, at break of day." You could say "arose early," "got up early," "arose early," things like that.

76 ***A na primjer kada ti kažeš Ja sam Bašić, što je to?***
76a *And for instance, when you say "I am Bašić," what is that?*

77 **Neznam Bogami.**
77a God knows! I don't.

78 ***Neznaš ti to?***
78a *You don't know this?*

79 **Ja jok Bogami. Jer ja njesam školovan tako, pa ja sam Bašić, ja to,**
79a No way, by God. I'm not schooled in such, I'm just Bašić, I, well—
80 **jer treba tu čojek školovan pa da sve to istomači,**
80a you need somebody with schooling to explain all that to you.
81 **a ja neumijem to istomačit ono materinijem jezikom.**
81a Me, I don't know how to explain that, not in my mother tongue.

82 ***A jeli to riječ na primjer kazati sam?***
82a *So is it a word, for instance, to say "am"/"oneself"?*

83 **Jes.**
83a Yes.

84 ***Jes, to je riječ?***
84a *It is? That's a word?*

85 **Ja, sam čojek, jes.**
85a Yes, I—I, myself, a person. Yes.

86 ***Ali kako onda može biti ono riječ, Podranijo od Kladuše Mujo?***
86a *But then how can this "Mujo of Kladuša arose early" be a word [too]?*

87 **Ama ja neznam, tako je to reć, tako je to.**
87a Well I don't know, that's just how you say it, that's just how it is.

## F. Return to Song texts (88–)

88 ***U redu moj Iro [sic].***
88a *O.K., my Ibro.*

89 **Ja.**
89a Yeah.

90 ***A znaš li ti još štogod o Gazi Hrustanbegu?***
90a *So do you know some other piece about Gazi Hrustanbeg?*

This selection is of special interest since it contains a particularly eloquent discussion of the concept of *riječ* (the singer's speech act),[20] one which has been frequently quoted. Parry's interest in the concept of "word for word" fidelity, a topic which comes up frequently in his conversations with the singers, is the central concern of section A. The conversation then moves to the process of transmission and learning (section B) and the singer's repertoire (section C). Sections D and E return to the idea of "word for word." Although section D is the one most frequently quoted, both are critical in this regard; indeed, the near breakdown of communication in section E contributes significantly to our understanding of the concept in the mind of the singer. In section F, Nikola moves to re-establish a communicative equilibrium with the singer; due to space limitations, only the beginning of this section has been included.

Comparison of the transcription with the audio records, which contain non-verbal information such as pauses, laughter, and intonational cues, is highly instructive. For one thing, although Parry's words are only infrequently marked in the transcript, they are much more frequently heard in the background. Furthermore, it is clear from the authoritative tone of his voice, even if his words

[20] For unknown reasons, John Foley consistently used the Serbian-marked form *reč* "word" to designate this concept, despite the fact that all the singers Parry worked with used the form *riječ* in the meaning "word," and that nearly all of them were from regions (Bosnia, Herzegovina, and Montenegro) where *riječ* was the accepted standard form.

are not always intelligible, that he is in control of the conversation. Nikola and Ibro appear to accept this fact of control though there are certain instances of discomfiture, heard both in non-verbal cues and in one purposeful word choice made by Nikola. Even the transcription itself provides evidence of this discomfiture. Most of it is accurate, but there are certain errors. Two rather significant ones concern omissions that occur relatively early in the text: in line 42, Ibro says not just *ono tačno* but *ono tačno koju znam* "exactly *the one I know,*" and in line 44 he says not just *pa prebaci* but *pa ono nije pa prebaci* "but *if it isn't* then you mix ...."

Nearly all the errors, however, occur during a segment of the conversation when Nikola appeared to be caught between his need to obey his employer and his knowledge (as a singer himself) that Parry's question will make no sense to Ibro. Because it is known that Nikola made the transcription of the conversation at least three (and perhaps four) years after it took place,[21] it would appear that his unease about this culture clash was still present at some level of his consciousness. I have included the correction for each of the errors in the translation and will summarize the most significant of them below.

The sections of relevance are D and E. After line 50 (the end of section C), there is a long pause. Parry's words in the background are not audible, but he is clearly directing Nikola to return to the issue of "word for word." Both Nikola and Ibro seem disoriented at this: they appear to feel that the question had been settled already (in section A). Nikola transcribes his own speech incorrectly in line 51, adding an extra instance of *za riječ* (as if he had said the equivalent of "word for word for word,"which he clearly did not say), and Ibro's intonation in line 52 conveys a clear sense of mistrust. Further on, Nikola writes for Ibro's speech in line 56 *tebi sad* instead of *sad tebi* ("[talking] to you now"): there is no essential change in meaning, but the lapse is unusual for Nikola, who usually makes a very faithful transcription of what is on the record.

In line 57, however, his error is more significant: he leaves out an entire phrase in one of Ibro's most significant speeches. Thus, Ibro says not just *to je kaže to je riječ to je naš jezik sve ono*, but rather *to je kaže to je riječ to je naš jezik riječ kaže to je besjede sve ono* "That's, you know, that's a word, you know, that's our language. *A word, you know, like speech*, all that." This new element, the idea of speech (or utterance), becomes the center of the next few lines (59–62), especially line 62, where Ibro illustrates the idea of a self-contained utterance very clearly (*jeli to knjiga Nikola? Jeli to ibrik Nikola* "Is that a book, Nikola? Is that an *ibrik*, Nikola?"). Parry's voice is heard in the background immediately after this, and it is right at this point that Nikola again leaves out an entire phrase of Ibro's.

[21] The conversation took place in June 1935, and Nikola made the transcription at some point during his eighteen-month stay at Harvard, between 1938 and 1940.

Thus, the conclusion of line 62 is not *E tako je to je reć*, but *E tako je to je reći reć riječ* (There, that's how to say—*how to say, to say a word*). Then in the next line, when Parry's words are heard in the background again, Nikola once more omits to transcribe several words from his own speech. This time there is no change in the meaning, but the smoothness of the transcription hides the fact that Nikola was, at this point, feeling some unease. Thus, instead of *Što je recimo jedna riječ u pjesmi, Kažimi jednu riječ iz pjesme?*, Nikola says *Što je recimo jedna riječ jedna riječ u pjesmi, Kažimi jednu riječ kaži iz pjesme?* ("Well, what's a word, *a word* in a song? Tell me a word, *tell me*, from a song"). In short, Nikola's transcription of this whole section conveys his own apparent discomfort as he recalls the situation. Once he and Ibro agree on the all-important distinction between "words" and "verses," however, in lines 66–67, equilibrium appears to be restored. Indeed, the intonational patterns at this point convey that all three sides (singer, singer/investigator, and scholar) are happy with this distinction.

But then Parry decides to push the issue further. After line 69, we hear his words clearly in the background as he says to Nikola the equivalent of "Ask him if *ja* ['I'] is a word, *ja sam* ['I am']." This puts Nikola in a quandary. As a singer himself, he knows this question will make no sense to Ibro, so he not only omits to transcribe altogether the clearly audible line of Parry's speech, but he also—after a notable pause—substitutes a different word, *podranio* "arose early" (line 70). But then, Parry repeats the request, after line 75, and Nikola is forced to put the question directly to Ibro (line 76). Ibro's response (line 77) is accompanied by derisive laughter, followed by his highly significant observation about the incongruence between the worlds of orality and literacy (lines 79–81), at which point the conversation seems almost in danger of breaking down altogether. But Parry is still not satisfied: we hear his directions again in the background, in response to which Nikola asks Ibro again (line 82) whether *sam* is a word. In doing so, however, Nikola pronounces the word not in the meaning "am" (quite naturally, since the rules of the language do not allow this word to be pronounced in isolation) but rather with a long vowel, in the meaning "oneself." After this exchange, even Parry seems to acknowledge the dead end, and he directs Nikola to shift the conversation back to Ibro's repertoire (section F).

The intent of the above excursus, comprising a brief description of the social situation of the conversations in general and an examination of a specific portion of one of these conversations, has been to demonstrate that the conversational speech of singers (as recorded by Parry) cannot be taken as exemplary of a neutral register, an "unmarked conversational standard." What this speech is, however, is much more interesting than what it is not. First, it is an example of the type of discourse which sociolinguists analyze in terms of participant manipulation, in terms of the choices made by each participant in a conversation as he negotiates the constant trade-off between the achievement of his own individual goals and the maintenance of the conversational flow. Space does not permit a full conversational analysis of this excerpt, though a few elements have been mentioned above. Second, this situation gives us valuable insight into the actual means by which Parry both obtained his remarkable collection and derived the significant insights which Lord then brought to full expression. It is paramount to remember as well that Parry also obtained nearly all of the most valuable epic song texts in his collection in this very same recording situation, one in which the two-person audience, though clearly a knowledgeable one, was not representative of the social situation in which singers normally performed.

This, of course, reminds us that the performance situation represented by the Parry-Lord material is one which we must largely reconstruct and that we have relatively little direct information about the neutral context of South Slavic epic performance at the time Parry did his recordings. We have what Murko (1929, 1951) and Parry have told us about their observations, and we have a few isolated narratives by the singers themselves (indeed, at another point in his conversation with Nikola,[22] Ibro tells a vivid tale, replete with epic hyperbole, of how he out-sang several other singers on a particular occasion). But without actual videotape evidence or multiple detailed first-hand reports, we simply do not have enough information about the performance situation to achieve a full-fledged description of the performance register. At the same time, we can and must use the insights of modern scholarship to deepen and enhance our understanding of what the epic register must have been like in those portions of the South Slavic world of which Milman Parry and Albert Lord have left us such a vivid record.

22 PN 6598, discs 4403–4404.

## Bibliography

Agha, A. 2006. *Language and Social Relations*. Cambridge.

Bauman, R. 1977. *Verbal Art as Performance*. Prospect Heights, IL.

Bauman, R., and C. L. Briggs. 1990. "Poetics and Performance as Critical Perspectives on Language and Social Life." *Annual Review of Anthropology* 19:59–88.

———. 1991. "Genre, Intertextuality, and Social Power." *Journal of Linguistic Anthropology* 2:131–172.

Biber, D., and S. Conrad. 2009. *Register, Genre, and Style*. Cambridge.

Chomsky, N. 1965. *Aspects of the Theory of Syntax*. Cambridge, MA.

Halliday, M. A. K. 1978. *Language as Social Semiotic: The Social Interpretation of Language and Meaning*. Baltimore.

Hymes, D. 1966. "Two Types of Linguistic Relativity." In *Sociolinguistics*, ed. W. Bright, 114–158. The Hague.

———. 1994. "Ethnopoetics, Oral-Formulaic Theory, and Editing Texts." *Oral Tradition* 9:330–370.

Foley, J. M. 1992. "Word-power, Performance, and Tradition." *Journal of American Folklore* 105/417:275–301.

———. 1995. *The Singer of Tales in Performance*. Bloomington.

———. 1996. "*Guslar* and *Aoidos*: Traditional Register in South Slavic and Homeric Epic." *Transactions of the American Philological Association* 126:11–41.

———. 1999. *Homer's Traditional Art*. University Park, PA.

Lord, A. B. 2019. *The Singer of Tales*. 3rd ed. Ed. D. F. Elmer. Hellenic Studies 77. Publications of the Milman Parry Collection of Oral Literature 4. Washington, DC. Orig. pub. Cambridge, MA, 1960.

Murko, M. 1929. *La poésie populaire épique en Yougoslavie au début du XXe siècle*. Paris.

———. 1951. *Tragom srpskohrvatske epike*. Zagreb.

Parry, M. 1971. "Ćor Huso: A Study of Southslavic Song, Extracts." In *The Making of Homeric Verse: The Collected Papers of Milman Parry*, ed. A. Parry, 437–464. Oxford.

Peco, A. 1964. "Istočnohercegovački govor." *Srpski dijalektološki zbornik* 14:1–200.

Reid, T. B. W. 1956. "Linguistics, Structuralism and Philology." *Archivum Linguisticum* 8:28–37.

Ure, J. 1982. "Introduction: Approaches to the Study of Register Range." *International Journal of the Sociology of Language* 35:5–24.

# 22

# There Are No Oral Media?

## Multisensory Perceptions of South Slavic Epic Poetry

Peter McMurray

Oral poetry sounds. In other words, it is also aural poetry. This claim serves as the foundation of this essay, and while it may not seem particularly revolutionary, such a notion has considerable potential not only to bring studies of oral poetry into fruitful dialogue with other emerging fields of academic inquiry—for example, sound studies, media studies, and the anthropology of the senses—but also to offer some meaningful reflection, in this age of digitization and hypermedia, on what we actually mean by "oral poetry." Stated succinctly, we cannot understand orality without consideration of sound. In particular, the histories of sound and listening at stake here are closely connected to recording technologies that simultaneously respond to but also shape our sensory experiences of oral poetry. Furthermore, those histories of mediated sound likewise point to a multisensory realm that extends far beyond the oral and aural. These claims emerge from that most canonical of corpora, South Slavic epic song, one of the most important sources for generating our current notions of "oral poetry." Somewhat paradoxically, listening carefully to this tradition and its sonic qualities makes clear that oral poetry is less exclusively oral than its name indicates, begging the question: how oral is oral poetry?

To set the stage for this sensory exploration of oral poetry, I turn to Miloš Velimirović, Albert Lord's assistant during his 1950 and 1951 fieldwork in the former Yugoslavia. As an aspiring musicologist and Byzantinist without particularly good standing with the government at the time, Velimirović did not consider himself a natural candidate to act as Lord's assistant. But the linguistic problems of describing oral poetry led to just such an outcome, which he described in an interview shortly before his death:

> [After Albert Lord] completed his dissertation[1] ... he got an interesting idea, which was apparently never before tested or explored: namely, to try to find the very same singers from whom they recorded texts, whether in dictation or on the recording machine, and record them again and see whether these texts remained the same in length, and whether there was any change, as well. So in early 1950, I gather Albert wrote a letter to the Yugoslav government, asking that he be assigned an assistant because Parry and Lord did have an assistant in 1934–35 by the name of Nikola Vujnović. And apparently it was not possible to establish contact with Vujnović at that point, so Albert asked the government to assign somebody.
>
> Now here comes an interesting story. The letter was received in the Committee for Cultural Relations with Foreign Countries ... and they said, 'Well, let's not send again one of our men with him again. The man wants to record songs.' See, the term *pesma* means song, but it can also be used for epic poetry. And they understood that Albert was interested in music ... They just founded a musicological institute in 1948. So the letter came to the Serbian Academy of Sciences, in Belgrade, and they looked at the letter, read that Albert was interested in *pesma*, songs, so they said, 'Well, we've got the Musicological Institute.' They sent the letter to the Musicological Institute, which came into the hands of Petar Konjević, the composer and director of the Institute, [who] was to make a recommendation for somebody to the Committee for Cultural Relations with Foreign Countries to be [an] assistant to Albert. And Albert said that he had brought with him a wire recorder, and that he also brought two—I don't know how many-voltage batteries—six- or twelve-volt batteries that had to be charged every night in some garage. They were actually car batteries. So he needed somebody

1 Albert Lord, "The Singer of Tales: A Study in the Processes of Composition of Yugoslav, Greek, and Germanic Oral Narrative Poetry" (1949). In the same interview, Velimirović highlights some of the delays Lord faced in sifting through the massive archive left to him after Parry's passing, including his service in the Navy. This period of Lord's life and work from 1935 to 1949, including also his collecting work in Albania, his processing of Parry's archive, and his work with various collaborators (Parry's assistant Nikola Vujnović; ethnomusicologist George Herzog; and composer/ethnomusicologist Béla Bartók, to name a few) to begin transcribing the archive's contents all warrant further examination. In many ways, this period would set the scope and trajectory for much of Lord's work over the half century to follow, as well as having a marked influence on the directions his many students would then pursue.

> who was going to help both carry this stuff and operate the recording machine, the wire recorder.[2]

Velimirović seems baffled that he, as a musicologist, was brought along rather than, say, a folklorist, philologist, or anthropologist. Certainly, the Academy of Sciences, which had itself collected such "songs" in the past, should have understood what was being requested. And yet, somehow, the uncertain valence of *pesma* (or *pjesma*) as "song" but also "poem"—and etymologically, an abstract noun, "that which is sung"—was sufficient in 1950 to lead Lord to Velimirović.[3]

In addition to this ontological ambiguity (what is a *pesma*?), which I will return to shortly, Velimirović's comments suggest a number of other avenues of interest for the question of oral poetry. For example, he highlights three institutions that mediate this encounter: the Committee for Cultural Relations with Foreign Countries, the Academy of Sciences, and the Musicological Institute. But this isolated example suggests that these institutions were not simply forwarding along mail to one another; rather, they were (at least implicitly, if not consciously) engaging in a conversation about the definitions, significance, and aesthetics of poetry. The politics of collecting and fieldwork often fades into the background, overshadowed by heroicizing accounts in which the collector is an unrestricted agent, able to impose his or her will around the globe in the name of science and knowledge. But certainly, a newly-formed "second Yugoslavia," standing on a major fault line of the Cold War, had reason to be wary of any kind of agent, literary or otherwise, roaming through the countryside with recording equipment. Indeed, one of the great counterfactual tales of Parry's work was his failed attempt to go to Soviet Central Asia because of the politics of the early 1930s (Mitchell and Nagy 2000:xiii), following in the footsteps of the nineteenth-century Turkologist Vasiliy (Wilhelm) Radloff (1885). As several scholars have pointed out since, Radloff had already explored their practices of orality (or "art of improvisation") and also made explicit comparison between Kyrgyz epic singers and ancient Greek *aoidoi* (Schoeler 2006:87–88, also A. Parry 1971:xxx,

2 Miloš Velimirović, interview with author, July 16, 2007. Video of this interview segment can be seen here: https://vimeo.com/104102200.

3 Petar Skok writes the following in his 1971 (Croato-Serbian) etymological dictionary: "Old derivatives [*izvedenice*] from the base [*osnova*] *pê-* are numerous: with the suffix *-sn* for an abstract noun (compare *basna*, v.) *pjêsan*, genitive *-sni*...From there also Vuk's *pjesnarica*. In this form the assimilation p – n > p – m appears...*pjesma* = (in ikavijan dialect) *pisma* (Kačić), the appearance common in written language" (1971:672). Just as interesting as the formal linguistic trajectory here are the examples Skok gives: Vuk Karadžić and Andrija Kačić-Miošić, both of whom play important roles in the cultural space between orality and writing. Indeed, Parry's and Lord's efforts are often (always?) responding to Karadžić, while the writings of authors like Kačić-Miošić leave traces of a rich oral culture that hint at the fluid movements between these two (too rigid) categories.

Lord 1948:36, Reichl 2000:12–13).[4] But, more significantly, given Parry's fascination with bilingual singers like Salih Ugljanin and singers with knowledge of particularly long songs, one can only imagine his astonishment had he encountered the trilingual bards of Khorasan or performers of the massive *Manas* epic, which, in its longest iterations, dwarfs the Homeric epic.[5] While Parry's eventual choice of Yugoslavia obviously proved tremendously fruitful, it should be remembered that such choices are always brokered through relationships of politics and power, whether through formal institutions (as with Lord) or not.

In this essay, I explore the slippery ontology of oral poetry as suggested by these examples and by Lord's exchange with the Yugoslavian authorities. As my title suggests, I will argue that there is, in effect, no such thing as oral poetry. Or, put less polemically, I suggest that orality is a multisensory phenomenon, whether as sung poetry, as poetry heard in live performance, or as poetry encountered archivally through writing, audio recording, video, or other media. My thoughts here, originally delivered (fittingly) in an oral form in 2010, resonate strongly with the ethnographic history Haun Saussy has laid out in his 2016 book, *The Ethnography of Rhythm: Orality and Its Technologies.* Saussy's formulations of the "human gramophone" and oral tradition as "a particular kind of writing, an inscription on other human minds" (156) might be seen as a kind of inversion of my arguments here: he focuses on transmission and the tradition, and I am especially interested in what the tradition leaves behind and even excises from itself.

Put crudely, Saussy re-imagines orality as a kind of technological process without the technologies. For my part, I will be especially interested in how orality is, in fact, co-constructed with material recording technologies. There is no singular sensory experience of orality; but to the degree "orality" as such exists, I would argue that it is bound up with the documentary machinery that allowed it to be inscribed in places besides "other human minds." In what follows, I first explore briefly the question: what kind of medium or art form

4 In his own writings, Milman Parry highlights three scholars whose writings on epic he deemed reliable, while also hinting at the political pragmatics of his choice: "I found myself in the position of speaking about the nature of oral style almost purely on the basis of a logical reasoning from the characteristics of Homeric style, whereas what information I had about oral style as it could be seen in actual practice was due to what I had been able to gather here and there from the remarks of different authors who, save in a few cases—that of Murko and Gesemann for the Southslavic poetries, and of Radloff for the Kirgiz-Tartar poetry—were apt to be haphazard and fragmentary—and I could well fear, misleading. Of the various oral poetries for which I could obtain enough information the Southslavic seemed to be the most suitable for a study which I had in mind, to give that knowledge of a still living oral poetry which I saw to be needed if I were to go on with any sureness in my study of Homer" (1971:440).

5 On bards of (Iranian) Khorasan, see Youssefzadeh 2002. On *Manas* see Reichl 2000, Köçümkulkïzï 2005, and van der Heide 2008.

is oral poetry? To answer that, I turn to the longstanding debate in art history about medium specificity. I then look to specific examples from the Milman Parry Collection of Oral Literature to capture some of the ontological slipperiness of orality in the context of the South Slavic traditions Milman Parry and Albert Lord documented and analyzed: pictures that sound, voices that map space, and videos that reveal the inescapable contingency of performance.

## On *pesma*; or, the Multisensory Poetics of Poetics

To return to the word *pesma*, Velimirović's comments underscore not only the word's political and linguistic ambiguities but also its multiple sensory meanings: in other words, what kind of art form was Lord in fact seeking? Certainly Lord was under no illusions about the complexity of his request or its nominalism, as exemplified by his vacillation between titles around that time: his collaborative book with Béla Bartók was titled *Serbo-Croatian Folk Songs* (1951), featuring mostly "women's" (i.e. lyric) songs; the series of epic texts published from 1953 onward, *Serbocroatian Heroic Songs*; and his dissertation (1949) and the resultant book (1960), both called *The Singer of Tales*. Folk songs, heroic songs, sung tales: Lord seems quite cognizant of the challenge of naming this sonic art. That Velimirović, who would go on to become an eminent scholar of Byzantine chant—another genre of verbal practice that poses many similar questions of musical definitions—would draw such amusement from this anecdote suggests that the confusion here did not originate in Lord's misuse of the term in his letter (presumably written in Serbian, using the word "*pesma*"). Rather, the humor stems from the misunderstanding (or perhaps lack of awareness) on the part of government officials with regard to such a tradition. Yet their bafflement and Lord's continual tweaking of terminology in his titles highlight a critical sonic reality of this repertoire: not just its definition as a practice of sung poetry or verbal arts but its ontology more broadly.

In recent decades, art historians have taken up similar challenges with regards to visual arts. One influential line of thinking has been that of "medium specificity": what makes painting, or sculpture, or film, unique relative to each other? And, by extension, how does an artist fulfill the aesthetic possibilities of a given medium? Perhaps the most famous advocate of this notion was Clement Greenberg (and to a lesser degree Michael Fried), who used it to elaborate a powerful argument privileging painting as the purest of visual mediums and, therefore, the natural bedrock for the discipline of art history (Greenberg 1940). Sculpture and architecture raise too many ontological/sensory problems to fulfill that task. Outside the visual arts, poetry—which has never proved easily reducible to music or to literature—created even more problems for this idea, some of which I will discuss below. Yet, for many, "medium specificity" remained a compelling explanation for the visual power of painting and a plausible yardstick for aesthetic judgments (however circular): a given art form (e.g. painting) was successful to the degree it fulfilled but also confined itself to the possibilities of its particular medium. More recently, however, the emergence of a broader discipline of visual studies has necessitated a rethinking of medium specificity that offers insight into the question of oral poetry too. In his rebuttal of scholars like Greenberg, W.J.T. Mitchell argues that *all* art forms are multimedia and, therefore, must lack medium specificity. He opens his provocatively titled essay, "There Are No Visual Media," as follows:

> "Visual media" is a colloquial expression used to designate things such as television, film, photography and painting, etc. But it is highly inexact and misleading. On closer inspection, all the so-called visual media turn out to involve the other senses (especially touch and hearing). All media are, from the standpoint of sensory modality, "mixed media."
>
> Mitchell 2005:257

Mitchell goes on to suggest that even seeing itself has a complicated relationship to the visual, with numerous ways in which the two terms are *not* concomitant, whether because of physiological processes or disabilities.[6] Furthermore, he places poetry at the opposite end of the medium-specific spectrum, drawing on the centuries-old practice of ekphrastic poetry, in which an object (his example is Achilles' shield in the *Iliad*) is described as a palpable, visible thing—"a kind of action-at-distance between two rigorously separated sensory and semiotic tracks, one which requires completion in the mind of the reader. This is why poetry remains the most subtle, agile master-medium of the *sensus communis*, no matter how many spectacular multimedia inventions are devised to assault our collective sensibilities" (Mitchell 2005:263).

Strikingly, however, Mitchell's understanding of sensory mingling in poetry apparently presumes a fixed, written form of poetry—even when speaking of Homeric ekphrasis. Friedrich Kittler, on the other hand, sees that interchange

[6] Caroline Jones (2006) also explores Greenberg's ideas of "opticality" and "eyesight alone," situating the formation of these ideas in a process she terms "the bureaucratization of the senses." Whether disciplined (Mitchell) or bureaucratized (Jones), the assumption of clear-cut distinctions between the senses that prevailed through much of twentieth-century art history proves poorly suited to deal with the multisensory complexities of oral poetry. There is a certain irony in these theories that proved so adept at explaining some of the most avant-garde modern art of the century yet failed to adequately explain genres like oral poetry that have been the subject of such discussions for millennia, dating back at least to Aristotle's *Poetics*.

between the sonic and the written and the incommensurability of those two "sensory and semiotic tracks" (to use Mitchell's description again) as the fundamental starting point of German, if not all European, poetry. His reading of Goethe's *Faust* as a struggle to capture the sighs and non-inscribable utterances of the world into codified, solidified writing sets the table for his theory of *Aufschreibesysteme* (1985), more literally "writing-down systems" or, more commonly in English, "discourse networks" (1990). Kittler highlights the profound transformations of meaning that come through speech, writing, the writing of speech, and the speaking of writing. The entire possibility of enunciation at this juncture (c. 1800) relies on a back-and-forth between writing and speaking as a core practice in poetry, such that "the magic power of signs [is able] to liberate sensual and intoxicating powers in the reader once the signs have disappeared into the fluid medium of their signified—the voice" (Kittler 1990:7). In other words, the voice becomes the point of media transfer in the Romantic Era, whether reading words and thus (at least implicitly, though literally for Faust) sounding by means of the voice or uttering/singing/speaking as a precondition for inscription.

It seems fitting, then, that the introduction of South Slavic poetry to Germany and Western European elites in general came around the same moment as Kittler is describing, with Goethe, the Grimms, and other figures championing the poetry—once it was made available in written form by South Slavic collectors (i.e. inscribers-of-poetry) like Vuk Karadžić. This media malleability of poetry highlights what must have been immediately obvious to all nineteenth-century readers: that such poetry, oral-turned-written (but still entailing voice, if Kittler is correct) as it was, destabilized the emergent categories of literature that Goethe and others were simultaneously producing. In other words, since the first attempts to make oral poetry legible in a graphocentric culture, such poetry has always vacillated richly (or awkwardly, for those who would muscle it into the debates of medium specificity) between music and literature, sound and text. The confusion of the Yugoslav government only confirms what a threat verbal arts posed to any universalizing notion of "medium specificity" that might try to subsume them. Furthermore, to echo the arguments of several of the authors in this volume, oral poetry often blurs these distinctions of medium even more stubbornly than its written counterpart: it has a strongly visual component, and I will show here other sensory modes that are implicated as well.

To move from "medium specificity" to the specificities of oral poetry requires a few observations. First, as alluded to above, oral poetry is much more than a singular medium and defies much of the discourse surrounding "medium specificity."

Second, if an art form cannot be reduced to a single, specific medium, and the medium and the message are intimately connected, or at least (and less clichéd) this multiplicity of media has some impact on the singularity of that "message," we can expect the *meaning* of oral poetry to call for (if not outright demand) a multisensory mode of perception. The multisensory qualities of oral poetry include the poetics of audition—of being a capable audience member, not only in terms of physical ability (i.e. being able to hear) but, far more importantly, in terms of knowing the tradition and its aesthetic criteria (at least in passing), allowing audiences to recognize, respond to, and reward singers in different ways (Lord 2019:14–17).

Third, the history of oral poetry is inextricably linked with the history of its recording—its integration into "writing-down systems"—such that the poetry shaped the kinds of technologies used for recording and, in turn, these recording apparatuses have long (if not always) impacted the way such poetry is performed. These technologies of inscription might encompass large-scale institutions and technologies like the vocalic alphabet (Powell 1996) but come into clearer focus with recording technologies like the phonograph (first used to record a nursery rhyme and quickly taken up in the service of the anthropology of sound/music) or even, more specifically, the sound-recording apparatus that Milman Parry commissioned from Lincoln Thompson to circumvent the limits of commercial phonographs, gramophones, parlographs, etc. (Mitchell and Nagy 2000:xv–xvi).

And, finally, as a result of what I call the *synaesthetics of recording*, these recordings, by their nature, document certain aspects of the total sensory experience of these performances, while reducing or totally eliding others. Sound within a certain proximity of a microphone is preserved, while other so-called ambient sounds are lost, along with most visual, olfactory, and spatial information. Perhaps some photos are taken, thus fixing some other set of sensory data while also necessarily eliding so much else. (It bears mention that Parry and Lord both used photography and, to a very limited degree for Parry, film, in important ways in their research.) But recording is not just a reductive fixing; it simultaneously produces new sensory possibilities. Once fixed as recorded objects, these discs or photographs in turn engender new synaesthestic, multisensory experiences: listening in an archive that smells of its paper-based transcriptions; looking at photographs of musical performance or, even more significantly, performances for documentation through particular sound technologies; or pressing play on an old (but not too old) tape recorder to find that the last tape to be recorded was still there with no metadata to be had to indicate names and dates but, instead, with the tactile resistance of heavy, slightly sticky buttons and the minor heft of a much smaller, more portable apparatus.[7]

These broad points about oral poetry and its mediality can perhaps better be understood with three concrete examples from the Milman Parry Collection which will make up the remainder of this essay. The first is a set of photographs that explore senses of sound; the second, a sound recording that explores senses of place; and the third, a video recording that suggests how sound, sight, and place give rise to sensory-mediated forms of knowledge and meaning, a multisensory version of what Steven Feld calls "acoustemology" (1996, 2015). All these media, taken together, exemplify the kinds of multisensory perception I have described above as well as the intertwined histories of oral poetry and recording itself. At the same time, they also exemplify the sensory reduction I mentioned—they bear obvious traces of sensory data they have failed to preserve. Yet, as I hinted above, this sensory reduction is part of a larger synaesthetics of recording that allows some of these media objects—after having been concretized, materialized, *aufgeschrieben* in writing-down systems—to lead very fruitful lives since their initial recording, exemplifying the kind of sensory pluripotentiality of recordings when played back.

## Media as Synaesthetic Reduction

### 1. Images of sound

Photography is a multisensory activity, as Roland Barthes reminds us: "For me, the Photographer's organ is not his eye (which terrifies me) but his finger: what is linked to the trigger of the lens, to the metallic shifting of the plates (when the camera still has such things)" (1981:15). He then shifts from the haptic to the sonic as a key marker of photographic time rooted in the camera apparatus itself:

> I love these mechanical sounds in an almost voluptuous way, as if, in the Photograph, they were the very thing—and the only thing—to which my desire clings, their abrupt click breaking through the

7 Arlette Farge (2013) and Carolyn Steedman (2001) address some of these sensory configurations of the archive itself, including smell and taste (Farge's book, *The Allure of the Archives*, is originally titled in French *Le Goût de l'archive* [The taste of the archive], 1989). I thank Wolfgang Ernst for his relentless curiosity during a visit to the Milman Parry Collection in which he asked repeatedly to try each of the dozen or so wire and tape recorders tucked in the physical corners of the archive. He finally found a playable piece of media on the very last try—a tape recording that sounds like Bulgarian poetry but, again, with no metadata to tell a more complete story. I discuss this interaction as well as related cases in McMurray 2015.

> mortiferous layer of the Pose. For me the noise of Time is not sad: I love bells, clocks, watches—and I recall that at first photographic implements were related to techniques of cabinetmaking and the machinery of precision: cameras, in short, were clocks for seeing, and perhaps in me someone very old still hears in the photographic mechanism the living sound of the wood.
>
> (Barthes 1981:15)

In photography, Barthes *hears* time passing—an emergent archive rooted not only in vision but also in sound, touch, and decay. Following in the footsteps of Matthias Murko, whom he met while completing his doctoral studies at the Sorbonne, Milman Parry actively photographed the singers he recorded and the cities and landscapes which surrounded them. Unlike Murko (1951), however, Parry—or perhaps, in some instances, Albert Lord or one of his assistants—was also able to photograph a number of performances, in addition to the portrait photographs of singers that mark both Parry's and Murko's collections. That collection of photographs exhibits the passage of time through sound quite literally.

Nicola Scaldaferri and Zymer Neziri's chapter in this volume considers the kinds of bodily technics employed by Albanian epic singers for mnemonics and performance. (These examples of contemporary Albanian poetry offer a compelling corroboration of Haun Saussy's arguments.) Milman Parry's photograph of singer Jusuf Smajić from September 27, 1934, illustrates a similar bodily technics (Figure 1).[8] For all the innovations of Parry's commissioned audio apparatus, considering the audio recording being made here in isolation risks obscuring what I consider a very important, if silent, aspect of the epic being performed here: the cane as *gusle*. This photo, in fact, is part of a larger sequence, but it also serves as an iconic reminder of the many things that recordings do not capture within the context of a performance. The audio recording alone sounds like a performer sitting in front of a microphone—presumably with empty hands. The image, however, resonates with observations made by the late author and cultural critic, Ismet Rebronja (whose grandfather, incidentally, sang for and was recorded by Albert Lord in 1950). In conversations I had with him, he mentioned repeatedly what a physical process epic performance was, and that it was not uncommon for singers who did not have *gusle* at hand to find some other objects

[8] In addition to the archival afterlife of the Smajić images I discuss here, these photographs have also led to an important expansion of the archive through conversations and correspondence with descendants and relatives of Smajić who have been able to share more about his musical skills and verbal artistry. (He was also renowned for his Islamic recitation skills.) I discuss this further in McMurray 2019.

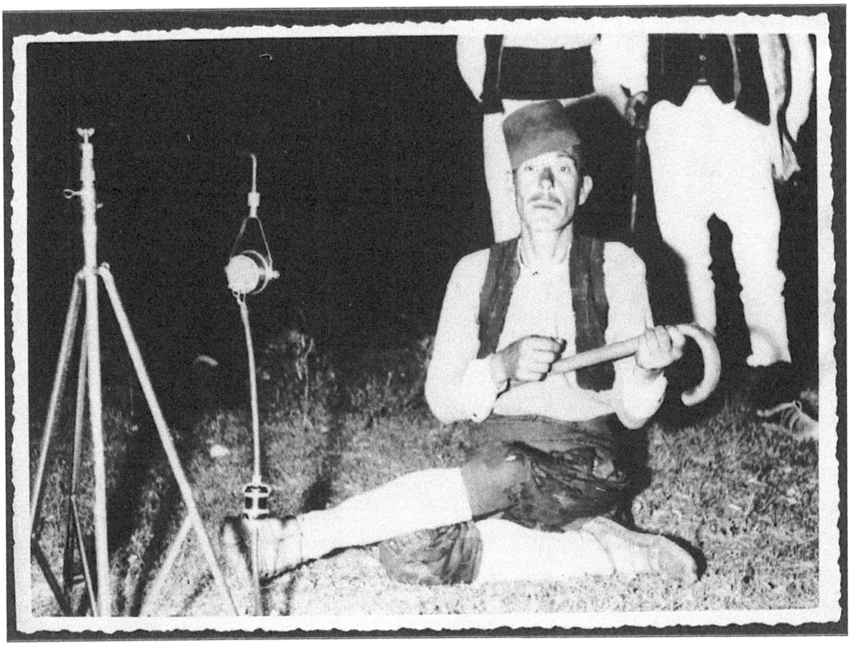

Figure 1. Jusuf Smajić recording for Milman Parry, September 1934 (MPC 0054). All photographs from the Milman Parry Collection of Oral Literature, Harvard University.

(rubbing sticks together, for example) to generate the kinds of kinetic rhythms that self-accompaniment provides.[9]

Milman Parry's photographic efforts have received little attention, yet they offer significant insight both into the performance tradition and into Parry's research methodologies. Two general observations about the photographs have relevance for my discussion here: first, many of them occur in series, creating a kind of proto-cinematic sense of temporal visuality; and second, a significant number depict not only the singers (an obvious choice) but also the recording technologies used, ranging from the common and (relatively) rudimentary (pen and notebook) to the idiosyncratic and complex (the famed two-turntable apparatus Parry commissioned from Lincoln Thompson). For my present purposes, I am especially interested in the intersection of these two groupings of photos: sequential images of the recording devices, which function as a |meta-documentary medium consisting of moving pictures about recording.

One of the features of the photos Parry took—and perhaps a more general phenomenon in taking photos—is that photos often come in series. This

[9] Interview with author, June 7, 2004.

Figure 2. Nikola Vujnović recording at Parry's parlograph (MPC 0345).

sequential aspect of photography is built into the medium, with the constraint of only being able to take a single picture at once. It also emerges from the flow of activities: I pull out my camera and take a photograph right now in this room, then in the hallway with a colleague, then outside, and so on. The logical sequencing of action is mundane—we hardly think about it and all the less when we are taking photographs with a digital camera that barely limits the quantity of pictures we take. And yet, such series clarify much of what is happening temporally and spatially beyond the frame of a single image, bridging the space between the photograph and moving pictures. Parry's documentation of the recording apparatuses he used—and the implications of sound, and the reproduction of sound embedded visually in them—is of particular interest to me as evidence of recording devices whose whereabouts are no longer known. Yet, in several cases, he created not just a single image of recording but a brief sequence—a burst of images that animate the act of recording, highlighting the kinds of sonic temporalities inherent in photography, especially photography of sound, and the temporalities of recording more generally.

For example, a whole series of near-identical photographs were taken of Parry's assistant, Nikola Vujnović, recording in front of a parlograph at the Pansion Viktorija in Dubrovnik, essentially variations of this photograph (Figure 2), all depicting Vujnović sitting with slight movements of his head and body.

Figure 3. Jusuf Smajić recording in a field near Glamoč, Bosnia (MPC 0035).

Figure 4. Jusuf Smajić recording in a field near Glamoč, Bosnia (MPC 0036).

Figure 5. Jusuf Smajić recording in a field near Glamoč, Bosnia (MPC 0037).

Figure 6. Jusuf Smajić recording in a field near Glamoč, Bosnia (MPC 0038).

Before Parry commissioned his famous two-turntables-and-a-microphone from Lincoln Thompson, he used a parlograph as seen here with Vujnović. The photograph not only offers a compelling visual portrait of one of the most important figures in the entire project, it also makes clear how unwieldy such a device would have been for recording singers like Smajić, who appears behind a much smaller microphone while sitting outdoors.

In addition to the photograph looking straight on at Smajić, another cinematic series (Figures 3–6) photographed at that recording session gives a sense of one possible configuration for recording, especially outdoors. While the order of these images depicting Smajić is difficult to ascertain, several significant points arise. First, Milman Parry's car can be seen, a critical vehicle (literally) for traveling and for powering the recording device. The microphone is set up at considerable remove from the actual recording equipment, allowing for a quieter recording (and also giving some indication of what kinds of distances were possible and perhaps necessary for recording). Second, several people gather around for the performance, but for the most part, they seem to be seated at some remove from Smajić, presumably to minimize other sounds in the recording. (The question of audience interactivity or lack thereof in Parry's work remains unclear, but there are clear traces throughout the archive that it was not unheard of to have various kinds of audiences at a recording session.) Third, Vujnović can be seen lying on the ground next to Smajić, suggesting that his role was not always one of immediate engagement with the singer—these could be lengthy songs and presumably recording created additional technical and logistical delays—though he is the only one who remains at Smajić's side throughout the series of photos.

Another such series from the village of Kijevo pod Dinarom features the *guslar*/singer Ante Cicvarić. This sequence of images (Figures 7–11) shows a similar set of circumstances and photography: outdoor recording; villagers (and probably family members) gathered around (though this time women are present in sizable numbers); a portrait of the singer; and an image of the act of recording itself, though this time the singer is nestled away in a stone hut, perhaps an attempt to mitigate wind noise. (The caption to image MPC 0499 states, "In the picture, the apparatus with which we worked is seen. At right, the singer is inside the hut and the microphone is in front of the door. The hut is a storehouse for hay, and the singer, Ante Cicvarić, is seen with the *gusle*.") Five distinct boxes can be seen as part of the recording apparatus, apart from the microphone—the clearest image of the apparatus. The caption from photograph MPC 0042 states that "the apparatus is ready for work," and Vujnović can be seen at the edge of the frame adjusting the microphone on its stand.

Figure 7. Recording at Kijevo with Ante Cicvarić (MPC 0041).

Figure 8. Recording at Kijevo with Ante Cicvarić (MPC 0042).
Original caption: "*aparat spreman za rad*." [The apparatus is ready for work.]

Figure 9. Recording at Kijevo with Ante Cicvarić (MPC 0043).

Figure 10. Recording at Kijevo with Ante Cicvarić (MPC 0044).

Figure 11. Recording at Kijevo with Ante Cicvarić (MPC 0499).

The order of the photographs is not necessarily apparent from their captioning alone (and the numbering system given to them is a relatively recent development). But the cinematic logic of these images gives a strong indication of their likely ordering: the photographer, probably Milman Parry, stands back and photographs the entire scene (MPC 0041), including a young boy who has pulled his jacket over his head; the next photograph (MPC 0042) comes closer, focusing on the women to the far left and the recording apparatus, just as Vujnović is adjusting the microphone—a reminder of his integral role intellectually and technically; the scene shifts back toward the performer, Cicvarić, who has now picked up his *gusle* from the ground while the camera rotates its orientation (MPC 0043); the photographic zoom then continues, settling on Cicvarić's face, with its furrowed brow, thick moustache, and salt-and-pepper beard (MPC 0044). The sequence comes to a close after a demonstrable break as Cicvarić moves into the hut, the microphone is set up there, and the crowd repositions itself near the hut, presumably to listen during the performance (MPC 0499).

Strikingly, these two sequences of images were taken within a week of each other: Cicvarić on September 22, 1934, Smajić on September 27, 1934. Another iconic photograph of the apparatus at Kulen Vakuf (MPC 0714) was taken in the intervening days. Such a clustering of meta-documentary seems to be intentional—a sudden upsurge in interest or ability to document process. Whatever the reasons, these photographs show the complex intersection between material technology, the aural and visual realms, the emplacement of recording, and the cinema of "still" photography. The apparatus becomes a social mediator too, bringing together women and children as well as men, albeit with a tentative gender separation.

## 2. Sounds of place

Just as the visual encodes sound, so too can sound encode other senses. The best-known case of this phenomenon is the poetic texts themselves in which sound conveys all kinds of imagery, smells, and even self-reflexive, poetic descriptions of the poetry's own sonic workings. For example, Murat Kurtagić's invocations to his own *gusle* (see Čolaković 2004) might be fruitfully understood as an extension of the kinds of engravings on some *gusle* themselves, with scenes of battles and so forth. But even the interviews Parry and Vujnović conducted with nearly every singer transmit an abundance of sensory information as well. Returning to Ugljanin and Vujnović's conversations, the sixth conversation/interview (*pričanje*, PN 659) they recorded has a number of interesting features that situate sound as a feature of place. First, it starts with a lengthy digression about a certain manuscript (presumably of written poetry) that Parry had apparently been trying to obtain through Ugljanin—a manuscript (*rukopis*) also described as a *ćitab* or *jazija* (Arabic/Turkish *kitāb/kitap*, Turkish *yazı*). The exchange maps out a variety of spaces: first, the space of the room in which they are speaking, as Parry occasionally interjects, at an audible remove from the microphone, during the conversation that is otherwise taking place between Ugljanin and Vujnović; second, the neighborhood, which Ugljanin verbally maps (with some reluctance), explaining a route to the shop of the woman who has this text; and finally, a larger cultural map, as they discuss the language of the text—whether it is in Bosnian, Turkish, or Arabic, all of which Vujnović claims to know, jokingly comparing himself to the Bosnian hero Halil Hrnjica, whose brother Mujo was also a major hero: "Mujo's brother Halil knew 24 languages. I know 25!" (PN 659, disc 1043).

Once they have resolved the location of the manuscript, they then begin the interview proper, as it were, with Vujnović immediately asking Ugljanin what the experience of war is like. Ugljanin's response verbally recreates the space and sounds of the battlefield, setting the stage for him to then recite a short epic song, "Velagić Selim i Nukić [or more commonly, Đulić] Bajraktar." Much of this macabre conversation focuses on Ugljanin's supposedly having cut off someone's head during war:

> NV: Salja, tell me, was it during the war, that you cut someone's head off?
>
> SU: Yes, it was during the war.
>
> NV: Where did that happen?
>
> SU: It was in Montenegro.
>
> NV: In what place?
>
> SU: Over near Andrijevica.
>
> NV: Tell me what that was like, tell me everything, in case I ever go to war, so I know what war is like [*kako ratovati*, literally "how to do battle"], how to take off someone's head.
>
> SU: What war is like? The army goes this way, that way, and then this army of ours goes that way, and then all at once they light up, ka ka ka ka ka, guns are shooting. Then ha! On our feet to get our knives. And

> you rush and get settled, and then strike, and whichever has the better knife, klap klap klap klap....
>
> (PN 659, disc 1043)[10]

Ugljanin's use of oral sound effects is striking, interjected spontaneously, suggesting the verbal repertoire available to a seasoned raconteur like him, despite a line of questioning from Vujnović that likely has no clear connection to poetry (and is ethically questionable, though the martial experience of singers themselves is an important theme for Parry). Vujnović presses on for several minutes in a similar manner, with prying questions about this act of violence that seems to have no connection to songs (what did the body do afterward? did you pray to God and repent?). Ugljanin responds with further verbal sound effects, such as the body's response ("the back springs and lurches back, *ruub*," disc 1043) and the sound of blood ("like whiskey pouring out, *brrrrrr*," disc 1044).[11]

These sound effects also suggest a physical, bodily language to enhance the accounts. Of course, one can only speculate, but from my conversations with *guslar*s and other storytellers in more recent years, I suspect each of these sounds may well have been accompanied by physical gestures, suggesting a strong gestural dimension to these ostensibly verbal performances.

Other sonic aspects beyond the text of the interview itself emerge as well: again, Parry interjects occasionally from some physical distance, occasionally feeding questions to Vujnović or asking Ugljanin directly, and during this particular story of the beheading (just before Vujnović asks if he prayed to God for forgiveness), asking Ugljanin to speak up: "Louder, I can't hear well." Vujnović repeats similar encouragements just before Ugljanin begins reciting the story of Velagić Selim in an odd exchange between the two:

> SU: I can't [sing it] until I rest, my God, it's long ... Let me stand up and take a break.
>
> NV: Fine, fine, if you're tired, take a break.
>
> SU: And should I keep count as well?
>
> NV: Yes, yes, every syllable [*slovo*], if you don't tell it exactly—I know the whole thing.
>
> SU: Yes, alright.

10 https://sds.lib.harvard.edu/sds/audio/462511918, disc 1043. Audio recordings are from the Milman Parry Collection of Oral Literature, Harvard University.

11 In response to the question about praying, Ugljanin asserts that he was acting in self-defense.

> NV: If you don't tell it exactly, we won't pay you anything.
>
> SU: Oh, I don't know how others sing it, but the way I sing it, I won't leave anything out.
>
> NV: Good! Now let's go, *bismillah*!
>
> SU: *Bismillah* [laughing] and may God help!
>
> NV: But sing it cleanly, clearly, and loudly!
>
> SU: Alright. "In olden times and seasons / One morning had just dawned..."
>
> (PN 659, disc 1044)

The exchange shows a certain intimacy as Vujnović (a Christian) seems to be joking with his Islamic invocation of Allah (*bismillah*), which elicits a brief laugh from Ugljanin (a Muslim). At the same time, the economic threats over performance suggest a power dynamic underlying the exchange. All of this is further complicated by the physicality of recording, which would necessitate that both interlocutors sit closely to the microphone—a physical intimacy demanded technologically (Figure 12). In other words, the recording has organized the spatialization of bodies and bodily sound in this session, not unlike what we see with Smajić and Vujnović sitting in the field above or Cicvarić near the hut. The "apparatus" of these recordings thus expands beyond just the technical devices to include the space beyond them, the economic exchange involved, and the (largely unprecedented) social dynamics that inevitably would have emerged while Parry recorded in small villages around the Yugoslav countryside. Slavica Ranković has highlighted the complex, multi-party performativity that marks these interviews (2012), and while I am less inclined to characterize them as full-fledged acts of "epistemic violence" as she does, these interactions certainly warrant further study as performances in their own right with their own sensory priorities.

## 3. Acoustemology and Obrov

Having viewed sound by way of apparatus photography and then heard space by way of sound effects, off-microphone interjections, and larger linguistic, religious, and cultural references, I turn now to a third and final medium/case study: video, especially as it relates to memory as well as performance context more generally. In June 2004, I had the tremendous opportunity of spending time conversing with and recording Zaim Međedović, the son of Avdo Međedović, a

Figure 12. Salih Ugljanin and Nikola Vujnović share the microphone during a recording (MPC 0525).

bard from Bijelo Polje, Montenegro, who became the central figure in Parry's and Lord's research because of his abilities to perform extraordinarily lengthy tales. Zaim offered to perform an epic song for me, but with a set of conditions: first, that I arrange for a *gusle* for him to play, since he no longer owned one; second, that we record the performance, preferably with video (which I was unprepared to do but ultimately managed, thanks to the help of a relative, the late Tule Međedović, who lent me his camera); and third, that the performance take place in Obrov, a hillside village opposite the town of Bijelo Polje, in front of the house where his father had lived when Albert Lord visited him again in the 1950s.

Video camera in hand, I joined Zaim and traveled around a massive hillside to Obrov with a couple other family members and friends. The warm June morning was alive with the hum of cicadas and other bugs, while a slight wind gave the whole hillside a sense of inhaling and exhaling. Zaim insisted on beginning his performance with a speech addressed to me and, by extension, to previous generations of researchers:[12]

[12] Video of Zaim's speech can be seen at: https://vimeo.com/104101820. His performance of an epic song can be seen at: https://vimeo.com/104101821.

> First let's talk, and then [I'll sing] the song. Dear Peter, esteemed *gospodin* [gentleman] Peter, student from the American university, you have set out and come to Yugoslavia in Montenegro to visit the home of the singer, the great singer Avdo Međedović, as well as his remaining family members. As the last remaining son in the family of the singer Avdo Međedović, I have the duty to thank you for having come from America, from where your professors Milman and Albert Lord [came and] recorded in 1935. And after that, in 1950, your professor Albert Lord returned...

At this point, a neighbor walked up—the current owner of the house, as I understood it—and interrupted Zaim. The two then briefly argued about what we were doing. As the years pass since I made that recording, this interruption seems increasingly central to the entire performance, though at the time I found it immensely frustrating (Figure 13). (I distinctly remember thinking in the moment: He just ruined my video! Now I see this interaction as precisely the kind of ethnographic reality that Parry and Lord are pushing against, yet inadvertently documenting, in the Smajić and Cicvarić performances.)

After placating the neighbor, Zaim continued with his speech, recounting Albert Lord's return to Bijelo Polje in 1950:

> Your professor Albert Lord, who came in 1952, that is, 1950, to the home of my aging father, at which I was present when I was twenty years old, and he asked my father again, he called him *poočime* [adopted father] and asked him to sing the same song from 1935, when he had sung for him in the hotel in Bijelo Polje. My father had become extremely weak with illness, but his memory soared to great heights, so he took it [the *gusle*] and he sang him a song, which he had sung for him in 1935. Albert recorded it again, his verses, which his professor Parry had recorded before him. He hugged him and kissed the singer Međedović and said, "O dear friend, in 18 years you have neither left out a single word nor added one. Such is your genius! [*Takav si um.*]" He cried, hugged him, all of this in the hotel in Bijelo Polje. Three days he sang for him again in 1950 in such old age, and his son Zaim Međedović listened as his father sang live for Professor Albert Lord. And he stayed here in the hotel. The professor left for America, while my father died half a year later. His son, Zaim Međedović, remained, and now along with *gospodin* Peter who came to my home to visit the son of singer Avdo Međedović. I'm thankful that *gospodin* Peter wanted to record the son of singer Avdo

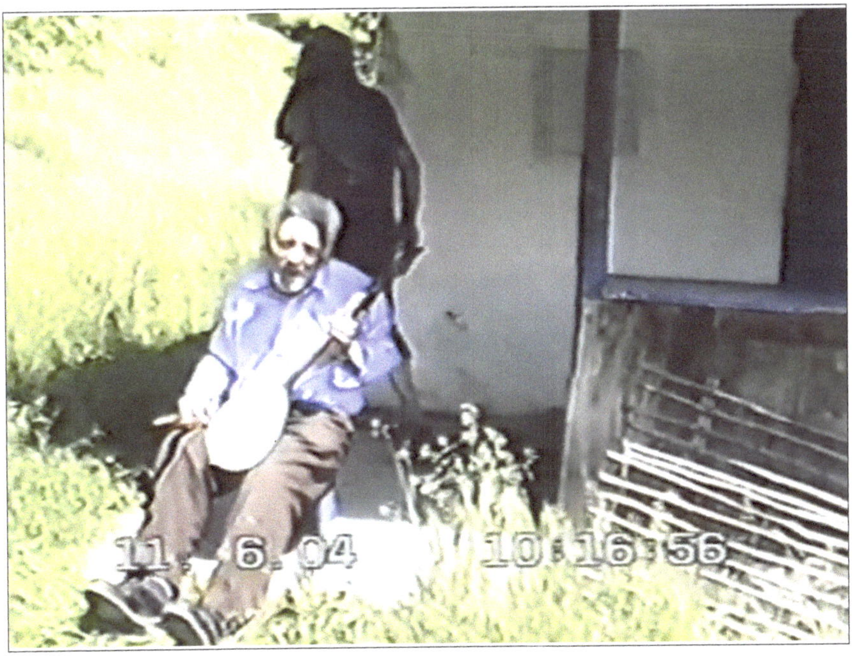


Figure 13. Zaim Međedović at former family home in Obrov, with (interrupting) neighbor in background (video still, June 2004).

> Međedović, who followed and listened to his father in person. I most graciously thank you for your coming.
>
> And now, I'll sing a short passage of one song, which my dear father, may he rest in peace, Avdo Međedović, sang. Now I'll begin the song. This is just the prologue to thank *gospodin* Peter and Albert Lord and his family, if there are any of them still alive.

I had not expected any such speech, let alone one that entangled me in the legacy of Milman Parry and Albert Lord: generations of the Međedović family, on the one hand, bound up with generations of American (and many other) scholars, on the other. The comments were gratifying but also foreshadowed a kind of mediated responsibility that I would only discover months later. For the time being, Zaim launched into the epic song, "The Wedding of Alija Bojičić":

| | |
|---|---|
| Riječ prva: "Bože nam pomozi." | Let the first word be: "O God, help us!" |
| Evo druga: "Hoće ako bogda." | And the second: "It shall be if God wills." |
| Samo da ga često pominjemo, | So long as we call on him often |
| da se Bogu krivo ne kunemo. | and do not swear falsely before him |
| Pa će nama Allah pomagati, | Then Allah will help us, |
| od svake muke zaklanjati, | shelter us from every torment, |
| svake muke i kaurske ruke, | from every torment and the hand of the unbeliever, |
| sačuvat nas hala i belaja, | preserve us from misery and misfortune |
| a i bijede gore od belaja. | and from poverty worse than misfortune. |
| ................................................... | ................................................... |
| A sad stari gosti i uvaženi, | And now old and esteemed guests, |
| da vi jednu pesmu zapevamo. | may we sing a song for you. |
| Od kako je Bosna postanula | From the time when Bosnia was formed |
| nije bolji cvijet procvateo... | no better flower bloomed... |

The song's opening ("Let the first word be...") is based on the opening Zaim's father, Avdo, so often sang, a kind of expansion of the sentiments of the brief *bismillah* invocation made by Salih Ugljanin. Due to the physical exertion of singing, Zaim Međedović was only able to sing for about ten minutes—a far cry from the hours-long performances his father recorded for Milman Parry. So we continued the following day at the home of a relative, as I continued to film. The video camera, able to capture sound and image (with a reasonable degree of verisimilitude), had served to catalyze a certain type of performance and a whole network of activities of memory. But even video is only able to collect an exteriority of those memories: an index through speech, as when Zaim recounts his experience; or a facade, literally and figuratively, of the house on that hillside and its rich family history; or even, simply, a framed viewing whereby Zaim is visible but friends and relatives gathered (as well as myself, as camera operator) are not. Memory is sheared, even as it is preserved.

## Media as Synaesthetic Catalyst

If these media inherently pare down the sensory experiences they document—reducing a rich world of sound, sight, and likely smell and taste—they paradoxically also catalyze new sensory experiences as they are played back in the present. Or, in other words, while recording violently severs much of our sensory world in the name of documentation, it prompts or gives back a whole new set of possible sensory and social possibilities. These media almost literally have a life of their own.

For example, one of the most interesting aspects of my work with Zaim Međedović was my first return to Bijelo Polje in December 2004, a few months after first meeting him. For me, it afforded an opportunity to follow up on a number of issues relating to his performance; but for him, the central priority was clear—he wanted to get a copy of the video recording I had made. This exchange opened up a whole new set of conversations, explicitly about his perceptions of the ethics of the numerous "collectors" and other researchers who had visited his father and him over the years. In particular, he expressed disappointment about the failure of any of those scholars, but especially Albert Lord, to bring back a recording. Furthermore, this failure was not just an oversight, in his opinion, but a lack of scholarly integrity. While it would be all but impossible to verify such a claim—and my next example suggests that Lord actively *did* return copies of media, even to much less central figures in the collection—I found the exchange academically interesting, and if I may be permitted a personal note, frankly touching as he thanked me profusely for bringing him these copies. In our conversations, he kept fixating on the *trake* (recorded "tracks") I had left him and, to a lesser degree, on the recordings of his father included with the copy of the *Singer of Tales* I brought. I thus return to my earlier comment: recorded media can and do mediate relationships between people, not just between an object and its mechanical reproduction.[13] Indeed, in this case, media not only mediated but caused our relationship to flourish, contrary to a certain notion within anthropology and ethnomusicology that imagines media as primarily disrupting otherwise "natural" interactions.

A strangely similar experience—but with very different implications for the material legacy of Parry and Lord—took place in 2009 while I was doing research in North Macedonia. Impressed by my exchanges with Zaim, I thought I would try to track down other singers who had recorded for Lord in the 1950s. As Miloš Velimirović had recalled, much of Lord's focus by 1950 was on North Macedonia, and I hoped I might find more people like Zaim who were still alive and remembered his visits. After failure in a couple villages, I made one last attempt, traveling to Pletvar, near the city of Prilep, where Lord had recorded several members

13 This social aspect of media is increasingly obvious in the years that have passed since this essay was first written. But even well before "social media," it has long been clear that media mediated people and their relationships (among other things). Lisa Gitelman's pithy formulation of media as "socially realized structures of communication" (2006:7) thus seems especially useful here, not only for recordings of oral poetry but also the poetry itself.

of the same family in both years, and was pleased to find Rampo Šijakoski alive and in good physical health.

After some conversation, Šijakoski retrieved a photo of himself, his brother, and his father, all of whom recorded for Albert Lord. The photograph was signed on the back: "Greetings from Professor Albert Lord, Harvard University."[14] Of course, people keep all sorts of photos. But returning to Zaim's comments, the fact that Lord had apparently distributed photos to singers he worked with even only briefly suggests that he shared what he gathered with the singers he met. The Šijakoskis only recorded a few songs for Lord (LN 141–145b, 182–185); presumably Lord would have been even more likely to bring/send back duplicate recordings to other singers with whom he worked more extensively, like Avdo Međedović. (Perhaps Zaim never received such media remittances because Lord's attentions were focused on Avdo, the main singer of the family, rather than his son Zaim). In any case, I was struck to hear Zaim criticize me during a visit in May 2012 for not bringing back copies of the media I had made. I reminded him that I had already done so and offered to make another copy if needed, but he assured me it would not be necessary. The entire exchange offered a sobering reminder that the writing-down systems of media can both prompt memory and also displace it, much as Plato's King Thamous argues in the *Phaedrus* (see also Derrida 1981).[15] As if an emblem of the whole tradition, Zaim was fighting against (literal) oblivion, or *zaborav*, a longstanding component of Bosnian oral poetry (see Kunić 2012).

As my 2009 conversation with Rampo Šijakoski progressed, he eventually offered to sing a number of short songs. I had simply (and inaccurately) presumed he would *want* to sing. Only much later in our conversation did he bring out more photos, this time of his son, who had passed away over a decade earlier, and whose death had affected him such that he stopped singing songs until that visit and reminiscence of past singing. Of course, I had little to do with this complex performance, apart from showing up—like many writing in this volume, I was simply reaping the fruits of seeds planted by previous generations of scholars, particularly Albert Lord. And again, the immediate catalyst for this exchange was a piece of media that somehow indexed a sensory moment of the past, reduced to a 3" x 3" black-and-white photographic image, but that nevertheless led to a very rich and very different sensory moment years later.

14 Personal interview/visit, June 20, 2009.

15 Prior to my 2012 visit, Zaim had sadly suffered from a stroke and struggled to converse with the same clarity as he had eight years earlier (which I discuss briefly in McMurray 2012). I hesitate to read too much into any conversation from that visit given his health circumstances. But it was a poignant reminder of how crucial a role memory, both personal and cultural, plays in this tradition.

My final example, or set of examples, is a number of music compositions inspired by the materials of the Parry Collection, dating back to Béla Bartók's *Concerto for Orchestra*, and the second movement's "Game of Pairs," which some musicologists have attributed to his hearing Dalmatian vocal music (Suchoff 1995, 2004). More recently, a number of composers have set texts from the Parry Collection to music, or simply created new compositions with loose musical connections. Composer Ketty Nez wrote an entire cycle of pieces based on these materials, *Postcards from the 1930's* (premiered 2008; recorded and released 2009b) as well as a "folk opera" with similar inspirations, *The Fiddler and the Old Woman of Rumelia* (2009a). The interest of Bartók, Aida Vidan (2003), and Ketty Nez (among others) in songs sung by women highlights, quite explicitly, the way that recordings—and their afterlives—can also actively include and exclude certain voices.

Let me conclude by returning to McLuhan's formulation of media and message (1964), which I alluded to earlier in passing, by way of Mladen Dolar. In his book, *A Voice and Nothing More,* Dolar writes: "'The medium is the message'—this notorious slogan should perhaps be twisted in such a way that the message of the medium pertains to its voice" (2006:191). I would like to twist this idea still once more: whatever messages a voice-as-medium may have conveyed are reduced and then expanded again through the process of recording. The medium indeed pertains to the voice in this case—it is, after all, oral poetry—but through the transformations of recording, we are left with a totally different sensory experience, an aural poetry—as in a poetry of the ear, not the voice. And, then again, much more than the ear, or aurality, is engaged. Photographs become sonic, sound recording becomes spatial and geographic, video becomes memory and oblivion. The oral—the voice—remains but only as a single component in a much larger assemblage of body parts, media, and human entanglements.

## Abbreviations

LN Lord Number, for objects recorded/collected by Albert Lord 1950–51.
MPC Milman Parry Collection, for photographs taken by/for Milman Parry 1933–1935.
PN Parry Number, for objects recorded/collected by Milman Parry 1933–1935.

## Bibliography

Barthes, R. 1981. *Camera Lucida: Reflections on Photography*. Trans. R. Howard. New York.

Bartók, B., and A. B. Lord. 1951. *Serbo-Croatian Folk Songs. Texts and Translations of Seventy-Five Folks Songs from the Milman Parry Collection and a Morphology of Serbo-Croatian Folk Melodies.* With a foreword by G. Herzog. New York.

Čolaković, Z. 2004. *Mrtva Glava Jezik Progovara*. Podgorica.

Derrida, J. 1981. *Dissemination*. Trans. B. Johnson. Chicago.

Dolar, M. 2006. *A Voice and Nothing More*. Cambridge, MA.

Farge, A. 1989. *Le Goût de l'archive*. Paris.

———. 2013. *The Allure of the Archives*. New Haven.

Feld, S. 1996. "Waterfalls of Song: An Acoustemology of Place Resounding in Bosavi, Papua New Guinea." In *Senses of Place*, ed. S. Feld and K. H. Basso, 91–135. Santa Fe.

———. 2015. "Acoustemology." In *Keywords in Sound*, ed. D. Novak and M. Sakakeeny. Durham, NC.

Gitelman, L. 2006. *Always Already New: Media, History, and the Data of Culture*. Cambridge, MA.

Greenberg, C. 1940. "Towards a Newer Laocoon." *Partisan Review.* 7:296–310.

Jones, C. 2006. *Eyesight Alone: Clement Greenberg's Modernism and the Bureaucratization of the Senses*. Chicago.

Kittler, F. 1985. *Aufschreibesysteme 1800/1900*. Munich.

———. 1990. *Discourse Networks 1800/1900*. Trans. M. Metteer with C. Cullens. Stanford.

Köçümkulkïzï, E. 2005. "The Kyrgyz Epic Manas." www.silkroadfoundation.org/folklore/manas/manasintro.html.

Kunić, M. 2012. *Usmeno pamćenje i zaborav: krajiška epika i njeni junaci*. Tešanj.

Lord, A. B. 1948. "Homer, Parry, and Huso." *American Journal of Archaeology* 52:34–44.

———. 1949. *The Singer of Tales: A Study in the Processes of Composition of Yugoslav, Greek, and Germanic Oral Narrative Poetry*. PhD diss., Harvard University.

Lord, A. B., ed. 1954. *Serbocroatian Heroic Songs*. Vol. 1, *Novi Pazar: English Translations*. With musical transcriptions by B. Bartók and prefaces by J. H. Finley, Jr. and R. Jakobson. Cambridge, MA.

———. 1960. *The Singer of Tales*. Cambridge, MA.

———. 2019. *The Singer of Tales*. 3rd ed. Ed. D. F. Elmer. Hellenic Studies 77. Publications of the Milman Parry Collection of Oral Literature 4. Washington, DC. Orig. pub. Cambridge, MA, 1960.

McLuhan, M. 1964. *Understanding Media: The Extensions of Man*. New York.

McMurray, P. 2012. "Fathers and Sons; or, Recalling the Sound of Time." In *Donum natalicium digitaliter confectum Gregorio Nagy septuagenario a discipulis collegis familiaribus oblatum*, ed. V. Bers et al. https://chs.harvard.edu/peter-mcmurray-fathers-and-sons/.

———. 2015. "Archival Excess: Sensational Histories beyond the Audiovisual." *Fontes Artis Musicae* 62:262–275.

———. 2019. "After the Archive: An Archaeology of Bosnian Voices." In *The Oxford Handbook of Musical Repatriation*, ed. F. D. Gunderson, R. C. Lancefield, and B. D. Woods, 607–626. New York.

Mitchell, S., and G. Nagy. 2000. "Introduction to the Second Edition." In Lord 2019, xi-xxxviii.

Mitchell, W. J. T. 2005. "There Are No Visual Media." *Journal of Visual Culture* 4:257–266.

Murko, M. 1951. *Tragom srpsko-hrvatske narodne epike: putovanja u godinama 1930–1932*. Zagreb.

Nez, K. 2008. *Postcards from the 1930's*. Chamber music composition.

———. 2009a. *The Fiddler and the Old Woman of Rumelia*. Folk opera.

———. 2009b. *Listen to a Wonder Never Heard Before!* Albany Records, TROY1169.

Parry, A. 1971. "Introduction." In M. Parry 1971, ix–lxi.

Parry, M. 1971. *The Making of Homeric Verse: The Collected Papers of Milman Parry*. Ed. A. Parry. Oxford.

Powell, B. 1996. *Homer and the Origin of the Greek Alphabet*. Cambridge.

Radloff, W. 1885. *Proben der Volksliteratur der nördlichen türkischen Stämme V: Der Dialekt der Kara-Kirgisen*. St. Petersburg.

Ranković, S. 2012. "Managing the 'Boss': Epistemic Violence, Resistance, and Negotiations in Milman Parry's and Nikola Vujnović's *Pričanja* with Salih Ugljanin." *Oral Tradition* 27:5–66.

Reichl, K. 2000. *Singing the Past: Turkic and Medieval Heroic Poetry*. Ithaca.

Saussy, H. 2016. *The Ethnography of Rhythm: Orality and Its Technologies*. New York.

Schoeler, G. 2006. *The Oral and the Written in Early Islam*. Trans. U. Vagelpohl, ed. J. Montgomery. London.

Skok, P. 1971. *Etimologijski rječnik hrvatskoga ili srpskoga jezika*. Zagreb.

Suchoff, B. 1995. *Bartók: Concerto for Orchestra: Understanding Bartók's World*. New York.

———. 2004. *Béla Bartók: A Celebration*. Lanham, MD.

van der Heide, N. 2008. *Spirited Performance: The Manas Epic and Society in Kyrgyzstan*. Amsterdam.

Vidan, A. 2003. *Embroidered with Gold, Strung with Pearls: The Traditional Ballads of Bosnian Women*. Milman Parry Collection of Oral Literature 1. Cambridge, MA.

Youssefzadeh, A. 2002. *Les Bardes du Khorassan Iranien: Le Bakhshi et son Répertoire*. Leuven.

# Index